Frommer's®
Scotland

Our Scotland

by Darwin Porter & Danforth Prince

YEAR AFTER YEAR, WE VISIT SCOTLAND—AS "STERN AND WILD" TODAY as when Sir Walter Scott described its "brown heath and shaggy wood" in the 18th century. But it's not just the blue-tipped mountains, spring-green meadows filled with sheep, mysterious lochs, or even *uisge-beatha* (whisky) that keep drawing us back. It's the people.

Central casting would have trouble assembling a more colorful and out-spoken brood: the male punk rocker, in tartanry-à-go-go, inviting us to hear his band that night in an Edinburgh pub; the elegantly attired Duke of Roxburghe asking us to "set beside his hound dog for a wee dram of Drambuie"; the weather-beaten crofter near Applecross who asked us "lad-dies" into his thatched roof stone cottage for a "cuppa" tea; the gap-toothed, red-headed Glaswegian 12-year-old street girl who tells us she's going to be the first prime minister of a completely independent Scotland.

Once you start meeting these friendly, rugged folk—who exported 20 million of their sons and daughters to change the face of the world with their hard work and inventive minds—you won't be surprised to learn that the greeting *Ceud Mile Fàite*, plastered across the land, means "A Hundred Thousand Welcomes."

© Cephas Picture Library/Alamy

Like the thistle, the kipper, porridge, and haggis, **PEAT (left)** is an integral part of Scottish life. In the West Highlands, a peat cutter gathers the decomposing and partially carbonized vegetable tissue as fuel for winter. Many a Scot has endured a blustery night through the warmth of a long-burning peat fire and, perhaps, a *wee goldie* (Scotch). Scotch itself gets its warm, smoky flavor from peat, used to dry the malted barley before distillation.

On the Isle of Lewis in the Outer Hebrides, the **CALLANDISH STANDING STONES (above)** are Britain's most important prehistoric monument after Stonehenge. Laid out like a Celtic cross in 1800 B.C., the 13 monoliths stand 3m (12 ft.) tall, encircling a burial cairn like ghostly sentinels. Their origins and function remain a mystery; some have speculated they were the seat of a Viking parliament, a site for predicting eclipses, or even a UFO landing site.

During the Cold War, writer Hugh McIlvanney claimed that **SCOTIA (above)**, Glasgow's oldest pub, could be taken by the Red Army in 3 days—or maybe a day and a half, if they used nuclear weapons. For decades, Glaswegian pubs were Britain's toughest, known as "blood buckets." Today, however, it's artists and writers who flock to Scotia, on 112 Stockwell St. Featuring live folk music, it's the most authentic place in Glasgow for a *wee hauf* (small whisky).

When Dr. Johnson reached the Isle of Mull, the Hebrides' third largest, he lamented the lack of trees. But, with all that extra grass, this **ULVA HIGHLAND BULL (right)** finds the grazing just fine—which is probably why cattle and more red deer than people preside over Scotland's greenest island. With its wild and mountainous countryside, sea lochs, and sandy bars, Mull was the setting for many of David Balfour's adventures in Robert Louis Stevenson's *Kidnapped*.

PRINCES STREET, Edinburgh's main thoroughfare, lights up for the oncoming night as the sun sets. This view, dominated by the Balmoral Hotel clock tower, is from Calton Hill in the east (Robert Louis Stevenson's favorite vantage), which rises 106m (350 ft.). Running parallel to the Royal Mile, Princes Street has been fashionable since 1805. It's still the capital's finest address for shopping, and it's home to the Scott Monument and Royal Scottish Academy.

Students of **ST. ANDREWS UNIVERSITY** (above) take their traditional pier walk along the North Sea after Sunday morning services. As a student, Prince William joined in this parade, with paparazzi on standby, waiting for gusts of wind to flap his red robes for the ultimate shot. Founded in 1411 in the "kingdom" of Fife, north of Edinburgh, St. Andrews is the oldest university in Scotland. Incidentally, the burgh of St. Andrews is also the birthplace of golf.

At the **EDINBURGH FRINGE FESTIVAL** (right), contortionist Bendyem (real name, Emma Tunbridge) escapes a straitjacket, as did her more famous predecessor, Houdini. The festival—which began in 1947 to take advantage of the crowds and press attending the capital's International Festival—now sells more than a million tickets a year for some 28,000 performances throughout the month of August.

Often called the Oatmeal Olympics, the **BRAEMAR GAMES GATHERING (right)** takes place in the Grampian Mountains the first Saturday in September. This tug-of-war is one of many face-offs among brawny men, often kilted, competing to the sound of bagpipes. The queen attends religiously, pronouncing it "a keen and fair contest" every year.

In the enclave of Edinburgh's Old Town, **VICTORIA STREET (below)** is undergoing a renaissance. In its 1600s' heyday, a dozen people shared a bed in these old stone tenements. Today, young professionals have taken over the properties, yet many of the original businesses are still thriving.

When St. Columba sailed across **LOCH NESS** in 565 A.D., he became the first person to allegedly behold the lake's resident monster. Since then, dozens of eyewitnesses have claimed to catch sight of Nessie—one very old beast by now, after 1,500 years. Whether or not she exists, Nessie is Scotland's most famous resident. Even hardened skeptics can't resist scanning the water surface, watching for a head to rise from the murky depths. See it?

© David Cooknell/Alamy

Frommer's®

Scotland

10th Edition

by Darwin Porter & Danforth Prince

Here's what the critics say about Frommer's:

"Amazingly easy to use. Very portable, very complete."

—Booklist

"Detailed, accurate, and easy-to-read information for all price ranges."
—Glamour Magazine

"Hotel information is close to encyclopedic."

—Des Moines Sunday Register

"Frommer's Guides have a way of giving you a real feel for a place."
—Knight Ridder Newspapers

Wiley Publishing, Inc.

Published by:

Wiley Publishing, Inc.
111 River St.
Hoboken, NJ 07030-5774

ISBN: 978-0-470-18187-4

Editor: Christina Summers
Production Editor: Suzanna R. Thompson
Cartographer: Roberta Stockwell
Photo Editor: Richard Fox
Anniversary Logo Design: Richard Pacifico
Production by Wiley Indianapolis Composition Services

Front cover photo: Man playing bagpipes, wearing traditional Scottish dress
Back cover photo: Argyll: Kilchurn Castle

Contents

12   The Hebridean Islands   363

13   The Orkney & Shetland Islands   402

Appendix: Scotland in Depth   432

Index   449

List of Maps

About the Authors

An experienced team of veteran travel writers, **Darwin Porter** and **Danforth Prince** have produced numerous titles for Frommer's, including best-selling guides to Italy, France, the Caribbean, England, Germany, and Portugal. A noted Hollywood biographer, Porter is the author of *Brando Unzipped* and *Jacko: His Rise and Fall,* which documents the saga of Michael Jackson. Porter is also a widely respected film critic, entertainment columnist, and radio commentator, with broadcasts heard in all 50 states. Prince, formerly of the *New York Times* Paris bureau, is president of Blood Moon Productions (www.BloodMoonProductions. com) and other media-related firms.

An Invitation to the Reader

In researching this book, we discovered many wonderful places—hotels, restaurants, shops, and more. We're sure you'll find others. Please tell us about them, so we can share the information with your fellow travelers in upcoming editions. If you were disappointed with a recommendation, we'd love to know that, too. Please write to:

Frommer's Scotland, 10th Edition
Wiley Publishing, Inc. • 111 River St. • Hoboken, NJ 07030-5774

An Additional Note

Please be advised that travel information is subject to change at any time—and this is especially true of prices. We therefore suggest that you write or call ahead for confirmation when making your travel plans. The authors, editors, and publisher cannot be held responsible for the experiences of readers while traveling. Your safety is important to us, however, so we encourage you to stay alert and be aware of your surroundings. Keep a close eye on cameras, purses, and wallets, all favorite targets of thieves and pickpockets.

Other Great Guides for Your Trip:

Scotland For Dummies
Frommer's Britain's Best-Loved Driving Tours
Frommer's Edinburgh & Glasgow
Frommer's European Cruises & Ports of Call

Frommer's Star Ratings, Icons & Abbreviations

Every hotel, restaurant, and attraction listing in this guide has been ranked for quality, value, service, amenities, and special features using a **star-rating system.** In country, state, and regional guides, we also rate towns and regions to help you narrow down your choices and budget your time accordingly. Hotels and restaurants are rated on a scale of zero (recommended) to three stars (exceptional). Attractions, shopping, nightlife, towns, and regions are rated according to the following scale: zero stars (recommended), one star (highly recommended), two stars (very highly recommended), and three stars (must-see).

In addition to the star-rating system, we also use **seven feature icons** that point you to the great deals, in-the-know advice, and unique experiences that separate travelers from tourists. Throughout the book, look for:

Finds	Special finds—those places only insiders know about
Fun Fact	Fun facts—details that make travelers more informed and their trips more fun
Kids	Best bets for kids and advice for the whole family
Moments	Special moments—those experiences that memories are made of
Overrated	Places or experiences not worth your time or money
Tips	Insider tips—great ways to save time and money
Value	Great values—where to get the best deals

The following **abbreviations** are used for credit cards:

AE	American Express	DISC	Discover	V	Visa
DC	Diners Club	MC	MasterCard		

Frommers.com

Now that you have this guidebook to help you plan a great trip, visit our website at **www. frommers.com** for additional travel information on more than 3,600 destinations. We update features regularly to give you instant access to the most current trip-planning information available. At Frommers.com, you'll find scoops on the best airfares, lodging rates, and car rental bargains. You can even book your travel online through our reliable travel booking partners. Other popular features include:

- Online updates of our most popular guidebooks
- Vacation sweepstakes and contest giveaways
- Newsletters highlighting the hottest travel trends
- Online travel message boards with featured travel discussions

What's New in Scotland

Visitors justifiably flock to Scotland for its medieval castles, dramatic countryside, world-class golf, and Highland Gatherings. But travelers will delight in the country's new offerings, too, many of which incorporate the best of Scotland's past with modern entertainment, luxury, and style. Here are some of the latest developments.

EDINBURGH **Accommodations** The famous hotel **George,** 19–21 George St. (© **0131/225-1251**), broke from its link with the Inter-Continental chain and recently underwent a £12-million restoration, making it better than ever. See p. 85.

The Scotsman, 20 N. Bridge St. (© **0131/556-5565**), installed the best hotel spa in Scotland. It's The Cowshed Spa, taking its name from the original in Somerset, England. Employing organic flower and plant oils, the spa staff uses ingredients blended in-house, which are applied to the scent of rose and jasmine candles. See p. 85.

Old Waverley Hotel, 43 Princes St. (© **0131/556-4648**), has been given a new lease on life under the management of the Kapoor family. They have extensively modernized this relic, the oldest operating hotel in the land. In addition to the rejuvenated bedrooms, drinking and dining facilities have also found vast improvement. See p. 87.

Kew House & Apartments, 1 Kew Terrace (© **0131/313-0700**), lying near a rugby field 1 mile (.6km) west of the center, is one of Edinburgh's most successful Victorian restorations. Each room is individually furnished, and there are also well-furnished apartments that are ideal for families. See p. 88.

In the more affordable range, **Stuart Guest House,** 12 E. Claremont St. (© **0131/557-9030**), has been converted from a Georgian town house into an excellent B&B, with the original architectural features intact. See p. 89.

Dining Emerging as the best Indian restaurant in town, **Roti,** 70 Rose St. (© **0131/225-1233**), is installed behind a Georgian town house facade. Its owner, former head chef aboard the Queen's *Britannia* royal yacht, is in charge. He uses the best of regional produce from Scotland and exotic spices from India to produce a superb cuisine, with many dishes based on "secrets" of his home country. See p. 98.

Shopping The queen of cashmere, **Brenda Robertson** opened a store at 13A Dundas St. (© **0131/557-8118**), where she sells the city's finest collection of cashmeres, often in vibrant colors. To make these couture styles, she employs some of the most skilled artisans in Scotland. See p. 117.

After Dark Prince William made **Opal Lounge,** 51A George St. (© **0131/226-2275**), famous when he visited frequently while a student at St. Andrews. Even though he's gone, this chic bar has emerged as *the* place to be seen in Edinburgh, attracting a 20s and 30s crowd. There is a dance floor plus many hidden nooks where you can get to know your partner of the evening a lot better. See p. 123.

ST. ANDREWS   At the famous old golf hotel here, **St. Andrews Old Course Hotel,** Old Station Rd. (© **01334/ 474-371**), the Kohler company has opened its first "Waters Spa" outside of its flagship center in Wisconsin. The deluxe spa uses "remineralizing treatments" that involve freeze-dried seawater and other ingredients. See p. 258.

ABERYFOLE   A country house overlooking Loch Ard, **Forest Hills,** Kinlochard (© **0870/194-2105**), won "The Scottish Family Hotel of the Year" award in 2007. In the foothills of the Trossachs, arguably the most beautiful part of Scotland, the resort stands in 10 hectares (25 acres) of private grounds. With its excellent local cuisine and beautifully restored bedrooms, it is a sure-fire winner. See p. 274.

GLASGOW Accommodations   An elegantly restored Edwardian building has been turned into the **ABode Hotel,** 129 Bath St. (© **0141/221-6789**). Renovated from top to bottom with stunning results, it offers a wide variety of bedrooms, including some called "fabulous" that live up to their name. ABode is also the setting for one of Glasgow's most sophisticated restaurants, **Michael Caines** (see below). See p. 178.

Dining   Ayr-born **Brian Maule** at **Chardon d'Or,** 176 W. Regent St. (© **0141/248-3801**), was hailed in 2006 and 2007 as "one of the finest chefs in Scotland." Some serious local foodies call him the finest chef in the land. At the age of 24, he became head chef at Le Gavroche, still considered London's finest restaurant. Today he has returned to his native roots and shares his superlative take on a French and Scottish cuisine with his fellow Glaswegians. Each dish

from his kitchen bears his original and creative stamp. See p. 183.

The celebrated London designer, Sir Terrence Conran, has moved outside of England to open **étain** in The Glass House, Springfield Court, Queen St. (© **0141/225-5630**). His staff serves a superb French and Scottish cuisine in a glamorous setting, using market-fresh regional produce whenever possible. One visitor told us that dining at étain is reason enough to go to Glasgow. See p. 183.

The famous West Country (England) chef, **Michael Caines** at **ABode Glasgow,** in the ABode Hotel (© **0141/ 572-6011**), has expanded northward. In this chic restaurant, he serves some of the city's finest and most refined Continental and Scottish cuisine. He makes use of top-quality regional produce to turn out award-winning dinners. See p. 187.

KINTYRE PENINSULA   Scotland's newest long-distance walk, the **Kintyre Way,** opened in 2006, stretching for 113km (90 miles), beginning in the town of Tarbert in the north of the peninsula and stretching to the village of Southend in the south. It takes most hikers anywhere from 4 to 7 days to walk this stunning and scenic route. Along the way, they pass much wildlife, especially birds inhabiting the coastline. See p. 224.

BRAEMAR   This town in Grampian has long been celebrated for its **Braemar Castle** (© **01339/741-219**), attracting visitors from all over the world. However, at presstime, the castle had shut down for much-needed renovations, with no date announced for reopening. Check with tourist authorities in Scotland before making a special trip here to see this venerated old castle. See p. 313.

ISLE OF MULL   The restored **Glengorm Castle,** Route B8073 (© **01688/ 302-321**), has been turned into the premier B&B on this historic island. Built in

1860, it rents out only five handsomely furnished bedrooms, so reserve well in advance. The castle stands on the northern tip of the island near Tobermory, overlooking the Atlantic. See p. 383.

JOHN O'GROATS   A legacy of the late Queen Mother, **Castle of Mey,** lying 9.6km (6 miles) west of John o' Groats on A836 (© **01847/851-473**), has been opened to the public. Her Majesty restored the castle when she discovered that it was going to be abandoned in 1952, and came here every summer of her life. Today that tradition is carried on by her heir, Prince Charles. See p. 359.

1

The Best of Scotland

Scotland is permeated with legend and romance. Its ruined castles standing amid fields of heather and bracken bespeak a past of heroic struggle. Its two great cities—the ancient seat of Scottish royalty, Edinburgh, and even more ancient Glasgow, boasting Victorian splendor—are among Europe's most dynamic centers. And equally alluring is the picturesque countryside, with Highlands, mountains, lochs, salmon-filled rivers, incomparable golf courses, and so much more.

1 The Best Travel Experiences

- **Checking Out the Local Pub:** You're in a Scottish pub, talking to the bartender and choosing from a dizzying array of single-malt whiskies. Perhaps the wind is blowing fitfully outside, causing the wooden sign to creak above the battered door, and a fire is flickering against the blackened bricks of the old fireplace. As the evening wanes and you've established common ground with the locals, you'll realize you're having one of your most authentic Scottish experiences. We list our favorite pubs in the destination chapters that follow.

- **Visiting Edinburgh at Festival Time:** The Edinburgh International Festival has become one of Europe's most prestigious arts festivals. From mid-August to early September, a host of singers, dancers, musicians, and actors descends on the city, infusing it with a kind of manic creative energy. If you're planning to sample the many offerings, get your tickets well in advance, and make your hotel and flight reservations early. Call ℂ **0131/473-2000** or go to www.eif.co.uk. See p. 122.

- **Haunting the Castles:** The land of Macbeth contains more castles than anywhere else in the world. Many are in ruins, but dozens of the foreboding royal dwellings are intact and open to the public. Some, such as **Culzean** (p. 211), built by Robert Adam, are architectural masterpieces filled with paintings and antiques. Travelers who can't get enough of Scotland's castles should consider staying in one of the many relics that have been converted into comfortable, though sometimes drafty, hotels.

- **Horseback Riding Through the Highlands & Argyll:** There's nothing like an equestrian excursion through the Highlands' fragrant heather and over its lichen-covered rocks. One of Scotland's biggest stables is the **Highland Riding Centre,** Drumnadrochit (ℂ **01456/450-220**). See p. 336. For scenic rides across the moors, Highlands, and headlands of the Argyll, try the **Ardfern Riding Centre,** Loch Gilphead (ℂ **01852/500-632**). See p. 221.

- **Cruising Along the Caledonian Canal:** In 1822, a group of enterprising Scots connected three of the Highlands' longest lakes (lochs Ness, Lochy, and Oich) with a canal linking Britain's east and west coasts. Since then, barges have hauled everything from grain to building supplies without having to negotiate the wild storms off Scotland's northernmost tips. Now cabin cruisers tote a different kind of cargo along the Caledonian Canal: people seeking a spectacular waterborne view of the countryside that was tamed centuries ago by the Camerons, the Stewarts, and the Mac-Donalds. **Caley Cruisers,** based in Inverness (© **01463/236-328;** www.caleycruisers.co.uk), rents out skippered-boats by the week. See p. 337.

- **Attending a Highland Game:** Unlike any other sporting event, a Highland Game emphasizes clannish traditions rather than athletic dexterity, and the centerpiece is usually an exhibition of brute strength (tossing logs and the like). Most visitors show up for the men in kilts, the bagpipe playing, the pomp and circumstance, and the general celebration of all things Scottish. The best known (and most widely televised) of the events is Braemar's **Royal Highland Gathering,** held near Balmoral Castle in late August or early September. For details, call the **Braemar Tourist Office** (© **01339/741-600**). See p. 313.

- **Ferrying to the Isle of Iona:** It's an otherworldly rock, one of Europe's most evocative holy places, anchored solidly among the Hebrides off Scotland's west coast. St. Columba established Iona as a Christian center in A.D. 563, and used it as a base for converting Scotland. You'll find a ruined Benedictine nunnery and a fully restored cathedral where 50 Scottish kings were buried during the early Middle Ages. Hundreds of Celtic crosses once adorned Iona; today, only three of the originals remain. Now part of the National Trust, the island is home to an ecumenical group dedicated to the perpetuation of Christian ideals. Reaching Iona requires a 10-minute ferry ride from the hamlet of Fionnphort, on the nearby island of Mull. See p. 388.

- **Exploring the Orkneys:** Archaeologists say the Orkneys, an archipelago comprising some 70 islands, hold the richest trove of prehistoric monuments in the British Isles—an average of three sites per square mile. Ornithologists claim that about 16% of all winged animals in the United Kingdom reside here, and linguists have documented an ancient dialect that still uses Viking terms. Northwest of the Scottish mainland, closer to Oslo than to faraway London, these islands are on the same latitude as St. Petersburg but much more exposed to the raging gales of the North Sea. The late-spring sunsets and the aurora borealis have been called mystical, and in midsummer the sun remains above the horizon for 18 hours a day. An equivalent twilight—and even total darkness—envelops the islands in winter. Only 19 of the Orkneys are inhabited; the others, often drenched with rain, seem to float above primordial seas. See "The Orkney Islands: An Archaeological Garden" in chapter 13.

2 The Best Golf

For full details about golfing in Scotland, see "Teeing Off: Golfing in Scotland" in chapter 3.

- **Turnberry Hotel Golf Courses** (Ayrshire; © **01655/334-032**): Established in 1903, the Ailsa is one of the world's preeminent courses. It's not, however, for the faint of heart—although the links are verdant, many are marked by bunkers, salt-resistant rough grasses, and powerful winds blasting in from the nearby ocean. See p. 211.

Scotland

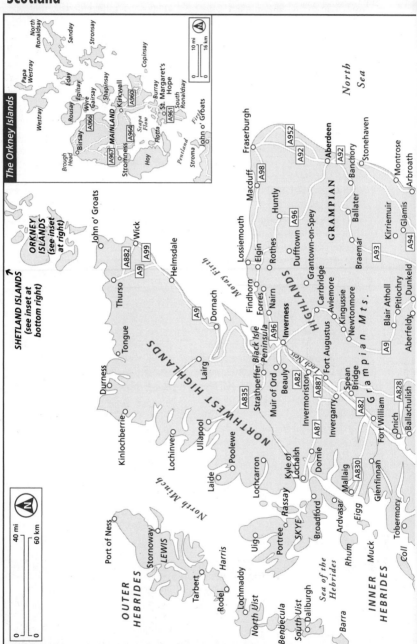

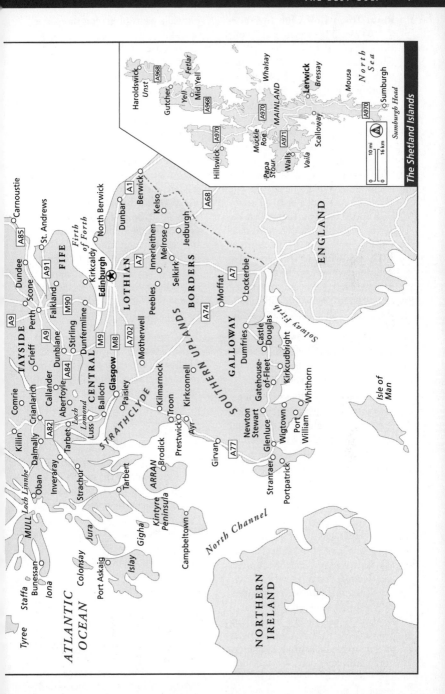

The Shetland Islands

- **Royal Troon Golf Club** (Ayrshire; *©* **01292/311-555**): Laid out along lines paralleling the Firth of Clyde, this club fills a flat lowland terrain whose fairways are almost breathtakingly green despite their foundations on sandy soil. This is lowland Scotland at its most seductive, a 7,097-yard course (one of Scotland's longest), with a par of 71. See p. 213.
- **Old Course** (St. Andrews; *©* **01334/466-666**): Sometime during the late 14th century, a group of bored aristocrats started hitting a ball around the nearby meadows. By the time their activities were officially recorded in 1552, the bylaws of the game were well on their way to being part of Scotland's lore. Old Course is indeed a golf shrine, one whose difficulty is shaped not only by nature but by the erstwhile paths of grazing sheep. See p. 254.
- **Carnoustie Golf Links** (Tayside; *©* **01241/802-270**): Site of six British Opens, Carnoustie is considerably more difficult than most players anticipate at first glance. U.S. champions Tom Watson and Gary Player have referred to it as their favorite, and much of the town of Carnoustie was built because of the stream of world-class golfers who migrated here. See p. 57.
- **Royal Dornoch Golf Club** (Sutherland; *©* **01862/810-219**): Located only 6° south of the Arctic Circle, this is the most northerly of the world's great golf courses. Despite its location, Royal Dornoch enjoys a microclimate more akin to the fens around Norfolk, England, than to the Arctic. See p. 353.

3 The Best Fishing

For more details about fishing in Scotland, see "Fishing" in chapter 3.

- **The Borders & Galloway Regions:** Sea fishing is pure heaven in the Solway Firth, especially near Port William and Portpatrick villages, in the vicinity of Loch Ryan, and also along the shore of the Isle of Whithorn. The elusive salmon is best pursued along the River Tweed, and the lesser-known hill lochans are ideal for trout fishermen. Local tourist offices distribute two helpful guides: *A Comprehensive Guide to Scottish Borders Angling* and *Castabout Anglers Guide to Dumfries and Galloway.* See chapter 6.
- **Argyll & the Southern Hebrides:** This much-visited area in western Scotland is split in two by the long peninsula of Kintyre. The topography is decidedly northern Atlantic, distinguished by open sea and loch, and the Firth of Clyde separates the region from the Inner Hebrides. Along with about 50 prime freshwater-angling sites, Argyll and the Southern Hebrides contain some two dozen villages with fantastic sea fishing. See chapter 8.
- **Tayside:** The northeast section of Scotland is filled not only with major rivers—the Don, Dee, Ythan, and Deverson—but with smaller ones, too, like the Ugie, all ideal for salmon fishing. Besides the rivers, numerous estuaries and lochs make this one of the country's best areas for game fishing. Local tourist offices keep abreast of the details about boat rentals and permit prices, and some country hotels offer fishing packages. See chapter 10.
- **The Great Glen:** Anglers from all over the world flock to the Great Glen, with its many lochs and rivers, to cast their flies in search of Scottish trout and salmon. Sea fishing from boat or shore is also permitted.

Salmon season runs from February to September; brown trout season is mid-March to early October. Anglers can catch rainbow trout here year-round. See chapter 11.

- **Sutherland & Northern Highlands:** Sutherland's myriad lochs provide endless possibilities for anglers. Trout fishing is the big lure, and local tourist offices will tell you all about boats and permits. Not only is the fishing superb, but your hotel cook may also prepare your catch for you. See chapter 11.

- **The Orkney Islands:** These northern islands are major fishing grounds. At least seven outfitters offer charters, and you can rent equipment. Loch fishing is also a popular pastime in the Orkneys, especially in Loch of Stenness and Loch of Harray, where hopeful anglers go after salmon, trout, sea trout, and salmon trout, although porbeagle shark, cod, halibut, bass, hake, skate, and turbot also turn up. See chapter 13.

4 The Best Countryside Drives

- **The Valley of the Tweed:** The waters originate in Scotland, define the border with England for part of their length, and are noted for some of Britain's top salmon fishing. Ruins of once-wealthy abbeys dot the landscape like beacons of long-lost power and prestige. Most travelers begin in Kelso and move west through Dryburgh, Selkirk, Melrose, Innerleithen, and Peebles. Although the total distance is less than 81km (50 miles), with a bit of backtracking en route, the many historic sites call for at least a full day's exploration. See chapter 6.

- **The Isle of Arran:** Situated off Scotland's southwestern edge, Arran combines radically different climates and topographies in a relatively small space. Lush, temperate vegetation grows in its southern tier—which is warmed by the Gulf Stream—while the moors and hills of its northern edge are as wild and craggy as the Highlands. You'll find prehistoric monuments, a redsandstone pile beloved by medievalists, and sweeping vistas of Northern Ireland. Allow half a day, not including stopover times, for the 90km (56-mile) circumnavigation of the island's coastal road. See "The Isle of Arran: Scotland in Miniature" in chapter 8.

- **The Lochs & Mountains South of Oban:** In this solitary but dramatic area are Scotland's longest freshwater lake (Loch Awe), one of its longest saltwater fjords (Loch Fyne), some of its most historic buildings (Kilchurn Castle, Carnasserie Castle, and the Kilmartin Church), and one of its most notorious battlefields (the slopes of Ben Cruachan). Locals refer to it as the Hinterlands near Oban, though the 140km (87-mile) route follows an excellent network of highways along the jagged coast. Major towns through which it passes are Dalmally, Inveraray, Lochgilphead, and Oban. See chapter 8.

- **The Trossachs:** Located at the narrowest point of the mainland, just north of Glasgow, the Trossachs have been famous for their scenery since Queen Victoria called them lovely in 1869. Mystery seems to shroud the waters of lochs Lomond and Katrine. According to legend, the region's highest mountain, Ben Venue, is the traditional meeting point for Scotland's goblins. Ruled for generations by the MacGregor clan, this is the setting of Sir Walter Scott's *Rob Roy* and *The Lady of the Lake*. A tour through the region, beginning at

Callander and meandering through Aberfoyle, Stronachlacher, and Inversnaid, should take about half a day. In summer, expect lots of traffic, often from tour buses. See chapter 9.

- **The Road to the Isles (Hwy. A830):** It begins in Fort William, western terminus of the Caledonian Canal, and ends at Mallaig, the departure point for ferries servicing several offshore islands, including Mull, 74km

(46 miles) northwest. Along the way, it passes both the highest mountains in Britain and one of the Victorian Age's engineering triumphs—Neptune's Staircase, a network of eight lochs that raise the level of the canal 19m (64 ft.) in a span of less than 455m (1,500 ft.). Although summer traffic can be heavy, services en route are scarce, so start with a full tank of gas. See chapters 11 and 12.

5 The Best Bike Rides

For details on biking around the country, see "Biking, Walking & Other Outdoor Pursuits" in chapter 3.

- **The Galloway Region:** Southwestern Scotland doesn't draw the most visitors, but its beauty is unrivaled. A land of fields, verdant forests, and mist-shrouded hills, Galloway offers endless biking possibilities. All tourist offices in the area carry *Cycling in Dumfries and Galloway,* which describes the best routes. A free leaflet published by the Scottish Forest Enterprise gives trail routes through the various forests. See chapter 6.

- **The Isle of Arran:** The largest of the Clyde Islands, Arran has been called "Scotland in miniature." And indeed, if you don't have time to see the whole country, you can get a preview of its various regions by biking this island. The northern part is mountainous like the Highlands, while the south, with scenery akin to the Borders, resembles the Lowlands. The full circuit around the island takes about 9 hours. The tourist office distributes the free *Cycling on Arran,* which indicates the best routes. See "Exploring the Island" in chapter 8.

- **The Trossachs:** Scotland's most scenic stretch for biking (not to mention for driving and bucolic walks) is the Trossachs, famed as Rob Roy MacGregor country. The ideal biking spot is along Loch Katrine, 16km (10 miles) long and 3km (2 miles) at its widest. See chapter 9.

- **Glencoe:** Site of a famous 1692 massacre, Glencoe features stark and grandiose mountain scenery. Rent a bike in the village and embark on an adventure, though you're likely to get rained on, as some 100 inches of rain a year are recorded. But as one local said, "Biking through Glencoe in the rain is when it's at its most mystical—we Scots have done that for years." See "Glencoe: Scenery & Sorrow" in chapter 11.

- **The Isle of Skye:** Part of the Hebrides, Skye is the land of the Cuillins, a brooding mountain range you see at every turn as you pedal along. The most unusual place to bike is the 32km (20-mile) Trotternish Peninsula. It's known for its odd rock formations, and its coastal road passes an area of beautiful but often rocky seascapes, opening onto Loch Snizort and the Sound of Raasay. See chapter 12.

6 The Best Hikes

- **The Southern Upland Way:** Rivaling the West Highland Way (see below), this is the second of Scotland's great walks. The footpath begins at Portpatrick and runs 341km (212 miles) along the southwest coast to Cockburnspath, on the east coast. It passes through some of the most dramatic scenery in the Borders, including Galloway Forest Park. Contact the **Edinburgh & Scotland Information Centre,** Princes Mall, 3 Princes St., Edinburgh (© **0131/473-3800**). See chapter 6.

- **East Neuk:** Directly south of St. Andrews lie some of Scotland's loveliest fishing villages, collectively known as East Neuk. The most enchanting walk is between the villages of Pittenweem and Anstruther. It's often breezy here, with wind from the sea, so dress accordingly. The path begins at the bottom of West Braes, a cul-de-sac off the main road in Anstruther. See chapter 9.

- **The Trossachs:** The Trossachs Trail extends from Loch Lomond, in the west, to Callander, in the east, and also from Doune to Aberfoyle and the Lord Ard Forest, to the south. In the north, it's bounded by the Crianlarich Hills and Balquhidder, the site of Rob Roy's grave. Ever since Sir Walter Scott published *The Lady of the Lake* and *Rob Roy,* the area has attracted hikers in search of unspoiled natural beauty. Our favorite start for walks is the village of Brig o' Turk, between lochs Achray and Venachar, at the foot of Glen Finglas. From here you can set out in any direction, including one signposted toward the Achray Forest. There's also the Glen Finglas circular walk, and many hikers leave Brig o' Turk heading for Balquhidder via Glen Finglas. See "Callander & a Trio of Lochs" in chapter 9.

- **The West Highland Way:** Unquestionably one of Scotland's great walks, the West Highland Way begins north of Glasgow, in Milngavie. The footpath stretches 153km (95 miles) northward along Loch Lomond, going through Glencoe to Fort William and eventually to Ben Nevis, Britain's highest mountain. Even if you only want to walk part of this path, you need to make plans in advance. Contact the **Edinburgh & Scotland Information Centre,** Princes Mall, 3 Princes St., Edinburgh (© **0131/473-3800**). See p. 206.

- **Ben Nevis:** Six kilometers (4 miles) southeast of the town of Fort William looms Ben Nevis, Britain's highest mountain. At 1,342m (4,406 ft.), the snow-capped granite mass dominates this entire region of Scotland. This trip can be done in a day, but you'll need to massage your feet in the evening at a local pub. See chapter 11.

7 The Best Castles & Palaces

- **Edinburgh Castle** (Edinburgh): Few other buildings symbolize the grandeur of an independent Scotland as clearly as this one. Begun around A.D. 1000 on a hilltop high above the rest of Edinburgh, it witnessed some of the bloodiest and most treacherous events in Scottish history, including a doomed 1573 defense by Kirkaldy of Grange in the name of Mary Queen of Scots. See p. 102.

- **Palace of Holyroodhouse** (Edinburgh): Throughout the clan battles for independence from England, this palace served as a pawn between opposing forces. In its changing fortunes, it has housed a strange assortment of monarchs involved in traumatic events: Mary Queen of Scots, Bonnie Prince Charlie, James VII (before his ascendancy to the throne), and French King Charles X (on his forced abdication after an 1830 revolution). The building's present form dates from the late 1600s, when it was rebuilt in a dignified neo-Palladian style. Today, Holyrood-house is one of Queen Elizabeth's official residences. See p. 107.

- **Drumlanrig Castle** (Dumfries): Begun in 1679, this castle took 12 years to build and so much money that its patron, the third earl and first duke of Queensbury, complained that he deeply resented its existence. Later, it was embroiled in dynastic inheritance scandals worthy of a Gothic novel. One of the most prestigious buildings in Scotland, it houses the antiques and artwork of four illustrious families. See p. 157.

- **Culzean Castle** (near Maybole): Designed for comfort and prestige, this castle was built in the late 1700s by Scotland's most celebrated architect, Robert Adam, as a replacement for a dark, dank tower that had stood for longer than anyone could remember. Culzean was donated to the National Trust for Scotland just after World War II. A suite was granted to General Eisenhower for his lifetime use, in gratitude for his role in staving off a foreign invasion of Britain. See p. 211.

- **Stirling Castle** (Stirling): Stirling is a triumph of Renaissance ornamentation, a startling contrast to the severe bulk of many other Scottish castles. Despite its beauty, after its completion in 1540 the castle was one of the most impregnable fortresses in the British Isles, thanks partly to its position on a rocky crag. See p. 262.

- **Scone Palace** (Scone): As early as A.D. 900, Scottish kings were crowned here on a lump of granite so imbued with ancient magic that, in the 13th century, the English hauled it off to Westminster Abbey. (The Stone of Scone was returned to Scotland in 1996 and is now found in Edinburgh Castle.) The palace you see today was rebuilt in 1802 from ruins that incorporated a 1580 structure with stones laid during the dim early days of Scottish and Pictish union. See p. 295.

- **Glamis Castle** (Glamis): This castle's core was built for defense against rival clans during the 1400s, but over the centuries it evolved into a luxurious dwelling. The seat of the same family since 1372, Glamis is said to be haunted by the ghost of Lady Glamis, a former owner, whom James V had burnt as a witch when she resisted his annexation of her castle. It also figured into the ambitions of Macbeth, thane of Glamis. See p. 307.

- **Crathes Castle & Gardens** (Grampian): Crathes evokes the luxury of a 15th- and 16th-century Scottish laird. The style focuses on high heraldry, with frequent references to the persistent Scottish hope of an enduring independence. The gardens' massive yew hedges were originally planted in 1702. See p. 290.

- **Balmoral Castle** (Ballater): Scotland offers far greater castles to explore, but Balmoral, the rebuilt castle of Prince Albert and Queen Victoria, draws hordes of visitors, who no doubt hope to glimpse Prince William. That's because it's still the Scottish residence of the queen. Although inside you can visit only the ballroom, the sprawling manicured grounds and gardens also await you. See p. 310.

- **Braemar Castle** (Grampian): Built by the earl of Mar in 1628 as a hunting lodge, Braemar was burned to the ground, and then rebuilt by Farquharson of Invercauld, an ancestor of the present owner. It's often photographed as a symbol of Scottish grandeur and the well-upholstered aristocratic life. See p. 313.

- **Cawdor Castle** (Cawdor): From its heavily fortified origins in the 1300s, Cawdor evolved into the Campbell clan's luxurious seat. According to legend and Shakespearean plot lines, three witches promised this castle to Macbeth to tempt him into the deeds that led to his destruction. See p. 348.

8 The Best Cathedrals

- **Melrose Abbey** (the Borders): If it weren't for the abbey's location in the frequently devastated Borders, this would be one of the world's most spectacular ecclesiastical complexes. Founded in the 1100s, Melrose acquired vast wealth and was the target of its covetous enemies; it was burned and rebuilt several times before the Protestant takeover of Scotland. Today, it's one of the world's most beautiful ruins, a site immortalized by Robert Burns, who advised people to visit it only by moonlight. See p. 145.

- **Cathedral of St. Kentigern** (Glasgow): In the 7th century, St. Mungo built a wooden structure here, intending it to be his headquarters and eventual tomb. It burned down but was rebuilt in the 1300s. St. Kentigern is mainland Scotland's only complete medieval cathedral, with a form based extensively on the pointed arch. In the 1600s, the Calvinists stripped it of anything hinting at papist idolatry, though a remarkable set of sculptures atop its stone nave screen, said to be unique in Scotland, still represent the seven deadly sins. See p. 195.

- **Dunfermline Abbey and Palace** (Fife): During the 1100s, in its role as Scotland's Westminster Abbey, Dunfermline became one of Europe's wealthiest churches. Three kings of Scotland were born here, and 22 members of the Scottish royal family were buried here. In the early 1800s, its ruined premises were partially restored to what you see today. Several years later, Andrew Carnegie, a markedly different kind of benefactor, was born within the cathedral's shadow. See p. 243.

- **Dunblane Cathedral** (Fife): Partly because the site had been holy since the days of the Celts, David I founded a church here in 1150. Despite later alterations and additions, Dunblane is still one of the country's best examples of Gothic architecture from the 1200s. See p. 267.

- **St. Magnus Cathedral** (the Orkney Islands): The most spectacular medieval building in the Orkneys, St. Magnus features an odd imposition of the Norman Gothic style on a territory administered during the time of its construction (the 1100s) by the Norwegians. The bodies of St. Magnus, patron saint of the Orkneys, and his nephew Earl Rognvald, the church's builder, are buried inside. See p. 405.

9 The Best Ruins

- **Linlithgow Palace** (Lothian): These ruins brood over an island in a loch, an unhappy vestige of what was the most glamorous royal residence during Scotland's golden age of independence, in the early 1500s. Mary Queen of Scots was born here, but tragedy seemed to permeate the palace, as roofs collapsed from lack of maintenance, and early deaths in the royal family hastened an inevitable union of Scotland with England. In 1745, after Linlithgow was occupied by Bonnie Prince Charlie and his troops, a mysterious fire swept over the palace. See p. 126.

- **Dryburgh Abbey** (the Borders): Begun in 1150 along a meandering curve of the River Tweed, Dryburgh was once home to thousands of monks who transformed the surrounding forests into arable fields, and drained many local swamps. The abbey's location, astride the much-troubled border with England, resulted in its destruction in three episodes (1322, 1385, and 1544), the last of which included the burning of the nearby village (Dryburgh). Today, the red-sandstone rocks are dim reminders of a long-ago monastic age. See p. 143.

- **Elgin Cathedral** (Grampian): This cathedral was built during the 1100s, and although many other churches were erected in Scotland at the time, Elgin was reputedly the most beautiful. Burned and rebuilt twice (in 1290 and 1370), it—along with many other Catholic churches—deteriorated after the Reformation; the belfry collapsed in 1711, shattering most of the roof and some of the walls. Efforts were undertaken to repair the damage, yet the place remains an evocative ruin. See p. 321.

- **Skara Brae** (the Orkney Islands): Last occupied around 2500 B.C., and far humbler than the feudal castles you'll find on the Scottish mainland, this cluster of fortified stone buildings is the best-preserved Neolithic village in northwestern Europe. Buried beneath sand for thousands of years, Skara Brae was uncovered by a storm in 1850. See p. 409.

10 The Best Museums

- **National Gallery of Scotland** (Edinburgh): This museum boasts a small but choice collection whose presence in Edinburgh is firmly entwined with the city's self-image as the cultural capital of Scotland. (Glaswegians, however, will happily dispute that idea.) Gallery highlights include works by Velázquez, Zurbarán, Verrocchio, del Sarto, and Cézanne. See p. 109.

- **National Museum of Scotland** (Edinburgh): In 1998, the collections of the Royal Museum of Scotland and the National Museum of Antiquities were united into a coherent whole. Here you'll find everything you ever wanted to know about Scotland, from prehistory to the Industrial Age. Among its myriad items, the museum has a milk bottle once carried by Sean Connery and a 2.9-billion-year-old rock from the Isle of South Uist. See p. 110.

- **The Burrell Collection** (Glasgow): Sir William Burrell (1861–1958), a wealthy industrialist who devoted much of his life to accumulating art, is responsible for this collection. Set in a postmodern building in a suburb of Glasgow, it's one of Scotland's most admired museums, with a strong focus on medieval art, 19th-century French paintings, and Chinese ceramics. See p. 191.

- **Hunterian Art Gallery** (Glasgow): This museum owns much of the artistic estate of James McNeill Whistler, as well as a re-creation of the home of Scotland's most famous designer, Charles Rennie Mackintosh. On display are grand oils by Whistler, Rubens, and Rembrandt, not to mention one of the country's best collections of 19th-century Scottish paintings. See p. 194.

- **Aberdeen Art Gallery** (Aberdeen): A treasure-trove of art from all over the world, this prestigious gallery has exhibits ranging from the 1700s to the present, from Hogarth to Reynolds to Picasso. The museum is also home to the most important temporary exhibits in northeast Scotland. See p. 282.

11 The Best Luxury Hotels

- **The Howard** (Edinburgh; © **0131/ 557-3500;** www.thehoward.com): Three adjacent Georgian-style town houses in an upscale neighborhood have undergone millions of pounds' worth of renovations, creating the most alluring accommodations in a city filled with fine hotels. A restaurant in one of the cellars serves meals inspired by Scottish traditions. See p. 85.

- **Holyrood Hotel** (Edinburgh; © 0131/550-4500; www.holyrood-hotel.com): This deluxe charmer launched itself into the millennium when it was designated "Hotel of the Year in Scotland" by the Automobile Association. Located near the new Scottish Parliament, the Holyrood is a bastion of comfort with luxury furnishings. See p. 91.

- **The Malmaison** (Leith, outside Edinburgh; © **0131/468-5000;** www.malmaison.com): Malmaison is at the port of Leith, about a 15-minute ride northeast of Edinburgh's center. Named after Joséphine's mansion outside Paris, it celebrates the Auld Alliance of France and Scotland, and was created from a 1900 Victorian building. Malmaison once housed indigent seamen, but today it's an oasis of chic. See p. 93.

- **Greywalls Hotel** (East Lothian; © **01620/842-144;** www.greywalls. co.uk): Although Sir Edward Lutyens designed dozens of opulent Edwardian homes throughout Britain, this is one of the few that's been converted into a hotel. Built in 1901 in what architects praise as perfect harmony with its setting, Greywalls features walled gardens designed by the doyenne of eccentric turn-of-the-20th-century landscape architects, Gertrude Jekyll. This national treasure, representing the Empire's most ostentatious days, is eccentric but eminently comfortable. See p. 129.

- **Knockinaam Lodge** (Portpatrick; © **01776/810-471;** www.knockinaam lodge.com): Memories of Winston Churchill's clandestine meetings with General Eisenhower, a beacon of hope during the darkest days of World War II, pervade the Knockinaam. Today, the late-Victorian country house is as well upholstered and wryly sedate as you'd expect from a top-notch hotel with such a pedigree. Its restaurant is always included on critics' lists of the best of Scotland. See p. 165.

- **Hotel du Vin** (Glasgow; © **0141/ 339-2001;** www.onedevonshire gardens.com): This is the best-groomed building in a neighborhood filled with similar sandstone-fronted town houses. Ring the doorbell and an Edwardian-costumed maid will answer, curtsy, and usher you inside as if you're an extra in a Merchant-Ivory film. This re-creation of a high-bourgeois Scottish home from the early 1900s boasts antique furnishings and discreetly concealed modern comforts. See p. 180.

- **Fairmont St. Andrews Bay Golf Resort & Spa** (St. Andrews; © **01334/837-000;** www.fairmont. com): This is the premier government-rated five-star hotel of eastern Scotland, lying right outside "the home of golf," as the town of St. Andrews is so often called. Boasting two championship golf courses, the finest rooms and cuisine in the area, and a to-die-for spa and health club, the resort is the creation of two entrepreneurs from the southern U.S. state of Georgia. Did we mention that Prince William is a member of the health club? See p. 256.

- **The Gleneagles Hotel** (Auchterarder; $\textcircled{C}$ **01764/662-231;** www.gleneagles.com): This is Britain's greatest golf hotel, a government-rated five-star resort that also offers such extras as a deluxe spa and hunting excursions. Better than ever after major renovations and expansion, it is also a gourmet citadel with one of Scotland's most awarded chefs, Andrew Fairlie, overseeing those pots and pans. See p. 297.

- **Kinnaird Estate** (Dunkeld; $\textcircled{C}$ **01796/482-440;** www.kinnairdestate.com): An 18th-century hunting lodge for the duke of Atholl, Kinnaird dominates an enormous estate—3,646 hectares (9,000 acres) of moor, mountain, and forest. You'll find all the accouterments of a British country house in high-Edwardian style. The supremely comfortable interiors contrast dramatically with the tempests of the great outdoors, and the dining room is among the finest in Scotland. See p. 300.

- **Inverlochy Castle** (near Fort William; $\textcircled{C}$ **01397/702-177;** www.inverlochycastlehotel.com): This castle was built in 1863 by Lord Abinger in a style that set into stone the most high-blown hopes of Scottish Romantics. Today, lovers can follow in the footsteps of Queen Victoria amid the frescoed walls of this Scottish baronial hideaway. See p. 329.

- **Culloden House** (Inverness; $\textcircled{C}$ **01463/790-461;** www.cullodenhouse.co.uk): If you'd like to sleep where Bonnie Prince Charlie did, head for this Adam-style Georgian mansion on 16 hectares (40 acres) of parkland. Scottish tradition appears at every turn, from the grand lounge to the sound of a bagpiper on the grounds. Dinner in the Adam Room is an elegant affair, with French culinary skills applied to the finest Scottish produce. See p. 342.

- **Carnegie Club at Skibo Castle** (Dornoch; $\textcircled{C}$ **01862/894-600;** www.carnegieclub.co.uk): Andrew Carnegie called his glorious Highland castle and estate Heaven on Earth, and so it is. A private residential golf-and-sporting club, it stands on a 2,835-hectare (7,000-acre) estate in one of Europe's last great wilderness areas. It was owned by the Carnegie family until the early 1980s, and is one of the few places left where you can see how the privileged of the Gilded Age lived. See p. 354.

12 The Best Moderately Priced Hotels

- **Brasserie Malmaison** (Glasgow; $\textcircled{C}$ **0141/572-1000;** www.malmaison.com): Linked to a hotel with the same name in Edinburgh (see above), this Malmaison dates from the 1830s, when it was built as a Greek Orthodox church. Now converted into one of the best of Glasgow's moderately priced hotels (though its prices are creeping up into the expensive range), it welcomes visitors with a distinct Scottish hospitality. See p. 186.

- **Inn at Lathones** (St. Andrews; $\textcircled{C}$ **01334/840-494;** www.theinn.co.uk): Located in the golf capital of Scotland, this 2-century-old manor has been lovingly restored with excellent accommodations. Scottish hospitality and tradition permeate the place, also known for its "Taste of Scotland" menu. See p. 259.

- **Polmaily House Hotel** (Drumnadrochit; ℭ **01456/450-343;** www.polmaily.co.uk): While you search for Nessie, the Loch Ness Monster, you can lodge comfortably at this inn. The building dates from the 18th century and offers tasteful Edwardian-style living on a farm of mixed gardens and woodland.

- **The Cuillin Hills Hotel** (Portree, Isle of Skye; ℭ **01478/612-003;** www.cuillinhills.demon.co.uk): Built in the 1820s as a hunting lodge for the MacDonald clan, this manor house has been skillfully converted into a small hotel. It attracts nature lovers to its nearby hills of heath and heather, and offers lovely rooms and great food that uses some of the best Highland produce. See p. 371.

13 The Best Restaurants

- **The Tower** (Edinburgh; ℭ **0131/225-3003**): The town's hot dining ticket lies on the top floor of the Museum of Scotland, an unlikely venue for one of Edinburgh's best restaurants. Featuring fresh seafood and an innovative modern British cuisine, The Tower serves some of the city's tastiest fare, made with the freshest ingredients. See p. 98.

- **Martin Wishart** (Edinburgh; ℭ **0131/553-3557**): Many food critics hail this dining room as the best restaurant in Scotland. If it's not that, it ranks among the top five. Out in Leith, Greater Edinburgh's port-bordering town, it serves a modern French cuisine—dishes composed with quality products and filled with flavor. See p. 101.

- **Ostlers Close** (Cupar, near St. Andrews; ℭ **01334/655-574**): Chef Jimmy Graham is one of the finest in the St. Andrews area, and he's known to pick his own wild mushrooms. Golfers with discriminating palates flock to this modestly appointed

place, which makes the best use of fish and seafood from the Fife Coast, as well as ducks from a local free-range supplier. Everything is delectable. See p. 260.

- **The Cross** (Kingussie; ℭ **01540/661-166**): Housed in a cleverly converted 19th-century tweed mill, The Cross is a lot more chic than you'd imagine. The menu items are a celebration of Scottish ingredients, prepared with modern international palates in mind. An example is the West Coast seafood salad with ultra-fresh monkfish, scallops, prawns, and asparagus. See p. 320.

- **Inverlochy Castle** (near Fort William; ℭ **01397/702-177**): Cherubs cavort across frescoed ceilings, and chandeliers drip with Venetian crystal in a dining room created in the 1870s for a mogul. A Relais & Châteaux member, Inverlochy is likely to draw aristocrats and movie stars with a cuisine focusing on flavorful and natural interpretations of Scottish delicacies. See p. 331.

14 The Best Pubs

- **Café Royal Circle Bar** (Edinburgh; ℭ **0131/556-1884**): The Café Royal Circle stands out in a city famous for its pubs. This longtime favorite, boasting lots of atmosphere and Victorian

trappings, attracts a sea of drinkers, locals as well as visitors. See p. 124.

- **Deacon Brodie's Tavern** (Edinburgh; ℭ **0131/225-6531**): This is the best spot for a wee dram or a pint

along Edinburgh's Royal Mile. It perpetuates the memory of Deacon
Brodie, good citizen by day and robber by night, the prototype for
Robert Louis Stevenson's *Dr. Jekyll
and Mr. Hyde.* It's been around since
1806 and has a cocktail-lounge bar
and a large, rowdy tavern. See p. 124.

- **Globe Inn** (Dumfries; ✆ **01387/
252-335**): Located in the Borders,
this was Robert Burns's favorite *howff*
(small, cozy room). Today, you can
imbibe as he did in a pub that's been
in business since 1610. He liked the
place so much that he had a child
with the barmaid. A small museum is
devoted to Burns. See p. 159.

- **Corn Exchange** (Glasgow; ✆ **0141/
248-5380**): There was a time when
it took a bit of courage or a foolish
heart to enter a Glasgow pub. Those
bad old days are long forgotten at
this reliable pub in the city center. In
the mid-1800s, the Corn Exchange
was here (hence the name), but
today it's a watering hole with good
drinks and modestly priced bar platters. See p. 205.

- **Rabbie's Bar** (Ayr; ✆ **01292/
262-112**): Robert Burns didn't confine his drinking to Dumfries. Ayr
was also one of his hangouts, and this
favorite pub is a nostalgic reminder of
another era. Bits of pithy verse by
Burns adorn the walls, and the collection of imported beers is the best in
the area. See "Side Trips from Glasgow: The Best of the Strathclyde
Region" (p. 209).

- **Dreel Tavern** (Anstruther; ✆ **01333/
310-727**): This 16th-century wood-
and-stone coaching inn is now a pub
where old salts from the harbor and
other locals gather to unwind on
windy nights. Try the Orkney Dark
Island, on hand pump. Anstruther,
74km (46 miles) northeast of Edinburgh, is a gem of a Scottish seaside
town. See "East Neuk's Scenic Fishing
Villages" in chapter 9.

- **Ship Inn** (Elie; ✆ **01333/330-246**):
Down at the harbor in this little port
town is the Ship Inn, one of the best
places along the east coast for a pint.
The building dates from 1778, and
the pub from 1830. In summer, you
can enjoy your pint outside with a
view over the water, but on blustery
winter days, the blazing fireplace is
the attraction. Stick around for
dinner—the menu ranges from
pheasant to venison to fresh seafood,
not your typical pub grub. See "East
Neuk's Scenic Fishing Villages" in
chapter 9.

- **Prince of Wales** (Aberdeen;
✆ **01224/640-597**): Furnished with
church pews and antiques, the Prince
of Wales features the city's longest bar
counter. Oilmen from the North Sea
join the regulars to ask for tap beers
like Courage Directors and sample the
chef's Guinness pie. You'll find real flavor and authentic atmosphere; it's a
good place to mingle with the locals in
a mellow setting. See "Aberdeen: The
Castle Country" (p. 290).

15 The Best Shopping

- **Celtic Jewelry:** Modern reproductions of Celtic jewelry are one of
Scotland's most creative craft forms.
Some pieces reflect early Christian
themes, like the Gaelic cross so often
displayed in Presbyterian churches.
Others are pure pagan, and sometimes

Nordic, rich with symbols like dragons, intertwined ovals, and geometrics
that would gladden the heart of a
Celtic lord. Another common theme
commemorates the yearnings for a
politically independent country
(Luckenbooths, entwined hearts

surmounted by a monarch's crown). Clan brooches, kilt pins, and other jewelry are often adorned with the Highland thistle and sometimes rendered in fine gold, silver, or platinum.

- **Sheepskins:** In some of Scotland's rocky districts, sheep are more numerous than people. Tanned sheepskins are for sale in hundreds of shops, usually accompanied by advice from the sales staff on what to do with them once you return home. *Note:* Black sheepskins are much rarer than white ones.

- **Sweaters, Tartans & Fabrics:** Sweaters come in every style and design, from bulky fishermen's pullovers to silky cashmere cardigans. Some factories pride themselves on duplicating the tartans of every Scottish clan; others stick to 50 or so of the more popular designs. A meter of fine tartan fabric sells for around £35 ($67). For a more authentic experience, buy your garment directly from whoever sewed or knitted it. You'll find ample opportunities at crofts and crafts shops around the countryside.

- **Liquor:** One of the most famous liquors in the world is named after the country that produces it: Scotch whisky (spelled without the "e") is distilled and aged throughout the country. Use your trip to Scotland as an opportunity to try new single malts (Laphroaig and MacCallan are our favorites), and bring a bottle or two home.

2

Planning Your Trip to Scotland

This chapter is devoted to the where, when, and how of your trip—the advance planning required to get it together and take it on the road. Because you may not know exactly where in Scotland you want to go or what surrounds the major city you want to see, we begin with a quick rundown on the various regions.

1 The Regions in Brief

Scotland is Great Britain's oldest geological formation, and is divided into three major regions: the **Southern Uplands,** smooth, rolling moorland broken with low crags and threaded with rivers and valleys, between the central plain and the English border; the **Central Lowlands,** where three valleys and the estuaries (firths) of the Clyde, Forth, and Tay rivers make up a fertile belt from the Atlantic Ocean to the North Sea; and the granite **Highlands,** with lochs (lakes), glens, and mountains, plus the hundreds of islands to the west and north. Each of these regions is then made up of smaller regions (see below).

Consult the map on p. 6 to visualize the areas described below.

EDINBURGH & THE LOTHIAN REGION

This area includes not only the country's capital but also West Lothian, most of Midlothian, and East Lothian. Half medieval and half Georgian, **Edinburgh** is at its liveliest every August during the International Arts Festival, but you can visit Edinburgh Castle and Holyroodhouse and walk the Royal Mile year-round. This is one of Europe's most beautiful capitals, and in 3 days you can do it royally, taking in the highlights of the Old Town and the New Town, which include some of the country's major museums. Edinburgh is surrounded by major attractions like the village of **Cramond,** the ancient town of **Linlithgow,** and **Dirleton,** the "prettiest village in Scotland."

THE BORDERS & GALLOWAY REGIONS

Witness to a turbulent history, the Borders and Galloway regions between England and Scotland are rich in castle ruins and Gothic abbeys.

Home of the cashmere sweater and the tweed suit, **Borders** proved a rich mine for the fiction of Sir Walter Scott. Highlights are **Kelso,** which Scott found "the most beautiful," and **Melrose,** site of the ruined Melrose Abbey and Scott's former home of Abbotsford. Ancient monuments include Jedburgh Abbey and Dryburg Abbey, Scott's burial place. At Floors Castle, outside Kelso, you can see one of the great mansions designed by William Adam.

Southwestern Scotland is known as the **Galloway region.** It consists of much of the former stamping ground of Robert Burns and includes centers like **Dumfries, Castle Douglas,** and **Moffat.** Highlights are the artists' colony of **Kirkcudbright,** the baronial Threave Garden, Sweetheart Abbey outside Dumfries (the ruins of a Cistercian abbey from 1273), and the Burns Mausoleum at Dumfries.

GLASGOW & THE STRATHCLYDE REGION

A true renaissance has come to the once-grimy industrial city of **Glasgow,** and we recommend you spend at least 2 days in "the greatest surviving example of a Victorian city." Of course, part of the fun of going to Glasgow is meeting Glaswegians and, if only temporarily, becoming part of their lives. But there are plenty of museums and galleries, too, notably The Burrell Collection, a wealthy ship-owner's gift of more than 8,000 items from the ancient world to the modern; and the Hunterian Art Gallery, with its array of masterpieces by everybody from Rembrandt to Whistler. The Kelvingrove Art Gallery and Museum, home of Britain's finest civic collection of British and European paintings, reopened in mid-2006 following significant restoration.

Glasgow is at the doorstep of one of the most historic regions of Scotland. You can explore Robert Burns Country in the **Strathclyde region,** especially the district around Ayr and Prestwick, or visit a string of famous seaside resorts (including Turnberry, which boasts some of the country's greatest golf courses). An especially worthwhile destination in this region is **Culzean Castle,** overlooking the Firth of Clyde and designed by Robert Adam in the 18th century.

ARGYLL & THE SOUTHERN HEBRIDES

Once the independent kingdom of Dalriada, the **Argyll Peninsula** of western Scotland is centered at **Oban,** a bustling port town and one of Scotland's leading coastal resorts. Ace attractions here are **Argyll Forest Park,** actually three forests—Benmore, Ardgartan, and Glenbranter—covering some 24,300 hectares (60,000 acres). You can also visit **Loch Awe,** a natural moat that protected the Campbells of Inveraray from their enemies to the north, and explore some of Scotland's most interesting islands,

including the **Isle of Arran,** called "Scotland in miniature." The **Isle of Islay** is the southernmost of the Inner Hebrides, with lonely moors, lochs, tranquil bays, and windswept cliffs. The **Isle of Jura,** the fourth largest of the Inner Hebrides, is known for its red deer, and it was on this remote island that George Orwell wrote his masterpiece *1984.* Finally, you can visit **Kintyre,** the longest peninsula in Scotland, more than 97km (60 miles) of beautiful scenery, sleepy villages, and sandy beaches.

FIFE & THE CENTRAL HIGHLANDS

The "kingdom" of **Fife** is one of the most history-rich parts of Scotland, evocative of the era of romance and pageantry during the reign of the early Stuart kings. Its most enchanting stretch is a series of fishing villages called **East Neuk.** And **Culross,** renovated by the National Trust, could well be the most beautiful village in Scotland. Opening onto the North Sea, **St. Andrews,** the "Oxford of Scotland," is the capital of golf and boasts many great courses. The area is rich in castles and abbeys, notably Dunfermline Abbey, burial place of 22 royal personages, and Falkland Palace and Gardens, where Mary Queen of Scots came for hunting and hawking. You can also visit **Stirling,** dominated by its castle, where Mary Queen of Scots lived as an infant monarch. **Loch Lomond,** largest of the Scottish lakes, is fabled for its "bonnie bonnie banks," and the **Trossachs** is perhaps the most beautiful area in Scotland, famed for its moors, mountains, and lakes.

ABERDEEN & THE TAYSIDE & GRAMPIAN REGIONS

Carved from the old counties of Perth and Angus, **Tayside** takes its name from its major river, the Tay, running for 192km (119 miles). One of the loveliest regions, it's known for salmon and trout fishing. Major centers are **Perth,** former capital of Scotland, standing where the Highlands meet the Lowlands; **Dundee,** an old seaport and royal burgh on the north shore of the Firth of Tay; and **Pitlochry,** a popular resort that's an ideal base for touring the Valley of the Tummel. The area abounds in castles and palaces, including Glamis, linked to British royalty for 10 centuries, and Scone, an art-filled palace from 1580. The great city of the north, **Aberdeen** is called Scotland's "granite city" and ranks third in population. It's the best center for touring "castle country." **Braemar** is known for its scenery as well as for being the site of every summer's Royal Highland Gathering, and Balmoral Castle at Ballater was the "beloved paradise" of Queen Victoria and is still home to the royal family. Finally, you can follow the **Whisky Trail** to check out some of Scotland's most famous distilleries, including Glenlivet and Glenfiddich.

INVERNESS & THE WEST HIGHLANDS

Land of rugged glens and majestic mountain landscapes, the Highlands is one of the great meccas of the United Kingdom. The capital is **Inverness,** one of the oldest inhabited localities in Scotland; another city of great interest is **Nairn,** old-time royal burgh and seaside resort. Top attractions are **Loch Ness,** home of the legendary "Nessie," and **Cawdor Castle,** the most romantic in the Highlands, linked with Macbeth. The **Caledonian Canal,** launched in 1803, stretches for 97km (60 miles) of man-made canal, joining the natural lochs. As you proceed to the north you can visit the **Black Isle,** a historic peninsula, before heading for such far northern outposts as **Ullapool,** an 18th-century fishing village on the shores of Loch Broom (and for some, a gateway to the Outer Hebrides), and **John o' Groats,** the most distant point to which you can drive, near the northernmost point of mainland Britain, **Dunnet Head.**

THE HEBRIDEAN ISLANDS

The chain of the Inner Hebrides lies just off the west coast of the mainland. The major center is the **Isle of Skye,** a mystical island and subject of the Scottish ballad "Over the Sea to Skye." If you have time to visit only one island, make it Skye—it's the most beautiful and intriguing. However, the **Isle of Mull,** third largest of the Inner Hebrides, is also rich in legend and folklore, including ghosts, monsters, and the "wee folk." **Iona,** off the coast of Mull, is known as the "Grave of Kings," with an abbey dating from the 13th century. Those with time remaining can also explore the Outer Hebrides, notably **Lewis,** the largest and most northerly. Along with the island of **Harris,** Lewis stretches for a combined length of some 153km (95 miles). This is relatively treeless land of marshy peat bogs and ancient relics.

THE ORKNEY & SHETLAND ISLANDS

These northern outposts of British civilization are archipelagos consisting of some 200 islands, about 40 of which are

---

Okay for a Wee Dram, but Not for a Fag

Pub devotees in Scotland had to give up smoking in March 2006, so no more fags (the slang term for cigarettes). A wee dram—or a lot more—is still acceptable, of course. The ban, which applies not only to pubs but also to restaurants, workplaces, and public transport, was designed to protect fellow workers, other diners, and even bartenders from inhaling secondhand smoke. Ignoring the ban will cost violators £50 ($95). The British Heart Foundation proclaimed the moment the ban went into effect as a "historic day for Scotland."

inhabited. With a rich Viking heritage, they reward visitors with scenery and antiquities. Major centers of the Orkneys are **Kirkwall,** established by Norse invaders and the capital of the Orkneys for 9 centuries, and **Stromness,** the main port of the archipelago and once the last port of call before the New World. **Lerwick** is the capital of the Shetlands and has been since the 17th century. All these islands are filled with ancient monuments: The most outstanding are Midhower Broch (brochs are fortified structures, often called "castles of the Picts"); tombs on Rousay, dating from the Iron Age and called the "great ship of death"; Quoyness Chambered Tomb, on Sanday, a spectacular chambered cairn from 2900 B.C.; the Ring of Brodgar between Loch and Stenness, a stone circle of some 36 stones dating from 1560 B.C. and called the "Stonehenge of Scotland"; and Skara Brae, a Neolithic village joined by covered passages, last occupied about 2500 B.C.

2 Visitor Information & Maps

Before you go, you can get information and maps from the **British Tourist Authority** (**Visit Britain;** www.visit britain.com). In the **United States:** 551 Fifth Ave., Suite 701, New York, NY 10176-0799 (© **800/462-2748,** or 212/ 986-2266 in New York; fax 212/ 986-1188). In **Canada:** 5915 Airport Rd., Mississauga, ON L4V 1T1 (© **888/ VISIT-UK** in Canada; fax 905/405-1835 in Toronto). In **Australia:** Level 2, 15 Blue St., North Sydney NSW 2060 (© **02/ 9021-4400;** fax 02/9021-4499). In **New Zealand:** Fay Richwite Blvd., 17 Floor, 151 Queen St., Auckland 1 (© **09/ 303-1446;** fax 09/377-6965).

If you're in London and are contemplating a trip north, you can visit the **Scottish Tourist Board,** 19 Cockspur St., London SW1 Y5BL (© **0845/225-5121;** www.visit scotland.com); it's open Monday through Friday from 9:30am to 5:30pm and Saturday from noon to 4pm. Once you're in Scotland, you can stop by the **Edinburgh & Scotland Information Centre,** Princes Mall, 3 Princes St., Edinburgh EH2 2QP (© **0131/473-3800;** www.edinburgh.org; bus: 3, 7, 14, 31, or 69). July and August, it's open Monday through Saturday from 9am to 8pm and Sunday from 10am to 8pm. May, June, and September, hours are Monday through Saturday from 9am to 7pm and Sunday from 10am to 7pm. From October to April, hours are Monday through Saturday from 9am to 6pm and Sunday from 10am to 6pm.

There are more than 170 **tourist centers** in Scotland, all well signposted in their cities or towns; some are closed in winter, however.

WHAT'S ON THE WEB? The most useful site was created by a very knowledgeable source, the British Tourist Authority itself, with U.S. visitors targeted. A wealth of information is tapped at **www.travelbritain.org**, which lets you order brochures online, provides tripplanning hints, and even allows e-mail questions for prompt answers. All of Great Britain is covered.

If you're surfing the Web for accommodations, a good site to browse is **www.visitscotland.com** (site of the Scotland Tourist Board).

A lot of individual tourist board websites are helpful. The best of these include information on the Borders at **www.scotborders.co.uk**; on the Highlands at **www.visithighlands.com**; on Ayrshire and Arran at **www.ayrshire-arran.com**; on Argyll and the Isles, Lock Lomond, Stirling, and the Trossachs at **www.visit scottishheartlands.com**; on Perthshire at **www.perthshire.co.uk**; on Angus and Dundee at **www.angusanddundee.co.uk**; on Glasgow at **www.seeglasgow.com**; and on Aberdeen and the Grampian region at **www.agtb.org**.

MAPS Good ones are available from the **Royal Automobile Club** (© **0800/730-1104;** www.rac.co.uk) or from the **Automobile Association** (© **0870/600-0371;** www.theaa.co.uk). The best road map, especially if you're trying to locate some obscure village, is *The Ordnance Survey Motor Atlas of Great Britain,* revised annually and published by Temple Press. It's available at most bookstores in Scotland. If you're in London and plan to head north to Scotland, go to W. & G. Foyle Ltd., 113 and 119 Charing Cross Rd. (© **020/7434-1574;** www.foyles.co.uk).

Other excellent maps include the *Collins Touring Map of Scotland* and *Frommer's Road Atlas.*

3 Entry Requirements

ENTRY REQUIREMENTS

All U.S. citizens, Canadians, Australians, New Zealanders, and South Africans must have a passport with at least 2 months' validity remaining. No visa is required. The immigration officer will also want proof of your intention to return to your point of origin (usually a round-trip ticket) and visible means of support while you're in Scotland. If you're planning to fly from the United States or Canada to the United Kingdom and then on to a country that requires a visa (India, for example), you should secure that visa before you arrive in Britain.

Your valid driver's license and at least 1 year of driving experience is required to drive personal or rented cars.

For information on how to get a passport, go to the "Fast Facts: Scotland" section, later in this chapter—the websites listed provide downloadable passport applications as well as the current fees for processing passport applications. For an up-to-date country-by-country listing of passport requirements around the world, go the "Foreign Entry Requirement" Web page of the U.S. State Department at http://travel.state.gov.

MEDICAL REQUIREMENTS

For information on medical requirements and recommendations, see "Health" on p. 36.

CUSTOMS

For information on what you can bring into and take out of Scotland, go to "Customs" in the "Fast Facts" section of this chapter.

4 When to Go

WEATHER

Seasonal weather should be given careful consideration when planning your trip to Scotland. The Lowlands usually have a moderate temperature year-round. In spring, the average temperature is 53°F (12°C), rising to about 65°F (18°C) in summer. By the time the crisp autumn has arrived, the temperatures have dropped to spring levels. In winter, the average temperature is 43°F (6°C). Temperatures in the north of Scotland are lower, especially in winter, and you should dress accordingly. It rains a lot in Scotland, but perhaps not as much as age-old myths would have it: The rainfall in Edinburgh is exactly the same as that in London. September is often the sunniest month.

WHEN YOU FIND BARGAINS

The cheapest time to travel to Scotland is off season: **November 1 to December 12** and **December 26 to March 14.** In the past few years, airlines have been offering irresistible fares during these periods. And

Average Temperature & Rainfall in Scotland

		Jan	Feb	Mar	Apr	May	June	July	Aug	Sept	Oct	Nov	Dec
Edinburgh	Temp. (°F)	38	38	42	44	50	55	59	58	54	48	43	40
	Temp. (°C)	3	3	6	7	10	13	15	14	12	9	6	4
	Rainfall (in.)	2.2	1.6	1.9	1.5	2.0	2.0	2.5	2.7	2.5	2.4	2.5	2.4

		Jan	Feb	Mar	Apr	May	June	July	Aug	Sept	Oct	Nov	Dec
Aberdeen	Temp. (°F)	38	38	41	44	49	54	58	57	53	48	42	39
	Temp. (°C)	3	3	5	7	9	12	14	14	11	9	6	4
	Rainfall (in.)	2.5	2.0	2.1	1.9	2.1	2.0	2.8	2.8	2.5	3.0	3.1	2.9

weekday flights are cheaper than weekend fares, often by 10% or more.

Rates generally increase **March 14 to June 5** and in **October,** and then hit their peak in the high seasons from **June 6 to September 30** and **December 13 to December 24.** July and August are when most Britons take their holidays, so besides the higher prices, you'll have to deal with crowds and limited availability of accommodations.

Sure, in winter Scotland is usually rainy and cold—but it doesn't shut down when the tourists leave. In fact, the winter season gives visitors a more honest view of Scottish life. Additionally, many hotel prices drop by 20%, and cheaper accommodations offer weekly rates (unheard of during peak travel times). By arriving after the winter holidays, you can take advantage of post-Christmas sales to buy your fill of woolens, china, crystal, silver, fashion, handicrafts, and curios.

In short, spring offers the countryside at its greenest, autumn brings the bright colors of the northern Highlands, and summer's warmth gives rise to the many outdoor music and theater festivals. But winter offers savings across the board and a chance to see Scots going about their everyday lives, largely unhindered by tourist invasions.

HOLIDAYS

The following holidays are celebrated in Scotland: New Year's Day (Jan 1–2), Good Friday and Easter Monday, May Day (May 1), spring bank holiday (last Mon in May), summer bank holiday (first Mon in Aug), Christmas Day (Dec 25), and Boxing Day (Dec 26).

SCOTLAND CALENDAR OF EVENTS

You can get details of specific events at many of the festivals below by going to **www.edinburgh-festivals.com**.

For an exhaustive list of events beyond those listed here, check http://events.frommers.com, where you'll find a searchable, up-to-the-minute roster of what's happening in cities all over the world.

January

Celtic Connections, Glasgow. During this celebration of the Celtic roots that combined with other cultures to form modern Scotland, concerts are staged in churches, auditoriums, and meeting halls throughout the city. A prime venue is the Old Fruit Market on Albion Street, drawing dance troupes from throughout Scotland, Wales, and Ireland. For tickets and details, call ℂ **0141/353-8000** (www.celticconnections.com). Mid January to late February.

Burns Night, Ayr (near his birthplace) and Dumfries. Naturally, during the celebrations to honor Robert Burns, there's much toasting with scotch and eating of haggis (spiced intestines), whose arrival is announced by a bag-pipe. For details, call ℭ **01292/ 443-700** in Ayr, or 01387/253-862 in Dumfries. The website www.burns heritagepark.com also has information. January 25.

Up Helly Aa, Lerwick, in the Shetland Islands. The most northerly town in Great Britain still clings to tradition by staging an ancient Norse fire festival whose aim is to encourage the return of the sun after the pitch-dark days of winter. Its highlight is the burning of a replica of a Norse longboat. Call ℭ **01595/693-434** (www.visitshetland. com). Last Tuesday in January.

February

Aberdeen Angus Cattle Show, Perth. This show draws the finest cattle raised in Scotland. Sales are lively. Call ℭ **01738/622-477.** Early February.

March

Whuppity Scourie, Lanark. Residents of the Strathclyde get so tired of winter that they stage this traditional cere-mony to chase it away. Call ℭ **01555/ 661-661.** March 1.

April

C'eilidh Culture, at various venues, Edinburgh. For details on this feast of Scottish folk tunes, call ℭ **0131/ 228-1155** (www.ceilidhculture.co.uk). Generally April 1.

Kate Kennedy Procession & Pageant, St. Andrews. This historic university pageant is staged annually in the uni-versity city of St. Andrews, in eastern Scotland. Call ℭ **01334/472-021.** Second Saturday in April.

May

Scottish Motorcycle Trials, Fort William. The trials are run for 6 days at the beginning of the month, drawing aficionados from all over Europe. Call ℭ **01397/703-781** (www.ssdt.org). Early May.

Highland Games & Gatherings, at various venues throughout the coun-try, including Aberfeldy, Perth, Crieff, Ballater, Oban, and Portree on the Isle of Skye. Details are available from the Edinburgh & Scotland Information Centre (see "Visitor Information," ear-lier in this chapter). Early May to mid-September.

Exhibitions at the Royal Scottish Academy, Edinburgh. Changing exhibits of international interest are offered here annually. Call ℭ **0131/ 225-6671** (www.royalscottishacademy. org). Early May to late June.

June

Promenade Concerts, Glasgow. These concerts by the Scottish National Orchestra are given at the Glasgow Royal Concert Hall. Call ℭ **0141/ 353-8000** (www.grch.com). Through-out June (sometimes into July).

Pitlochry Festival Theatre, Pitlochry. Scotland's "theater in the hills" launches

---

Tips Hot Line to Scotland

Travel information for the whole of Scotland is offered on Visit Scotland's national telephone hot line, available for inquiries from the U.K. and overseas. Travel advisors are available to help you book accommodations throughout Scotland—hotels, guesthouses, or bed-and-breakfasts—or find out about special offers, events, and attractions to visit. You can order brochures as well. Advisors are available Monday to Friday 8am to 8pm and Saturday 9am to 5:30pm (U.K. time). In the U.K., ℭ **0845/225-5121**; from overseas, ℭ **011-44-845/225-5121**; www.visitscotland.com.

its season in June. Call ✆ **01796/ 484-626** (www.pitlochry.org.uk). June to early November.

Lanimer Day, Lanark. This week of festivities features a ritual procession around the town's boundaries, the election of a Lanimer Queen and a Cornet King, and a parade with floats, along with Highland dances and bagpipe playing. Call ✆ **01555/663-251** (www. lanarklanimers.co.uk). The Thursday between June 6 and 12.

Guid Nychburris (Good Neighbors), Dumfries. This age-old festival is an event similar to (but less impressive than) the Selkirk Common Riding (see below). Call ✆ **01387/253-862** (www. guidnychburris.co.uk). Mid-June.

Royal Highland Show, at the Ingliston Showground, outskirts of Edinburgh. This show is devoted to agriculture and commerce. For details, call ✆ **0131/335-6200** (www.royal highlandshow.org). Mid- to late June.

Selkirk Common Riding, Selkirk. This is Scotland's most elaborate display of horsemanship, remembering Selkirk's losses in the 1560 Battle of Flodden—only one Selkirk soldier returned alive from the battle to warn the town before dropping dead in the marketplace. Some 400 horses and riders parade through the streets, and a young unmarried male is crowned at the sound of the cornet, representing the soldier who sounded the alarm. Call ✆ **01750/200-54.** Mid-June.

Beltane Day, Peebles. A town "Cornet" rides around to see if the boundaries are safe from the "invading" English, a young girl is elected Festival Queen, and her court is filled with courtiers, sword bearers, guards, and attendants. Children of the town dress in costumes for parade floats through the streets. Call ✆ **0870/608-0404.** Mid-June.

Gay Pride, Edinburgh or Glasgow. Scotland's annual gay pride celebration alternates between Edinburgh and Glasgow. You'll see a quirky, boisterous parade through the heart of Glasgow or along Princes Street in Edinburgh. For details, call Pride Scotia (✆ **0131/556-9471;** www.pridescotia.org). Sometime in June.

Glasgow International Jazz Festival, Glasgow. Jazz musicians from all over the world come together to perform at various venues around the city. Call ✆ **0141/552-3552** (www.jazzfest. co.uk). Late June to early July.

August

Lammas Fair, St. Andrews. Although there's a dim medieval origin to this 2-day festival, it's not particularly obvious. Temporary Ferris wheels and whirligigs are hauled in, cotton candy and popcorn are sold, palm readers describe your past and your future, and flashing lights and recorded disco music create something akin to Blackpool-in-the-Highlands. There's even an opportunity for bungee-jumping. Call ✆ **01334/472-021.** Early August.

World Pipe Band Championships, Glasgow. Bagpipe bands from around the world gather on the parklike Glasgow Green in the city's East End. From 11am to about 6pm, there's a virtual orgy of bagpiping, as kilted participants strut their stuff in musical and military precision. Call ✆ **0141/221-5414** (www.rspba.org). Mid-August.

Edinburgh International Festival, Edinburgh. Scotland's best-known festival is held for 3 weeks (see chapter 5 for more information). Called an "arts bonanza," it draws major talent from around the world, with more than a thousand shows presented and a million tickets sold. Book, jazz, and film festivals are also staged at this time, but nothing tops the Military Tattoo against the backdrop of spot-lit Edinburgh Castle. Contact the Festival Society, 21 Market St., Edinburgh, Scotland EH1 1BW (© **0131/473-2099;** www.eif.co.uk). Three weeks in August.

September

Ben Nevis Mountain Race, Fort William, in the Highlands. A tradition since 1895, when it was established by a member of the MacFarlane clan, the race assembles as many as 500 runners who compete for the coveted MacFarlane Cup, a gold medal, and a prize of £50 ($95). Runners congregate at the base of Ben Nevis (Britain's highest peak) to tackle a course that takes them up narrow footpaths to the summit and back. Bagpipes rise in crescendos at the beginning and end of the experience. Call © **01397/700-707** (www.visitfortwilliam.co.uk). First Saturday in September.

Highland Games & Gathering, Braemar. The queen and many members of the royal family often show up for this annual event, with its massed bands, piping and dancing competitions, and performances of great strength by a tribe of gigantic men. Contact © **013397/ 55377** (www.braemargathering.org). First Saturday in September.

Hamilton Flat Races, Hamilton, near Glasgow. The races take place over a period of 2 to 3 days. Call the Hamilton race course at © **01698/283-806** (www.hamilton-park.co.uk).

October

Highland Autumn Cattle Show, Oban, in western Scotland. Since the days of Rob Roy, Oban has been a marketplace for the long-haired, tawny cattle whose elongated horns have been associated with the toughness of the Highlands. For this show, buyers and sellers from Britain, as well as from such cold-weather climes as Sweden, Norway, and Canada, come to buy cattle (either for stud or for beef purposes). Everything is rather businesslike (but still colorful) in the industrial-looking Caledonian Auction Mart, 5km (3 miles) south of Oban. Call © **01631/ 563-122.** Mid-October.

November

Winter Antiques & Collector's Fair, Edinburgh. This fair draws dealers and buyers from all over Europe and America. Call © **0131/335-6200.** Second week in November.

Christmas Shopping Festival, Aberdeen. For those who want to shop early for Christmas. Call © **01224/ 288-828.** Third week of November to December.

St. Andrews Week, St. Andrews. This annual festival of exhibits, concerts, sporting events, fireworks displays, and local foods takes place over the week leading up to St. Andrews Day on November 30. Call © **01334/472-021.** The week ending November 30.

December

Flambeaux Procession, Comrie, Tayside. This torchlight parade takes place on New Year's Eve. For details, call © **01764/652-578** in Crieff. December 31.

Hogmanay, Edinburgh. Hogmanay begins on New Year's Eve and merges into New Year's Day festivities. Events include a torchlight procession, a fire festival along Princes Street, a carnival, and a street-theater spectacular. Call © **0845/225-5121.** December 31.

5 Getting There

BY PLANE
Visitors will find frequent flights available from London to Scotland. **British** Airways (© **800/247-9297** or 0870/ 850-9850; www.britishairways.com) offers 22 nonstop flights daily from

Value **Travel Accommodations**

BritRail (© 866/BRIT-RAIL; www.britrail.com) has a new offer for visitors to Scotland that promises to save money. When going from London to Scotland, a typical traveler often pays not only for a train ticket but for that night's sleeping accommodations as well. But BritRail has created the Caledonian Sleeper Packages to eliminate the excess spending. Passengers travel overnight from London to either Scotland's Lowlands or Highlands and sleep on the train. Travelers receive a wake-up call the next morning, along with tea or coffee. The sleepers have all the basics: air-conditioning, toiletries, a sink, and an electric outlet. Nonsmoking units are available. Travelers should make reservations for sleeper cars.

London's Heathrow Airport to both Edinburgh and Glasgow. British Airways can make a visit to Scotland cheaper than you might have expected. Ask about packages that include both airfare and discounted hotel accommodations in Scotland. **Ryanair** (© 353/1-249-7791; www.ryanair.com) flies from Stansted outside London to Prestwick on the west coast of Scotland, and **British Midland** (© 0870/6070-555; www.flybmi.com) flies from Heathrow to both Edinburgh and Glasgow.

Known for consistently offering excellent fares, **Virgin Atlantic Airways** (© 800/862-8621; www.virgin-atlantic. com) flies daily to either Heathrow or Gatwick from Boston; Newark, New Jersey; New York's JFK; Los Angeles; San Francisco; Washington's Dulles; Las Vegas; Miami; and Orlando. **American Airlines** (© 800/433-7300; www.aa.com) offers daily flights to Heathrow from half a dozen U.S. gateways—New York's JFK, Newark, Chicago, Boston, Miami, and Los Angeles.

Depending on the day and season, **Delta Air Lines** (© 800/241-4141; www.delta.com) runs two daily nonstop flights between Atlanta and Gatwick. Delta also offers nonstop daily service from Cincinnati.

Northwest Airlines (© 800/225-2525 or 800/447-4747; www.nwa.com) flies nonstop from Minneapolis and Detroit to Gatwick, with connections possible from other cities, such as Boston or New York.

Continental Airlines (© 800/525-0280; www.continental.com) has daily flights to London from Houston and Newark.

United Airlines (© 800/241-6522; www.united.com) flies nonstop from Chicago to Heathrow three times daily, depending on the season. United also offers nonstop service three times a day from Dulles Airport, near Washington, D.C.

For travelers departing from Canada, **Air Canada** (© 888/247-2262; www. aircanada.com) flies daily to London's Heathrow nonstop from Vancouver, Montreal, and Toronto. There are also frequent direct flights from Calgary and Ottawa. **British Airways** (© 800/247-9297) has direct flights from Toronto, Montreal, and Vancouver.

For travelers departing from Australia, **British Airways** (© 800/247-9297) has flights to London from Sydney, Melbourne, Perth, and Brisbane. **Qantas** (© 852/2822-9000; www.qantas.com) offers flights from Australia to London's Heathrow. Direct flights depart from Sydney and Melbourne. Some have the bonus of free stopovers in Bangkok or Singapore.

Departing from New Zealand, **Air New Zealand** (© 800/028-4149; www. airnewzealand.com) has direct flights to

London from Auckland. These flights depart daily.

Short flights from Dublin to London are available through **British Airways** (© 800/247-9297), with four flights daily into London's Gatwick airport; **Aer Lingus** (© 800/IRISH-AIR; www.aerlingus.com), which flies into Heathrow; **Ryanair** (© 353/1-249-7791; www.ryanair.com); and **British Midland** (© 0870/6070555; www.flybmi.com).

Some Scotland-bound passengers opt for flights into Manchester, England—it's closer than London to Scotland's Highlands and islands. British Airways offers frequent flights into Manchester, many nonstop, from various parts of the United States.

FLYING FOR LESS: TIPS FOR GETTING THE BEST AIRFARE

- Passengers who can book their ticket either **long in advance or at the last minute,** or who **fly midweek** or **at less-trafficked hours** may pay a fraction of the full fare. If your schedule is flexible, say so, and ask if you can secure a cheaper fare by changing your flight plans.

- Search **the Internet** for cheap fares. The most popular online travel agencies are **Travelocity.com** (www.travelocity.co.uk); **Expedia.com** (www.expedia.co.uk and www.expedia.ca); and **Orbitz.com.** In the U.K., go to **Travelsupermarket** (© 0845/345-5708; www.travelsupermarket.com), a flight search engine that offers flight comparisons for the budget airlines whose seats often end up in bucket-shop sales. Other websites for booking airline tickets online include **Cheapflights.com, SmarterTravel.com, Priceline.com,** and **Opodo** (www.opodo.co.uk). Meta search sites (which find and then direct you to airline and hotel websites for booking) include **Sidestep.com** and **Kayak.com**—the latter includes fares for budget carriers like Jet Blue and Spirit as well as the major airlines. **Site59.com** is a great source for last-minute flights and getaways. In addition, most **airlines** offer online-only fares that even their phone agents know nothing about. British travelers should check **Flights International** (© 0800/0187050; www.flights-international.com) for deals on flights all over the world.

- Keep an eye on local newspapers for **promotional specials** or **fare wars,** when airlines lower prices on their most popular routes.

- **Consolidators,** also known as bucket shops, are wholesale brokers in the airline-ticket game. Consolidators buy deeply discounted tickets ("distressed" inventories of unsold seats) from airlines and sell them to online ticket agencies, travel agents, tour operators, corporations, and, to a lesser degree, the general public. Consolidators advertise in Sunday newspaper travel sections (often in small ads with tiny type), both in the U.S. and the U.K. They can be great sources for cheap international tickets. On the down side, bucket shop tickets are often rigged with restrictions, such as stiff cancellation penalties (as high as 50%–75% of the ticket price). And keep in mind that most of what you see advertised is of limited availability. Several reliable consolidators are worldwide and available online. **STA Travel** (www.statravel.com) has been the world's leading consolidator for students since purchasing Council Travel, but their fares are competitive for travelers of all ages. **Flights.com** (© 201/541-3826; www.flights.com) has excellent fares worldwide, particularly to Europe. They also have "local" websites in 12 countries. **FlyCheap** (© 800/FLY-CHEAP; www.1800flycheap.com) has especially good fares to sunny destinations. **Air Tickets Direct** (© **888/858-8884;** www.airtickets direct.com) is based in Montreal and leverages the currently weak Canadian dollar for low fares; they also book trips to places that U.S. travel agents won't touch, such as Cuba.

- Join **frequent-flier clubs.** Frequent-flier membership doesn't cost a cent, but it does entitle you to free tickets or upgrades when you amass the airline's required number of frequent-flier points. You don't even have to fly to earn points; **frequent-flier credit cards** can earn you thousands of miles for doing your everyday shopping. But keep in mind that award seats are limited, seats on popular routes are hard to snag, and more and more major airlines are cutting their expiration periods for mileage points—so check your airline's frequent-flier program so you don't lose your miles before you use them. *Inside tip:* Award seats are offered almost a year in advance, but seats also open up at the last minute, so if your travel plans are flexible, you may strike gold. To play the frequent-flier game to your best advantage, consult the community bulletin boards on **FlyerTalk** (www.flyertalk.com) or go to Randy Petersen's **Inside Flyer** (www.insideflyer.com). Petersen and friends review all the programs in detail and post regular updates on changes in policies and trends.

BY CAR

If you're driving north to Scotland from England, it's fastest to take the **M1 motorway** north from London. You can reach M1 by driving to the ring road from any point in the British capital. Southeast of Leeds, you'll need to connect with **A1** (not a motorway), which you take north to Scotch Corner. Here M1 resumes, ending south of Newcastle-upon-Tyne. Then you can take **A696,** which becomes **A68,** for its final run north into Edinburgh.

If you're in the west of England, go north along **M5,** which begins at Exeter (Devon). Eventually this will merge with **M6.** Continue north on M6 until you reach a point north of Carlisle. From Carlisle, cross into Scotland near Gretna Green. Continue north along **A74** via Moffat. A74 will eventually connect with **M74** heading toward Glasgow. If your goal is Edinburgh, not Glasgow, various roads will take you east to the Scottish capital, including **M8,** which goes part of the way, as do **A702, A70,** and **A71** (all these routes are well signposted).

BY TRAIN

From England, two main rail lines link London to Scotland. The most popular and fastest route is London's **King's Cross Station** to Edinburgh, going by way of Newcastle and Durham. Trains cross from England into Scotland at Berwick-upon-Tweed. Fifteen trains a day leave London for Edinburgh between 8am and 6pm; night service is more limited, and you must reserve sleepers. Three of these trains go on to Aberdeen.

If you're going on to the western Highlands and islands, Edinburgh makes a good gateway, with better train connections to those areas than Glasgow.

If you're going via the west coast, trains leave London's **Euston Station** for Glasgow, by way of Rugby, Crewe, Preston, and Carlisle, with nearly a train per hour during the day. Most of these trains take about 5 hours to reach Glasgow. You can also take the *Highland Chieftain,* going direct to Stirling and Aviemore and terminating in Inverness, capital of the Highlands. There's overnight sleeper service from Euston Station to Glasgow, Perth, Stirling, Aviemore, Fort William, and Inverness. It's possible to book a family compartment.

Scotland is served by other trains from England, including regular service from such cities as Birmingham, Liverpool, Manchester, Southampton, and Bristol. If you're in Penzance (Cornwall), you can reach Glasgow or Edinburgh directly by train without having to return to London.

Orient Express Trains & Cruises has launched its fifth train in Britain, the *Northern Belle.* You get great luxury, except for one oversight: There are no berths. Making about 20 departures a week, the *Northern Belle* carries 252 passengers and feeds them in six stately dining rooms evocative of a Scottish country home. In addition to its runs in England, the train features weekend jaunts up to Scotland, with departures from Liverpool, Manchester, and York. What about taking a bath? Stays in hotels will be part of the itinerary. For reservations, call (C) **0845/077-2222** in the U.K., or 800/ 524-2420 in the U.S. You can also go to **www.orient-express.com**.

See "Getting Around Scotland," below, for information on rail passes.

BY TRAIN FROM CONTINENTAL EUROPE

Britain's isolation from the rest of Europe led to the development of an independent railway network with different rules and regulations from those observed on the Continent. That's all changing now, but one big difference that may affect you still remains: If you're traveling to Britain from the Continent, *your Eurailpass will not be valid when you get there.*

In 1994, Queen Elizabeth and President François Mitterand officially opened the Channel Tunnel, or Chunnel, and the *Eurostar* express passenger train began twice-daily service between London and both Paris and Brussels—a 3-hour trip. The $15-billion tunnel, one of the great engineering feats of all time, is the first link between Britain and the Continent since the Ice Age.

So if you're coming to London from say, Rome, your Eurailpass will get you as far as

the Chunnel. At that point, you can cross the English Channel aboard the *Eurostar,* and you'll receive a discount on your ticket. Once in England, you must use a separate BritRail pass or purchase a direct ticket to continue on to your destination.

Rail Europe (C) **877/272-RAIL; www.raileurope.com**) sells direct-service tickets on the *Eurostar* between Paris or Brussels and London. A one-way fare between Paris and London costs £107 to £210 ($205–$399) in first class and £49 to £146 ($94–$277) in second class.

In London, make reservations for *Eurostar* by calling (C) **08705/186-186** and in the United States, it's (C) **800/ EUROSTAR** (www.eurostar.com). *Eurostar* trains arrive and depart from London's Waterloo Station, Paris's Gare du Nord, and Brussels's Central Station.

BY BUS (COACH)

Long-distance buses, called "motorcoaches" in Britain, are the least expensive means of reaching Scotland from England. Some 20 coach companies run services, mainly from London to Edinburgh or Glasgow. The major operators are **National Express, Scottish Omnibuses, Western SMT, Stagecoach,** and **Eastern Scottish.** It takes 8 to 8½ hours to reach Edinburgh or Glasgow from London.

It's estimated that coach fares are about one-third of the rail charges for comparable trips to Scotland. Most coaches depart from London's **Victoria Coach Station.** If you're visiting between June and August, it's wise to make seat reservations at least 3 days in advance (4 or 5 days if possible). For timetables, available from London to Edinburgh, call **National Express** (C) **08705/808-080;** www.national express.com) or **Rapsons** (C) **0870/608-2608;** www.rapsons.com), or check on all other companies by calling (C) **08705/ 505-050.** Travel centers and travel agents also have details. Most travel agents in London sell coach seats and can make reservations for you.

If you're traveling by bus in the United Kingdom, consider purchasing a Britexpress Card, which entitles you to a 30% discount on National Express (England and Wales) and Caledonian Express (Scotland) buses. Contact a travel agent for details.

6 Money & Costs

POUNDS & PENCE

Britain's monetary system is based on the pound Sterling (£), which is made up of 100 pence (written as "p"). Britons also call pounds "quid." Scotland issues its own pound notes, but English and Scottish money are interchangeable. There are £1 and £2 coins, as well as coins of 50p, 20p, 10p, 5p, 2p, and 1p. Banknotes come in denominations of £5, £10, £20, and £50.

As a general guideline, the price conversions in this book have been computed at the rate of £1 = $1.90 (U.S.). Bear in mind, however, that exchange rates fluctuate daily. For more exact ratios between these and other currencies, check an up-to-date source at the time of your arrival in Europe.

ATMs

The easiest and best way to get cash away from home is from an ATM (automated teller machine), sometimes referred to as a "cash machine," or a "cashpoint." The Cirrus (℡ 800/424-7787; www.master card.com) and PLUS (℡ 800/843-7587; www.visa.com) networks span the globe. Go to your bank card's website to find ATM locations at your destination. Be sure you know your personal identification number (PIN) and your daily withdrawal limit before you depart. *Note:*

Many banks impose a fee every time you use a card at another bank's ATM, and that fee can be higher for international transactions (up to $5 or more) than for domestic ones (where they're rarely more than $2). In addition, the bank from which you withdraw cash may charge its own fee. For international withdrawal fees, ask your bank.

Note: Banks that are members of the **Global ATM Alliance** charge no transaction fees for cash withdrawals at other Alliance member ATMs; these include Bank of America, Scotiabank (Canada, Caribbean, and Mexico), Barclays (U.K. and parts of Africa), Deutsche Bank (Germany, Poland, Spain, and Italy), and BNP Paribus (France).

CREDIT CARDS

Credit cards are another safe way to carry money. They also provide a convenient record of all your expenses, and they generally offer relatively good exchange rates. You can withdraw cash advances from your credit cards at banks or ATMs, but high fees make credit card cash advances a pricey way to get cash. Keep in mind that you'll pay interest from the moment of your withdrawal, even if you pay your monthly bills on time. Also, note that many banks now assess a 1% to 3%

The U.S. Dollar, the British Pound & the Euro

You will not see Europe's newest currency, the euro (currently worth approximately $1.30), used in Great Britain, which steadfastly refuses to give up the British pound. As a result, all prices in this book are noted only in pounds and dollars at a rate of £1 = $1.90. For up-to-the-minute exchange rates for all three currencies, check this currency-converter website: **www.xe.com/ucc**.

Tips Small Change

When you change money, ask for some small bills or loose change. Petty cash will come in handy for tipping and public transportation. Consider keeping the change separate from your larger bills so that it's readily accessible and you'll be less of a target for theft.

"transaction fee" on *all* charges you incur abroad (whether you're using the local currency or your native currency).

TRAVELER'S CHECKS

You can buy traveler's checks at most banks. They are offered in denominations of $20, $50, $100, $500, and sometimes $1,000. Generally, you'll pay a service charge ranging from 1% to 4%.

The most popular traveler's checks are offered by **American Express** (© **800/807-6233** or 800/221-7282 for card holders—this number accepts collect calls, offers service in several foreign languages, and exempts Amex gold and platinum cardholders from the 1% fee); **Visa** (© **800/732-1322**)—AAA members can obtain Visa checks for a $9.95 fee (for checks up to $1,500) at most AAA offices or by calling © **866/339-3378**; and **MasterCard** (© **800/223-9920**).

Be sure to keep a record of the traveler's checks serial numbers separate from your checks in the event that they are stolen or lost. You'll get a refund faster if you know the numbers.

American Express, Thomas Cook, Visa, and **MasterCard** offer **foreign currency traveler's checks,** useful if you're traveling to one country or to the Euro zone; they're accepted at locations where dollar checks may not be.

Another option is the new prepaid traveler's check cards, reloadable cards that work much like debit cards but aren't linked to your checking account. The **American Express Travelers Cheque Card,** for example, requires a minimum deposit, sets a maximum balance, and has a one-time issuance fee of $14.95. You can withdraw money from an ATM (for a fee of $2.50 per transaction, not including bank fees), and the funds can be purchased in dollars, euros, or pounds. If you lose the card, your available funds will be refunded within 24 hours.

7 Travel Insurance

The cost of travel insurance varies widely, depending on the destination, the cost and length of your trip, your age and health, and the type of trip you're taking, but expect to pay between 5% and 8% of the vacation itself. You can get estimates from various providers through **InsureMy Trip.com**. Enter your trip cost and dates, your age, and other information, for prices from more than a dozen companies.

U.K. citizens and their families who make more than one trip abroad per year may find an annual travel insurance policy works out cheaper. Check **www. moneysupermarket.com**, which compares prices across a wide range of providers for single- and multi-trip policies.

Most big travel agents offer their own insurance and will probably try to sell you their package when you book a holiday. Think before you sign. **Britain's Consumers' Association** recommends that you insist on seeing the policy and reading the fine print before buying travel insurance. **The Association of British Insurers** (© **020/7600-3333;** www.abi.org.uk)

gives advice by phone and publishes *Holiday Insurance,* a free guide to policy provisions and prices. You might also shop around for better deals: Try **Columbus Direct** (© **0870/033-9988;** www.columbusdirect.net).

TRIP-CANCELLATION INSURANCE

Trip-cancellation insurance will help retrieve your money if you have to back out of a trip or depart early, or if your travel supplier goes bankrupt. Trip cancellation traditionally covers such events as sickness, natural disasters, and State Department advisories. The latest news in trip-cancellation insurance is the availability of **expanded hurricane coverage** and the **"any-reason"** cancellation coverage—which costs more but covers cancellations made for any reason. You won't get back 100% of your prepaid trip cost, but you'll be refunded a substantial portion. **TravelSafe** (© **888/885-7233;** www.travelsafe.com) offers both types of coverage. Expedia also offers any-reason cancellation coverage for its air-hotel packages.

For details, contact one of the following recommended insurers: **Access America** (© 800/729-6021; www.accessamerica.com); **Travel Guard International** (© 800/826-4919; www.travelguard.com); **Travel Insured International** (© 800/243-3174; www.travelinsured.com); and **Travelex Insurance Services** (© 800/228-9792; www.travelex-insurance.com).

MEDICAL INSURANCE

For travel overseas, most U.S. health plans (including Medicare and Medicaid) do not provide coverage, and the ones that do often require you to pay for services upfront and reimburse you only after you return home.

As a safety net, you may want to buy travel medical insurance, particularly if you're traveling to a remote or high-risk area where emergency evacuation might be necessary. If you require additional medical insurance, try **MEDEX Assistance** (© **800/732-5309;** www.medexassist.com) or **Travel Assistance International** (© **800/821-2828;** www.travelassistance.com; for general information on services, call the company's **Worldwide Assistance Services, Inc.,** at © **800/777-8710**).

Canadians should check with their provincial health plan offices or call **Health Canada** (© **866/225-0709;** www.hc-sc.gc.ca) to find out the extent of their coverage and what documentation and receipts they must take home in case they are treated overseas.

LOST-LUGGAGE INSURANCE

On international flights (including U.S. portions of international trips), baggage coverage is limited to approximately

---

Tips Dear Visa: I'm Off to Aberdeen!

Some credit card companies recommend that you notify them of any impending trip abroad so that they don't become suspicious when the card is used numerous times in a foreign destination and your charges are blocked. Even if you don't call your credit card company in advance, you can always call the card's toll-free emergency number (see "Fast Facts: Scotland," later in this chapter) if a charge is refused—a good reason to carry the phone number with you. But perhaps the most important lesson here is to carry more than one card with you on your trip; a card might not work for any number of reasons, so having a backup is the smart way to go.

$9.07 per pound, up to approximately $635 per checked bag. If you plan to check items more valuable than what's covered by the standard liability, see if your homeowner's policy covers your valuables, or get baggage insurance as part of your comprehensive travel-insurance package.

If your luggage is lost, immediately file a lost-luggage claim at the airport, detailing the luggage contents. Most airlines require that you report delayed, damaged, or lost baggage within 4 hours of arrival. The airlines are required to deliver luggage, once found, directly to your house or destination free of charge.

8 Health

STAYING HEALTHY

You'll encounter few health problems while in Scotland. If you need a doctor, your hotel can recommend one, or you can contact your embassy or consulate. *Note:* U.S. visitors who become ill while in England are eligible for free emergency care only. For other treatment, including follow-up care, you'll be asked to pay.

Contact the **International Association for Medical Assistance to Travelers (IAMAT;** © **716/754-4883,** or 416/652-0137 in Canada; www.iamat.org) for tips on travel and health concerns in the

countries you're visiting, and for lists of local, English-speaking doctors. The United States **Centers for Disease Control and Prevention** (© **800/311-3435;** www.cdc.gov) provides up-to-date information on health hazards by region or country and offers tips on food safety. **Travel Health Online** (www.tripprep. com), sponsored by a consortium of travel medicine practitioners, may also offer helpful advice on traveling abroad. You can find listings of reliable medical clinics overseas at the **International Society of Travel Medicine** (www.istm.org).

9 Safety

Like all big cities, Edinburgh and Glasgow have their share of crime. Compared to most large European cities, however, they are relatively safe, and violent crime against visitors is extremely rare. The same precautions prevail in these larger cities as they do elsewhere in the world. Rural Scotland is quite safe.

Crime, however, has increased over the past few years. Tourists are typically prey to incidents of pickpocketing; mugging; "snatch and grab" theft of mobile phones,

watches, and jewelry; and theft of unattended bags, especially at airports and from cars parked at restaurants, hotels, and resorts.

Pickpockets target tourists at historic sites and restaurants, as well as on buses, trains, and the Underground (subway). Unattended cars are targeted, too. Visitors in Scotland are not expected to produce identity documents for police authorities and thus may secure their passports in hotel safes or residences.

Healthy Travels to You

The following government websites offer up-to-date health-related travel advice:

- **Australia:** www.dfat.gov.au/travel
- **Canada:** www.hc-sc.gc.ca/index_e.html
- **U.K.:** www.dh.gov.uk/PolicyAndGuidance/HealthAdviceForTravellers
- **U.S.:** www.cdc.gov/travel

10 Specialized Travel Resources

TRAVELERS WITH DISABILITIES

Many Scottish hotels, museums, restaurants, and sightseeing attractions have wheelchair ramps, less so in rural areas. Persons with disabilities are often granted special discounts at attractions and, in some cases, nightclubs. These are called "concessions" in Britain. It always pays to ask. Free information and advice is available from **Holiday Care,** Imperial Building, 2nd floor, Victoria Road, Horley, Surrey RH6 7PZ (℗ **0845/124-9971;** www.holidaycare.org.uk).

Flying Wheels Travel (℗ **507/451-5005;** www.flyingwheelstravel.com) offers escorted tours and cruises that emphasize sports and private tours in minivans with lifts. **Access-Able Travel Source** (℗ **303/232-2979;** www.access-able.com) offers extensive access information and advice for traveling around the world with disabilities. **Accessible Journeys** (℗ **800/846-4537** or 610/521-0339; www.disabilitytravel.com) caters specifically to slow walkers and wheelchair travelers and their families and friends.

Organizations that offer assistance to travelers with disabilities include the **Moss Rehab Hospital** (℗ **800/CALL-MOSS;** www.mossresourcenet.org), which provides a library of accessible-travel resources online; and the **SATH** (Society for Accessible Travel and Hospitality; ℗ **212/447-7284;** www.sath.org), which is now partnered with **AirAmbulanceCard.com** and allows you to preselect top-notch hospitals in case of an emergency. **Flying with Disability** (www.flying-with-disability.org) is a comprehensive information source on airplane travel, and the **American Foundation for the Blind** (AFB; ℗ **800/232-5463;** www.afb.org) provides information on traveling with Seeing Eye dogs.

Also check out the quarterly magazine *Emerging Horizons* ($16.95 per year, $21.95 outside the U.S.; www.emerginghorizons.com), and *Open World Magazine,* published by the Society for Accessible Travel and Hospitality (see above; subscription $13 per year, $21 outside the U.S.).

GAY & LESBIAN TRAVELERS

Bars, clubs, restaurants, and hotels catering to gays are confined almost exclusively to Edinburgh, Glasgow, and Inverness. Gay males can call the **Lothian Gay and Lesbian Switchboard** (℗ **0131/556-4049;** www.lgls.co.uk) or the **Glasgow Gay and Lesbian Switchboard** (℗ **0141/847-0447;** www.sgls.co.uk) for information on local events. Lesbian visitors in Edinburgh can call ℗ **0131/557-0751** for information.

Scotland doesn't boast much of a gay scene. Gay-bashing happens, especially in the grimy industrial sections of Glasgow, where neo-Nazi skinheads hang out. Although it's a crime, it's rarely punished. Open displays of affection between same-sex couples usually invite scorn in rural Scotland.

The best guide is *Spartacus Britain and Ireland.* Although the third edition of *Frommer's Gay & Lesbian Europe* doesn't include Scotland, it does include London and Brighton, in case you're heading to England before or after Scotland. For up-to-the-minute activities in Britain, we recommend *Gay Times* (London).

The **International Gay & Lesbian Travel Association** (IGLTA; ℗ **800/448-8550** or 954/776-2626; www.iglta.org) is the trade association for the gay and lesbian travel industry, and offers an online directory of gay and lesbian–friendly travel businesses; go to their website and click on "Members."

Many agencies offer tours and travel itineraries specifically for gay and lesbian travelers. **Above and Beyond Tours**

(© **800/397-2681;** www.abovebeyond tours.com) are gay tour operators. **Now, Voyager** (© **800/255-6951;** www. nowvoyager.com) is a well-known San Francisco–based gay-owned and -operated travel service.

SENIOR TRAVEL

Many discounts are available to seniors. Be advised that in Scotland you often have to be a member of an association to get discounts. Public-transportation reductions, for example, are available only to holders of British Pension books. However, many attractions do offer discounts for seniors (women 60 or over and men 65 or over). Even if discounts aren't posted, ask if they're available.

If you're over 60, you're eligible for special 10% discounts on **British Airways (BA)** through its Privileged Traveler program. You also qualify for reduced restrictions on APEX cancellations. Discounts are also granted for BA tours and for intra-Britain air tickets booked in North America. **British Rail** offers seniors discounted rates on first-class rail passes around Britain. See "By Train from Continental Europe," in "Getting There," earlier in the chapter.

Don't be shy about asking for discounts, but carry some kind of identification that shows your date of birth. Also, mention you're a senior when you make your reservations. Many hotels offer seniors discounts. In most cities, people over the age of 60 qualify for reduced admission to theaters, museums, and other attractions, and discounted fares on public transportation.

Many reliable agencies and organizations target the 50-plus market. **Elderhostel** (© **800/454-5768;** www.elder hostel.org) arranges study programs for those age 55 and over (and a spouse or companion of any age) in the U.S. and in more than 80 countries around the world. Most courses last 2 to 4 weeks abroad, and many include airfare, accommodations in university dormitories or modest inns, meals, and tuition.

Recommended publications offering travel resources and discounts for seniors include: the quarterly magazine *Travel 50 & Beyond* (www.travel50andbeyond. com); and the bestselling paperback *Unbelievably Good Deals and Great Adventures That You Absolutely Can't Get Unless You're Over 50 2005–2006, 16th Edition* (McGraw-Hill), by Joann Rattner Heilman.

FAMILY TRAVEL

If you have enough trouble getting your kids out of the house in the morning, dragging them thousands of miles away may seem like an insurmountable challenge. But family travel can be immensely rewarding, giving you new ways of seeing the world through smaller pairs of eyes.

When booking rooms, ask whether family suites are available. Accommodations in more rural areas sometimes have self-catering cottages or apartments, which might be an ideal solution for families trying to save some money and looking for a bit more space than a typical hotel room. Throughout this book, look for our kids icon, which indicates attractions, restaurants, or hotels and resorts that are especially family friendly. Note that some castles and more private luxury accommodations do not accept young children as guests. Such instances are noted in all reviews.

Recommended family travel websites include **Family Travel Forum** (www. familytravelforum.com), a comprehensive site that offers customized trip planning; **Family Travel Network** (www. familytravelnetwork.com), an award-winning site that offers travel features, deals, and tips; **Travel with Your Kids** (www.travelwithyourkids.com), a comprehensive site offering sound advice for long-distance and international travel

Traveling with Minors

It's always wise to have plenty of documentation when traveling with children. For up-to-date details on entry requirements for children traveling abroad, go to the U.S. State Department website: travel.state.gov/foreignentryreq.html. All children must have their own passport. In the United States, any questions parents or guardians might have can be answered by calling the **National Passport Information Center** at ℰ 877/487-2778.

with children; and **Family Travel Files** (www.thefamilytravelfiles.com), which offers an online magazine and a directory of off-the-beaten-path tours and tour operators for families.

STUDENT TRAVEL

The **International Student Travel Confederation** (**ISTC**; www.istc.org) was formed in 1949 to make travel around the world more affordable for students. Check out its website for comprehensive travel services information and details on how to get an **International Student Identity Card** (**ISIC**), which qualifies students for substantial savings on rail passes, plane tickets, entrance fees, and more. It also provides students with basic health and life insurance and a 24-hour helpline. The card is valid for a maximum

of 18 months. You can apply for the card online or in person at **STA Travel** (ℰ 800/781-4040 in North America; www.statravel.com), the biggest student travel agency in the world; check out the website to locate STA Travel offices worldwide. If you're no longer a student but are still under 26, you can get an **International Youth Travel Card** (**IYTC**) from the same people; this card entitles you to some discounts. **Travel CUTS** (ℰ 800/592-2887; www.travelcuts.com) offers similar services for both Canadians and U.S. residents. Irish students may prefer to turn to **USIT** (ℰ 01/602-1904; www.usit.ie), an Ireland-based specialist in student, youth, and independent travel.

11 Sustainable Tourism/Ecotourism

Each time you take a flight or drive a car CO_2 is released into the atmosphere. You can help neutralize this danger to our planet through "carbon offsetting"—paying someone to reduce your CO_2 emissions by the same amount you've added. Carbon offsets can be purchased in the U.S. from companies such as **Carbonfund.org** (www.carbonfund.org) and **TerraPass** (www.terrapass.org), and from **Climate Care** (www.climatecare.org) in the U.K.

Although one could argue that any vacation that includes an airplane flight can't be truly "green," you can go on holiday and still contribute positively to the environment. You can offset carbon

emissions from your flight in other ways. Choose forward-looking companies that embrace responsible development practices, helping preserve destinations for the future by working alongside local people. An increasing number of sustainable tourism initiatives can help you plan a family trip and leave as small a "footprint" as possible on the places you visit.

Responsible Travel (www.responsibletravel.com) contains a great source of sustainable travel ideas run by a spokesperson for responsible tourism in the travel industry. **Sustainable Travel International** (www.sustainabletravelinternational.org) promotes responsible tourism practices and issues an annual Green Gear & Gift Guide.

Frommers.com: The Complete Travel Resource

For an excellent travel-planning resource, we highly recommend **Frommers.com** (www.frommers.com). We're a little biased, of course, but we guarantee that you'll find the travel tips, reviews, monthly vacation giveaways, and online-booking capabilities thoroughly indispensable. Among the special features are our popular **Message Boards,** where Frommer's readers post queries and share advice (sometimes even our authors show up to answer questions); **Frommers.com Newsletter,** for the latest travel bargains and insider travel secrets; and **Frommer's Destinations Section,** where you'll get expert travel tips, hotel and dining recommendations, and advice on the sights to see for more than 3,000 destinations around the globe. When your research is done, the **Online Reservations System** (www.frommers.com/book_a_trip) takes you to Frommer's preferred online partners for booking your vacation at affordable prices.

You can find eco-friendly travel tips, statistics, and touring companies and associations—listed by destination under "Travel Choice"—at The International Ecotourism Society (TIES) website, www.ecotourism.org. Also check out **Conservation International** (www.conservation.org)—which, with *National Geographic Traveler,* annually presents **World Legacy Awards** (www.wlaward.org) to those travel tour operators, businesses, organizations, and places that have made a significant contribution to sustainable tourism. **Ecotravel.com** is part online magazine and part ecodirectory that lets you search for touring companies in several categories (water-based, land-based, spiritually oriented, and so on).

In the U.K., **Tourism Concern** (www.tourismconcern.org.uk) works to reduce social and environmental problems connected to tourism and find ways of improving tourism so that local benefits are increased.

The **Association of British Travel Agents** (**ABTA;** www.abtamembers.org/responsibletourism) acts as a focal point for the U.K. travel industry and is one of the leading groups spearheading responsible tourism.

The **Association of Independent Tour Operators** (**AITO;** www.aito.co.uk) is a group of interesting specialist operators leading the field in making holidays sustainable.

12 Staying Connected

TELEPHONES

To call Scotland from North America, dial **011** (international code), **44** (Britain's country code), the local area codes (usually three or four digits and found in every phone number we've given in this book), and the local phone number. The local area codes found throughout this book all begin with "0"; you drop the "0" if you're calling from outside Britain, but you need to dial it along with the area code if you're calling from another city or town within Britain. For calls within the same city or town, the local number is all you need.

For **directory assistance** in London, dial © **142;** for the rest of Britain, **192.**

There are three types of public pay phones: those taking only coins, those accepting only phone cards (called

Cardphones), and those taking both phone cards and credit cards. At coin-operated phones, insert your coins before dialing. The minimum charge is 10p (20¢).

Phone cards are available in four values—£2 ($3.80), £4 ($7.60), £10 ($19), and £20 ($38)—and are reusable until the total value has expired. Cards can be purchased from newsstands and post offices. Finally, the credit card pay phone—Access (MasterCard), Visa, American Express, and Diners Club—is most common at airports and large railway stations.

To make an international call from Britain, dial the international access code **(00),** then the country code, then the area code, and finally the local number. Or call through one of the following long-distance access codes: **AT&T USA Direct** (ⓒ 1800/CALL-ATT), **Canada Direct** (ⓒ 0800/890016), **Australia** (ⓒ 0800/ 890061), and **New Zealand** (ⓒ 0800/ 890064). Common country codes are U.S. and Canada, **1;** Australia, **61;** New Zealand, **64;** and South Africa, **27.**

For calling **collect** or if you need an international operator, dial **155.**

Caller beware: Some hotels routinely add outrageous surcharges onto phone calls made from your room. Inquire before you call! It may be a lot cheaper to use your own calling-card number or to find a pay phone.

CELLPHONES

The three letters that define much of the world's wireless capabilities are **GSM** (Global System for Mobile Communications), a big, seamless network that makes for easy cross-border cellphone use throughout Europe and dozens of other countries worldwide. In the U.S., T-Mobile, and AT&T use this quasi-universal system; in Canada, Microcell and some Rogers customers are GSM, and all Europeans and most Australians use GSM. GSM phones function with a removable plastic SIM card, encoded with your phone number and account information. If your cellphone is on a GSM system, and you have a world-capable multiband phone such as many Sony Ericsson, Motorola, or Samsung models, you can make and receive calls across civilized areas around much of the globe. Just call your wireless operator and ask for "international roaming" to be activated on your account. Unfortunately, per-minute charges can be high—usually $1 to $1.50 in Western Europe and up to $5 in places like Russia and Indonesia.

For many, **renting** a phone is a good idea. While you can rent a phone from any number of overseas sites, including kiosks at airports and at car-rental agencies, we suggest renting the phone before you leave home. North Americans can rent one before leaving home from **InTouch USA** (ⓒ **800/872-7626;** www.intouchglobal. com) or **RoadPost** (ⓒ **888/290-1616** or 905/272-5665; www.roadpost.com). InTouch will also, for free, advise you on whether your existing phone will work overseas.

Buying a phone can be economically attractive, as many nations have cheap

---

Tips **Calling Scotland**

To call Scotland from the United States, dial the **international prefix, 011;** then Scotland's **country code, 44;** then the **city code** (for example, **131** for Edinburgh and **141** for Glasgow—minus the initial zero, which is used only if you're dialing from within the United Kingdom); then dial the **phone number.**

prepaid phone systems. Once you arrive at your destination, stop by a local cellphone shop and get the cheapest package; you'll probably pay less than $100 for a phone and a starter calling card. Local calls may be as low as 10¢ per minute, and in many countries incoming calls are free.

VOICE-OVER INTERNET PROTOCOL (VOIP)

If you have Web access while traveling, you might consider a broadband-based telephone service (in technical terms, **Voice over Internet protocol, or VoIP**) such as Skype (www.skype.com) or Vonage (www.vonage.com), which allows you to make free international calls if you use their services from your laptop or in a cybercafe. The people you're calling must also use the service for it to work; check the sites for details.

INTERNET/E-MAIL
WITHOUT YOUR OWN COMPUTER

To find cybercafes in your destination check **www.cybercaptive.com** and **www.cybercafe.com**.

Most major airports have **Internet kiosks** that provide basic Web access for a per-minute fee that's usually higher than cybercafe prices. Check out copy shops like **Kinko's** (FedEx Kinko's), which offers computer stations with fully loaded software (as well as Wi-Fi).

WITH YOUR OWN COMPUTER

More and more hotels, resorts, airports, cafes, and retailers are going **Wi-Fi** (wireless fidelity), becoming "hotspots" that offer free high-speed Wi-Fi access or charge a small fee for usage. Most laptops sold today have built-in wireless capability. To find public Wi-Fi hotspots at your destination, go to **www.jiwire.com**; its Hotspot Finder holds the world's largest directory of public wireless hotspots.

For dial-up access, most business-class hotels throughout the world offer dataports for laptop modems, and a few thousand hotels in Europe now offer free high-speed Internet access.

Wherever you go, bring a **connection kit** of the right power and phone adapters, a spare phone cord, and a spare Ethernet network cable—or find out whether your hotel supplies them to guests.

For the electrical current, refer to "Fast Facts," below.

13 Getting Around Scotland

BY CAR

Scotland has many excellent roads, often "dual carriageways" (divided highways), as well as fast trunk roads, linking the Lowlands to the Highlands. In more remote areas, especially the islands of western Scotland, single-lane roads exist. Here caution while driving is important.

Passing places are provided. However, many of the roads are unfenced, and livestock can be a serious hazard when you're driving, either day or night. Drive slowly when you're passing through areas filled with sheep.

CAR RENTALS It's best to shop around, compare prices, and have a clear idea of your needs before you reserve a car. All companies give the best rates to those who reserve at least 2 business days in advance and who agree to return the car to its point of origin, and some require drivers be at least 23 years old (in some cases 21). It's also an advantage to keep the car for at least a week, as opposed to 3 or 4 days. Be warned that all car rentals in the United Kingdom are slapped with a whopping 17.5% government tax known as VAT.

To rent a car in Scotland, you must present your passport and driver's license along with your deposit. No special British or international license is needed.

Rentals are available through **Avis** (📞 800/331-1084; www.avis.com),**British Airways** (📞 800/AIRWAYS; www.british-airways.com), **Budget** (📞 800/472-3325; www.budget.com), and **Hertz** (📞 800/654-3001; www.hertz.com). **Kemwel Drive Group** (📞 877/820-0668; www.kemwel.com) is among the cheapest and most reliable of the rental agencies. **AutoEurope** (📞 888/223-5555 in the U.S., or 0800/223-5555 in London; www.autoeurope.com) acts as a wholesale company for rental agencies in Europe.

Car-rental rates vary even more than airline fares. The price you pay depends on the size of the car, where and when you pick it up and drop it off, length of the rental period, where and how far you drive it, whether you purchase insurance, and a host of other factors. A few key questions could save you hundreds of dollars:

- Are weekend rates lower than week-day rates? Ask if the rate is the same for pickup Friday morning, for instance, as it is for Thursday night.
- Is a weekly rate cheaper than the daily rate? If you need to keep the car for 4 days, it may be cheaper to keep it for 5, even if you don't need it for that long.
- Does the agency assess a drop-off charge if you do not return the car to the same location where you picked it up? Is it cheaper to pick up the car at the airport compared to a downtown location?
- Are special promotional rates available? If you see an advertised price in your local newspaper, be sure to ask for that specific rate; otherwise, you may be charged the standard cost. The terms change constantly, and phone operators may not volunteer information.

- Are discounts available for members of AARP, AAA, frequent-flier programs, or trade unions? If you belong to any of these organizations, you are probably entitled to discounts of up to 30%.
- What is the cost of adding an additional driver's name to the contract?
- How many free miles are included in the price? Free mileage is often negotiable, depending on the length of your rental.
- How much does the rental company charge to refill your gas tank if you return with the tank less than full? Though most rental companies claim these prices are "competitive," fuel is almost always cheaper in town. Try to allow enough time to refuel the car yourself before returning it.

GASOLINE   There are plenty of gas ("petrol") stations in the environs of Glasgow and Edinburgh. However, in remote areas they're often few and far between, and many are closed on Sunday. If you're planning a lot of Sunday driving in remote parts, always make sure your tank is full on Saturday.

Note that gasoline costs more in Britain than in North America, and to encourage energy saving the government has imposed a new 25% tax on gas.

DRIVING RULES & REQUIREMENTS   In Scotland, *you drive on the left* and pass on the right. Road signs are clear and the international symbols are unmistakable.

It's a good idea to get a copy of the *British Highway Code,* available from almost any gas station or newsstand (called a "news stall" in Britain).

(*Tips* **Look Both Ways!**

Visitors from the U.S. should remember that in Great Britain, cars drive on the left. Always look both ways before stepping off a curb.

(Value) Budgeting Adventure

If you're going to be visiting a large number of Scotland's historic properties, your best bet is the **Explorer Pass.** It gives you savings on 75 of Scotland's most visited historic attractions, including Edinburgh, Stirling, and Urquhart castles. There are three types of passes. The first is good for 3 days within a 5-day period and costs adults £19 ($36) and seniors and children £15 ($28). The second pass is available for 7 days within a 14-day period and costs adults £27 ($51) and seniors and children £21 ($39). For those who are uncertain of when they'll be traveling, the third pass, which allows for 10 days in a 30-day period, is a good choice. However, it is the most expensive alternative, costing adults £32 ($61) and seniors and children £24 ($46). The pass is available at all of Scotland's historical sites, the tourist information centers, and on the Web at www. historic-scotland.gov.uk.

Another good choice for visitors on a budget is **The Great Britain Heritage Pass,** which is accepted all over Great Britain. The pass will allow you free entry to more than 600 tourist attractions in Ireland, Wales, Scotland, and England, including Stonehenge, Palace of Holyroodhouse, Edinburgh Castle, and the Roman Baths. In addition to the free entry, pass holders also get a 40-page guidebook and a map of Great Britain. The 4-day pass costs £28 ($53). For 7 days, it's £39 ($74) and 15 days is £52 ($99). The month-long pass costs £70 ($133). You must use the pass on consecutive days. It can be purchased at a tourist office or online at www.gbheritagepass.com.

Warning: Pedestrian crossings are marked by striped lines (zebra striping) on the road; flashing lights near the curb indicate that drivers must stop and yield the right of way if a pedestrian has stepped out into the zebra zone to cross the street.

BREAKDOWNS Membership in one of the two major auto clubs can be helpful: the **Automobile Association (AA)** at Norfolk House, Priestly Road, Basingstoke, Hampshire RG24 9NY (© **0870/5444-444**), or the **Royal Automobile Club (RAC),** P.O. Box 700, Bristol, Somerset BS99 1RB (© **08000/966-999;** www.rac.co.uk). You can join these clubs through your car-rental agent. (Members of AAA in the U.S. can enjoy reciprocity overseas.) There are roadside emergency telephone boxes about every mile along the motorways. If you don't see one, walk down the road for a bit to the blue-and-white marker with an arrow that points to the nearest

box. The 24-hour number to call for the AA is © **0800/887-766;** for the RAC, it's © **0800/82-82-82.** In addition, you can call a police traffic unit that will contact either of the auto clubs on your behalf.

BY PLANE

Scotland's relatively small scale makes flights between many cities inconvenient and impractical. Although **British Airways** (© **800/247-9297;** in the U.K. 0870/859-9850; www.britishairways.com) offers regular flights between Glasgow and Edinburgh, the excellent rail and highway connections usually deter most passengers from flying that route—unless their plane just happens to stop en route to other, more distant, points in Scotland. Frankly, except for visits to the far-distant Shetlands and Orkneys, we prefer to drive to all but the most inaccessible points. However, British Airways is by far the largest intra-Britain carrier since its

Tips **Eurailpass Warning**

Note that your Eurailpass is *not* valid on trains in Great Britain.

merger with regional carriers Logan Airways and British Express. From Edinburgh, you can fly British Airways to Inverness, Wick, Kirkwall (the Orkneys), and Lerwick (the Shetlands).

BY TRAIN

The cost of rail travel in Scotland is often quite low, and trains are generally punctual. Timetables are available at all stations, with free timetables covering only certain regions available at various stations. For £20 ($38), a **Scottish Youth rail card** (ages 16–18) is sold at major stations. Two passport-size photos are needed. It's estimated this card reduces all fares by one-third for 1 year.

If you plan much travel on European railroads, get the latest copy of the *Thomas Cook European Timetable of Railroads.* This 500-plus-page book documents all of Europe's main passenger-rail services with detail and accuracy. It's available on the Web at www.thomascooktimetables.com.

The Royal Scotsman (*©* **401/351-7518;** www.royalscotsman.com) is one of the most luxurious trains in the world—called "a country house hotel on wheels." The train passes by ancient mountains and mysterious lochs, through glens and across villages as you live in sumptuous surroundings. It's like being the guest at a private party. The train carries a maximum of 36 guests, each passenger enjoying plenty of space. Plush beds and opulent bathrooms are the order of the day. The classic tour calls for 4 nights aboard, and goes from the panoramic Southern Highlands to the more rugged grandeur of the Western Highlands. Superb cuisine and a long list of fine wines and choice malt whiskies are more reasons to hop aboard.

For information on rail travel in Scotland, contact **First ScotRail,** Caledonian

Chambers, 87 Union St., Glasgow G1 3TA, Scotland (*©* **0845/601-5929;** www.firstgroup.com).

BRITRAIL TRAVEL PASSES

BritRail Passes allow unlimited travel in England, Scotland, and Wales on any British Rail scheduled train over the whole of the network during the validity of the pass without restrictions. **BritRail Consecutive Pass** allows you to travel for a consecutive number of days for a flat rate. In first class adults pay $327 for 4 days, $469 for 8 days, $702 for 15 days, $891 for 22 days, and $1,054 for 1 month. In second class, fares are $218 for 4 days, $311 for 8 days, $469 for 15 days, $592 for 22 days, and $702 for 1 month. Seniors (60 and over) qualify for discounts in first class travel and pay $278 for 4 days, $375 for 8 days, $597 for 15 days, $757 for 22 days, and $896 for 1 month of first class travel. Passengers under 26 quality for a **Youth Pass:** $142 for 4 days, $206 for 8 days, $307 for 15 days, $388 for 22 days, and $459 for 1 month. One child (under age 15) can travel free with each adult or senior pass by requesting the **BritRail Family Pass** when buying the adult pass. Additional children pay half the regular adult fare.

A more versatile pass is the **BritRail FlexiPass** allowing you to travel when you want, during a 2-month period of time. In first class, it costs $409 for 4 days, $598 for 8 days, and $901 for 15 days of travel. Second class costs $275 for 4 days, $399 for 8 days, and $604 for 15 days of travel.

A pass for travel in England only, the **BritRail England Consecutive Pass** is sold at a price 20% lower than regular BritRail Passes which cover rail travel throughout the U.K. (Britain, Scotland, Wales, and Northern Ireland). Starting at

Getting Your VAT Refund

You can get a VAT refund if you shop at stores that participate in the Retail Export Scheme. (Signs are posted in the window.) When you make a purchase, show your passport and request a Retail Export Scheme form (VAT 407) and a stamped, pre-addressed envelope. Show the VAT form and your sales receipt to British Customs when you leave the country—they may also ask to see the merchandise. After Customs has stamped it, mail the form back to the shop in the envelope provided *before you leave the country.* Your VAT refund will be mailed to you.

Remember: Keep your VAT forms with your passport; pack your purchases in a carry-on bag so you'll have them handy; and allow yourself enough time at your departure point to find a mailbox.

Several readers have reported a VAT refund scam. Some merchants allegedly tell customers they can get a refund form at the airport on their way out of the country. *This is not true.* The form must be completed by the retailer on the spot, or you won't get a refund later.

For information, contact **Global Refund,** 707 Summer St., Stamford, CT 06901 (© **800/566-9828;** www.globalrefund.com).

$262 for 4 consecutive days of travel in standard class, the BritRail England Pass is also offered for 8, 15, or 22 consecutive days or 1 month or as a FlexiPass (days may be consecutive or nonconsecutive) for 4, 8, or 15 days within a 2-month period. It is also available in first class, starting at $327 and at discounted prices for seniors (60 and over) in first class and youth (under 26) in standard class. As with other BritRail Passes, one child under 15 may travel free when accompanied by an adult or senior purchasing a BritRail England Pass and requesting the Family Pass.

To call BritRail in the United States, dial © **877/677-1066.** On the Web, BritRail Passes and vacation packages are presented at www.britrail.net and www.BritainSecrets.com.

TRAVELPASSES FOR SCOTLAND
If you plan to travel primarily in Scotland, the Scottish Tourist Authorities offer the **Scottish Freedom Pass,** with unlimited transportation on trains and most ferries throughout Scotland and discounts for bus travel. It includes access to obscure bus routes to almost forgotten hamlets, free rides on ferries operated by Caledonian MacBrayne, and discounted fares with P&O Scottish Lines. The ferries connect to the Western Islands, the islands of the Clyde, and the Orkneys.

The Freedom Pass covers the entire Scottish rail network and is usable from Carlisle, England (near the western Scotland-England border), and from Berwick-upon-Tweed, England (near the eastern Scotland-England border). In addition, if you have to fly into London and want to go straight to Scotland from there, a reduced rate is available for a round-trip ticket between London and Edinburgh or Glasgow for Travelpass holders.

The Freedom Pass is available for 4 days' travel over an 8-day period for $217 and 8 days' travel over a 15-day period for $292. For more information, contact **BritRail** (see above).

BY BUS (COACH)

No doubt about it, the cheapest means of transport from London to Scotland is the bus (coach). It's also the least expensive way to travel within Scotland.

All major towns have a **local bus service,** and every tourist office can provide details about half- or full-day bus excursions to scenic highlights. If you want to explore a particular area, you can often avail yourself of an economical bus pass. If you're planning to travel extensively in Scotland, see the Scotland Freedom Pass, described above.

Many adventurous travelers like to explore the country on one of the **postal buses,** which carry not only mail but also a limited number of passengers to rural areas. Ask at any local post office for details. A general timetable is available at the head post office in Edinburgh.

Scottish Citylink Coaches are a good bet. They link the major cities (Glasgow and Edinburgh) with the two most popular tourist centers, Inverness and Aviemore. Travel is fast and prices are low. For example, it takes only 3 hours to reach Aviemore from Edinburgh, and Inverness is just 3½ hours from Edinburgh. A direct Scottish Citylink overnight coach makes the run from London to Aviemore and Inverness at reasonable fares.

Coaches offer many other popular runs, including links between Glasgow and Fort William, Inverness and Ullapool, and Glasgow and Oban. For details, contact **Rapsons,** 1 Seafield Rd., Inverness (ⓒ **01463/710-555;** www.rapsons.co.uk), or **Scottish Citylink,** Buchanan Street Bus Station, Glasgow (ⓒ **08705/505-050;** www.citylink.co.uk).

FAST FACTS: Scotland

American Express There's an office at 69 George St. in Edinburgh (ⓒ **0131/ 718-2505**); hours are Monday through Friday from 9am to 5:30pm and Saturday from 9am to 4pm. Another office is at 115 Hope St. in Glasgow (ⓒ **0141/ 222-1405**); it's open Monday through Friday from 8:30am to 5:30pm, Saturday from 9am to noon (9am–4pm June–July).

Area Codes The country code for Britain is **44.** The area code for Edinburgh is **0131;** for Glasgow **0141.**

Business Hours With many, many exceptions, business hours are Monday through Friday from 9am to 5pm. In general, stores are open Monday through Saturday from 9am to 5:30pm. In country towns, there is usually an early closing day (often on Wed or Thurs), when the shops close at 1pm.

Car Rentals See "Getting Around Scotland," earlier in this chapter.

Climate See "When to Go," earlier in this chapter.

Currency See "Money & Costs," earlier in this chapter.

Customs **Non-E.U. Nationals** can bring in, duty-free, 200 cigarettes, 100 cigarillos, 50 cigars, or 250 grams of smoking tobacco. This amount is doubled if you live outside Europe. You can also bring in 2 liters of wine and either 1 liter of alcohol over 22 proof or 2 liters of wine under 22 proof. In addition, you can bring in 60 cc's (2.03 oz.) of perfume, a quarter liter (250ml) of eau de toilette, 500 grams (1 lb.) of coffee, and 200 grams (½ lb.) of tea. Visitors 15 and over may also bring in other goods totaling £145 ($276); the allowance for those 14 and under is £73 ($138). (Customs officials tend to be lenient about general merchandise, realizing the limits are unrealistically low.)

Returning **U.S. citizens** who have been away for at least 48 hours are allowed to bring back, once every 30 days, $800 worth of merchandise duty-free. You'll be charged a flat rate of 4% duty on the next $1,000 worth of purchases. Be sure to have your receipts handy. On mailed gifts, the duty-free limit is $200. With some exceptions, you cannot bring fresh fruits and vegetables into the United States. For specifics on what you can bring back, download the invaluable free pamphlet *Know Before You Go* online at **www.cbp.gov**. (Click on "Know Before You Go!") Or contact the **U.S. Customs & Border Protection (CBP),** 1300 Pennsylvania Ave., NW, Washington, DC 20229 (© **877/287-8867**) and request the pamphlet.

For a clear summary of **Canadian** rules, write for the booklet *I Declare*, issued by the **Canada Border Services Agency** (© **800/461-9999** in Canada, or 204/983-3500; www.ccra-adrc.gc.ca). Canada allows its citizens a C$750 exemption, and you're allowed to bring back duty-free one carton of cigarettes, 1 can of tobacco, 40 imperial ounces of liquor, and 50 cigars. In addition, you're allowed to mail gifts to Canada valued at less than C$60 a day, provided they're unsolicited and don't contain alcohol or tobacco (write on the package "Unsolicited gift, under $60 value"). All valuables should be declared on the Y-38 form before departure from Canada, including serial numbers of valuables you already own, such as expensive foreign cameras. *Note:* The C$750 exemption can only be used once a year and only after an absence of 7 days.

Citizens of the U.K. who are **returning from a European Union (E.U.) country** will go through a separate Customs Exit (called the "Blue Exit") especially for E.U. travelers. There is no limit on what you can bring back from an E.U. country, as long as the items are for personal use (this includes gifts), and you have already paid the necessary duty and tax. However, customs law sets out guidance levels. If you bring in more than these levels, you may be asked to prove that the goods are for your own use. Guidance levels on goods bought in the E.U. for your own use are 3,200 cigarettes, 200 cigars, 3 kilograms of smoking tobacco, 10 liters of spirits, 90 liters of wine (of this not more than 60 liters can be sparkling wine), and 110 liters of beer.

The duty-free allowance in **Australia** is A$400 or, for those under 18, A$200. Citizens can bring in 250 cigarettes or 250 grams of loose tobacco, and 1,125 milliliters of alcohol. If you're returning with valuables you already own, such as foreign-made cameras, you should file form B263. A helpful brochure available from Australian consulates or Customs offices is *Know Before You Go.* For more information, call the **Australian Customs Service** at © **1300/363-263,** or log on to www.customs.gov.au.

The duty-free allowance for **New Zealand** is NZ$700. Citizens over 17 can bring in 200 cigarettes, 50 cigars, or 250 grams of tobacco (or a mixture of all three if their combined weight doesn't exceed 250 grams); plus 4.5 liters of wine and beer, or 1.125 liters of liquor. New Zealand currency does not carry import or export restrictions. Fill out a certificate of export, listing the valuables you are taking out of the country; that way, you can bring them back without paying duty. Most questions are answered in a free pamphlet available at New

Zealand consulates and Customs offices: *New Zealand Customs Guide for Travellers, Notice no. 4*. For more information, contact **New Zealand Customs Service,** The Customhouse, 17–21 Whitmore St., Box 2218, Wellington (© **04/ 473-6099** or 0800/428-786; www.customs.govt.nz).

Drug Laws Great Britain is becoming increasingly severe in enforcing drug laws. People arrested for possession of even tiny quantities of marijuana have been deported, forced to pay stiff fines, or sentenced to jail for 2 to 7 years. Possession of drugs like heroin and cocaine carries even more stringent penalties.

Drugstores In Britain, they're called "chemists." Every police station in the country has a list of emergency chemists. Dial "0" (zero) and ask the operator for the local police, who will give you the name of one nearest you.

Electricity British electricity is 240 volts AC (50 cycles), roughly twice the voltage in North America, which is 115 to 120 volts AC (60 cycles). American plugs don't fit British wall outlets. Always bring suitable transformers and/or adapters—if you plug an American appliance directly into a European electrical outlet without a transformer, you'll destroy your appliance and possibly start a fire. Tape recorders, VCRs, and other devices with motors intended to revolve at a fixed number of revolutions per minute probably won't work properly even with transformers.

Embassies & Consulates All embassies are in London. There's a **U.S. Consulate** in Edinburgh at 3 Regent Terrace (© **0131/556-8315**), open Monday through Friday from 1 to 5:30pm. All other nationals have to use London to conduct their business: The **Canadian High Commission** is at 50 Lothian Rd. (© **0131/ 473-6320**), open Monday through Friday from 8am to 4pm. The **Australian High Commission** is at 69 George St. (© **0131/624-3333**), open Monday through Friday from 9:30am to 3:30pm. The **New Zealand Consulate** is at 5 Rutland Sq. (© **0131/222-8109**), open Monday to Friday 9am to 5pm. The **Irish Consulate** is at 16 Randolph Crescent (© **0131/226-7711**), open Monday through Friday from 9:30am to 1pm and 2:15 to 5pm.

Emergencies For police, fire, or ambulance, dial © **999.** Give your name, address, phone number, and the nature of the emergency. Misuse of the 999 service will result in a heavy fine (cardiac arrest, yes; dented fender, no).

Holidays See "When to Go," earlier in this chapter.

Information See "Visitor Information," earlier in this chapter, and the individual city/regional chapters that follow.

Legal Aid Your consulate, embassy, or high commission (see above) will give you advice if you run into trouble. They can advise you of your rights and even provide a list of attorneys (for which you'll have to pay if services are used), but they can't interfere on your behalf in the legal processes of Great Britain. For questions about American citizens arrested abroad, including ways of getting money to them, call the **Citizens Emergency Center of the Office of Special Consulate Services,** in Washington, D.C. (© **202/647-5225**). Other nationals can go to their nearest consulate or embassy.

Liquor Laws The legal drinking age is 18. Children under 16 aren't allowed in pubs, except in certain rooms, and then only when accompanied by a parent or guardian. Don't drink and drive; the penalties are stiff. Basically, you can get a drink from 11am to 11pm, but this can vary widely, depending on the discretion of the local tavern owner. Certain licensed premises can have hours extended in some areas up to 4am, on a "local need" basis. Not all pubs are open on Sunday; those that are generally stay open from noon to 3pm and 7 to 10:30 or 11pm. Restaurants are allowed to serve liquor during these hours, but only to people who are dining on the premises. The law allows 30 minutes for "drinking-up time." A meal, incidentally, is defined as "substantial refreshment." And you have to eat and drink sitting down. In hotels, liquor may be served from 11am to 11pm to both guests and nonguests; after 11pm, only guests may be served.

Mail Post offices and subpost offices are open Monday through Friday from 9am to 5:30pm and Saturday from 9:30am to noon.

Sending an airmail letter to North America costs 54p ($1.05) for 10 grams (.35 oz.), and postcards require a 54p ($1.05) stamp. British mailboxes are painted red and carry a royal coat of arms. All post offices accept parcels for mailing, provided they are properly and securely wrapped.

Newspapers & Magazines Each major Scottish city publishes its own newspaper. All newsagents (newsstands) carry the major London papers as well. In summer, you can generally pick up a copy of the *International Herald Tribune,* published in Paris, along with the European editions of *USA Today, Time,* and *Newsweek.*

Passports **For Residents of the United States:** Whether you're applying in person or by mail, you can download passport applications from the U.S. State Department website at **http://travel.state.gov**. To find your regional passport office, check the U.S. State Department website.

For Residents of Canada: Passport applications are available at travel agencies throughout Canada or from the central **Passport Office,** Department of Foreign Affairs and International Trade, Ottawa, ON K1A 0G3 (✆ **800/567-6868;** www.ppt.gc.ca).

For Residents of Ireland: You can apply for a 10-year passport at the **Passport Office,** Setanta Centre, Molesworth Street, Dublin 2 (✆ **01/671-1633;** www.irl gov.ie/iveagh). Those under age 18 and over 65 must apply for a €12 3-year passport. You can also apply at 1A South Mall, Cork (✆ **021/272-525**) or at most main post offices.

For Residents of Australia: You can pick up an application from your local post office or any branch of Passports Australia, but you must schedule an interview at the passport office to present your application materials. Call the **Australian Passport Information Service** at ✆ **131-232,** or visit the government website at www.passports.gov.au.

For Residents of New Zealand: You can pick up a passport application at any New Zealand Passports Office or download it from their website. Contact the **Passports Office** at ✆ **0800/225-050** in New Zealand or 04/474-8100, or log on to www.passports.govt.nz.

Pets Great Britain has finally eased a 100-year-old mandatory pet quarantine, but rigid requirements are still in place. Now pets need no longer fear a long separation from their Britain-bound families if they pass several tests and can wait long enough. The animal must also be coming from a country that is approved by Britain. All countries in the European Union such as Germany, Switzerland, Austria, Spain, Italy, and France are participants in the PETS program, but the United States is not. For information, check out www.defra.gov.uk/animalh/quarantine/index.htm.

Police The best source of help and advice in emergencies is the police. For non-life-threatening situations, dial "0" (zero) and ask for the police, or 999 for emergencies. If the local police can't assist, they'll have the address of a person who can. Losses, thefts, and other crimes should be reported immediately.

Restrooms Public toilets are clean and often have an attendant. Hotels can be used, but they discourage nonguests. Garages (filling stations) don't always have facilities for the use of customers. There's no need to tip, except to a hotel attendant.

Safety See "Safety," earlier in this chapter.

Taxes There's no local sales tax. However, Great Britain imposes a standard value-added tax (VAT) of 17.5%. Hotel rates and meals in restaurants are taxed 17.5%; the extra charge will show up on your bill unless otherwise stated. This can be refunded if you shop at stores that participate in the Retail Export Scheme (signs are posted in the window); see "Getting Your VAT Refund," earlier in this chapter.

Britain imposes a departure tax of £40 ($76) on short-haul flights or £80 ($152) for longer international flights including those to the United States. Economy class passengers pay £10 ($19) for short-haul flights or £40 ($76) for most international flights. This tax is accounted for in your ticket.

There is also a 25% tax on gasoline ("petrol").

Telephone To call the United Kingdom from North America, dial 011 (international code), 44 (Britain's country code), the local area codes (usually three or four digits and found in every phone number we've given in this book), and the seven-digit local phone number. The local area codes found throughout this book all begin with "0"; you drop the "0" if you're calling from outside Britain, but you need to dial it along with the area code if you're calling from another city or town within Britain. For calls within the same city or town, the local number is all you need.

For **directory assistance** in London, dial ✆ **142;** for the rest of Britain, **192.**

There are three types of public pay phones: those taking only coins, those accepting only phonecards (called Cardphones), and those taking both phonecards and credit cards. At coin-operated phones, insert your coins before dialing. The minimum charge is 10p (20¢).

Phone cards are available in four values—£2 ($3.80), £4 ($7.60), £10 ($19), and £20 ($38)—and are reusable until the total value has expired. Cards can be purchased from newsstands and post offices. Finally, the credit-call pay phone operates on credit cards—Access (MasterCard), Visa, American Express, and Diners Club—and is most common at airports and large railway stations.

To make an international call from Britain, dial the international access code **(00),** then the country code, then the area code, and finally the local number.

Or call through one of the following long-distance access codes: **AT&T USA Direct** (*©* 1800/CALL-ATT), **Canada Direct** (*©* 0800/890-016), **Australia** (*©* 0800/890-061), and **New Zealand** (*©* 0800/890-064). Common country codes are: USA and Canada, **1**; Australia, **61**; New Zealand, **64**; and South Africa, **27**.

For calling **collect** or if you need an international operator, dial *©* **155**.

Caller beware: Some hotels routinely add outrageous surcharges onto phone calls made from your room. Inquire before you call! It'll be a lot cheaper to use your own calling-card number or to find a pay phone.

Time England follows Greenwich Mean Time (GMT), which is 5 hours ahead of Eastern Standard Time, with British summertime lasting (roughly) from the end of March to the end of October. For most of the year, including summer, Britain is 5 hours ahead of the time observed in the eastern United States. Because of different daylight-savings-time practices in the two nations, there's a brief period (about a week) in autumn when Britain is only 4 hours ahead of New York, and a brief period in spring when it's 6 hours ahead.

Tipping For **cab drivers,** add about 10% to 15% to the fare as shown on the meter. If the driver personally unloads or loads your luggage, add 50p (95¢) per bag.

Hotel **porters** get 75p ($1.45) per bag even if you have only one small suitcase. Hall porters are tipped only for special services. **Maids** receive £1 ($1.90) per day. In top-ranked hotels, the **concierge** often submits a separate bill, showing charges for newspapers and the like; if he or she has been particularly helpful, tip extra.

Hotels often add a **service charge** of 10% to 15% to bills. In smaller B&Bs, the tip isn't likely to be included. Therefore, tip for special services, such as the waiter who serves you breakfast. If several people have served you in a B&B, a 10% to 15% charge will be added to the bill and divided among the staff.

In **restaurants** and **nightclubs,** a 15% service charge is added to the bill. To that, add another 3% to 5%, depending on the quality of the service. **Waiters** in deluxe restaurants and clubs are accustomed to the extra 5%, which means you end up tipping 20%. If that seems excessive, remember that the initial service charge reflected in the fixed price is distributed among all the help. **Sommeliers** (wine stewards) get about £1 ($1.90) per bottle of wine served. Tipping in **pubs** is not common, although in cocktail bars the waiter or barmaid usually gets about £1 ($1.90) per round of drinks.

Barbers and **hairdressers** expect 10% to 15%. **Tour guides** expect £2 ($3.80), but it's not mandatory. **Petrol station attendants** are rarely tipped. **Theater ushers** also don't expect tips.

Water Tap water is considered safe to drink throughout Scotland.

The Active Vacation Planner

If you're headed to Scotland to enjoy the outdoors, you can get guidance from **Sport Scotland,** Caledonian House, South Gyle, Edinburgh EH12 9DQ (© **0131/317-7200;** fax 0131/317-7202; www.sportscotland.org.uk), open Monday to Friday 9am to 5pm. It can supply names of nature areas, playing fields, prices, and facilities, as well as send a copy of *Arena,* a bulletin packed with advice on sporting programs and facilities.

1 Teeing Off: Golfing in Scotland

Although golf has become Scotland's pride, the sport hasn't always been so well received. Monks around St. Andrews weren't applauded when they diverted themselves from a schedule of felling trees and praying to play *gowff,* and James I and James II rather churlishly issued edicts prohibiting its practice. Despite that, by the mid-1700s the game was firmly entrenched in Scotland and viewed as a bucolic oddity by Englishmen chasing hounds in the milder climes to the south.

Scotland has more than 440 golf courses, many of them municipal courses open to everyone. Some are royal and ancient (such as St. Andrews), others modern and hip. An example of a well-received relative newcomer is the Loch Lomond course in the Trossachs, established as a private club in 1993. Although they lie as far north as Sutherland, only 6 degrees south of the Arctic Circle, most of Scotland's courses are in the Central Belt, stretching from Stirling down to Edinburgh and Glasgow.

Fortunately, you don't need to lug a set of clubs across the Atlantic if you don't want to, because many courses rent full or half sets. If you're female or plan on playing golf with someone who is, be aware that some courses are restricted to men only, while others limit female play to designated days. Despite this tradition-bound holdover from another era, women's golf thrives in Scotland, with about 33,000 members in the Scottish Ladies Golfing Association. The Ladies British Open Amateur Championship was first held in 1893. (The U.S. equivalent was first held in 1895.) Contact Mrs. L. H. Park, Secretary, **Scottish Ladies Golfing Association** (© **01738/442-357;** www.slga.co.uk), for information on tournaments or finding women golf partners.

Sharing offices with the Scottish Ladies Golfing Association is the **Scottish Golf Union,** established in 1920 to foster and maintain a high standard of amateur golf in Scotland.

Any serious golfer who will be in Scotland for a long stay should consider joining a local club. Membership makes it easier to get coveted tee times, and attending or competing in a local club's tournaments can be both fun and sociable. If you won't be staying long, you might not bother, but remember to bring a letter from a golf club in your home country—it can open a lot of doors otherwise closed to the general public.

Scotland's Best Golf Courses

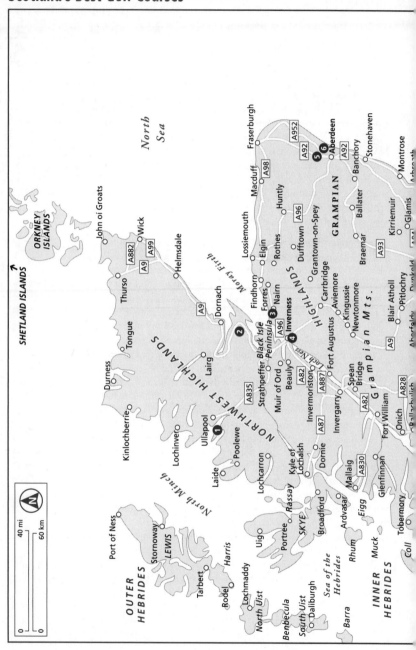

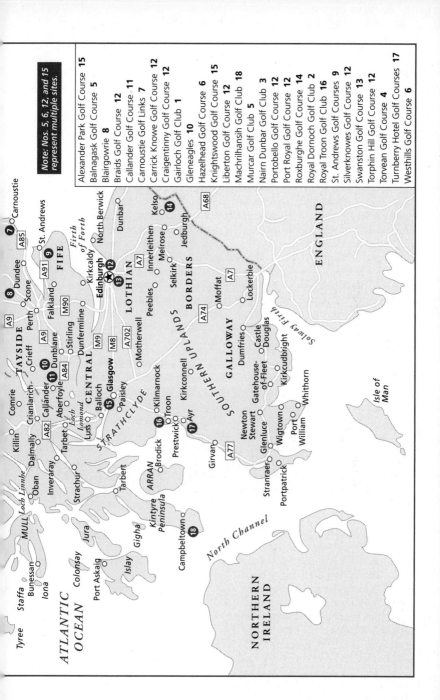

Note: Nos. 5, 6, 12, and 15 represent multiple sites.

Alexander Park Golf Course **15**
Balnagask Golf Course **5**
Blairgowrie **8**
Braids Golf Course **12**
Callander Golf Course **11**
Carnoustie Golf Links **7**
Carrick Knowe Golf Course **12**
Craigentinny Golf Course **12**
Gairloch Golf Club **1**
Gleneagles **10**
Hazelhead Golf Course **6**
Knightswood Golf Course **15**
Liberton Golf Course **12**
Machrihanish Golf Club **18**
Murcar Golf Club **5**
Nairn Dunbar Golf Club **3**
Portobello Golf Course **12**
Port Royal Golf Course **12**
Roxburghe Golf Course **14**
Royal Dornoch Golf Club **2**
Royal Troon Golf Club **16**
St. Andrews Golf Courses **9**
Silverknowes Golf Course **12**
Swanston Golf Course **13**
Torphin Hill Golf Course **12**
Torvean Golf Course **4**
Turnberry Hotel Golf Courses **17**
Westhills Golf Course **6**

Access to many private clubs can be dicey, however, particularly those boasting so much tradition that waiting lists for tee-off times can stretch on for up to a year in advance. You can always stay in a hotel (Gleneagles or Turnberry) that has its own course, thereby guaranteeing the availability of tee times. Or you can arrange a golf tour (see below).

Abandon forever any hope of balmy tropical weather, azure skies, and lush fairways. Scotland's rains and fogs produce an altogether different kind of golf-related aesthetic, one buffeted by coastal winds, sometimes torn by gales and storms, and (in some places) accented only with salt-tolerant tough grasses and wind-blown stunted trees and shrubs like gorse and heather.

Knowing a term or two in advance might help in picking your golf course. The Scots make a strong distinction between their two types of courses: links and upland. **Links courses** nestle into the sandy terrain of coastal regions, and although years of cultivation have rendered their fairways and putting greens emerald colored, there's a vague sense that eons ago the terrain was submerged beneath the water. Links courses are among the famous names in Scotland and include Royal Troon, Turnberry, Prestwick, North Berwick, and Glasgow Gailes. All links courses are on or near the sea. **Upland courses,** by contrast, are based inland and invariably consist of hilly terrain. They're usually drier and less windy than links courses. Nonetheless, it rains a lot in Scotland, so a sweater and raingear are recommended for *all* courses. Examples of upland courses are Gleneagles, Loch Lomond, and Pitlochry.

GOLF TOURS

Access for nonmembers to the country's maze of golf courses hasn't always been possible. All that changed in 1988, however, with the establishment of **Golf International,** 14 E. 38th St., New York, NY 10016 (© **800/833-1389** or 212/986-9176; www.golf international.com), which maintains a branch office in St. Andrews, the ivy-clad *sanctum sanctorum* of the golfing world. The company caters to golfers from moderate to advanced levels and, against hitherto impossible odds, will guarantee its clients starting times at 40 or so of Scotland's most sought-after courses, including St. Andrews, Carnoustie, Royal Troon, Prestwick, and Gullane.

Potential clients, in self-organized groups of 2 to 12, produce a wish list of the courses they'd like to play. Starting times are prearranged (sometimes rigidly) with an ease that an individual traveler or even a travel agent would find impossible. Packages can be arranged for anywhere from 5 to 14 days (the average is about 7 days) and can include as much or as little golf, at as many courses, as you want. Weekly prices, including hotels, breakfasts, car rentals, greens fees, and the services of a greeter and helpmate at the airport, range from £1,069 ($2,056) to £5,288 ($10,169) per person. Discounted airfares to Scotland can also be arranged.

Other companies specializing in golf tours are **Adventures in Golf,** 22 Greeley St., 7 Medallion Center, Merrimack, NH 03054 (© **877/424-7320** or 603/424-7320; www. adventures-in-golf.com); **Classic Golf & Leisure,** 75-770 McLachlin Circle, Palm Desert, CA 92211 (© **800/283-1619** in the U.S. or 760/772-2560; www.classic-golf.com); **ITC Golf Tours,** 2428 Lewis Ave., Signal Hill, CA 90755 (© **800/257-4981** or 562/595-6905; www.itcgolf-africatours.com); **Perry Golf,** 1904 Eastwood Rd., Suite 315, Wilmington, NC 28403 (© **800/344-5257** or 910/795-1048; www.perry golf.com); and **Tayleur Mayde Golf Tours,** 21 Castle St., Edinburgh EH2 3DA (© **800/ 847-8064** or 0131/225-9114; www.tayleurmayde.com).

A Beginner's Warning

Neophytes unfamiliar with the rules of the game simply aren't allowed to play the country's most legendary golf courses. Many courses will want evidence of your familiarity with the game before you're allowed on the links. Depending on the setting and the season, this could include a letter from your club back home citing your ability and experience, or visual proof that you've mastered a basically sound swing and an understanding of golf-related etiquette.

THE CLASSIC COURSES

For more details on these fabled golf courses, refer to "The Best Golf," in chapter 1. In addition to the big names below, many additional courses are listed in the appropriate destination chapters that follow.

The **Carnoustie Golf Links,** Links Parade, Carnoustie, Angus (© **01241/802-270;** www.carnoustiegolflinks.co.uk), has a par of 72. This 6,941-yard championship course requires the use of a caddy, costing £40 ($76) for 18 holes. As with most championship courses, electric golf carts aren't allowed, but you can rent a trolley for £4 ($7.60) per round (trolleys permitted May–Oct only). Greens fees are £115 ($219), and club rentals, available at the pro shop, cost £35 ($67).

The par-72 **Old Course, St. Andrews,** Golf Place, St. Andrews, Fife (© **01334/466-666**), is a 6,566-yard, 18-hole course. Golf was first played here around 1400, and it's billed as the Home of Golf. This fabled course hosted the 2000 British Open and witnessed history when Tiger Woods became the youngest golfer to complete a grand slam (and only the fifth golfer to ever perform the feat). In 2005, the Open returned to St. Andrews—and Woods once again was its champion. Greens fees are £125 ($238), a caddy costs £40 ($76) plus tip, and clubs rent for £20 to £30 ($38–$57) per round. Electric carts are not allowed, and you can rent a trolley on afternoons only between May and October for £3 ($5.70). Reservations must be made in advance.

The 18-hole **Royal Dornoch Golf Club,** Dornoch, Sutherland (© **01862/810-219;** www.royaldornoch.com), 65km (40 miles) north of Inverness, has a par of 70. At this 6,514-yard course, the greens fees are £52 to £78 ($99–$148) Monday to Friday and £58 to £88 ($110–$167) on Saturday and Sunday (members only). Golf club and trolley rentals are £15 to £25 ($29–$48) and £3 to £5 ($5.70–$9.50), respectively. Caddy service is available for £35 ($67) plus tip.

The par-71 **Royal Troon Golf Club,** Craigend Road, Troon, Ayrshire (© **01292/311-555;** fax 01292/318-204; www.royaltroon.co.uk), has one of the largest courses in Scotland, with 7,079 yards of playing area. The greens fees of £220 ($418) for a day include a buffet lunch and two 18-hole sets. For one round of play, a trolley rents for £3 ($5.70) and a caddy £35 ($67); club rental is £25 ($48) per round or £40 ($76) per day.

The **Turnberry Hotel Golf Courses,** Ayrshire (© **01655/334-032;** www.turnberry. co.uk), gives priority at its 6,976-yard, par-70 course to guests of the hotel. The greens fees—£45 to £135 ($86–$257) for guests and £60 to £200 ($114–$380) for nonguests—include 18 holes on the Ailsa course and an 18-hole round on the less-desirable Kintyre course. For one round, clubs rent for £50 ($95) and caddy service costs £40 ($76) plus tip. If you're not staying here, call in the morning to check on any unclaimed tee times—but it's a long shot.

2 Fishing

Anglers consider Scotland a paradise. Its fast-flowing rivers harbor Atlantic salmon (the king of all game fish). The rivers and numerous pristine lochs allow you to enjoy some of Europe's most beautiful scenery, and local innkeepers are extremely hospitable. Note that permits for fishing (often arranged by your hotel) can be expensive. For one of the grand beats on the River Tay, a week's permit could run as much as hundreds of pounds. However, there are many lesser-known rivers where a club ticket costs only a few pounds a day.

The **Tweed** and the **Tay** are just two of the famous Scottish salmon rivers. In Perthshire, the Tay is the broadest and longest river in the country. The **Dee** is the famous salmon-fishing river of Aberdeenshire. The royal family fishes this river, and the queen herself has been seen casting from these banks. Other anglers prefer to fish the **Spey,** staying at one of the inns along the Malt Whisky Trail. Certain well-heeled fishermen travel every year to Scotland to fish in the lochs and rivers of the **Outer Hebrides.**

In general, Scotland's season for salmon fishing runs from late February until late October, but these dates vary from region to region.

TYPES OF FISHING

Here's a breakdown of terms you're likely to hear even before you cast your first line into the country's glittering waters:

COARSE FISHING   This means going after any species of freshwater fish except salmon and trout. Especially prized trophies, known for putting up a spirited fight, are carp, tench, pike, bream, roach, and perch. Because few lochs actually freeze during winter, the sport can be practiced throughout the year. Local tourist boards all over the country can provide advice.

GAME FISHING   Salmon and trout (brown, rainbow, or sea) are the most desired of the game fish and the ones that have inspired the image of a fly fisherman whipping a lure and line in serpentine arcs above a loch. Many vacationers dream of donning bulky rubber waders up to their waists and trying their luck in streams and freshwater lochs. Fly-fishing for salmon and trout is subject to seasonal controls and sometimes requires a permit. For details on game fishing, contact the **Salmon & Trout Association (Scottish Branch),** The National Game Angling Centre, The Pier, Loch Leven, Kinross KY138UF (© **01577/861-116;** fax 01577/864-769; www. salmon-trout.org).

SEA FISHING   This simply means fishing from a beach, a rocky shoreline, or a pier. Inshore fishing involves dropping a line into ocean waters within 5km (3 miles) of any Scottish coastline; deep-sea fishing is done from a boat, more than 5km (3 miles) offshore, in a style made popular by cigar-chomping tycoons and Hemingway clones. Offshore waters have produced several species of shark, including porbeagle, thresher, mako, and blue shark. For information on what to expect from offshore waters, contact the **Scottish Tourist Board,** 95 Ocean Dr., Edinburgh EH6 6JH (© **0845/225-5121;** www.visitscotland.com).

FISHING CLUBS

Getting permits and information on worthwhile places to fish is easier if you join one of the more than 380 fishing clubs headquartered in Scotland. (The oldest angling club in the world, the Ellem Fishing Club, was founded in Scotland in 1829.) Each of its

---

(*Fun Fact* **Death Chimes for the Fox Hunt**

Some old-time Scots are rolling over in their graves, but the Scottish Parliament in 2002 outlawed traditional fox hunting with dogs in Scotland. The passage of the Protection of Wild Mammals Bill brings to an end a centuries-old hunting tradition. A last-ditch demonstration by fox hunters failed. Heavy fines or a 6-month prison sentence will be imposed on violators.

---

activities is supervised by the **Scottish Anglers National Association** (*©* **01577/ 861-116;** www.sana.org.uk), which firmly believes that newcomers should learn at the side of the more experienced. Courses in the fine art of fishing are offered in or around Scotland. For details, contact the Scottish Tourist Board (see above).

3 Biking, Walking & Other Outdoor Pursuits

BIKING

Scotland is one of the most gorgeous settings in Europe for a bike trip, but note that bicycles are forbidden on most highways and trunk roads and on what the British call dual carriageways (divided highways). May, June, and September are the best months for cycling, in spite of the often bad weather. Many of the narrow and scenic roads are likely to be overcrowded with cars in July and August. For the best biking routes, see chapter 1.

Your first source of information should be the **Scottish Cyclists Union,** which provides an annual handbook and a regular newsletter for members. It's also one of the most potent lobbying groups in Scotland for the inauguration and preservation of cyclists' byways. It distributes maps showing worthwhile bike routes and supports the publication of technical material of interest to cyclists. Nonmembers are welcome for a small fee. Scottish Cyclists Union, The Velodrome, Meadowbank Stadium, London Road, Edinburgh EH7 6AD (*©* **0131/652-0187;** fax 0131/661-0474; www.scuonline.org).

Although based in England, the **Cyclists Tourist Club,** Parklands, Railton Road, Guildford, Surrey GU2 9JX (*©* **0870/873-0060;** fax 0870/873-0064; www.ctc. org.uk), offers details on cycling holidays in Scotland. Membership is £34 ($65) a year for adults and £12 ($23) for those 17 and under. A family of three or more can get a membership for £55 ($105). This organization gives advice on where to rent or buy a bike; it also offers free legal advice to members involved in cycle-related accidents and information on available medical insurance for members.

You may take your bike without restrictions on car and passenger ferries in Scotland. It's rarely necessary to make arrangements in advance. However, the transport of your bike is likely to cost £2 to £8 ($3.80–$15), plus the cost of your own passage. On trains, there is no charge for bicycles.

The best biking trips in Scotland are offered by **Bespoke Highland Tours,** Tigh Na Creig, Garve Road, Ullapool, Ross-shire IV26 2SX (*©*/fax **01854/612-628;** www. highland-tours.co.uk), and **Scottish Border Trails,** Drummore, Venlaw High Road, Peebles EH45 8RL (*©* **01721/722-934;** fax 01721/723-004).

Local rental shops offer a wide range of bicycles, from three-speeds to mountain bikes, and may offer organized trips, ranging from tours of several hours to full-fledged weeklong itineraries. We've listed the best local rental shops, with their rates, in the destination chapters that follow.

BIRD-WATCHING

The moors and Highlands of Scotland, partly because of their low population density, attract millions of birds. For reasons not fully understood by ornithologists, the Orkneys shelter absolutely staggering numbers of birds. Bird-watchers cite the Orkneys as even richer in native species than the more isolated Shetlands, with species like the hen harrier, short-eared owl, and red-throated diver (a form of Arctic loon) not frequently seen in the Shetlands.

Any general tour of the Orkneys will bring you into contact with thousands of birds, as well as with Neolithic burial sites, cromlechs, dolmens, and other items rich in intrigue and history. A worthy tour operator is **Wild About,** 5 Cloustons Corner, Stenness, Stromness Orkney KW16 3LD (℅ **01856/851-011;** www.wildaboutorkney. com). Tour guides in minivans will help you spot the sites. The per-person cost is £45 ($86) for a full day, £30 ($57) for a half-day. In summer, reserve in advance.

A bird-watching specialist is **Orkney Island Wildlife,** Shapinsay 20, Orkney KW17 2DY (℅ **01856/711-373;** www.orkneyislandholidays.com). Between May and August, it leads 5-day bird-watching tours that include full board, housing, and exposure to the fields, moors, and wetlands of Shapinsay and Orkney. Tours are conducted from a rustic croft or farmstead that was upgraded and enlarged into a center in 1990. Your hosts are Paul and Louise Hollinrake, both qualified wardens at the Mill Dam Wetlands Reserve and accredited by the Royal Society for the Protection of Birds. Tours depart every morning around 9am (allowing participants to either sleep late or embark on sunrise expeditions of their own). Lunches are box-lunch affairs. Touring is by minivan or by inflatable boat, allowing close-up inspection of offshore skerries (small islets without vegetation) and sea caves. No more than six participants are allowed on any tour. All-inclusive rates are £899 ($1,708) per person for the 5-day/6-night experience.

During winter and early spring, the entire Solway shoreline, Loch Ryan, Wigtown Bay, and Auchencairn Bay are excellent locations for observing wintering wildfowl and waders. Inland, Galloway has a rich and varied range of bird life, including British barn owls, kestrels, tawnies, and merlins. Bird-watching fact sheets are available at tourist offices in Galloway.

CANOEING

Several canoe clubs offer instruction and advice. Supervising their activities is the **Scottish Canoe Association (SCA),** Caledonia House, South Gyle, Edinburgh EH12 9DQ (℅ **0131/317-7314;** fax 0131/317-7319; www.canoescotland.com). It coordinates all competitive canoeing events in Scotland, including slaloms, polo games, and white-water races. It also offers a handbook and a range of other publications, plus promotional material like its own magazine, *Scottish Paddler.* (An equivalent magazine published in England is *Canoe Focus.*)

HIKING & WALKING

Scotland is unsurpassed for those who like to walk and hike across mountain and dale, coming to rest on the bonnie, bonnie banks of a loch.

In all of Scotland, there are no finer long-distance footpaths than the **West Highland Way** and the **Southern Upland Way,** both previewed in chapter 1. The West Highland Way begins north of Glasgow, in the town of Milngavie, the Southern Upland Way in Portpatrick, in the Dumfries and Galloway region. Information on these paths is provided by the **Scottish Tourist Board,** 94 Ocean Dr., Edinburgh

EH6 6JH (© **0845/225-5121;** www.visitscotland.com). Nearly all bookstores in Scotland sell guides documenting these paths.

The **Borders** (see chapter 6) is one of the greatest places for walks. All tourist boards in the area provide a free guide, *Walking in the Scottish Borders,* detailing half-day scenic walks around the various towns. Scotland's longest footpath, the 341km (212-mile) **Southern Upland Way,** also extends through the Borders.

The magnificent coastline of **Galloway,** southwest of the Borders, is ideal for walks. Tourist offices distribute a free guide to 30 walks, *Walking in Dumfries and Galloway.* They also offer a helpful pamphlet called *Ranger-Led Walks and Events,* outlining scenic hikes through the forests of the southwest.

In central Scotland, the **Cairngorm region** offers the major concentration of ski resorts in the country, including Ben Macdui, the second-highest peak in Britain at nearly 1,304m (4,300 ft.). In the Cairngorm Ski Area, Cairngorm Rangers offer guided walks through the forest to both skilled and beginning hikers. The **Glenmore Forest Park Visitors Centre** (© **01479/861-220**) dispenses information on great walks in the area. It's open daily from 9am to 5pm.

The best self-led tours of the Scottish Highlands and islands are offered by **Bespoke Highland Tours,** Tigh Na Creig, Ross-shire (© **01854/334-3662;** www.highland-tours.co.uk). It has devised a series of treks, lasting from 5 to 12 days, including the **West Highland Way,** that take in the finest scenery in Scotland. Their tours are reasonably priced, ranging from £350 to £470 ($665–$893).

You can arrange with a company such as **Easyways,** Haypark Business Centre, Marchmont Ave., Polmont, Falkirk (© **01324/714-132;** www.easyways.com), to make all your bookings during an extended hike along trails like the West Highland Way, the Great Glen Way, Rob Roy Way, and St. Cuthbert's Way. The staff will take care of sending your luggage ahead, so you don't have to walk with heavy backpacks.

With **North-West Frontiers,** Tigh Na Crieg, Garve Road, Ullapool, Ross-shire (© **01854/612-628;** www.nwfrontiers.com), you can explore remote glens, magnificent mountains and lochs, and isolated islands and beaches. You're likely to see seals, deer, and many species of birds, including divers and golden eagles. Unlike Bespoke (see above), these tours are led by experienced hikers who know the countryside as if it were their backyard.

Some of the most memorable walks in Scotland are along **Loch Lomond** and the **Trossachs.** At tourist centers and various bookstores in Scotland, you can purchase a copy of *Walk Loch Lomond and the Trossachs* to guide you on your way.

An organization that can put you in touch with like-minded hikers is the **Ramblers Association (Scotland),** Kingfisher, Auld Mart Business Park, Milnathort, Kinross KY13 9DA (© **01577/861-222;** www.ramblers.org.uk/scotland). To book a rambling tour before you go to Scotland, contact the **English Lakeland Ramblers,** 15404 Beachview Dr., Montclair, VA 22025 (© **800/724-8801** or 703/680-4276; www.ramblers.com).

Offering guided walking and hiking tours on a daily basis from Edinburgh, **Walkabout Scotland,** 2F2, 70 Strathearn Rd., Edinburgh (© **0845/686-1344;** www.walkaboutscotland.com), specializes in jaunts through the Highlands. A different tour for each day of the week is offered, tackling different grades of walks. From backpackers to millionaires, the ages of clients range from 16 to 69. Longer walking holidays throughout Scotland can also be booked, including to such fabled spots as Glen Nevis, Glencoe, Loch Lomond, and the Isle of Arran.

C-N-Do Scotland (*📞* **01786/445-703;** www.cndoscotland.com) has been organizing hiking tours since 1984. It knows the Scottish landscapes well, and hooks up its patrons with the best in hiking, good Scottish food, wildlife viewing, and what it terms (accurately) "a palette-full of panoramas."

English Lakeland Ramblers (*📞* **800/724-8801** or 703/680-4276; www.ramblers. com) features a walking tour of Skye and the Outer Isles. The tour spends 2 nights on Skye, plus 3 on the Outer Hebridean Islands of Lewis and Harris. Passengers walk along hills and dales, mountain screes and grassy moors, and lakes and gushing waterfalls. Later they can explore old Scottish villages, stopping off perhaps at a pub for a wee dram of Scotch.

HORSEBACK RIDING & PONY TREKKING

Horseback riding and trekking through the panoramic countryside—from the Lowlands to the Highlands and through all the in-between lands—can be enjoyed by most everyone, from novices to experienced riders.

Although more adventurous riders prefer the hillier terrain of the Highlands, the Borders in the southeast (see chapter 6) is the best for horseback riding—in fact, it's often called Scotland's horse country. Its equivalent in the United States would be Kentucky. On the western coastline, Argyll (see chapter 8) is another great center for riding while taking in dramatic scenery. The Argyll Forest Park, stretching almost to Loch Fyne, encompasses 24,300 hectares (60,000 acres) and contains some of the lushest scenery in Scotland. Its trails lead through forests to sea lochs cut deep into the park, evoking the fjords of Norway.

Pony trekking across moors and dales is reason enough to come to Scotland. Pony trekking originated as a job for Highland ponies that weren't otherwise engaged in toting dead deer off the hills during deer-stalking season. Most treks last from 2½ hours to a full day, and most centers have ponies suitable for nearly all age groups. You find operators in Kirkudbright and on Shetland, plus several in the Hebrides.

MOUNTAINEERING

Mountain climbing can range from fair-weather treks over heather-clad hilltops to demanding climbs up rock faces in wintry conditions of snow and ice.

The **Southern Uplands,** the **offshore islands,** and the **Highlands** of Scotland contain the best mountaineering sites. Regardless of your abilities, treat the landscape with respect. The weather can turn foul during any season with almost no advance notice, creating dangerous conditions. If you're climbing rock faces, you should be familiar with basic techniques and the use of such specialized equipment as carabiners, crampons, ice axes, and ropes. Don't even consider climbing without proper instruction and equipment.

Ben Nevis is the highest (but by no means the most remote) peak in Scotland. Despite its loftiness at 1,336m (4,406 ft.), it has attracted some daredevils who have driven cars and motorcycles to points near its top; one eccentric even arranged the transport of a dining table with formal dinner service and a grand piano.

If you want to improve your rock-climbing skills, consider joining a club or signing on for a mountaineering course at a climbing center maintained by the Scottish Sports Council. Also contact the **Mountaineering Council of Scotland,** Perth (*📞* **01738/ 493-942;** www.mountaineering-scotland.org.uk). Membership allows overnight stays at the club's climbing huts on the island of Skye (in Glen Brittle), in the Cairngorms (at Glen Feshie), and near the high-altitude mountain pass at Glencoe. True rock-climbing aficionados looking to earn certification might contact the **Scottish Mountain Leader Training Board,** at Glenmore, Aviemore, Inverness-shire PH22 1QU (*C* **01479/861-248;** www.mltuk.org).

SAILING & WATERSPORTS

Wherever you travel in Scotland, you're never far from the water. Windsurfing, canoeing, water-skiing, and sailing are just some of the activities available at a number of sailing centers and holiday parks. You'll find it easy to rent boats and equipment at any of the major resorts along Scotland's famous lakes.

4

Suggested Scotland Itineraries

For visitors to Europe, one of the great pleasures is getting "lost" in the Highlands and islands of Scotland: wandering about at random, making new discoveries off the beaten path, and finding charming towns and Brigadoon-like villages such as Pittenweem or Crail. Unfortunately, few of us have unlimited time. That's why you may find "Scotland in 1 Week" or "Scotland in 2 Weeks" helpful for skimming the highlights. If you've been to Scotland before and explored the well-trodden meccas of Glasgow and Edinburgh, you may want to visit a different area of the country this time. See "The High Road to History & Natural Wonder," later in this chapter.

You might also want to review this guide's "Best of" recommendations (in chapter 1) to see what experiences or sights have special appeal to you, and adjust the itineraries to suit your travel plans. If you stick to the main highways, you'll find that Scotland has some of the best-maintained roads in Europe. But when you wander off the beaten track, you may have to open and shut a fence to keep the sheep from wandering astray.

The itineraries that follow take you to some major attractions, such as Edinburgh, but also direct you to more secluded spots like the Trossachs. The pace may be a bit breathless for some visitors, so skip a town or sight occasionally to have some down time—after all, you're on vacation. *Note:* Each itinerary requires the use of a car.

1 Scotland in 1 Week

While it's impossible to see all of Scotland in 1 week, if you budget your time well, you'll have a memorable trip—and you'll see quite a lot. One week provides just enough time to get acquainted with the attractions in **Edinburgh,** its museums and castles, as well as with those in **Glasgow,** Scotland's largest city and home to some of Britain's greatest museums. With time remaining, you can head to the bonnie, bonnie banks of **Loch Lomond,** and even visit such centers of the famed Highlands as **Fort William** and **Inverness,** which is the capital.

Days ❶ & ❷: Edinburgh, Gateway to Scotland ★★★

Most arrivals in the capital of Scotland are from London, either by rail, plane, or bus. Hit town as early as possible in the morning to get in a full round of the city's attractions. After checking into a hotel, head for the Old Town's **Royal Mile** (p. 77), stretching from one of the city's major sights,

Edinburgh Castle (p. 102), to the **Palace of Holyroodhouse** (p. 107). You can probably visit only one of these attractions before lunch, saving the other for the afternoon. We suggest you go to Edinburgh Castle in the morning and Holyroodhouse in the afternoon. Then, during the latter visit, you can also check out the new **Scottish Parliament** building (p. 108).

Scotland Itineraries: Weeks 1 & 2

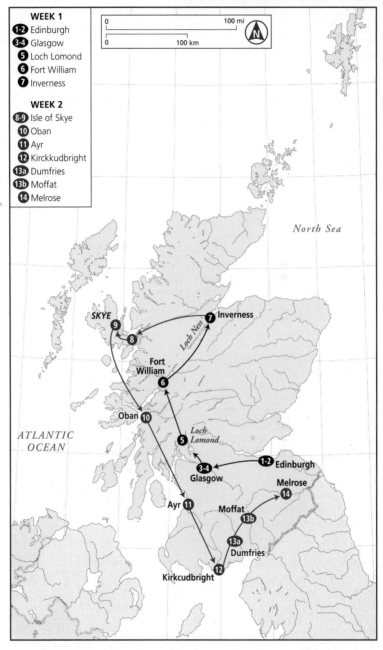

WEEK 1
- 1-2 Edinburgh
- 3-4 Glasgow
- 5 Loch Lomond
- 6 Fort William
- 7 Inverness

WEEK 2
- 8-9 Isle of Skye
- 10 Oban
- 11 Ayr
- 12 Kirckkudbright
- 13a Dumfries
- 13b Moffat
- 14 Melrose

0 — 100 mi
0 — 100 km

N

North Sea

SKYE

9

8

7 Inverness

Loch Ness

Fort William

6

Oban 10

5 *Loch Lomond*

ATLANTIC OCEAN

3-4

Glasgow

1-2 Edinburgh

Melrose

14

Ayr 11

Moffat

13b

13a

Dumfries

12

Kirkcudbright

As the afternoon wanes, head down into the New Town for a walk and some shopping along the fabled **Princes Street.** In the early evening, drop into an Edinburgh pub for a pint or a wee dram—and for a sample of some local life. Have dinner in one of the New Town's wide variety of restaurants (coverage begins on p. 94).

On **Day 2,** which could turn into a very busy day, check out the artistic masterpieces in the **National Gallery of Scotland** (p. 109) and see the artifactloaded **National Museum of Scotland** (p. 110). Both of these treasure troves can be seen in one busy morning. In the afternoon, and for a change of pace, visit **Calton Hill** (p. 112) in the east of Edinburgh—it looks like Athens—and the **Royal Botanic Garden** (p. 113), one of Britain's greatest botanical gardens. For your final night in Edinburgh, have dinner in one of the ancient restaurants of the Old Town, following in the footsteps of Robert Louis Stevenson.

Days ❸ & ❹: Glasgow, Scotland's Largest City ⟨★★★⟩

On **Day 3,** get an early morning start and drive to Glasgow, which is only 65km (40 miles) west of Edinburgh. You can arrive in time to check into a hotel and see **The Burrell Collection** (p. 191) before lunch. In the afternoon, visit the **Kelvingrove Art Gallery and Museum** (p. 194), one of the finest in Britain, and the **Glasgow Science Centre** (p. 191), on the banks of the River Clyde. After a visit to a Glaswegian pub, if that's your style, head to dinner in one of Glasgow's restaurants (coverage beings on p. 183).

On the morning of **Day 4,** visit the **Cathedral of St. Kentigern** (p. 195), which dates from the Middle Ages. You'll still have time to check out the masterpieces at the **Hunterian Art Gallery** (p. 194) before lunch. For the afternoon, you can explore Glasgow's fascinating **Museum of Transport** (p. 195) and visit some minor attractions, such as **The Tall**

Ship at Glasgow Harbour (p. 196), or take in some shopping along **Sauchiehall Street** or **Argyle Street.** In the evening, should you wish, you can attend a performance of opera or ballet at **Theatre Royal** (p. 202).

Day ❺: Loch Lomond

From Glasgow, on **Day 5,** you can head northwest for 32km (20 miles) to **Balloch** (p. 276), a good center for exploring the bonnie, bonnie banks of Loch Lomond. The best way to spend a day touring the lake is to take one of **Sweeney's Cruisers** (p. 276). If you return in time, you can also explore **Balloch Castle Country Park** (p. 276). Overnight in Balloch, which lies at the southern end of the Loch.

Day ❻: Fort William, Gateway to the Highlands ⟨★⟩

From Glasgow (or Balloch if you spent the night there), you can strike out for **Fort William,** 167km (104 miles) north of Glasgow. Located on the shores of Loch Linnhe, Fort William is the best stopover for those traveling between Glasgow and Inverness, in the north. You can arrive in time for lunch, taking in views of **Ben Nevis,** the highest mountain in Scotland. In the afternoon, visit the ruins of **Old Inverlochy Castle** (p. 327) and **Neptune's Staircase** (p. 328). Overnight in Fort William.

Day ❼: Inverness, Capital of the Highlands ⟨★⟩

Fort William to Inverness is a drive of 109km (68 miles). Before reaching Inverness, drive along the western bank of **Loch Ness** (p. 335), keeping your eye out for the elusive monster. At Drumnadrochit, there is the official **Loch Ness Monster Exhibition** (p. 337), and you can also explore the ruins of **Urquhart Castle** (p. 337).

Have lunch in Inverness, then set out to see the **Culloden Battlefield** (p. 340), with its Graves of the Clans, and also visit the

Fort George/Queen's Own Highlanders Regimental Museum (p. 341). Spend the rest of the afternoon walking around and exploring the center of Inverness, which lies on both sides of the Ness River, with scenic walks in all directions. Overnight in Inverness.

2 Scotland in 2 Weeks

With 2 weeks to explore Scotland, you have a bit more breathing time, and you can take in some of the more esoteric destinations, such as the **Isle of Skye,** the most mystical and evocative of the Hebridean islands. The second week will also allow you to explore some of the history-rich towns of the **Borders,** which face a once-hostile England across the boundary.

Days ❶ to ❼
Follow the itinerary outlined above in "Scotland in 1 Week."

Days ❽ & ❾: Isle of Skye ⋒⋒
On **Day 8,** from your last stopover in Inverness (see above), drive west along A832 to the **Kyle of Lochalsh,** the gateway to the Isle of Skye; it's 132km (82 miles) southwest of Inverness. You can now drive from Kyle to Skye, over a bridge, which will allow more time for sightseeing.

Once on Skye check into a hotel for 2 nights. Although it's the largest of the Hebridean islands, Skye is relatively small, only 77km (48 miles) long, so you can stay almost anywhere and use the town as your headquarters for exploring the entire island. Some of the best places for lodgings include **Kyleakin** (p. 368), **Sligachan** (p. 369), and **Portree** (p. 371). Portree is the capital of the island. For complete coverage of the Isle of Skye, refer to p. 367.

Assuming you base yourself in the center of the island, at the lochside village of Sligachan, you can order lunch and then spend the afternoon driving A856 to the north of Skye, taking in the scenic beauty along the way. You ultimately reach the village of **Uig,** where you should visit the **Skye Museum of Island Life** (p. 372). After leaving Uig, traverse the entire northeastern part of Skye by following A855 in a half-moon crescent, finally heading back to Sligachan for the night.

On the morning of **Day 9,** set out from Sligachan (or whichever village you've lodged in) to explore the **Sleat Peninsula,** in the south, following A850 (which becomes A851). Once at Sleat, visit **Knock Castle** (p. 374), the former stronghold of the MacDonalds, now some of the most evocative ruins in the Hebridean islands. You can also explore **Armadale Castle Gardens & Museum of the Isles** (p. 374). Allow an hour or so for a visit here.

Sleat is known as the garden of Skye, and you can wander at leisure, taking in its woodland glens, cliffs, and waterfalls, especially enjoying the dramatic beauty of the jagged **Cuillin Hills** (p. 371). For your afternoon adventure, take a 3-hour cruise at Elgol (see **Bella Jane Boat Trips** on p. 368), and you'll see some of the island's grandest natural beauty. Finally, return to your hotel for a well-deserved dinner.

Day ❿: Oban ⋒
On **Day 10,** take the bridge from Skye back to the mainland and head south to the coastal resort of **Oban** (coverage begins on p. 237). On the way to Oban, you'll pass through the previously visited Fort William (see above). Oban lies another 81km (50 miles) southwest of Fort William. Check into a hotel here, and, after lunch, visit such attractions as **McCaig's Tower** (p. 239), enjoying the panoramic view across the Firth of Lorn to the Sound of Mull. You should also have

time to visit **Dunstaffnage Castle** (p. 237) and to walk along the harborfront before dinner; later in the evening, stop at **McTavish's Kitchens** (p. 242), where you might see some Highland dancing.

Day ⓫: Ayr, Ode to Robert Burns

Leave Oban on the morning of **Day 11,** continuing along the coastline to the town of **Ayr** (coverage begins on p. 205). You'll bypass Glasgow to your east as you arrive in the town of Ayr, which has many associations with Robert Burns, Scotland's national poet.

Ayr itself lies at a point 56km (35 miles) southeast of Glasgow. Check into a hotel at Ayr and use it as a base for exploring nearby **Alloway,** the birthplace of Burns, which is 3km (2 miles) south. Once here, visit the **Burns Cottage and Museum** (p. 210) and the **Burns Monument and Gardens** (p. 210). Allow at least 2 hours.

You can also make it to **Culzean Castle** (p. 211), 19km (12 miles) southwest of Ayr, that afternoon. Designed by Scottish architect Robert Adam, this is one of the grandest castles in the west of Scotland. General Eisenhower was a former guest. For the night, return to Ayr.

Day ⓬: Kirkcudbright, an Artists' Colony 𝒜

On **Day 12,** leave Ayr in the morning and drive into the Borders country, scheduling a stop at the old sheep-market town of **Castle Douglas,** 79km (49 miles) southeast of Ayr. Visit the 14th-century ruins of **Threave Castle** (p. 161), and have lunch later in town.

Instead of overnighting here, we recommend that you continue for 16km (10 miles) to the southwest until you reach the old town of Kirkcudbright, which is the center of a flourishing artists' colony. In the afternoon, you stroll around for an hour or two, taking in such attractions as **Broughton House** (p. 163) and the **Tolbooth Art Centre** (p. 163). Stay at the famous **Selkirk Arms** (p. 164), where

Burns composed his fabled "Selkirk Grace."

Day ⓭: Dumfries 𝒜 & Moffat

On **Day 13,** after a night in Kirkcudbright, head north until you reach A75, continuing northeast into the town of Dumfries. At this point, you'll be 129km (80 miles) southwest of Edinburgh and about the same distance from Glasgow.

Like Ayr, Dumfries also has associations with Robert Burns, and you can visit **Burns House** (p. 157) before taking in **Drumlanrig Castle** (p. 157) and the **Dumfries Museum** (p. 157). You might also want to view the ruins of **Sweetheart Abbey** (p. 158) before heading for the town of **Moffat,** a drive of only 35km (22 miles) to the northeast. Check into a hotel and spend the rest of the afternoon exploring **Devil's Beef Tub** (p. 154), the **Grey Mare's Tail** (p. 154), and **Annan Water Valley Road** (p. 154) before returning to Moffat for the night.

Day ⓮: Melrose, Highlight of the Borders 𝒜

For your final look at the Borders, leave Moffat on **Day 14,** which promises to be busy. The best place to stop today is **Melrose,** northeast of Moffat and only 60km (37 miles) southeast of Edinburgh. Check into a hotel at Melrose and use it as a base for exploring nearby attractions. In the town itself, visit **Abbotsford House** (p. 145), former home of Sir Walter Scott; **Melrose Abbey** (p. 145), which embraces some of the most beautiful ruins in Europe; and **Traquair House** (p. 146), Scotland's oldest and most romantic house.

In the afternoon, drive 19km (12 miles) east of Melrose, to the town of **Kelso.** Here it is but an 11km (7-mile) jaunt to **Mellerstain,** one of the most famous mansions designed by Robert Adam. Allow 2 hours for a visit. Return to Melrose for the night and plan an early morning departure for Edinburgh and your return home.

3 Scotland for Families

Scotland has never been known as the most kid-friendly destination in Europe. And indeed, many of its pleasures and pastimes, such as playing golf or drinking whisky, are adult-oriented. Nevertheless, there are a number of attractions that all the family can enjoy, especially in Edinburgh and Glasgow. Perhaps the main concern with having children along is pacing yourself, particularly in the museums. Our suggestion is to spend 2 days each in Edinburgh and Glasgow before venturing into the countryside. Children generally delight in exploring spooky old castles, heading up to the Highlands—where there are all those bagpipe players—and looking for the Loch Ness monster in Inverness.

Days ❶ & ❷: Edinburgh, Gateway to Scotland ✦✦✦

By train, plane, or bus—usually from London—families descend on the capital of Scotland. Try to arrive as early in the day as you can and check into a hotel. If your timing is right, you'll have virtually a full day of sightseeing in the capital instead of spending it in transit. Start at **Edinburgh Castle** (p. 102) at the beginning of the Royal Mile in the Old Town. Kids may be a bit bored with the State Apartments where Mary Queen of Scots once lived, but they delight in the spooky 18th-century prisons and the batteries of cannons that used to protect the fortress. After a visit, pay a call on the **Museum of Childhood** (p. 106), found along High Street. Everything is here, from antique toys to games. Kids also enjoy the nearby **Outlook Tower and Camera Obscura** (p. 106), especially those who like their history told with an optical theme.

After lunch in the Old Town, descend on **Princes Street,** the main drag in the New Town. At the **Scott Monument** (p. 110), it's fun for the whole family to climb the 287 steps for the most panoramic view of the city. Before the afternoon ends, spend at least 1½ hours taking in **Dynamic Earth** (p. 111), whose exhibits have been compared to an interpretation by Walt Disney. Kids push buttons to simulate everything from earthquakes to meteor showers.

On **Day 2** in Edinburgh, get an early start for another busy round of sightseeing. Take your kids aboard the luxury yacht *Britannia* (p. 112), once used by Queen Elizabeth II herself. After that, a visit to **Edinburgh Zoo** (p. 111) is called for, with its more than 1,500 animals, including some endangered species. Have lunch in the New Town, then visit the spectacular **Royal Botanic Garden** (p. 113), one of the best and grandest in Britain, before ending your day by wandering through **The Real Mary King's Close** (p. 108), which stays open until 9pm in summer. This was the once-thriving underground part of the Old Town, where the "deepest secrets" are hidden in the warren of almost buried streets, or "closes." Kids seem to expect Robert Louis Stevenson's "Mr. Hyde" to emerge at any minute.

Day ❸: Deep Sea World ✦ & Stirling Castle ✦✦

On **Day 3,** after checking out of your hotel in Edinburgh, drive to **Deep Sea World** (p. 131) to visit Scotland's most comprehensive and dramatic menagerie of water creatures, including its most ferocious sharks. Allow 90 minutes for this attraction, which is 19km (12 miles) west of Edinburgh's center.

Next, make your way to **Stirling** (coverage begins on p. 261). This ancient town, lying between the rivers Forth and Clyde, is famed for its castle. After checking into a hotel, you'll want to have lunch.

In the afternoon take your kids to **Stirling Castle** (p. 262), where Mary Queen of Scots lived as an infant monarch. Children especially enjoy going through the on-site **Museum of the Argyll and Sutherland Highlanders,** with all the pipe banners and other paraphernalia. For the rest of the afternoon, you can drive to **Bannockburn** (p. 262) nearby, where Robert the Bruce once summoned his "Braveheart" army to defeat Edward II in 1314. Kids find the audiovisual presentation of this violent story at the **Bannockburn Heritage Centre** as fascinating as Mel Gibson's own *Braveheart* movie. Return to Stirling for the night.

Days ❹ & ❺: Glasgow ☆☆☆

On **Day 4,** drive 45km (28 miles) southwest to Glasgow. Make a bargain with your kids: If they'll accompany you to **The Burrell Collection** (p. 191), you'll fill up the rest of the day with amusements designed primarily for them. The collection is one of the greatest repositories of art in Britain. Allow about 2 hours here—less if your kids get bored looking at such art as Rodin's *The Thinker.*

Now take the kids on a trip aboard the **Waverley** (p. 197), the world's last seagoing paddle steamer, which will carry you to scenic places along the Firth of Clyde. You can have lunch aboard. Back in Glasgow, spend 2 hours visiting the **Glasgow Science Centre** (p. 191), a kid-friendly favorite complete with a Space Theatre and plenty of hands-on activities for children.

On the morning of **Day 5,** make another compromise with your kids so you can spend at least an hour and a half at the **Kelvingrove Art Gallery and Museum** (p. 194). Even if your children aren't interested in art, they'll be intrigued by the ethnography collections, which display everything from artifacts from the Eskimos to Oceania, with mammoth galleries devoted to natural history. Later in the morning, spend an hour or so wandering about the **Museum of Transport** (p. 195).

The varied ship models seem to intrigue kids the most here. Follow these visits with lunch at the **Willow Tea Room** (p. 188), where kids especially enjoy the homemade pastries and ice-cream dishes.

In the afternoon, take the family to the **Scottish Maritime Museum** (p. 196), before descending on **Linn Park** (p. 197), spread across 86 hectares (212 acres). There are many attractions for kids here, including a special children's zoo and pony rides.

Day ❻: Oban ☆ & Fort William ☆

On the morning of **Day 6,** drive northwest from Glasgow along the western banks of **Loch Lomond** (coverage begins on p. 275), heading for the town of **Oban** (coverage begins on p. 237). The distance between Glasgow and Oban is 81km (50 miles). Once in Oban, take your kids on a tour of **Dunstaffnage Castle** (p. 237) and up to **McCaig's Tower** (p. 239), an unfinished replica of the Coliseum of Rome. After taking in the panoramic view from **Pulpit Hill** here, descend on the town for a kitschy lunch at **McTavish's Kitchens** (p. 242), which is Highland tartan with a vengeance.

After lunch, proceed north to the town of Fort William, 81km (50 miles) from Oban. Check into a hotel in the shadow of Ben Nevis, Scotland's highest mountain. In the afternoon you can drive through the hauntingly beautiful **Glencoe** (p. 325), scene of the famous massacre of 1692, when the Campbells did in the MacDonalds. Kids are fascinated by the audiovisual presentation shown at the Glencoe Visitor Center. Return to Fort William for the night.

Day ❼: Loch Ness ☆☆ & Inverness ☆

On **Day 7,** leave Fort William and continue north to **Inverness,** the capital of the Highlands, a distance of 109km (68 miles). Along the way you can stop at the little village of **Drumnadrochit** to see the official **Loch Ness Monster Exhibition**

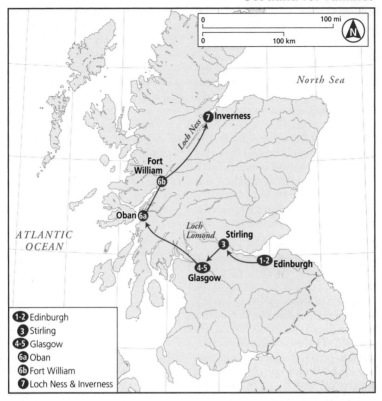

North Sea

ATLANTIC
OCEAN

Loch Ness

7 Inverness

Fort
William
6b

Oban 6a

Loch
Lomond   Stirling
3

4-5   1-2 Edinburgh
Glasgow

1-2 Edinburgh
3 Stirling
4-5 Glasgow
6a Oban
6b Fort William
7 Loch Ness & Inverness

(p. 337). With its lasers and visual effects, this exhibition is definitely a kid-pleaser. After seeing the exhibition, it's great fun for families to explore the ruins of **Urquhart Castle,** which overlooks the loch. It is from here that most sightings of the Loch Ness Monster are reported.

Proceed north, to Inverness, and check into a hotel. After lunch, families can explore the **Culloden Battlefield** (p. 340), where Bonnie Prince Charlie and his Jacobite army were crushed by the English. Kids also like to walk the ramparts, a distance of 1.6km (1 mile), found at the **Fort George/Queen's Own Highlanders Regimental Museum** (p. 341). Inverness has a variety of options for dining that evening. Following a night in Inverness, most visitors drive back to Glasgow or Edinburgh for their *adieu* to Scotland.

4 The High Road to History & Natural Wonder

The following tour is one of the most history-rich in the country. It could be called "Scotland in a nutshell" in that it leaves from Edinburgh and includes everything from beautiful scenery, such as the Trossachs, to historic palaces, such as Scone, and even the royal castles of Glamis and Balmoral. The tour also includes the home of golf at St. Andrews and the country's most charming fishing villages at East Neuk.

Day ❶: Stirling ★★ & Its Castle ★★

Set out on **Day 1** to visit the ancient town of **Stirling,** lying 56km (37 miles) to the northwest; it's located in the midst of Mel Gibson's *Braveheart* country. Explore **Stirling Castle** (p. 262) in the morning, have lunch, and then head for the **Bannockburn Heritage Centre** (p. 263) in the afternoon. This is on the site of the battleground where Robert the Bruce's army defeated the forces of Edward II in 1314. Back in Stirling, if time remains, visit the 15th-century **Church of the Holy Rude** (p. 262). That night you might check to see if a cultural presentation is being staged at the **Macrobert Arts Centre** (p. 266), on the campus of Stirling University.

Day ❷: Callander ★ & Aberfoyle ★

On the morning of **Day 2,** drive 26km (16 miles) northwest of Stirling, to the town of **Callander,** which is set in a thickly wooded valley of lochs. Stop in at the Rob Roy & Trossachs Visitor Centre and pick up a map that directs you to the scenic highlights of the area. These include **Leny Park** (p. 269) and **Leny Falls** (p. 269).

After lunch in Callander, drive over to the little town of **Aberfoyle,** 23km (14 miles) to the southwest. Check into a hotel, then stop into the **Trossachs Discovery Centre** (p. 273) for a map of the area's scenic attractions. At Aberfoyle you're on the doorstep of the **Trossachs,** arguably the most beautiful natural attraction in Scotland. From here you can spend the afternoon exploring a section of **Queen Elizabeth Forest Park** (p. 273), on the eastern shore of Loch Lomond, as well as **Loch Katrine** (p. 273), fabled because of the Sir Walter Scott poem *The Lady of the Lake.* After stopping off at **Dukes Pass** (p. 273) for a panoramic view, return to Aberfoyle for the night.

Day ❸: Perth ★ & Scone Palace ★★

Leave Aberfoyle on **Day 3** in the morning, driving east to the ancient city on the Tay, the town of **Perth,** the former capital of Scotland. The distance is 92km (57 miles). Check into a hotel here and set out to explore the city that is the gateway to the Highlands. For orientation, visit **Kinnoull Hill** (p. 291), which is the geographic dividing point between the Highlands and the Lowlands. Follow a nature trail here before having a "pre-lunch lunch" at the 16th-century **Balhousie Castle** (p. 292), after which you can walk through the **North Inch** (p. 292), a 41-hectare (100-acre) park along the west bank of the Tay River.

Following lunch in Perth, drive 3km (2 miles) to Old Scone, site of **Scone Palace** (p. 295), with its precious antiques, art work, and grand architecture. After a visit you can wander the gardens and woodlands around the palace before returning to Perth for the night. That evening, check out the offerings of the **Perth Repertory Theatre** (p. 295).

Day ❹: East Neuk Fishing Villages ★★

Leaving Perth in the morning of **Day 4,** drive 87km (54 miles) east. Here you can begin to explore East Neuk, a generic name used to describe a series of the most beautiful and unspoiled fishing villages in Scotland. Begin your voyage of discovery at **Elie** (p. 251), which is our favorite village along the coast, with its picture-postcard harbor and step-gabled houses. If the weather is warm, you can swim from one of the golden sand beaches. After a walk around the village for an hour or so, continue north to **Pittenweem** (p. 248), where you can attend a fish auction down by the water, Monday to Saturday morning. After a look-see, drive immediately north along A917 to **Anstruther** (p. 249), a fishing port and summer resort. Explore the **Scottish Fisheries Museum** (p. 249), down by the harbor, and later take a charming walk over to the tiny hamlet of **Cellardyke** (p. 249). Lunch at Anstruther.

The High Road to History & Natural Wonder

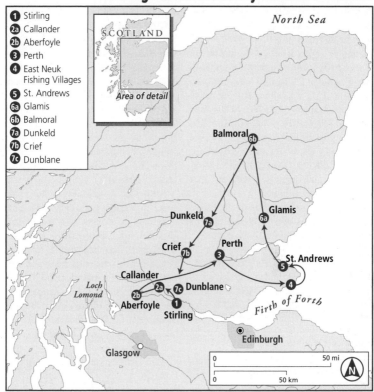

1. Stirling
2a. Callander
2b. Aberfoyle
3. Perth
4. East Neuk Fishing Villages
5. St. Andrews
6a. Glamis
6b. Balmoral
7a. Dunkeld
7b. Crief
7c. Dunblane

For the day's final destination, head north into **Crail** (p. 252). Check into a hotel here and spend the rest of the afternoon strolling through this port with its little fishermen's cottages. Pay a visit to its **Crail Museum & Heritage Centre** (p. 252), marked by an array of fishing memorabilia. Find a local pub and anchor in with a pint and dinner of fish and chips before returning to your hotel.

Day ❺: St. Andrews, Birthplace of Golf ✸✸

On the morning of **Day 5,** leave Crail and drive the short distance 15km (9 miles) north to St. Andrews. Golfers will spend the rest of the day playing on this hallowed turf; others can explore the attractions in the area—for example, the grounds of the **University of St. Andrews** (p. 254), which Prince William attended. Also, explore the ruins of the **Castle of St. Andrews** (p. 255). After lunch, visit **St. Andrews Cathedral and Priory** (p. 255) before descending on the **Secret Bunker** (p. 255), the place where Britain would have been commanded in the event of a nuclear attack. If you like lager, check out some of the local pubs, or attend a performance—perhaps a Shakespearean play—at the **Byre Theatre** (p. 260).

Day ❻: Royal Castles Glamis ✸✸ & Balmoral ✸

Leave St. Andrews on the morning of **Day 6,** heading north toward Dundee, where you link up with the A90 into Glamis, a distance of 133km (83 miles).

For 600 years, **Glamis Castle** (p. 307) was linked to the British Royal Family, and the late Queen Mother was brought up here. This is the castle where Macbeth is said to have murdered King Duncan. Allow at least 1½ hours for a look around.

If you have extra time, drive north of Glamis for 6.5km (4 miles), to the little town of **Kirriemuir.** Here you can visit **Barrie's birthplace** (p. 308). He, of course, was the author of *Peter Pan,* the eternal children's favorite, and his body was buried in the local cemetery. See p. 308 for more details.

After a quick lunch, drive from Kirriemuir to **Ballater,** site of the Queen's **Balmoral Castle** (p. 310). The distance is 98km (61 miles). Built in the Scottish baronial style, this was the summer home of Queen Victoria, and it's still used in late summer by Queen Elizabeth and her family. Since it closes at 5pm, you have to time your afternoon carefully. If you're running late, you should skip Kirriemuir.

If indeed Kirriemuir doesn't fit your itinerary, spend your time wandering around the towns of Ballater or Braemar. Overnight in either one and fortify yourself for one of your busiest days—your final day in Scotland.

Day ❼: Dunkeld 🅰, Crief 🅰 & Dunblane

Leave Ballater early on the morning of **Day 7,** heading southwest to **Dunkeld,** a distance of 108km (67 miles). On the doorway to the Perthshire Highlands, explore **Dunkeld Cathedral** (p. 299), one of the most historic in Britain, dating from A.D. 815. After a visit, wander around to see the old houses and shops around the cathedral and the marketplace, walking along both High and Cathedral streets.

After your visit, continue southwest to **Crief,** a distance of 46km (29 miles). Here you can spend 1½ hours seeing **Drummond Castle Gardens** (p. 298), which date from the early 17th century. Before lunch, also visit **The Glenturret Distillery** (Scotland's oldest).

Lunch in Crief before setting out in the afternoon to **Dunblane,** a distance of 69km (43 miles) to the south. At Dunblane, see **Dunblane Cathedral** (p. 267), one of the best examples of 13th-century Gothic architecture in Britain. Allow an hour for a visit. When finished, drive southeast to Edinburgh—a distance of 68km (42 miles)—for your final night in Scotland.

5

Edinburgh & the Lothian Region

Edinburgh ★★★ (pronounced *edin-burra*) has been called one of Europe's fairest cities, the Athens of the North, and the gateway to central Scotland. You can use it as a base for excursions to the Borders, the Trossachs (Scotland's Lake District), the silver waters of Loch Lomond, and the Kingdom of Fife, on the opposite shore of the Firth of Forth.

Edinburgh's past is filled with historic and literary icons: John Knox, Mary Queen of Scots, Robert Louis Stevenson, Sir Arthur Conan Doyle, Alexander Graham Bell, Sir Walter Scott, and Bonnie Prince Charlie. In modern times, the city has become famous for hosting the ever-growing **Edinburgh International Festival,** with its world-class list of cultural events. But remember that the treasures of this ancient seat of Scottish royalty are available year-round; in fact, when festival-hoppers have gone home, the pace is more relaxed, the prices are lower, and the people themselves, under less pressure, return to their traditional hospitable ways.

Built atop extinct volcanoes on an inlet from the North Sea (the Firth of Forth), and enveloped by rolling hills, lakes, and forests, Edinburgh is a city made for walking. The Old Town and the New Town sport elegant streets, cobbled alleys, lovely squares, and enough circuses and crescents to rival Bath in England. Hilltops unveil panoramic views, and Edinburgh's sunsets are spectacularly romantic—Scots call the fading evening light the "gloaming."

The city was once the cultural capital of the north, but it has lost that distinction to Glasgow. However, Edinburgh is trying to reclaim its former reputation. In fact, if you could visit only two cities in Great Britain, we'd recommend London first and Edinburgh second. But you may want to budget some time for side trips, too. Notable attractions on the doorstep of Edinburgh are the royal burgh of Linlithgow, where Mary Queen of Scots was born at Linlithgow Palace; the port of North Berwick (today a holiday resort); and lovely Dirleton, with its 13th-century castle ruins.

1 Essentials

ARRIVING

BY PLANE   Edinburgh is about an hour's flying time from London, which lies 633km (393 miles) south. **Edinburgh Airport** (© **0870/040-0007**) is 12km (8 miles) west of the city center, receiving flights from within the British Isles and the rest of Europe. Before heading into town, you might want to stop at the **information and accommodation desk** (© **0131/473-3800**); it's open Monday to Saturday 8am to 8pm and Sunday 9am to 4:30pm. A double-decker Airlink bus makes the trip from the airport to Edinburgh every 15 minutes, letting you off near Waverley Bridge, between the Old Town and the New Town; the fare is £3 ($5.70) one-way or £4.50 ($8.55) round-trip, and the ride takes about 25 minutes. A taxi into the city costs £13 ($25) or more, depending on traffic, and the trip is about 25 minutes.

BY TRAIN   InterCity trains that link London with Edinburgh are fast and efficient, providing both restaurant and bar service as well as air-conditioning. Trains from London's Kings Cross Station arrive in Edinburgh at **Waverley Station,** at the east end of Princes Street (✆ **08457/484-950** in London for rail info). Trains depart London every hour or so, taking about 4½ hours and costing about £100 ($190) one-way. Overnight trains have a sleeper berth, which you can rent for an extra £40 ($76). Taxis and buses are right outside the station in Edinburgh.

BY BUS   The least expensive way to go from London to Edinburgh is by bus, but it's an 8-hour journey. Nevertheless, it'll get you there for only about £30 ($57) one-way or £40 ($76) round-trip. Scottish Citylink coaches depart from London's Victoria Coach Station, delivering you to Edinburgh's **St. Andrews Square Bus Station,** St. Andrews Square (✆ **08705/505-050** in London, or 0181/663-9233 in Edinburgh).

BY CAR   Edinburgh is 74km (46 miles) east of Glasgow and 169km (105 miles) north of Newcastle-upon-Tyne, in England. No express motorway links London and Edinburgh. The M1 from London takes you part of the way north, but you have to come into Edinburgh along secondary roads: A68 or A7 from the southeast, A1 from the east, or A702 from the north. The A71 or A8 comes in from the west, A8 connecting with M8 just west of Edinburgh; A90 comes down from the north over the Forth Road Bridge. Allow 8 hours or more for the drive north from London.

VISITOR INFORMATION

Edinburgh & Scotland Information Centre, Princes Mall, 3 Princes St., at the corner of Princes Street and Waverley Bridge (✆ **0131/473-3800;** www.edinburgh.org; bus: 3, 7, 14, 31, or 69), can give you sightseeing information and also help find lodgings. The center sells bus tours, theater tickets, and souvenirs of Edinburgh. It's open year-round, Monday to Saturday 9am to 8pm. There's also an information and accommodations desk at Edinburgh Airport.

CITY LAYOUT

Edinburgh is composed of the New Town and the Old Town. Chances are, you'll find lodgings in the New Town and visit the Old Town only for dining, drinking, shopping, and sightseeing.

The **New Town,** with its world-famous **Princes Street,** came about in the 18th century, during the Golden Age of Edinburgh. Everybody from Robert Burns to James Boswell visited in that era. The first building went up here in 1767, and by the end of the century, classical squares, streets, and town houses had been added. Princes Street is known for both its shopping and its beauty—it opens onto the Princes Street Gardens with panoramic views of the Old Town.

North of and running parallel to Princes Street is the New Town's second great street, **George Street.** It begins at Charlotte Square and extends east to St. Andrews Square. Directly north of George Street is another impressive thoroughfare, **Queen Street,** opening onto Queen Street Gardens on its north side. You'll also hear a lot about **Rose Street,** directly north of Princes Street, which boasts more pubs per square block than any other place in Scotland, and is filled with shops and restaurants.

It seems everyone has heard of the **Royal Mile,** the main thoroughfare of the **Old Town,** beginning at Edinburgh Castle and running all the way to the Palace of Holyroodhouse. A famous street to the south of the castle is **Grassmarket,** where convicted criminals were once hanged on the dreaded gallows.

Greater Edinburgh

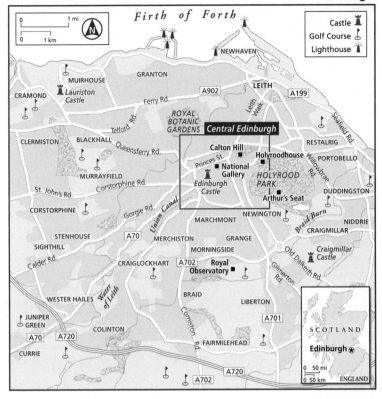

Firth of Forth

Castle
Golf Course
Lighthouse

NEWHAVEN

GRANTON

MUIRHOUSE
Lauriston Castle
CRAMOND

LEITH
A902   A199

Ferry Rd.

Leith Walk

Telford Rd.

ROYAL
BOTANIC
GARDENS   Central Edinburgh

Scaffeld Rd.

CLERMISTON   BLACKHALL
Queensferry Rd.

Calton Hill

RESTALRIG

Holyroodhouse   PORTOBELLO

MURRAYFIELD

Princes St.   National
Gallery

Willowbrae Rd.

St. John's Rd.   Corstorphine Rd.

Edinburgh
Castle

HOLYROOD
PARK

CORSTORPHINE

Gorgie Rd.

Arthur's Seat

DUDDINGSTON

Union Canal

MARCHMONT   NEWINGTON

Braid Burn

NIDDRIE

STENHOUSE   A70   MERCHISTON   GRANGE

CRAIGMILLAR

SIGHTHILL

MORNINGSIDE

Craigmillar
Castle

Calder Rd.

CRAIGLOCKHART   A702   Royal
Observatory

Old Dalkeith Rd.

Gilmerton Rd.

Water of Leith

BRAID

WESTER HAILES

LIBERTON

JUNIPER
GREEN

Comiston Rd.

A701

A70   A720
COLINTON

SCOTLAND

CURRIE

FAIRMILEHEAD

Edinburgh

A720

A702

0   50 mi
0   50 km   ENGLAND

0   1 mi
0   1 km

N

THE NEIGHBORHOODS IN BRIEF

The Old Town This area is where Edinburgh began. Its backbone is the **Royal Mile,** a medieval thoroughfare stretching for about 1.6km (1 mile) from Edinburgh Castle and running downhill to the Palace of Holyroodhouse. It comprises four connected streets: Castlehill, Lawnmarket, High Street, and Canongate. "This is perhaps the largest, longest, and finest street for buildings and number of inhabitants in the world," wrote English author Daniel Defoe. And the same might be said of the Royal Mile today.

The New Town Lying below the Old Town, the New Town burst into full bloom between 1766 and 1840 and became one of the largest Georgian developments in the world. It contains most of the northern heart of the city, covering some 320 hectares (790 acres). With about 25,000 residents, it's the largest government-protected area in Britain. The New Town is made up of a network of squares, streets, terraces, and circuses, reaching from Haymarket in the west to Abbeyhill in the east. The New Town also goes from Canonmills on the northern perimeter down to Princes Street, its main artery, along the southern tier.

Marchmont About 1.5km (1 mile) south of High Street, this suburb was

> ## *Tips* Finding an Address
>
> Edinburgh's streets often follow no pattern, and both names and house numbers seem to have been created purposely to confuse. First, the city is checkered with innumerable squares, terraces, circuses, wynds, and closes, which will jut into or cross or overlap or interrupt whatever street you're trying to follow, usually without the slightest warning.
>
> Then the house numbers run in sequences of odds or evens, or they run clockwise or counterclockwise at random—that is, when such numbers exist at all. Many establishments don't use street numbers. (This is even more prevalent when you leave Edinburgh and go to provincial towns.) Before heading out, get a detailed map of Edinburgh and ask for specific directions; locals are generally glad to assist a bewildered visitor. If you're looking for an address, try to get the name of the nearest cross street.

constructed between 1869 and 1914 as a massive building program of new housing for people who could no longer afford to live in the New Town. It borders a public park, the Meadows. Although Marchmont is not a tourist area, visitors sometimes find an affordable B&B in one of the little homes that receive guests.

Bruntsfield This suburb to the west is named for Bruntsfield Links. Now a residential district, it was the ground on which James IV gathered the Scottish army he marched to its defeat at Flodden in 1513. Plague victims were once brought here for burial; now suburban gardens have grown over those graves. Many low-cost B&Bs are found in this area.

Churchill Churchill is known as "holy corner" because of the wide array of Scottish churches within its borders at the junctions of Colinton, Chamberlain, and Bruntsfield roads. These churches are primarily for local worshipers and not of artistic interest.

Leith Only a few kilometers north of Princes Street is the Port of Leith, the city's major harbor, which opens onto the Firth of Forth. The area is currently being gentrified, and visitors come here for the restaurants and pubs, many of which specialize in seafood. The port doesn't flex the maritime muscle that it used to; its glory days were back when stevedores unloaded cargoes by hand.

Newhaven Newhaven is the fishing village adjacent to Leith. Founded in the 1400s, this former little harbor with its bustling fish market was greatly altered in the 1960s. Many of its "bow-tows" (a nickname for closely knit, clannish residents) were uprooted, like the Leithers, in a major gentrification program. Many of the old houses have now been restored, and the fishwife no longer goes from door to door hawking fish from her basket. Today the harbor is mostly filled with pleasure craft instead of fishing boats. If your time is limited, you can skip this area.

2 Getting Around

Because of its narrow lanes, wynds, and closes, you can only explore the Old Town in any depth on foot. Edinburgh is fairly convenient for the visitor who likes to walk—most of the attractions are along the Royal Mile, Princes Street, or one of the major streets of the New Town.

BY BUS   The bus will probably be your chief method of transport. The fare is £1 ($1.90) for one journey, any distance. Children ages 5 to 15 are charged a flat rate of 60p ($1.15), but teenagers ages 16 to 18 must carry a **teen card** (available where bus tickets are sold—see below) as proof of age and their fare is 65p ($1.25); children 4 and under ride free. Exact change is required if you're paying your fare on the bus.

The **Edinburgh Day Saver Ticket** allows 1 day of unlimited travel on city buses at a cost of £2.50 ($4.75) adults and £2 ($3.80) children.

For daily commuters or die-hard Scottish enthusiasts, a **RidaCard** season ticket allows unlimited travel on all buses. For adults, the price is £13 ($25) for 1 week and £35 ($67) for 4 weeks; tickets for children cost £9 ($17) for 1 week and £23 ($44) for 4 weeks. Travel must begin on Sunday.

You can get these tickets and further information in the city center at the **Waverley Bridge Transport Office,** Waverley Bridge (© **0131/554-4494;** bus: 3 or 31), open Monday to Saturday 8:30am to 6pm and Sunday 9:30am to 5pm, or at the Hanover Street office (bus: 3 or 31), open Monday to Saturday 8:30am to 6pm. For details on timetables, call © **0131/555-6363.**

BY TAXI   You can hail a taxi or pick one up at a taxi stand. Meters begin at £2 ($3.80) and increase £2 ($3.80) every 1km (½ mile). Taxi ranks are at Hanover Street, North St. Andrews Street, Waverley Station, Haymarket Station, and Lauriston Place. Fares are displayed in the front of the taxi, including extra charges for night drivers or destinations outside the city limits. You can also call a taxi, which costs 60p ($1.15). Try **City Cabs** at © **0131/228-1211** or **Central Radio Taxis** at © **0131/229-2468.**

BY CAR   Don't think about driving in Edinburgh—it's a tricky business, even for natives. Parking is expensive and difficult to find. Metered parking is available, but you need the right change and have to watch out for traffic wardens who issue tickets. Some zones are marked PERMIT HOLDERS ONLY—your vehicle will be towed if you have no permit. A yellow line along the curb indicates no parking. Major car parks (parking lots) are at Castle Terrace, convenient for Edinburgh Castle and the west end of Princes Street; at Lothian Road, near the west end of Princes Street; at St. John Hill, convenient to the Royal Mile, the west end of Princes Street, and Waverley Station; and at St. James Centre (entrance from York Place), close to the east end of Princes Street.

You may want a rental car for touring the countryside or for heading onward. Many agencies give discounts to those who reserve in advance (see chapter 2 for more information). They will usually accept your U.S. or Canadian driver's license, provided you've held it for more than a year and are over 21. Most of the major car-rental companies maintain offices at the Edinburgh airport. Call **Avis** (© **0131/333-1866**), **Hertz** (© **0131/333-1019**), or **Europcar** (© **0131/333-2588**).

BY BICYCLE   Biking in town isn't a good idea for most visitors because the city is constructed on a series of high ridges and terraces. You may, however, want to rent a bike for exploring the flatter countryside around the city. Try **Central Cycle Hire,** 13

Lochrin Place (℃ **0131/228-6333;** bus: 10), off Home Street in Tollcross, near the Cameo Cinema. Depending on the type of bike, charges average around £22 ($42) per day. A deposit of £100 ($190) is required. June to September, the shop is open Monday to Saturday 9:30am to 6pm and Sunday noon to 7pm; October to May, hours are Monday to Saturday 10am to 5:30pm.

FAST FACTS: Edinburgh

American Express The office is at 139 Princes St. (℃ **0131/225-9179;** bus: 3, 39, or 69), 5 blocks from Waverley Station. It's open Monday to Friday 9am to 5:30pm and Saturday 9am to 4pm; on Thursday, the office opens at 9:30am.

Babysitters The most reliable services are provided by Guardians Baby Sitting Service, 13 Eton Terrace (℃ **0131/337-4150**), and Care Connections, 45 Barclay Place (℃ **01506/856-106**).

Business Hours In Edinburgh, banks are usually open Monday to Wednesday 9:30am to 3:45pm and Thursday and Friday 9:30am to 5 or 5:30pm. Shops are generally open Monday to Saturday 10am to 5:30 or 6pm; on Thursday, stores are open to 8pm. Offices are open Monday to Friday 9am to 5pm.

Currency Exchange Try the **Clydesdale Bank,** 5 Waverley Bridge at Waverley Market.

Dentists If you have a dental emergency, go to the **Edinburgh Dental Institute,** 39 Lauriston Place (℃ **0131/536-4931;** bus: 23 or 41), open Monday through Friday from 9am to 3pm.

Doctors You can seek help from the **Edinburgh Royal Infirmary,** 1 Lauriston Place (℃ **0131/536-1000;** bus: 23 or 41). Medical attention is available 24 hours.

Embassies & Consulates See "Fast Facts: Scotland," in chapter 2.

Emergencies Call ℃ **999** in an emergency to summon the police, an ambulance, or firefighters.

Hospitals See "Doctors," above.

Internet Access The **International Telecom Centre,** 52 High St. (℃ **0131/559-7114;** bus: 1 or 6), charges £1 ($1.90) for 15 minutes. Open daily from 9am to 10pm.

Laundry & Dry Cleaning For your dry-cleaning needs, go to **Johnson's Cleaners,** 23 Frederick St. (℃ **0131/225-8095;** bus: 23 or 41), open Monday to Friday 8:30am to 5:30pm and Saturday 8am to 4pm.

Luggage Storage & Lockers Luggage lockers are available at **Waverley Station,** at Waverley Bridge (℃ **0131/550-2031**), open Monday to Saturday 7am to 11pm and Sunday 8am to 11pm.

Newspapers Published since 1817, *The Scotsman* is a quality daily newspaper. Along with national and international news, it's strong on the arts.

Pharmacies There are no 24-hour pharmacies (also called chemists) in Edinburgh. The major drugstore is **Boots,** 48 Shandwick Place (℃ **0131/225-6757;** bus: 3 or 31), open Monday to Friday 8am to 9pm, Saturday 8am to 6pm, and Sunday 10am to 4pm.

Police See "Emergencies," above.

Post Office The **Edinburgh Branch Post Office,** St. James's Centre, is open Monday to Friday 9am to 5:30pm and Saturday 8:30am to noon. For postal information and customer service, call © **0131/556-0478.**

Restrooms These are found at rail stations, terminals, restaurants, hotels, pubs, and department stores. Don't hesitate to use the system of public toilets, often marked WC, at strategic corners and squares throughout the city. They're perfectly safe and clean, but likely to be closed late in the evening.

Safety Edinburgh is generally safer than Glasgow—in fact, it's one of Europe's safest capitals for strolling at any time of day or night. But crimes, especially muggings, do occur, largely because of Edinburgh's shockingly large drug problem.

Weather For weather forecasts and road conditions, call © **0845/300-0300.** This number also provides weather information for Lothian, the Borders, Tayside, and Fife.

3 Where to Stay

Edinburgh offers a full range of accommodations throughout the year. But it should come as no surprise that during the 3-week period of the Edinburgh International Festival, in August, the hotels fill up; if you're coming at that time, be sure to reserve far in advance.

The **Edinburgh & Scotland Information Centre,** Princes Mall, 3 Princes St., at the corner of Princes Street and Waverley Bridge (© **0131/473-3800;** fax 0131/473-3881; www.edinburgh.org; bus: 3, 7, 14, 31, or 69), compiles a lengthy list of small hotels, guesthouses, and private homes providing a bed-and-breakfast for as little as £20 ($38) per person. A £3 ($5.70) booking fee and a 10% deposit are charged. Allow about 4 weeks' notice, especially during summer and during the festival weeks. July and August, hours are Monday to Saturday 9am to 8pm and Sunday 10am to 8pm; May, June, and September, hours are Monday to Saturday 8am to 7pm and Sunday 9am to 5pm; October to April, hours are Monday to Saturday 9am to 6pm and Sunday 10am to 6pm.

If you have an early flight out and need a hotel convenient to the airport, consider the 244-unit **Edinburgh Marriott,** 111 Glasgow Rd. (© **0131/334-9191**), off A8 on Edinburgh's western outskirts. It offers doubles for £110 to £175 ($209–$333), including breakfast. Facilities include an indoor pool, gym, sauna, and two restaurants.

THE NEW TOWN
VERY EXPENSIVE
Balmoral Hotel 🌟🌟🌟   This legendary place opened in 1902 as the grandest hotel in northern Britain. After a $35-million restoration, it reopened in 1991 under the name Balmoral, and it was refurbished several times since. Almost directly above the Waverley Rail Station, it features a soaring clock tower that many locals consider one of their city's landmarks. Kilted doormen and a bagpiper supply the Scottish atmosphere. Each unit comes with a commodious bathroom with combination tub/shower. Dining options include the elegant No. 1 Princes Street (see "Where to Dine," later in this chapter) and the more convivial brasserie Hadrian's. Afternoon tea is served in

Edinburgh Accommodations & Dining

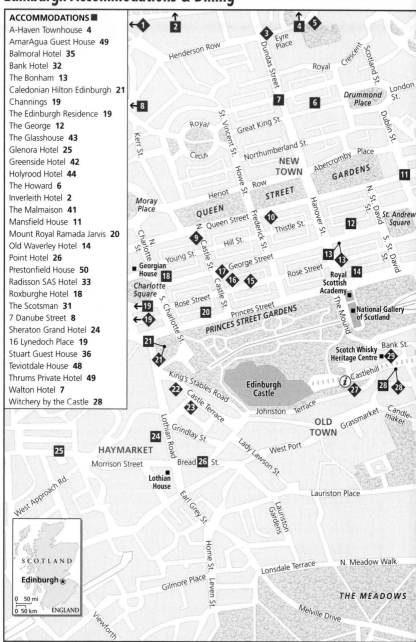

ACCOMMODATIONS ■

A-Haven Townhouse **4**
AmarAgua Guest House **49**
Balmoral Hotel **35**
Bank Hotel **32**
The Bonham **13**
Caledonian Hilton Edinburgh **21**
Channings **19**
The Edinburgh Residence **19**
The George **12**
The Glasshouse **43**
Glenora Hotel **25**
Greenside Hotel **42**
Holyrood Hotel **44**
The Howard **6**
Inverleith Hotel **2**
The Malmaison **41**
Mansfield House **11**
Mount Royal Ramada Jarvis **20**
Old Waverley Hotel **14**
Point Hotel **26**
Prestonfield House **50**
Radisson SAS Hotel **33**
Roxburghe Hotel **18**
The Scotsman **31**
7 Danube Street **8**
Sheraton Grand Hotel **24**
16 Lynedoch Place **19**
Stuart Guest House **36**
Teviotdale House **48**
Thrums Private Hotel **49**
Walton Hotel **7**
Witchery by the Castle **28**

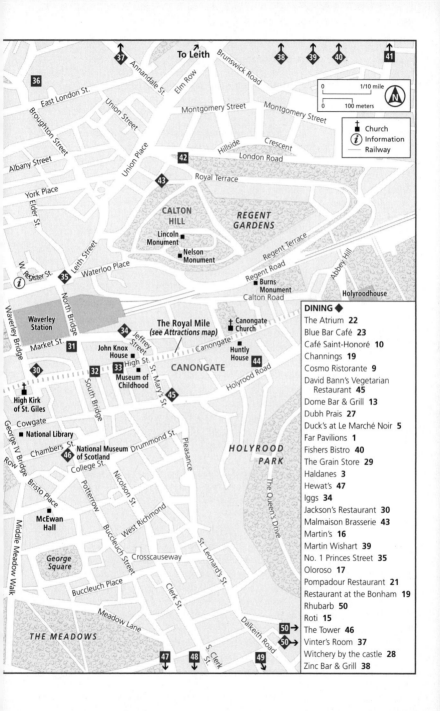

DINING ◆

The Atrium **22**
Blue Bar Café **23**
Café Saint-Honoré **10**
Channings **19**
Cosmo Ristorante **9**
David Bann's Vegetarian Restaurant **45**
Dome Bar & Grill **13**
Dubh Prais **27**
Duck's at Le Marché Noir **5**
Far Pavilions **1**
Fishers Bistro **40**
The Grain Store **29**
Haldanes **3**
Hewat's **47**
Iggs **34**
Jackson's Restaurant **30**
Malmaison Brasserie **43**
Martin's **16**
Martin Wishart **39**
No. 1 Princes Street **35**
Oloroso **17**
Pompadour Restaurant **21**
Restaurant at the Bonham **19**
Rhubarb **50**
Roti **15**
The Tower **46**
Vinter's Room **37**
Witchery by the castle **28**
Zinc Bar & Grill **38**

the high-ceilinged Palm Court. Foremost among the several bar areas is N.B.'s, a Scottish pub with an entrance directly on Princes Street.

1 Princes St., Edinburgh EH2 2EQ. © 800/223-6800 in the U.S., or 0131/556-2414. Fax 0131/557-3747. www.the balmoralhotel.com. 188 units. £345–£510 ($656–$969) double; from £640 ($1,216) suite. AE, DC, MC, V. Valet parking £20 ($38). Bus: 50. **Amenities:** 3 restaurants; 2 bars; indoor pool; health club; spa; sauna; business center; room service; laundry service; dry cleaning; nonsmoking rooms. *In room:* A/C, TV, fax, minibar, hair dryer, safe, trouser press, Wi-Fi.

The Bonham 🏨🏨   One of Edinburgh's most stylish hotels occupies three connected town houses that functioned since the 19th century as a nursing home and as dorms for the local university. In 1998, all that changed when a team of entrepreneurs poured millions of pounds into refurbishment, pumped up the style, and outfitted the high-ceilinged guest rooms with a hip blend of old and new. Each has an individual theme, plush upholsteries, and a TV with a keyboard hooked up to the Internet—the first setup of its kind in Europe. Bathrooms are cutting edge, with checkered floors, Molton Brown toiletries, and combination tub/showers. The Restaurant at the Bonham is reviewed under "Where to Dine," later in this chapter.

35 Drumsheugh Gardens, Edinburgh EH3 7RN. © 0131/226-6050. Fax 0131/226-6080. www.thebonham.com. 48 units. £105–£245 ($200–$466) double; £190–£350 ($361–$665) suite. Rates include continental breakfast. AE, DC, DISC, MC, V. Bus: 23 or 27. **Amenities:** Restaurant; room service; nonsmoking rooms. *In room:* TV, minibar, coffeemaker, hair dryer, iron, trouser press, Wi-Fi.

Caledonian Hilton Edinburgh 🏨🏨   The hotel remains one of the city's landmarks and offers commanding views of Edinburgh Castle and the Princes Street Gardens. The public rooms are reminiscent of Edwardian splendor, and the guest rooms (many of which are exceptionally spacious) are conservatively styled with reproduction furniture. The fifth-floor rooms are the smallest. Bathrooms come with combination tub/showers. Although the accommodations are superior to those of many first-class hotels in Edinburgh, the Caledonian lacks the leisure facilities of its major competitor, the Balmoral. The hotel contains a traditional pub, Henry J. Beans, and Chisholms Bar. More formal meals are served in Pompadour Restaurant (see "Where to Dine," later in this chapter). A traditional tea is featured in the high-ceilinged lounge.

Princes St., Edinburgh EH1 2AB. © 0131/222-8888. Fax 0131/222-8889. www.caledonian.hilton.com. 249 units. £164–£250 ($312–$475) double; from £244 ($464) suite. Children age 15 and under stay free in parent's room. AE, DC, MC, V. Bus: 33. Parking £10 ($19). **Amenities:** 3 restaurants; bar; indoor pool; exercise room; room service; laundry service; dry cleaning; limited-mobility rooms; nonsmoking rooms. *In room:* TV, minibar, hair dryer, iron, trouser press, Wi-Fi.

The Edinburgh Residence 🏨🏨🏨   If Robert Burns, who liked his luxuries, were checking into a hotel in Edinburgh today, he no doubt would come here. One of the finest luxury hotels in Scotland, it's a series of elegant town-house suites installed in a trio of architecturally beautiful and sensitively restored Georgian buildings. As you enter, grand staircases and classic wood paneling greet you. A stay here is like lodging in an elegant town house from long ago, but with all the modern conveniences. This hotel is on the same level or better than its siblings, The Howard, The Bonham, and Channings. Accommodations are the ultimate in local comfort; each of a trio of classic suites has a private entrance. All units are spacious.

7 Rothesay Terrace, Edinburgh EH3 7RY. © 0131/226-3380. Fax 0131/226-3381. www.theedinburghresidence.com. 29 units. £130–£295 ($247–$561) suite; £210–£410 ($399–$779) apt. Rates include continental breakfast. AE, MC, V. Free parking. Bus: 19 or 37. **Amenities:** Bar; room service; nonsmoking rooms. *In room:* TV, minibar, microwave, hair dryer, iron, Wi-Fi.

The George ⭐ Designed by famed architect Robert Adam and only yards from St. Andrews Square, the city's financial center, The George opened in 1755 and was turned into a hotel in 1972. In 2007 it underwent a £12-million restoration and is looking better than ever. The public rooms have retained the style, elegance, and old-fashioned comfort of a country house. The guest rooms come in various sizes and have undergone frequent refurbishments. The best units are those with views: on the fourth floor and above in the new wing.

19–21 George St., Edinburgh EH2 2PB. © **0131/225-1251.** Fax 0131/226-5644. www.edinburghgeorgehotel.co.uk. 195 units. £119 ($226) double; from £399 ($758) suite. AE, DC, MC, V. Limited free parking. Bus: 41 or 42. **Amenities:** Restaurant; bar; room service; babysitting; laundry service; dry cleaning; nonsmoking rooms. *In room:* TV, minibar, coffeemaker, hair dryer, iron, safe, trouser press, Wi-Fi.

The Howard ⭐⭐⭐ Dubbed the most discreet government-rated five-star hotel in the city, The Howard comprises a trio of Georgian-terraced houses that once were private homes of rich burghers. The landmark is pricier and more refined than its sibling, Channings (see later in this chapter). Service is a staple of the hotel, with a dedicated butler tending to your needs, even unpacking your luggage if you desire. Some of the aura of a private home remains in the buildings. Accommodations are midsize to spacious, each individually and rather elegantly decorated, with some of the best bathrooms in town, featuring power and double showers and, in some, a Jacuzzi. The decor is traditional and modern, using both antiques and reproductions. Three of the units are terraced suites, and the accommodations are named after Edinburgh streets.

34 Great King St., Edinburgh EH3 6QH. © **0131/557-3500.** Fax 0131/557-6515. www.thehoward.com. 18 units. £140–£275 ($266–$523) double; £220–£395 ($418–$751) suite. Rates include breakfast. AE, DC, MC, V. Bus: 13, 23, 27, or C5. **Amenities:** Restaurant; room service; laundry service; dry cleaning; butler/valet service; nonsmoking rooms. *In room:* TV, hair dryer, Wi-Fi.

Paramount Carlton Highland Hotel ⭐ *Kids* A century ago, this was one of Edinburgh's leading department stores, with 4 of its 10 stories below sidewalk level. In 1984, the baronial pile was converted into a plush hotel. In spite of its overhaul, the architectural charm of 1900 still remains. Its Victorian turrets, Flemish gables, and severe gray stonework rise from a corner on the Royal Mile, near Waverley Station. The Paramount investment group substantially improved this hotel with an influx of pounds. Some bedrooms were done away with to make the units larger and more comfortable, with private bathrooms that feature tub and shower. Furnishings are tasteful with a subdued modern simplicity. Offering more facilities than the landmark Caledonian, the Carlton is known for its top-notch service and both formal and informal dining venues.

19 North Bridge, Edinburgh, Lothian EH1 1SD. © **0131/472-3000.** Fax 0131/556-2691. www.paramount-hotels. co.uk. 189 units. £190–£200 ($361–$380) executive double. Children age 14 and under stay free in parent's room. AE, DC, MC, V. Parking £18 ($34). Bus: 55 or 80. **Amenities:** Restaurant; bar; indoor pool; health club; Jacuzzi; sauna; room service; babysitting; squash courts; limited-mobility rooms; nonsmoking rooms. *In room:* TV, coffeemaker, hair dryer, iron, safe, Wi-Fi.

The Scotsman ⭐⭐⭐ Located on the historic North Bridge, only minutes from the Royal Mile and Princes Street, this is one of the brightest and most stylish hotels to open in Edinburgh in many a year. Its name honors the famous newspaper that was published here for nearly a century. One reviewer noted when it opened: "Think native son Sir Arthur Conan Doyle getting a reverent makeover from Gucci's Tom Ford." Traditional styling and cutting-edge design are harmoniously wed in the 1904 baronial limestone pile, a city landmark since it was first constructed. Guest rooms, in honor of their former roles as newspaper offices, are categorized by size and given masthead ranks such as assistant editor, editor, or publisher. They include state-of-the-art bathrooms and such extras as two-way service closets, which means your laundry is picked up virtually unnoticed. Our favorite retreat here is Room 399, a cozy bar named for its number of single-malt whiskies.

The Cowshed Spa here is the finest in Edinburgh. The name sounds odd, of course, but is taken from the original Cowshed at Babington House in Somerset, England. It was named for its former occupants. As you enter you'll be enveloped in various scents ranging from jasmine to rose candles. The 80-minute Stoned Cow massage uses both hot and cold stones and organic flower and plant oils, all blended in-house.

20 N. Bridge, Edinburgh EH1 1DF. © 0131/556-5565. Fax 0131/652-3652. www.thescotsmanhotel.co.uk. 68 units. £250 ($475) double; from £380 ($722) suite. AE, DC, MC, V. Bus: 7, 8, 21, 31, or 33. **Amenities:** 2 restaurants; bar; indoor pool; health club; spa; sauna; salon; room service; massage; babysitting; laundry service; dry cleaning; nonsmoking rooms. *In room:* TV, minibar, coffeemaker, hair dryer, iron, safe, Wi-Fi.

Sheraton Grand Hotel *finds finds*   This former railway siding, a short walk from Princes Street, is now a six-story postmodern structure housing a glamorous hotel and an office complex. The hotel is elegant, with soaring public rooms and carpeting in tones of thistle and mauve. Boasting a central location and a well-chosen staff, this is the most appealing modern hotel in the capital. The spacious, well-furnished guest rooms have double-glazed windows; glamorous suites are available, as are rooms for non-smokers and travelers with disabilities. The castle-view rooms on the top three floors are the best. The main restaurant, with views of the Festival Square Fountain, presents well-prepared meals and a lavish Sunday buffet. The plushly modern cocktail bar is a favorite rendezvous for locals.

1 Festival Sq., Edinburgh, Lothian EH3 9SR. © 800/325-3535 in the U.S. and Canada, or 0131/229-9131. Fax 0131/228-4510. www.sheraton.com. 260 units. £239–£380 ($454–$722) double; £400 ($760) suite. AE, DC, MC, V. Bus: 4, 15, or 44. **Amenities:** 4 restaurants; 2 bars; indoor and outdoor pools; exercise room; spa; sauna; room service; massage; babysitting; laundry service; dry cleaning; nonsmoking rooms; rooms for those w/limited mobility. *In room:* A/C, TV, minibar, coffeemaker, hair dryer, iron, trouser press, Wi-Fi.

EXPENSIVE
The Glasshouse *finds (Finds*   This unique hotel is not only one of the most modern but one of the best so-called boutique hotels in Edinburgh. It combines the old and the new. At the foot of Carlton Hill, within walking distance of Princes Street, The Glasshouse has an impressive church facade—the actual entrance to the hotel—which coexists in surprising harmony with a modern glass structure. The well-furnished bedrooms open onto panoramic views of Edinburgh. A special feature is the residential rooftop bar. The bedrooms are as modern as tomorrow, with sleek, well-styled furnishings, the beds closed off from the sitting area by wood panels.

2 Greenside Place, Edinburgh EH1 3AA. © 0131/525-8200. Fax 0131/525-8205. www.theetoncollection.com/hotels/glasshouse. 65 units. £160–£215 ($304–$409) double; £215–£345 ($409–$656) suite. AE, DC, MC, V. Parking £18 ($34). Bus: 10, 11, 15, 16, 17, or 22. **Amenities:** Restaurant; bar; health club; room service; babysitting; laundry service; dry cleaning; nonsmoking rooms; rooms for those w/limited mobility. *In room:* A/C, TV, minibar, coffeemaker, hair dryer, safe, trouser press, Wi-Fi.

Mount Royal Ramada Jarvis *finds*   The Mount Royal, a remake of an 1860s hotel, is right in the middle of Princes Street. A modern world emerges as you climb the spiral staircase, or take an elevator, to the second floor, with its reception rooms, lounges, and floor-to-ceiling windows opening onto views of the Old Town and the castle. There aren't a lot of frills, but the comfort is genuine in the streamlined guest rooms.

Be aware this is a tour-group favorite. The lounge, with views of the Scott Memorial and Princes Street, provides a wide range of savory and sweet snacks and beverages throughout the day.

53 Princes St., Edinburgh EH2 2DG. © **0131/225-7161**. Fax 0131/220-4671. www.ramadajarvis.co.uk. 158 units. £84–£180 ($160–$342) double; £180–£250 ($342–$475) suite. AE, DC, MC, V. Bus: 15 or 100. Parking. **Amenities:** Restaurant; bar; room service; laundry service; dry cleaning; nonsmoking rooms; rooms for those w/limited mobility. *In room:* TV, coffeemaker, hair dryer, trouser press, Wi-Fi.

Old Waverley Hotel ✯   The first teetotal hotel in Scotland, this old timer is much improved and restored. In 1848 it opened opposite Waverley Station when it catered to passengers arriving on the newfangled rail tracks. It remains the oldest operating hotel in Scotland but over the decades became less grand. That changed with the takeover by the Kapoor family who have been modernizing and giving the hotel a new lease on life in yet another century.

The high ceilings and narrow corridors remain, and the owners are restricted to what they can do to a landmark building. As befits the era of its construction, bedrooms come in all shapes and sizes. The views have remained the same from the front rooms, opening onto the Princes Street Gardens with Edinburgh Castle in the distance. If you have to skip the view, rooms are much quieter in the rear. Of course, the accommodations, even though restored, are hardly in the category of The Balmoral or The Caledonian, but Old Waverley is better on your pocketbook. Dining and drinking facilities have been vastly improved. Both Kapoor's Restaurant and Cranston's specialize in Scottish regional dishes among other offerings.

43 Princes St., Edinburgh EH2 2BY. © **0131/556-4648**. Fax 031/557-6316. www.oldwaverley.co.uk. 66 units. £189–£199 ($359–$378) double. Rates include breakfast. Children 12 and under stay free in parent's room. AE, MC, V. Parking £10 ($19) for 24 hr. Bus: 15 or 100. **Amenities:** Restaurant; bar; spa; sauna; room service; laundry service; dry cleaning; nonsmoking rooms. *In room:* TV, hair dryer, coffeemaker, Wi-Fi.

Roxburghe Hotel ✯   The heart of the Roxburghe is a stately gray-stone Robert Adam town house on a tree-filled square, a short walk from Princes Street. The atmosphere is traditional, reflected in the drawing room with its ornate ceiling and woodwork, antique furnishings, and tall arched windows. In 1999, the hotel was enlarged into two neighboring buildings, tripling the original number of guest rooms, which vary in size. The largest are in the original building and maintain features like their imposing fireplaces. The newer rooms have more recent furnishings and more up-to-date plumbing. The elegant Consort Restaurant is a good place to congregate for drinks.

38 Charlotte St. (at George St.), Edinburgh EH2 4HQ. © **0131/240-5500**. Fax 0131/240-5555. www.the roxburghe.com. 197 units. £170–£250 ($323–$475) double; from £250 ($475) suite. Rates include breakfast. AE, DC, MC, V. Parking £11 ($21). Bus: 100. **Amenities:** Restaurant; bar; indoor pool; health club; sauna; room service; massage; steam room; laundry service; dry cleaning; nonsmoking rooms. *In room:* TV, minibar, coffeemaker, hair dryer, iron, trouser press, Wi-Fi.

MODERATE
A-Haven Townhouse *Kids*   A-Haven is a semi-detached gray-stone Victorian, a 15-minute walk or a 5-minute bus ride north of the rail station in an up-and-coming neighborhood. The guest rooms are various sizes (the biggest on the second floor) and outfitted with traditional furnishings and shower-only bathrooms. Some units in back overlook the Firth of Forth, and those in front open onto views of Arthur's Seat. Some units are large enough to accommodate family bedrooms with cots, and a playground is available for children. Ronnie Murdock extends a Scottish welcome in this family-type place. He has a licensed bar (for guests only), but breakfast is the only meal served.

180 Ferry Rd., Edinburgh, EH6 4NS. ✆ **0131/554-6559**. Fax 0131/554-5252. www.a-haven.co.uk. 14 units. £60–£150 ($114–$285) double. Rates include breakfast. AE, MC, V. Free parking. Bus: 7, 11, 14, or 21. **Amenities:** Bar; children's playground; nonsmoking rooms. *In room:* TV, hair dryer, coffeemaker, trouser press.

Glenora Hotel   Only a 10-minute walk from Princes Street and the city center is this refurbished bed-and-breakfast. Its convenient location and comfortable rooms, all of which are nonsmoking, make this a favorite among visitors and business clients alike. The reception area's white walls, potted plants, and hanging paintings evoke a doctor's office waiting room. But the rest of the hotel has much nicer decor. Victorian touches, such as brass servant's bells and speaking tubes, are everywhere you look. The rooms are nothing special, just clean and cozy with a TV, beverage maker, and toiletries. Each unit has a small bathroom with shower.

Morning meals are innovative, with the kitchen serving a vegetarian breakfast, an all-organic breakfast, a buffet continental breakfast, and a traditional Scottish breakfast.

14 Rosebury Crescent, Edinburgh EH12 5JY. ✆ **0131/337-1186**. Fax 0131/337-1119. www.glenorahotel.co.uk. 12 units. £90–£145 ($171–$276) double; £120–£156 ($228–$296) triple. Rates include Scottish breakfast. MC, V. Bus: 4, 15, or 44. **Amenities:** Dining room; nonsmoking rooms. *In room:* TV, beverage maker, hair dryer.

Inverleith Hotel   Across from the Royal Botanic Gardens, on the street that Robert Louis Stevenson once called home, is a charming, family-run bed-and-breakfast. Steve and Adrienne Case, the owners, are congenial and helpful people who run the place with care. The rooms are all small to midsize, and comfortable, with basic British decor and direct-dial telephones.

The large Scottish breakfast usually includes cereal, bacon, eggs, sausage, tomato, hash browns, mushrooms, baked beans, haggis, and porridge. A bar on-site specializes in malt whisky. For those who want a more self-sufficient vacation, Inverleith also has a first-floor apartment. This completely separate living arrangement, known as the Brandon Apartment, has a drawing room with a dining area, a kitchen complete with an electric oven, gas hob, refrigerator, utensils, laundry machines, and linens.

5 Inverleith Terrace, Edinburgh EH3 5NS. ✆ **0131/556-2745**. www.inverleithhotel.co.uk. 12 units. £59–£79 ($112–$150) double; £89–£159 ($169–$302) apt. Rates include Scottish breakfast. Weekday parking £4.30 ($8.15). Free parking on weekends. AE, MC, V. Bus: 8, 23, or 27. **Amenities:** Dining room; bar; nonsmoking rooms. *In room:* TV.

Kew House & Apartments ⊙ *Kids*   One of the New Town's most successful Victorian restorations, this complex near the Murrayfield Rugby Stadium lies 1 mile (.6km) west of Princes Street and is easily reached by public transportation, a 10-minute walk from Haymarket rail station. Each bedroom has been furnished in an individual style, with much comfort, including private bathrooms with shower. Thoughtful touches abound, including the gift of chocolates and sherry upon your arrival. In all, there are six bedrooms here plus two well-furnished apartments, which lie a 5-minute walk from the main house. The apartments, ideal for families, also contain full kitchens and sitting rooms.

1 Kew Terrace, Murrayfield, Edinburgh EH12 5JE. ✆ **0131/313-0700**. www.kewhouse.com. 8 units. Off season £85–£95 ($162–$181) double, £110 ($209) triple, £100 ($190) apt; Summer £140–£150 ($266–$285) double, £160 ($304) triple, £180 ($342) apt. Rates include breakfast. Free parking. AE, MC, V. Bus: 12, 26, or 31. **Amenities:** Lounge; nonsmoking rooms. *In room:* TV, kitchen (in some), fridge (in some), beverage maker, hair dryer, trouser press.

Point Hotel   This stylish place, in the shadow of Edinburgh Castle, has one of the most dramatic contemporary interiors of any hotel in Edinburgh. The decor has appeared in a book detailing the 50 premier hotel designs in the world, with a great emphasis on color and innovation, including a black stone floor at the front that's marked by "dusty footprints." In one place, blue walls are spotted neon red, creating a brilliant optical fantasy. Sometimes, for a dramatic minimalist effect, a lone armchair and sofa will occupy 92 sq. m (1,000 sq. ft.) of space. Bedrooms are large and attractively furnished. Most of the guest rooms have views of the castle; however, those in the rear do not, so be duly warned. If you like stainless steel, laser projections, and chrome instead of Scottish antiques, this might be an address for you. Standard rooms are a bit small, while the premium rooms are more comfortable and spacious.

34 Bread St., Edinburgh EH3 9AF. ⓒ **0131/221-5555.** Fax 0131/221-9929. www.point-hotel.co.uk. 140 units. £130–£160 ($247–$304) double; £360 ($684) suite. Rates include English breakfast. AE, DC, MC, V. Bus: 4 or 31. **Amenities:** Restaurant; bar; room service; laundry service; dry cleaning; nonsmoking rooms. *In room:* TV, hair dryer, iron.

7 Danube Street ☆   This 1825 B&B, run by Fiona and Colin Mitchell-Rose, is in Stockbridge, a stylish residential neighborhood, 10 minutes' walk north of the commercial center. It was designed by architect James Milne and was once the home of painter Horatio McCulloch. The public rooms and spacious guest rooms boast artfully draped chintzes. The most desirable room has a four-poster bed and direct access to the garden. All units are well stocked with such sundries as perfumed soaps, adapters, dental floss, and nail files. A lavish breakfast in the formal dining room may include venison sausages, omelets made from free-range eggs, homemade scones, and jams and marmalades put up by Fiona.

7 Danube St., Edinburgh EH4 1NN. ⓒ **0131/332-2755.** Fax 0131/343-3648. www.aboutedinburgh.com/danube.html. 3 units. £100–£145 ($190–$276) double. Rates include breakfast. MC, V. Free parking nearby. Bus: 28. **Amenities:** Laundry; nonsmoking rooms. *In room:* TV, coffeemaker, hair dryer.

16 Lynedoch Place   This stone-fronted 1821 Georgian row house, run by affable hosts Andrew and Susie Hamilton, has a flower-filled front garden, unusual for a house of this type. Inside are high ceilings with deep cove moldings, a cantilevered staircase illuminated by a glassed-in cupola, and family antiques. The midsize guest rooms are cozy and decorated with charm (three with shower only and one with bath only). The elaborate breakfasts are served in a formal dining room. Andrew is an expert in planning itineraries through the Highlands, thanks to the time he spent there as a member of the elite Black Watch Infantry.

16 Lynedoch Place, Edinburgh EH3 7PY. ⓒ **0131/225-5507.** Fax 0131/226-4185. www.16lynedochplace.co.uk. 4 units. £75–£120 ($143–$228) double. Rates include breakfast. MC, V. Bus: 19. **Amenities:** Nonsmoking rooms *In room:* TV, coffeemaker, no phone.

Stuart Guest House   This Georgian town house has been successfully converted to receive overnight guests. The location is a 15-minute walk from the center of town. The property dates from 1830 but has been completely modernized, although its fine plasterwork remains. Many other original features are intact, including cornices in the high-ceilinged rooms, a large open staircase, and fireplaces. Bedrooms are restored and tastefully furnished, each with a private bathroom with shower. Although breakfast is provided, there is no evening meal; many good restaurants, however, lie within walking distance. There is no elevator, so be prepared to mount stairs (there are no ground-floor bedrooms). In the dining room/sitting area a computer is available for the use of guests wanting to check their e-mail. There is also Wi-Fi access.

12 East Claremont St., Edinburgh EH7 4JD. ⓒ **0131/557-9030.** Fax 0131/557-0563. www.stuartguesthouse.com. 5 units. £70–£100 ($133–$190) double. Rates include breakfast. AE, MC, V. Bus: 8 or 17. **Amenities:** Nonsmoking rooms. *In room:* TV, hair dryer, Wi-Fi.

(Kids) Family-Friendly Hotels

A-Haven Townhouse (p. 87) With some guest rooms large enough to accommodate families, and a playground for children, any family should feel right at home here.

Paramount Carlton Highland Hotel (p. 85) Kids love the indoor pool. Parents love the availability of extra-large units and the fact that kids 14 and under stay free in parent's room.

Teviotdale House (p. 92) Some enthusiastic visitors rate this place the best B&B in Edinburgh. Three rooms are large enough for families with up to four members. A great value.

Thrums Private Hotel (p. 92) This hotel takes its name from J. M. Barrie's fictional name for his hometown of Kirriemuir. Barrie is known to children as the author of *Peter Pan*. Kids are made especially welcome here and are housed in family rooms with their parents.

INEXPENSIVE

AmarAgua Guest House This bed-and-breakfast, a favorite of the Scottish Tourist board, is located in an 1880s Victorian residential a little over 1.6km (1 mile) from Princes Street. The quaint rooms are not for those who seek modern accommodations, but are well kept. Amenities in the small to midsize rooms—all nonsmoking—include a heating system, beverage maker, alarm clock, toiletries, hair dryer, television, a book, and playing cards. After a good night's sleep, visitors can head downstairs for breakfast in the dining room. Guests choose their meals a la carte, a rarity for a small bed-and-breakfast. Before you leave for the day, owners Dawn-Ann and Tony will give suggestions about what to visit, and what to avoid.

10 Kilmaurs Terrace, Edinburgh EH16 5DR. ℂ 0131/667-6775. Fax 0131/667-7687. www.amaragua.co.uk. 7 units. £66–£106 ($125–$201) double. Rates include breakfast. Free parking. MC, V. Bus: 30 or 33. **Amenities:** Dining room; nonsmoking rooms. *In room:* TV, beverage maker, hair dryer.

Greenside Hotel Behind a chiseled sandstone facade on the back side of Carlton Hill, this four-story Georgian, although recently renovated, has retained such features as its high ceilings, cove moldings, and elaborate trim. Guests access their rooms via a winding staircase, illuminated by a skylight. The rooms are so large that 10 of them contain a double bed and two singles. All have shower-only bathrooms. The Firth of Forth, the yacht *Britannia,* and the dramatic Forth Road Bridge are visible from the uppermost front floors; the rear windows overlook a sloping tiered garden with a patio at the bottom. Breakfast is served in a formal dining room.

9 Royal Terrace, Edinburgh EH7 5AB. ℂ/fax 0131/557-0022 or -0121. www.townhousehotels.co.uk. 16 units. £45–£130 ($86–$247) double. Rates include breakfast. AE, MC, V. Bus: 4, 15, or 44. **Amenities:** Restaurant; bar; nonsmoking rooms. *In room:* TV, coffeemaker, hair dryer, Wi-Fi.

Mansfield House Well located in the New Town, this friendly gay guesthouse offers individually decorated rooms of reasonable size. The best rooms, nos. 9 and 10, are two superior king-size units with sumptuous beds. Bathrooms contain showers only. The hotel is within walking distance of all the gay bars, clubs, and restaurants. It's always busy, so early booking is advised.

57 Dublin St., Edinburgh EH3 6NL. © 0131/556-7980. Fax 0131/466-1315. 9 units, 6 with private bathroom. £60 ($114) double without bathroom; £60–£75 ($114–$143) double with bathroom. Rates include continental breakfast. MC, V. Bus: 19 or 39. *In room:* TV, fridge (in some), coffeemaker, iron, no phone.

Walton Hotel   This little hotel, a well-restored 200-year-old town house, lies right in the heart of Edinburgh. A complete renovation has maintained the Walton's essential Georgian character, but has revitalized and modernized the entire hotel. Bedrooms are midsize, nonsmoking, cozy, comfortable, and tranquil. Don't expect much here in the way of service. The location is only a few minutes' walk from Princes Street.

79 Dundas St., Edinburgh EH3 6SD. © 0131/556-1137. Fax 0131/557-8367. www.waltonhotel.com. 10 units. £79–£149 ($150–$283) double. Rates include breakfast. MC, V. Bus: 23 or 27. Free parking. *In room:* TV, coffeemaker, hair dryer, iron.

THE OLD TOWN
VERY EXPENSIVE
The Witchery by the Castle ★★★ *Finds*   An offbeat offshoot of a famous Edinburgh restaurant (p. 100), this is a sumptuous, theatrically decorated address that houses Gothic antiques and elaborate tapestries. *Cosmopolitan* and other media have called The Witchery one of the "world's most wonderful places to stay." Each lavishly decorated suite features splendid furnishings—"fit for a lord and his lady"—and such extras as books, mood lighting, chocolates, a Bose sound system, and a free bottle of champagne. All the hype about the suites at this hotel is true—"the perfect lust-den," "Scotland's most romantic hotel," "a jewel-box setting," and "one of the 50 best places in the world for honeymooners." Each suite has its own character. Expect a huge rolltop bath built for two. The building is 17th century, filled with open fires, luxurious sitting areas, a galley kitchen, and wall-to-wall luxury. And the beds were broken in by the likes of Michael Douglas, Catherine Zeta-Jones, Pierce Brosnan, and Andrew Lloyd Webber.

Castlehill, The Royal Mile, Edinburgh EH1 2NF. © 0131/225-5613. Fax 0131/220-4392. www.thewitchery.com. 7 suites. From £295 ($561) double. AE, DC, MC, V. Rates include continental breakfast. Bus: 1 or 6. **Amenities:** 2 restaurants; nonsmoking rooms. *In room:* A/C, TV, fridge, coffeemaker, hair dryer, iron, safe, Wi-Fi.

EXPENSIVE
The Bank Hotel ★ *Value*   This imposing hotel offers better value than many of its competitors in this congested neighborhood beside the Royal Mile. Until around 1990, it was a branch of the Royal Bank of Scotland, and the past is still evident in its Greek Temple design. High ceilings, well-chosen furnishings, and king-size beds provide comfort; all but one guest room has a tub/shower bathroom. Each bedroom celebrates the work of a famous Scot, including rooms dedicated to Robert Burns, Robert Louis Stevenson, and Alexander Graham Bell.

Royal Mile at 1 S. Bridge St., Edinburgh EH1 1LL. © 0131/622-6800. Fax 0131/622-6822. www.festival-inns.co.uk. 9 units. £100 ($190) double without bathroom; £110–£140 ($209–$266) double with bathroom. Rates include breakfast. AE, MC, V. Nearby parking £8 ($15). Bus: 4, 15, 31, or 100. **Amenities:** Bar; laundry service; nonsmoking rooms. *In room:* TV, coffeemaker, hair dryer, trouser press.

Holyrood Hotel ★★★   We prefer this deluxe charmer to the grand palace hotels of Edinburgh. Holyrood launched itself into the millennium as the Automobile Association's "Hotel of the Year for Scotland." This impressive and exceedingly stylish hotel stands near the Scottish Parliament, the Palace of Holyroodhouse, and Dynamic

Earth, and is only 5 minutes from Princes Street. Bedrooms are luxurious, with deluxe furnishings and elegant toiletries. The Club Floor is one of the best retreats in Edinburgh for luxury-minded guests: It has its own private elevator, lounge, and library along with butler and business services.

Holyrood Rd., Edinburgh EH8 8AU. © **0131/550-4500.** Fax 0131/550-4545. www.holyrood-hotel.com. 157 units. £145–£245 ($276–$466) double; from £245 ($466) suite. Rates include buffet breakfast. AE, DC, MC, V. Bus: 25. **Amenities:** Restaurant; bar; indoor pool; health club; sauna; room service; laundry service; dry cleaning; club-level rooms; nonsmoking rooms. *In room:* A/C, TV, fax, minibar, coffeemaker, hair dryer, iron, safe, trouser press, Wi-Fi.

Radisson SAS Hotel 🏕   This is the best major hotel in the Old Town close to "Royal Edinburgh." This restored and mellow brick building lies midway along the Royal Mile, halfway between Edinburgh Castle and Palace of Holyroodhouse. In spite of the antique geography, the hotel is thoroughly modernized and offers first-class facilities, though it lacks the old-world charm of some of Edinburgh's grand dame hotels. It's also one of the best-equipped hotels in the area, with such luxuries as a leisure club and a jet-stream pool. Most of the bedrooms are spacious and well decorated; bathrooms contain tubs and showers as well as heated floors for those chilly Scottish mornings.

80 High St., Edinburgh EH1 1TH. © **0131/557-9797.** Fax 0131/557-9789. www.radissonsas.com. 238 units. £154–£179 ($293–$340) double; £219–£269 ($416–$511) suite. AE, DC, MC, V. Bus: 1 or 6. Parking £5 ($9.50). **Amenities:** Restaurant; bar; indoor pool; health club; sauna; business center; room service; massage; laundry service; dry cleaning; nonsmoking rooms; rooms for those w/limited mobility. *In room:* TV, minibar, coffeemaker, hair dryer, iron, safe, trouser press, Wi-Fi.

BRUNTSFIELD
EXPENSIVE

Teviotdale House 🏕🏕 *Kids* *Value*   Some visitors rate this three-story 1848 house—10 minutes by bus from Princes Street, Waverley Station, and Edinburgh Castle—as the finest B&B in the city. Elizabeth and Willy Thiebaud's attention to detail has earned them an enviable reputation. The house is furnished with antiques. The three largest rooms can accommodate up to four beds. The home-cooked breakfast may be the highlight of your day's dining, and can include smoked salmon, kippers, and fresh-baked bread and scones.

53 Grange Loan, Edinburgh EH9 2ER. © **0131/667-4376.** Fax 0131/667-4763. www.teviotdalehouse.com. 7 units. £62–£116 ($118–$220). AE, MC, V. Bus: 42. **Amenities:** Nonsmoking rooms. *In room:* TV, coffeemaker, hair dryer.

Thrums Private Hotel *Kids*   Located about 1.6km (1 mile) south of Princes Street, Thrums is a pair of connected antique buildings, one a two-story 1820 Georgian and the other a small inn (ca. 1900). The hotel contains high-ceilinged guest rooms with furnishings that are either contemporary (in the inn) or reproduction antique (in the Georgian). Children are especially welcome here, and some accommodations are set aside as family rooms. Six rooms come with a shower-only bathroom—the rest are equipped with combination tub/shower. The Thrums restaurant serves fixed-price and a la carte menus of British food; there's also a bar and a peaceful garden.

14–15 Minto St., Edinburgh EH9 1RQ. © **0131/667-5545.** Fax 0131/667-8707. www.thrumshotel.com. 5 units. £55–£110 ($105–$209) double; £180–£230 ($342–$437) family room. Rates include breakfast. MC, V. Free parking. Bus: 3, 7, 8, 31, 81, or 87. **Amenities:** Restaurant; bar; laundry service; nonsmoking rooms; rooms for those w/limited mobility. *In room:* TV, coffeemaker, hair dryer.

NEWINGTON
INEXPENSIVE

Aonach Mor 🏕 *Finds*   In the Newington district of the city, a mile (.6km) from the center, this small, family-run guest house is a restored Victorian terraced building run by Edinburgh natives, Ross and Kathleen. It is an informal, friendly home that is exceedingly comfortable, and offers one of the best home-cooked breakfasts in town. Rooms, each with private bathroom, open onto views either of Arthur's Seat or else walled gardens. Each room is individually decorated and refurbished, the most spectacular—and obviously the most expensive—being a luxurious Jacobean style double with an elegant four-poster.

14 Kilmaurs Terrace, Newington, Edinburgh EH16 5DR. ✆ 0131/667-8694. www.aonachmor.com. 7 units. £27–£70 ($51–$133) double. Rates include breakfast. MC, V. Free parking. Bus: 30 or 33. Children under 5 are not accepted. **Amenities:** Dining room/lounge; Internet access. *In room:* TV, beverage maker, hair dryer, iron.

LEITH

The Malmaison 🐾🐾   This is Leith's most stylish boutique hotel, located in the dockyard district, a few steps from Leith Water. It was converted from an 1883 seamen's mission/dorm, and is capped by a stately stone clock tower. Its owners have created a hip, unpretentious place with minimalist decor. The color schemes vary by level; the purple-and-beige floor has been favored by touring rock bands. Rooms are average size though well equipped. The facilities are sparse, but you'll find the Malmaison Brasserie (see "Where to Dine," below) and a cafe and wine bar favored by locals.

1 Tower Place, Leith, Edinburgh EH6 7DB. ✆ 0131/468-5000. www.malmaison.com. 100 units. £165 ($314) double; £235–£265 ($447–$504) suite. AE, DC, MC, V. Free parking. Bus: 16 or 22. **Amenities:** Restaurant; bar; exercise room; rooms for those w/limited mobility. *In room:* TV, minibar, coffeemaker, hair dryer, Wi-Fi.

PRESTONFIELD

EXPENSIVE

Prestonfield House 🐾🐾   The Prestonfield, rising in Jacobean splendor above 5.3 hectares (13 acres) of grounds, and a 5-minute drive from the city center, is more celebrated as a restaurant than as a hotel. It was designed by Sir William Bruce, who also designed Holyroodhouse. Guests appreciate the traditional atmosphere and 1680s architecture, as well as the peacocks and Highland cattle that strut and stroll across the grounds. The spacious bedrooms are decorated in country-house style and open onto a view of Arthur's Seat, a golf course surrounding the hotel, and the gardens. In 1997, the five rooms in the main house were supplemented by a three-story annex that matches the original structure; these up-to-date rooms get lots of sun thanks to the large windows. The hotel's dining room, Rhubarb, is one of the city's finest. (See "Where to Dine," below.)

Priestfield Rd., Edinburgh EH16 5UT. ✆ 0131/668-3346. Fax 0131/668-3976. www.prestonfield.com. 31 units. £160–£235 ($304–$447) double; from £375 ($713) suite. Rates include breakfast. AE, DC, MC, V. Free parking. Bus: 21 or 33. RV/truck parking available. **Amenities:** Restaurant; 2 bars; secretarial service; room service; babysitting; laundry service; dry cleaning; nonsmoking rooms. *In room:* AC, TV, coffeemaker, hair dryer, iron.

DEAN VILLAGE

Channings 🐾🐾   Five Edwardian terrace houses combine to create this hotel, 7 blocks north of Dean Village in a tranquil residential area. Although it's a 5-minute drive from the city center, it maintains the atmosphere of a Scottish country house, with oak paneling, ornate fireplaces, molded ceilings, and antiques. The guest rooms are modern; the front units get the views, but the rear ones get the quiet. The most desirable rooms are the "Executives," most of which have bay windows and wingback chairs. Even if you're not a guest, consider a meal here, as Channings offers some of the best hotel food in Edinburgh (see "Where to Dine," below).

South Learmonth Gardens 15, Edinburgh EH4 1EZ. © **0131/315-2226.** Fax 0131/332-9631. www.channings.co.uk. 46 units. £170–£205 ($323–$390) double; from £250 ($475) suite. Rates include breakfast. Children age 14 and under £30 ($57) extra. AE, DC, DISC, MC, V. Bus: 18, 19, 41, or 81. **Amenities:** 2 restaurants; bar, room service; laundry service; dry cleaning; nonsmoking rooms. *In room:* TV, coffeemaker, hair dryer, iron, trouser press.

4 Where to Dine

Rivaled only by Glasgow, Edinburgh boasts the finest restaurants in Scotland, and the choices are more diverse now than ever before. Even if you don't care for some of the more exotic regional fare, like *haggis* (spicy intestines), you'll find an array of top French dining rooms along with other foreign cuisines, especially Indian. And more and more restaurants have begun to cater to vegetarians. But we advise you go native and sample many of the dishes for which Edinburgh is known, like fresh salmon and seafood, game from Scottish fields, and Aberdeen Angus steaks. What's the rage at lunch? Stuffed potatoes (baked potatoes with a variety of stuffings). Many Scots make a lunch out of just one of these.

Some restaurants have sections reserved for nonsmokers; others don't. If smoking and dining (or nonsmoking and dining) are very important to you, inquire when making your reservation.

Note: For the locations of the restaurants below, see the "Edinburgh Accommodations & Dining" map, on p. 82.

THE NEW TOWN
EXPENSIVE
The Atrium ⚸ MODERN SCOTTISH/INTERNATIONAL   Since 1993, this has been one of the most emulated restaurants in Edinburgh. No more than 60 diners can be accommodated in the "deliberately moody" atmosphere that's a fusion of Argentine hacienda and stylish Beverly Hills bistro. Flickering oil lamps create shadows on the dark-colored walls while patrons enjoy dishes prepared with taste and flair. Although offerings vary according to the inspiration of the chef, one of our favorites is the organic sea trout with pea and artichoke risotto and tomato oil. The desserts are equally superb, especially the lemon tart with berry coulis and crème fraîche.

10 Cambridge St. (beneath Saltire Court in City Center, a 10-min. walk from Waverley Train Station). © **0131/ 228-8882.** Reservations recommended. Fixed-price lunch £20 ($37); main courses lunch £11–£23 ($20–$44); fixed-price dinner £27 ($51); main courses dinner £11–£25 ($20–$48). AE, DC, MC, V. Mon–Fri noon–2pm and 6–10pm; Sat 6:30–10pm. Closed for 1 week at Christmas. Bus: 11 or 15.

Channings ⚸ SCOTTISH/INTERNATIONAL   This is the main dining room of an Edwardian charmer of a hotel, offering traditional decor and elegant service from a well-trained staff. The exemplary cuisine allows the natural flavors of the superior-quality Scottish ingredients to shine through. The chefs know, for example, to go to the Baines of Tarves for free-range Aberdeen chickens, or to Iain Mellis for cheese. For dinner, you might opt for the herb crusted Borders lamb. To finish, try the caramelized orange tart with basil sorbet. The restaurant is proud of its extensive wine list, which incorporates the old standards and newer, more exciting choices.

A less formal brasserie, with a log fireplace and a casual atmosphere, serves bar meals, light lunches, and dinners.

In Channings Hotel, 15 S. Learmonth Gardens. © **0131/315-2225.** Reservations recommended. Fixed-price lunch £12 ($23) for 2 courses, £15 ($29) for 3 courses; dinner main courses £13–£25 ($24–$48). AE, MC, V. Tues–Sat noon–2:30pm and 6:30–10pm; Sun 6:30–10pm. Closed Dec 26–29. Bus: 41 or 42.

Cosmo Ristorante ☆ ITALIAN   Even after more than 30 years in business, Cosmo is still one of the most popular Italian restaurants in town, where courtesy, efficiency, and good cooking draw the crowds. The soups and pastas are always reliable. The kitchen is known for its *saltimbocca* (veal with ham) and Italian-inspired preparations of fish. Justifiably favorite dishes include chargrilled sea bass with mint, marjoram, and rocket served on a bed of lentils or medallions of filet mignon in a brandy sauce. This isn't the greatest Italian dining in Scotland, but the restaurant certainly offers a good, filling meal.

78A N. Castle St. ✆ **0131/226-6743**. Reservations required. Lunch main courses £15–£19 ($29–$36). Main courses dinner £20–£26 ($38–$49). AE, MC, V. Mon–Fri 12:30–2:30pm; Mon–Sat 7–10:30pm. Bus: 31 or 33.

Dome Bar & Grill ☆ INTERNATIONAL   Located in a restored Georgian building with an elaborate domed ceiling, this bar and grill is part of the Dome entertainment complex. Throughout are elaborate columns, pedimental sculptures, and marble mosaic floors. The menu is ambitious and creative, with dishes like duck liver pâté with Cumberland sauce and oat cakes, king prawn brochettes, and tortellini in a broccoli-and-cheese sauce.

14 George St. ✆ **0131/624-8624**. Reservations required for lunch and dinner. Main courses lunch £9.50–£17 ($18–$32); dinner £13–£22 ($25–$42). AE, MC, V. Restaurant daily noon–10pm; bar Sun–Thurs 10am–11pm, Fri–Sat 10am–1am. Bus: 3, 21, 26, 31, or 85.

Duck's at Le Marché Noir ☆ SCOTTISH/FRENCH   This place's cuisine is more stylish, and more tuned to the culinary sophistication of London, than many other restaurants in Edinburgh. A handful of dishes honor the traditions of Scotland—for example, the baked haggis and truffled parsnip and red sauce. More modern dishes include breast of duck with choucroute, duck boudin, thyme, and morel *jus*. A classic favorite is Angus beef with a red-onion confit and port *jus*. We recommend the rhubarb crumble tart for dessert.

2–4 Eyre Place. ✆ **0131/558-1608**. Reservations recommended. Fixed-price lunch £10–£15 ($19–$29) for 2 courses; dinner main courses £14–£25 ($26–$48). AE, DC, MC, V. Tues–Fri noon–2:30pm; daily 7–10:30pm. Bus: 23 or 27.

Haldanes Restaurant ☆ SCOTTISH   In another location for more than a decade, Haldanes earned a reputation for authentic Scottish fare. Today it lies at the top end of Dundas Street set among a series of art galleries and enjoying an elegant setting of white linen tablecloths, plush carpets, art prints on the wall, and a refined service. Locals view dining here as a special occasion. The chefs are known for their light touch in the kitchen, their freshness in their selection of ingredients, and their skill in "harmonizing" flavors.

The menu changes to reflect the best in any season. To get you going, try the terrine of wild rabbit and a wild mushroom sauce or else the baked goats' cheese with glazed beetroot and an artichoke salad. A superb main course is the roast breast of duck with balsamic-glazed figs, as well as the filet of prime Scottish beef with roasted celeriac gratin and a black pepper sabayon. A rump of Scottish lamb appears with portobello mushrooms, plus an herb gnocchi with a port wine reduction. For dessert, we'd recommend the sugar-glazed lemon tart with a brandy basket of sorbet.

13 B. Dundas St. ✆ **0131/556-8407**. Reservations required. Main courses dinner £18–£28 ($34–$53); fixed-price lunch and pre-theater meal £19 ($35) for 2 courses. DC, MC, V. Mon–Fri noon–1:45pm; daily 6–9pm. Bus: 15.

Martin's ☆ SCOTTISH   Owners Gay and Martin Irons and their trio of top chefs are deeply committed to wild, organically grown foods, which are often featured on a menu that changes daily. Martin's father provides herbs from his own garden. The best

Oh, Give It a Try!

Haggis, the much-maligned national dish of Scotland, is certainly an acquired taste. But you've come all this way—why not be brave and have a taste? **Macsween of Edinburgh Haggis** is a long-established family business specializing in haggis. Macsween haggis includes lamb, beef, oatmeal, onions, and a special blend of seasonings and spices cooked together. There's also an all-vegetarian version. Both are sold in vacuum-packed plastic bags that require only reheating in a microwave or regular oven. You can find this company's product at food stores and supermarkets throughout Edinburgh. Two central distributors are **Peckham's Delicatessen,** 155–159 Bruntsfield Place (© **0131/229-7054**), open daily from 8am to midnight, and **Jenners Department Store,** 2 East Princes St. (© **0131/260-2242**), open Monday, Wednesday, Friday, and Saturday 9am to 6pm, Tuesday 9:30am to 6pm, Thursday 9am to 8pm, and Sunday 11am to 5pm.

of the country's venison, fish (especially salmon), and shellfish appear regularly; wild mushrooms are a particular favorite. You might try pan-fried filet of sea trout with caramelized fennel, or roast loin of wild venison in a red-wine *jus.*

70 Rose St., North Lane. © **0131/225-3106.** Reservations required. Main courses lunch £8–£19 ($15–$36), 2 courses £14 ($27); dinner £8–£19 ($15–$36), for 3 courses £35 ($67). AE, DC, MC, V. Tues–Fri noon–2pm; Tues–Sat 7–10pm. During festival in Aug Mon–Sat 6:30–11pm. Closed Dec 24–Jan 23, 1 week in May/June, and 1 week in Sept/Oct. Bus: 2, 4, 15, 21, or 44. No children under 8.

No. 1 Princes Street ☆ SCOTTISH/CONTINENTAL   This is the Balmoral's premier restaurant, an intimate, crimson-colored enclave whose walls are studded with Scottish memorabilia. You can sample the likes of roast monkfish with caramel polenta, or perhaps Gressingham duck breast with braised lentils. Dessert brings a variety of sorbets, cheeses, and more exotic choices like a fig tatin with lavender ice cream. There's a wide-ranging wine list with celestial tariffs.

In the Balmoral Hotel, 1 Princes St. © **0131/556-2414.** Reservations recommended. Main courses £25–£35 ($48–$67); fixed-price lunch £20 ($38) for 3 courses; tasting menu £69 ($131). AE, DC, MC, V. Mon–Fri noon–2pm; Sun–Thurs 7–10pm; Fri–Sat 7–10:30pm.

Oloroso ☆☆☆ MODERN BRITISH   At the west end of Princes Street, this citadel of fine food sits atop the landmark Basil Spencer Building, opening onto a roof terrace, with views of Edinburgh Castle and Fife in the distance. The restaurant is a high-fashion setting that would be more at home in Los Angeles than in Edinburgh. Chef Tony Singh doesn't follow trends—so "expect the unexpected," as the staff says.

Creative cookery with quality ingredients characterizes this über-restaurant. Expect the best of Highland beef, venison, and freshly caught salmon. The meat, including all forms of steak, comes with a wide choice of accompaniments, ranging from anchovy butter to red-wine *jus.* The selection of starters is the capital's finest. We love the chicken liver parfait with Cumberland sauce and melba toast. For dessert, you can hardly go wrong with the white chocolate mousse, kumquat marmalade, and blood orange sorbet.

33 Castle St. © **0131/226-7614.** Reservations required. Main courses £15–£22 ($29–$42). AE, MC, V. Daily noon–2:30pm and 7–10:30pm. Bus: 33.

Pompadour Restaurant ✸ SCOTTISH/FRENCH   On the mezzanine of the Caledonian Hilton Edinburgh, the Pompadour is one of Edinburgh's best. The restaurant has been refurbished in a Louis XV decor. The chef blends *cuisine moderne* with traditional menus, and his daily offerings reflect the best available from the market, including Scottish salmon, venison, and other game. The menu also features items like filet of lemon sole and roasted loin of lamb. The wine list is lethally expensive.

In the Caledonian Hilton Edinburgh, Princes St. ℂ **0131/222-8777.** Reservations required. Fixed-price lunch £15 ($29); main courses £18–£32 ($34–$61). AE, DC, MC, V. Tues–Fri 12:30–2pm; Tues–Sat 7–10pm. Bus: 4, 15, or 44.

MODERATE

Blue Bar Café INTERNATIONAL   Located in the building containing the Traverse Theatre, this attractive bistro is the less expensive sibling of The Atrium (see above). You'll find a mostly white, minimalist decor (with touches of blue); solid oaken tables; and a cheerful staff. The sophisticated menu might feature delectable filet of sea trout with pickled cucumber or lamb Gigot chops with mint pesto.

10 Cambridge St. ℂ **0131/221-1222.** Reservations recommended. Main courses lunch £8–£15 ($15–$29); fixed-price lunch £12 ($23) for 2 courses; dinner main courses £12–£15 ($23–$29); fixed-price dinner £15 ($29) for 2 courses. AE, DC, MC, V. Mon–Sat noon–2:30pm; Mon–Thurs 5:30–10:30pm; Fri–Sat 5:30–11pm. Bus: 10, 11, 16, or 27.

Café Saint-Honoré FRENCH/SCOTTISH   This French-inspired bistro is a deliberately rapid-paced place at lunchtime, then becomes much more formal at dinner. The menu is completely revised each day, based on what's fresh and what the chefs feel inspired to cook. An upbeat and usually enthusiastic staff serves a combination of Scottish and French cuisine that includes venison with juniper berries and wild mushrooms, local pheasant in wine and garlic sauce, and lamb kidneys with broad beans.

34 NW Thistle St. Lane. ℂ **0131/226-2211.** Reservations recommended. Fixed-price lunch £15 ($29); main courses £12–£40 ($23–$76); fixed-price dinner 20 ($38); fixed-price pre-theater meal £16 ($30) for 2 courses. AE, DC, MC, V. Mon–Fri noon–2:15pm; Mon–Fri (pre-theater meal) 5–7pm; Mon–Sat 7–10pm (sometimes 11pm). Bus: 3, 16, 17, 23, 27, or 31.

Hewat's ✸ SCOTTISH/INTERNATIONAL   Hewat's is ideally located near the theater and offers reasonably priced pre- and post-performance dinners. Owned by Lara Kearney, John Rutter, and Glyn Stevens, all formerly of The Atrium, this is a

---

⸻ *Moments* **Tea for Two**

If you're looking for a bit of refreshment while sightseeing, try **Clarinda's Tea Room,** 69 Canongate (ℂ **0131/557-1888**), for the very British experience of afternoon tea. This cubbyhole of a tearoom is only steps from Holyroodhouse and decorated in the manner you'd expect, with lace tablecloths, bone china, and antique Wedgwood plates on the walls. There are plenty of teas from which to choose, plus a long list of tempting sweets. Homemade soup, lasagna, baked potatoes with cheese, salads, and similar dishes are also offered. It's open Monday to Saturday 9am to 4:45pm and Sunday 10am to 4:45pm.

Another choice is **Ryan's Bar,** 2 Hope St. (ℂ **0131/226-6669**), near the northwestern corner of the West Princes Street Gardens. It serves tea daily 10:30am to 1am. If you want a more formal tea ceremony, try the Palm Court at the **Balmoral Hotel,** Princes Street (ℂ **0131/556-2414**), serving tea daily noon to 3pm.

fast-growing, popular place. The bold yellow walls and black-and-white floor give this converted antiques shop a unique, contemporary look. The cuisine is ambitious and seductive. Main courses include sea bass and salmon with lime; chargrilled sirloin; and chicken. The sticky toffee pudding with butterscotch sauce is a great way to end an enjoyable meal.

19–21 Causewayside. (C) **0131/466-6660.** Reservations recommended. Main courses £12–£18 ($23–$34); fixed-price lunch £15 ($29) for 3 courses; pre- and post-theater dinner £18 ($34) for 3 courses. AE, MC, V. Wed–Sat noon–2pm; Sun 12:30–3pm; Tues–Thurs 6–9pm; Fri–Sat 6–10:30pm. Bus: 42.

Restaurant at the Bonham ✹✹ SCOTTISH/CONTINENTAL   The setting at one of Edinburgh's most charming restaurants marries 19th-century oak paneling and deep ceiling coves with modern paintings and oversize mirrors. Chef Michel Bouyer has greatly improved the cuisine here, creating a stimulating menu in his own style. Though classically trained in Paris, he adds his own creative touches to favorites such as grilled filet of halibut; grilled gnocchi and roasted crepes; and roast rack of Border lamb with anchovy potatoes and green olive *jus.*

In The Bonham Hotel, 35 Drumsheugh Gardens. (C) **0131/274-7444.** Reservations recommended. Fixed-price lunch £16 ($30) for 3 courses; main courses £15–£21 ($29–$40). AE, DC, MC, V. Mon–Sat 12:30–2:30pm and 6:30–10pm; Sun noon–3pm. Bus: 23 or 27.

Roti ✹✹ INDIAN   This restaurant behind a Georgian facade serves the best Indian cuisine in town. Its owner is Tony Singh, who was head chef aboard the *Britannia,* Britain's last royal yacht. In his latest endeavor, he welcomes guests in to a sleek, modern interior decorated with elegant artifacts from the subcontinent. Once you taste the first dish here, you'll realize this is no Indian food joint going heavy on the curry. Dishes, full of flavor and prepared with subtlety, are based on the best of regional produce. One of our favorite mains here is lamb *roganjosh,* a fork-tender shank with spicy Kashmiri sauce and deep-fried lotus stems. Another intriguing dish is *tawewalli macchi,* seared halibut with a coconut-flavored sauce. The chicken roulate comes with a quail's egg, rice vermicelli, and an eggplant compote. Roasted pickled salmon with saffron yogurt is a treat, as is chargrilled chicken with a red pepper confit. The dessert specialty is *kesari kulfi,* a saffron- and cardamom-spiced parfait.

70 Rose St., North Lane. (C) **0131/225-1233.** Reservations required. Main courses £12–£20 ($23–$38). AE, MC, V. Daily noon–2pm and 6–11pm. Bus: 2, 4, 15, 21, or 44.

The Tower ✹✹ SEAFOOD/MODERN BRITISH   This is the town's hot new dining ticket, set at the top of the Museum of Scotland. The chef uses local ingredients to create some of the capital's tastiest fare. The inventive kitchen will regale you with hearty portions of steak, roast beef, and excellent seafood. We still remember fondly the grilled sea bass with warm king prawns and seaweed. The tuna is perfectly seasoned and grilled.

In the Museum of Scotland, Chambers St. (C) **0131/225-3003.** Reservations required. Main courses lunch £13 ($24); main courses dinner £17–£24 ($31–$46). AE, DC, MC, V. Daily noon–11pm. Bus: 3, 7, 21, 30, 31, 53, 69, or 80.

INEXPENSIVE

Far Pavilions INDIAN/CONTINENTAL   Established in 1987, this Indian restaurant offers finely tuned service. You might appreciate a drink in the bar before confronting the long menu that features dishes from the former Portuguese colony of Goa and the northern Indian province of Punjab. Highly recommended is the house specialty, Murgh Massala, concocted with tandoori chicken that falls off the bone thanks to slow cooking in a garlic-based butter sauce.

Kids Family-Friendly Restaurants

Mr. Boni's Ice Cream Parlour   Mr. Boni's is at 4 Lochrin Bridge (☎ **0131/ 229-2740**). Every kid comes away loving Mr. Boni, who makes the best homemade ice cream in Edinburgh, plus sandwiches, jumbo hot dogs, and beef burgers with french fries.

Henderson's Salad Table   Edinburgh's leading vegetarian restaurant has an array of nutritious salads, followed by some of the most delectable home-made desserts in the city. Located at 94 Hanover St. (☎ **0131/225-2131**).

Baked Potato Shop   Children delight in being taken to this worker's favorite lunch spot, where they can order flaky baked potatoes with a choice of half a dozen hot fillings along with all sorts of other dishes, including chili and 20 kinds of salads. It's cheap, too. 56 Cockburn St. (☎ **0131/225-7572**).

10 Craighleith Rd., Comely Bank. ☎ 0131/332-3362. Reservations recommended. Main courses lunch £8–£16 ($15–$30); lunch buffet £6.95 ($13) per person; main courses dinner £10–£18 ($19–$34). AE, MC, V. Mon–Fri noon–2pm; Mon–Sat 5:30pm–midnight. Bus: 19, 39, 55, 81, or X91.

THE OLD TOWN
EXPENSIVE
Dubh Prais ✪ SCOTTISH   Dubh Prais (Gaelic for "The Black Pot") conjures up an image of old-fashioned Scottish recipes bubbling away in a stewpot above a fire-place. In dining rooms adorned with stenciled thistles, the restaurant serves time-tested, and not at all experimental, meals that are flavorful nonetheless. Examples include smoked salmon; saddle of venison with juniper sauce; and a suprême of salmon with grapefruit-flavored butter sauce. The chef is known for turning out an array of game meats as well as ostrich and rabbit dishes.

123B High St., Royal Mile. ☎ 0131/557-5732. Reservations recommended. Main courses dinner £13–£19 ($25–$36). AE, MC, V. Tues–Sat noon–4pm and 6:30–10:30pm. Bus: 11.

Iggs ✪ SPANISH/SCOTTISH   Just off the Royal Mile in the Old Town, this Vic-torian-style establishment is the domain of a dynamic chef, Andrew McQueen, who is not afraid to experiment but also seems well grounded in the classics. Dinner here is made more charming by the attention from the waitstaff, clad in black polo shirts. For a main course you might choose the more traditional rack of Highland lamb with spring vegetables; if you want to go more exotic, opt for the loin of veal on a truffle and Gruyère risotto given extra flavor by a Madeira sauce. After you think you've had every dessert in the world, along comes a honey-roasted butternut-squash cheesecake with a caramel sauce.

15 Jeffrey St. ☎ 0131/557-8184. Reservations recommended. Main courses £15–£30 ($29–$57); fixed-price lunch £10–£15 ($19–$29) for 3 courses. AE, DC, MC, V. Mon–Sat noon–2:30pm and 6–10:30pm. Bus: 1 or 35.

Jackson's Restaurant ✪ SCOTTISH   Serving a cuisine described as "Scottish with a French flair," this bustling restaurant is in the stone cellar of a 300-year-old building. Choose your drink from almost 40 kinds of Highland malts, and then select from a menu featuring dinners made from local ingredients. A specialty is roast rack of lamb, black pudding, and apple fondont. For dessert, we recommend the mixed berry pudding with cinnamon cream.

209 High St., Royal Mile. © 0131/225-1793. Reservations recommended. Fixed-price lunch £13 ($25) for 3 courses; main courses £16–£19 ($30–$36); fixed-price dinner £25 ($48) for 3 courses. AE, DC, MC, V. Daily noon–2:30pm and 6–10:30pm. Bus: 35.

The Witchery by the Castle ⊀ SCOTTISH/FRENCH   This place bills itself as the oldest, most haunted restaurant in town, and the Hellfire Club supposedly met here during the Middle Ages. The building has been linked with witchcraft since the period between 1470 and 1722, when more than 1,000 people were burned alive on Castlehill; one of the victims is alleged to haunt The Witchery. The chef uses creative flair to create classy Scottish food, such as Angus beef, Scottish lobster, and Loch Fyne oysters. Such well-prepared old-time favorites as confit of wild rabbit with bacon appear on the menu, as does roast halibut; herb-crusted rack of Borders lamb; seared sea bass with wild mushrooms and butternut squash. One restaurant critic called the vast slabs of bloody beef and venison politically incorrect—that and the cigar smoke.

352 Castlehill, Royal Mile. © 0131/225-5613. Reservations recommended. Fixed-price lunch and pre-theater menu £13 ($25) for 2 courses; main courses £18–£35 ($34–$67). AE, DC, MC, V. Daily noon–4pm and 5:30–11:30pm. Bus: 1 or 6.

MODERATE
The Grain Store ⊀⊀ SCOTTISH   Just below the Royal Mile stands one of the most unpretentious places to eat in Edinburgh, a local favorite serving some of the best food based on regional produce. The decor is rustic, with exposed stonework, a large clock, dried flower garlands, and polished wooden floors. Each dish is individually prepared to order, and the menu changes regularly. From field and stream comes an array of market-fresh ingredients, including game birds in the autumn, forest-fresh mushrooms, lamb from the Borders, Scottish salmon from the rivers, Angus beef, and perhaps the best venison we've ever tasted in Scotland. Some dishes are prepared simply to preserve their natural flavors; others are fancier including West Coast king scallops with almond and chive velouté. For dessert, try one of the specialties such as warm pear dartois with an apricot brandy ice cream or vanilla pannacotta with honey-roasted figs.

30 Victoria St., 1st Floor. © 0131/225-7635. www.grainstore-restaurant.co.uk. Reservations recommended. Fixed-price lunch £10 ($19) 2 courses, £13 ($25) 3 courses; fixed-price dinner £19 ($36); main courses £18–£26 ($34–$49). AE, MC, V. Daily noon–2pm and 6–10pm. Bus: 35 or 41.

INEXPENSIVE
David Bann's Vegetarian Restaurant ⊀ *Value* VEGETARIAN   This is the city's best vegetarian restaurant—even carnivores often come here to sample the well-flavored dishes made with market-fresh ingredients, often shipped in that day from the fertile fields of Scotland. Located a short walk off the Royal Mile, the restaurant has steadily gained in popularity since its opening in the Old Town.

Chef Bann roams the world for inspiration for his meat-free recipes. A dish might be from Mexico, definitely from Thailand. The restaurant is popular with students, among others, and they can be seen avidly perusing the menu that features such dishes as a mushroom, smoked cheese, and ale strudel blended with free-range eggs or a risotto of asparagus with green peas and blue cheese. The menu is strong on freshly made salads and "sides," including a soup of the day served with homemade bread, or Thai fritters, a spicy blend of tofu, ginger, green chile, sesame, and mango chutney among other ingredients. The desserts are also reason enough to visit, especially if you sample the malt whisky pannacotta served with a homemade orange sorbet, or the rhubarb cheesecake with a ginger-laced rhubarb sauce.

56–58 St. Mary's St. © **0131/556-5888.** Reservations required. Main courses £8.50–£12 ($16–23); fixed-price brunch £5.50 ($11). AE, MC, V. Sun–Thurs 11am–9:45pm; Fri–Sat 11am–10:15pm. Bus: 35.

LEITH

In the northern regions of Edinburgh, the old port town of Leith opens onto the Firth of Forth. After decades of decay, it has become an arty neighborhood with a collection of restaurants, wine bars, and pubs.

EXPENSIVE

Martin Wishart ✶✶✶ MODERN FRENCH   Several gourmet associations claim this as the best restaurant in Edinburgh. Chef and owner Martin Wishart takes it all in stride and continues to improve the quality of his establishment in a fashionable part of the Leith docklands. The minimalist decor features white walls and modern art. The menu is short but sweet, taking advantage of the best of the season. The gratin of sea bass arrives aromatically with a soft, herby crust. Many dishes are simply prepared, the natural flavors coming through; others show a touch of fantasy. Try the braised shin and short rib of beef with veal shortbreads and mushroom ravioli. And after eating the strawberry soufflé with basil cappuccino, the day is yours.

54 The Shore, Leith. © **0131/553-3557.** Reservations required. Main courses £20–£50 ($38–$95); set lunch £23 ($43) for 3 courses; tasting menu £60 ($114) for 6-course dinner. AE, MC, V. Tues–Sat noon–2pm and 7–10pm. Bus: 7 or 10.

Vintner's Rooms ✶ FRENCH/SCOTTISH   This stone-fronted building down by the waterfront was constructed around 1650 as a warehouse for barrels of bordeaux (claret) and port that came in from Europe's mainland. Near the entrance, beneath a ceiling of venerable oaken beams, a wine bar serves platters and drinks beside a large stone fireplace. Most people, however, head for the dining room, decorated with elaborate Italianate plasterwork and lit with flickering candles. The menu might feature such robust cuisine as seared foie gras with caramelized fruits, new season lamb, and venison in a bitter-chocolate sauce. Halibut stuffed with braised fennel and sauce antiboise is one of the chef's specialties.

The Vaults, 87 Giles St., Leith. © **0131/554-6767.** Reservations recommended. Set price lunch £16–£20 ($30–$37); main courses dinner £17–£25 ($32–$48). AE, MC, V. Mon–Sat noon–2pm and 7–10:30pm. Closed 2 weeks at Christmas. Bus: 7 or 10.

MODERATE

Fishers Bistro ✶ INTERNATIONAL/SEAFOOD   This place is noted for its outstanding seafood and its setting next to a 17th-century windmill with a panoramic view of the harbor at Leith. It's well known among locals, who praise it for its selection of seafood and the quality of its fresh fish. You can dine in the main restaurant or at a specialty seafood bar. Naturally, a nautical aura prevails with fish nets, pictures of the sea, and various marine memorabilia. The Miller family founded the restaurant in the early '90s, and their chefs offer such enticing appetizers as fresh Loch Fyne oysters, reputedly among Britain's finest. For your main course, sample the lemon sole with spinach, basil, and pine nut butter, or Greek sea bass served with salsa verde. One of the most commendable main courses is pan-fried Aegean Marlin with a mussel and vegetable Malaysian curry.

1 The Shore, Leith. © **0131/554-5666.** Reservations required. Main courses £15–£26 ($29–$49). AE, MC, V. Mon–Sat noon–4pm and 5–10pm; Sun noon–4pm and 5–10:30pm. Bus: 22.

Malmaison Brasserie TRADITIONAL FRENCH   Located in the previously rec-ommended hotel (p. 93), this unpretentious brasserie is charming enough to merit a trip out from Edinburgh. The setting is simple: lots of polished wood and wrought iron. The bistro-inspired menu includes fried steak with *pommes frites* (french fries), seared wild trout with crushed spring peas and Feve's citrus dressing, and stuffed sad-dle of rabbit with linguine and pommery mustard sauce. Everyone's favorite dessert is the crème brûlée. Regrettably, the restaurant doesn't have a view of the harbor but faces a side street.

In The Malmaison Hotel, 1 Tower Place, Leith. ℂ **0131/468-5000.** Reservations recommended for dinner. Fixed-price menu £14 ($27) for 2 courses; £16 ($30) for 3 courses. AE, DC, MC, V. Mon–Fri 7am–10am; daily noon–2:30pm and 6–10:30pm; Sun brunch noon–3pm. Bus: 6, 16, or 22A.

INEXPENSIVE
Zinc Bar & Grill INTERNATIONAL   No one does modern chic better than pro-prietor Sir Terence Conran. You dine at metal tables while enjoying (perhaps) the abstract wall hangings. This brasserie-grill opens onto vast picture windows with a view of the harbor. For warm days, there is an outdoor terrace. It's a good choice for lunch—especially before or after visiting the Royal Yacht *Britannia*. Food is prepared to order, and it includes an array of burgers, roast lamb, grilled chicken, fried sole, or salmon, along with tender Scottish steaks made from Angus beef. You might opt for such good-tasting dishes as poached salmon with couscous, or else a tender sirloin steak. Pasta fans gravitate to the spaghetti with a lemon basil sauce and pine nuts.

The restaurant is part of the £120-million ($213-million) leisure resort, Ocean Terminal, which opened in 2001 and features a cinema, bars, dining choices, and shops. To reach Zinc, take the escalator upstairs. Unit 42, Ocean Termi-nal, Leith. ℂ **0131/553-8070.** Reservations recommended. Main courses lunch £8–£15 ($15–$29); 2-course lunch £13 ($25); 3-course lunch £15 ($29); main courses dinner £12–£20 ($23–$38). AE, DC, MC, V. Mon–Sat noon–mid-night; Sun noon–11:30pm. Bus: 22.

PRESTONFIELD
EXPENSIVE
Rhubarb ⚑ BRITISH   Hidden amid 5.3 hectares (13 acres) of private parkland and gardens, 5km (3 miles) south of Edinburgh's center, this elegant restaurant often hosts locals celebrating special occasions. It's an old-fashioned choice, certainly, but it still offers the same fine quality as always. Menu items include roast filet of Angus beef Rossini and pan-fried filet of sea bass with artichoke ravioli. To top off your meal, try an assiette of rhubarb desserts.

Prestonfield House, Priestfield Rd., Edinburgh EH16 5UT. ℂ **0131/225-1333.** Reservations preferred. Main courses £18–£30 ($34–$57); table d'hôte menu £17 ($32) lunch. AE, DC, MC, V. Daily noon–3pm and 6–11pm. Bus: 2, 14, or 31.

5 Exploring the City
ALONG THE ROYAL MILE
The Old Town's **Royal Mile** ⚑⚑⚑ stretches from Edinburgh Castle all the way to the Palace of Holyroodhouse and bears four names along its length: Castlehill, Lawnmar-ket, High Street, and Canongate. Walking along, you see some of the most interest-ing old structures in the city, with turrets, gables, and towering chimneys. Take bus nos. 1, 6, 23, 27, 30, 34, or 36 to reach the Royal Mile.

Edinburgh Castle ⚑⚑   No place in Scotland is filled with as much history, legend, and lore as Edinburgh Castle, one of the highlights of a visit to this little country. It's believed the ancient city grew up at the base of an extinct volcano, Castle Rock. The early history is vague, but it's known that in the 11th century, Malcolm III (Canmore) and his Saxon queen, later venerated as St. Margaret, founded a castle on this spot. The only fragment left of their original castle—in fact, the oldest structure in Edinburgh—is St. Margaret's Chapel, built in the Norman style and dating principally from the 12th century. After hundreds of years of demolitions and upheavals, the buildings that stand today are basically those that resulted from the castle's role as a military garrison during the past 2 or 3 centuries.

You can visit the State Apartments, particularly Queen Mary's Bedroom, where Mary Queen of Scots gave birth to James VI of Scotland (later James I of England). Scottish Parliaments used to convene in the Great Hall. The highlight is the Crown Chamber, housing the Honours of Scotland (Scottish Crown Jewels), used at the coronation of James VI, along with the scepter and sword of State of Scotland. The French Prisons were put to use in the 18th century, and these great storerooms housed hundreds of Napoleonic soldiers in the early 19th century. Many of them made wall carvings you can see today. Among the batteries of cannons that protected the castle is Mons Meg, a 15th-century cannon weighing more than 5 tons.

Castlehill. ℂ 0131/225-9846. Admission £11 ($21) adults, £9 ($17) seniors, £3.50 ($6.65) children age 15 and under. Apr–Oct daily 9:30am–6pm; Nov–Mar daily 9:30am–5pm. Bus: 1 or 6.

Gladstone's Land ✿ This 17th-century merchant's house has been furnished and kept in its original style. On the ground floor is a reconstructed shop booth displaying replicas of goods from the period, and an upstairs apartment is furnished as it might have been in the 17th century. It's worth a visit on your journey along the Royal Mile, if only to get the impression of just how confined living conditions were, even for the reasonably well off, before the construction of the New Town.

477B Lawnmarket (10-min. walk from Waverley Train Station). ℂ 0131/226-5856. Admission £5 ($9.50) adults, £4 ($7.60) students, seniors, and children. Mar–June and Sept–Oct daily 10am–5pm; July–Aug daily 10am–7pm.

High Kirk of St. Giles ✿✿ Built in 1120 a short walk downhill from Edinburgh Castle, this church is one of the most important architectural landmarks along the Royal Mile. It combines a dark and brooding stone exterior with surprisingly graceful flying buttresses. One of its outstanding features is Thistle Chapel, housing beautiful stalls and notable heraldic stained-glass windows.

High St. ℂ 0131/225-9442. Free admission, but £2 ($3.80) donation suggested. Easter–Sept Mon–Sat 9am–5pm. Sun services at 8, 10, and 11:30am and 6 and 8pm. Bus: 23 or 27.

Huntly House Across from the Canongate Tolbooth is this fine example of a restored 16th-century mansion, whose builders preferred a bulky, relatively simple design that suited its role as a secular building. Today, it functions as Edinburgh's principal museum of local history. Inside are faithfully crafted reproductions of rooms inspired by the city's traditional industries, including glassmaking, pottery, wool processing, and cabinetry.

142 Canongate. ℂ 0131/529-4143. Free admission. June–Sept Mon–Sat 10am–6pm; Oct–May Mon–Sat 10am–5pm; Aug also open Sun 2–5pm. Bus: 35.

John Knox House Even if you're not interested in the reformer who founded the Scottish Presbyterian church, you may want to visit his late-15th-century house, characteristic of the "lands" that used to flank the Royal Mile. The Oak Room is noteworthy for its frescoed ceiling and for its Knox memorabilia. Born into a prosperous East Lothian middle-class family, John Knox is acknowledged as the first Moderator of the

Edinburgh Attractions

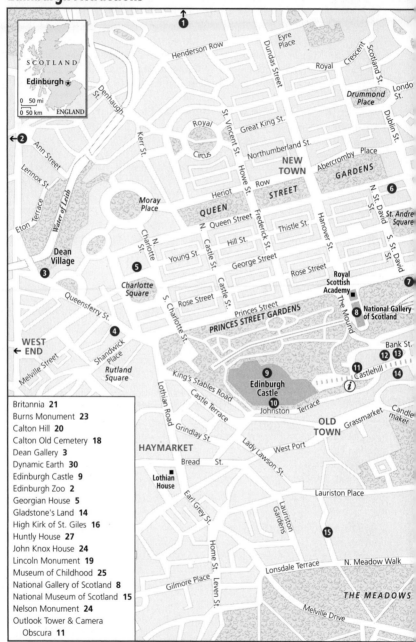

Britannia **21**
Burns Monument **23**
Calton Hill **20**
Calton Old Cemetery **18**
Dean Gallery **3**
Dynamic Earth **30**
Edinburgh Castle **9**
Edinburgh Zoo **2**
Georgian House **5**
Gladstone's Land **14**
High Kirk of St. Giles **16**
Huntly House **27**
John Knox House **24**
Lincoln Monument **19**
Museum of Childhood **25**
National Gallery of Scotland **8**
National Museum of Scotland **15**
Nelson Monument **24**
Outlook Tower & Camera
  Obscura **11**

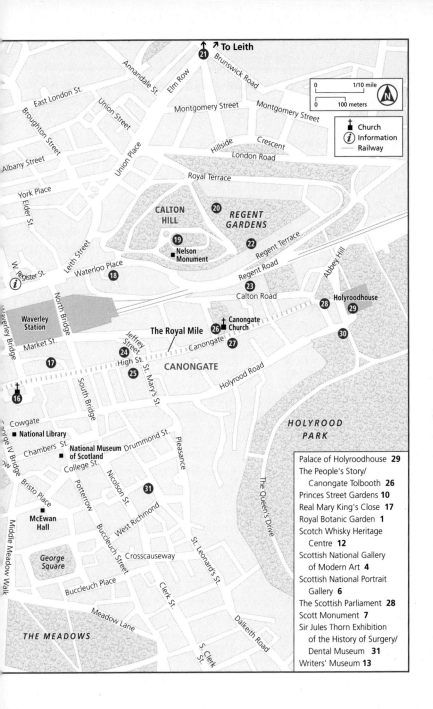

To Leith

Annandale St.

Brunswick Road

East London St.

Union Street

Montgomery Street

Montgomery Street

Elm Row

Broughton Street

Union Place

Hillside

Crescent

London Road

Albany Street

Royal Terrace

York Place

Elder St.

CALTON
HILL

REGENT
GARDENS

Leith Street

Nelson
Monument

Regent Terrace

Waterloo Place

Regent Terrace

Regent Road

W. Register St.

Calton Road

Abbey Hill

Holyroodhouse

North Bridge

Waverley
Station

Jeffrey
Street

The Royal Mile

Canongate
Church

Canongate

Market St.

High St.

St. Mary's St.

CANONGATE

Holyrood Road

Cowgate

HOLYROOD
PARK

National Library

Chambers St.

Drummond St.

National Museum
of Scotland

College St.

Nicolson St.

Pleasance

The Queen's Drive

George IV Bridge

Bristo Place

Porterrow

McEwan
Hall

West Richmond

Buccleuch Street

George
Square

Crosscauseway

St. Leonard's St.

Buccleuch Place

Clerk St.

Meadow Lane

Dalkeith Road

THE MEADOWS

S. Clerk
St.

Middle Meadow Walk

Church
Information
Railway

0	1/10 mile
0	100 meters

Palace of Holyroodhouse **29**
The People's Story/
   Canongate Tolbooth **26**
Princes Street Gardens **10**
Real Mary King's Close **17**
Royal Botanic Garden **1**
Scotch Whisky Heritage
   Centre **12**
Scottish National Gallery
   of Modern Art **4**
Scottish National Portrait
   Gallery **6**
The Scottish Parliament **28**
Scott Monument **7**
Sir Jules Thorn Exhibition
   of the History of Surgery/
   Dental Museum **31**
Writers' Museum **13**

Frommer's Favorite Edinburgh Experiences

Contemplating the City & Environs from Arthur's Seat. At 250m (823 ft.) atop Arthur's Seat (which you reach by climbing up Holyrood Park), you see the Highlands in miniature—the view is magical. Scots congregate here to await the solstice.

Visiting Dean Village. About 30m (100 ft.) below the rest of the city, Dean Village is an 800-year-old grain-milling town on the Water of Leith. Come here to soak up local color and enjoy a summertime stroll on the path by the river; it makes for great people-watching.

Shopping along Princes Street. This is the main thoroughfare in Edinburgh, the local equivalent of New York's Fifth Avenue. Flower-filled gardens stretch along the street's whole south side. When not admiring the flowers, you can browse the country's finest merchandise, everything from kilts to Scottish crystal.

Downing a Pint in an Edinburgh Pub. Sampling a pint of McEwan's real ale or Tennent's lager is a chance to soak up the special atmosphere of Edinburgh. Our favorites are The Abbotsford (p. 124) and the Bow Bar (p. 124).

Presbyterian Church of Scotland, the tenets of which he established in 1560. He's regarded as the prototype Puritan, but actually started his professional life as a Catholic priest and was renowned for his sharp wit and sarcasm. Knox lived at a time of great religious and political upheaval, and although he escaped execution, he spent 2 years as a galley slave in France for agitating against papal authority. On his release, he worked tirelessly with the English Crown to ensure Protestant victory in Scotland, then closely aligned to Catholic France. Knox was also a writer/historian—his *History of the Reformation* was his greatest literary achievement, but he's better known for the inflammatory treatise *The First Blast of the Trumpet Against the Monstrous Regiment of Women,* largely inspired by his opposition to the reign of Mary Queen of Scots. The title, however, did very little to endear him to Mary's cousin Elizabeth I, who insisted his particular brand of crusading zeal remain north of the border.

43–45 High St. (5-min. walk from Waverley Train Station.) ⓒ 0131/556-9579. Admission £2.25 ($4.30) adults, £1.75 ($3.35) seniors and students, 75p ($1.45) children under 15. Mon–Sat 10am–4:30pm (July–Aug also Sun 10am–4:30pm).

Museum of Childhood *Kids*   The world's first museum devoted solely to the history of childhood stands just opposite the John Knox House. Contents of its four floors range from antique toys to games to exhibits on health, education, and costumes, plus video presentations and an activity area. Not surprisingly, this is usually the noisiest museum in town.

42 High St. ⓒ 0131/529-4142. Free admission. Mon–Sat 10am–5pm; during the Edinburgh Festival, also Sun noon–5pm.

Outlook Tower and Camera Obscura   The 1853 periscope at the top of the Outlook Tower throws a revolving image of nearby streets and buildings onto a circular table. Guides point out the landmarks and talk about Edinburgh's fascinating history.

In addition, there are several entertaining exhibits, all with an optical theme, plus a well-stocked shop selling books, crafts, and CDs.

Castlehill. ℂ **0131/226-3709.** Admission £7.50 ($14) adults, £6 ($11) seniors, and £5 ($9.50) students and children. Apr–Oct daily 9:30am–6pm; Nov–Mar daily 10am–5pm. Bus: 1 or 6.

Palace of Holyroodhouse ✮✮

James IV built this palace in the 16th century adjacent to an Augustinian abbey that David I had established in the 12th century. The nave of the abbey church, now in ruins, still remains, but only the north tower of James's palace is left. Most of what you see today was built by Charles II after Scotland and England were united in the 17th century. The palace suffered long periods of neglect, but it basked in glory at the ball thrown by Bonnie Prince Charlie in the mid–18th century, during the peak of his feverish (and doomed) optimism about uniting the Scottish clans in their struggle against the English. Queen Elizabeth II and Prince Philip stay here whenever they visit Edinburgh; when they're not in residence, the palace is open to visitors.

The old wing was the scene of Holyroodhouse's most dramatic episode: Lord Darnley, the jealous husband of Mary Queen of Scots, murdered his wife's Italian secretary on March 9, 1566; the incident is memorialized with a plaque. And one of the more curious exhibits is a piece of needlework done by Mary depicting a cat-and-mouse scene. (Her cousin, Elizabeth I, is the cat.)

Highlights of the palace are the oldest surviving section, King James Tower, where Mary Queen of Scots lived on the second floor, with Lord Darnley's rooms below. Some of the rich tapestries, paneling, massive fireplaces, and antiques from the 1700s are still in place. The Throne Room and other drawing rooms are still used for state occasions. In the rear of the palace is the richly furnished King's Bedchamber. The Picture Gallery boasts many portraits of Scottish monarchs by Dutch artist Jacob De Witt, who in 1684 signed a contract to turn out one potboiler portrait after another, at the rate of one a week for 2 years. But don't take all the portraits too seriously: Some of these royal figures may have never existed, and the likenesses of some aren't known, so the portraits are from the artist's imagination.

Behind Holyroodhouse begins **Holyrood Park,** Edinburgh's largest. With rocky crags, a loch, sweeping meadows, and the ruins of a chapel, it's a wee bit of the Scottish countryside in the city, and a great place for a picnic. If you climb up Holyrood Park, you'll come to 250m-high (823-ft.) **Arthur's Seat,** from which the panorama is breathtaking. (The name doesn't refer to King Arthur, as many people assume, but perhaps is a reference to Prince Arthur of Strathclyde or a corruption of *Ard Thor,* Gaelic for "height of Thor." No one knows for sure.) If you visit on a winter morning, you'll think you're in the heart of the Highlands. Arthur's Seat dates from prehistoric times; you can see clusters of cultivated terraces from the Dark Ages, especially on the east flank of the hill, both above and below Queen's Drive.

Canongate, at the eastern end of the Royal Mile. ℂ **0131/556-5100.** Admission £9.50 ($18) adults, £8.50 ($16) seniors, £5.50 ($10) children age 15 and under, £20 ($38) families (up to 2 adults and 2 children). Apr–Oct daily 9am–6pm, Nov–Mar 9am–4:30pm. Closed 2 weeks in May and 3 weeks in late June and early July (dates vary). Bus: 1 or 6.

The People's Story

If you continue walking downhill along Canongate toward Holyroodhouse (see below), you'll see one of the handsomest buildings on the Royal Mile: Built in 1591, the Canongate Tolbooth was once the courthouse, prison, and center of municipal affairs for the burgh of Canongate. It now contains this museum, which celebrates the social history of the inhabitants of Edinburgh from the late 18th

---

For Fans of Mr. Hyde

Near Gladstone's Land is **Brodie's Close,** a stone-floored alleyway. You can wander into the alley for a view of old stone houses that make you think you've stepped into a scene from a BBC production of a Dickens novel. It was named in honor of the notorious Deacon Brodie, a respectable councilor by day and a thief by night. (He was the inspiration for Robert Louis Stevenson's *The Strange Case of Dr. Jekyll and Mr. Hyde,* although Stevenson set his story in foggy London, not in Edinburgh.) Brodie was hanged in 1788. The mechanism used for the hangman's scaffolding had previously been improved by Brodie himself—for use on others, of course. Across the street is the most famous pub along the Royal Mile: **Deacon Brodie's Tavern,** 435 Lawnmarket (© 0131/225-6531).

---

century to the present, with an emphasis on the cultural displacements of the Industrial Revolution.

163 Canongate. © 0131/529-4057. Free admission. Mon–Sat 10am–5pm. Bus: 1.

The Real Mary King's Close *(Finds)*   Beneath the City Chambers on the Royal Mile lies the Old Town's deepest secret, a warren of hidden streets where people lived and worked for centuries. This new attraction allows you to go back to the 17th century, the turbulent days of plague-ridden Edinburgh. Today visitors can see a number of underground "closes," originally very narrow walkways with houses on either side, some dating back centuries. When the Royal Exchange (now the City Chambers) was constructed in 1753, the top floors of the buildings of the Close were torn down, although the lower sections were left standing and used as the foundations of the new building, leaving a number of dark and mysterious passages intact. In April 2003, guided parties were allowed to visit these dwellings for the first time. Subtle lighting and audio effects add to the experience. You can see everything from a grave-digger's family, stricken with the plague, to a grand 16th-century town house. The haunted shrine room is the best surviving 17th-century house in Scotland.

Writers' Court, off the Royal Mile. © 0870/243-0160. www.realmarykingsclose.com. Admission £9.50 ($18) adults, £8.50 ($16) seniors and students, £6 ($11) children, £22 ($42) family ticket. Nov–Mar Sun–Fri 10am–4pm, Sat 10am–9pm; Apr–Oct daily 10am–9pm. Closed Dec 25. Bus: 1 or 6.

Scotch Whisky Heritage Centre   Privately funded by a conglomeration of Scotland's biggest distillers, the Centre highlights the economic effect of whisky on both Scotland and the world, and illuminates the centuries-old traditions associated with whisky making. You get to see a 7-minute audiovisual show and ride an electric car past 13 sets showing historic moments in the whisky industry. A tour entitling you to sample five whiskies and take away a miniature bottle costs £13 ($25) per person.

354 Castlehill (10-min. walk from Waverley Train Station). © 0131/220-0441. Admission £9.25 ($18) adults; £7 ($13) seniors and students with ID; £4.95 ($9.40) children ages 5–17; children age 4 and under free. Sept–May 10am–6pm; June–Aug 9:30am–6:30pm. Closed Dec 25.

The Scottish Parliament   Modern architecture has come to Edinburgh thanks to the late Spanish architect Enric Miralles, who died in 2000 and never got to see his vision completely materialize. After years of delay and £470 million ($893 million) spent, the first Scottish Parliament in nearly 300 years was opened to much controversy over the price and the design. Some called it a "granite monstrosity," while others felt that it was just what Scotland needed to shed the stereotype of tartan and bagpipes. Both the London *Times* and *Guardian* called the new building a masterpiece, but some traditionalists have likened it to a "collection of coffins, bananas, and boomerangs." There is one thing that everyone can agree on, however: The Scottish Parliament is unique. That feature is what has made the building one of Edinburgh's top attractions. Guided tours are recommended, and you get colorful anecdotes along the way. If you can go when Parliament is in session, you'll often hear heated debates about Scotland's relationship with England.

Canongate. (*) **0131/348-5200.** www.scottish.parliament.uk. Free admission. Guided Tours £5 ($9.50) adults, £3 ($5.70) children 5–16, students, and seniors, free for children under 5. Parliament in session Mon, Wed, and Fri 10am–6pm (until 4pm Nov–Mar); Tues–Thurs 9am–7pm; Sat–Sun 10am–4pm. Bus: 1 or 6.

Writers' Museum This 1622 house is a treasure trove of portraits, relics, and manuscripts relating to three of Scotland's greatest men of letters: Robert Burns (1759–96), Sir Walter Scott (1771–1832), and Robert Louis Stevenson (1850–94). The Burns collection includes his writing desk, rare manuscripts, portraits, and many other items. Also on display are some of Sir Walter Scott's possessions, including his pipe, chess set, and original manuscripts. The museum holds one of the most significant Stevenson collections anywhere, featuring personal belongings, paintings, photographs, and early editions.

In Lady Stair's House, off Lawnmarket (10-min. walk from Waverley Train Station). (*) **0131/529-4901.** Free admission. Mon–Sat 10am–5pm; Sun noon–5pm Aug only.

THE TOP MUSEUMS & MONUMENTS

Dean Gallery ★ *(Finds)* Across from the Scottish Gallery of Modern Art, the Dean Gallery opened mainly to house the larger museum's vast collection of Dada and Surrealism. A lot of the pieces come from Edinburgh-born sculptor Sir Eduardo Paolozzi, who gave an extensive body of his private collection to the National Galleries of Scotland, including prints, drawings, plaster maquettes, and molds. The works of Salvador Dalí, Max Ernst, and Joan Miró overflow, as does a large selection of Paolozzi's own sculptures. The artist's mammoth composition of the robotic Vulcan dominates the entrance hall. In the gallery is a re-creation of Paolozzi's London studio. The gallery also hosts traveling or changing exhibitions.

73 Belford Rd. (*) **0131/624-6200.** www.nationalgalleries.org. Free admission to permanent collection; variable prices to special exhibitions. Daily 10am–5pm. Closed Dec 25–26. Bus: 13.

National Gallery of Scotland ★★★ Located in the center of Princes Street Gardens, this gallery is small as national galleries go, but the collection has been chosen with great care and expanded considerably by bequests, gifts, and loans. A recent major acquisition was Giulio Romano's *Vièrge à la Légende.* Other important Italian paintings are Verrocchio's *Ruskin Madonna,* Andrea del Sarto's *Portrait of a Man,* Domenichino's *Adoration of the Shepherds,* and Tiepolo's *Finding of Moses.* There are also works by El Greco and Velázquez.

The Duke of Sutherland has lent the museum two Raphaels, Titian's two Diana canvases and *Venus Rising from the Sea,* and Nicolas Poussin's *The Seven Sacraments.* On loan from the queen is Hugo van der Goess's *Trinity Altarpiece,* an early Netherlandish masterpiece historically linked to Edinburgh. Notable also are Rubens's *The Feast of Herod* and *The Reconciliation of Jacob and Esau,* and Rembrandt's *Woman in Bed,* as well as superb landscapes by Cuyp and Ruisdael. In 1982, the gallery made one of its most prized acquisitions, Pieter Saenredam's *Interior of St. Bavo's Church, Haarlem,* his largest, and arguably finest, painting.

Tips **A Note on Museum Hours**

Be aware that many museums that are usually closed on Sunday *are* open on Sunday during the Edinburgh Festival. Some museums that open only in summer are also open on public holidays.

The most valuable gift to the gallery, the Maitland Collection, includes one of Cézanne's *Mont St-Victoire* series, as well as works by Degas, van Gogh, Renoir, Gauguin, and Seurat. In 1980, two rare works were added: an early Monet, *Shipping Scene—Night Effects,* and a stunning landscape, *Niagara Falls, from the American Side,* by 19th-century American painter Frederic Church. In the new wing (opened in 1978), Henry Raeburn is at his best in the whimsical *The Rev. Robert Walker Skating on Duddingston Loch.*

2 The Mound. © **0131/624-6200.** www.nationalgalleries.org. Free admission. Daily 10am–5pm; Thurs 10am–7pm (extended hours during the festival). Closed Dec 25–26. Bus: 3, 21, or 26.

National Museum of Scotland (NMS) ★★★   In 1998, two long-established museums, the Royal Museum of Scotland and the National Museum of Antiquities, were united into this single institution 2 blocks south of the Royal Mile. The museum showcases exhibits in the decorative arts, ethnography, natural history, geology, archaeology, technology, and science. Six modern galleries distill billions of years of Scottish history—a total of 12,000 items range from rocks, dating back 2.9 billion years, found on the island of South Uist to a Hillman Imp, one of the last 500 cars manufactured at the Linwood plant near Glasgow before it closed in 1981. One gallery is devoted to Scotland's role as an independent nation before it merged with the United Kingdom in 1707. Another gallery, highlighting industry and empire from 1707 to 1914, includes exhibits on shipbuilding, whisky distilling, the railways, and such textiles as the tartan and paisley.

Chambers St. © **0131/247-4422.** www.nms.ac.uk. Free admission. Mon and Wed–Sat 10am–5pm; Tues 10am–8pm; Sun noon–5pm. Walk south from Waverley Station for 10 min. to reach Chambers St. or take bus nos. 3, 7, 21, 30, 31, 53, 69, or 80.

Scott Monument ★   Looking more like a church spire than a monument to a writer, the Gothic-inspired Scott Monument is Edinburgh's most famous landmark, completed in the mid–19th century. In the center of the more than 60m (200-ft.) spire is a large seated statue of Sir Walter Scott and his dog, Maida, with Scott's heroes carved as small figures in the monument. You can climb 287 steps to the top for a spectacular view. From here, you can also see the **Burns Monument,** dedicated to Robert Burns and designed by Thomas Hamilton in 1830, clearly visible along Regent Road.

In the East Princes St. Gardens. © **0131/529-4068.** Admission £3 ($5.70). Apr–Sept Mon–Sat 9am–6pm and Sun 10am–6pm; Oct–Mar Mon–Sat 9am–3pm and Sun 10am–3pm. Bus: 1 or 6.

Scottish National Gallery of Modern Art ★   Scotland's national collection of 20th-century art occupies a gallery converted from an 1828 school set on 4.8 hectares (12 acres) of grounds, a 15-minute walk from the west end of Princes Street. The collection is international in scope and quality, despite its modest size. Major sculptures outside include pieces by Henry Moore and Barbara Hepworth. Inside, the collection ranges from Braque and Picasso to recent works by Paolozzi. English and Scottish art are strongly represented, and you also find artists from Europe and America, notably Matisse, Miró, Kirchner, Ernst, Balthus, Lichtenstein, and Hockney. The cafe sells light refreshments and salads.

Belford Rd. ⓒ 0131/556-8921. www.nationalgalleries.org. Free admission, except for some temporary exhibits. Fri–Wed 10am–5pm; Thurs 10am–7pm. Closed Dec 25–26. Bus: 13 stops by the gallery but is infrequent; 18, 20, and 41 pass along Queensferry Rd., a 5-min. walk up Queensferry Terrace and Belford Rd. from the gallery.

Scottish National Portrait Gallery ⓕ   Housed in a red-stone Victorian Gothic building designed by Rowand Anderson, this portrait gallery gives you a chance to see what the famous people of Scottish history looked like. The portraits, several by Ramsay and Raeburn, include everybody from Mary Queen of Scots to Flora Macdonald to Sean Connery.

1 Queen St. ⓒ 0131/624-6200. www.nationalgalleries.org. Free admission, except for some temporary exhibits. Daily 10am–5pm (Thurs 10am–7pm). Closed Dec 25–26. Bus: 18, 20, or 41.

ADDITIONAL ATTRACTIONS

Dynamic Earth ⓕ Kids   This former brewery has been converted into a stone amphitheater capped by a futuristic translucent tent. Its galleries celebrate the natural diversity of the physical earth, with emphasis on the seismological and biological processes that led from the Big Bang to the world we know today. The presentation has been called "physical evolution as interpreted by Disney"—audio and video clips; buttons you can push to simulate earthquakes, meteor showers, and views of outer space; replicas of the slimy green primordial soup where life began; time capsules winding their way back through the eons; and a series of specialized aquariums, some with replicas of primordial life forms, some with actual living sharks, dolphins, and coral. You wander through simulated terrains, like polar ice caps, tundras, deserts, and grasslands. The most dramatic is a tropical rainforest where skies darken at 15-minute intervals and torrents of rain fall as creepy-crawlies appear underfoot. Hands down the most fun is the exhibit in which you can jump on a monitored platform while your movements are amplified to duplicate an earthquake; seismic instruments record what it would have registered on the Richter scale. On the premises are a restaurant, a cafe, a children's play area, and a gift shop. Plan to spend at least 1½ hours here.

Holyrood Rd. (10-min. walk from Waverley Train Station.) ⓒ 0131/550-7800. www.dynamicearth.co.uk. Admission £8.95 ($17) adults, £6.95 ($13) seniors, £5.75 ($11) children age 5–15, £1.95 ($3.70) children 2–4. Nov–Mar Wed–Sun 10am–5pm; Apr–Oct daily 10am–5pm; Jul–Aug daily 10am–6pm.

Edinburgh Zoo ⓕⓕ Kids   Scotland's largest animal collection is 10 minutes from Edinburgh's center on 32 hectares (80 acres) of hillside parkland offering unrivaled views from the Pentlands to the Firth of Forth. It contains more than 1,500 animals, including many endangered species: snow leopards, white rhinos, pygmy hippos, and others. The zoo boasts the largest penguin colony in Europe, with four species, plus the world's largest penguin enclosure. From April to September, a penguin parade is held daily at 2pm.

134 Corstorphine Rd. ⓒ 0131/334-9171. www.edinburghzoo.org.uk. Admission £11 ($20) adults, £8 ($15) seniors and students, £7.50 ($14) children. Apr–Sept daily 9am–6pm; Oct and Mar daily 9am–5pm; Nov–Feb daily 9am–4:30pm. Parking £2.50 ($4.75). Bus: 2, 26, 69, 85, or 86.

Georgian House   The most architecturally interesting district of the New Town is the north side of Charlotte Square, designed by Robert Adam. Together with his brother, James, he developed a symmetrical but airy style with an elegant reworking of Greek and Roman classical motifs. The Adams' influence was widespread in Britain

Britannia: The People's Yacht

In case Queen Elizabeth II never invited you to sail aboard her 125m (412-ft.) yacht, you still have a chance to board this famous vessel; the gangplank has been lowered for the public. The luxury *Britannia* ⊛ was launched on April 16, 1953, sailed more than a million miles, and was decommissioned on December 11, 1997. Today, the ship rests at anchor in the port of Leith, 3km (2 miles) from Edinburgh's center. You reach the vessel by going through a visitor center designed by Sir Terence Conran. Once aboard, you're guided around all five decks by an audio tour. You can walk the decks where Prince Charles and Princess Diana strolled on their honeymoon, visit the drawing room and the Royal Apartments, and explore the engine room, the galleys, and the captain's cabin.

Tickets can be booked in advance by calling ℂ **0131/555-5566** (www.royal yachtbritannia.co.uk). The yacht is open daily except Christmas, with the first tour beginning at 10am, the last at 3:30pm. Each tour (approximately 90–120 min.) is self-guided with the use of a headset lent to participants. Adults pay £9.50 ($18), seniors £7.50 ($14), and children ages 5 to 17 £5.50 ($10); those age 4 and under visit for free. A family ticket, good for two adults and up to two children, is £26.50 ($50). From Waverley Bridge, take either city bus (Lothian Transport) X50, or else the Guide Friday tour bus, which is marked all over its sides with the words BRITANNIA.

and the United States, especially in the American South. Georgian House has been refurbished and opened to the public by Scotland's National Trust. The furniture is mainly Hepplewhite, Chippendale, and Sheraton, all from the 18th century. A sturdy old four-poster with an original 18th-century canopy occupies a ground-floor bedroom. The dining-room table is set with fine Wedgwood china and the kitchen stocked with gleaming copper pots and pans.

7 Charlotte Sq. ℂ **0131/225-2160.** Admission £5 ($9.50) adults, £4 ($7.60) children, students, and seniors, £14 ($27) per family. Mar daily 11am–3pm; Apr–June and Sept–Oct daily 10am–5pm; July–Aug daily 10am–7pm; Nov daily 11am–3pm. Bus: 2, 12, 26, or 31.

Sir Jules Thorn Exhibition of the History of Surgery/Dental Museum   Edinburgh's rich medical history and associations make the Exhibition of the History of Surgery well worth a visit. On the upper floors of a 19th-century town house in a tucked-away square, you can chart the development of surgery from 1505 to the 20th century. The sometimes macabre exhibits include such gems as a pocketbook made from the skin of the notorious body snatcher William Burke. The Dental Museum, its gleaming glass cases full of every conceivable dentistry tool, is certainly not for the squeamish or those experiencing dental problems!

9 Hill Sq. ℂ **0131/527-1649.** Free admission. Mon–Fri 2–4pm. Bus: 31 or 33.

THE MONUMENTS ON CALTON HILL

Calton Hill ⊛⊛⊛, rising 106m (350 ft.) off Regent Road in the eastern sector, is often credited with giving Edinburgh a look somewhat like that of Athens. It's a hill of monuments; when some of them were created, they were called "instant ruins" by critics. People visit the hill not only to see its monuments but also to enjoy the panoramic views of the Firth of Forth and the city spread beneath it. The Parthenon was partially reproduced on this location in 1824. The intention of the builders was to honor the brave Scottish dead killed in the Napoleonic wars. However, the city fathers ran out of money and the monument (often referred to as "Scotland's shame") was never finished.

The **Nelson Monument** (© **0131/556-2716**), containing relics of the hero of Trafalgar, dates from 1815 and rises more than 30m (100 ft.) above the hill. A time ball at the top falls at 1pm Monday to Saturday. The monument is open April to September, Monday from 1 to 6pm and Tuesday to Saturday ˜)m 10am to 6pm; and October to March, Monday to Saturday from 10am to 3pm. Admission is £3 ($5.70). Take bus nos. 26, 85, or 86.

For Americans, the curiosity here is the **Lincoln Monument,** which Edinburghers erected in 1893. It was dedicated to the thousands of American soldiers of Scottish descent who lost their lives in America's Civil War. Below Waterloo Place, on the flatter slope of Calton Hill, you can walk through the **Calton Old Cemetery,** dating from the 1700s. Many famous Scots were buried here, often with elaborate tombs honoring their memory (notably the Robert Adam–designed tomb for philosopher David Hume).

DEAN VILLAGE

Beautiful Dean Village is one of the city's most photographed sights. Dating from the 12th century, this former grain-milling center occupies a valley about 30m (100 ft.) below the rest of Edinburgh. It's a few minutes from the West End, at the end of Bells Brae off Queensferry Street, on the Water of Leith. You can enjoy a celebrated view by looking downstream, under the high arches of Dean Bridge (1833), designed by Telford.

The village's old buildings have been restored and converted into apartments and houses. You don't come here for any one particular site but to stroll around, people-watch, and enjoy the village. You can also walk for kilometers along the Water of Leith, one of the most tranquil strolls in the greater Edinburgh area.

GARDENS

The **Royal Botanic Garden** , Inverleith Row (© **0131/552-7171**), is one of the grandest outdoor spaces in Great Britain. Sprawling across 28 hectares (70 acres), it dates from the late 17th century, when it was originally used for medical studies. In spring, the rhododendrons alone are reason enough to visit Scotland. Admission to the glasshouses is £3.50 ($6.65) for adults, £3 ($5.70) for seniors, and £1 ($1.90) for children under 10. It's open daily: January to February 10am to 4pm, March 10am to 6pm, April to September 10am to 7pm, and October to December 10am to 6pm.

As the New Town grew, the city fathers decided to turn the area below Edinburgh Castle into the **Princes Street Gardens,** now one of the city's main beauty spots. The area was once Nor Loch, a body of water in the city center, but it was drained to make way for a railway line. (When it was still a bog, the great philosopher David Hume fell into it, couldn't remove himself, and called for help from a passing woman. She recognized him, pronounced him an atheist, and wouldn't offer her umbrella to pull him out of the mire until he recited the Lord's Prayer.)

ORGANIZED TOURS

For a quick introduction to the principal attractions in and around Edinburgh, consider the tours offered from April to late October by **Lothian Region Transport,** 14 Queen St. (© **0131/555-6363**). You can see most of the major sights of Edinburgh, including the Royal Mile, the Palace of Holyroodhouse, Princes Street, and Edinburgh Castle, by double-decker motor coach for £9 ($17) for adults, £8 ($15) for seniors and students, and £3 ($5.70) for children. This ticket is valid all day on any **LRT Edinburgh Classic Tour bus,** which allows passengers to get on and off at any of the 15 stops along its routes. Buses start from Waverley Bridge every day beginning at 9:40am, departing every 15 minutes in summer and about every 30 minutes in winter, then embark on a circuit of Edinburgh, which takes about 1 hour. Commentary is offered along the way.

Tickets for any of these tours can be bought at LRT offices, at Waverley Bridge or at 14 Queen St., or the tourist information center in Waverley Market. Reservations are a good idea. For more information, call © **0131/220-0770,** 24 hours a day.

McEwan's Literary Pub Tour (© **0131/226-6665**) follows in the footsteps of such literary greats as Robert Burns, Robert Louis Stevenson, and Sir Walter Scott. The *Edinburgh Evening News* has called this tour "vivid, erudite, and entertaining" (and we concur). It goes into the city's famous or infamous taverns and *howffs* (Scottish pubs), highlighting, among other things, tales of Dr. Jekyll and Mr. Hyde, and the erotic love poetry of Burns. Tours depart from the Beehive Pub on Grassmarket in the Old Town, going along the Royal Mile. The 2-hour tour costs £10 ($19) for adults, £8 ($15) for children. From May to September tours leave nightly at 7:30pm; March, April, and October, Thursday to Sunday at 7:30pm; and December, January, February, and November Friday at 7:30pm. Reservations are recommended.

The Witchery Tours (© **0131/225-6745**) are filled with ghosts, gore, and witchcraft, enlivened by "jumper-outers"—actors who jump out to scare you. Two tours— "Ghost & Gore" and "Murder & Mystery"—are a bit similar and overlap in parts. Scenes of many horrific tortures, murders, and supernatural happenings in the historic Old Town are visited, all under the cloak of darkness. The ghost tour departs daily at 7pm and 7:30pm, with the murder tour leaving daily at 9pm and again at 10pm year-round. Tours last 1 hour and 15 minutes, costing £7.50 ($14) for adults, £5 ($9.50) for children. Departures are from outside the Witchery Restaurant on Castlehill. Reserve early.

Mercat Tours (© **0131/557-6464**) conducts the city's best walking tours, which are topical: They cover everything from "Secrets of the Royal Mile" to a "Haunted Underground Experience." Tours meet outside the Tourist Office on Princes Street. "Secrets of the Royal Mile" leaves daily at 10:30am with the "Grand Tour" departing at 10am daily. "Hidden Vaults" runs hourly from May to September noon to 4pm, off season daily at 2pm and 4pm. The cost of these tours begins at £7.50 ($14) for adults, £4 ($7.60) for children. Reservations are recommended for these 1-hour tours.

Guide Friday (© **0131/556-2244**) is good for a quick overview. You can later follow up with more in-depth visits. You're taken around the city in one of the company's fleet of open-top, double-decker buses, with informed and often amusing running commentaries. Highlights include the Royal Mile, Princes Street, Palace of Holyroodhouse, and Edinburgh Castle, as well as the New Town. Tours run between 9:20am and dusk, costing £9 ($17) for adults, £3 ($5.70) for kids ages 5 to 15. Reservations are recommended for these 1-hour tours, which depart from Waverley Bridge.

6 Special Events & Festivals

Hogmanay begins on New Year's Eve and merges into New Year's Day festivities. It's celebrated throughout Scotland with the ritual kissing of everyone in sight, and is followed by the time-honored practice of "first footing" with a lump of coal, a bun, and (needless to say) a drop of the hard stuff. In 1993, the Edinburgh City Council began a 3-day festival that now features street theater, lively processions illuminated by firebrands, and the burning of a long boat. By 1997, the crush to attend Europe's largest winter festival forced Edinburgh to limit attendees; you now have to get tickets to enter the city center after 8pm on New Year's Eve. For details, call © **0131/ 473-3800.**

January 25 is **Burns Night,** *the* night when Scots the world over gather to consume the traditional supper of haggis, *neeps* (turnips), and *tatties* (potatoes), accompanied by a wee dram of whisky, while listening to recitals of the works of Scotland's Bard, Robert "Rabbie" Burns, whose birthday is being celebrated. Burns suppers are held all over town.

By far, the highlight of Edinburgh's year comes in the last weeks of August during the **Edinburgh International Festival.** Since 1947, the festival has attracted artists and companies of the highest caliber in music, opera, dance, theater, poetry, and prose. One of the most exciting spectacles is the **Military Tattoo** on the floodlit esplanade in front of Edinburgh Castle, high on its rock above the city. First performed in 1950, the Tattoo features the precision marching of not only the British Army's Scottish regiments but also performers from some 30 countries, including bands, dancers, drill teams, gymnasts, and motorcyclists—and even horses, camels, elephants, and police dogs. The music ranges from ethnic to pop, military to jazz. Schedules are released each year about 6 months before the festival, but they're subject to change. Mail-order bookings are available from the Edinburgh Military Tattoo, Tattoo Office, 32 Market St., Edinburgh EH1 1QB (© **0131/225-1188**). You can check schedules and buy tickets online at **www.eif.co.uk**.

Running simultaneously with the festival, but less predictable in quality, is the **Edinburgh Festival Fringe,** an opportunity for anybody—professional or amateur, individual, group, or company—to put on a show wherever they can find an empty stage or street corner. Late-night revues, outrageous contemporary drama, university theater presentations, even full-length opera—Edinburgh gives them all free rein. As if that weren't enough, Edinburgh has a **Film Festival,** a **Jazz Festival,** a **Television Festival,** and a non-annual **Book Festival** at the same time.

Ticket prices vary from £6 to £10 ($11–$19). You can get information from **Edinburgh International Festival,** The Hub, Castle Hill, Edinburgh EH1 7ND (© **0131/ 473-2000;** fax 0131/473-2002), open Monday to Friday from 9:30am to 5:30pm. Other information sources are the **Edinburgh Festival Fringe,** 180 High St., Edinburgh EH1 1BW (© **0131/226-0026**); **Edinburgh Book Festival,** Scottish Book Centre, 137 Dundee St., Edinburgh EH11 1BG (© **0131/228-6866**); and **Edinburgh Film Festival,** 88 Lothian Rd., Edinburgh EH3 9BZ (© **0131/228-4051;** www.edfilmfest.org.uk).

For visitors traveling from the U.S., the most convenient, but slightly more expensive, way to order tickets for the festival is to purchase them stateside from **Global Tickets, Inc.,** 234 W. 44th St., Suite 100, New York, NY 10036 (© **800/223-6108**).

7 Spectator Sports & Outdoor Pursuits

SPECTATOR SPORTS

HORSE RACING   Place your bets at the **Musselburgh Racecourse,** Musselburgh Park (© **0131/665-2859**), about 6.5km (4 miles) east of Edinburgh. In summer, the races are on a flat circular track, but in winter, the more elaborate National Hunt format challenges horses and riders to a series of jumps and obstacle courses of great technical difficulty. Admission is £8 to £20 ($15–$38), or £20 ($38) for club stand on Saturday.

RUGBY   Home of the National Rugby Team of Scotland, **Murrayfield Stadium,** Murrayfield (© **0131/346-5000;** www.sru.org.uk), is about 1.6km (1 mile) west of Edinburgh. The sport is played from September to April, usually on Saturdays. Some of the most passionate matches are those among teams from the five-nation bloc comprising Scotland, Wales, England, Ireland, and France. These matches occur only between January and March, when sports enthusiasts in Scotland seem to talk about little else. Ticket prices range from £15 to £30 ($29–$57).

SOCCER   You might quickly get swept up in Edinburghers' zeal for their local soccer (referred to as "football") clubs. Both teams, when not battling each other, challenge other teams from throughout Europe. The home of the Edinburgh Hearts (more formally known as the Heart of Midlothian Football Club) is **Tynecastle Park,** Gorgie Road (© **0131/337-7200**); the home of the Hibs (short for the Hibernians) is **Easter Road Park,** Easter Road (© **0131/661-2159**). The traditional playing times are Saturday afternoons, when games are likely to be televised in pubs throughout Scotland. Tickets range from £12 to £24 ($23–$46).

OUTDOOR ACTIVITIES

GOLF   Note that none of the following courses has caddy service.

The par-71 **Silverknowes Golf Course,** Silverknowes Parkway (© **0131/336-3843**), is a 6,202-yard course. Greens fees for 18 holes are £16 ($29) Monday to Friday and £18.50 ($35) Saturday and Sunday, with club and cart rentals costing £16 ($30) and £3 ($5.70), respectively.

The par-67 **Craigentinny,** Craigentinny Gold, Fillyside Road (© **0131/554-7501**), 5km (3 miles) east of Edinburgh, features 5,413 yards of playing area. Clubs rent for £16 ($30) per round and carts for £3 ($5.70). Greens fees for 18 holes are £14 ($27) Monday to Friday and £17 ($31) Saturday and Sunday.

The par-67, 5,306-yard **Liberton Golf Course,** Kingston Grange, 297 Gilmerton Rd. (© **0131/664-3009**), requires 2 days' notice if you want to rent clubs, the price of which is included in the greens fees of £25 ($48) Monday to Friday for 18 holes. On Saturday and Sunday, fees are £30 ($57). Carts can be rented for £3 ($5.70).

The par-70 **Braids,** Braid House Golf Course, Approach Road (© **0131/447-6666**), is 5km (3 miles) south of Edinburgh's city center. The greens fees at this 5,731-yard course are £19 ($35) Monday to Friday and £23 ($44) Saturday and Sunday. Clubs rent for £16 ($30) including deposit; carts go for £3 ($5.70) plus a £15 ($29) deposit per 18 holes of play.

The par-66 **Swanston Golf Course,** Swanston Road (© **0131/445-2239**), is an 18-hole, 4,825-yard course located 15km (9 miles) southwest of Edinburgh. Clubs go for £10 ($19) and trolleys for £3 ($5.70); greens fees are £17 ($32) per round Monday to Friday and £28 ($53) Saturday and Sunday. The per-day rates are £2 to £27 ($3.80–$51).

The **Portobello,** Stanley Street (© **0131/669–4361**), is a 9-hole course with a par of 32. The greens fees at this 2,252-yard course are £7 ($13) Monday to Friday and £9 ($17) Saturday and Sunday. A deposit of £10 ($19) is required for club rental, costing £16 ($30). Carts go for £3 ($5.70) plus a £10 ($19) deposit.

Carrick Knowe, Glen Devon Park (© **0131/554-1096**), is one of Scotland's larger courses, featuring 5,697 yards of playing area. Eight kilometers (5 miles) west of Edinburgh, this 18-hole, par-70 course was redesigned in 1998 and offers club rentals at £16 ($30) and trolleys at £3 ($5.70). The greens fees for 18 holes are £16 ($29) Monday to Friday and £19 ($35) Saturday and Sunday.

The par-66 **Torphin Hill Golf Course,** Torphin Road (© **0131/441-4061**), is a 4,648-yard, 18-hole course, offering no club rentals or trolleys. The greens fees are £15 ($29) per round Monday to Friday. Visitors are only welcome Monday to Friday.

SAILING   Visit the Firth of Forth firsthand by contacting the **Port Edgar Sailing Centre,** Port Edgar, South Queensferry (© **0131/331-3330**), about 15km (9 miles) west of the city center. Between Easter and mid-October, it offers instruction in smallcraft sailing, canoeing, and powerboating, as well as half-day rentals. The rate for a dinghy, suitable for four adults, is £30 ($57) for 2 hours. April to September, the center is open daily 9am to 6:30pm, and boats can be hired until 9pm. In winter, it's open daily 9am to 4:30pm.

TENNIS   Reservations are necessary for the courts at the **Craiglockhart Sports Centre,** 177 Colinton Rd. (© **0131/444-1969**), which also has badminton courts and a gym. Indoor courts cost £12 to £20 ($23–$38) per hour for adults and £3.20 to £5.70 ($6.10–$11) for children; they're available daily 7am to 10:30pm. The outdoor courts cost £5.20 to £7.20 ($9.90–$14) per hour for adults and £5 ($9.50) for children; these are available daily 7am until 10:30pm. They're closed when the weather turns cold. Racquet rental is free. More convenient, and sometimes more crowded, are a handful of concrete-surfaced **public tennis courts** behind George Square, on the north side of the public park known as the Meadows.

8 Shopping

The New Town's **Princes Street** is the main shopping artery. **George Street** and the Old Town's **Royal Mile** are also major shopping areas. The best buys are in tartans and woolens, along with bone china and Scottish crystal.

Shopping hours are generally Monday to Saturday 9am to 5 or 5:30pm and Sunday 11am to 5pm. On Thursdays, many shops remain open until 7 or 8pm.

BRASS RUBBINGS

Scottish Stone and Brass Rubbing Centre   You can rub any of the brass or stones on display here to create your own wall hangings, or buy them ready made. Those commemorating King Robert the Bruce are particularly impressive. The brass you choose is covered in white or black paper, silver wax is used to outline the brass, and then you fill it in with different colors of wax. You can visit the center's collection of replicas molded from ancient Pictish stones, rare Scottish brasses, and medieval church brasses. Trinity Apse, Chalmers Close, near the Royal Mile. © 0131/556-4364. Bus: 1.

CASHMERE

Brenda Robertson ⟲⟲   In Edinburgh Ms. Robertson is known as "the queen of cashmere." Her cashmere couture collection is the finest in the city. The fabric is spun,

---

Tips **Bring That Passport!**

If you are a non-U.K. resident, take your passport when you go shopping in case you make a purchase that entitles you to a **VAT (value-added tax) refund.** For details, see "Getting Your VAT Refund" under "Fast Facts: Scotland," in chapter 2.

---

dyed, and knitted in Scotland by the most skilled artisans. The colors of the cashmeres are often vibrant. You can order any of the couture styles from an amazing collection of 131 different colors—and at no extra charge. Classic British shirts and luxury jersey T-shirts are also sold. On the lower level look for sales all year round. 13A Dundas St. © 0131/557-8118. Bus: 3, 8, or 22.

CRYSTAL

Edinburgh Crystal   This place is devoted to handmade crystal glassware. The visitor center (Mon–Sat 9am–5pm, Sun 11am–5pm) contains the factory shop where the world's largest collection of Edinburgh Crystal (plus inexpensive factory seconds) is on sale. Although Waterford is the more prestigious name, Edinburgh Crystal is a serious competitor, its most popular design being the thistle, symbolizing Scotland. It can be traced back to the 17th century, when the glassmaking art was brought here by the Venetians. The center also has a gift shop and a coffee shop specializing in home baking. Thirty-minute tours of the factory to watch glassmakers at work are given Monday to Friday 10am to 4pm; April to September, weekend tours are given 10am to 2:30pm. Tours cost £3.50 ($6.65) for adults, £2.50 ($4.75) for children, £9.50 ($18) for a family ticket. Eastfield, Penicuik (16km/10 miles south of Edinburgh, just off A701 to Peebles). © 01968/675-128. Bus: 37, 37A, or 62 (Lowland), 64 or 65 (green), or 81 or 87 (red) Waverley bus link.

DEPARTMENT STORES & A MALL

Debenham's   Old reliable Debenham's is still perhaps the best department store in Edinburgh, with a wide array of Scottish and international merchandise displayed in a marble-covered interior. 109–112 Princes St. © 0131/225-1320. Bus: 3, 31, or 69.

Jenners   Everyone in Edinburgh has probably been to Jenners at least once. Its neo-Gothic facade, opposite the Scott Monument, couldn't be more prominent. The store's selection of Scottish and international merchandise is astounding. Jenners sells much the same merchandise as Debenham's, but has a wider selection of china and glassware, not to mention a popular food hall featuring, among other items, heather honey, Dundee marmalade, and Scottish shortbreads and cakes. A wide variety of tartans, cashmere, and lambs wool knits is also available. 48 Princes St. © 0131/225-2442. Bus: 3, 31, or 69.

Princes Mall   There's something for everyone at this tri-level mall. You can browse through some 60 shops selling fashions, accessories, gifts, books, jewelry, and beauty products. Unique handmade items are sold in the Scottish crafts center. The food court has tempting snacks, while the food hall boasts top-quality produce. Next to Waverley Station, Princes St. © 0131/557-3759. Bus: 3, 31, or 69.

DOLLS

Doll Hospital (Geraldine's of Edinburgh)   Lined with glass-fronted cases, this is a basement showroom for Edinburgh's only doll factory, with more than 100 dolls on display. Each of the heirloom-quality dolls requires about 10 days' labor to create, and has a hand-painted porcelain head and sometimes an elaborate coiffure. Also available are fully jointed, all-mohair teddy bears that children love. 133–135 Canongate. ℭ **0131/ 556-4295**. Bus: 23 or 27.

FASHION

Bill Baber   Ten to fifteen highly creative craftspeople work here, creating artfully modernized adaptations of traditional Scottish patterns for both men and women. Expect to find traditional Scottish jacquard-patterned knits spiced up with strands of Caribbean-inspired turquoise or aqua; rugged-looking blazers, jackets, and sweaters suitable for treks or bike rides through the moors; and tailored jackets a woman might feel comfortable wearing to a glamorous cocktail party. 66 Grassmarket, near the Royal Mile. ℭ **0131/225-3249**. Bus: 2 or 12.

Corniche   Designer Nina Grant operates the most sophisticated boutique in Edinburgh. If it's the latest in Scottish fashion, expect to find it here, even "Anglomania kilts" designed by that controversial lady of fashion herself, Vivienne Westwood. Relative newcomer Jackie Burke has made a splash with her fur-trimmed Harris tweed riding jackets. 2 Jeffrey St. ℭ **0131/556-3707**. 10-min. walk from Waverley Train Station.

Edinburgh Woollen Mill   One of about 30 such shops throughout the United Kingdom, the Edinburgh Woollen Mill sells good Scottish woolens, knitwear, skirts, gifts, and travel rugs. Note, however, that most of the merchandise is made in England. 139 Princes St. ℭ **0131/226-3840**. Bus: 3, 31, or 69.

Ragamuffin   The staff here sells what is termed "wearable art" created by some 150 fashion designers from all over the U.K. Along the Royal Mile, Lesley Robertson and her staff sell what they amusingly call "clothes for clowns" in jazzy, bright, and bulky knits, many of which contain Celtic motifs. This is one of the most unusual designer-label shops in Edinburgh. The apparel here is unique. Canongate, Royal Mile. ℭ **0131/557- 6007**. Bus: 1 or 6.

Schuh   Schuh has the latest in unique footwear, specializing in the yellow, red, and blue plaid boots made famous by the local rugby team. Expect funky finds. 6 Frederick St. ℭ **0131/220-0290**. Bus: 11, 15, 16, or 25.

Shetland Connection   Owner Moira-Ann Leask promotes Shetland Island knitwear, and her shop is packed with sweaters, hats, and gloves in colorful Fair Isle designs. She also offers hand-knitted mohair, Aran, and Icelandic sweaters. Items range from fine-ply cobweb shawls to bulky ski sweaters in high-quality wool. A large range of Celtic jewelry and gifts makes this shop a top-priority visit. 491 Lawnmarket. ℭ **0131/225-3525**. Bus: 1.

GIFTS

Ness Scotland   Along the Royal Mile, Ness Scotland is filled with whimsical accessories searched out by Gordon MacAulay and Adrienne Wells. They have scoured the country from the Orkney Islands to the Borders for that unique item. You'll see hand-loomed cardigans, tasteful scarves, and charming Dinky bags made during the long winters on the Isle of Lewis. 367 High St. ℭ **0131/226-5227**. A 5-min. walk from Waverley Train Station.

JEWELRY

Alistir Tait   This is one of the most charming jewelry stores in Edinburgh, with a reputation for Scottish minerals like agates; Scottish gold; garnets, sapphires, and freshwater pearls; and estate jewelry. Ask to see the artful depictions of Luckenbooths.

Tracing Your Ancestral Roots

If you have a name beginning with Mac (which simply means "son of") or one of the other Scottish names, you may have descended from a clan, a group of kinsmen claiming a common ancestry. Clans and clan societies have their own museums throughout Scotland, and local tourist offices provide details about where to locate them. Bookstores throughout Scotland sell clan histories and maps.

Scotland's densest concentration of genealogical records is at the **General Register Office,** New Register House, 3 W. Register St., Edinburgh EH1 3YT (© 0131/334-4433; www.gro-scotland.gov.uk; bus: 3, 26, 33, or 86). Opened in 1863 in a black-brick Victorian headquarters, it contains hundreds of thousands of microfiche and microfilm documents and a computerized system that tells you where to begin looking for whatever records interest you. The strictly self-service system is open Monday to Friday from 9am to 4:30pm; it gets crowded in summer. The fee you pay for a full day's access to the records is £17 ($32); if you enter after 1pm, you'll pay £10 ($19).

The house has detailed records of every birth, marriage, and death in Scotland since 1855. There are also old parish registers, the earliest dating from 1553, listing baptisms, marriages, and burials, but these are far from complete. It also has census returns for every decade from 1841 to 1891 and such data as the foreign marriages of Scots, adopted children's registers, and war registers.

Fashioned as pendants, usually as two entwined hearts capped by a royal crest, they're associated with the loves and tragedies of Mary Queen of Scots, and are often accessorized with a baroque pearl. They come in subtle hues of petal, orange, brown, and (most desirable and rare) purple. Prices for Luckenbooths are £28 to £250 ($45–$400). 116A Rose St. © 0131/225-4105. Bus: 3, 31, or 69.

Hamilton & Inches   Since 1866, the prestigious Hamilton & Inches has sold gold and silver jewelry, porcelain and silver, and gift items. You'll find everything you'd want for an upscale wedding present, all sorts of jewelry, and two memorable kinds of silver dishes—weighty plates, copied from items found in the Spanish Armada wrecks during Elizabeth I's reign, and endearingly folkloric *quaichs* (drinking vessels). The quaichs originated in the West Highlands as whisky measures crafted from wood or horn and were later gentrified into something like silver porringers or chafing dishes, each with a pair of lugs (ears) fashioned into Celtic or thistle patterns. 87 George St. © 0131/225-4898. Bus: 41 or 42.

LINENS & BEDS

And So To Bed   The danger of popping into this store is you might make a much larger investment than you'd intended when you see the fine-textured sheets and pillowcases. Most feature Italian and British cotton (not linen), usually in white and cream. There's also a beautiful collection of ornate brass, iron, and wooden beds you can order in several sizes and have shipped anywhere. 30 Dundas St. © 0131/652-3700. Bus: 23 or 27.

LIQUORS

Demijohn ★★ A cross between a liquor store and an apothecary, this shop is lined with bottles (called demijohns) filled with various spirits, including artisanal wines and meads. The staff allows customers to taste the products fully before a purchase. Customers can also choose a demijohn of their choice, and their selection of a bottle will be filled right on the spot. Our recommendation? Pick up a demijohn of an amber-colored 12-year-old whisky called Caol Ila. It's waiting your selection in a mellow old cask. Although the shop is known mainly for its mature and very rare single malt whiskies, it also has a unique collection of products from around the globe, including unusual spices, rare vinegars, and the best collection of virgin olive oils in Scotland. Herbs and several unique gift items are also for sale. 32 Victoria St. ⓒ **0131/225-3265.** Bus: 35 or 41.

TARTANS & KILTS

Anta Some of the most stylish tartans are found at Anta, where Lachian and Anne Stewart, the creative design team behind Ralph Lauren's home tartan fabrics, present a series of tartans newly invented in unique styles. The woolen blankets with hand-purled fringe are woven on old-style looms. 32 High St. ⓒ **0131/557-8300.**

Clan Tartan Centre This is one of the leading tartan specialists in Edinburgh, regardless of which clan you claim as your own. If you want help in identifying a particular tartan, the staff will assist you. 70–74 Bangor Rd., Leith. ⓒ **0131/553-5161.** Bus: 7 or 10.

Geoffrey (Tailor) Highland Crafts This is the most famous kiltmaker in the Scottish capital. Its customers have included Sean Connery, Charlton Heston, Dr. Ruth Westheimer, members of Scotland's rugby teams, and Mel Gibson (who favors the tartan design Hunting Buchanan and wore his outfit when he received an award from the Scottish government after filming *Braveheart*). Expect 4 to 8 weeks for your costume to be completed. The company sets up sales outlets at Scottish reunions and Highland Games around the world, and maintains a toll-free number (ⓒ **800/566-1467**) for calls from the United States or Canada. It stocks 200 of Scotland's best-known tartan patterns and is revolutionizing the kilt by establishing a subsidiary called 21st Century Kilts, which makes them in fabrics ranging from denim to leather.

Geoffrey is also one of the few kiltmakers to actually weave the garment, a process that you can watch at the **Edinburgh Old Town Weaving Company,** 555 Castlehill (ⓒ **0131/26-1555;** bus: 1), Monday to Friday 9am to 5pm. Note that the factory doesn't sell kilts directly to visitors. 57–59 High St. ⓒ **0131/557-0256.** Bus: 1.

James Pringle Woolen Mill The mill produces a large variety of top-quality wool items, including cashmere sweaters, tartan and tweed ties, travel rugs, tweed hats, and tam o' shanters. In addition, it boasts one of Scotland's best Clan Tartan Centres, with more than 5,000 tartans accessible. A free audiovisual presentation shows the history and development of the tartan. You can visit for free, and there's even a free taxi service to the mill from anywhere in Edinburgh (ask at your hotel). 70–74 Bangor Rd., Leith. ⓒ **0131/553-5161.** Bus: 7 or 10.

Tartan Gift Shops Tartan Gift Shops has a chart indicating the place of origin (in Scotland) of family names, accompanied by a bewildering array of both hunt and dress tartans for men and women, sold by the yard. There's also a line of lambswool and cashmere sweaters and all the accessories. 54 High St. ⓒ **0131/558-3187.** Bus: 1.

Tartan Weaving Mill & Exhibition This is both a shopping venue and an attraction. You can view powerlooms blending together different wools, and can also see a display of Highland dress down through the centuries. At this outlet, you can look up your clan tartan and buy the appropriate kilt right on the spot. 55 Castlehill, Royal Mile. © **0131/226-1555.** Bus: 1 or 6.

9 Edinburgh After Dark

Every year in late August, the **Edinburgh International Festival** brings numerous world-class cultural offerings to the city, but year-round there are plenty of choices, whether you prefer theater, opera, ballet, or other diversions. The waterfront district, featuring many jazz clubs and restaurants, is especially lively in summer, and students flock to the pubs and clubs around Grassmarket. Discos are found off High and Princes streets, and in the city's numerous pubs you often hear traditional Scottish folk music for the price of a pint.

For a thorough list of entertainment options during your stay, pick up a copy of *The List,* a free biweekly paper available at the tourist office. Before you leave home, you might want to check *Time Out* (www.timeout.com/edinburgh) for the latest listings.

THE PERFORMING ARTS

THEATER Edinburgh has a lively theater scene. In 1994, the **Festival Theatre,** 13–29 Nicolson St. (© **0131/662-1112** for administration, 0131/529-6000 for tickets during festival times with an additional phone line [0131/473-2000] that's operational during the August festival; bus: 3, 31, or 33), opened in time for some aspects of the Edinburgh Festival. Set on the eastern edge of the city, near the old campus of the University of Edinburgh, it has since been called "Britain's de facto Dance House" because of its sprung floor, its enormous stage (the largest in Britain), and its suitability for opera presentations of all kinds. Tickets are £6 to £60 ($11–$114).

Another major theater is the **King's Theatre,** 2 Leven St. (© **0131/529-6000;** bus: 10 or 11), a 1,600-seat Victorian venue offering a wide repertoire of classical entertainment, including ballet, opera, and West End productions. The **Netherbow Arts Centre,** 43 High St. (© **0131/556-9579;** bus: 1), has been called "informal," and productions here are often experimental and delightful—new Scottish theater at its best.

The resident company of **Royal Lyceum Theatre,** Grindlay Street (© **0131/248-4848;** bus: 11 or 15), also has an enviable reputation; its presentations range from the works of Shakespeare to new Scottish playwrights. The **Traverse Theatre,** Cambridge Street (© **0131/228-1404;** bus: 11 or 15), is one of the few theaters in Britain funded solely to present new plays by British writers and first English translations of international works. The Traverse now offers two theaters under one roof: Traverse 1 seats 250, and Traverse 2 seats 100.

BALLET, OPERA & CLASSICAL MUSIC The **Scottish Ballet** and the **Scottish Opera** perform at the **Playhouse Theatre,** 18–22 Greenside Place (© **0870/606-3424;** bus: 7 or 14), which, with 3,100 seats, is the town's largest theater. The **Scottish Chamber Orchestra** makes its home at **Queen's Hall,** Clerk Street (© **0131/668-2019;** bus: 3, 33, or 31), also a major venue for the Edinburgh International Festival.

FOLK MUSIC & CEILIDHS Folk music is performed in many clubs and pubs in Edinburgh, but these musicians tend to appear sporadically. It's best to read notices in pubs and talk to the tourist office to see where the ceilidhs will be on the night of your visit.

Moments A Wee Dram for Fans of Malt Whisky

It requires a bit of an effort to reach it (take bus no. 10A, 16, or 17 from Princes St. to Leith), but for fans of malt whisky, the **Scotch Malt Whisky Society** has been called "The Top of the Whisky Pyramid" by distillery-industry magazines in Britain. It's on the second floor of a 16th-century warehouse at 87 Giles St., Leith (© **0131/554-3451**) that was originally designed to store bordeaux and port wines from France and Portugal. All you can order are single-malt whiskies, served neat, usually in a dram (unless you want yours watered down with branch water), and selected from a staggering choice of whiskies from more than 100 Scottish distilleries. Hours are Monday and Tuesday 10am to 5pm, Thursday to Saturday 10am to 11pm, and Sunday 11am to 10pm.

Some hotels regularly feature traditional Scottish music in the evenings. You might check with the **George Hotel,** 19–21 George St. (© **0131/225-1251;** bus: 3, 31, or 33). **Jamie's Scottish Evening** is presented daily at the King James Hotel on Leith Street (© **0131/556-0111;** bus: 7 or 14) Tuesday to Sunday at 7pm, costing £50 ($94) for a four-course dinner, wine, and show.

THE CLUB & MUSIC SCENE

The Cavendish   This isn't necessarily where you go to hear the next Oasis or Blur, but who knows? A rock legend might be born here any Friday or Saturday, when bands take the stage. The bar is open Wednesday to Sunday from 10pm to 3am. *Note:* No tennis shoes or jeans allowed. 3 W. Tollcross. © 0131/228-3252. Cover £8 ($15) Fri–Sat. Bus: 11, 15, or 23.

Club Mercado   The glamorous Club Mercado, once the headquarters of the Scottish branch of British Rail, hangs suspended over the rail tracks behind the city's main station. On Friday, the action kicks off with no-cover TFIS, which stands for a somewhat saltier version of "Thank God It's Friday"; it runs from 5 to 10pm and caters to youngish workers who indulge in cut-price drinks. Other special nights are alternate-Saturday Viva (eclectic music attracting all sorts from toughs to drag queens) and Eye Candy (basically a rave featuring the latest house music). Open daily from 10:30pm to 3am. 36–39 Market St. © 0131/226-4224. Cover £4–£12 ($7.60–$23), depending on what's on. Bus: 1.

Opal Lounge ★★   After the sun goes down, head for this chic rendezvous which for a while became the stamping ground of Prince William when he visited Edinburgh while attending St. Andrew's University. The handsome heir to the British throne set female and gay male hearts fluttering when he walked in the door. Attracting a young and affluent crowd in their 20s and 30s, the bar boasts one of the longest cocktail lists in town, priced from £4 to £9 ($7.60–$17). This is an underground retreat with many hidden nooks, plus a dance floor. You can order "small plates" here, including chile-flavored prawns, tuna sashimi, and other Asian-style fast food. Open Sunday to Friday 5pm to 3am, Saturday noon to 3am. 51A George St. © 0131/226-2275. Bus: 13, 19, or 41.

Po Na Na   Po Na Na is the Edinburgh branch of the most successful chain of clubs in Britain. The theme is a Moroccan casbah, thanks to wall mosaics, brass lanterns, and artifacts shipped in from Marrakech. You dance to a mix of house and funk in the cellar of a transformed 19th-century building, beneath a tented ceiling illuminated with strobes. Po Na Na isn't specifically gay, but does draw a strong gay following. Open daily from 8pm to 3am. 26 Frederick St. ✆ **0131/226-2224.** Cover £3–£5 ($5.70–$9.50). Bus: 80.

Revolution Popular with an under-25 crowd, this is Edinburgh's largest club, with a capacity of 1,500. Mainstream dance music (plus five bars) attracts the crowds, and there are theme and student nights as well. Open Wednesday to Sunday 10:30pm to 2am. 31 Lothian Rd. ✆ **0131/229-7670.** Cover £4–£10 ($7.60–$19). Bus: 11 or 15.

The Venue Behind the main post office and Waverley Station is The Venue, the principal stage for live music. Some of the biggest bands in the United Kingdom perform here. 15–17 Calton Rd. ✆ **0131/557-3073.** Bus: 26.

Whynot In the basement of the Dome Bar & Grill (see "Where to Dine," earlier in this chapter), Whynot is a hot entertainment complex that opened in the former Bank of Scotland building. It has low ceilings with veil-like curtains above the dance floor and lots of seating coves tucked away for privacy. The club swings Thursday to Sunday 10pm to 3am. On Thursday, there's dancing to the music of the 1960s, 1970s, and 1980s; Friday features mainstream pop; and Saturday brings the best in contemporary dance music. 14 George St. ✆ **0131/624-8633.** Cover £8–£10 ($15–$19). Bus: 41 or 42.

PUBS & BARS

The Abbotsford Near the eastern end of Rose Street, a short walk from Princes Street, The Abbotsford has served stiff drinks and oceans of beer since 1887. The gaslight era is alive here, thanks to a careful preservation of the original dark paneling, battered tables, and ornate plaster ceiling. The beers on tap change about once a week, supplementing the roster of single malts. Drinks are served Monday to Saturday 11am to 11pm. Platters of food are dispensed from the bar Monday to Saturday noon to 3pm and 5:30 to 10pm. 3–5 Rose St. ✆ **0131/225-5276.** Bus: 3, 31, or 33.

Bow Bar Near Edinburgh Castle, the Victorian Bow Bar is arranged around a series of tall beer pulls, antique phonographs, pendulum clocks, and as many as 140 single-malt whiskies from virtually every corner of the country. The only food offerings are simple snacks like steak or minced pie. Open Monday to Saturday noon to 11:30pm and Sunday 12:30 to 11pm. 80 West Bow. ✆ **0131/226-7667.** Bus: 2 or 12.

Café Royal Circle Bar ⨍ This is Edinburgh's most famous pub. One part is now occupied by the Oyster Bar of the Café Royal, but life in the Circle Bar continues as usual, with the opulent trappings of the Victorian era. Hours for the bar are Monday to Wednesday 11am to 11pm, Thursday 11am to midnight, Friday and Saturday 11am to 1am, and Sunday 12:30 to 11pm. The restaurant is open Sunday to Wednesday noon to 2pm and 7 to 10pm (also Thurs until midnight, Fri–Sat until 1am). 19 W. Register St. ✆ **0131/556-1884.** Bus: 3, 31, or 33.

Deacon Brodie's Tavern ⨍ Opened in 1806, Deacon Brodie's is the neighborhood pub along the Royal Mile. It perpetuates the memory of Deacon Brodie, good citizen by day and robber by night. The tavern and wine cellars offer a traditional pub setting and lots of atmosphere. The tavern is open Sunday to Thursday 10am to midnight and Friday and Saturday 10am to 12:30am. Light meals are served in the bar from 10am to 10pm; in the restaurant upstairs, more substantial food is served from noon to 10pm. 435 Lawnmarket. ✆ **0131/225-6531.** Bus: 1.

Guildford Arms   This place got a face-lift back to the mauve era of the 1890s, although a pub has stood here for 200 years. The Victorian Italianesque pub has seven arched windows with etched glass and an ornate ceiling. It's large, bustling, and at times a bit rough, but has plenty of character. Upstairs is a fish-and-chips shop run by the same company. At festival time, folk music is presented nightly. Open Monday to Thursday 11am to 11pm, Friday and Saturday 11am to midnight, and Sunday 12:30 to 11pm. 1 W. Register St. ✆ **0131/556-4312.** Bus: 3, 31, or 33.

GAY BARS & CLUBS

The heart of the gay community is centered on **Broughton Street** around the Playhouse Theatre (take bus no. 8, 9, or 19). Be sure to check "The Club & Music Scene" (see above) for the heavily gay crowd at **Po Na Na.**

C. C. Bloom's   Named after Bette Midler's character in *Beaches,* C. C. Bloom's is one of Edinburgh's most popular gay spots. The upstairs bar offers drinks and camaraderie; on Thursday and Sunday at 11pm, there's karaoke, and Sunday afternoons heat up with a male stripper. The downstairs club offers dancing to a wide range of music, with no cover. Open Monday to Saturday 6pm to 3am and Sunday 3pm to 3am. 23–24 Greenside Place. ✆ **0131/556-9331.**

Next door is **Habana,** 22 Greenside Place (✆ **0131/556-4349**), drawing a mixed gay crowd daily from noon to 1am.

New Town Bar   Adjacent to the corner of Queen Street is the New Town Bar, a street-level pub where everyday blokes clad in everything from jeans to suits gather for a pint of lager. It's open daily from noon to 2am. If you're looking for something a bit less conventional, and it happens to be Wednesday to Sunday between 10pm and 2am, head into the basement for the **Intense Cruise Bar,** where the crowd dons its own interpretations of Tom of Finland combat gear, leather, and uniforms. Depending on the crowd, this can be intense, amusing, or both. 26B Dublin St. ✆ **0131/538-7775.**

Planet Out   This place hosts a mixed crowd, but attracts more women than most gay bars. It describes itself as a friendly and unpretentious neighborhood bar where you're likely to run into your favorite gay uncle or aunt and share a bit of family gossip, and then meet either the love of your life or a decent building contractor. There's an occasional drag night. Open Monday to Friday 4pm to 1am and Saturday and Sunday 12:30pm to 1am. 6 Baxters Place. ✆ **0131/524-0061.**

10 Side Trips from Edinburgh: The Best of the Lothian Region

Armed with a good map, you can explore the major attractions of the countryside south of the Firth of Forth in just a day. Most attractions are no more than an hour's drive from the city. The highlights are **Hopetoun House** of Robert Adam fame and the impressive ruins of **Linlithgow Palace,** birthplace of Mary Queen of Scots in 1542.

One of the best day trips from the Scottish capital is to the ancient town of **Dunfermline,** north of Edinburgh. It can easily be visited in a day, which also gives you time to see its famous abbey and palace as well as the Andrew Carnegie Birthplace Museum. See chapter 9 for details.

LINLITHGOW & ITS PALACE

In 1542, Mary Queen of Scots was born in the royal burgh of Linlithgow, in West Lothian, 29km (18 miles) west of Edinburgh. You can visit the site of her birth, Linlithgow

Palace. Buses and trains depart daily from Edinburgh for the 20- to 25-minute ride, which costs £10 ($19) round-trip. If you're driving from central Edinburgh, follow A8 toward Glasgow and then merge with M9, following the signs to Linlithgow.

Linlithgow Palace 𝒜   Birthplace of Mary Queen of Scots, this was once a favorite residence of Scottish kings and is now one of the country's most poignant ruins. Although the palace is roofless, its pink-ocher walls climb five floors and are supported on the lower edge by flying buttresses. It's most dramatic and evocative when floodlit at night. Many of the former royal rooms are still remarkably preserved, so you get a clear idea of how grand it used to be. In one of the tragic events associated with Scottish sovereignty, the palace burned to the ground in 1746, along with many of the hopes and dreams of Scottish independence. A small display in the first floor Great Hall shows some of the more interesting architectural relics.

On A706, on the south shore of Linlithgow Loch, 1km (½ mile) from Linlithgow Station. ℂ **01506/842-896.** Admission £5 ($9.50) adults, £4 ($7.60) seniors, £2.50 ($4.75) children. Apr–Sept daily 9:30am–5:30pm; Oct–Mar Mon–Sat 9:30am–4:30pm, Sun 2:30–4:30pm.

St. Michael's Parish Church   South of the palace stands the medieval kirk of St. Michael the Archangel, site of worship of many a Scottish monarch since its consecration in 1242. Despite being ravaged by the disciples of John Knox (who then chided his followers for their "excesses") and transformed into a stable by Cromwell, this remains one of Scotland's best examples of a parish church.

Adjacent to Linlithgow Palace. ℂ **01506/842-188.** Free admission. Apr–Sept daily 10am–4:30pm; Oct–Mar Mon–Fri 10am–3pm.

Hopetoun House 𝒜   Set amid beautifully landscaped grounds, à la Versailles, Hopetoun is Scotland's greatest Robert Adam mansion and a fine example of 18th-century architecture (note its resemblance to Buckingham Palace). Seven bays extend across the slightly recessed center, and the classical style includes a complicated tympanum, as well as hood molds, quoins, and straight-headed windows. A rooftop balustrade with urns completes the ensemble. You can wander through splendid reception rooms, filled with 18th-century furniture, paintings, statuary, and other artwork, and check out the panoramic view of the Firth of Forth from the roof. After touring the house, take the nature trail, explore the deer parks, see the Stables Museum, or stroll through the formal gardens. Refreshments are available near the Ballroom Suite.

3km (2 miles) from the Forth Road Bridge near South Queensferry, 16km (10 miles) from Edinburgh off A904. ℂ **0131/331-2451.** Admission £8 ($15) adults, £7 ($13) seniors, £4.25 ($8.10) children, £22 ($42) families of up to 6. Apr 9–Sept 26 Mon–Sun 10am–5:30pm (last admission 4:30pm). Closed Sept 27–Apr 8.

WHERE TO DINE

Champany Inn 𝒜𝒜 SCOTTISH   You'll find the best steaks in Britain in this converted farmhouse. Owner Clive Davidson is an expert on beef and insists his steaks be 3 centimeters (1¼ in.) thick; his meat is hung for at least 4 weeks, adding greatly to its flavor. He also prepares an assortment of oysters, salmon, and lobsters kept in a pool on the premises. Next to the main dining room is a chophouse that has less-expensive options; you can choose your own cut and watch it being grilled. The wine list has won an award for excellence from *Wine Spectator*.

The inn also rents 16 handsomely furnished guest rooms, each with TV, minibar, hair dryer, and phone. The rate of £135 ($257) for a double includes a full breakfast.

Side Trips from Edinburgh

Map legend:

- Andrew Carnegie Birthplace Museum **2**
- *Britannia* **6**
- Deep Sea World **3**
- Dirleton Castle **10**
- Dumferline Abbey & Palace **1**
- Hopetoun House **4**
- Linlithgow Palace **5**
- Muirfield Golf Course **9**
- Newhailes **7**
- Rosslyn Chapel **8**
- St. Michael's Parish Church **5**
- Tantallon Castle **11**

127

Champany Corner, Linlithgow. Take M9 until junction 3, then A904 until you reach the restaurant. ℂ **01506/834-532.** Fax 01506/834302. www.champany.com. Reservations required. Main courses £22–£50 ($42–$95); fixed-price lunch £19 ($36). AE, DC, MC, V. Mon–Fri noon–2pm and 6:30–10pm. Closed Jan 1–2 and Dec 25.

Livingston's ☆ MODERN SCOTTISH/FRENCH   Chef Julian Wright reigns supreme in this cottagelike restaurant of converted stables with sandstone walls and Black Watch tartan carpets. A conservatory overlooks a neat little garden, and candle-light makes the atmosphere warm and romantic. The chef is inventive and imaginatively uses quality ingredients. The saddle of venison is the most requested dish, and rightly so. It comes in a cassis sauce with glazed shallots and a cassoulet of lentils. Pigeon pie and brambles often appear on the menu, as does a risotto of wild mushrooms and truffles made all the more delectable by a shaving of Parmesan. Elegant dessert selections may feature a chilled soup of strawberries and champagne accompanied by a chocolate mousse. There is an ample wine list, including bottles from California.

52 High St. (opposite the post office), Linlithgow. ℂ **01506/846-565.** Reservations recommended. Fixed-price 2-course lunch £15 ($29), 3-course lunch £18 ($34); fixed-price dinner £30 ($57) for 2 courses, £35 ($67) for 3 courses. MC, V. Tues–Sat noon–2pm and 6–9pm. Closed first 2 weeks in Jan.

NORTH BERWICK

This royal burgh dating from the 14th century is an upmarket holiday resort, drawing visitors to its golf courses, beaches, and harbor on the Firth of Forth. Located in East Lothian, 39km (24 miles) east of Edinburgh, the town is on a direct rail line from the capital; the trip takes 30 minutes. There's also bus service from Edinburgh, taking 1¼ hours. Both cost £3 ($5.70) one-way. If you're driving, take A1 in the direction marked THE SOUTH and DUNBAR; then turn onto A198, following the signs to North Berwick.

At the **tourist office,** Quality Street (ℂ **01620/892-197**), you can get information on boat trips to the offshore islands, including **Bass Rock,** a breeding ground for about 10,000 gannets. The gannets return from Africa in the spring, usually around April, to nest here until fall. It's possible to see the rock from the harbor, but the view-ing is even better at **Berwick Law,** a volcanic lookout point.

Some 3km (2 miles) east of North Berwick and 40km (25 miles) east of Edinburgh on A198 stand the ruins of the 14th-century diked and rose-colored **Tantallon Cas-tle** (ℂ **01620/892-727**). This was the ancient stronghold of the Douglases until their defeat by Cromwell's forces in 1651. Overlooking the Firth of Forth, the ruins are still formidable, with a square five-story central tower and a dovecote, plus the shell of its east tower. It's open April to September, daily 9:30am to 5:30pm; and October to March, Saturday to Wednesday 9:30am to 4:30pm. Admission is £4.50 ($8.55) for adults, £3.50 ($6.65) for seniors, £2.25 ($4.30) for children.

WHERE TO STAY & DINE

The Glebe House   This dignified 1780 home belongs to Gwen and Jake Scott, who have worked hard to preserve its original character as the residence of the pastor for the nearby Presbyterian Church. Glebe House is near many golf courses and is just a minute's walk south of the town's main street, near the edge of the sea. Each cozy guest room boasts part of Mrs. Scott's collection of hand-painted porcelain, artfully arranged on tabletops, in wall niches, and on hanging shelves. (She'll point out the various manufacturers, which include Quimper, Rouen, and Staffordshire.) Views include 1.6 hectares (4 acres) of field, garden, and horse paddock. The breakfasts are served in a formal, high-ceilinged dining room.

4 Law Rd., North Berwick, East Lothian EH39 4PL. ℂ/fax **01620/892-608**. www.aboutscotland.com/glebe/house.html. 4 units, 3 with private bathroom. £70–£90 ($133–$171) double. Rates include breakfast. No credit cards. *In room:* TV, coffeemaker, hair dryer.

The Marine   This turreted Victorian commands panoramic views across the West Links Course, some of whose putting greens are near the hotel's foundations. It's a home for players such as Tiger Woods, Phil Mickelson, and Chris DiMarco during the Open, and it's close to almost 20 golf courses. The hotel feels like an elegant country house. Although its guest rooms vary in size, all are clean and comfortable. The bar is lined with antique golf photos. The dining room is open to nonguests and serves the best food in town: international cuisine, with many Scottish specialties.

18 Cromwell Rd., North Berwick, East Lothian EH39 4LZ. ℂ **800/225-5843** in the U.S., or 0870/400-8129. Fax 01620/894-480. www.macdonaldhotels.co.uk. 83 units. £125–£210 ($238–$399) double; £180–£315 ($342–$599) suite. AE, DC, MC, V. **Amenities:** Restaurant; bar; outdoor heated pool; tennis court; sauna; room service; laundry service; nonsmoking rooms. *In room:* TV, coffeemaker, hair dryer, iron.

GULLANE & THE MUIRFIELD GOLF COURSE

Lying 31km (19 miles) east of Edinburgh in East Lothian, Gullane, with a population of around 2,000, is an upscale resort with a fine sandy beach and one of Scotland's great country hotels. There's no rail service into Gullane. Buses, including nos. 124 and 125, depart from the St. Andrews Square station in Edinburgh (ℂ **0800/505-050** for information). They take 20 to 25 minutes and cost £3 ($5.70) each way. If you're driving, take A1 in the direction marked THE SOUTH and DUNBAR; then turn onto A198 and follow the signs to Gullane.

On the western edge of the village, **Gullane Hill** is a nature reserve and bird sanctuary, where some 200 species of birds have been spotted. You cross a small wood footbridge from the car park to enter the reserve.

What really puts Gullane on the tourist map, besides its fine dining and accommodations, is the 1891 **Muirfield Golf Course** (ℂ **01620/842-123**), ranked 6th among the world's 100 greatest golf courses by the editors of *GolfWeb*. Developed from a boggy piece of low-lying links, Muirfield has hosted 10 Open Championships, and is a par-70, 6,801-yard course. A round costs £120 to £150 ($228–$285). Nonmembers can play on Tuesday and Thursday.

WHERE TO STAY & DINE

Greywalls Hotel 𝄐𝄐   This is an elegant, exclusive retreat. The Edwardian country house was designed in 1901 as a private home by the most renowned architect of his day, Sir Edwin Lutyens. It was visited from time to time by Edward VII, who admired the views across the Firth of Forth and south to the Lammermuir Hills. The gardens were laid out by one of England's most respected landscape architects, Gertrude Jekyll. In the paneled library, guests relax on comfortable sofas before a blazing log fire. The guest rooms vary in size; some smaller ones are simply decorated, while the more spacious units are furnished with period pieces. Each comes with a beautifully kept bathroom. The light French-style dishes served in the elegant dining room are almost as appealing to the eye as to the palate; specialties include fresh seafood.

Muirfield, Duncur Rd., Gullane, East Lothian EH31 2EG. ℂ **01620/842-144.** Fax 01620/842-241. www. greywalls.co.uk. 23 units. £240–£300 ($456–$570) double. Rates include Scottish breakfast. AE, DC, MC, V. Closed Oct 15–Apr 15. Follow the signs from A198 about 8km (5 miles) from North Berwick. **Amenities:** Restaurant; bar; putting green; 2 tennis courts; room service; babysitting; laundry service; nonsmoking rooms. *In room:* TV, hair dryer.

La Potinière ⭑⭑ MODERN BRITISH This cozy dining room in the center of the village, the recipient of a Michelin star, has been taken over by Keith Marley and Mary Runciman. Not only do they maintain the high standards of the past, but their kitchen is even better than in old days. The restaurant serves sublime food made from the freshest and finest ingredients. The menu is seasonally adjusted, and only set menus are offered.

Our lunch began with pea-and-mint soup and a warm Parmesan custard, followed by grilled lemon sole served with smoked salmon. It was finished off with a raspberry and strawberry crème brûlée. Other culinary delights likely to be enjoyed at dinner include a duck, foie gras, and Armagnac parfait with a rhubarb and cinnamon compote. Our favorite dessert here is a trilogy of apple: caramelized apple and vanilla crème brûlée with apple juice, apple sorbet, and, yes, a plain apple.

Main St. ℂ 01620/843-214. Reservations required. Set dinner £37 ($70); fixed-price lunch £17 ($32) for 2 courses, £19 ($36) for 3 courses. MC, V. Wed–Fri and Sun 12:30–2pm; Wed–Sat 7–9pm.

DIRLETON ⭑⭑: THE PRETTIEST VILLAGE IN SCOTLAND

Midway between North Berwick and Gullane is Dirleton, often cited as the prettiest village in Scotland (and it is indeed a contender). The town was drafted in the early 16th century, and remains little changed today. It's picture perfect, not like a real town at all, but one that appears to have been created for a movie set. Since the main A198 bypasses the village, there is little traffic. The village green is the hub of local life. In the center is a ghostly castle abandoned by its residents in 1663. Even the rail station is closed; the last train passed through in 1954. The biggest news occurred in the 1940s, when President Roosevelt and Sir Winston Churchill met in Dirleton to plan D-day landings.

It's on the Edinburgh–North Berwick road (A198); North Berwick is 8km (5 miles) east and Edinburgh 31km (19 miles) west. There's no train service. Buses, including nos. 124 and 125, depart from the St. Andrews Square station in Edinburgh (ℂ 0800/505-050 for information). The trip takes 25 minutes and costs £3 ($5.70) one-way. If you're driving, take A1 in the direction marked THE SOUTH and DUNBAR; then turn onto A198 and follow the signs to Dirleton.

Dirleton Castle ⭑ A rose-tinted 13th-century castle with surrounding gardens, Dirleton Castle looks like a fairy-tale fortification, with towers, arched entries, and an oak ramp similar to the drawbridge that used to protect it. Reputed to have been fully sacked by Cromwell in 1650, the building was in fact only partially destroyed by him and was further torn down by the Nesbitt family, who, after building nearby Archiefield House, wanted a romantic ruin on their land. You can see the remains of the Great Hall and kitchen, as well as what's left of the lord's chamber: windows and window seats, a wall with a toilet and drains, and other household features. The 16th-century main gate has a hole through which boiling tar or water was poured to discourage unwanted visitors. The castle's country garden and a bowling green are still in use.

Dirleton, East Lothian. ℂ 01620/850-330. Admission £4.50 ($8.55) adults, £3.50 ($6.65) seniors, £2.25 ($4.30) children. Apr–Sept daily 9:30am–5:30pm; Oct–Mar Mon–Sat 9:30am–4:30pm, Sun 2:30–4:30pm.

WHERE TO STAY & DINE

Castle Inn Opposite the village green and the castle, and unspoiled by modernization, this is a most satisfactory inn, with 10 dormer windows and a pair of entrances. The small guest rooms are pleasant and comfortably furnished. The most desirable units are in the main house, with smaller and more modestly furnished rooms in an adjoining modern annex (all with shower-only bathrooms). Guests are welcome in a lounge with rugged stone walls and a free-standing stone fireplace where, during the day, light snacks are served.

Off A198, Dirleton, East Lothian EH39 5EP. ✆ 01620/850-221. infocastleinn@aol.com. 8 units. £30–£60 ($57–$114) double. MC, V. Pet friendly. **Amenities:** Restaurant; 2 bars; babysitting; nonsmoking rooms. *In room:* Coffeemaker, hair dryer.

Open Arms The Open Arms will receive you with you know what. This old stone hostelry, off A198 overlooking the castle ruins, has been transformed into a handsome hotel that serves the finest food in the area. The average-size guest units come with small tub/shower bathrooms. Log fires crackle and blaze, and golfers will find 20 courses within a 32km (20-mile) radius. The owners have built a local reputation for serving Scottish dishes using regional venison, beef, lamb, and freshly caught salmon. The whiskies used in the sauces are of the region, too.

Main St., Dirleton, East Lothian EH39 5EG. ✆ 01620/850-241. Fax 01620/850-570. www.openarmshotel.com. 10 units. £100–£140 ($190–$266) double. Rates include Scottish breakfast. MC, V. Free parking. Pet friendly. **Amenities:** 2 restaurants; bar; room service; babysitting; laundry service. *In room:* TV, coffeemaker, hair dryer.

INTO THE DEEP AT DEEP SEA WORLD

Although it's in the Fife region, another popular day trip from Edinburgh is to Deep Sea World. From central Edinburgh, drive 19km (12 miles) west, following the signs to Inverkeithing and the Forth Road Bridge. By train, go to either the Waverley or the Haymarket stations in Edinburgh and take any train stopping at North Queensferry (departing at 35-min. intervals); from the North Queensferry station, follow the signs to Deep Sea World, about a 10-minute walk. Round-trip fare is £10 to £12 ($19–$23).

Deep Sea World ✦ *Kids* In the early 1990s, a group of entrepreneurs flooded a quarry with a million gallons of seawater, stocked it with a menagerie of water-dwelling creatures, and opened it as Scotland's most comprehensive aquarium. You walk through underwater microclimates featuring views of a kelp forest; sandy flats that shelter bottom-dwelling schools of stingray, turbot, and sole; murky caves favored by conger eels and small sharks; and a scary trench whose sponge-encrusted bottom careens abruptly away from view. Schools of shark and battalions of as many as 5,000 fish stare back at you. On the premises are a cafe, a gift shop, and an audiovisual show. Allow at least 90 minutes for your visit, and try to avoid the weekend crowds.

North Queensferry, in Fife. ✆ 01383/411-880. Admission £10 ($19) adults, £7.50 ($14) students, £7 ($13) children 3–15, £33 ($63) per family. Mon–Fri 10am–5pm; Sat–Sun 11am–6pm.

ROSLIN

The town of Roslin lies 9.6 km (6 miles) south of Edinburgh's Princes Street and can be reached by bus nos. 15A and 62. The town's Biocenter (not open to the public) became world famous when "Dolly," a sheep, was cloned here.

But mainly, Roslin is visited by those wishing to see **Rosslyn Chapel** ✦✦✦ (note the different spelling). One of the alleged sites of the Holy Grail, the chapel played a pivotal role in Dan Brown's international bestseller, *The Da Vinci Code.* Sir William St. Clair founded the chapel in 1446, and it's been the subject of legend and lore ever since. Although never finished, the chapel is famous for having every corner and cornice adorned with elaborate stonework, depicting almost anything, certainly devils, dragons, animals, knights, and their ladies fair. Its most celebrated work is the Apprentice

Pillar. The chapel (© **0131/440-2159;** www.rosslyn-chapel.com) is open April to September Monday to Saturday 9:30am to 6pm, Sunday noon to 4:45pm; October to March Monday to Saturday 9:30am to 5pm, Sunday noon to 4:45pm. Admission is £7 ($13) for adults, £6 ($11) for students and seniors. Children under 17 enter free.

NEWHAILES

On the outskirts of Edinburgh, **Newhailes** ⭑, Newhailes Rd., Musselburgh in East Lothian (© **0131/653-5599**), is an impressive late-17th-century mansion that lay dormant for years, a remarkable Palladian villa with views of the Firth of Forth. Presented to the National Trust of Scotland, it has been restored and is now open to the public. Much of it has survived intact, including a 7,000-volume library hailed by Samuel Johnson as "the most learned room in Europe." Often called "The Sleeping Beauty," the house is ornately decorated, including rich furnishings, gilding, antique wallpaper, damask, and needlepoint. Why has Newhailes remained much as it used to be? A National Trust official said the reason's simple—"nobody in this house earned a penny after 1790 and subsequent owners couldn't afford to change anything." Newhailes is open April to September Thursday to Monday noon to 5pm. Tours of the house take 1 hour, and admission is £10 ($19) for adults, £7 ($13) for students and children. Children under 5 go free. From the center of Edinburgh, take bus no. 40. The location is 6.4km (4 miles) to the east of Edinburgh.

6

The Borders & Galloway Regions

The romantic castle ruins and skeletons of Gothic abbeys in the **Borders** region stand as reminders of the battles that once raged between England and Scotland. For a long time, the "Border Country" was a no-man's land of plunder and destruction, lying south of the line of the Moorfoot, Pentland, and Lammermuir hill ranges, and east of the Annandale Valley and the upper valley of the River Tweed.

The Borders is the land of Sir Walter Scott, master of romantic adventure, who topped the bestseller list in the early 19th century. The remains of four great mid-12th-century abbeys are here: Dryburgh (where Scott is buried), Melrose, Jedburgh, and Kelso. And because of its abundant sheep-grazing land, the Borders is the home of the cashmere sweater and the tweed suit. Ask at the tourist office for a *Borders Woollen Trail* brochure, detailing where you can visit woolen mills, shops, and museums and follow the weaving process from start to finish.

Southwest of the Borders is the often-overlooked **Galloway** region (also known as Dumfries and Galloway), a land of unspoiled countryside, fishing harbors, and romantic ruins. Major centers to visit are the ancient city of Dumfries, perhaps the best base for touring Galloway, and the artists' colony of Kirkcudbright, an ancient burgh filled with color-washed houses. In the far west, Stranraer is a major terminal for those making the 56km (35-mile) ferry crossing into Northern

Ireland. Among the major sights are Sweetheart Abbey, outside Dumfries, and the Burns Mausoleum at Dumfries. If you have time, explore Threave Garden, outside Castle Douglas.

Edinburgh Airport is about 64km (40 miles) northwest of Selkirk in the Borders, and **Glasgow Airport** is about 121km (75 miles) north of Dumfries in the Galloway region. Trains from Glasgow run south along the coast, toward Stranraer, stopping along the way at Ayr and Girvan. Another rail line from Glasgow extends south to Dumfries, depositing and picking up passengers before crossing the border en route to the English city of Carlisle. In contrast, southbound trains from Edinburgh almost always bypass most of the Borders towns, making direct transits to Berwick, England. Consequently, to reach most of the Borders towns covered here, you'll probably rely on a rental car or on bus service from Edinburgh or Berwick to reach Peebles, Selkirk, Melrose, and Kelso. For train information and schedules, call **National Rail Enquiries** (*©* **08457/484-950**).

Trains from London's King's Cross Station to Edinburgh's Waverley Station make their first stop in Scotland at Berwick-upon-Tweed; travel time is 6 hours. From Berwick, a network of buses runs among the villages and towns. Three rail lines pass through the region from London's Euston Station en route to Glasgow. Dumfries or Stranraer is the best center if you're traveling by rail in the Uplands. Bus travel isn't recommended for reaching the region, but once you get here, you'll find it a reliable means of public transportation.

1 Jedburgh: Gateway to the Borders ★

77km (48 miles) SE of Edinburgh, 92km (57 miles) N of Newcastle-upon-Tyne, 21km (13 miles) S of Melrose

The little town of Jedburgh, divided by the River Jed, developed around Jedburgh Abbey on a Roman road called Dere Street. Today the market town gives little hint of its turbulent early history as home for royalty in the beleaguered Borders area.

If you have limited time to spend in the region, note that Jedburgh is a typical Borders town and makes a good base: It not only boasts some of the most impressive and evocative abbey ruins around, but it's also the home of a fortified town house once inhabited by Mary Queen of Scots. In its environs you can enjoy some of the area's loveliest walks and excursions.

ESSENTIALS

GETTING THERE   There's no direct rail link to Jedburgh. The nearest **rail station** is at Berwick-upon-Tweed (✆ **08457/484-950** for information and tickets), from which you must take two buses (see below). Depending on the day's schedule, it's sometimes more practical to take a train to Newcastle-upon-Tyne (England), and from there take a bus to Jedburgh (see below).

There are daily **buses** from Edinburgh; a 9:15am bus arrives in Jedburgh at 10:55am and costs £8 ($15) one-way or £13 ($25) round-trip. Call ✆ **08705/808-080** for schedules. From England, take the train to Berwick and then the bus (a 75-min. trip) from Berwick to Kelso. In Kelso, transfer to another bus (six to eight per day) that continues to Jedburgh, a 25-minute ride. One-way fares are £4 ($7.60). For information, call the Jedburgh tourist office (which has all the schedules) or the Kelso bus station (✆ **01573/224-141**). Two buses a day run from Newcastle-upon-Tyne to Jedburgh, taking 90 minutes and charging £11 to £13 ($21–$25) one-way.

If you're **driving,** at Corbridge (England), continue north into Scotland along A68, using Jedburgh as your gateway into the Borders. From Edinburgh, take A7 and then A68, following the signs to Jedburgh. From the center of Edinburgh, expect a driving time of around 75 minutes.

VISITOR INFORMATION   The **Jedburgh Visitor Centre** (✆ **01835/863-435**) is at Murray's Green, near the police station, adjacent to the spot where buses pull in, behind the Town Hall, and very close to the famous abbey. It's open March 24 to October 31 daily 10am to 5pm.

SEEING THE SIGHTS

Castle Gaol   This museum stands on the site of Jedburgh Castle, a 12th-century royal residence and—because the ancient Jed Forest once surrounded the area—the scene of many a hunting party. The castle was torn down in the 15th century to keep it from falling under English control. In the 1820s, a Georgian prison was built in its place and became the most modern in the country; its cells even had central heating, a far cry from the typical dungeon prisons of the day.

Castlegate. ✆ 01835/864-750. Admission £2 ($3.80) adults, £1.50 ($2.85) seniors and students, free for children. Easter–Oct Mon–Sat 10am–4pm, Sun 1–4pm. Closed Nov–Easter.

Jedburgh Abbey ★★   This famous ruined abbey, founded by David I in 1138, is one of Scotland's finest. Under the Augustinian canons from Beauvais, France, it

The Borders & Galloway Regions

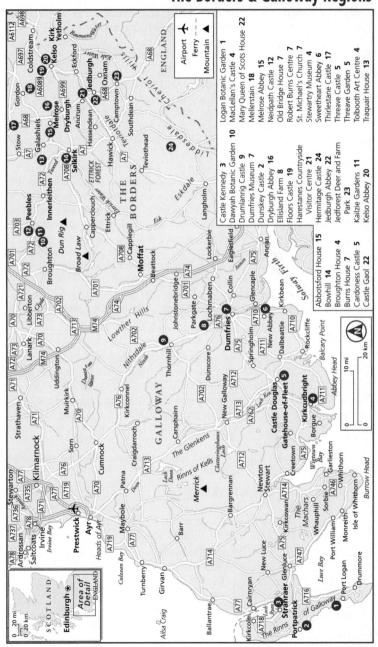

Airport ✈
Ferry --- ■
Mountain ▲

Logan Botanic Garden **1**
MacLellan's Castle **4**
Mary Queen of Scots House **22**
Mellerstain **18**
Melrose Abbey **15**
Neidpath Castle **12**
Old Bridge House **7**
Robert Burns Centre **7**
St. Michael's Church **7**
Stewartry Museum **6**
Sweetheart Abbey **17**
Thirlestane Castle **17**
Threave Castle **5**
Threave Garden **5**
Tolbooth Art Centre **4**
Traquair House **13**

Castle Kennedy **3**
Dawyck Botanic Garden **10**
Drumlanrig Castle **9**
Dumfries Museum **7**
Dunskey Castle **2**
Dryburgh Abbey **16**
Ellisland Farm **8**
Floors Castle **19**
Harestanes Countryside Visitor Centre **21**
Hermitage Castle **24**
Jedburgh Abbey **22**
Jedforest Deer and Farm Park **23**
Kailzie Gardens **11**
Kelso Abbey **20**

Abbotsford House **15**
Bowhill **14**
Broughton House **4**
Burns House **7**
Cardoness Castle **5**
Castle Gaol **22**

achieved abbey status in 1152 (when enough of its infrastructure was complete to allow a formal endorsement by the Augustinian hierarchies in Rome), and went on to witness much royal pageantry, like the coronation of the founder's grandson, Malcolm IV (1153–65), and the marriage of Alexander III (1249–86) to his second wife, Yolande de Dreux.

The abbey was sacked by the English in 1544 and 1545 during the frequent wars that ravaged the villages along the Scotland-England border. Its roof was burned, allowing rains to penetrate and further destroy much of the interior detailing. After 1560, the ascendancy of the straitlaced Church of Scotland acted as a disincentive for rebuilding any grand-scale "papist monuments," so no efforts were made to repair the abbey.

For about 300 years, a small section of the abbey was the town's parish church, but in 1875 other premises were found for day-to-day worship. Then teams of architects set to work restoring the place to its original medieval design. The abbey is still roofless but otherwise fairly complete, with most of its exterior stonework still in place. You can view the late-12th-century west front; three pedimented gables remain at the doorway; and the solid buttresses and rounded arches in the Norman style are relatively intact. You can also walk through the nave and the ruins of the former cloister. In a century-old outbuilding is the **Jedburgh Abbey Visitor Centre,** Abbey Place (© **01835/863-925**), open the same hours as the abbey.

Abbey Place. © **01835/863-925**. Admission £5 ($9.50) adults, £4 ($7.60) seniors, £2.50 ($4.75) children under 16. Apr–Sept daily 9:30am–5:30pm; Oct–Mar daily 9:30am–4:30pm. Last entrance 30 min. before closing.

Mary Queen of Scots House ⓡ   Here, in 1566, Mary Stuart spent 6 weeks and almost died of a mysterious ailment after a tiring 64km (40-mile) return ride from a visit to her wounded beloved, the earl of Bothwell, at Hermitage Castle (see "Exploring the Countryside," below). In a later lament, commenting on the emotional agonies of the last 20 years of her life, she wrote, "Would that I had died at Jedburgh." The house, in the center of High Street, contains paintings, engravings, and articles dealing with Mary's life. Ancient pear trees still stand on the grounds, a reminder of the days when Jedburgh was famous for its fruit. "Jethard pears" were once hawked in the streets of London.

Queen St. © **01835/863-331**. Admission £3 ($5.70) adults, £2 ($3.80) seniors and children. Mar–Nov Mon–Sat 10am–4:30pm, Sun 11am–4:30pm. Closed Dec–Feb.

EXPLORING THE COUNTRYSIDE

You can rent a bike in the nearby town of Hawick, at the **Hawick Cycle Centre,** 45 N. Bridge St. (© **01450/373-352**), where you pay £13 ($25) per day or £57 ($108) per week, plus a £55 ($105) deposit. It's open Monday to Saturday 9am to 5pm.

Harestanes Countryside Visitor Centre   For another experience with nature, head north of Jedburgh (it's signposted) to this visitor center. You can follow marked trails or take guided walks through one of the most beautiful spots in the Borders. The center houses a Discovery Room with wildlife displays, a gift shop that sells local crafts, and a tearoom.

At the junction of A68 and B6400, Monteviot. © **01835/830-306**. Free admission. Mar–Oct daily 10am–5pm. Closed Nov–Feb.

Hermitage Castle   If you want to follow in the footsteps of Mary Queen of Scots, you can drive from Jedburgh to Hermitage Castle. It was to Hermitage that Mary was headed when she made her famous 64km (40-mile) ride from Jedburgh to rush to the bedside of her lover, the earl of Bothwell (1535–78), who was wounded by English troops. Still mired in the misty gloom of the 1300s, this medieval castle was restored in the early 1800s. Its original owner, Lord Soulis, was accused of devil worship and was boiled alive by the angry townspeople.

On an unclassified road (the castle is signposted) between A7 and B6399, 16km (10 miles) south of Hawick in Liddes-dale. (✆ 01387/376-222. Admission £3 ($5.70) adults, £2.80 ($5.30) seniors, £1.75 ($3.35) children 15 and younger. Apr–Sept daily 9:30am–6:30pm. Closed Oct–Mar.

Jedforest Deer and Farm Park *(Finds* You'll find the area's best walks and nature experiences at this deer and farm park. Approximately 32 hectares (80 acres) of this 405-hectare (1,000-acre) farm are open to the public and dotted with unusual species of pigs, chickens, and especially deer. Owner Marion Armitage prides herself on her herds of red fallow and Asian Sitka deer (bred for food), which either nuzzle or flee from visitors. You can buy a bag of special deer food for 30p (55¢) and follow one of the two trails along the softly undulating, partially forested terrain. The trail marked with brown signposts requires 30 minutes; the trail marked with green signposts takes an hour. Each is peppered with signs explaining the flora and fauna you'll see en route.

An unusual side attraction in the park is Diana Durman-Walters and her **Birds of Prey Experience.** The staff members exercise the owls, buzzards, eagles, hawks, and falcons at periodic intervals every day, feeding them raw rabbit meat or chicken—but not so much that they lose their incentive to catch rats, rabbits, and field mice during their exercise regimens. If the art of falconry interests you, you can participate in a half-day Hawk Walk for £50 ($95) or a full-day Hawk Walk for £75 ($143). Participation requires a reservation (call the number below) and is limited to no more than six people. Wear sturdy walking shoes and sensible clothing that won't wilt in a rain shower. If you're willing, you can handle one of these temperamental birds and experience the way it returns to the glove after spotting, catching, and killing a rodent or rabbit.

Camptown, 8km (5 miles) south of Jedburgh along A68. (✆ 01835/840-364. Admission £4.50 ($8.55) adults, £2.50 ($4.75) children 3–16. Easter–Aug daily 10am–5:30pm; Sept–Oct daily 11am–4:30pm. Other times by appointment.

WHERE TO STAY

Ancrum Craig Most of this place dates from the 1830s, when a simple farmhouse (built in 1722) was massively expanded into a red-sandstone Victorian home. Surrounded by landscaped gardens, with views stretching out over the valley of the Teviot, Ancrum Craig is a fine example of baronial, somewhat chilly, Scottish living. It's called "the perfect first stop in Scotland." The guest rooms are cozy, one with a tub and the other two with a shower-only bathroom. The largest is the Gold Room, with a bay window boasting a sweeping view. The smallest is the Heather Room, which overlooks the original medieval core, long ago made into an outbuilding. The breakfasts are generous.

Ancrum, Jedburgh, Roxburghshire TD8 6UN. (✆ 01835/830-280. Fax 01835/830-259. www.ancrumcraig.co.uk. 3 units. £58–£66 ($110–$125) double. Rates include breakfast. MC, V. Free parking. Call for directions. Dogs welcome. **Amenities:** Nonsmoking rooms. *In room:* TV, coffeemaker, hair dryer.

Ferniehirst Mill Lodge Built in 1980, this chalet-inspired modern guesthouse is in a quiet neighborhood away from the town center and attracts those (including hunters and anglers) seeking quiet and rural charm. A haven for wild fowl on 10 hectares

(25 acres) of private land, it stands in a secluded valley beside the fast-moving Jed Water. Its pine-paneled guest rooms are functional but comfortable, each with a private shower-only bathroom. Horseback riding (for experienced riders only) costs about £19 ($36) per hour (minimum of 2 hr.), and riders must supply their own riding habits. Picnic lunches are available with advance notice £5 ($9.50).

Hwy. A68, Jedburgh, Roxburghshire TD8 6PQ. ⓒ/fax **01835/863-279.** www.ferniehirstmill.co.uk. 9 units. £20–£25 ($38–$48) per person. Rates include breakfast; dinner £15 ($29) extra. Riding packages available for those willing to stay 1 week. MC, V. Free parking. Take A68 4km (2½ miles) south of Jedburgh. **Amenities:** Bar. *In room:* Coffeemaker.

Glenfriar's Hotel   This small private hotel is in a Georgian house on a quiet corner next to St. John's Church. It features antique wooden furnishings, including four-poster beds in two rooms, and well-maintained bathrooms with showers.

The Friars, Jedburgh, The Borders TD8 6BN. ⓒ **01835/862-000.** Fax 01835/862-112. www.edenroad.demon.co.uk. 6 units. £60 ($114) double. Rates include breakfast. AE, MC, V. *In room:* TV, coffeemaker, hair dryer.

Jedforest Hotel ⓐⓐ   For a motorist coming into Scotland, this country hotel would be a good introduction to the hospitality of the land. Lying on the A68, the main artery linking Newcastle to Edinburgh, the hotel is called "the first hotel in Scotland." Rated four stars by the government, it stands on 14 hectares (35 acres) with private fishing on Jed Water flowing into the rivers Teviot and Tweed. Many sportsmen check in here just to fish. Bedrooms come in a wide range of sizes and styles, from standard to king size, even a four-poster suite. Four ground floor rooms, equally as comfortable as those in the main house, lie in the river cottage adjacent to the hotel. Built in the 1800s, the hotel was originally a shooting lodge which has been extended over the years into the massive sprawl that greets you today. A team of skilled chefs prepares a Scottish and international cuisine in the hotel's bistro, the food served on fine china to both residents and visitors who call to reserve a table.

The location is 4.8km (3 miles) south of Jedburg and 11km (7 miles) north of the border. Camptown TD8 6PJ Jedburgh. ⓒ **01835/840-364.** Fax 01835/840-226. 12 units. £100–£140 ($190–$266) double; £160 ($304) suite. AE, DC, MC, V. **Amenities:** Restaurant; bar; room service; fishing; nonsmoking rooms; rooms for those w/limited mobility. *In room:* TV.

The Spinney Guest House and Lodges ⓐ ⓕⁱⁿᵈˢ   Run by Mr. and Mrs. Fry, this B&B complex includes a main house, a modernized cottage with three doubles, and three pinewood chalets with bathrooms, sitting rooms, and kitchens. Leather and wood furnishings are found throughout the well-maintained guest rooms. The Scottish Tourist Board recently bestowed upon the guesthouse a deluxe rating.

Langlee, Jedburgh, The Borders TD8 6PB. ⓒ **01835/863-525.** Fax 01835/864-883. www.thespinney-jedburgh.co.uk. 3 units, 3 chalets. £26–£65 ($49–$124) per person. Rates for regular double rooms include breakfast. MC, V. Free parking. Main house B&B closed Dec–Feb; chalets open year-round. Take A68 3km (2 miles) south of Jedburgh. Pets welcome in chalets by prior arrangement. **Amenities:** Nonsmoking rooms. *In room:* TV, coffeemaker, hair dryer.

WHERE TO DINE

Carter's Rest SCOTTISH/CONTINENTAL   This pub, with a downstairs dining room built of old abbey stones, is the favorite gathering place for locals. Mr. Jonentz, the owner, serves wholesome and hearty food and drink. The simple but tasty menu includes dishes like steaks, scampi, chicken cordon bleu, pork and lamb chops, as well as fresh vegetables in season. The pub also has eight regional beers on tap.

Abbey Place. ⓒ **01835/863-414.** Main courses £8–£16 ($15–$30); bar lunches £6–£10 ($11–$19). MC, V. Restaurant daily noon–2:30pm and 6–9pm; pub Mon–Sat 11am–11pm, Sun 11am–10:30pm.

Simply Scottish SCOTTISH   In the heart of town, amid stripped pinewood floors and heavy pine furniture, is this decent, well-scrubbed restaurant, which serves savory lunches and dinners, plus countless pots of tea for all the locals who drop by. Menu items, made entirely from Scottish ingredients, are likely to include a salad of smoked chicken and avocado, haggis with white onion sauce, grilled Borders lamb steak with Arran mustard, and roasted salmon with herb-flavored butter sauce. Preferred desserts are raspberry-and-apple crumble with vanilla ice cream and sticky toffee pudding.

6–8 High St. ✆ **01835/864-696.** Reservations recommended for dinner. Lunch main courses £3.50–£9 ($6.65–$17); pot of tea with scones and jam £3.75 ($7.15); fixed-price dinner £12 ($23); main courses dinner £7–£14 ($13–$27). MC, V. Sun–Fri 10am–8:30pm; Sat 10am–9pm.

2 Kelso: Abbey Ruins & Adam Architecture ⊀

71km (44 miles) SE of Edinburgh, 19km (12 miles) NE of Jedburgh, 110km (68 miles) NW of Newcastle-upon-Tyne, 19km (12 miles) E of Melrose, 39km (23 miles) W of Berwick-upon-Tweed

A typical historic border town like Jedburgh, Kelso lies at the point where the River Teviot meets the River Tweed. Sir Walter Scott called it "the most beautiful, if not the most romantic, village in Scotland." The settlement that grew up here developed into a town around Kelso Abbey.

Kelso today is a flourishing market town at the center of an agricultural district. But for visitors, the reasons to come are the ruined abbey and the palatial Floors Castle (by the great architect William Adam) and Mellerstain (begun by William but finished by his son Robert). The town is also one of the best centers for touring the Borders because it's near Jedburgh, Dryburgh Abbey, and Melrose.

ESSENTIALS
GETTING THERE   The nearest rail station connection is Berwick-upon-Tweed, from which you can take a bus to Kelso (see below). For information, call ✆ **8457/ 484-950.**

From Edinburgh, board the bus to Saint Boswells, with connecting service to Kelso; the full trip lasts about 80 minutes and costs £8 ($15) one-way and £13 ($25) round-trip. Phone ✆ **8705/808-080** for more information. From Berwick to Kelso, there are between six and eight buses a day, depending on the day of the week and the season. Transit costs £4 ($7.60) each way and takes an hour. Because three bus companies make the run, it's best to call the local tourist office at ✆ **01573/223-464** for the schedules.

From Edinburgh, take A7 and follow the signs to Hawick; then change to A68, follow the signs to Jedburgh, and take A6089 to Kelso.

VISITOR INFORMATION   The **tourist office** is at Town House, The Square (✆ **01573/223-464**). It's open year-round Monday to Saturday 10am to 5pm and Sunday 10am to 2pm.

SEEING THE SIGHTS
Floors Castle ⊀   Located on the banks of the Tweed, the home of the dukes of Roxburghe was designed in 1721 by William Adam and remodeled in the mid–19th century by William Playfair. Part of the castle contains superb French and English furniture, porcelain, tapestries, and paintings by Gainsborough, Reynolds, and Canaletto. You'll also find a licensed restaurant, a coffee shop, and a gift shop, as well as a walled garden and garden center. You might recognize Floors: It was a major location for the Tarzan film *Greystoke*.

Hwy. A697, 3km (2 miles) north of Kelso. ℂ **01573/223-333**. www.floorscastle.com. Admission £6.50 ($12) adults, £5.50 ($10) seniors and students, £3.50 ($6.65) children ages 5-16, free for children age 4 and under. Apr–Oct daily 11am–5pm (last admission 4:30pm). Closed Nov–Mar. Follow the signs north from Kelso center.

Kelso Abbey 𝒜   Once a great ecclesiastical center, Kelso Abbey has lain in ruins since the late 16th century, when it suffered its last and most devastating attack by the English, who ripped off its roofs, burned it, and declared it officially defunct. The lands and remaining buildings were given to the earl of Roxburghe. The oldest (1128) and probably largest of the Border abbeys, it was once one of the richest, collecting revenues and rents from granges, fisheries, mills, and manor houses throughout the region. In 1919, the abbey was given to the nation.

Although the remains of this abbey may not be as impressive as those of Jedburgh (see "Jedburgh: Gateway to the Borders," earlier in this chapter), Kelso has had its moments in history, including the crowning of the infant James III. At the entrance is part of the south recessed doorway, where some of the sculpture on the arches is still fairly intact. The west transept tower still suggests its original massive construction, and a trio of building sections with round-headed openings remains. The west front and tower are visible, the whole flanked by buttresses crowned with rounded turrets. A partial cloister here dates from 1933, when it was built as the Roxburghe family vault. Sir Walter Scott knew Kelso Abbey well, because he spent time here studying at Waverley Cottage, which you can see from the abbey's parking area; it was once the Kelso Grammar School, where the famous author learned how to read and write.

Bridge St. Free admission. Apr–Sept daily 9:30am–6:30pm; Oct–Mar daily 9:30am–4:30pm.

Mellerstain 𝒜𝒜   Eleven kilometers (7 miles) northwest of Kelso stands Mellerstain, the seat of the earls of Haddington. This is one of the most famous mansions designed by Robert Adam and one of Scotland's greatest Georgian residences. William Adam built two wings on the house in 1725; the main building was designed by his more famous son, Robert, some 40 years later. (For more details on the Adam family of architectural geniuses, see "Robert Adam: Architect to the King," below.)

Mellerstain is associated with Lady Grisell Baillie (born Grisell Hume). When she was 13 years old, in 1689, her father was suspected of plotting to assassinate Charles II. The young Giselle showed great courage by hiding her father in the village church's crypt, bringing him food and supplies in the dead of night, and facing down the English. She eventually fled to Holland but returned in triumph with William of Orange (later William I of England) and subsequently married into the Baillie family, scions of Mellerstain. You can see the interior, with its impressive library, paintings, and antique furniture. The garden terrace offers a panoramic view south to the lake, with the Cheviot Hills in the distance. Afternoon tea is served, and souvenir gifts are on sale.

Gordon. From Edinburgh, follow A68 to Earlston, then follow the signs to Mellerstain for another 8km (5 miles); from Kelso, head northwest along A6089 until you see the signposted turn to the left. ℂ **01573/410-225**. Admission £6 ($11) adults, free for kids 16 and under. May–June and Sept Sun, Wed, and bank holidays 12:30–5pm; July–Aug Sun–Mon and Wed–Thurs 12:30–5pm; Oct Sun 12:30–5pm.

OUTDOOR PURSUITS

The 18-hole **Roxburghe Golf Course** (ℂ **01573/450-331**) is the only championship course in the region. Designed by Dave Thomas, one of Britain's leading golf-course architects, it's 7,111 yards. Guests of The Roxburghe Hotel (see "Where to Stay & Dine," below) can most easily get tee times, but the course is open to nonmembers as well. Greens fees are £30 to £65 ($57–$124) for 18 holes.

Our favorite countryside spot is the nearby village of **Kirk Yeetholm,** 11km (7 miles) southeast of Kelso on B6352. This is the northern terminus of the **Pennine Way,** a 403km (250-mile) hike that begins down in Yorkshire, England. Today Kirk Yeetholm is filled with tired hikers at the end of the trail, but it was once the Gypsy capital of Scotland—until 1883, a Gypsy queen was crowned here. You can see (at least from the outside) the "Gypsy palace," really a tiny cottage in the center of the village.

Another place for walking and hiking is around **Smailholm Tower** (© **01573/460-365**), on a ridge 13km (8 miles) west of Kelso and 3km (2 miles) south of Meller-stain (see listing, above), signposted off B6404. A so-called peel tower (fortified tower) from the 1500s, it has been restored and rises 18m (60 ft.) above a loch, providing some of the best views of the Borders. Open October Saturday to Wednesday 9:30am to 4:30pm; November to March Saturday and Sunday 9:30am to 4:30pm. April to September, it's open daily 9:30am to 5:30pm, charging £3.50 ($6.65) admission for adults, £2.80 ($5.30) for seniors and students, and £1.75 ($3.35) for children.

WHERE TO STAY & DINE

The Cross Keys Hotel   Facing the cobbled main square of the town, the facade of this hotel is a stately Georgian style from 1769. Since then, guests have included Bonnie Prince Charlie and Beatrix Potter. The public areas are comfortable and busy, vaguely inspired by Scottish Art Nouveau master Charles Rennie Mackintosh. The midsize guest rooms are well appointed and have double-glazed windows; each has a shower-only bathroom. The superior rooms are larger and sport sofas; all are non-smoking. The restaurant serves lunch and dinner daily, while the cozy Scottish-style bar, The 36, boasts an impressive collection of single-malt whiskies.

36 The Square, Kelso, The Borders TD5 7HL. © **01573/223-303.** Fax 01573/225-792. www.cross-keys-hotel.co.uk. 28 units. £67–£99 ($127–$188) double. Rates include breakfast. AE, MC, V. **Amenities:** Restaurant; bar; rooms for those w/limited mobility. *In room:* TV, coffeemaker, hair dryer (superior rooms only), iron.

Edenwater House ✸✸ *(Finds)*   This former private manor house opening onto the Edenwater lies in the village of Ednam, 3.2km (2 miles) north of Kelso. It enjoys one of the most tranquil settings in the Borders, and is an exceedingly comfortable small private hotel known for its excellent cuisine and personal service. Guests meet each other in the formal and spacious drawing room where a log fire burns on chilly nights. In fair weather they can stroll through the garden and grounds. Bedrooms are large and airy and beautifully furnished. Units, all of which are nonsmoking, contain a private bathroom, three with tub and one with shower. The food is among the best in the area, but the restaurant is open to nonresidents only for dinner on Friday and Saturday. A fixed-price menu costs £35 ($67).

Ednam (off the B6461), Kelso TD5 7QL. © **01573/224-070.** Fax 01573/226-615. www.edenwaterhouse.co.uk. 4 units. £70–£90 ($133–$171) double. Rates include full breakfast. MC, V. Closed Jan 1–14. **Amenities:** Restaurant. *In room:* TV, coffeemaker, iron, hair dryer.

Ednam House Hotel ✸✸   The Ednam, on the fringe of Kelso, is a conversion of a mid-18th-century Georgian house often referred to as "that lovely place beside the river." In the oldest section is an unusual collection of antiques. The so-called Principal Rooms—the original master bedrooms of the manor—are on the third floor and offer a view of the river; less expensive and scenic are those on the first and second floors. The rooms vary in size, but all come with shower or bath and bathrobes.

The Georgian style Orangerie, a building where oranges were once grown, lies only a few meters from the main house. Often rented to families or groups of friends, it

Robert Adam: Architect to the King

In the field of architecture, one Scottish name towers over all the rest: **Robert Adam** (1728–92), whose adaptations of the Italian Palladian style have been admired and duplicated in public and private buildings around the world. He has emerged as Britain's most prestigious neoclassical architect in a century that produced dozens of talented competitors. Today, owning an Adam building is an honor akin to being knighted by the queen, but (if you happen to be selling the building) infinitely more profitable.

Adam's genius derived from his synthesis of the decorative traditions of the French and Italian Renaissance with those of ancient Greece and Rome. His designs are particularly notable for their lavish use of color, inspired by Grecian vase paintings and by what was being excavated from archaeological digs in places like Pompeii. Almost as important, Adam seemed to have a well-developed business sense and a knack for decorating the right house at the right time, and his moneyed clients helped propel him into the spotlight.

Throughout much of his career, he collaborated with his capable but less talented younger brother, **James** (1730–94), who handled many of the workaday details of the projects they executed together. And when, say, a Scottish lord hired the Adam brothers, he got more than an intensely detailed building—in most cases, the commission included every aspect of the interior decoration and most of the furnishings. The brothers' education in the visual arts began early: Their father, **William Adam** (1689–1748), was the leading Scottish architect of his day and designed dozens of manor houses in what has been called a crude but vigorous Palladian style.

Robert was born in Kirkcaldy, in Fife, but soon emigrated to London, the source of most of his large commissions. He laboriously studied the architecture

contains two elegantly furnished and most comfortable upstairs bedrooms with a shared living room downstairs overlooking the river. These accommodations are very private and exclusive and feature loads of antiques.

Bridge St., Kelso, The Borders TD5 7HT. ℭ **01573/224-168.** Fax 01573/226-319. www.ednamhouse.com. 32 units. £101–£190 ($192–$361) double. Rates include breakfast. MC, V. **Amenities:** Restaurant; babysitting. *In room:* TV, coffeemaker, hair dryer, trouser press.

The Roxburghe Hotel and Golf Course ✦✦   This late-19th-century castle stands on 81 hectares (200 acres) of woodland, lawns, and gardens. It was built as the family home of the Roxburghes, who valued its location on the trout-filled Teviot. In 1982, it was converted into a country hotel: The old stable block contains six guest rooms; another 16 are in the main house. All are well appointed; suites and a few doubles have four-poster beds. Amid a subdued but elegant interior, the hotel has four log-burning fireplaces going, even in summer. It also offers a number of leisure and sporting activities, from archery to biking to fishing. From April to October a complimentary visit to Floors Castle is given to guests.

Hwy. A698, Helton, Kelso, The Borders TD5 8JZ. ℭ **01573/450-331.** Fax 01573/450-611. www.roxburghe.net. 22 units. £178 ($338) double; £210 ($399) double with four-poster bed; £296 ($562) suite. Rates include breakfast. AE, of imperial Rome under the supervision of then-famous French antiquarian C. L. Clérisseau, with whom he toured widely in Italy and Dalmatia (later part of Yugoslavia). In 1764, he compiled the information he gathered during these tours in the widely acclaimed *The Ruins of the Palace of the Emperor Diocletian at Spalatro.* In 1761, Robert, along with architect William Chambers, was appointed architect of the king's works, at the time the most prestigious post in Britain. In 1773, an illustrated volume, *The Works of Robert and James Adam,* documented the brothers' vision; they justifiably claimed credit for revolutionizing the principles of English aesthetics.

The Adam style, a richly detailed yet airy interpretation of neoclassicism, was a radical departure from the more ponderous and sometimes ecclesiastical forms that preceded it. Almost immediately, the Adam style of ceiling decorations and mantelpieces was widely copied throughout Britain. And within less than a generation, this vision radically influenced furniture styles throughout Europe and North America, most notably France's Louis XVI style. Looser derivations are the Directoire, Sheraton, and Empire styles.

Adam buildings in Scotland include the **Old Quad** at Edinburgh University and **Mellerstain** in the Borders (described earlier in this chapter). Many more of his works remain in England, especially in London, thanks to his careful cultivation of the wealthy English. Examples are **Kenwood House** (1767–69) in London, **Osterly Park** (1761–80) and **Syon House** (1762–69) in Middlesex, and **Luton Hoo** (1768–75) in Bedfordshire. Much more widespread than Adam buildings, however, are examples of their furniture and interior decor (especially chairs, sideboards, and mantelpieces), which are proudly displayed in museums and private homes across the United Kingdom and North America.

DC, MC, V. Take A698 5km (3 miles) southwest of Kelso. **Amenities:** Restaurant; bar; golf course; tennis court; spa; room service. *In room:* TV, hair dryer, robes, slippers.

A SIDE TRIP TO DRYBURGH ABBEY

Sixteen kilometers (10 miles) west of Kelso and 6km (4 miles) southeast of Melrose (off A68), you'll find the town of **Dryburgh** and its ruined abbey. The adjoining town is **St. Boswells,** an old village on the Selkirk–Kelso road. Near Dryburgh is **Scott's View** ☞ (take B6356 north) over the Tweed to Sir Walter's beloved Eildon Hills; it's the most glorious vista in the region.

Dryburgh Abbey ☞☞   These Gothic ruins are surrounded by gnarled yew trees and cedars of Lebanon, said to have been planted by knights returning from the Crusades. It's still a lovely ruin, and its setting in a loop of the Tweed is memorable. The cloister buildings are relatively intact, but not much remains of the church itself, except a few foundation stones. You can see enough fragments to realize that the architectural style was transitional, between the Romanesque and the pointed Early English style. Sir Walter Scott is buried here in a pillared side chapel.

Hwy. A68, Dryburgh, Roxburghshire. © **01835/822-381.** Admission £4.50 ($8.55) adults, £3.50 ($6.65) seniors, £2.25 ($4.30) children ages 5–15, free for children age 4 and under. Apr–Sept daily 9:30am–6:30pm (July–Aug to

7:30pm); Oct–Mar daily 9:30am–4:30pm. Closed Dec 25–26 and Jan 1–2. Drive south from Dryburgh along B6356 (it's signposted); from Edinburgh take A68 to St. Boswells and turn onto B6404 and then left onto B6356.

WHERE TO STAY & DINE

Clint Lodge Guest House Scotland _Finds_ This former lodge has been carefully converted into a small guesthouse of charm and grace. In the 18th century, the establishment was a sports lodge, and the setting is still tranquil, with panoramic views over the valley. The midsize bedrooms are comfortable and traditionally furnished, often with a treasure trove of family heirlooms. Each room has a private bathroom with shower; two rooms also have the original "deep fill" tubs. The menu features real "taste of Scotland" fare with such dishes as curried apple soup; Border lamb with onions in raisin sauce; filet of salmon with lemon sauce; and pears poached in a white-wine syrup.

St. Boswells, Melrose TD6 0DZ. ℃ **01835/822-027.** Fax 01835/822-656. www.clintlodge.co.uk. 5 units. £100 ($190) double with breakfast; £155 ($295) double with breakfast and dinner. MC, V. At St. Boswells, take B6404, continue 3.2km (2 miles) across Mertoun Bridge, and turn left onto B6356 through Clint Mains village, veering left. This road leads to Clint Lodge, 1.6km (1 mile) away on the right. _In room:_ TV, coffeemaker.

Dryburgh Abbey Hotel Located next to the abbey ruins, this hotel is the best in the area. It was built in 1845 as the home of Lady Grisell Baillie and remained in her family until 1929. It's said to be haunted by the "gray lady," who had an ill-fated affair with a monk that led to his execution and her suicide by drowning. After restoration, the deteriorated property was the first in the Borders to be awarded five crowns by the Scottish Tourist Board. The accommodations—named for fishing lures—include both deluxe rooms with half-tester or four-poster beds (some have small balconies) and standard abbey- or river-view rooms. The Tower Suites have separate sitting rooms and abbey or river views.

Hwy. B6404, outside St. Boswells, The Borders TD6 0RQ. ℃ **01835/822-261.** Fax 01835/823-945. www.dryburgh. co.uk. 38 units. £120–£150 ($228–$285) double; £200–£230 ($380–$437) suite for 2. Rates include full Scottish breakfast. AE, MC, V. **Amenities:** Restaurant; bar; heated indoor pool; room service; babysitting; laundry service; nonsmoking rooms. _In room:_ TV, coffeemaker, hair dryer, iron, trouser press.

3 Melrose

60km (37 miles) SE of Edinburgh, 113km (70 miles) NW of Newcastle-upon-Tyne, 65km (40 miles) W of Berwick-upon-Tweed

Rich in sights, Melrose is a highlight of the Borders: It offers one of the most beautiful ruined abbeys in the region, as well as diverse shopping. Abbotsford House, former home of Sir Walter Scott, is only 3km (2 miles) west, and Melrose is close to the Southern Upland Way, which passes to the north. Even if you can follow only part of this trail, take a day hike on the section along the River Tweed outside Melrose—it's one of the most delightful and scenic walks in Scotland.

ESSENTIALS

GETTING THERE The nearest rail station is in Berwick-upon-Tweed, where you can catch a bus to Melrose. From Berwick, about five buses per day travel to Melrose; travel time is about 90 minutes. Fares are about £5 ($9.50) one-way and £10 ($19) round-trip. Call the tourist office in Berwick-upon-Tweed at ℃ **01289/330-733** for bus schedules and ℃ **8457/484-950** for train schedules.

Many visitors prefer to take the bus into Melrose directly from Edinburgh. Travel time by bus from Edinburgh is 90 minutes, and buses depart every 1½ hours throughout the day. Phone ℃ **0870/580-8080** for more information.

Driving from Edinburgh, you can reach Melrose by going southeast along A7 and following the signs to Galashiels. From Kelso, take A699 west to St. Boswells and at the junction with A6091 head northwest.

VISITOR INFORMATION   The tourist office is at **Abbey House,** Abbey Street (© **01896/822-555**). In April, May, and October, it's open Monday to Saturday 10am to 5pm and Sunday 10am to 1pm. June and September hours are Monday to Saturday 10am to 5:30pm and Sunday 10am to 2pm. July and August, hours are Monday to Saturday 9:30am to 6:30pm and Sunday 10am to 6pm.

SEEING THE SIGHTS

Abbotsford House 𝕲𝕲   This was the home Sir Walter Scott built, and lived in, from 1812 until he died. Designed in the Scottish baronial style and considered, after his literary works, Scott's most enduring achievement, it contains many relics, including artifacts, and mementos the famous author collected from the Waterloo battlefield. Other exhibits include his clothes and his death mask. Especially interesting is his study, with his writing desk and chair. In 1935, two secret drawers were found in the desk. One of them contained 57 letters, part of the correspondence between Sir Walter and his wife-to-be.

Scott purchased Cartley Hall farmhouse, on the banks of the Tweed, in 1812. In 1822, he had the old house demolished and replaced it with the building you see today. Scott was one of Britain's earliest souvenir hunters, scouring the land for artifacts associated with the historical characters he rendered in his novels. One of his proudest possessions was a sword given to the duke of Montrose by English king Charles I for his cooperation (some say collaboration) during the struggles between Scotland and England. The sword is proudly displayed near a gun, sword, dagger, and small knife owned by the sworn enemy of the duke, cattle herder Rob Roy, whose exploits were later depicted in an eponymous drama penned by Sir Walter Scott. (You may remember the Liam Neeson film from a few years back.) You can see Scott's study, library (with 9,000 rare volumes), drawing room, entrance hall, and armories—even the dining room overlooking the Tweed, where he died on September 21, 1832. There are also extensive gardens and grounds to visit, plus the private chapel, added after Scott's death.

Hwy. B6360, Melrose. © **01896/752-043**. www.melrose.bordernet.co.uk/abbotsford. Admission £6 ($11) adults, £3 ($5.70) students and children. Mar–Oct Mon–Sat 9:30am–5pm, Sun 2–5pm. Head just off A7, south of the junction with A72, onto B6360, some 4km (2½ miles) southeast of Galashiels.

Melrose Abbey 𝕲𝕲   These lichen-covered ruins, among the most beautiful in Europe, are all that's left of the ecclesiastical community established by Cistercian monks in 1136. The complex's pure Gothic lines were made famous by Sir Walter Scott, who was instrumental in getting the decayed remains repaired and restored in the early 19th century. In *The Lay of the Last Minstrel,* Scott wrote, "If thou would'st view fair Melrose aright, go visit in the pale moonlight." You can still view its redsandstone shell, built in the Perpendicular style and filled with elongated windows and carved capitals with delicate tracery. The heart of Robert the Bruce is supposed to be interred in the abbey, but the location is unknown. Look for the beautiful carvings and the tombs of other famous Scotsmen buried in the chancel.

Abbey St. © **01896/822-562**. Admission £5 ($9.50) adults, £4 ($7.60) seniors, £2.50 ($4.75) children. Apr–Sept daily 9:30am–5:30pm; Oct–Mar daily 9:30am–4:30pm. Closed Dec 25–26 and Jan 1–2.

Thirlestane Castle $\mathcal{A}$ One of Scotland's most imposing country houses, Thirlestane has been owned by the Lauderdale family since 1218. A T-shaped building, the castle has a keep from the 16th century, and was much altered after Queen Victoria took the throne. The interior is known for its ornamental plaster ceilings, the finest in the country from the Restoration period. In the old nurseries is the Historic Toy Collection, and Border Country Life exhibits depict life in the Borders from prehistoric times to the present.

16km (10 miles) north of Melrose, overlooking Leader Water, about 1km (½ mile) from Lauder. ℂ 01578/722-430. www.thirlestanecastle.co.uk. Admission £7 ($13) adults, £6 ($11) seniors, £5 ($9.50) children, £20 ($38) families (2 adults and children). Apr 11–June 28 Sun and Wed–Thurs 10:30am–3pm; July–Aug Sun–Thurs 10am–3pm; Sept Sun and Wed–Thurs 10am–3pm. Open Easter weekend. Take A68 to Lauder in Berwickshire, 16km (10 miles) north of Melrose and 45km (28 miles) south of Edinburgh on A68.

Traquair House $\mathcal{A}\mathcal{A}$ Dating from the 10th century, this is perhaps Scotland's oldest and most romantic house, rich in associations with Mary Queen of Scots and the Jacobite uprisings. The great house is occupied by the Stuarts of Traquair. One of the most poignant exhibits is an ornately carved oak cradle in the King's Room, in which Mary rocked her infant son, who later became James VI of Scotland and James I of England. Other treasures here are glass, embroideries, silver, manuscripts, and paintings. Of particular interest is a brew house equipped as it was 2 centuries ago and still used regularly. On the grounds are craft workshops as well as a maze and woodland walks.

Hwy. A72, 26km (16 miles) west of Melrose. ℂ 01896/830-323. www.traquair.co.uk. Admission £6.30 ($12) adults, £5.70 ($11) seniors, £3.40 ($6.45) students and children, £18 ($34) families of 5. Mar 25–May 31 and Sept Mon–Sat noon–5pm; June–Aug daily 10:30am–5pm; Oct daily 11am–4pm; Nov Sat–Sun noon–4pm guided tours only. Closed Dec to mid-Mar.

SHOPPING

Melrose is one of the best destinations for shopping in the Borders. Most shops are open Monday to Saturday 9:30am to 5pm and Sunday noon to around 4pm.

The Country Kitchen, Market Square (ℂ 01896/822-586), displays a comprehensive choice of English, French, and Scottish cheeses, along with pâtés and meat products. You can buy them prepackaged or order up gourmet sandwiches and picnic fixings. **Abbey Wines,** Abbey Street (ℂ 01896/823-224), stocks the town's largest wine selection, plus at least 150 malt whiskies, some from the most obscure distilleries in Scotland.

The town's most complete collection of books is for sale at **Talisman Books,** 9 Market Square (ℂ 01896/822-196), in an old-fashioned Edwardian shop. Gifts, especially impractical-but-charming items in porcelain and china, are available at **Butterfly,** High Street (ℂ 01896/822-045).

Feeling chilly in the Scottish fog? A meticulously crafted wool or cashmere sweater from **Anne Oliver Knitwear,** 1 Scott's Place (ℂ 01896/822-975), might provide the extra warmth you need. **Lochcarron of Scotland,** 5 Market Sq. (ℂ 01896/823-823), is larger, but stocks only its own goods. Designers like Calvin Klein, Ralph Lauren, and Jean-Paul Gaultier have ordered bulk amounts here for relabeling and distribution. For tartan and other fabrics, visit **The Fabric Shop,** High Street (ℂ 01896/823-475), which both high-class couturiers and homegrown dressmakers find appealing.

WHERE TO STAY

Burts Hotel Value Nestled on the banks of the River Tweed and within walking distance of the abbey, this family-run inn dates from 1722. The traditional three-story

A Walk Along the Borders: St. Cuthbert's Way

If you're feeling particularly saintly, you can walk in the footsteps of 7th-century St. Cuthbert along the Scotland-England border. The 101km (62-mile) path stretches from Melrose, 60km (37 miles) southwest of Edinburgh, across the border into northeast England to the Holy Island of Lindisfarne on the Northumberland coast. St. Cuthbert began his ministry in Melrose in about A.D. 650 and later was appointed prior at Lindisfarne. The walk passes many places linked to his legend, prehistoric relics, Roman ruins, and historic castles. The high point is Wideopen Hill, 434m (1,430 ft.) above sea level. Permission from landowners along the route has been obtained, and the walk is clearly marked. A leaflet suggests distances you can comfortably cover in a day and makes recommendations for overnight stops. Contact Roger Smith, Walking Development Officer, **Scottish Border Enterprise Center,** Bridge Street, Galashiels TB1 ISW (© **01896/758-991;** fax 01896/758-625), for information.

town house offers a taste of small-town Scotland. The decor is modern, with an airy and restful feel. All guest rooms are well furnished and equipped with a shower. In the attractive bar, which sports Windsor chairs and a coal-burning fireplace, tasty lunches and suppers are served (as well as 90 different single-malt whiskies). The Restaurant (that's its name) has a clublike atmosphere with hunting scenes and classic Tartans. A classic Scottish cuisine is served using regional produce, with meals costing from £25 ($47) to £36 ($68).

Market Square, Melrose, The Borders TD6 9PN. © **01896/822-285.** Fax 01896/822-870. www.burtshotel.co.uk. 20 units. £112 ($213) double. Rates include Scottish breakfast. AE, DC, MC, V. Free parking. **Amenities:** Restaurant; bar; room service; laundry. In room: TV, coffeemaker, hair dryer.

King's Arms Hotel *(Kids)*   One of Melrose's oldest commercial buildings still in use, this 17th-century coaching inn has a three-story stone-and-brick facade that overlooks the pedestrian traffic of the main street. Inside is a series of cozy but slightly dowdy public rooms and half a dozen simple but comfortably furnished small guest rooms, each with a shower. One suite has a kitchen and is large enough for families, and a cottage is available in summer. The nonsmoking restaurant serves an odd mix of international offerings, including Mexican tacos and enchiladas, Indian curries, British steak pies, and giant Yorkshire puddings.

High St., Melrose, The Borders TD6 9PB. © **01896/822-143.** Fax 01896/823-812. www.kingsarmsmelrose.co.uk. 7 units. £64 ($122) double. MC, V. **Amenities:** Restaurant; bar. In room: TV, kitchen (in family suite only), coffeemaker.

Millars of Melrose *(R)*   This well-maintained family-owned hotel is in the heart of Melrose and easily identified by the colorful window boxes adorning its facade in summer. Most accommodations are medium-size and rather functionally but comfortably furnished. The most spacious unit comes with a traditional four-poster bed and a Jacuzzi; honeymooners sometimes stay here and are welcomed in style with a complimentary bottle of champagne, flowers, and chocolates. One room is set aside for families. Bathrooms are equipped either with tub or shower.

The split-level dining room offers tasty, reasonably priced meals which are also served in the bar, along with a fine assortment of beers, wines, and whiskies.

Market Square, Melrose TD6 9PQ. ☏ 01896/822-645. Fax 01896/823-474. www.millarshotel.co.uk. 11 units. £100 ($190) double; £120 ($228) family room. Rates include breakfast. MC, V. Follow the A68 into Melrose to the center of town. **Amenities:** Restaurant; bar. *In room:* TV, coffeemaker, hair dryer, trouser press.

Traquair Arms Hotel ☆   This is the area's most tranquil retreat for those seeking a country-house atmosphere. The small hotel was built as a coaching inn around 1780, with Victorian additions added later. Open fires in the bar lounge and fresh flowers in the dining room create a pleasant ambience. The cozy guest rooms come with comfortable furnishings, well-maintained bathrooms, and views of the valley. The hotel is known for fine pub food; vegetarians and others with special dietary needs can be accommodated. All dishes are freshly prepared by chefs Hugh Anderson and Sara Currie. The hotel is within a 5-minute walk of the River Tweed and salmon and trout fishing can be arranged.

Traquair Rd., Innerleithen, The Borders EH44 6PD. ☏ 01896/830-229. Fax 01896/830-260. 15 units. £75–£95 ($143–$181) double. Rates include breakfast; dinner £32 ($61). AE, MC, V. Take E69 from Melrose for 23km (14 miles). **Amenities:** Restaurant; bar; 1 room for those w/limited mobility. *In room:* TV, coffeemaker, hair dryer.

WHERE TO DINE

Don't miss the pastries at Melrose's best bakery, **Jackie Lunn, Ltd.,** High Street (☏ 01896/822-888).

Two of the town's most likable pubs are the one in the **King's Arms,** High Street (☏ 01896/822-143), where you'll generally find lots of rugby players hoisting a pint or two, and the somewhat more sedate one in **Burts Hotel,** Market Square (☏ 01896/822-285).

Marmion's Brasserie SCOTTISH   Across from the post office in a 150-year-old building, this tasteful restaurant is a cross between a brasserie and a coffee shop. The kitchen likes to use all-Scottish ingredients. The cheerful staff will offer menu items that frequently change, but might include escallops of monkfish with tomatoes and fresh herb dressing; organic aubergine stuffed with tomato, garlic, fresh herbs, and Taleggio cheese; and cassoulet of local pork and Fiageolet beans with Greshingham duck.

2 Buccleuch St. ☏ 01896/822-245. Reservations recommended for dinner. Main courses lunch £5–£13 ($9.50–$25); main courses dinner £10–£18 ($19–$34). MC, V. Mon–Sat 9am–10pm.

4 Selkirk: At the Heart of Scott Country

65km (40 miles) SE of Edinburgh, 118km (73 miles) SE of Glasgow, 11km (7 miles) S of Galashiels

In the heart of Sir Walter Scott country is Selkirk, a great base if you want to explore many of the region's historic homes, including Bowhill (see below) and Traquair House (see "Melrose," above). Jedburgh and Melrose offer more to see and do, but this ancient royal burgh can easily occupy a morning of your time.

Selkirk was the hometown of the African explorer Mungo Park (1771–1806), whose exploits could have made a great Harrison Ford movie. Park was a doctor, but won fame for exploring the River Niger; he drowned while escaping in a canoe from hostile natives. A statue of him is at the east end of High Street in Mungo Park.

ESSENTIALS

GETTING THERE   Berwick-upon-Tweed is the nearest rail station, where you can get a connecting bus to Selkirk, some of which require a connection in Kelso. The bus ride is just under 2 hours, costing £8 ($15) one-way or £15.80 ($30) round-trip. Call the tourist office in Selkirk at © **01750/205-55** for bus schedules or © **08457/484-950** for rail information.

Buses running between Newcastle-upon-Tyne and Edinburgh make stops at Selkirk. The trip takes about 2½ hours and costs £9 ($17) one-way or £13 ($25) round-trip.

Driving from Edinburgh, head southeast along A7 to Galashiels, then cut southwest along B6360. The trip takes about an hour. To get here from Melrose, take B6360 southwest to Selkirk; it's a 15-minute drive.

VISITOR INFORMATION   A **tourist office** is located at Halliwell's House Museum (© **01750/720-054**). March to September, it's open Monday to Saturday 10am to 5pm and Sunday 10am to noon; July and August, hours are Monday to Saturday 10am to 5:30pm and Sunday 10am to 1pm; October hours are Monday to Saturday 10am to 4pm and Sunday 10am to 1pm.

EXPLORING THE AREA

In Selkirk, the former royal hunting grounds and forests have given way to textile mills along the river banks, but there are many beautiful spots in the nearby countryside—notably **St. Mary's Loch,** 23km (14 miles) southwest. Sailors and fishermen love this bucolic body of water, as did literary greats like Thomas Carlyle and Robert Louis Stevenson. A panoramic segment of the Southern Upland Way, one of Scotland's great backpacking trails (see chapter 1), skirts the east shore of St. Mary's Loch. You can take a day hike on the 13km (8-mile) stretch from the loch to Traquair House (see "Melrose," earlier in this chapter).

Bowhill 🐾🐾   This 18th- and 19th-century Border home of the Scotts (Sir Walter's family), as well as the dukes of Buccleuch, contains a rare-art collection, French furniture, porcelain, silverware, and mementos of Sir Walter Scott, Queen Victoria, and the duke of Monmouth. Its paintings include works by Canaletto, Claude, Gainsborough, and Reynolds. In the surrounding Country Park, you find an Adventure Woodland play area, a Victorian kitchen, an audiovisual presentation, a gift shop, and a tearoom/restaurant. Sotheby's "Works of Art" courses are offered at Bowhill.

Hwy. A708, 5km (3 miles) west of Selkirk. © **01750/222-04.** Admission to house £7 ($13) adults, £5 ($9.50) seniors, £3 ($5.70) children; admission to Country Park £2 ($3.80). House: July daily 1–5pm. Country Park: Apr daily 11am–5pm; May weekends 11am–5pm; June and Aug Sat–Thurs 11am–5pm; July daily 11am–5pm. Closed other months.

WHERE TO STAY & DINE

Heatherlie House Hotel   An imposing stone-and-slate Victorian mansion with steep gables and turrets, this hotel is set on .8 hectares (2 acres) of wooded lands and mature gardens, west from the center along the Green and a short walk from Selkirk. The guest rooms are immaculately maintained, furnished with reproductions of older pieces. The lone single room has no bathroom of its own.

A coal-burning fireplace adds warmth to the lounge, where reasonably priced bar meals are available daily. The high-ceilinged dining room is open for dinner. Golf, fishing, and shooting packages can be arranged, and about half a dozen golf courses are within a reasonable drive.

Heatherlie Park, Selkirk, The Borders TD7 5AL. © **01750/721-200.** Fax 01750/720-005. www.heatherlie.freeserve. co.uk. 7 units, 6 with private bathroom. £90 ($171) double with bathroom. Rates include breakfast. MC, V. **Amenities:** Restaurant; bar. In room: TV, coffeemaker, hair dryer.

5 Peebles

37km (23 miles) S of Edinburgh, 85km (53 miles) SE of Glasgow, 32km (20 miles) W of Melrose

Peebles, a royal burgh and county town, is a market center in the Tweed Valley, noted for its large woolen mills and fine knitwear shopping. Scottish kings used to come here when they hunted in Ettrick Forest, 35km (22 miles) away. It's one of hundreds of forests scattered throughout the Borders, and is very pretty, but no more so than forested patches closer to the town.

Peebles is known as a writer's town. It was home to Sir John Buchan (Baron Tweedsmuir, 1875–1940), a Scottish author who later was appointed governor-general of Canada. He's remembered chiefly for the adventure story *Prester John* and was the author of *The Thirty-Nine Steps,* the first of a highly successful series of espionage thrillers and later a Hitchcock film. Robert Louis Stevenson lived for a time in Peebles and drew on the surrounding countryside in his novel *Kidnapped* (1886).

ESSENTIALS

GETTING THERE   The nearest rail station is in Berwick-upon-Tweed, but bus connections from there into Peebles are quite inconvenient. It's easier to get from Edinburgh to Peebles by a 50-minute bus ride. Bus fares from Edinburgh are around £5 ($9.50) one-way. Call ✆ **08457/484-950** for rail and bus information.

If you're driving, take A703 south from Edinburgh. Continue west along A6091 from Melrose.

VISITOR INFORMATION   The **tourist office** is at the Chamber Institute, 23 High St. (✆ **0870/608-0404**). April 1 to June 1, it's open from Monday to Saturday 9am to 5pm and Sunday 11am to 4pm; June 2 to June 29, hours are Monday to Saturday 9am to 5:30pm and Sunday 10am to 4pm; June 30 to August 31 hours are Monday to Saturday 9am to 6pm and Sunday 10am to 4pm; September 1 to September 28, hours are Monday to Saturday 9am to 5:30pm and Sunday 10am to 4pm; September 29 to November 1, hours are Monday to Saturday 9am to 5pm and Sunday 11am to 4pm; November 2 to December, hours are Monday to Saturday 9:30am to 5pm and Sunday 11am to 3pm; January to March, hours are Monday to Saturday 9:30am to 4pm.

EXPLORING THE TOWN & THE COUNTRYSIDE

The tourist office (see above) provides pamphlets describing the best walking tours in the region. The £1 ($1.90) pamphlet *Walks Around Peebles* describes 20 walks, including one along the Tweed. The **Tweed Walk** begins in the center of Peebles, and—with the twists and turns described in the pamphlet—takes you downstream along the river, then upstream along the opposite bank for a return to Peebles. You can follow the path for segments of 4km (2½ miles), 7km (4½ miles), or 12km (7½ miles). Regardless of the length of your walk, you'll pass the stalwart walls of Neidpath Castle.

Glentress Bicycle Trekking Centre, Glentress, Peebles (✆ **01721/721-736**), is the place to rent a bike. You'll have to leave a refundable deposit of £55 ($105). Daily rates range from £14 ($27) for a half-day and £17 ($32) for a full day, and rentals must be arranged in advance. It's open daily April to October 9am to 7pm (Sat–Sun from 10am); November, Wednesday noon to 10pm and Saturday and Sunday 10am to 5pm.

Dawyck Botanic Garden   This botanical garden, run by the Royal Botanic Garden in Edinburgh, has a large variety of conifers, some exceeding 30m (100 ft.) in height, as well as many species of flowering shrubs. There's also a fine display of early-spring bulbs, plus wooded walks rich in wildlife interest.

Hwy. B712, 13km (8 miles) southwest of Peebles. ℂ **01721/760-254**. Admission £3.50 ($6.65) adults, £3 ($5.70) seniors and students, £1 ($1.90) children. Daily 10am–5pm.

Kailzie Gardens   These 6.8 hectares (17 acres) of formal walled gardens, dating from 1812, include a rose garden, woodlands, and *burnside* (streamside) walks. Restored during the past 20 years, it provides a stunning array of plants from early spring to late autumn and has a collection of waterfowl and owls. There's also an art gallery, a shop, and a restaurant.

Kailzie on B7063, 4km (2½ miles) southeast of Peebles. ℂ **01721/720-007**. Admission £2.50 ($4.75) adults, 75p ($1.45) children; gardens only £1 ($1.90). Apr–Oct daily 10am–5:30pm; Nov–Mar daily daylight hours.

Neidpath Castle   Once linked with two of the greatest families in Scotland (the Frasiers and the Hayes), Neidpath, a summer attraction, hasn't been occupied since 1958. Part of the interest here is the way the castle's medieval shell was transformed during the 1600s into a residence, using then-fashionable architectural conceits. Enormous galleries were divided into smaller, cozier spaces, with the exception of the Great Hall, whose statuesque proportions are still visible. The hall's medieval stonework is decorated with 11 batik panels crafted in the mid-1990s by noted artist Monica Hanisch; they depict the life and accomplishments of Mary Queen of Scots. Other parts of the museum are devoted to the role the castle has played as the setting for films like *The Bruce* (an English movie that had the bad luck to be released simultaneously with *Braveheart*) and *Merlin: The Quest Begins.* Also recently filmed here were the courtyard scene in the TV miniseries *Joan of Arc,* where the heroine was burned at the stake, and new British versions of *Hamlet* and *King Lear.*

Tweeddale, on A72, 1.6km (1 mile) west of Peebles. ℂ **01721/720-333**. Admission £3 ($5.70) adults, £2.50 ($4.75) seniors, £1 ($1.90) children, £7.50 ($14) families. May 1–Sept 30 Wed–Sat 10:30am–5pm, Sun 12:30–5pm. Also open Easter weekend and bank holidays. Closed Oct–Apr.

SHOPPING

Knitwear, crafted from yarn culled from local sheep, is the best buy in Peebles, and easily found as you stroll along High Street. General shopping hours are Monday to Saturday 10am to 5:30pm. On Sundays in July and August, some shops open from 10am to 5pm.

Woolgathering, 1 Bridge House Terrace (ℂ **01721/720-388**), offers knitwear and all kinds of sweaters. Three sprawling branches of **Castle Warehouse,** at 1 Greenside (ℂ **01721/723-636**), 7–13 Old Town (ℂ **01721/720-348**), and 29–31 Northgate (ℂ **01721/720-814**), sell gift items with a Scottish flavor as well as clothing, such as traditional Scottish garb and anything you might need for a fishing trip.

Caledonian Countrywear, Ltd., 74 High St. (ℂ **01721/723-055**), and **Out & About,** 2 Elcho St. Brae (ℂ **01721/723-590**), are sporting-goods stores with lots of durable clothing and hiking boots.

For Border handicrafts like pinewood furniture, stoneware, and porcelain, go to **Peebles Craft Centre,** 9 Newby Court (ℂ **01721/722-875**), or the **Couchee Righ,** 26 Northgate (ℂ **01721/721-890**).

Fewer than 10km (6 miles) from Walkerburn at Galashiels (head east along A72) is the **Peter Anderson Company,** Nether Mill (ℂ **01896/752-091**). This factory outlet sells more than 750 types of tartan fabrics, all made on the premises on modernized looms. The shop is open Monday through Saturday from 9am to 5pm and also

Sunday noon to 5pm, June to September. Dozens of other shops are in the nearby textile town of Galashiels.

WHERE TO STAY

Castle Venlaw Hotel 🔆 *Kids*   Originally built in 1782 and enlarged in 1854, Castle Venlaw lies among 1.6 hectares (4 acres) of woodlands and offers lovely views of the surrounding countryside. The hotel's round tower and craw-stepped gables are an evocative example of the Scottish baronial style.

Castle Venlaw has 12 spacious and individually decorated rooms—each named for a different malt whisky—that all offer excellent views and a selection of books and magazines. A four-poster room has especially nice views, and the hotel's two suites have a sitting room with a VCR in addition to the bedroom. In the tower at the top of the castle is a spacious family room with a children's den containing bunk beds, games, TV, and VCR.

Edinburgh Rd., Peebles EH45 8QG. ℘ **01721/720-384.** Fax 01721/724-066. www.venlaw.co.uk. 14 units. £126–£170 ($239–$323) double; £146–£175 ($277–$333) deluxe; £180–£200 ($342–$380) suite. Rates include breakfast. Children under 12 staying in parent's room £20 ($38); children ages 13–16 £25 ($48). MC, V. Free parking. Take A703 to Peebles. **Amenities:** Restaurant; bar; room service; laundry service. *In room:* TV, coffeemaker.

Cringletie House Hotel 🔆🔆🔆   This imposing 1861 red-sandstone Victorian mansion with towers and turrets is one of the most delightful country-house hotels in the Borders. Known for its charming setting and its luxurious rooms, the hotel stands on 11 hectares (28 acres) of well-manicured grounds, featuring a 17th-century walled garden that in itself is worth a visit. The tasteful house is immaculately maintained, with public rooms that range from an elegant cocktail lounge to an adjacent conservatory. There's even a small library, an elevator (thankfully), and a large lounge where guests from all over the world meet and chat. Each of the spacious bedrooms is individually decorated; several units contain their own original fireplaces, and a few have four-poster beds. All accommodations open onto views of the extensive grounds. The bathrooms are well maintained and come with luxurious toiletries.

Eddleston, Peebles, The Borders EH45 8PL. ℘ **01721/725-750.** Fax 01721/725-751. www.cringletie.com. 14 units. £165–£245 ($314–$466) double. Rates include breakfast. AE, MC, V. Take A703 for 4km (2½ miles) north of Peebles. **Amenities:** Restaurant; bar; putting green; tennis court; babysitting; nonsmoking rooms. *In room:* TV, coffeemaker, hair dryer.

The Tontine 🔆 *Finds*   The Tontine has been around since 1807, when it was built as a private club by a group of hunters who sold their friends shares in its ownership. French prisoners of war did the construction during the Napoleonic era; later enlargements were made by the Edwardians. Flower boxes adorn its stone lintels, and a stone lion guards the forecourt fountain. The modestly furnished guest rooms are in an angular modern wing in back of the building's 19th-century core; they come with shower-only bathrooms. The most expensive rooms have river views. The Adam-style dining room is one of the town's architectural gems, with tall fan-topped windows and a minstrels' gallery. The Tweeddale Shoot Bar is cozily rustic. Perhaps you'll encounter the resident ghost, who, many visitors report, lives and sleeps outside the hotel wine cellar.

39 High St., Peebles, The Borders EH45 8AJ. ℘ **01721/720-892.** Fax 01721/729-732. www.tontinehotel.com. 36 units. £110–£150 ($209–$285) double. Children under 5 stay free in parent's room; ages 5–10 £10 ($19); ages 11–13 £20 ($38). Rates include breakfast. AE, DC, MC, V. Free parking. **Amenities:** Restaurant; bar. *In room:* TV, coffeemaker, hair dryer, trouser press.

Whitestone House   Located on the eastern fringe of Peebles, this dignified dark stone dwelling was built in 1892. It used to house the pastor of a Presbyterian church—which has been demolished—and is now the genteel domain of Mrs. Margaret Muir. Its windows overlook a pleasant garden and the glacial deposits of Whitestone Park. The high-ceilinged guest rooms are large and comfortable, evoking life in a quiet private home. Of the two shared bathrooms, one is large and has a tub/shower combination; the other only a shower. Mrs. Muir speaks French and German flawlessly, but presides over breakfast with a Scottish brogue.

Innerleithen Rd., Peebles, The Borders EH45 8BD. ℂ/fax **01721/720-337.** 5 units, none with private bathroom. £44–£64 ($84–$122) double. Rates include breakfast. No credit cards. Free parking. Closed Christmas and part of Jan. **Amenities:** Nonsmoking rooms. *In room:* TV, coffeemaker, hair dryer.

WHERE TO DINE

Horse Shoe Inn SCOTTISH   In the center of the nearby village of Eddleston, this country restaurant serves top-quality beef and steaks. Appetizers include everything from the chef's own pâté with oat cakes to smoked Shetland salmon with brown bread. House favorites are braised ham shank with honey-roasted vegetables and seared Scottish salmon on a nest of Rocket salad. Food and drink are served in the bar most days, but the staff opens up a more formal dining room for dinner on Friday and Saturday nights and Sunday lunch.

The owners, Mr. and Mrs. Hathoway, bought the old school next door and converted it into a guesthouse with eight rooms at £60 to £90 ($114–$171) per person, depending on the season; the rates include breakfast.

Eddleston. ℂ **01721/730-225.** Reservations recommended Sat. Main courses £8–£20 ($15–$38). MC, V. Easter–Oct Mon–Thurs 11am–11pm, Fri–Sun 11am–midnight; Nov–Easter Mon–Thurs 11am–2:30pm and 5:30–11pm, Fri–Sat 11am–2:30pm and 5:30pm–midnight. Take A701 7km (4½ miles) north of Peebles.

PEEBLES AFTER DARK

Peebles has many options for drinking and dining, and some of the most appealing are in the hotels on the town's edge, even though they may seem rather staid at first glance. On Innerleithen Road, the **Park Hotel** (ℂ **01721/720-451**) and the nearby **Hotel Hydro** (ℂ **01721/720-602**) contain pubs and cocktail lounges.

For an earthier atmosphere, we highly recommend dropping into the town's oldest pub, at **The Cross Keys Hotel,** 24 Northgate (ℂ **01721/724-222**), where you'll find 300-year-old smoke-stained panels, a blazing fireplace, and an evocatively crooked bar. Ask the bartender about the resident ghost. Like the Loch Ness monster, she's taken on an almost mythical identity since her last sighting, but the rumor goes that she's the spirit of Sir Walter Scott's former landlady, Marian Ritchie. No one will be shy about telling you his or her theory, especially if you're buying.

6 Moffat

98km (61 miles) S of Edinburgh, 35km (22 miles) NE of Dumfries, 97km (60 miles) SE of Glasgow

A small town at the head of the Annandale Valley, Moffat thrives as the center of a sheep-farming area, symbolized by a statue of a ram on the wide High Street. It's been a holiday resort since the mid–17th century because of the curative properties of its water, and it was here that Robert Burns composed the drinking song "O Willie Brewd a Peck o' Maut." Today, people visit this town on the banks of the Annan River for its great fishing and golf.

ESSENTIALS

GETTING THERE   The nearest rail station is in Lockerbie, 24km (15 miles) south of Moffat. Call ℂ 08457/484-950 for train information. Getting to Lockerbie sometimes requires a change of train in Dumfries, so passengers from Edinburgh or Glasgow often transfer to a **National Express** bus at Dumfries for the 35-minute trip straight to Moffat's High Street, which costs £3.50 ($6.65) one-way. If you are coming from the Lockerbie rail station, though, you can get a National Express bus to Moffat; they run four times a day, and the fare is £5 ($9.50) each way. For more bus information, call ℂ **8705/808-080.**

If you're driving from Dumfries, head northeast along A701. From Edinburgh, head south along A701; from Peebles, drive west, following the signs to Glasgow, then turn south on A702 and merge onto M74, following the signs to Moffat.

VISITOR INFORMATION   A **tourist office** is a 5-minute walk south of the town center, at Unit One, Ledyknowe, off Station Road (ℂ **01683/220-620**). Hours are as follows: April 1 to June 29 Monday to Saturday 9:30am to 5pm, Sunday noon to 4pm; June 30 to September 14 Monday to Saturday 9:30am to 6pm, Sunday noon to 5pm; September 15 to October 19 Monday to Saturday 9:30am to 5pm, Sunday noon to 4pm; and October 20 to March 31 Monday to Friday 10am to 5pm, Saturday 9:30am to 4pm.

EXPLORING THE AREA

North of Moffat is a lot of panoramic hill scenery. Eight kilometers (5 miles) northwest is a sheer-sided 152m-deep (500-ft.), 3km (2-mile) wide hollow in the hills called the **Devil's Beef Tub,** where cattle thieves (reivers) once hid their loot. This hollow is of interest to geologists because of the way it illustrates Ice Age glacial action, and it makes for a good day hike in the quiet countryside. To reach it, walk north from Moffat along the **Annan Water Valley Road,** a rural route with virtually no vehicular traffic. In 6.5km (4 miles), the road will descend a steep slope whose contours form an unusual bowl shape. No signs mark the site, but you'll know it when you get there.

Northeast along Moffat Water, past 818m-high (2,696-ft.) White Coomb, is the **Grey Mare's Tail,** a 61m (200-ft.) hanging waterfall formed by the Tail Burn dropping from Loch Skene; it's part of the National Trust for Scotland.

GOLF

The region's most famous course is the **Moffat Golf Club Course,** Coates Hill (ℂ **01683/220-020**), about 1.6km (1 mile) southwest of the town center. Nonmembers can play if they call in advance except for Wednesday afternoon after 3pm. Greens fees are £22 ($42) per round or £28 ($53) per day during the week. On Saturday and Sunday greens fees are £30 ($57) per round or £36 ($68) per day. The tourist office has a free brochure called *Golfing in Dumfries & Galloway.*

WHERE TO STAY

You can also find accommodations at **Well View** (see "Where to Dine," below).

Auchen Castle Hotel ℱ   Located about 1.6km (1 mile) north of the village of Beattock, the area's most luxurious accommodations are at the Auchen, a Victorian mock-castle. It's really a country house built in 1849 on the site of Auchen Castle, with terraced gardens and a trout-filled loch. Most of the guest rooms are spacious, and all units are nonsmoking. Ask for a room in the main house (which is known as the castle); the others are in the Cedar Lodge, a less desirable annex built in the late 1970s.

Beattock, Dumfriesshire DG10 9SH. ✆ **01683/300-407.** Fax 01683/300-667. www.auchen-castle-hotel.co.uk. 25 units. £164–£229 ($312–$435) double in main house, £235–£300 ($447–$570) suite; £136–£201 ($258–$382) double in Cedar Lodge. Breakfast included. AE, DC, MC, V. Take A74 for 3km (2 miles) north of Moffat. **Amenities:** Restaurant; bar; room service; laundry service. *In room:* TV, coffeemaker, hair dryer.

Moffat House Hotel   The red- and black-stone Moffat House is one of the town's most architecturally noteworthy buildings; it was constructed in 1751 by John Adam. This Best Western affiliate's modernized guest rooms are comfortable and functional, each with a tub/shower bathroom. A few rooms have four-poster beds. Some rooms are equipped for families, others for travelers with disabilities.

Note: The hotel offers a selection of the best food in town, especially at night, when the chef prepares an international menu.

High St., Moffat, Galloway DG10 9HL. ✆ **01683/220-039.** Fax 01683/221-288. www.moffathouse.co.uk. 20 units. £100 ($190) double. Rates include breakfast. AE, DC, MC, V. Free parking. **Amenities:** Restaurant; bar; room service; rooms for those w/limited mobility. *In room:* TV, coffeemaker, hair dryer.

Star Hotel   With a 17th-century brick facade, this place bears the quirky fame of being the narrowest free-standing hotel in the United Kingdom—it's only 6m (20 ft.) wide (and is in the *Guinness Book of World Records*). The guest rooms, last refurbished in 1996, are small and unpretentious, with contemporary furnishings, and bathrooms with either a tub or a shower. The food here is popular; menu items are simple and straightforward but savory. The hotel also rents a two-bedroom cottage (good for families) for £110 ($209) per night.

44 High St., Moffat, Galloway DG10 9EF. ✆ **01683/220-156.** Fax 01683/221-524. www.famousstarhotel.co.uk. 8 units. £60 ($114) double. Rates include breakfast. AE, MC, V. **Amenities:** Restaurant; 2 bars. *In room:* TV, coffeemaker, hair dryer.

WHERE TO DINE

Other dining options include the restaurants in the hotels listed above.

Well View ⋆⋆ BRITISH/CONTINENTAL   Come to this hotel for some of the best food in the region. The setting is mid-Victorian, with Laura Ashley country-cottage charm and views of the kitchen garden. The set-price menus vary almost daily, depending on the season, and may include Thai smoked salmon with melon and tarragon dressing, or filet of Aberdeen Angus beef with roasted root vegetables, red-wine sauce, and Dauphinois potatoes.

Upstairs are five guest rooms and a junior suite, with modern furniture and reproduction antiques (including a four-poster bed), Laura Ashley fabrics, free sherry and fresh fruit, TVs, clock radios, tea/coffeemakers, trouser press, sewing kits, and hair dryers. Doubles are £110 ($209).

Ballplay Rd., Moffat DG10 9JU. ✆ **01683/220-184.** Fax 01683/220-088. www.wellview.co.uk. Reservations recommended. Fixed-price 3-course lunch £22 ($42); fixed-price 6-course dinner £35 ($67; includes wine). AE, MC, V. Sun–Fri 12:30–1:15pm; daily 7–8:30pm. Take A708 1.2km (¾ mile) east of Moffat.

7 Dumfries: An Ode to Burns ⋆

129km (80 miles) SW of Edinburgh, 127km (79 miles) SE of Glasgow, 55km (34 miles) NW of Carlisle

A county town and royal burgh, the Galloway center of Dumfries enjoys associations with national poet Robert Burns and *Peter Pan* author James Barrie. Burns lived in

Dumfries from 1791 until his death in 1796, and wrote some of his best-known songs here, including "Auld Lang Syne" and "Ye Banks and Braes of Bonnie Doon." A statue of Burns stands on High Street; you can visit his house, his favorite pub, and his mausoleum. Barrie was a pupil at the academy here and later wrote that he got the idea for *Peter Pan* from his games in the nearby garden.

The widest esplanade in Dumfries, **Whitesands,** flanks the edge of the River Nith. It was once the scene of horse and hiring fairs and is a fine place to park your car and explore this provincial town. The town center is reserved for pedestrians, and on the opposite bank of the Nith, the public Deer Park offers a small-scale manicured version of the wild majesty of Scotland. Allow a morning to visit the city's major sights, but there's even more to see in the surrounding countryside, including Sweetheart Abbey, Ellisland Farm, and Drumlanrig Castle at Thornhill, which is filled with artwork by Rembrandt and Leonardo da Vinci, among others.

ESSENTIALS

GETTING THERE   Seven trains per day make the run from Glasgow's Central Station, taking 1¾ hours. Tickets cost £12 ($23) one-way but only £13 to £20 ($25–$38) round-trip, depending on time of departure. For 24-hour information, call © **8457/ 484-950.**

Stagecoach buses depart from Glasgow (from Buchanan St. Station or Anderston Station); the trip is 2 hours and costs £7.80 ($15) one-way and £14 ($27) round-trip. Buses also run to Dumfries from Edinburgh's St. Andrew's Square. The prices are the same as from Glasgow, but the trip is 3 hours. For bus information, call © **01387/ 253-496.**

If you're driving from Edinburgh, take A701 to Moffat, then continue southwest to Dumfries. From Glasgow, take M74, which becomes A74 before it approaches Moffat. At Moffat, continue southwest along A701.

VISITOR INFORMATION   The **tourist office** is at 64 Whitesands (© **01387/ 245-550**), a 2-minute walk from High Street and adjacent to the big parking lots. September to March, it's open Monday to Friday 10am to 5pm and Saturday 10am to 4pm; April to August, hours are Monday to Saturday 10am to 6pm (July–Aug also Sun noon–4pm).

EXPLORING THE TOWN

The 18th-century **St. Michael's Church,** on St. Michael's Street, is the original parish church of Dumfries. Its foundation is ancient—the site was sacred before the advent of Christianity, and a Christian church has stood here for more than 1,300 years. The earliest written records date from 1165 to 1214. The church and the churchyard are interesting because of all their connections with Scottish history, continuing through World War II. You can still see the Burns family pew inside.

In St. Michael's Churchyard, a burial place for at least 900 years, stands the neo-Grecian **Burns Mausoleum.** Built of local sandstone and dripping with literary and patriotic nostalgia, the dome-capped mausoleum is one of the most important pilgrimage sites for Burns fans. The poet is buried here along with his wife, Jean Armour, and five of their children. Burns died in 1796, but his remains weren't moved to the tomb until 1815.

The **Mid Steeple** ℱ on High Street was built in 1707 as municipal buildings, a courthouse, and a prison. The old Scots "ell" measure, the equivalent of almost 1m (37 in.), is carved on the front, and a table of distances includes the mileage to Huntingdon,

England, which in the 18th century was the destination for Scottish cattle driven south for the London markets. Today the Mid Steeple is used mostly for municipal archives and government functions.

At Whitesands, the street paralleling the Nith's edge, **four bridges** span the river. The earliest was built by Devorgilla Balliol, widow of John Balliol. Their son, John, was made Scotland's "vassal king" by Edward I of England, the "Hammer of the Scots," who established himself as Scotland's overlord. The bridge (originally with nine arches but now with only six) is still in constant use as a footbridge.

The town's best **shopping** is along High Street, which is lined with turn-of-the-20th-century facades, and also along nearby Queensberry Street. **Alternatives,** 73–75 Queensberry St. (✆ **01387/257-467**), is an attractive new-age shop selling herbal remedies, artful wind chimes, and gift items, especially jewelry inspired by Celtic designs. At the **Edinburgh Woollen Mill,** 8 Church Place (✆ **01387/267-351**), you'll find men's and women's kilts in dozens of tartan patterns, as well as sweaters, overcoats, hats, and socks—all at reasonable prices.

If you want to explore the area on two wheels, the **Nithsdale Cycle Centre,** 46 Broon's Rd. (✆ **01387/254-870**), is the place to go. You'll have to leave a 25% deposit; rental rates are £9 ($17) for a half-day, £12 ($23) daily, or £37 ($70) weekly. It's open Monday to Saturday 10am to 5pm.

Burns House   In 1796, Scotland's national poet died in this unpretentious, terraced stone house off St. Michael's Street. Although he occupied the house only during the last 3 years of his life, it contains personal relics and mementos as well as much of the original furniture used by Burns during his creative years.

Burns St. ✆ **01387/255-297.** Free admission. Apr–Sept Mon–Sat 10am–5pm, Sun 2–5pm; Oct–Mar Tues–Sat 10am–1pm and 2–5pm.

Drumlanrig Castle 🦅 🅚ids   This pink castle, built between 1679 and 1689 in a parkland ringed by wild hills, is the seat of the dukes of Buccleuch and Queensberry. It's home to some outstanding paintings, including a famous Rembrandt and a Holbein, plus relics related to Bonnie Prince Charlie. In 2004 the castle made headlines around the world when two thieves, posing as sightseers, overpowered a castle guard and made off with the *Madonna with the Yarnwinder,* believed to have been an important work by Leonardo da Vinci. Valued at $50 million, the National Gallery of Scotland proclaimed the painting an authentic da Vinci in 1986, although skeptics remain. Even without da Vinci's *Madonna,* there are still works by Reynolds, Murillo, and other old masters, and the castle's architecture is splendid as well. There's a playground with amusements for kids and a working crafts center in the stable yard; the gardens are gradually being restored to their 1720 magnificence. Meals are served in the kitchen, which is hung with gleaming copper.

Thornhill, 5km (3 miles) north of Thornhill off A76 and 16 miles (26km) southwest of A74 at Elvanfoot. ✆ **01848/330-248** or 01848/331-555. Admission £7 ($13) adults, £6 ($11) seniors, £4 ($7.60) children, £12–£24 ($23–$46) families. May 1–June 30 Sat–Thurs noon–4pm; July 1–Aug 21 daily noon–4pm. Closed Sept–Apr.

Dumfries Museum   Southwestern Scotland's largest museum occupies a converted 18th-century windmill atop Corbelly Hill. Visit it only if you have extra time and an interest in the region's early geology, history, and archaeology. The museum is rich with collections ranging from early Christian stones to artifacts of 18th-century country life. Some exhibits suggest the site's role as an astronomical observatory in 1836; note the 20-centimeter (8-in.) telescope used to observe Halley's Comet in July

1836. The camera obscura provides panoramic views of the town and surrounding countryside.

Church St. ☎ **01387/253-374.** www.dumfriesmuseum.demon.co.uk. Museum free admission; camera obscura £1.90 ($3.60) adults, 95p ($1.80) children and seniors. Museum: Apr–Sept Mon–Sat 10am–5pm, Sun 2–5pm; Oct–Mar Tues–Sat 10am–1pm and 2–5pm. Camera obscura: Apr–Sept Mon–Sat 10am–5pm, Sun 2–5pm. Cross the river at St. Michael's Bridge Rd. and turn right onto Church St.

Ellisland Farm *Finds*   From 1788 to 1791, Robert Burns made his last attempt at farming at Ellisland Farm; it was here that he wrote *Tam o' Shanter*. After his marriage to Jean Armour, Burns leased the farm from Patrick Miller under the stipulation that he'd assist in erecting the building that's the centerpiece of the homestead. It's still a working farm for sheep and cattle, with many aspects devoted to a museum and shrine honoring Burns and his literary statements. On a circular 400m (.25-mile) trail ("the south trail") adjacent to the banks of the Nith, you can retrace the footsteps of Burns, who walked along it frequently during breaks from his writing.

10km (6 miles) north of Dumfries via A76 (follow the signs to Kilmarnock). ☎ **01387/740-426.** www.ellislandfarm. co.uk. Admission £2.50 ($4.75) adults, £1 ($1.90) students and seniors, children under 15 free. Apr–Sept Mon–Fri 10am–1pm and 2–5pm, Sun 2–5pm; Oct–Mar Tues–Sat 10am–4pm.

Old Bridge House   Associated with the Burns House (see above), this building dates from 1660, when it replaced a structure that had been on the site since 1431. It was occupied as a private house until as late as 1957 and has been restored and furnished in a style typical of the period between 1850 and 1900, with tons of worthy Victoriana. Devorgilla Bridge itself was constructed in the 16th century.

Mill Rd. at the far end of Devorgillas Bridge. ☎ **01387/256-904.** Free admission. Apr–Sept Mon–Sat 10am–5pm, Sun 2–5pm. From Whitesands, cross the river at Devorgillas Bridge.

Robert Burns Centre   You'll find this converted 18th-century water mill on the banks of the River Nith. Facilities include an exhibit on the poet, a restaurant, and an audiovisual theater showing films about Burns and the town of Dumfries.

Mill Rd. ☎ **01387/264-808.** Exhibition free admission; audiovisual theater £1.60 ($3.05) adults, 80p ($1.50) children, seniors, and students. Apr–Sept Mon–Sat 10am–8pm, Sun 2–5pm; Oct–Mar Tues–Sat 10am–1pm and 2–5pm. From Whitesands, cross the river at Devorgillas Bridge.

Sweetheart Abbey *𝒜*   The village of New Abbey is dominated by Sweetheart Abbey's red-sandstone ruins. The walls are mostly extant, even though the roof is missing. Devorgilla Balliol founded the abbey in 1273. With the death of her husband, John Balliol the Elder, she became one of Europe's richest women—most of Galloway, as well as estates and castles in England and Normandy, belonged to her. Devorgilla founded Balliol College, Oxford, in her husband's memory. For 21 years, she kept his embalmed heart in a silver-and-ivory casket, by her side, until her death in 1289 at age 80, when she and the casket were buried in front of the abbey altar. The abbey gained the name of "Dulce Cor," Latin for "sweet heart," a term that has become a part of the English language.

On A710, New Abbey. ☎ **01387/850-397** (regional office of Historic Scotland). Admission £3 ($5.70) adults, £2 ($3.80) seniors, £1.50 ($2.85) children under 16. Oct–Mar Sat–Wed 9:30am–4:30pm; Apr–Sept daily 9:30am–5:30pm. Drive 11km (7 miles) southwest from Dumfries on A710 (follow the signs saying SOLWAY FIRTH HERITAGE).

WHERE TO STAY

Cairndale Hotel & Leisure Club *𝒜*   This is the finest hotel in Dumfries, easily outdistancing The Station and all other competition. A four-story stone-fronted building from around 1900, the Cairndale is a fine choice with handsome public rooms. It's owned and managed by the Wallace family, who has carefully modernized the guest rooms. Executive rooms and suites have queen-size beds, trouser presses, and whirlpool baths. The hotel's leisure facilities are noteworthy—there's a 14m (46-ft.) heated pool—and the restaurant hosts a popular dinner dance on Saturday nights.

132–136 English St., Dumfries, Galloway DG1 2DF. ℂ **01387/254-111.** Fax 01387/250-555. www.cairndalehotel. co.uk. 91 units. £109 ($207) double; from £149 ($283) suite. Rates include breakfast. AE, DC, MC, V. Free parking. **Amenities:** Restaurant; bar; heated indoor pool; health club; Jacuzzi; 24-hr. room service; babysitting; laundry service; dry cleaning. *In room:* TV, minibar (in executive rooms and suites), coffeemaker, hair dryer.

The Station   This is among the most traditional hotels in Dumfries, a few steps from the gingerbread-fringed train station. It was built in 1896 of hewn sandstone, in a design of heavy timbers, polished paneling, and soaring ceilings. The modernized, but still somewhat dowdy, guest rooms contain comfortable beds and shower-only bathrooms. The four-poster rooms and the suite feature Jacuzzi tubs. A Garden Room lounge has been added, the creation of a Feng Shui consultant hoping to increase the *chi,* or "good feeling," of guests.

49 Lovers Walk, Dumfries, Galloway DG1 1LT. ℂ **800/780-7234** or 01387/254-316. Fax 01387/250-388. www.station hotel.co.uk. 32 units. £77–£125 ($146–$238) double; £145 ($276) suite. Rates include breakfast. AE, DC, MC, V. Free parking. **Amenities:** 2 restaurants; 2 bars; room service; babysitting; nonsmoking rooms; rooms for those w/limited mobility. *In room:* TV, minibar, coffeemaker, hair dryer, trouser press, Wi-Fi.

Trigony House Hotel   This pink-sandstone hotel was built around 1895 as the home of a local family. Its name *(trigony)* derives from the shape of the acreage, which is almost a perfect isosceles triangle. Today, it contains a handful of comfortable but unpretentious high-ceilinged guest rooms, each opening onto countryside views. Adam (the chef of the hotel's restaurant) and Jan Moore are your hosts and will tell you all about the building's occupant during the 1930s: Frances Shakerley. She lived to be 107 and was widely known as the oldest woman in Scotland.

The hotel operates a busy pub and a dinner-only restaurant. Drop into the pub for affordable platters of simple food at lunch or dinner. Meals may include filet of sea bass with a light fennel and white-wine sauce, or loin of Tamworth pork braised with white wine and mushrooms.

On the Dumfries-Ayr trunk road, Thornhill, Dumfries, Galloway DG3 5EZ. ℂ **01848/331-211.** Fax 01848/331-303. www.trigonyhotel.co.uk. 10 units. £90–£100 ($171–$190) double. Rates include breakfast. MC, V. From Dumfries, drive 21km (13 miles) north along A76, following the signs to Thornhill. Trigony House is 1.6km (1 mile) south of Thornhill. Dogs accepted. **Amenities:** Restaurant; bar. *In room:* TV, coffeemaker, hair dryer.

WHERE TO DINE

Bruno's ITALIAN   It may seem odd to recommend an Italian restaurant in the heart of Robert Burns territory, but Bruno's serves some of the best food in town. It's unassuming, but that's part of the charm. The chef's repertoire is familiar—first-rate minestrone, homemade pizza and pasta, veal with ham, and spicy chicken—but everything is done with flair.

3 Balmoral Rd. ℂ **01387/255-757.** Reservations required Sat–Sun. Main courses £8–£18 ($15–$34); fixed-price 3-course dinner £22 ($42); supper pasta menu £10 ($19). MC, V. Wed–Mon 5:30–10pm.

Globe Inn SCOTTISH   This is the traditional favorite, open since 1610. It was Burns's favorite haunt, and he used an old Scottish expression, *howff* (meaning a small, cozy room), to describe his local pub. He was definitely a regular: He had a child with the barmaid, Anna Park. You reach the pub down a narrow flagstone passage off High

Street, opposite the Marks & Spencer department store. You can go for a meal (perhaps roast lamb, steak pie, or chicken curry) or just to have a drink and play a game of dominoes. A little museum is devoted to Burns, and on window panes upstairs you can see verses he scratched with a diamond. Taps include Belhaven, Tennent's Lager, Galloway Ale, and Black Throne Cider.

56 High St. ℭ **01387/252-335.** Main courses £4–£6 ($7.60–$11). AE, MC, V. Mon–Thurs 10am–11pm; Fri–Sat 10am–midnight; Sun noon–midnight. Food served Mon–Sat 10–11:30am and noon–3pm.

Hullabaloo SCOTTISH   This is the most unusual restaurant in Dumfries. It's in a renovated grain mill, which you reach by taking a lovely 10-minute stroll across the Nith from the commercial heart of town. Built around 1780 by a prominent engineer, Thomas Sneaton, the mill also shelters a small movie house and the Robert Burns Centre (see above). The food is prepared with Scottish ingredients and changes with the seasons. A homemade soup of the day is always served along with freshly baked bread, and there are imaginative salads, including a Thai prawn and a tabbouleh-and-bean salad. Instead of elaborate main courses, you get various baguettes with such enticements as smoked salmon and cream cheese, or baked potatoes that are themselves almost meals. The aura is one of cafe dining with an emphasis on lighter fare than a major restaurant.

In the Robert Burns Centre, Mill Rd. ℭ **01387/259-679.** Reservations recommended. Main courses £7.25–£16 ($14–$30). MC, V. Easter–Sept Mon–Sat 11am–4pm, Tues–Sat 6–10pm, Sun 11am–3pm; Oct–Easter Tues–Sat 11am–4pm and 6–10pm.

DUMFRIES AFTER DARK

The town's most famous pub is the previously recommended **Globe Inn,** 56 High St. (ℭ **01387/252-335**), where Robert Burns tipped many a dram. An equally historic pub loaded with local color is **The Hole I' the Wa',** 156 High St. (ℭ **01387/252-770**), where an accordionist usually performs. If you want to go dancing, head for either of the town's two discos, **Chancers Nightclub,** 25 Munches St. (ℭ **01387/263-170**), or **The Junction,** 36 High St. (ℭ **01387/267-262**). The crowd and music at these two clubs change often, depending on the theme for the night, so it's best to call ahead.

8 Castle Douglas

26km (16 miles) SW of Dumfries, 158km (98 miles) SW of Edinburgh, 79km (49 miles) SE of Ayr

An old cattle- and sheep-market town, Castle Douglas, at the northern tip of Carlingwark Loch, is near such attractions as Threave Castle, Cardoness Castle, Kirkcudbright, and Sweetheart Abbey, and just southeast of the Galloway Forest Park. On one of the islets in the loch is an ancient lake dwelling known as a *crannog.*

ESSENTIALS

GETTING THERE   The nearest rail station is in Dumfries (see "Dumfries: An Ode to Burns," earlier in this chapter); from there, you can take a bus to Castle Douglas. Call ℭ **8457/484-950** for rail information.

The **Great Western Bus Co.** runs buses from Dumfries to Castle Douglas every hour throughout the day and early evening; travel time is about 30 minutes and costs £2 ($3.80) one-way. Call ℭ **8705/808-080** for bus information.

If you're driving from Dumfries, head southwest along A75.

VISITOR INFORMATION   A **tourist office** is at the Markethill Car Park (✆ **01556/ 502-611**). April to October, it's open Monday to Friday 10am to 6pm, Saturday 10am to 5pm (July–Aug also Sun 10am–5pm).

SEEING THE SIGHTS

Threave Castle ✦   This is the ruined 14th-century stronghold of the Black Douglases. The seven-story tower was built between 1639 and 1690 by Archibald the Grim, Lord of Galloway. In 1455, Threave was the last Douglas stronghold to surrender to James II, who employed some of the most advanced armaments of his day (including a cannon similar to Mons Meg, the massive cannon now displayed in Edinburgh Castle) in its subjection. Over the doorway is the gallows knob from which the Douglases hanged their enemies. In 1640, the castle was captured and dismantled by the Covenanters, the rebellious group of Scots who questioned the king's right to make laws.

To reach the site, you walk .8km (½ mile) through farmlands and then take a small boat across the Dee. When you get to the river, ring a bell signaling the custodian to come and ferry you across. The last boat is at 6pm. For information, contact Historic Scotland, Longmore House, Salisbury Place, Edinburgh (✆ **07711/223-101;** www. historic-scotland.gov.uk).

2.5km (1½ miles) west of Castle Douglas on an islet in the River Dee. Admission (including ferry ride) £4 ($7.60) adults, £3 ($5.70) seniors, £2 ($3.80) children under 16. Apr–Sept daily 9:30am–6:30pm. Last outward sailing at 4:30pm. Closed Oct–Mar.

Threave Garden ✦✦   About 1.6km (1 mile) southeast of Threave Castle, these gardens are built around Threave House, a Scottish baronial mansion constructed during the Victorian era. It's run by the National Trust for Scotland, which uses the complex as a school for gardening and as a wildfowl refuge. The garden is at its best in April, when the daffodils bloom, and in June, when the rhododendrons and the rock garden are in flower. On site are a visitor center and a restaurant.

Off A75 1km (½ mile) west of Castle Douglas. ✆ **01556/502-575.** www.nts.org.uk. Admission £5 ($9.50) adults, £3.75 ($7.15) children and seniors. Garden daily 9:30am–5:30pm; visitor center Feb–Mar daily 10am–4pm, Apr–Oct daily 9:30am–5:30pm, Nov–Dec 23 daily 10am–4pm.

WHERE TO STAY

Douglas Arms   Originally, a 17th-century coaching inn, this old favorite is surprisingly modern—it lies behind a rather stark two-story facade. The public rooms are bright and cheerful, giving you a toasty feeling on a cold night. The guest rooms were refurbished a few years ago and include shower-only bathrooms.

King St., Castle Douglas, Galloway DG7 1DB. ✆ **01556/502-231.** Fax 01556/504-000. www.douglasarmshotel.com. 24 units. £55–£100 ($105–$190) double. Rates include breakfast. AE, MC, V. **Amenities:** Restaurant; bar; nonsmoking rooms. *In room:* TV, coffeemaker, hair dryer, trouser press, Wi-Fi.

King's Arms   This inn provides reasonably priced accommodations ranging from single rooms to a family room. The guest rooms are touched up every year and in good shape; nine come with shower-only bathrooms. (Guests in the 10th room get a hallway bathroom with a tub reserved solely for their use.) The helpful staff will direct you to various activities in the area, including a 9-hole golf course a 45-minute drive away. The sun patio is a great place for tea or coffee or perhaps a sundowner of malt whisky. The cuisine is British with a Scottish emphasis; the range is extensive, featuring local produce, Solway salmon, and Galloway beef.

St. Andrew's St., Castle Douglas, Galloway DG7 1EL. © **01556/502-626.** Fax 01556/502-097. www.galloway-golf.
co.uk. 10 units, 9 with private bathroom. £76 ($144) double with bathroom. Rates include breakfast. MC, V. Free park-
ing. **Amenities:** Restaurant; bar. *In room:* TV, coffeemaker, hair dryer.

The Urr Valley Country House Hotel 🐾 *Finds*   Reached by a long drive, this country hotel in the scenic Urr Valley is set amid 5.6 hectares (14 acres) of lush woodlands
and gardens, 1.6km (1 mile) east of the center of Castle Douglas. You're welcomed
into a real Scottish macho atmosphere of stag heads and antique rods and reels, along
with paneled walls and log-burning fireplaces. Most of the guest rooms are spacious;
a few have four-poster beds and others are designed for families.

   You can have a drink or enjoy a pub meal in the lounge and bar. In the main restaurant, both French and Scottish cuisine are served, with an emphasis on fresh seafood
and local produce such as pheasant and Solway salmon. Dare you try the regional specialty, Scottish haggis?

Ernespie Rd., Castle Douglas, Galloway DG7 3JG. © **01556/502-188.** Fax 01556/504-055. www.scottish-inns.co.uk/
urrvalley. 17 units. £65–£70 ($124–$133) double; £75–£100 ($143–$190) family room. Rates include breakfast. AE,
MC, V. Free parking. Take A75 toward Castle Douglas. Dogs accepted by prior arrangement. **Amenities:** Restaurant;
bar; nonsmoking rooms. *In room:* TV, coffeemaker, hair dryer, trouser press.

WHERE TO DINE
Plumed Horse Restaurant 🐾🐾 SCOTTISH/INTERNATIONAL   Opened in
July 1998, this restaurant combines high-quality cuisine with a relaxed village atmosphere; it's set the rest of the local competition on its ear. The linen tablecloths, crystal, silver, and Villeroy & Boch tableware give the Plumed Horse an air of elegance.
Chef Tony Borthwick changes the menu regularly, but you might find roast Barbary
duck breast, crisp filet of salmon, scallop ravioli, and roast monkfish among the choices.
Desserts, such as pistachio and praline parfait and banana brûlée in butterscotch sauce,
are favorites. Ingredients used in the meals are often luxurious, including wild mushrooms and foie gras. The restaurant also has an extensive wine and champagne list.

Main St., Crossmichael (5km/3 miles from Castle Douglas). © **01556/670-333.** Reservations recommended. Main
courses £18–£21 ($34–$40). MC, V. Tues–Sun 12:30–1:30pm and 7–9:30pm (closed on Sat at lunch). Take A713
toward Ayr.

9 Kirkcudbright: An Artists' Colony 🐾

174km (108 miles) SW of Edinburgh, 45km (28 miles) SW of Dumfries, 166km (103 miles) S of Glasgow, 81km (50
miles) E of Stranraer, 16km (10 miles) SW of Castle Douglas

The ancient burgh of Kirkcudbright (kir-*coo*-bree) is at the head of Kirkcudbright Bay
on the Dee estuary. Many of this intriguing old town's color-washed houses belong to
artists; a lively group of weavers, potters, and painters live and work in the 18th-cen-
tury streets and lanes. What makes Kirkcudbright so enchanting isn't really its sights
(although it boasts several) but its artistic life and bohemian flavor. Various festivities
take place in July and August; expect to find anything from marching bagpipe bands
to exhibitions of Scottish country dancing to torchlight processions. And activities
range from raft races to nearby walks, from a floodlit tattoo in front of MacLellan's
Castle to a puppet festival. Check with the tourist office (see below) about what will
be happening when you visit.

ESSENTIALS
GETTING THERE   Kirkcudbright is on the same bus route that serves Castle
Douglas from Dumfries, with departures during the day about once per hour. The

40-minute ride from Dumfries is about £4 ($7.60) one-way, a day ticket is £5 ($9.50). For bus information, call ✆ **08705/808-080** or the local tourist office.

If you're driving from Castle Douglas, continue southwest along A75 until you come to the junction with A711, which takes you into Kirkcudbright.

VISITOR INFORMATION   A **tourist office** is at Harbour Square (✆ **01557/330-494**). April 1 to June 29 and September 15 to October 26, it's open Monday to Saturday 10am to 5pm and Sunday 11am to 4:30pm; June 30 to September 14, hours are Monday to Saturday 9:30am to 6pm and Sunday 10am to 5pm.

SEEING THE SIGHTS

In the old town **graveyard** are memorials to Covenanters and to Billy Marshall, the tinker (Gypsy) king who died in 1792 at age 120, reportedly having fathered four children after age 100.

Broughton House   Regular exhibits are displayed at this 18th-century mansion that once belonged to artist Edward Atkinson Hornel (1864–1933). His portrait by Bessie McNicol is displayed in the former dining room. Although largely forgotten today, Hornel was a famous artist in his day, known for his scenes depicting life in his native Galloway. With his bold and colorful style, he became one of the major figures of the Glasgow School of Art. Broughton contains a large reference library with a Burns collection, along with pictures by Hornel and other artists. One of the most appealing aspects of this place is Hornel's small but charming Japanese-style garden, whose plantings sometimes appeared in his paintings.

12 High St. ✆ **01557/330-437**. Admission £3.50 ($6.65) adults, £2.60 ($4.95) seniors and children, £9.50 ($18) per family. Apr–June Mon–Fri 11am–4pm; Sept–Oct Thurs–Mon noon–5:30pm; July–Aug daily noon–5pm. Closed Nov–Mar.

MacLellan's Castle   Dominating the center of town is this castle built in 1582 for the town's provost, Sir Thomas MacLellan. It has been a ruin since 1752, but it's impressive and worth a visit. A large staircase goes from the cellars on the ground floor to the Banqueting Hall, where a massive fireplace has what was called a "lairds lug" (spy hole). From almost anywhere in town, the jagged fangs of the castle loom overhead.

Off High St. ✆ **01557/331-856**. Admission £3.50 ($6.65) adults, £2.80 ($5.30) seniors, £1.75 ($3.35) children. Apr–Sept daily 9:30am–5:30pm. Closed Oct–Mar.

Stewartry Museum   Built by the Victorians in 1892 as a showcase for the region's distinctive culture, this museum contains an unusual collection of antiquities, tools, and artworks depicting the history, traditions, and sociology of this part of Galloway.

St. Mary St. ✆ **01557/331-643**. Free admission. July–Sept Mon–Sat 10m–5pm, Sun 2–5pmOct Mon–Sat 11am–4pm, Sun 2–5pm; Nov–June Mon–Sat 11am–4pm.

Tolbooth Art Centre   The Tolbooth (1629) has functioned as a prison, town hall, and courthouse. Out front is the MercatCross, from 1610, while inside is a memorial to John Paul Jones (1747–92), the gardener's son from Kirkbean who became a slave trader, a privateer, and, eventually, the father of the American navy. For a time before his emigration, he was imprisoned for murder here. In 1993, Queen Elizabeth inaugurated the building as a gallery displaying paintings by famous local artists. You'll find works by Jessie M. King, Lena Alexander, Robert Sivell, and S. J. Peploe.

High St. ✆ **01557/331-556**. Free admission. May–June and Sept Mon–Sat 11am–5pm, Sun 2–5pm; July–Aug Mon–Sat 10am–5pm, Sun 2–5pm; Oct Mon–Sat 11am–4pm, Sun 2–5pm; Nov–Apr Mon–Sat 11am–4pm.

WHERE TO STAY

Selkirk Arms ☞ This beloved old favorite—the finest inn in the area—is where Robert Burns stayed when he composed the celebrated "Selkirk Grace." It was built in the 1770s in a stone-fronted Georgian design with a slate roof. The guest rooms all have standard furniture and garden views. The restaurant/bistro offers a wide range of fresh local produce; bar lunches and suppers are also available. The lounge bar features an array of malt whiskies that would have warmed Burns's heart.

Old High St., Kirkcudbright, Galloway DG6 4JG. © **800/780-7234** or 01557/330-402. Fax 01557/331-639. www. selkirkarmshotel.co.uk. 16 units. £98 ($186) double. Rates include breakfast. Children under 17 in parent's room pay only for breakfast. AE, DC, MC, V. Free parking. **Amenities:** Restaurant; bar. *In room:* TV, coffeemaker, hair dryer.

WHERE TO DINE

Auld Alliance Restaurant SCOTTISH/FRENCH One of the most appealing restaurants in the region is this family-owned and -operated place. It's located in a pair of connected buildings that were constructed, in the 1880s, with stones from the ruins of Kirkcudbright Castle. The cooks are almost obsessed with the freshness of the fish they serve, and salmon (usually caught several hours before preparation in the Kirkcudbright estuary and its tributary, the Dee) are full of legendary flavor. A house specialty is *queenies* (queen-size scallops from deeper waters than the great scallop).

5 Castle St. © **01557/330-569.** Reservations recommended. Main courses £9–£16 ($17–$30). MC, V. Apr–Oct daily 6:30–9:30pm. Closed Halloween–Easter.

10 Portpatrick: Where the Southern Upland Way Begins

227km (141 miles) SW of Edinburgh, 13km (8 miles) SW of Stranraer, 156km (97 miles) SW of Glasgow, 129km (80 miles) W of Dumfries

Until 1849, steamers sailed the 34km (21 miles) from Donaghdee, in Northern Ireland, to Portpatrick, which became a "Gretna Green" for the Irish who wanted to marry quickly. Couples would land on Saturday, have the banns called on Sunday, and marry on Monday.

Today, you go to Portpatrick not because of its wealth of sights, although the Logan Botanic Gardens is worth the detour from Stranraer; you go, instead, because it's a major refueling stop for those driving along the Mull of Galloway. Portpatrick captures the flavor of an old Scottish fishing port as few other towns do. It's a land of cliffs and rugged seascapes, with a lighthouse here and there and even a bird reserve.

Hikers come because Portpatrick is the beginning of one of the greatest long-distance footpaths in Scotland, the **Southern Upland Way** (see "The Best Hikes," in chapter 1). Starting here, the 341km (212-mile) jaunt goes all the way to the Cockburnspath on the eastern coast of Scotland. Along the way, this path traverses the Galloway Forest Park and other scenic attractions of southern Scotland. Of course, very few have the time or the stamina for the entire hike. But you can enjoy one of the least-challenging stretches, going all the way from Portpatrick to Castle Kennedy, some 12km (7.5 miles).

ESSENTIALS

GETTING THERE Go to Stranraer by **train,** then take a bus to Portpatrick, 5 minutes away. For train information, call © **08457/484-950.** Bus no. 64 from Stranraer makes frequent runs throughout the day. The 5-minute ride costs around £1 ($1.90) one-way. For bus information, call © **08705/808-080.** If you're **driving** from Stranraer, take A77 southwest.

EXPLORING THE AREA

Commanding a cliff top 2.5km (1½ miles) south of the town center are the ruins of **Dunskey Castle,** a grim keep built in 1510. It's a dramatic site—the original stone walls and the chimney stacks, each rising abruptly from the top of the cliff, are all that remain. To walk or drive here from the town center, follow the clearly marked signs.

Some 16km (10 miles) south of Portpatrick is the little hamlet of Port Logan. In the vicinity is **Logan House** (not open to the public), the seat of the McDougall family, which claimed they could trace their ancestry so far back they were as old as the sun itself. The family laid out the gardens at Logan.

Approximately 23km (14 miles) south of Stranraer off B7065, the **Logan Botanic Garden** (✆ 01776/860-231), an annex of the Royal Botanic Garden in Edinburgh, contains a wide range of plants from the world's temperate regions. Cordylines, palms, tree ferns, and flowering shrubs grow well in the mild climate of southwestern Scotland. March to October, the garden is open daily 10am to 6pm. Admission is £3.50 ($6.65) for adults, £3 ($5.70) for seniors, £1 ($1.90) for children, and £8 ($15) for families. At the entrance is a pleasant refreshment room.

Portpatrick has become a magnet for artisans who produce charming handicrafts. You'll find handmade plant pots, slip-cast and glazed figurines, Spanish recycled glass, and Indian coffee tables at the port's largest gift shop, **Lighthouse Pottery,** South Pier (✆ 01776/810-284). The **Green Gillie Crafts Shop,** Main Street (✆ 01776/810-359), specializes in woolen jerseys and mittens, throw rugs, and calfskins.

WHERE TO STAY

The **Crown Hotel** (see "Where to Dine," below) also rents rooms.

Fernhill Hotel   This 19th-century gray-stone building stands above the village, looking down at the harbor; it's just a 5-minute walk from the first tee of the clifftop Dunskey Golf Course (which is scenic but not challenging). Renovated in 1990, the guest rooms are decorated with flair. Most desirable are the six executive rooms opening onto the sea; three have private balconies. Each unit comes with a small shower-only bathroom. The cocktail bar and the Victorian conservatory have a panoramic view of the town and the sea. The excellent cuisine, usually made from Scottish produce, is one of the reasons for staying here. The house specialty is fresh lobster.

Heugh Rd., Portpatrick, Galloway DG9 8TD. ✆ 01776/810-220. Fax 01776/810-596. www.mcmillanhotels.com. 23 units. £116–£180 ($220–$342) double. Rates include breakfast. MC, V. Free parking. On the approach to Portpatrick, turn right at the War Memorial. **Amenities:** Restaurant; bar; access to nearby health club; room service; laundry service. *In room:* TV, coffeemaker, hair dryer.

Knockinaam Lodge ★★★   Built in 1869, this three-story Victorian hunting lodge sits among towering cliffs. It's a country house of charm and grace in a coastal setting, boasting some of the finest cuisine served in southern Scotland. Since it's west of town, it is far more tranquil than any other hotel in the area. Indeed, you get an authentic feel for Scottish manorial living here, especially as you read your paper in the morning room, which overlooks the sea. The bedrooms are tastefully decorated and filled with thoughtful little extras, along with modernized bathrooms. This award-winning establishment also boasts luxurious lawns that lead down to a pristine, private beach. It was here on these 12 hectares (30 acres) of private woodland that Sir Winston Churchill met General Eisenhower and their chiefs of staff during the dark days of World War II.

Portpatrick Wigtownshire, Galloway DG9 9AD. ⓒ **01776/810-471.** Fax 01776/810-435. www.knockinaamlodge. com. 9 units. £135–£200 ($257–$380) double. Rates include breakfast and dinner. AE, DC, MC, V. Free parking. From A77 or A75, follow signs to Portpatrick. It's 3km (2 miles) west of Lochans; watch for hotel sign on right. **Amenities:** Restaurant; bar; dry cleaning. *In room:* TV, hair dryer, fireplace (in some).

WHERE TO DINE

The **Knockinaam Lodge** serves the area's best food (see "Where to Stay," above).

Crown Hotel SEAFOOD/INTERNATIONAL   One of the region's most popular restaurants occupies the ground floor of a century-old stone-sided hotel. You might enjoy a drink in the pub before heading into the dining room, which opens onto a wide-angled view of the ocean. Meat is available, but the biggest draw is seafood: scampi; monkfish; scallops in wine sauce; mullet; cod; and plaice, salmon, or sole filets. The Crown maintains 12 rooms upstairs, each with bathroom, TV, hair dryer, coffeemaker, and phone. Doubles rent for £75 ($143), which includes a hearty Scottish breakfast.

North Crescent, Portpatrick, Galloway DG9 8FX. ⓒ **01776/810-261.** Fax 01776/810-551. Reservations recommended. Main courses £13–£18 ($25–$34); fixed-price 3-course menu £18 ($34). MC, V. Daily noon–2:30pm and 6–10pm.

7

Glasgow & the Strathclyde Region

Glasgow ★★★ is only 65km (40 miles) west of Edinburgh, but there's a striking contrast between the two cities. Scotland's economic powerhouse and its largest city (Britain's third largest), up-and-coming Glasgow is now the country's cultural capital as well as home to half its population. It has long been famous for ironworks and steelworks; the local shipbuilding industry produced the *Queen Mary,* the *Queen Elizabeth,* and other fabled ocean liners.

Once polluted and plagued with some of the worst slums in Europe, Glasgow has been transformed. Urban development and the decision to locate the Scottish Exhibition and Conference Centre here have brought great changes: Grime is being sandblasted away, overcrowding has been reduced, and more open space and less traffic congestion mean cleaner air. Glasgow also boasts a vibrant and even edgy arts scene; indeed, it has become one of the cultural capitals of Europe.

John Betjeman and other critics have hailed Glasgow as "the greatest surviving example of a Victorian city." In the 19th century, planners thought on a grand scale when they designed the terraces and villas west and south of the city center.

Glasgow is ancient, making Edinburgh, for all its wealth of history, seem comparatively young. It began as a medieval ecclesiastical center beside a fjord, 32km (20 miles) from the mouth of the River Clyde. By the 17th century, the village started to grow and to prosper commercially, and it eventually engulfed the smaller medieval towns of Ardrie, Renfrew, Rutherglen, and Paisley.

Glasgow is part of **Strathclyde,** a populous district whose origins go back to the Middle Ages. Irish chroniclers wrote of the kingdom of Stratha Cluatha some 1,500 years ago, and Strathclyde was known to the Romans, who called its people Damnonii. The old capital, Dumbarton, on its high rock, provided a natural fortress in the days when locals had to defend themselves against enemy tribes.

The fortunes of Strathclyde changed in the 18th century, when the Clyde estuary became the gateway to the New World. Glasgow merchants grew rich on tobacco and then on cotton. It was Britain's fastest-growing region during the Industrial Revolution, and Glasgow was known as the Second City of the Empire. Until 1996, Strathclyde functioned as a government entity that included Glasgow, but it's now divided into several new districts: the City of Glasgow; Inverclyde, which includes the important industrial center of Greenock; and several others.

Glasgow is a good gateway for exploring the heart of **Burns country, Culzean Castle,** and the **resorts along the Ayrshire coast,** an hour away by frequent train service (see "Side Trips from Glasgow: The Best of the Strathclyde Region," later in this chapter). From Glasgow, you can also tour Loch Lomond, Loch Katrine, and the Trossachs (see chapter 9). After a day or so in Glasgow, you can head to Burns country for perhaps another night. Also on Glasgow's doorstep is the scenic estuary of the **Firth of Clyde,** which you can cruise on a paddle steamer. The Firth of Clyde, with its long sea lochs—Gareloch, Loch Long, Loch Goil, and Holy Loch—is one of the most scenic waterways in the world.

1 Essentials

ARRIVING

BY PLANE The **Glasgow Airport** is at Abbotsinch (© 0870/040-0008), 16km (10 miles) west of the city via M8. You can use the regular Glasgow Citylink bus service to get to the city center. From bus stop no. 1 or 2, take bus no. 905 to the Buchanan Street Bus Station, in the center of town. The ride takes about 25 minutes and costs £3.50 ($6.65). A taxi to the city center costs about £20 ($38). You can reach Edinburgh by taking a bus from Glasgow Airport to Queen Street Station and then changing to a bus for Edinburgh. The entire journey, including the change, takes about 2 hours and costs £9 ($17) one-way or £15 ($29) round-trip.

Monday to Friday, British Airways (www.ba.com) runs almost hourly shuttle service from London's Heathrow Airport to Glasgow. The first flight departs London at 7:15am and the last at 8:25pm; service is reduced on weekends, depending on volume. For flight schedules and fares, call British Airways in London at © **0845/779-9977.**

From mid-May through October, **American Airlines** (© 800/433-7300; www.aa.com) offers a daily nonstop flight to Glasgow from Chicago; the rest of the year, you'll make at least one transfer. **Northwest Airlines** (© 800/225-2525; www.nwa.com) operates nonstop flights between Boston and Glasgow daily in summer, somewhat less frequently in winter.

British Midland (© 0818/365-000; www.flybmi.com) flies from Heathrow to Glasgow. **Aer Lingus** (© 800/223-6537 or 01/844-4711 in Ireland; www.aerlingus.ie) flies daily from Dublin to Glasgow.

BY TRAIN Headquarters for British Rail is at Glasgow's Central Station and Queen Street Station. For **National Rail Enquiries,** call © 08457/484-950. The **Queen Street Station** serves the north and east of Scotland, with trains arriving from Edinburgh every 30 minutes during the day; the one-way trip between the two cities costs £9 ($17) and takes 50 minutes. You can also travel to such Highland destinations as Inverness and Fort William from here.

The **Central Station** serves southern Scotland, England, and Wales, with trains arriving from London's Euston and King's Cross Stations (call © 08457/484-950 in London for schedules) frequently throughout the day (trip time: about 5½ hr.). The trains leave Euston Monday to Saturday from 6:20am until 6:25pm, and the night

---

Value A First Day Bargain for Glasgow

For only £5 ($9.50), you can buy a FirstDay Tourist Ticket that allows you to hop on and off buses and to receive discounts to such select attractions as the House for an Art Lover. A pocket-size city map is also provided. The ticket is valid daily from 9:30am to midnight. It's available at tourist information centers, underground or bus stations, and at certain attractions. For more information, check www.seeglasgow.com.

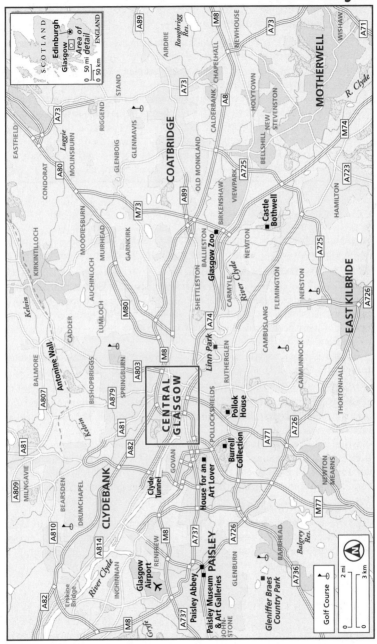

> **Tips** **Finding an Address**
>
> Glasgow was built in various sections and districts over the years, and massive sections have been torn down—some for slum clearance, others to make way for new highways. Following a consistent street plan is tough, as squares or terraces can suddenly interrupt your route.
>
> House numbers can run in odds or evens and clockwise or counterclockwise, and sometimes Glaswegians don't even use numbers at all. So don't be surprised to see something like "Blackfriars Street," without a number, given as an address. Get a detailed map of Glasgow before setting out. Always find the nearest cross street, and then look for your location from there. If it's a hotel or restaurant, the sign for the establishment is likely to be more prominent than the number anyway.

train departs at 11:40pm, getting into Glasgow at 7:16am. From Glasgow, trains leave for London every hour 6:15am to 5pm. The night train leaves at 11:55pm. Try to avoid Sunday travel—the frequency of trains is considerably reduced and the duration of the trip lengthened to at least 7 hours because of more stopovers en route.

BY BUS The **Buchanan Street Bus Station** is 2 blocks north of the Queen Street Station on Killermont Street (© **0141/333-3708**). **National Express** runs daily coaches from London's Victoria Coach Station to Buchanan frequently throughout the day. Buses from London take 8 hours and 40 minutes to reach Glasgow, depending on the number of stops. Scottish Citylink (© **08705/505-050**) also has frequent bus service to and from Edinburgh, with a one-way ticket costing £5 to £7.50 ($9.50–$14).

Contact National Express Enquiries at © **0990/808-080** for more information.

BY CAR Glasgow is 65km (40 miles) west of Edinburgh, 356km (221 miles) north of Manchester, and 625km (388 miles) north of London. From England in the south, Glasgow is reached by M74, a continuation of M8 that goes right into the city, making an S curve. Call your hotel and find out what exit you should take. M8, another express motorway, links Glasgow and Edinburgh.

Other major routes into the city are A77 northeast from Prestwick and Ayr and A8 from the west (this becomes M8 around the port of Glasgow). A82 comes in from the northwest (the Highlands) on the north bank of the Clyde, and A80 also goes into the city. (This route is the southwestern section of M80 and M9 from Stirling.)

VISITOR INFORMATION

The **Greater Glasgow and Clyde Valley Tourist Board,** 11 George Sq. (© **0141/566-0800;** Underground: Buchanan St.), is the country's most helpful office. October to May it's open Monday to Saturday 9am to 6pm; June to September hours are daily 9am to 6pm; August daily 9am to 8pm.

CITY LAYOUT

The monumental heart of Glasgow—the Victorian City and the Merchant City, along with the Central Station—lies on the north bank of the **River Clyde.** The ancient center has as its core the great Cathedral of St. Kentigern, a perfect example of pre-Reformation Gothic architecture that dates in part to the 12th century. Behind the cathedral is the Necropolis, burial ground of many Victorians, while across the square is Provand's Lordship, the city's oldest house, built in 1471. Down **High Street** you find the Tolbooth Steeple (from 1626) at Glasgow Cross, and nearer the River Clyde is **Glasgow Green** (from 1622), Britain's first public park.

From Ingram Street, South Frederick Street will take you to **George Square,** with its many statues, including one dedicated to Sir Walter Scott. This is the center of modern Glasgow.

The **Merchant City,** a compact area of imposing buildings, is the location of the National Trust for Scotland's shop and visitor center at Hutcheson's Hall. The broad pedestrian thoroughfares of **Buchanan, Argyle,** and **Sauchiehall streets** are the heart of the shopping district.

Glasgow's **West End** is Britain's finest example of a great Victorian city. The West End is just a short taxi journey from the city center, easily accessible from any part of the city and close to M8 and the Clydeside Expressway. An extensive network of local bus routes serves the West End. The Glasgow Underground operates a circular service; by boarding at any station on the system, you can reach the four stations serving the district: Kelvinbridge, Hillhead (the most central), Kelvin Hall, and Partick. The terraces of the Park Conservation Area have excellent views. Across Kelvingrove Park is the **Art Gallery and Museum.** And nearby, the tower of Glasgow University dominates Gilmorehill. Beyond is the **Hunterian Art Gallery,** home to a famous collection of Whistlers. Just a few strides away is Byres Road, a street of bars, shops, and restaurants. To the north is the **Botanic Gardens.**

A little more than 5km (3 miles) southwest of the city center is the heavily wooded **Pollok Country Park,** which is home to **The Burrell Collection Gallery.** This museum is Scotland's top tourist attraction and the focal point of any visit to the South Side. Nearby is the 18th-century Pollok House. An extensive network of bus routes passes close to the area, which is also served by two suburban rail stations. An electric bus service is in operation from the Country Park gates on Pollokshaws Road to Pollok House and The Burrell Collection Gallery. Extensive parklands and greenery characterize the city's southern environs. In addition to the Pollok Country Park, there are **Haggs Castle Golf Club,** home of the Glasgow Open, and **Bellahouston Park,** scene of the historic papal visit in 1983. En route to The Burrell Collection Gallery, you cross by the 59-hectare (148-acre) **Queens Park,** honoring Mary Queen of Scots. Near **Maxwell Park** is the Haggs Castle Museum, housed in a 400-year-old building.

THE NEIGHBORHOODS IN BRIEF

To locate the following neighborhoods, see the "Glasgow Attractions" map on p. 192.

Medieval Glasgow Also referred to as Old Glasgow, this is where St. Mungo arrived in A.D. 543 and built his little church in what's now the northeastern part of the city. At the top of High Street are the **Cathedral of St. Kentigern** and one of Britain's largest Victorian cemeteries. You enter the **Necropolis** by crossing the Bridge of Sighs, patterned after the famous bridge by the same name in Venice. Old Glasgow's major terminal is the High Street Station, near the former site of the University of Glasgow. **Glasgow Green,** opening onto the River Clyde, has been a public park since 1662. Today, vastly restored medieval Glasgow is the best place for strolls; however, it's not a popular place to stay because of limited accommodations.

Along the River Clyde It was once said that "The Clyde made Glasgow; Glasgow made the Clyde." Although the city is no longer so dependent on the river, you can still enjoy a stroll along the **Clyde Walkway** *, which stretches from King Albert Bridge, at the western end of Glasgow Green, for 3km (2 miles) downstream to Stobcross, now the site of the **Scottish Exhibition and Conference Centre.** This is one of the city's grandest walks; on these waters, Glasgow once shipped its manufactured goods around the world. However, if time is limited, you may want to concentrate instead on the major museums and historic Glasgow.

The Merchant City Glasgow spread west of High Street in the 18th century, largely because of profits made from sugar, cotton, and tobacco in trade with the Americas. The Merchant City extends from Trongate and Argyle Street in the south to George Street in the north. Its major terminal is the Queen Street Station; its major shopping venue, **Argyle Arcade.** It's also the site of City Hall and Strathclyde University and boasts some of Britain's most **elegant Georgian and Victorian buildings,** as well as **Greek Revival churches.** Tobacco barons once occupied much of the area, but their buildings have been recycled for other uses.

Glasgow Center Continuing its western progression, the city center of Glasgow is now dominated by the Central Station on Hope Street. This is the major shopping district, including such venues as the **Princes Square Shopping Mall.** Also here are the Stock Exchange and the Anderston Bus Station (near the Central Station).

The West End Beyond Charing Cross in the West End are the University of Glasgow and several major galleries and museums, some of which are in **Kelvingrove Park.** The West End mixes culture, art, and parks, and is dominated by the University of Glasgow, with the university structures idyllically placed in various parks. The city itself has more green spaces per resident than any other in Europe; 16 hectares (40 acres) of the West End are taken up by the **Botanic Gardens.**

2 Getting Around

The best way to explore Glasgow is on foot. The center is laid out on a grid system, which makes map reading relatively easy. Many major attractions, however, such as The Burrell Collection, are in the surrounding environs, and for those you need to rely on public transportation. *Remember:* Cars drive on the left, so when you cross streets make certain to look both ways.

BY BUS

Glasgow is serviced by **First Glasgow Bus Company** (✆ **0141/423-6600**). The buses come in a variety of colors, with the lighter ones (blue and yellow) tending to serve the Kelvin Central and Strathclyde rural areas, and the darker ones covering the urban zones. Service is frequent throughout the day, but greatly curtailed after 11pm. The major bus station is the **Buchanan Street Bus Station,** Killermont Street (call ✆ **0141/333-3708** for schedules), 2 blocks north of the Queen Station. Fares are £3.75 ($7.15), but you must have exact change.

BY UNDERGROUND

Called the "Clockwork Orange" (from the vivid orange of the trains) by Glaswegians, a 15-stop subway services the city. Most Underground trains operate from these stops every 5 minutes, with longer intervals between trains on Sunday and at night. The fare is £1 ($1.90). Service is Monday to Saturday 6:30am to 10pm and Sunday 11am to 6pm.

The **Travel Centre** at St. Enoch Square (© **0141/333-3708**), 2 blocks from the Central Station, is open Monday to Saturday 8:30am to 5:30pm. Here you can buy a £9 ($17) **Underground pass**—valid for a week's access to all the tube lines of Glasgow, as well as access to all the trains serving routes between Central Station and the southern suburbs—or a £8.50 ($16) **daytripper card,** covering one adult and one child for a day. For details, call © **0141/332-7133.**

BY TAXI

Taxis in Glasgow are as excellent as those found in Edinburgh or London. You can hail them on the street or call **TOA Taxis** at © **0141/429-7070.** Fares are displayed on a meter next to the driver. When a taxi is available on the street, a taxi sign on the roof is lit a bright yellow. Most taxi trips within the city cost £5 to £7 ($9.50–$13). The taxi meter starts at £2 ($3.80) and increases by 25p (50¢) every 61m (200 ft.), with an extra 15p (30¢) assessed for each additional passenger after the first two. A £1 ($1.90) surcharge is imposed midnight to 6am. Tip at least 10% of the fare shown on the meter.

BY CAR

Driving around Glasgow is tricky business, even for locals. You're better off with public transportation. The city is a warren of one-way streets, and parking is expensive and difficult to find. Metered parking is available, but you'll need 20p (40¢) coins, entitling you to only 20 minutes. And you must watch out for zealous traffic wardens issuing tickets. Some zones are marked PERMIT HOLDERS ONLY—your vehicle will be towed if you have no permit. A yellow line along the curb indicates no parking. Multistory car parks (parking lots), open 24 hours a day, are found at Anderston Cross, Cambridge, George, Mitchell, Oswald, and Waterloo streets.

If you want to rent a car to explore the countryside, it's best to do so before leaving home (see chapter 2). But if you want to rent a car locally, most companies will accept your American or Canadian driver's license. All the major rental agencies are represented at the airport. In addition, **Avis Rent-a-Car** is at 70 Lancefield St. (© **0141/221-2827**; bus: 6 or 6A), **Budget Rent-a-Car** at Glasgow Airport (© **0141/887-2261**; bus: 38, 45, 48, or 57), and **Europcar** at 38 Anderson Quay (© **0141/248-8788**; bus: 38, 45, 48, or 57).

BY BICYCLE

Parts of Glasgow are fine for biking, and you might want to rent a bike to explore the surrounding countryside. For what the Scots call cycle hire, go to a well-recommended shop about a kilometer (½ mile) west of the town center, just off Great Western Road: **West End Cycles,** 16–18 Chancellor St., in the Hillhead district (© **0141/357-1344;** Underground: Kelvin Bridge or Hillhead). It rents 21-speed trail and mountain bikes that conform well to the hilly terrain of Glasgow and its surroundings. The cost of £14 ($27) per day must be accompanied by a cash deposit of £100 ($190) or the imprint of a valid credit card. You can also rent weekly for £50 ($95).

FAST FACTS: Glasgow

American Express The office is at 115 Hope St. (© **0141/226-3077**; bus: 38, 45, 48, or 57), open Monday to Friday 8:30am to 5:30pm and Saturday 9am to noon (June–July to 4pm on Sat).

Business Hours Most **offices** are open Monday to Friday 9am to 5 or 5:30pm. Most **banks** are open Monday to Wednesday and Friday 9:30am to 4pm, Thursday 9:30am to 5:30pm, and Saturday 10am to 7pm. Opening times can vary slightly from bank to bank. **Shops** are generally open Monday to Saturday 10am to 5:30 or 6pm. On Thursday, stores remain open until 7pm.

Currency Exchange The tourist office and the American Express office (see above) will exchange most major foreign currencies. City-center banks operate *bureaux de change,* and nearly all will cash traveler's checks if you have the proper ID.

Dentists If you have an emergency, go to the Accident and Emergency Department of **Glasgow Dental Hospital & School NHS Trust,** 378 Sauchiehall St. (© **0141/211-9600;** bus: 57). Its hours are Monday to Friday 9:15am to 3:15pm and Sunday and public holidays 10:30am to noon.

Doctors The major hospital is the **Royal Infirmary,** 82–86 Castle St. (© **0141/211-4000;** bus: 2 or 2A).

Embassies & Consulates See "Fast Facts: Scotland," in chapter 2.

Emergencies Call © **999** in an emergency to summon the police, an ambulance, or firefighters.

Hospitals See "Doctors," above.

Hot Lines Women in crisis may want to call **Women's Aid** at © **0141/553-2022.** Gays and lesbians can call the **Gay and Lesbian Switchboard** at © **0141/322-8372,** daily 7 to 10pm. The **Rape Crisis Centre** is at © **0141/331-1990.**

Internet Access You can send or read e-mail and surf the Net at **EasyEverything Internet Café,** 57–61 St. Vincent St. (© **0141/222-2365;** Underground: Buchanan St.). This outlet offers 400 computers and good rates. Only £1 ($1.90) can buy 40 minutes or even 3 hours, depending on demand. Open Monday to Friday 7am to 10pm, Saturday to Sunday 8am to 9pm.

Laundry & Dry Cleaning Try the **Park Laundrette,** 14 Park Rd. (© **0141/337-1285;** Underground: Kelvin Bridge), open Monday to Friday 8:30am to 7:30pm and Saturday and Sunday 9am to 5pm.

Library The **Mitchell Library** is on North Street at Kent Road (© **0141/287-2999;** bus: 57). One of the largest libraries in Europe, it's a massive 19th-century pile. Newspapers and books, as well as miles of microfilm, are available. It's open Monday to Thursday 9am to 8pm and Friday and Saturday 9am to 5pm.

Pharmacies The best is **Boots,** 200 Sauchiehall St. (© **0141/332-1925;** bus: 57), open Monday to Saturday 8:30am to 6pm and Sunday 11am to 5pm.

Newspapers & Magazines Published since 1783, the *Herald* is the major newspaper with national, international, and financial news, sports, and cultural listings; the *Evening Times* offers local news.

Police In a real emergency, call © **999.** For other inquiries, contact police headquarters at © **0141/532-2000.**

Post Office The main branch is at 47 St. Vincent's St. (© **0141/204-3689;** Underground: Buchanan St.; bus: 6, 8, or 16). It's open Monday to Friday 8:30am to 5:45pm and Saturday 9am to 5pm.

Restrooms They can be found at rail stations, bus stations, air terminals, restaurants, hotels, pubs, and department stores. Glasgow also has a system of public toilets, often marked wc. Don't hesitate to use them, but they're likely to be closed late in the evening.

Safety Glasgow is the most dangerous city in Scotland, but it's relatively safe when compared to cities of its size in the United States. Muggings do occur, and often they're related to Glasgow's rather large drug problem. The famed razor gangs of Calton, Bridgeton, and the Gorbals are no longer around to earn the city a reputation for violence, but you still should stay alert.

3 Where to Stay

It's important to reserve your room well in advance (say, 2 months beforehand), especially in late July and August. Glasgow's rates are generally higher than those in Edinburgh, but many business hotels offer bargains on weekends. The airport and the downtown branches of Glasgow's tourist office offer an **Advance Reservations Service**—with 2 weeks' notice, you can book your hotel by calling ✆ **0141/221-0049.** The cost for this service is £3 ($5.70).

MERCHANT CITY
VERY EXPENSIVE
Millennium Hotel Glasgow ✮✮✮ Following a £9.5-million ($18-million) upgrade, this striking landmark, the original Copthorne from 1810, is now better than ever. It stands near Queen Street Station, where trains depart for the north of Scotland. When its high-ceilinged public rooms were renovated, designers searched out antiques and glistening marble panels to give it the aura of the Victorian era. Even though the building is old, it has been completely modernized with all the amenities and services you'd expect of such a highly rated hotel.

The decor is lighter and more comfortable than before. Guest rooms are among the finest in Glasgow, with new furnishings and first-class bathrooms. The best accommodations are at the front of the building, facing St. George Square; less desirable are those in the rear, which have no view.

The Millennium's managers have installed some of the best and most elegant drinking and dining facilities in Glasgow, including the classic Brasserie on George Square.

George Square, Glasgow G2 1DS. ✆ **0141/332-6711.** Fax 0141/332-4264. www.millenniumhotels.com. 117 units. £99–£305 ($188–$580) double; £220–£450 ($418–$855) suite. AE, DC, MC, V. Parking £5 ($9.50). Underground: Buchanan St. **Amenities:** Restaurant; 2 bars; car rental; business center; room service; babysitting; laundry service; dry cleaning; rooms for those w/limited mobility. *In room:* A/C, TV, minibar, coffeemaker, hair dryer, iron, safe, trouser press.

MODERATE
Babbity Bowster *Value* Located in Merchant City, this small but delightful Robert Adam–designed "five-bay house" is imbued with character. The guest rooms vary in size but are all attractive, with Victorian reproductions and white-lace bedding (some with shower only). The hotel attracts students and faculty from Strathclyde University and displays the work of Glaswegian artists (most are for sale). In summer, there's an outdoor barbecue area.

Glasgow Accommodations & Dining

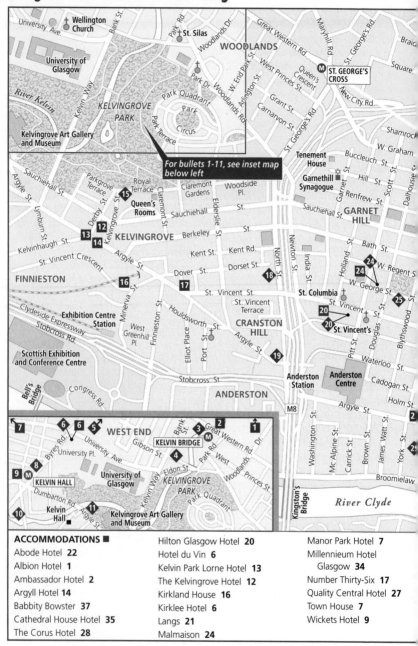

ACCOMMODATIONS ■

Abode Hotel **22**
Albion Hotel **1**
Ambassador Hotel **2**
Argyll Hotel **14**
Babbity Bowster **37**
Cathedral House Hotel **35**
The Corus Hotel **28**

Hilton Glasgow Hotel **20**
Hotel du Vin **6**
Kelvin Park Lorne Hotel **13**
The Kelvingrove Hotel **12**
Kirkland House **16**
Kirklee Hotel **6**
Langs **21**
Malmaison **24**

Manor Park Hotel **7**
Millennium Hotel
  Glasgow **34**
Number Thirty-Six **17**
Quality Central Hotel **27**
Town House **7**
Wickets Hotel **9**

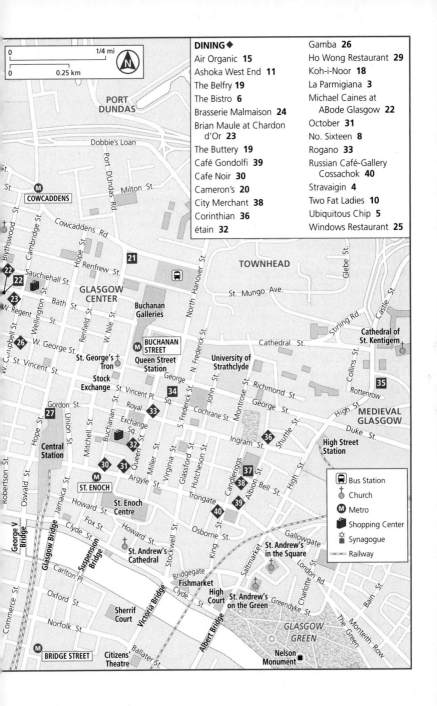

DINING ◆

Air Organic **15**
Ashoka West End **11**
The Belfry **19**
The Bistro **6**
Brasserie Malmaison **24**
Brian Maule at Chardon
  d'Or **23**
The Buttery **19**
Café Gondolfi **39**
Cafe Noir **30**
Cameron's **20**
City Merchant **38**
Corinthian **36**
étain **32**

Gamba **26**
Ho Wong Restaurant **29**
Koh-i-Noor **18**
La Parmigiana **3**
Michael Caines at
  ABode Glasgow **22**
October **31**
No. Sixteen **8**
Rogano **33**
Russian Café-Gallery
  Cossachok **40**
Stravaigin **4**
Two Fat Ladies **10**
Ubiquitous Chip **5**
Windows Restaurant **25**

Bus Station
Church
Metro
Shopping Center
Synagogue
Railway

16–18 Blackfriars St., Glasgow G1 1PE. ℂ **0141/552-5055.** Fax 0141/552-7774. 5 units. £80 ($152) double. Rates include Scottish breakfast. AE, MC, V. Free parking. Underground: Buchanan St. **Amenities:** Restaurant; bar; room service. *In room:* TV, coffeemaker, hair dryer, no phone.

Cathedral House Hotel *(Value)* We'd stay here for one reason alone—and that is the panoramic view of Glasgow Cathedral. But this well-run and affordable hotel has much more to recommend it than that. Standing on a tree-lined square adjacent to the cathedral, the hotel lies at the edge of Merchant City. It's small but choice, with a lot of atmosphere in a restored Glaswegian baronial-style building from the 1800s. All the rooms are individually designed and furnished comfortably and attractively in a minimalist style. In the morning you have a choice of a full Scottish breakfast or a vegetarian meal.

29–32 Cathedral Sq., Glasgow G4 0XA. ℂ **0141/552-3515.** Fax 0141/552-2444. www.cathedralhouse.com. 8 units. £65–£85 ($124–$162) double. Rates include breakfast. MC, V. Free parking. Underground: Queen St. Station. **Amenities:** Bistro; room service; laundry service. *In room:* TV, beverage maker, hair dryer.

GLASGOW CENTER *(★)*
VERY EXPENSIVE
Hilton Glasgow Hotel *(★★)* *(Kids)* Glasgow's only government-rated five-star hotel occupies Scotland's tallest building (20 floors). Dignified and modern, it rises in the heart of the city's business district, near the northern end of Argyle Street and exit 18 (Charing Cross) of M8. The good-size guest rooms—plush and conservative, popular with both vacationers and business travelers—offer fine views as far as the Clyde dockyards. The executive floors enjoy the enhanced facilities of a semiprivate club. The youthful staff is alert and helpful.

1 William St., Glasgow G3 8HT. ℂ **800/445-8667** in the U.S. and Canada, or 0141/204-5555. Fax 0141/204-5004. www.Glasgow.hilton.com. 331 units. £113–£204 ($215–$388) double; £160–£280 ($304–$532) suite. Weekend discounts often available. AE, DC, MC, V. Parking £5 ($9.50). Bus: 62. **Amenities:** 3 restaurants; bar; indoor heated pool; exercise room; sauna; business center; salon; room service; massage; babysitting; laundry service; dry cleaning; nonsmoking rooms; rooms for those w/limited mobility. *In room:* A/C, TV, minibar, coffeemaker, hair dryer, iron, safe, trouser press.

EXPENSIVE
ABode Hotel *(★★)* *(Finds)* This elegantly restored Edwardian building, 6 blocks northwest of Central Station, is one of the hotel charmers of Glasgow, though originally it housed school-board offices. It is also the setting for one of Glasgow's most sophisticated restaurants (Michael Caines; see below). The former Art Hotel has been renovated from top to bottom, and the results are stunning—for example, the grand staircase is ornamented with a campy motif of metallic copper painted bas-relief lions. Depending on the price range, rooms come in a number of sizes and styles and are ranked in four categories—"comfortable," "desirable," "enviable," and the truly fab "fabulous." The bathrooms are sleekly contemporary, with tub/shower combos. The address is preferred by photographers, fashionistas, and models.

129 Bath St., Glasgow G2 2SY. ℂ **0141/221-6789.** Fax 0141/221-6777. www.abodehotel.co.uk. 65 units. £125 ($238) double. AE, DC, MC, V. Underground: St. Enoch. **Amenities:** Restaurant; 2 bars; room service; laundry service; dry cleaning. *In room:* TV, minibar, hair dryer.

Langs *(★)* *(Finds)* If you're looking for Victorian Glasgow, head elsewhere. But if you gravitate to a minimalist Japanese style, check in at this trendy and exceedingly contemporary hotel, close to the Buchanan Galleries Shopping Mall and the Glasgow Royal Concert Hall. The Langs has a diverse medley of bedrooms in various shapes, sizes, and configurations, each with a certain flair. Nothing is overly adorned here, yet comfort and style, along with different colors and textures, make every unit a winner. The smallest are the studios, but you can also rent a duplex, a theme suite, or a very large suite. The beautifully kept bathrooms contain such extras as power showers with body jets. Nothing at the hotel evokes traditional Glasgow. And to emphasize the Asian theme all the more, Japanese body treatments are offered in the on-site Oshi Spa.

You can feast on both a Mediterranean cuisine as well as an array of light fusion foods, including teriyaki and sushi, in the hotel's two restaurants.

2 Port Dundas Place, Glasgow G2 3LD. ✆ **0141/333-1500.** Fax 0141/333-5700. www.langshotels.com. 100 units. £130–£170 ($247–$323) double; £180–£225 ($342–$428) suite. AE, DC, MC, V. Underground: Queen St. Station. **Amenities:** 2 restaurants; 2 bars; exercise room; spa; sauna; room service; massage; laundry service; dry cleaning. *In room:* TV, minibar, coffeemaker, hair dryer, iron, Wi-Fi.

Malmaison *★★ (Finds* This place beats all competitors in having the best contemporary interior. The hip hotel opened in 1994 in a historically important building, constructed in the 1830s as a Greek Orthodox church. Inside, few of the original details remain—the decor is sleek and ultramodern. In 1997, an annex—designed to preserve the architectural character of the church's exterior—was added to provide additional guest rooms. Bedrooms vary in size from smallish to average, but are chic and appointed with extras like CD players, specially commissioned art, and top-of-the-line toiletries.

278 W. George St., Glasgow G2 4LL. ✆ **0141/572-1000.** Fax 0141/572-1002. www.malmaison.com. 72 units. £150 ($285) double; from £225 ($428) suite. AE, DC, MC, V. Parking nearby £7 ($13). Bus: 11. **Amenities:** Restaurant; 2 bars; indoor heated pool; exercise room; 24-hr. room service; babysitting; laundry service; dry cleaning; rooms for those w/limited mobility. *In room:* A/C, TV, minibar, coffeemaker, hair dryer, iron, safe.

MODERATE
The Kelvingrove Hotel This family-run hotel gives off a certain air of sophistication. All 22 of its midsize rooms are well kept and decorated in an urbane fashion. Clean white is the color scheme for the rooms, while the reception area is a little more adventurous, with leather couches and hanging paintings. Being close to the city center, guests can easily get to top attractions like Kelvingrove Park and the Glasgow Museum of Transport. Staff here is especially helpful when it comes to giving directions and will arrange for a taxi to take you wherever you're going.

944 Sauchiehall St. Glasgow G3 7TH. ✆ **0141/339-5011.** Fax 0141/339-6566. www.kelvingrove-hotel.co.uk. 22 units. £60–£80 ($114–$152) double. Rates include breakfast. MC, V. Free parking. Underground: Queen St. Station. **Amenities:** Dining room; business services; laundry service; dry cleaning. *In room:* TV, beverage maker, hair dryer, iron.

Quality Hotel Glasgow When it opened in 1883 by the Central rail station, this was the grandest hotel in Glasgow and the landmark of the city's most famous street. Now restored to at least a glimmer of its former glory, the place may be too old-fashioned for some, but traditionalists like it. The baronial wooden staircase has been stripped and refinished, and sandblasting the facade revealed elaborate Victorian cornices and pilasters. The guest rooms, with an uninspired decor, are priced according to size and plumbing.

99 Gordon St., Glasgow G1 3SF. ✆ **0141/221-9680.** Fax 0141/226-3948. www.quality-hotels-glasgow.com. 222 units. £66–£120 ($125–$228) double; £140 ($266) suite. AE, DC, DISC, MC, V. Overnight parking £10 ($19). Underground: Central Station. **Amenities:** Restaurant; 2 bars; indoor pool; exercise room; Jacuzzi; sauna; room service; laundry service; dry cleaning; nonsmoking rooms. *In room:* TV, coffeemaker, hair dryer, iron, trouser press.

(Kids) Family-Friendly Hotels

Hotel du Vin (see below)   Although this elegant hotel is full of antiques, it's happy to cater to kids by providing toys, cots, and highchairs. There's an interconnecting bedroom that's perfect for families. Children are offered appropriate videos, and there are special facilities for heating food and sterilizing bottles. The restaurant is fully prepared to cook meals that kids adore, like pizza or fish fingers.

Hilton Glasgow Hotel (p. 178)   Children arriving on the weekend are presented with fun packs containing drawings, games, bubble bath, and comics. Kids enjoy the pool. Cots and highchairs are available. Minsky's, one of the hotel's restaurants, offers kids' meals, and room service is more than happy to provide sausages, chicken nuggets, or the like.

Kirklee Hotel (p. 182)   This small hotel lies in a safe area near the university and the Botanic Gardens, where guests often go for a stroll or for a picnic. Some of its comfortably and attractively furnished bedrooms are big enough to house small families.

INEXPENSIVE
Kirkland House   A 10-minute walk from the Glasgow Art Gallery and Museum, from the university, and from the Scottish Exhibition Centre, the Kirkland is an impeccably maintained Victorian crescent house, built in 1832. A mix of antiques and reproductions is used in the large guest rooms, each equipped with a shower-only bathroom. You get a warm welcome from owners Carole and Ewing Divers and their daughter Sally. Ewing is a keen admirer of American swing music and displays a collection of 78-rpm gramophone records, old photographs, and pictures. He's a member of the Harry James Appreciation Society. You're welcome to listen to recordings of Harry James, Benny Goodman, and many others.

42 St. Vincent Crescent, Glasgow G3 8NG. © **0141/248-3458.** Fax 0141/221-5174. www.kirkland.net43.co.uk. 5 units. £50–£65 ($95–$124) double. Rates include continental breakfast. No credit cards. Free parking. Underground: Exhibition Centre. *In room:* TV, coffeemaker, no phone.

THE WEST END
VERY EXPENSIVE
Hotel du Vin 🟊🟊🟊 *(Kids)*   Formerly called One Devonshire Gardens, this hotel beats out the Hilton Glasgow and all others as the most glamorous, most elegant, and most tranquil hotel in Scotland. Its Bistro restaurant also serves a finer cuisine than any of the major Glasgow restaurants (see "Where to Dine," below). In the Hyndland district just west of the center, the house at no. 1 was built in 1880 and is now even more elegant than it was in its heyday. At the ring of the doorbell, a pair of Edwardian chambermaids with frilly aprons and dust bonnets appears to welcome you. Each of the eight guest rooms in this building is furnished in period style, with lots of luxurious accessories. The success of no. 1 led to the acquisition of nos. 2 and 3. The newer rooms have the same elegant touches and high price tags.

1 Devonshire Gardens, Glasgow G12 0UX. © **0141/339-2001.** Fax 0141/337-1663. www.onedevonshiregardens.com. 38 units. £140–£190 ($266–$361) double; £275–£540 ($523–$1026) suite. AE, DC, MC, V. Free parking. Underground:

Historic Building to Become Hotel

Luxury Edinburgh hoteliers, The Town House Group, have invaded Glasgow. They have taken over the former Royal Scottish Automobile Club in Blythswood Square—built in 1823—and plan to open the 88-bedroom hotel, **Blythswood Square**, sometime in 2008. For more information check the website—www.blythswoodsquare.com—or call **0131/274-7450**.

The landmark is being renovated to its former glory, with restaurants, deluxe hotel rooms, and a first-class leisure club and spa. Included in the development is the restoration of the famous Rally Bar, named after the Monte Carlo Rally which once started from Blythswood Square. The building has some of the greatest architectural features (added early in the 20th c.) of all the buildings in Galsgow: wood paneling, grand staircases, marble floors, and many elegant Art Deco fittings and fixtures.

Hillhead. **Amenities:** 2 restaurants; bar; exercise room; room service; laundry service; dry cleaning. *In room:* TV, mini-bar, hair dryer, iron, safe.

MODERATE

Manor Park Hotel   This impressive West End town house was a private home when built in 1895, near the end of Victoria's reign. In 1947 it was converted into a hotel, and has been much improved and upgraded since that time. Owners Angus and Catherine MacDonald—true Scots to the core, both of whom speak Gaelic—offer grand Scottish hospitality. Naturally, they freely use the tartan when decorating. Their home is a blend of modern and traditional furnishings, including beechwood pieces set against a background of floral wallpaper. Each guest room comes with a neat little bathroom with either tub or shower.

28 Balshagray Dr., Glasgow G11 7DD. ℭ 0141/339-2143. Fax 0141/339-5842. www.manorparkhotel.com. 10 units. £67–£75 ($127–$143) double. Rates include full breakfast. AE, MC, V. Free parking. Underground: Partick Station. **Amenities:** Nonsmoking rooms; rooms for those w/limited mobility. *In room:* TV, coffeemaker, hair dryer, trouser press.

Town House ⟨⟨ *Value*   This is one of Glasgow's most upmarket and charming B&Bs. The stone-built Victorian terraced house has been successfully converted to receive guests at its tranquil little cul-de-sac location, tucked away in the West End. With a tennis club in the back and a rugby club out front, the place justifiably wins praise from its many repeat visitors. The hospitality, comfort level, and atmosphere are first-rate. Guests gather in the living room, with its many books and coal-burning fireplace. The large bedrooms have been faithfully restored and have first-rate private bathrooms with showers. The high-quality furnishings, including many traditional wooden pieces, are set against a decor of blue or yellow.

4 Hughenden Terrace, Glasgow G12 9XR. ℭ 0141/357-0862. Fax 0141/339-9605. www.thetownhouseglasgow.com. 10 units. £72 ($137) double. Rates include Scottish breakfast. MC, V. Free parking. Underground: Hillhead. **Amenities:** Bar; room service; laundry. *In room:* TV, coffeemaker, hair dryer, iron.

Wickets Hotel   Better known for its restaurant and bar than for its comfortable guest rooms, this hotel from the 1890s is an undiscovered West End gem, opposite one of the city's largest cricket grounds (the West of Scotland Cricket Club). The bedrooms are pleasantly spacious, each with cheerful decor.

The **Conservatory Restaurant** is a glamour spot, serving up moderately priced regional and Continental fare amid a setting of old photos of local cricket teams. Adjacent is one of the few open-air beer gardens in Glasgow, where meals can be eaten alfresco. Randall's Wine Bar sells wine by the glass in an Art Deco setting.

52–54 Fortrose St., Glasgow G11 5LP. ©/fax **0141/334-9334**. www.wicketshotel.co.uk. 11 units. £70–£85 ($133–$162) double; £80 ($152) family room. Rates include Scottish breakfast. AE, MC, V. Free parking. Underground: Partick. **Amenities:** Restaurant; 2 bars; room service; laundry service; dry cleaning. *In room:* TV, coffeemaker.

INEXPENSIVE

Albion Hotel   This unpretentious hotel was formed by connecting two nearly identical beige-sandstone row houses. In the heart of Glasgow's West End, it offers high-ceilinged guest rooms with modern furniture and small refrigerators. All the units contain a shower-only bathroom. If your hotel needs are simple, you'll likely be happy here.

405 N. Woodside Rd., Glasgow G20 6NN. © 0141/339-8620. Fax 0141/334-8159. www.glasgowhotelsandapartments. co.uk. 20 units. £70 ($133) double without breakfast; £78 ($148) double with breakfast; £84 ($160) triple without breakfast; £96 ($182) triple with breakfast; £104 ($198) quad without breakfast; £120 ($228) quad with breakfast. AE, DC, MC, V. Free parking. Underground: Kelvin Bridge. **Amenities:** Bar; laundry service; nonsmoking rooms. *In room:* TV, fridge, coffeemaker, hair dryer, iron, safe, trouser press, Wi-Fi.

Ambassador Hotel ★ *Value*   Located across from the BBC Studios and the Botanic Gardens, and overlooking the Kelvin River, this small hotel in an Edwardian town house (ca. 1900) is one of the better B&Bs in Glasgow. After being refurbished, the hotel looks quite stylish. Each of the individually decorated and attractively furnished bedrooms has a well-maintained bathroom with tub or shower. The hotel is well situated for exploring the West End's art galleries, restaurants, and brasseries.

7 Kelvin Dr., Glasgow G20 8QJ. © **0141/946-1018**. Fax 0141/945-5377. www.glasgowhotelsandapartments.co.uk. 16 units. £70 ($133) double without breakfast; £78 ($148) double with breakfast; £84 ($160) triple without breakfast; £96 ($182) triple with breakfast; £104 ($198) quad with breakfast; £120 ($228) with breakfast. AE, DC, MC, V. Free parking. Underground: Hillhead. **Amenities:** Bar; laundry service; nonsmoking rooms; mobile-phone rental. *In room:* TV, coffeemaker, hair dryer, iron, safe, trouser press, Wi-Fi.

Argyll Hotel   Small but special, this hotel is in a Georgian building near Glasgow University, the Art Gallery and Museum, the Kelvin Hall International Sports Arena, and the Scottish Exhibition Centre. Although completely modernized and comfortable, the Argyll shows a healthy respect for tradition.

973 Sauchiehall St., Glasgow G3 7TQ. © **0141/337-3313**. Fax 0141/337-3283. www.argyllhotelglasgow.co.uk. 38 units. £80–£95 ($152–$181) double. Rates include Scottish breakfast. MC, V. Parking on nearby streets. Underground: Kelvin Hall. Bus: 9, 16, 42, 57, 62, or 64. **Amenities:** Restaurant; bar; room service; babysitting; laundry service; dry cleaning; nonsmoking rooms. *In room:* TV, coffeemaker, hair dryer, iron, Wi-Fi.

Kirklee Hotel *Kids*   This red-sandstone Edwardian terraced house is near the university, the Botanic Gardens, and the major art galleries. It is graced with a rose garden that has won several awards. Guests arriving at the ornate stained-glass front door are welcomed by the owners. Most of the high-ceilinged guest rooms—all nonsmoking—are average size, but some are large enough to accommodate families. For guests who request it, breakfast is served in their room.

11 Kensington Gate, Glasgow G12 9LG. © **0141/334-5555**. Fax 0141/339-3828. www.kirkleehotel.co.uk. 9 units. £72 ($137) double; £80–£95 ($152–$181) family room. Rates include Scottish breakfast. MC, V. Parking nearby. Underground: Hillhead. **Amenities:** Bar. *In room:* TV, hospitality tray, hair dryer, trouser press.

Number Thirty-Six   This hotel, in the heart of the West End, occupies the two lower floors of a four-story sandstone building that was conceived as an apartment house in 1848. Hardworking entrepreneurs John and Julie MacKay keep the high-ceilinged pastel guest rooms in fine working order. All units are nonsmoking and equipped with a tidy shower-only bathroom.

36 St. Vincent Crescent, Glasgow G3 8NG. ✆ **0141/248-2086.** Fax 0141/221-1477. www.no36.co.uk. 5 units. £28–£33 ($53–$63) per person, per night double. Rates include continental breakfast. No credit cards. Bus: 42, 63, or 64. **Amenities:** Room service; nonsmoking rooms.

4 Where to Dine

The days are long gone when a meal out in Glasgow meant mutton pie and chips. Some of the best Scottish food is served here (especially lamb from the Highlands, salmon, trout, Aberdeen Angus steaks, and exotic delights like moor grouse), and there's an ever-increasing number of ethnic restaurants. This still being Britain, however, you'll find the usual fish-and-chips joints, burger outlets, fried-chicken eateries, and endless pubs. Many restaurants close on Sunday, and most are shut by 2:30pm, reopening again for dinner around 6pm. *Note:* For the locations of the restaurants below, see the "Glasgow Accommodations & Dining" map, on p. 176.

MERCHANT CITY
EXPENSIVE

Brian Maule at Chardon d'Or ✦✦✦ FRENCH/SCOTTISH   Ayr-born Brian Maule is hailed as one of the finest chefs in Scotland. He's earned that praise, having been elevated to head chef at the age of 24 at Le Gavroche, still hailed as London's best restaurant. Returning to his native roots north of the Border, he has brought all the skill and finesse that earned him fame in his homeland.

In Glasgow he prepares his cuisine with a passionate commitment, searching everywhere to find the best possible regional ingredients. Each dish is a creation of his own original style, beginning with such starters as pressed chicken, ham, and foie gras terrine with roast beetroot and a shallot salsa, or warm wood pigeon salad with celeriac and apple remoulade with a Madeira-laced dressing. We are dazzled by his light, full-flavored, and impertinently inventive mains, especially his roast filet of duck with a cabbage and potato cake or his chump of Scottish lamb with asparagus tips, and Puy green lentils flavored with sherry vinegar. Here he jazzes up Scottish pan-fried salmon with fresh tomatoes, virgin olive oil, broad beans, and a delectable aïoli sauce. His desserts are sumptuous, including baked raspberries in an almond cream or white chocolate mousse with a compote of blueberries.

176 W. Regent St. ✆ **0141/248-3801.** Reservations required. Main courses £20–£24 ($38–$45). AE, MC, V. Mon–Fri noon–2:30pm and Mon–Sat 6–10pm. Underground: Buchanan St.

étain ✦✦ FRENCH/SCOTTISH   The celebrated U.K. designer, Sir Terrence Conran, has moved outside of London to open his first "destination restaurant" in Britain. French for pewter, étain lies near the upmarket Princes Square Shopping Centre. The setting is intimate and elegant, and there is a definite sense of glamour in dining here. Though the culinary inspiration is definitely French, the market-fresh produce is Scottish regional whenever possible.

The creations here are sometimes simple, sometimes complex, but all in all the cooking is harmonious in its blending of textures and dishes are full of flavor. Some of the most exemplary offerings include grilled breast of wood pigeon with an endive compote and an Arran grain mustard potato salad. Other dishes we have savored include filet of monkfish with mussels and a basil *beurre blanc* or honey and spiced glazed duck leg confit with a celeriac purée and Madeira dressing. Desserts are made fresh daily and are sumptuous, including a dark chocolate concoction with coffee sauce and crème fraîche.

The Glass House, Springfield Ct., Queen St. ℂ **0141/225-5630.** Reservations required. Main course £16–£22 ($30–$42). AE, MC, V. Mon–Fri noon–2:30pm and Mon–Sat 7–11pm, Sun noon–3pm. Underground: Buchanan St.

Gamba 🕸🕸🕸 SEAFOOD   This restaurant, owned and "cheffed" by Derek Marshall, not only serves the best seafood in Glasgow, but it may also be the best restaurant, although locals will give you some sass about that claim. In a chic modern setting, with the best service in town, you sit back and are dazzled by the repertoire of dishes here. Although its specialty is fish and seafood, carnivores can also find palate pleasure here. The premium beef from the private Buccleuch Estate is among the best we've tasted in Scotland, and even vegetarians can find temptation. Gamba's fish soup with crab meat is clearly the best in town. It's flavored with ginger and served with prawn dumplings. Other winning starters include Marrbury smoked salmon with chili jam and crème fraîche (a heavenly dish) or mussels and oyster stew.

The main courses are wonderfully delicate and full of flavor, as evoked by the whole roasted sea bass with grilled red peppers and the pan-fried monkfish with crayfish tails and baby capers. Desserts sound simple but are marvelous in taste and texture. Try the spiced rum parfait with cinnamon and stewed apple or the raspberry ripple cheesecake.

225A W. George St. ℂ **0141/572-0899.** Reservations required. Main courses £12–£27 ($23–$51). AE, MC, V. Mon–Sat noon–2:30pm and 5–10:30pm. Underground: Buchanan St.

Rogano 🕸🕸 SEAFOOD   Rogano boasts a perfectly preserved Art Deco interior from 1935, when Messrs. Rogers and Anderson combined their talents and names to create a restaurant that has hosted virtually every star of the British film industry. You can enjoy dinner amid lapis-lazuli clocks, etched mirrors, ceiling fans, semicircular banquettes, and potted palms. The menu always emphasizes seafood, such as halibut in champagne-and-oyster sauce and lobster grilled or Thermidor. A less expensive menu is offered down in the **Cafe Rogano,** where main courses begin at £10 ($19).

11 Exchange Place. ℂ **0141/248-4055.** Reservations recommended. Main courses £20–£30 ($38–$57); fixed-price lunch £18–£24 ($33–$45). AE, DC, MC, V. Restaurant daily noon–2:30pm and 6:30–10:30pm; cafe Mon–Thurs noon–11pm, Fri–Sat noon–midnight, Sun noon–11pm. Underground: Buchanan St.

MODERATE

Cafe Noir 🕸 ECLECTIC   Originally this brasserie opened as Hemingways until the family of the legendary novelist stepped in and threatened legal action. Overlooking Glasgow's fabulous Princes Square, this is the enclave of Alan Dexter who gained fame for featuring the best tapas in Glasgow. The cafe occupies the second floor of Glasgow's most stylish shopping mall. A fashionable young crowd gathers here early in the evening for the town's best cocktails, which are consumed as they listen to each other and jazzy beats from the piano bar.

The venue is ideal for a snack or a complete dinner. The menu is full of flavor and designed for those with modern taste. A "taste of Scotland" is reflected in the homemade soup—smoked haddock and spring pea soup—or else you might enjoy a bloody mary cocktail of tiger prawns and pak choi. For mains, chefs offer everything from beer-battered fish and chips to chargrilled Aberfoyle rib-eye steak. You can even order a tuna BLT. Desserts are often old fashioned, including spiced date pudding with butterscotch sauce and vanilla ice cream or rhubarb crumble and clotted cream ice cream.

Princes Square, 48 Buchanan St. ✆ **0141/221-7800.** Main courses £8.50–£16 ($16–$30). AE, MC, V. Mon–Thurs noon–10pm; Fri–Sat noon–10:30pm. Underground: St. Enoch.

October ⚜ INTERNATIONAL   Located at the top of the Princes Square shopping district, this bar and restaurant offers a diverse menu. Of the several vegetarian dishes, one of the best is a type of potato sandwich filled with roasted vegetables. The array of choices includes everything from club sandwiches to mussels with white wine to bites like potato wedges and nachos. For dessert, try the raspberry tart.

The Rooftop, Princes Square, Buchanan St. ✆ **0141/221-0303.** Reservations recommended. Main courses £8–£11 ($15–$21). AE, MC, V. Mon–Wed 10am–11pm; Thurs–Sat 10am–midnight; Sun 12:30–5pm. Underground: St. Enoch.

Russian Café-Gallery Cossachok ⚜ *Finds* RUSSIAN   Before the opening of this restaurant near the Tron Theatre, Glasgow was about the last place you'd look for Russian cuisine. A favorite with actors from the nearby theater, this is an inviting oasis, with beautiful and authentic Russian decor, including plenty of mahogany pieces and ample use of the color of red.

The chefs concentrate mainly on Russian fare but are also adept at turning out a selection of Armenian, Georgian, and Ukrainian dishes. Come here to feast on famous Russian dishes such as borscht and savory blinis. The beef Stroganoff, served with fried straw potatoes, is the finest we've had in Scotland. Chicken Vladimir, a breaded breast of chicken with a mushroom sauce resting under a cheese topping, is another excellent offering. Cossachok's moussaka successfully blends eggplant, tomatoes, mushrooms, soy beans, garlic, and coriander spicing, and Zakuski Tzar is a tasty version of home-baked pork flavored with garlic and served with a dip inspired by the kitchens of Georgia.

10 King St., Merchant City. ✆ **0141/553-0733.** Reservations recommended. Main courses £8–£19 ($15–$36); pre-theater 2-course dinner Tues–Sat (5–7pm) £9.95 ($19). MC, V. Mon–Sat 10:30am–11pm; Sun 4–10pm. Underground: St. Enoch.

INEXPENSIVE

Cafe Gandolfi *Kids* SCOTTISH/FRENCH   Many students and young professionals will tell you this popular place in Merchant City is their favorite "caff"—you may sometimes have to wait for a table. A remake of a Victorian pub, it boasts rustic wooden floors, benches, and stools. If you don't fill up on soups and salads, try smoked venison with gratin dauphinois or smoked pheasant with an onion tartlet in winter. Vegetarians will find solace here.

64 Albion St. ✆ **0141/552-6813.** Reservations recommended on weekends. Main courses £6–£17 ($11–$32). MC, V. Mon–Sat 11am–midnight; Sun noon–11pm. Underground: St. Enoch/Cannon St.

Corinthian INTERNATIONAL   This restaurant in Lanarkshire House opened in 2000 with a 7.5m (25-ft.) illuminated glass dome as its stunning centerpiece. Crystal chandeliers and rococo friezes make for a luxurious atmosphere. The menu is based on the freshest products available. You might feast on pan-seared salmon filet; lentil Bolognese with herb fettuccini; or grilled breast of Grampian chicken. In the three bars (Lite Bar, Piano Bar, and Slouch Bar), you can relax on Italian leather sofas while listening to music spun by the local DJ.

191 Ingram St. ✆ **0141/552-1101.** Reservations recommended. Main courses £13–£22 ($25–$42); fixed-price pre-theater dinner £11 ($21) for 2 courses, £13 ($25) for 3 courses. AE, MC, V. Mon–Fri 5pm–3am; Sat–Sun noon–10pm. Underground: St. Enoch.

GLASGOW CENTER
VERY EXPENSIVE

Cameron's ✦✦ MODERN SCOTTISH   Outfitted like a baronial hunting lodge in the wilds of the Highlands, Cameron's is the most glamorous restaurant in Glasgow's best hotel. While the chef's conservative menu holds few surprises, it's a celebration of market-fresh ingredients deftly prepared. Small slip-ups sometimes mar the effect of a dish or two, but we have always gone away pleased. Your best bet is to stay Scottish when ordering. For example, choose whisky-cured Isle of Arran salmon, confit of Highland duck, or Firth of Lorne sea scallops—and those are only the appetizers. For a main course, we recommend the rack of Scottish lamb with a crust of whisky-steeped oatmeal and Arran mustard. A vegetarian menu is also available.

In the Glasgow Hilton Hotel, 1 William St. ✆ **0141/204-5555.** Reservations recommended. Fixed-price menu £20 ($38) for 2 courses, £35 ($67) for 3 courses. AE, DC, MC, V. Mon–Fri noon–10pm; Sat 7–10pm. Bus: 6A, 16, or 62.

EXPENSIVE

The Buttery ✦ SCOTTISH/FRENCH   This is the perfect hunter's restaurant, with oak panels and an air of baronial splendor, dating from 1870. The anteroom bar used to be the pulpit of a church, and the waitresses wear high-necked costumes, of which Queen Victoria would have approved. Menu items include smoked trout, rare roast beef, terrine of Scottish seafood, venison, and tuna steak with tarragon and tomato-butter sauce.

Adjacent is the Oyster Bar, outfitted in church-inspired Victoriana. The Belfry, which is less formal, is in the cellar (see below).

652 Argyle St. ✆ **0141/221-8188.** Reservations recommended. Fixed-price lunch menu £16 ($30) for 2 courses. Fixed-price dinner £36 ($68). AE, DC, MC, V. Tues–Fri noon–10pm; Sat 7–10pm. Underground: St. Enoch.

MODERATE

The Belfry ✦ SCOTTISH/FRENCH   The pews, pulpits, and stained glass that adorn this place are from a church in northern England. It's the only pub in Glasgow where you can contemplate Christ in Majesty while you enjoy a pint of ale. The kitchen produces daily specials like steak pie with roast potatoes; roast rack of lamb with rosemary, thyme, and caramelized shallots; and The Belfry mussel bowl with shallots. The cook is well known for making clever use of fresh Scottish produce.

In the basement of The Buttery (see above), 652 Argyle St. ✆ **0141/221-0630.** Reservations recommended. Main courses £10–£15 ($19–$29). AE, MC, V. Mon–Fri noon–2:30pm and 6–10:30pm; Sat 6–10:30pm. Underground: St. Enoch.

Brasserie Malmaison *(Kids)* SCOTTISH/CONTINENTAL   In a hip hotel converted from a Greek Orthodox church (see "Where to Stay," earlier in this chapter), this restaurant in the crypt, beneath the original vaults, serves imaginative food in a dark, masculine setting, with a large bar and wooden banquettes. Menu items arrive in generous portions and include French-style rumpsteak with garlic butter and pommes frites, monkfish au poivre, and grilled chicken with roasted red-pepper salsa. Sunday brunch menu items include eggs Benedict and corned beef hash.

In contrast, the greenhouse-inspired **Champagne Bar,** adjacent to the brasserie, has a menu of salads, sandwiches, pizzas, light platters, and—you guessed it—champagne.

In the Malmaison Hotel, 278 W. George St. ✆ **0141/572-1000.** Reservations recommended for dinner Thurs–Sun. Brasserie main courses £12–£23 ($23–$44). AE, DC, MC, V. Brasserie daily noon–2:30pm and 6–11pm; Champagne Bar daily 10am–midnight. Bus: 11.

Brasserie Malmaison (p. 186)   Dining here is like taking your kid to church—well, not really. The former Greek Orthodox church has given way to a Scottish and Continental cuisine. The chefs serve some of the city's best fries, salmon cakes, and grilled chicken dishes. Adjacent to the brasserie is a cafe with fresh salads, sandwiches, and pizzas.

Cafe Gandolfi (p. 185)   Children always find something to order here, and the staff offers half portions of all main courses. The chef also cooks up constantly changing plates for kids. Of course, the main course has to be followed by one of Cafe Gandolfi's homemade ice creams, the best in the city.

Willow Tea Room (p. 188)   Thousands of locals fondly remember coming here as children to enjoy delectable pastries and ice-cream dishes—and it's still a big treat for any kid.

City Merchant SCOTTISH/INTERNATIONAL   This cozy restaurant in the heart of the city offers friendly service, an extensive menu, and service throughout the day. The cuisine is more reliable than stunning, but it delivers quite an array of well-prepared fresh food at a good price. Try the roast breast of duck, rack of lamb, or medallions of venison. Also tempting are the fast-seared scallops and cockburns of Dingwall Haggis. Some of the desserts evoke old-time Scotland, such as the clootie dumpling, made with flour, spices, and fried fruit and served with home-churned butter.

97–99 Candlebiggs. ✆ 0141/553-1577. Reservations recommended. Main courses £8–£26 ($15–$49); fixed-price dinner £28 ($52). AE, DC, MC, V. Mon–Sat noon–11pm; Sun 5–11pm. Underground: St. Enoch.

Ho Wong Restaurant ASIAN/PACIFIC   This is one of the city's finest Chinese restaurants, 2 blocks from the Central Station; it's an outpost of Jimmy Ho and David Wong's Hong Kong establishment. There are at least eight duck dishes on the menu, along with four types of fresh lobster and some sizzling platters.

82 York St. ✆ 0141/221-3550. Reservations required. Main courses £11–£20 ($21–$38); fixed-price 2-course lunch £9.50 ($18); fixed-price banquet £29 ($55; 5 courses). AE, DC, MC, V. Mon–Sat noon–2pm and 6–11:30pm; Sun 6–11:30pm. Underground: Central Station.

Michael Caines at ABode Glasgow SCOTTISH/CONTINENTAL   The famous West Country (England) chef, Michael Caines, has expanded northward into Glasgow. In one of the city's most fashionable hotels (see ABode, above), he has opened this chic restaurant, serving some of the city's finest cuisine in a relaxed yet efficient style. He's appointed executive chef Martin Donnelly to oversee the day-by-day operation. The kitchen team makes expert use of Scottish regional produce to create their award-winning meals.

We find that the appetizers are some of the best in Glasgow, including roasted quail with a fricassee of artichokes and cepes (flap mushrooms) or else a salad of Scottish scallops with an endive marmalade (a first for us). Main courses will regale you, especially the saddle of wild red deer with mixed berries or the Loch Duart salmon with wild mushrooms. The desserts are a great way to finish off a good meal, especially the millefeuille of caramelized apples with a green apple sorbet or the milk chocolate mousse with hazelnuts and homemade ice cream. Luncheons are popular with the city's business community but at night the place takes on a more romantic ambience. A temperature-controlled Wine Room is a special feature of the restaurant, and it's supervised by perhaps the finest sommelier in Glasgow.

In the ABode Hotel, 129 Bath St. © **0141/572-6011.** Reservations required. Main courses £18–£23 ($33–$44). AE, DC, MC, V. Mon–Sat noon–2:30pm; Mon–Thurs 7–10pm; Fri–Sat 6:30–10pm. Underground: Buchanan St.

Two Fat Ladies ☆ MODERN BRITISH/SEAFOOD   This ranks high on the list of everybody's favorite restaurants, especially for irreverent diners who appreciate the unexpected. The "Two Fat Ladies" are its street number—a nickname for the number 88 in Scotland's church-sponsored bingo games (there's no connection to the "Two Fat Ladies" of TV Food Network fame). The custard-colored decor is minimalist and "post-punk." The restaurant packs in crowds for specialties like king prawns cooked in garlic and saffron butter, and medallions of Angus filet teriyaki. Vegetarian dishes are also available. The best dessert is the Pavlova (a chewy meringue) with raspberries and Drambuie sauce.

88 Dumbarton Rd. © **0141/339-1944.** Reservations recommended. Fixed-price lunch 2 courses £13 ($25); fixed-price pre-theater supper (6–7pm) £11–£13 ($21–$25); main courses £9–£17 ($17–$32). MC, V. Tues–Thurs noon–2pm; Fri–Sat 6–10pm. Bus: 16, 42, or 57.

Windows Restaurant ☆ SCOTTISH   Located on the 7th floor of the Carlton George Hotel, this restaurant is aptly named—it opens onto panoramic views of Glasgow. It doesn't stop there, however, as its chefs feature an innovative menu prepared with a high standard of ingredients. Diners get a true "Taste of Scotland" with such dishes as seared West Coast scallops or the grilled filet of Scottish beef with chanterelle mushrooms. You might also try other Scottish delights, like tomato and mozzarella stuffed in a pastry; grilled tuna steak with herb noodles and soy dressing; and leaves of smoked salmon and halibut with crème fraîche, capers, and chives. For dessert, opt for the freshly baked lemon tart or the fresh raspberries flavored with lime.

In the Carlton George Hotel, 44 West George St. © **0141/354-5070.** Reservations recommended. 2-course lunch £15–£17 ($29–$32); 3-course lunch £18 ($34); 2-course dinner £18–£20 ($34–$38); 3-course dinner £22–£24 ($42–$46). AE, MC, V. Mon–Fri 6:30am–11:30pm, Sat–Sun 7am–11:30pm. Underground: Buchanan St.

⌐Moments **Tea for Two**

For tea, a light lunch, or a snack, try the famed **Willow Tea Room,** 217 Sauchiehall St. (© **0141/332-0521;** Underground: Cowcaddens). When it opened in 1904, the Willow became a sensation because of its Charles Rennie Mackintosh design, and it has been restored to its original condition. Thousands of locals fondly remember coming here as children to enjoy delectable pastries and ice-cream dishes—and it's still a big treat for any kid.

On the ground floor is a well-known jeweler, M. M. Henderson Ltd. The "room de luxe" is in the heart of the building, and it's fashionable to drop in for tea at any time of day. Reservations are recommended, and afternoon tea with pastry is £10.50 ($20). It's open Monday to Saturday 9am to 5pm and Sunday 11am to 4:15pm.

THE WEST END
EXPENSIVE

The Bistro ✶✶ SCOTTISH/FRENCH   In one of Glasgow's most elegant hotels, the Bistro menu changes daily, but is a delight on any day you show up. It's that good. Why? The talented chefs take quality produce, often regional in origin, and cook it simply without destroying its natural flavor. Although influenced by Scottish and French recipes, the chefs also have adapted their food to more modern tastes.

You peruse the menu in an intimate, oak-paneled setting, most atmospheric. True foodies wanting regional flavors might select a starter such as a ravioli of John Dory with smoked eel and black pudding, although others might opt for the ballotine of foie gras wrapped in toasted pistachios. Wonderfully delicate mains include roast filet of roe deer and a boudin of guinea fowl or else poached line-caught turbot with Cantonese pork belly. One of our favorites is the butter-roasted loin of lamb from the Borders served with an anchovy beignet. For an original dessert, opt for the tonka bean crème brûlée with eucalyptus ice cream.

In Hotel du Vin, 1 Devonshire Gardens. ✆ **0141/339-2001.** Reservations required. Main courses £19–£20 ($36–$38). AE, MC, V. Daily 7–9:30pm. Underground: Hillhead.

Ubiquitous Chip ✶ SCOTTISH   This restaurant is inside the rough-textured stone walls of a former stable; its glass-covered courtyard boasts masses of climbing vines. Upstairs is a pub where simple platters are served with pints of lager and drams of whisky; the menu may include wood pigeon, or Orkney organic salmon. The downstairs bistro-style restaurant might feature free-range chicken, shellfish with crispy seaweed snaps, or wild rabbit. Vegetarians are catered to at both places.

12 Ashton Lane, off Byres Rd. ✆ **0141/334-5007.** Reservations recommended. Restaurant fixed-price lunch £23 ($44) for 2 courses, £29 ($55) for 3 courses; fixed-price dinner £35 ($67) for 2 courses, £40 ($76) for 3 courses; bar meals £4–£15 ($7.60–$29) at lunch, £8–£17 ($15–$32) at dinner. AE, DC, MC, V. Restaurant Mon–Sat noon–2:30pm, daily 5:30–11pm; bar only Sun 1–11pm. Underground: Hillhead.

MODERATE

Air Organic ✶ *(Finds)* ORGANIC FUSION   Space-age Air Organic is designed like an airport lounge, with white walls and sky-blue tables. The menu, designed to look like a plane ticket, features both organic and non-organic foods. The Thai seafood broth with coconut, lime, and coriander is exceptional, as is the Thai pumpkin curry. The restaurant also specializes in Japanese cooking, offering a variety of bento boxes. We were especially taken with the char-siu roast pork with sticky mustard apples. For dessert, there's nothing better than the steamed banana-and-ginger pudding. The friendly service, wide range of choices, and unique design make this place worth visiting.

36 Kelvingrove St. ✆ **0141/564-5200.** Reservations recommended. Main courses £10–£20 ($19–$38); fixed-price 2-course dinner (daily 5–7pm) £14 ($27); bento boxes £13–£18 ($25–$34). AE, DC, MC, V. Sun–Thurs 11am–11pm; Fri–Sat noon–midnight. Underground: Hillhead.

Ashoka West End ✶ INDIAN/PUNJABI   This is a culinary landmark in Glasgow, serving the finest cuisine of the subcontinent. Novice chapatti chompers and vindaloo veterans alike discover this restaurant with each new generation. Many Glaswegians learned to "eat Indian" at this very restaurant. The decor is a bit eclectic, involving rugs, brass objects, murals, and greenery.

The dishes are full of flavor and pleasingly fragrant. You might launch your repast with Pakora, which is deep-fried chicken, mushrooms, or fish. From there you can go on to order Jalandhri, a potent fusion of ginger, garlic, onions, peppers, coconut cream, and fresh herbs, served with a choice of chicken, lamb, or mixed vegetables. Sing Sing Chandni is a sweet and spicy Cantonese-style dish with crispy peppers, spring onions, and cashew nuts served most often with chicken. Those preferring something less robust enjoy Chasni, a light and smooth cream sauce served with chicken, lamb, or mixed vegetables.

1284 Argyle St. ✆ **0141/389-3371.** Reservations required. Main courses £10–£15 ($19–$29). AE, DC, MC, V. Sun–Thurs 5pm–12:30am; Fri–Sat 5pm–1am. Underground: Kelvin Hall.

No. Sixteen MODERN SCOTTISH   Chefs here decided to take old Scottish and European recipes and turn them on their heads. Innovation is all over the menu, which changes constantly. The restaurant is one room, evoking a French bistro, and a friendly and attentive staff enhances the dining experience. Two good choices that have graced past menus are the baked eggplant tart with goat's cheese quenelle and the baked sea bass stuffed with black olive tapenade and tomatoes in a lime beurre blanc. You might also opt for the tender grilled filet of Scottish beef with braised shallots.

16 Byres Rd. ✆ **0141/339-2544.** Reservations recommended. Fixed-price lunch £20 ($38) 2 courses, £22 ($42) 3 courses. Main courses dinner £14–£19 ($27–$36). DC, MC, V. Mon–Sat noon–2:30pm and 5:30–10pm; Sun 12:30–2:30pm and 5:30–9pm. Underground: Exhibition Centre.

INEXPENSIVE

Koh-i-Noor INDIAN/PUNJABI   This is one of the city's top Indian restaurants. The family who run this spacious place come from the Punjab in Pakistan, and, naturally, Punjabi specialties like *paratha* (flatbread) and *bhuna* (dry cooked) lamb are recommended. The Sunday Indian buffet is one of the great food values of the city; the Indian buffet held on weekdays is another treat. You can also order a three- or four-course business lunch.

235 North St., Charing Cross. ✆ **0141/221-1555.** Reservations recommended. Main courses £7.50–£17 ($14–$32); fixed-price business lunch £6 ($11) for 3 courses, £8 ($15) for 4 courses; pre-theatre meal £9.95 ($19) 3 courses; Sun–Thurs buffet £12.50 ($24); Fri–Sat buffet £13.50 ($26). AE, DC, MC, V. Sun–Thurs noon–midnight; Fri–Sat noon–1am. Underground: St. Georges.

La Parmigiana ⟨Value⟩ ITALIAN   This seems to be everyone's favorite trattoria, providing a cosmopolitan Continental atmosphere and a good change of pace from the typical Glasgow dining scene. Even Italians living in Glasgow swear by the food here. A long-established family dining room, it offers the usual array of pasta dishes, some especially delectable, like the lobster-stuffed ravioli in basil cream sauce. Also try the chargrilled scallops cooked quickly in olive oil and served with fresh lemon juice.

447 Great Western Rd. ✆ **0141/334-0686.** Reservations required. Main courses £15–£21 ($29–$40); fixed-price lunch £12 ($22); fixed-price dinner £13–£15 ($24–$28). AE, DC, MC, V. Mon–Sat noon–2:30pm and 6–11pm. Underground: Kelvinbridge.

Stravaigin ⟨★★⟩ GLOBAL   We've never seen any restaurant like this in Glasgow. The chef, who is also the owner, truly roams the globe for inspiration. Although some of his ideas might come from as far away as China or the Caribbean, he also knows how to use the finest of the regional Scottish bounty. Expect concoctions such as Vietnamese-inspired marinated quail served on a candy smoked eggplant concasse. Other menu items include Mexican tortilla cannelloni, Mancheyo and smoked tomato sauce; and roast filet of mullet, chorizo garlic roast potatoes, asparagus and Romesco sauce. Many locals finish with a selection of Scottish cheeses with quince jelly and bannocks. On the ground level is a pub/café.

28 Gibson St., Hillhead. ℂ **0141/334-2665**. Reservations required. Fixed-price menus (lunch or dinner) £12–£14 ($23–$27). AE, DC, MC, V. Mon–Sat 11am–10:30pm; Sun 11am–5pm. Underground: Kelvinbridge.

5 Seeing the Sights

THE TOP ATTRACTIONS

The center of Glasgow is **George Square,** dominated by the **City Chambers** that Queen Victoria opened in 1888. Of the statues in the square, the most imposing is that of Sir Walter Scott, atop a 25m (80-ft.) column. Naturally, you'll find Victoria along with her beloved Albert, plus Robert Burns. The **Banqueting Hall,** lavishly decorated, is open to the public on most weekdays.

The Burrell Collection 🏵🏵🏵 This museum houses the mind-boggling treasures left to Glasgow by Sir William Burrell, a wealthy ship owner who had a lifelong passion for art. Burrell started collecting art when he was 14, and his passion continued until he died at the age of 96, in 1958. His tastes were eclectic: Chinese ceramics, French paintings from the 1800s, tapestries, stained-glass windows from churches, even stone doorways from the Middle Ages. It is said that the collector "liked about everything," including one of the very few original bronze casts of Rodin's *Thinker.* He did, however, find some art distasteful, including avant-garde works ("Monet was just too impressionistic"). You can see a vast aggregation of furniture, textiles, ceramics, stained glass, silver, art objects, and pictures in the dining room, hall, and drawing room, which was reconstructed from Sir William's home, Hutton Castle at Berwick-upon-Tweed. Ancient artifacts, Asian art, and European decorative arts and paintings are featured. A restaurant is on-site, and you can roam through the surrounding park, 5km (3 miles) south of Glasgow Bridge.

Pollok Country Park, 2060 Pollokshaws Rd. ℂ **0141/287-2550**. www.glasgowmuseums.com. Free admission. Mon and Wed–Sat 10am–5pm; Sun 11am–5pm. Closed Jan 1 and Dec 25. Bus: 45, 48, or 57.

Glasgow Science Centre 🏵🏵🏵 *(Kids* This is Britain's most successful millennium project. It opened in 2001 and lies on the banks of the River Clyde, opposite the Scottish Exhibition and Conference Centre. The center is the focal point of Glasgow's drive to become one of Europe's major high-tech locations. In three landmark buildings, the center features the first titanium-clad structures in the United Kingdom, including Scotland's only Space Theatre. The complex also contains the only 360-degree rotating tower in the world. Other features include innovative laboratories, multimedia and science theaters, and interactive exhibits. The overall objective: to document the challenges facing Scotland in the 21st century. The center is also a showcase depicting Glasgow's contribution to science and technology in the past, present, and future.

Children love the hands-on activities: They can make their own soundtrack and animation, do a 3-D head scan and rearrange their own features, or star in their own digital video. At special shows and workshops, you see a glass smashed by sound, "catch" shadows, experience a million volts of indoor lighting, see liquid nitrogen, view bacteria, and build a lie detector.

At the IMAX Theatre are some 150 films that, for example, explore natural wonders like Deep Sea 3-D, the inside of an atom, or the magic of space. The theater charges separate admission: £6.95 ($13) for adults or £4.95 ($9.40) for students and children. It's open from 11am to 6pm Sunday to Wednesday and 11am to 8pm Thursday and Saturday.

Glasgow Attractions

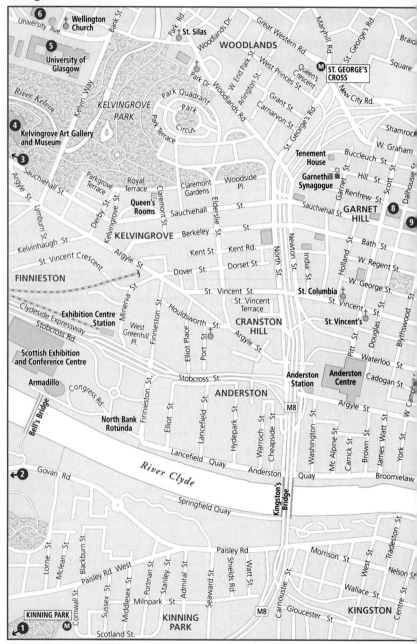

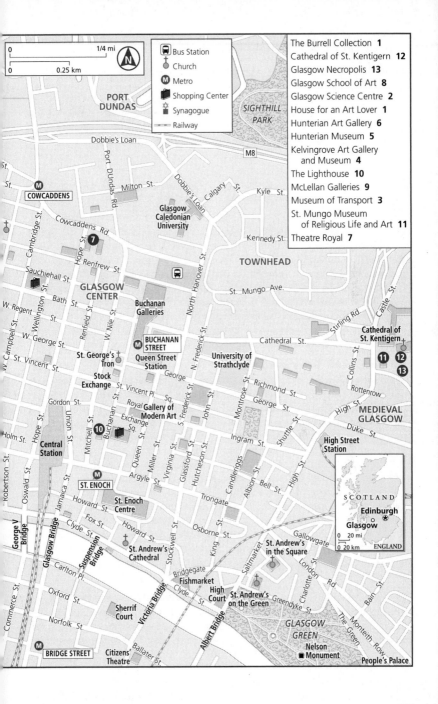

Legend:
- Bus Station
- Church
- Metro
- Shopping Center
- Synagogue
- Railway

The Burrell Collection **1**
Cathedral of St. Kentigern **12**
Glasgow Necropolis **13**
Glasgow School of Art **8**
Glasgow Science Centre **2**
House for an Art Lover **1**
Hunterian Art Gallery **6**
Hunterian Museum **5**
Kelvingrove Art Gallery and Museum **4**
The Lighthouse **10**
McLellan Galleries **9**
Museum of Transport **3**
St. Mungo Museum of Religious Life and Art **11**
Theatre Royal **7**

50 Pacific Quay. ℂ 0141/540-1000. www.gsc.org.uk. Admission £6.95 ($13) adults, £4.95 ($9.40) students and seniors. Daily 10am–6pm. Underground: Buchan St. Station to Cessnock, from which there's a 10-min. walk.

Hunterian Art Gallery 𝒢𝒢 This gallery owns the artistic estate of James McNeill Whistler, with some 60 of his paintings bestowed by his sister-in-law. It also boasts a Charles Rennie Mackintosh collection, including the architect's home (with his own furniture) on three levels, decorated in the original style. The main gallery exhibits 17th- and 18th-century paintings (Rembrandt to Rubens) and 19th- and 20th-century Scottish works. Temporary exhibits, selected from Scotland's largest collection of prints, are presented in the print gallery, which also houses a permanent display of print-making techniques.

University of Glasgow, 22 Hillhead St. ℂ 0141/330-5431. www.hunterian.gla.ac.uk. Free admission. Mon–Sat 9:30am–5pm (Mackintosh House closed 12:30–1:30pm). Closed Jan 1, July 21, Sept 29, and Dec 25. Underground: Hillhead.

Hunterian Museum This museum, Glasgow's oldest, opened in 1807. It's named after its early benefactor, William Hunter, who donated his private collections. Today the Hunterian contains a wide-range of interesting items, from dinosaur fossils to coins to relics of the Roman occupation, as well as plunder by the Vikings. The story of Captain Cook's voyages is pieced together in ethnographic material from the South Seas. The museum, which has a bookstall and an 18th-century-style coffeehouse, is located in the main Glasgow University buildings, 3km (2 miles) west of the city center.

University of Glasgow, Main/Gilbert-Scott Building. ℂ 0141/330-4221, ext. 4221. Free admission. Mon–Sat 9:30am–5pm; additional hours for special exhibits vary. Closed Jan 1, July 21, Sept 29, and Dec 25. Underground: Hillhead.

Kelvingrove Art Gallery and Museum 𝒢𝒢 Neil MacGregor, director of London's National Gallery, hailed this Glasgow landmark as "one of the greatest civic collections in Europe." Traditionally, more than a million people a year have come to this museum in the West End's Kelvingrove Park, making it the most visited museum in the United Kingdom (outside of London). You can view a wide range of exhibits consisting of fine and decorative arts and of 300-million-year-old marine-life fossils; one of the world's greatest collections of arms and armor is here as well.

Restored at a cost of £27.9 million ($53 million), the museum displays such important works as Salvador Dali's controversial painting *Christ of St. John of the Cross.* The galleries contain a superb collection from Dutch and Italian Old Masters, including Giorgione's *Adulteress Brought Before Christ,* Rembrandt's *Man in Armor,* and Millet's *Going to Work.* Scottish painting is well represented from the 17th century to the present. One of the gallery's major paintings is Whistler's *Arrangement in Grey and Black no. 2: Portrait of Thomas Carlyle,* the first Whistler to be hung in a British gallery.

Argyle St. ℂ 0141/276-9599. Free admission. Mon–Thurs and Sat 10am–5pm; Fri and Sun 11am–5pm. Underground: Kelvin Hall.

The Lighthouse (Scotland's Centre for Architecture, Design and the City) 𝒦𝒾𝒹𝓈 The Lighthouse, which opened in July 1999, is based in Charles Rennie Mackintosh's first public commission; from 1895 to 1980 it housed the *Glasgow Herald.* Unoccupied for 15 years, the building is now the site of a seven-story, state-of-the-art exhibition center with a blue neon-tracked escalator that leads to four galleries, lecture facilities, education suites, and a cafe.

The **Mackintosh Interpretation Centre** is the first facility to provide an overview of Mackintosh's art, design, and architecture. The impressive glass timeline wall illustrates his achievements. There are also interactive stations with models, drawings, and computer and video displays. Visitors can ride the lift up to the Mackintosh Tower and see a panorama of the city. The education program offers tours, lectures, films, and workshops for people of all ages. The Wee People's City is an interactive play area for children under 9. The IT Hotspot features Macintosh computers with printing facilities, video conferencing, and a large selection of software for research, training, and hands-on activities.

11 Mitchell Lane. ℂ 0141/221-6362. www.thelighthouse.co.uk. Admission to Lighthouse and Mackintosh Interpretation Center £3 ($5.70) adults, £1.50 ($2.85) students and seniors, £1 ($1.90) children 5 and over, free for children under 5. Mon and Wed–Sat 10:30am–5pm; Tues 11am–5pm; Sun noon–5pm. Underground: Buchanan Station.

McLellan Galleries The McLellan is the repository of an impressive collection of Italian works from the 16th and 17th centuries, and it is also a showcase for modern pop art. Many of its exhibits on loan from the Kelvingrove Art Gallery include a superb collection of Dutch and Italian Old Masters, featuring Giorgione and Rembrandt. Such international artists as Botticelli are also represented. Expect a rotating series of art.

270 Sauchiehall St. ℂ 0141/565-4137. www.glasgowmuseums.com. Free admission. Mon–Thurs and Sat 10am–5pm; Fri–Sun 11am–5pm. Underground: Cowcaddens and Buchanan St.

Museum of Transport ✸✸ This museum contains a fascinating collection of all forms of transportation and related technology. Displays include a simulated 1938 Glasgow street with period shopfronts, era-appropriate vehicles, and a reconstruction of one of the Glasgow Underground stations. The superb and varied ship models in the Clyde Room reflect the significance of Glasgow and the River Clyde as one of the world's foremost areas of shipbuilding and engineering.

1 Bunhouse Rd., Kelvin Hall. ℂ 0141/287-2720. www.glasgowmuseums.com. Free admission. Mon–Thurs and Sat 10am–5pm; Sun and Fri 11am–5pm. Closed Dec 25, Boxing Day, and Jan 1–2. Underground: Kelvin Hall.

ADDITIONAL ATTRACTIONS
Cathedral of St. Kentigern ✸✸✸ Also known as St. Mungo's, this cathedral was consecrated in 1136, burned down in 1192, and rebuilt soon after. The Laigh Kirk (lower church), whose vaulted crypt is said to be the finest in Europe, remains to this day and holds St. Mungo's tomb, where a light always burns. The edifice is mainland Scotland's only complete medieval cathedral from the 12th and 13th centuries. It was once a place of pilgrimage, but 16th-century zeal purged it of all monuments of idolatry.

Highlights of the interior include the nave, from the 1400s, with a stone screen showing the seven deadly sins. Both the choir and the lower church are in the mid-13th-century First Pointed style. The church itself, though a bit austere, is filled with intricate details left by long-ago craftspeople—note the tinctured bosses of the ambulatory vaulting in the back of the main altar. The lower church, reached via a set of steps north of the pulpit, is where Gothic reigns supreme, with an array of pointed arches and piers.

For the best view of the cathedral, cross the Bridge of Sighs into the **Glasgow Necropolis** (ℂ 0141/552-3145; bus: 2 or 27), the graveyard containing almost every type of architecture in the world. Built on a rocky hill and dominated by a statue of John Knox, this fascinating graveyard was opened in 1832. Typical of the mixing of all groups in this tolerant, cosmopolitan city, the first person to be buried here was a Jew, Joseph Levi. It is open daily from 8am to 4:30pm.

Cathedral Square, Castle St. ✆ 0141/552-6891. Free admission. Apr–Sept Mon–Sat 9:30am–6pm, Sun 2–5pm; Oct–Mar Mon–Sat 9:30am–4pm, Sun 1–4pm. Sun services at 11am and 6:30pm. Underground: Queen St. Station.

House for an Art Lover   This house, which opened in 1996, is based on an unrealized and incomplete 1901 competition entry of Charles Rennie Mackintosh. The impressive building, with its elegant interiors, was brought to life by contemporary artists and craftspeople. A tour begins in the main hall and goes through the dining room, with its lovely gesso panels, and on to the music room, which shows Mackintosh designs at their most inspirational. Also here are an art cafe and design shop (✆ **0141/353-4779**), and a striking parkland adjacent to Victorian walled gardens.

Bellahouston Park, 10 Dumbreck Rd. ✆ 0141/353-4770. www.houseforanartlover.co.uk. Admission £3.50 ($6.65) adults, £2.50 ($4.75) children, students, and seniors. Apr 1–Sept 30 Mon–Wed 10am–4pm, Thurs–Sun 10am–1pm; Oct 1–Mar 31 Sat–Sun 10am–4pm, call for weekday times. Cafe and shop daily 10am–5pm. Underground: Ibrox. Bus: 9A, 39, 54, 59, or 36.

St. Mungo Museum of Religious Life and Art 🖈 *Finds*   Opened in 1993, this is an eclectic and often controversial museum, close to the Glasgow Cathedral. It has a collection that spans the centuries and highlights various religious groups that have lived in Glasgow and the surrounding area. The museum is hailed as unique for its representation of Buddha, Ganesha, Shiva, and others. Also on display is the Chinese robe worn in the Bernardo Bertolucci film *The Last Emperor.* In back of the museum is the U.K.'s only Japanese Zen garden.

2 Castle St. ✆ 0141/552-2557. Free admission. Mon–Thurs and Sat 10am–5pm; Fri and Sun 11am–5pm. Bus: 11, 36, 37, 38, 42, 89, or 138.

MARITIME GLASGOW

Scottish Maritime Museum   Irvine Harbour outside Glasgow was once a major trading port, and its maritime history lives on at this restoration. Tours take you through a shipyard worker's tenement flat, and you can also see a collection of vessels moored at the harbor. These include the SV *Carrick,* the world's oldest colonial clipper, which made 22 passages between Scotland and Adelaide, Australia. You can also see the SY *Carola,* built on the Clyde in 1898 as a private family yacht, and the oldest seagoing steam yacht in Great Britain.

Harbourside, Irvine. ✆ 01294/278-283. www.scottishmaritimemuseum.org. Admission £3 ($5.70) adults, £2 ($3.80) seniors, students, and children, £7 ($13) family ticket (maximum 5 people). Apr–Oct daily 10am–5pm. Braehead bus from Central Station.

The Tall Ship at Glasgow Harbour   Here's a rare chance to explore one of the last remaining Clyde-built tall ships, the SV *Glenlee,* built in 1896, a vessel that rounded Cape Horn 15 times. Restored in 1999, *Glenlee* is one of only five Clyde-built sailing ships that remain afloat. While on board, take in an exhibition detailing the vessel's cargo-trading history. On the dock, the Victorian Pumphouse Centre contains a restaurant and a nautical gift shop, as well as exhibition galleries.

100 Stobcross Rd. ✆ 0141/222-2513. www.thetallship.com. Admission £4.95 ($9.40) adults, £3.75 ($7.15) seniors, students, and children. 1 free child admission with paying adult. Mar–Oct daily 10am–5pm; Nov–Feb daily 11am–4pm. Take the low-level train from Glasgow Central to Finnieston/SECC.

GARDENS & PARKS

Glasgow's **Botanic Gardens,** Great Western Road (✆ **0141/334-2422;** Underground: Hillhead), covers 16 hectares (40 acres); it's an extensive collection of tropical plants and herb gardens, and is especially acclaimed for its spectacular orchids and

Frommer's Favorite Glasgow Experiences

Touring The Burrell Collection The pièce de résistance of Glasgow (some say of Scotland), this gallery is the city's major attraction. See what good taste and an unlimited budget can acquire in a lifetime.

Following Walkways & Cycle Paths Greater Glasgow has an array of trails and bike paths cutting through areas of historic interest and scenic beauty, including the Paisley/Irvine Cycle and Walkway, 27km (17 miles) of unused railway line converted to a trail.

Riding the World's Last Seagoing Paddle Steamer From spring to early fall, the *Waverley* (© 0845/130-4647) makes day trips to scenic spots on the Firth of Clyde, past docks that once supplied more than half the tonnage of oceangoing ships.

Shopping Paddy's Market This daily market by the railway arches on Ship-bank Lane gives you the real flavor of the almost-vanished Glaswegian style of street vending.

begonias. It's open daily from 7am to dusk. The greenhouses are open March to October 10am to 4:45pm and November to February 10am to 4:15pm. Admission is free.

Linn Park, on Clarkston Road (bus: 24 or 36), is 86 hectares (212 acres) of pine and woodland, with many scenic walks along the river. Here you'll find a nature trail, pony rides for children, an old snuff mill, and a children's zoo. The park is open daily from 8am to dusk. **Gleniffer Braes Country Park** (© 0141/287-5108), Glenfield Road, in Paisley, covers 526 hectares (1,300 acres) of woodland and moorland and has picnic areas and an adventure playground. It's open daily from dawn to dusk.

ORGANIZED TOURS

The *Waverley* is the world's last seagoing paddle steamer, and from the last week of June to the end of August (depending on weather conditions), the Paddle Steamer Preservation Society conducts 1-day trips from Anderston Quay in Glasgow to historic and scenic places beyond the Firth of Clyde. As you sail along, you can take in what were once vast shipyards turning out more than half the earth's tonnage of oceangoing liners. You're welcome to bring your own sandwiches for a picnic aboard, or you can enjoy lunch in the Waverley Restaurant. Boat tours cost £7 to £33 ($13–$63). For details, contact **Waverley Excursions,** Waverley Terminal, Anderston Quay, Broomielaw (© 0141/243-2224).

There's also regular ferry service run by **Caledonian MacBrayne** (© 0870/565-0000) in Gourock on the banks of the Clyde. The ferry is close to the station in Gourock, connected to Glasgow Central Station by trains that leave every hour and take 30 to 45 minutes. The ferry service, which can accommodate cars, runs every hour to the attractive seaside resort of Dunoon at the mouth of the Clyde. The journey takes about 20 minutes, and ferries run every hour from 6:20am to 8:20pm, April to October 16; in winter the service is less frequent and visitors are advised to check beforehand as it's liable to change. The round-trip costs £5.60 ($11) per person.

The best Glasgow tours are run by **Scotguide Tourist Services (City Sighting Glasgow),** operated from 153 Queen St. at George Square, opposite the City Chambers

(© 0141/204-0444; Underground: Buchanan St.). April 1 to October 31, departures are every 15 minutes 9:30am to 4pm (Nov 1–Mar 31 every 30 min.). The price is £9 ($17) for adults, £7 ($13) for students and seniors, and £3 ($5.70) for children 5 to 14, £20 ($38) family ticket.

If you prefer to stay on terra firma, **Mercat Walks** (© 0141/586-5378) focuses on the city's ghostly past. Historians re-create macabre Glasgow with a parade of hangmen, ghosts, murderers, and body snatchers. Tours leave from the tourist information center on George Square at 7 and 8pm daily, costing £7 to £29.50 ($13–$56) depending on the type of tour you choose.

6 Special Events

The **Royal Bank Glasgow Jazz Festival** (www.jazzfest.co.uk) usually opens in midJune. This festival has attracted some big names in the past, including the late Miles Davis and Dizzy Gillespie. Tickets are available from the Ticket Centre, Candleriggs (© 0141/552-3552), but some free events are always announced.

On June 10, the **Bearsden** and **Milngavie Highland Games** are held at Burnbray in the small town of Milngavie (pronounced "*mill*-guy"), 10km (6 miles) from Glasgow. The games include tug-of-war, wrestling, caber tossing, piping, and Highland dancing, and offer a fun day out of the city. In case you were wondering, a caber is a young tree trunk used for tossing—the aim of the competition is to toss a 5.7m-long (19-ft.) pine tree into the air and have it land on a straight line. Check the website, www.bearsdenmilngaviehighlandgames.com for more information. The **Glasgow Fair** (held during most of the month of July) is likely to have carnivals, tea dances, European circuses, Victorian rides, and even a country-and-western stampede. For information, call © 0141/287-2000.

OUTDOOR PURSUITS

BIKING   The tourist office provides maps with detailed bike paths. Rentals are available from **West End Cycles,** 16–18 Chancellor St. (© 0141/357-1344; Underground: Kelvin Hall), charging £10 to £15 ($19–$29) per day and requiring a deposit of £100 ($190) or two pieces of ID.

GOLF   Several courses are near Glasgow, but there's a limited number actually in the city itself. Two 9-hole courses are **Alexandra Park,** Alexandra Parade (© 0141/556-1294), and **Knightswood,** Lincoln Avenue (© 0141/959-6358). Neither offers caddy service or rentals of clubs and carts. Both Alexandra, a 2,281-yard, par-31 course, and Knightswood, a 2,793-yard, par-34 course, charge greens fees between £4 to £5 ($7.60–$9.50) per round. Visitors must call 24 hours in advance to arrange tee times. Open daily from 10am to 5pm in winter, daily from 7am to 8pm in summer.

SPORTS COMPLEXES   The **Kelvin Hall International Sports Arena** is on Argyle Street (© 0141/357-2525; Underground: Kelvin Hall), near the River Kelvin. It offers volleyball and basketball courts, as well as an indoor track. Daily from 9am to 10:30pm, you can use the weight room for £3.50 ($6.65) or the fully equipped gym for £5 ($9.50). This is also the country's major venue for national and international sports competitions; check with the tourist office for any events scheduled for the time of your visit.

Scotstoun Leisure Centre, 72 Danes Dr., Scotstoun (© 0141/959-4000; bus: 9, 44, 62, or 64), is about 3km (2 miles) from the center of Glasgow. It's open Monday 7:30am to 10pm, Tuesday 9am to 10pm, Wednesday 7:30am to 10pm, Thursday

10am to 10pm, Friday 7:30am to 10pm, Saturday 9am to 5pm, and Sunday 9am to 9pm. There's an obligatory first-time fee of £7.20 ($14) for anyone wanting to use the gym; entry thereafter is £4.50 ($8.55).

WATERSPORTS & ICE-SKATING   The **Lagoon Leisure Centre,** Mill Street, Paisley (© 0141/889-4000), offers indoor facilities that include a free-form pool with a wave machine, fountains, and a flume. You'll also find sauna suites with sunbeds, Jacuzzis, and a Finnish steam room. The ice rink boasts an international ice pad with six curling lanes and is home to the Paisley Pirates hockey team. There are also bar and catering facilities.

The center is open Monday to Friday from 10am to 10pm and Saturday and Sunday from 9:30am to 5pm. Use of the sauna is £3.50 to £5 ($6.65–$9.50). There are frequent trains throughout the day from Glasgow Central Station to Paisley.

7 Shopping

One of the major hunting grounds is **Sauchiehall Street,** Glasgow's fashion center, where many shops and department stores frequently offer good bargains, particularly in woolen goods. About 3 blocks long, this street has been made into a pedestrian mall. **Argyle Street,** which runs by the Central Station, is another major shopping artery.

All dedicated world shoppers know of **Buchanan Street,** a premier pedestrian thoroughfare. This is the location of the famed Fraser's department store (see below). From Buchanan Street you can also enter **Princes Square,** an excellent shopping complex with many specialty stores, restaurants, and cafes.

In the heart of Glasgow is the city's latest and most innovative shopping complex, the **St. Enoch Shopping Centre** (Underground: St. Enoch; bus: 16, 41, or 44), whose merchandise is less expensive but a lot less posh than what you'd find at the Princes Square shopping center. You can shop under the biggest glass roof in Europe. The center is to the east of Central Station on St. Enoch Square.

The **Argyll Arcade** is at 30 Buchanan St. (Underground: Buchanan St.). Even if the year of its construction (1827) wasn't set in mosaic tiles above the entrance, you'd still know that this col-

> **Tips**   **Bring That Passport!**
>
> Take along your passport when you go shopping in case you make a purchase that entitles you to a **VAT (value-added tax)** refund.

lection of shops beneath a curved glass ceiling has been here for a while. The arcade contains what's possibly the largest concentration of retail **jewelers,** both antique and modern, in Europe, surpassing even Amsterdam. It's considered lucky to purchase a wedding ring here.

Dedicated fashion mavens should take a trip to the **Italian Shopping Centre** (Underground: Buchanan St.), a small complex in the Courtyard, off Ingram Street, where most of the units sell clothes, including Versace, Prada, Gucci, and Armani.

The latest contribution to mall shopping has come in the form of the **Buchanan Galleries** (Underground: Buchanan St.), which connects Sauchiehall, Buchanan, and Argyll streets, and was completed in 1999. This plush development includes an enormous **John Lewis department store** and the biggest **Habitat** in Europe—a paradise for anyone wanting reasonably priced contemporary furniture or accessories.

The Barras, held Saturday and Sunday 10am to 5pm, takes place about .5km (¼ mile) east of Glasgow Cross. This century-old market has some 800 traders selling their wares in stalls and shops. Not only can you browse for that special treasure, you can also become a part of Glasgow life and be amused by the *buskers* (colorfully and amusingly garbed street entertainers). If you want to see an old-fashioned slice of Glaswegian street vending, go to **Paddy's Market,** by the rail arches on Shipbank Lane.

General **shopping hours** are Monday to Saturday 9am to 5:30 or 6pm, depending on the merchant. On Thursdays, shops stay open to 8pm.

ANTIQUES
Victorian Village   This warren of tiny shops stands in a slightly claustrophobic cluster. Much of the merchandise isn't particularly noteworthy, but there are many exceptional pieces if you're willing to go hunting. Several of the owners stock reasonably priced 19th-century articles; others sell old jewelry and clothing, a helter-skelter of artifacts. 93 W. Regent St. ✆ **0141/332-0808**. Bus: 23, 38, 45, 48, or 57.

ART
Compass Gallery   This gallery offers refreshingly affordable pieces; you can find something special for as little as £25 ($48), depending on the exhibition. The curators tend to concentrate on local artists, often university students. 178 W. Regent St. ✆ **0141/221-6370**. Bus: 23, 38, 45, 48, or 57.

Cyril Gerber Fine Art   One of Glasgow's most respected art galleries veers away from the avant-garde, specializing in British paintings, sculptures, and ceramics crafted between 1880 and today, as well as in Scottish landscapes and cityscapes. Cyril Gerber is a respected art authority with lots of contacts in art circles throughout Britain. Pieces begin at around £200 ($380). 148 W. Regent St. ✆ **0141/221-3095**. Bus: 23, 38, 45, 48, or 57.

CLOTHING
James Pringle Weavers ✿   In business since 1780, this shop is owned by the Edinburgh Woollen Mill, known for its high-quality clothing that includes well-crafted sweaters from the Island of Arran, and a tasteful selection of ties, kilts, and tartans. Some of the merchandise is unique to this stop. Ever slept in a tartan nightshirt? 130 Buchanan St. ✆ **0141/221-3434**.

CRAFTS
Scottish Craft Centre ✿✿   The work of some of the finest craftspeople in Scotland is highlighted at this showcase. Most of the items are exquisitely crafted in porcelain, metal, glass, and wood. You can select from such items as metal candle holders, hand-carved wooden boxes, exquisite glasses and china, and porcelain vases. Princes Square Mall, 48 Buchanan St. ✆ **0141/248-2885**. Underground: St. Enoch. Bus 9, 12, 44, 66, or 75.

A DEPARTMENT STORE
Fraser's of Glasgow   Fraser's is Glasgow's version of Harrods. A soaring Victorian-era glass arcade rises four stories, and inside you'll find everything from clothing to Oriental rugs, from crystal to handmade local artifacts of all kinds. 21–45 Buchanan St. ✆ **0141/221-3880**. Underground: Buchanan St.

GIFTS & DESIGN
Catherine Shaw   Named after the long-deceased matriarch of the family that runs the place today, Catherine Shaw is a somewhat cramped gift shop that has cups, mugs,

postcards, and gift items based on the designs of Charles Rennie Mackintosh. There are also some highly evocative Celtic mugs called *quaichs* (welcoming cups or whisky measures, depending on whom you ask) and tankards in both pewter and silver. It's a great place for easy-to-pack and somewhat offbeat gifts. 24 Gordon St. ℭ 0141/204-4762. Underground: Buchanan St.

Mackintosh Shop ⭐⭐⭐   This tiny shop prides itself on its stock of books, cards, stationery, coffee and beer mugs, glassware, and sterling-and-enamel jewelry created from the original designs of Mackintosh. Although the shop doesn't sell furniture, the staff will refer you to a craftsman whose work they recommend: **Bruce Hamilton, Furnituremaker,** 4 Woodcroft Ave., Broomhill (ℭ **01505/322-550;** bus: 6, 16, or 44), has been involved in the restoration of many Mackintosh interiors and has produced a worthy group of chairs, sideboards, and wardrobes authentic to Mackintosh's designs. Expect to pay around £250 ($475), not including upholstery fabric, for a copy of the designer's best-known chair (the Mackintosh-Ingram chair); there is a delay of at least a month before customers receive their furniture. In the foyer of the Glasgow School of Art, 4 Napier St. ℭ 0141/353-4526. Underground: Queen St.

National Trust for Scotland Shop ⭐   Drop in here for maps, calendars, postcards, pictures, dish towels, bath accessories, and kitchenware. Some of the crockery is in Mackintosh-design styles. The neoclassical building, constructed as a charity and hospice in 1806, is on the site of a larger hospice built in 1641. Hutcheson's Hall, 158 Ingram St. ℭ 0141/552-8391. Underground: Buchanan St.

KILTS & TARTANS

Hector Russell ⭐⭐⭐   Founded in 1881, Hector Russell is Scotland's oldest kiltmaker. This elegant store might be the most prestigious in Scotland. The welcome of the experienced sales staff is genuinely warm-hearted. Crystal and gift items are sold on street level, but the real heart and soul of the place is on the lower level, where you'll find impeccably crafted and reasonably priced tweed jackets, tartan-patterned accessories, waistcoats, and sweaters of top-quality wool for men and women. Men's, women's, and children's hand-stitched kilts are available. 110 Buchanan St. ℭ 0141/221-0217. Underground: Buchanan St.

MUSIC

Fopp   In our view, this is the city's finest and coolest record outlet. It offers one of the best selections of DVDs on Glasgow, as well as CDs representing all musical styles. For some real values, search out the "bargain bin." Fopp's range of traditional Scottish music is a highlight. 19 Union St. ℭ 0141/222-2128. Underground: St. Enoch.

PORCELAIN & CRYSTAL

Stockwell Bazaar   This is Glasgow's largest purveyor of porcelain, its four floors bulging with Royal Doulton, Waterford, Lladro, Wedgwood, Noritake, and Royal Worcester, plus crystal stemware by many manufacturers. Anything you buy can be insured and shipped. 67 Glassford St. ℭ 0141/552-5781. Underground: St. Enoch.

SPIRITS

Demijohn   Let's call this a "liquid deli." If you're seeking unusual whiskies or liqueurs, head here. You'll even find a collection of rare spirits. There is a unique policy here of allowing customers the freedom to taste all of the products before they buy. The products are not just from Scotland, but include rare olive oils, vinegars, and spices from around the world. Other merchandise includes several intriguing gift items. 382 Byres Rd. (© 0141/337-3600. Underground: Hillhead.

8 Glasgow After Dark

Glasgow, not Edinburgh, is the cultural center of Scotland, and the city is alive with performances. Before you leave home, check *Time Out* (www.timeout.co.uk) for the latest round-up of who's playing in the clubs and concert halls. After you've arrived, pick up a copy of the free monthlies *Culture City* and *What's On* at the tourist office or your hotel. In addition, at most newsstands you can get a free copy of *The List,* published every other week. It details arts and other events for both Edinburgh and Glasgow.

THE PERFORMING ARTS

OPERA & CLASSICAL MUSIC   The **Theatre Royal,** Hope Street and Cowcaddens Road ((© **0141/332-9000;** box office 0870/060-6647; Underground: Cowcaddens; bus: 23, 48, or 57), is the home of the **Scottish Opera** ((© **0141/248-4567**) as well as of the **Scottish Ballet** ((© **0141/331-2931**). The theater also hosts visiting companies from around the world. Called "the most beautiful opera theatre in the kingdom" by the *Daily Telegraph,* it offers splendid Victorian Italian Renaissance plasterwork, glittering chandeliers, and 1,547 comfortable seats, plus spacious bars and buffets on all four levels. However, it's not the decor but the ambitious repertoire that attracts operagoers. Ballet tickets run £14 to £20 ($27–$38) and opera tickets cost £8.50 to £58 ($16–$110). On performance days, the box office is open Monday to Saturday 10am to 8pm; on nonperformance days, hours are Monday to Saturday 10am to 6pm. In winter, the **Royal Scottish National Orchestra** ((© **0141/226-3868**) offers Saturday-evening concerts at the **Glasgow Royal Concert Hall,** 2 Sauchiehall St. (box office (© **0141/353-8000;** Underground: Buchanan St.). The **BBC Scottish Symphony Orchestra** presents Friday-evening concerts at the **BBC Broadcasting House,** Queen Margaret Drive (Underground: St. Enoch), or at **City Halls,** Albion Street (Underground: St. Enoch). In summer, the Scottish National Orchestra has a short promenade season (dates and venues are announced in the papers). Tickets can only be purchased at individual venues.

THEATER   Although hardly competition for London, Glasgow's theater scene is certainly the equal of Edinburgh's. Young Scottish playwrights often make their debuts here, and you're likely to see anything from Steinbeck's *The Grapes of Wrath* to Wilde's *Salome* to *Romeo and Juliet* done in Edwardian dress.

The prime symbol of Glasgow's verve remains the **Citizens Theatre,** Gorbals and Ballater streets ((© **0141/429-0022;** bus: 12 or 66), founded after World War II by James Bridie, a famous Glaswegian whose plays are still produced on occasion there. It's home to a repertory company, with tickets at £5 to £16 ($9.50–$30). The box office hours are Monday 10am to 6pm and Tuesday to Saturday 10am to 9pm. The company is usually closed from June to the first week in August.

The **Strathclyde Arts Centre,** 12 Washington St. ((© **0141/221-4526;** bus: 2, 4, or 21), always seems to be doing something interesting, including children's productions and other theatrical performances. It's open Monday to Friday 9:30am to 5pm and 6:30 to 10pm; in summer, it's closed in the evening. The center is funded by the Glasgow Council and performances are free. The **King's Theatre,** 297 Bath St. ((© **0141/240-1111;** bus: 18, 42, or 57), offers a wide range of productions, including straight plays, musicals, and comedies. During winter it's noted for its pantomime presentations. Tickets are £10 to £28 ($19–$53), and the box office is open Monday to Saturday 10am to 8pm.

The **Mitchell Theatre,** 6 Granville St. (℃ **0141/287-5511;** bus: 57), has earned a reputation for staging small-scale entertainment—ranging from dark drama to dance—and for hosting conferences and seminars. A small, modern theater, it adjoins the well-known Mitchell Library. When there are performances, the theater box office is open from 4pm until the show. Ticket prices vary with each production. The **Pavilion Theatre,** 121 Renfield St. (℃ **0141/332-1846;** bus: 21, 23, or 38), specializes in modern versions of vaudeville (which, as they'll assure you around here, isn't dead). The Pavilion sells its own tickets for £10 to £25 ($19–$48) they're not available at City Centre. The box office is open Monday to Saturday 10am to 8pm.

The **Tron Theatre,** 63 Trongate (℃ **0141/552-4267;** Underground: St. Enoch), occupies one of the three oldest buildings in Glasgow, the former Tron Church. The church, with its famous Adam dome and checkered history, has been transformed into a small theater presenting the best contemporary drama, dance, and music events. The Tron also has a beautifully restored Victorian cafe/bar serving traditional home-cooked meals, including vegetarian dishes and a fine selection of beer and wine. The box office is open Monday to Saturday 10am to 6pm over the counter, and until 9pm by phone. Tickets are £6 to £18 ($11–$34) for adults and £1 to £8 ($1.90–$15) for children.

THE CLUB & MUSIC SCENE

Barrowland   This hall seats 2,000 and is open only on nights shows are booked. July and August are the quiet months, as most performances are geared toward a student audience. The cover runs highest when the hall hosts popular bands like The Proclaimers or Black Rebel Motorcycle Club. Gallowgate. ℃ 0141/552-4601. Cover £11–£26 ($21–$49). Underground: St. Enoch. Bus: 61 or 62.

The Ferry   This old car ferry once provided service on the River Clyde. Musical acts are booked infrequently during the year. 25 Anderston Quay. ℃ 0141/248-5376. Cover £8–£22 ($15–$42). Bus: 21, 23, 38, 45, 48, or 57.

Fury Murry's   Most of the crowd consists of students looking for nothing more than a good, and sometimes rowdy, time; the club's disco music is upbeat if not ultra-trendy. Fury Murry's is in a cellar, a 2-minute walk from the very central St. Enoch Shopping Centre. With its busy bar and dance floor, there are ample opportunities to meet the best and brightest in Scotland's university system. Jeans and T-shirts are the right garb. It's open Thursday to Sunday 11pm to 3am. Thursday and Friday feature live bands, and other nights are strictly for dancing or can be reserved for private parties. 96 Maxwell St. ℃ 0141/221-6511. Cover £5–£7 ($9.50–$13). Underground: St. Enoch.

The Garage   A big student crowd pushes the limits of the 1,478-person capacity here on weekends. In the downstairs area, surrounded by rough stone walls, you get the impression you're in a castle with a Brit pop and indie soundtrack. Most regulars, however, gravitate to the huge main dance floor, where lots of shiny metal fixtures stand out in contrast to the stone walls. There are three bars downstairs and two upstairs. Open daily 10:30pm to 3am. 490 Sauchiehall St. ℃ 0141/332-1120. Cover £2–£10 ($3.80–$19). Underground: Buchanan St.

Grand Ole Opry   In a sprawling sandstone building 2.5km (1½ miles) south of Glasgow's center is the Grand Ole Opry, the largest country-western club in Europe. There's a bar and dancing area on both levels and a chuck-wagon eatery serving affordable steaks and other such fare on the upper level. Live music is always performed from a large stage at the front. Performers are usually from the United Kingdom, but a handful of artists from the States turn up. Open Friday to Sunday and occasionally Thursday (if demand warrants it) from 6:30pm to 12:30am. 2–4 Govan Rd., Paisley Toll Rd. ℭ 0141/429-5396. Cover £3–£10 ($5.70–$19). Bus: 23 or 23A.

King Tut's Wah-Wah Hut   This sweaty, crowded rock bar has been in business for nearly a decade. It's a good place to check out the Glasgow music and arts crowd, as well as local bands and the occasional international act. Successful Scottish bands My Bloody Valentine and Teenage Fan Club got their starts here. Open Monday to Saturday noon to midnight and Sunday 6pm to midnight. 272-A St. Vincent St. ℭ 0141/221-5279. Cover £5–£15 ($9.50–$29). Bus: 6, 8, 9, or 16.

Nice 'n' Sleazy   This club books live acts Thursday to Sunday. The cover is usually quite reasonable, but it gets more expensive if you catch a band like The Cranberries, Alice Donut, or Helmet. Holding some 200 patrons, it provides a rare opportunity to see internationally popular bands in an intimate setting. Upstairs on Sunday and Monday nights, DJs spin an eclectic mix of dance music, but most people come for the bands. Open Monday to Saturday 11:30am to midnight and Sun 12:30pm to midnight. 421 Sauchiehall St. ℭ 0141/333-0900 or -9637. Cover usually £3.50 ($6.65); higher if a big name is playing. Bus: 23 or 48.

The Riverside Club   One of Glasgow's oldest music venues, this barnlike hall is known for staging its weekend ceilidhs (pronounced "*kay*-lees"), or Scottish folk dances. Visiting Scots (or rather their descendants), who have long left the old country, return here to brush up on toe-tappin' Scottish regional dances. The good-natured, often drunken Scottish dancers range in age from 20 to 60. You don't even have to dance to take to the floor. On other nights of the month, the club stages theme nights. One night might be called "Fusion," another "Saltlick." After midnight on the first Friday of every month a party is staged called "Goodfoot," when the soul sounds of the far north are presented live by various groups. Open Thursday to Saturday 6pm to midnight. Fox St., off Clyde St. ℭ 0141/248-3144. Cover usually £5 ($9.50), but that can vary. Underground: St. Enoch.

The 13th Note   This club has moved away from jazz in the past couple of years and now books mainly heavy-rock bands on Wednesday and Thursday nights, country on Monday. It is also a vegan and vegetarian café. Friday, Saturday, and Sunday are dedicated to ambient and alternative music. Open Sunday and Wednesday to Thursday 11pm to 3am, Friday and Saturday 9pm to 3am. 50–60 King St. ℭ 0141/553-1638. Bus: 21, 23, or 38.

FAVORITE PUBS

Archie's   One of several traditional Scottish pubs in its neighborhood, Archie's is outfitted with stone floors and rows of decorative barrels. At the self-service food counter you can order cheap steak pie, lasagna, and salads; at the bar you can choose from an impressive array of single malts. There's a live jazz band on Saturday afternoons. Open Monday to Saturday noon to midnight. 27 Waterloo St. ℭ 0141/221-3210. Bus: 21, 23, or 48.

Bon Accord   This amiably weathered pub is a longtime favorite. There's an array of hand-pumps—a dozen devoted to real British ales, the rest to beers and stouts from the Czech Republic, Belgium, Germany, Ireland, and Holland. The pub is likely to satisfy your taste in malt whisky as well, and offers affordable bar snacks. Open Monday to Saturday noon to midnight, Sunday noon to 11pm. 153 North St. ℂ **0141/248-4427.** Bus: 6, 8, or 16.

Corn Exchange ⚘   Opposite the Central Station, this place was really the Corn Exchange in the mid–19th century but now is one of Glasgow's most popular pubs. Amid dark paneling and high ceilings, you can enjoy a pint of lager until 11pm Sunday to Wednesday and until midnight Thursday to Saturday. Affordable pub grub is served daily noon to 9pm. 88 Gordon St. ℂ **0141/248-5380.** Bus: 21, 23, or 38.

The Pot Still   Here's the best place for sampling malt whisky. You can taste from a selection of more than 500 single malts, at a variety of strengths (perhaps not on the same night) and maturities (that is, years spent in casks). Many prefer the malt whisky that has been aged in a sherry cask. There's good bar food at lunch, including cold meat salads and sandwiches. Open Monday to Thursday noon to 11pm, Friday and Saturday noon to midnight. 154 Hope St. ℂ **0141/333-0980.** Bus: 21, 23, or 38.

The Scotia Bar ⚘   This is the oldest pub in Glasgow, established in 1792. Live performers, singers, and musicians perform almost nightly. If you're great on the guitar, you might be handed an instrument and asked to perform yourself. One group we like is called "Tons of Slobs." The pub has had a long and colorful history, once known as the socialist pub in the 1960s. There is a large collection of malt whisky, and you can even order pub grub here, such as steak burgers or macaroni and cheese with garlic bread. Food is served Monday to Friday noon to 3pm and on weekends until 4pm. The pub itself is open Monday to Saturday noon to midnight, Sunday noon to 11pm. 112–114 Stockwell St. ℂ **0141/552-8681.** Underground: St. Enoch.

THE GAY SCENE

There's no strongly visible lesbian bar or nightclub scene in Glasgow. Many lesbians who attend bars frequent those that cater mainly to males.

Bennet's, 90 Glassford St. (ℂ **0141/552-5761**) is one of the major gay/lesbian nightclubs in town. On certain nights it's the most fun and crowded gay disco in Scotland. The crowd includes men and women ages 17 to 60, and the music plays on and on, interrupted only by the occasional drag show. The **Court Bar,** 69 Hutcheson St. (ℂ **0141/552-2463**), is a small, cozy pub that's a popular meeting place for the gay/lesbian crowd. The pub gets decidedly more male after 7pm and is a good starting point for a gay evening on the town. Attracting a slightly older crowd, **Waterloo Bar,** 306 Argyle St. (ℂ **0141/229-5891**), gets most packed during happy hour (9pm–midnight), when you can make your drink a double for just £3 ($5.70).

9 Side Trips from Glasgow: The Best of the Strathclyde Region

Just as Sir Walter Scott dominates the Borders, the presence of **Robert Burns** is felt in the Strathclyde region around Ayr. A string of famous seaside resorts stretches from Girvan to Largs. Some of Britain's greatest golf courses, including **Turnberry,** are here. Glasgow makes a good gateway to Burns country, as it has excellent bus and rail connections to Ayr, which is your best bet for exploring the area. If you're driving, take A77 southwest from Glasgow to Ayr.

AYR: A POPULAR WEST COAST RESORT

The royal burgh of Ayr is the most popular resort on Scotland's west coast. Facing the Isle of Arran and the Firth of Clyde, it's 130km (81 miles) southwest of Edinburgh,

Backpacking the West Highland Way

One of Scotland's most legendary long-distance footpaths is the **West Highland Way** (see "The Best Hikes," in chapter 1), set aside by the government in 1967 to preserve its beauty. It begins north of Glasgow in the town of Milngavie and winds its way for 153km (95 miles) north along Loch Lomond, with its bonnie, bonnie banks. The trail continues through Glencoe, site of a famous passage, and goes on to Fort William and eventually to Ben Nevis, Scotland's highest mountain. The most dramatic part of this walk is from the Bridge of Orchy to Glencoe.

Trains run frequently throughout the day from the Queen's Street railway station in central Glasgow to Milngavie, starting point of the walk. The 15-minute trip costs £3 ($5.70) one-way. For information and a map of this footpath, contact the **Scottish Tourist Board,** 23 Ravelston Terrace, Edinburgh EH4 3EU (© 0845/2255-121; www.visitscotland.com; Underground: Buchanan St.).

and 56km (35 miles) southwest of Glasgow. A busy market town, it offers 4km (2½ miles) of beach (alas, spoiled by pollution), steamer cruises, fishing, and golf, and is a manufacturing center for fabrics and carpets. Ayr also boasts the top racecourse in Scotland.

Trains from Glasgow's Central Station (© **08457/484-950**) will whisk you to Ayr in 50 minutes; the fare is £5.60 ($11). Stagecoach Express (© **01292/613-500**) buses from Glasgow arrive in Ayr in 1 hour, costing £5.80 ($11) one-way.

The **tourist office** is at 22 Sandgate, Ayr (© **01292/288-688**). It's open April to June, Monday to Saturday 9am to 5pm; July and August, Monday to Saturday 9am to 6pm, Sunday 10am to 5pm; September, Monday to Saturday 9am to 5pm, Sunday 11am to 5pm; and October to March, Monday to Friday 9am to 5pm.

SEEING THE SIGHTS

Burns associations abound in Ayr. The 13th-century **Auld Brig o' Ayr,** the poet's "poor narrow footpath of a street where two wheelbarrows tremble when they meet," was renovated in 1910.

On Blackfriar's Walk, on the banks of the River Ayr, is the **Auld Kirk of Ayr;** it dates from 1653 to 1655, when it replaced the 12th-century Church of St. John, which had been seized by Cromwell and dismantled. Its greatest curiosity is a grim series of "mort safes" from 1655—they were used to cover freshly filled graves to discourage body-snatchers. Robert Burns was baptized in the kirk. The church is open Monday to Saturday 8:30am to 7pm and Sunday noon to 7pm. Sunday service is at 11am.

The **Wallace Tower,** on High Street, rises some 34m (112 ft.). Constructed in 1828, it has a statue of William Wallace (remember *Braveheart?*) by local sculptor James Thom. Tradition holds that Wallace was imprisoned here and made a daring escape.

Another architectural curiosity is **Loudoun Hall** (© **01292/286-385**), Boat Vennal, at the junction of Hope and High streets, off Cross Street, in the heart of town. A wealthy merchant had this town house built in the late 1400s, and it's one of the oldest examples of burgh architecture left in the country. From mid-July to the end of August, it's open Monday to Saturday from 11am to 6pm.

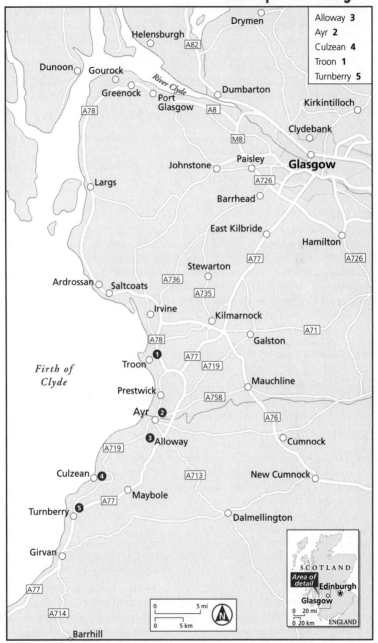

Side Trips from Glasgow

Alloway **3**
Ayr **2**
Culzean **4**
Troon **1**
Turnberry **5**

Drymen

Helensburgh

A82

Dunoon

Gourock

Greenock

River Clyde

Port Glasgow

Dumbarton

A8

Kirkintilloch

Clydebank

A78

M8

Johnstone

Paisley

Glasgow

A726

Largs

Barrhead

East Kilbride

Hamilton

A726

Stewarton

A77

Ardrossan

Saltcoats

A736

A735

Irvine

Kilmarnock

A71

A78

Troon **1**

A77

Galston

Firth of Clyde

A719

Prestwick

Mauchline

Ayr **2**

A758

A76

3 Alloway

A719

Cumnock

Culzean **4**

A713

New Cumnock

Turnberry **5**

A77

Maybole

Dalmellington

Girvan

A77

A714

Barrhill

0   5 mi
0   5 km

N

SCOTLAND

Area of detail

Edinburgh

Glasgow

0   20 mi
0   20 km

ENGLAND

Located about 2.5km (1½ miles) south of Ayr, on Monument Road in Rozelle Park (© 01292/443-708), the **Maclaurin Gallery and Rozelle House** are installed in what were once stables and servants' quarters. A Henry Moore bronze sculpture and a major collection of contemporary art are on display. A nature trail winds through the woodland. The park is off the road to the Burns Cottage at Alloway (see below), and is open Monday to Saturday from 10am to 5pm (Apr–Oct also Sun 2–5pm). Admission is free.

The **Ayr Racecourse** (© 0870/850-5666; www.ayr-racecourse.co.uk), about 2.5km (1½ miles) north of the town center (follow the signs on A77), is open year-round. Races are usually held Friday, Saturday, and Monday, generally at 2:15pm. Peak racing season is May to October, with jumping events held in November, January, and April. The Scottish Grand National is held mid-April.

There are three nearby golf courses; the best is the municipal **Belleisle Golf Course,** Doonfoot Road, Alloway (© 01292/441-258). There are some three dozen courses in the area.

WHERE TO STAY

Fairfield House 👍 This 1912 Edwardian town house, on the seafront near Low Green, has been restored to its original elegance and converted into Ayr's best hotel. The staff is especially attentive and will help you arrange tee times at nearby golf courses. Lady Henrietta Spencer-Churchill, noted designer of classic British interiors, decorated the rooms in a country-house style. The guest rooms are large and luxurious, many done in chintz; most of the bathrooms have bidets. The food at Fairfield has been called an oasis in a culinary desert.

12 Fairfield Rd., Ayr, Ayrshire KA7 2AR. © 01292/267-461. Fax 01292/261-456. www.fairfieldhotel.co.uk. 44 units. £115–£150 ($219–$285) double; £175–£200 ($333–$380) suite. Rates include Scottish breakfast. AE, DC, MC, V. Free parking. **Amenities:** 2 restaurants; bar; indoor pool; health club; spa; sauna; room service; laundry service; dry cleaning. *In room:* A/C, TV, coffeemaker, hair dryer, trouser press.

Glenapp Castle 👍👍👍 This beautifully decorated castle offers spectacular baronial living, and is run by Graham and Fay Cowan. All other accommodations in the area pale in comparison. The castle was constructed in 1870 by David Bryce, a celebrated architect of his day. This vast Victorian mansion stands high above a village overlooking the Irish Sea. Elegant lounges and dining rooms await you, as do 17 spacious and individually furnished bedrooms and suites. Antiques, oil paintings, and elegant Victorian touches are seen at every turn. Tall Victorian windows let in the Scottish sun, making the rooms bright and sunny on many days. Dining at Glenapp, which has some of the finest wine cellars in the area, is a gourmet experience. The castle is on 12 hectares (30 acres) of lovely, secluded grounds, with many rare plants. The kitchen uses fresh herbs and fruit from the garden.

Ballantrae, Ayrshire KA26 0NZ. © 01465/831-212. Fax 01465/831-000. www.glenappcastle.com. 17 units. £375–£475 ($713–$903) double; £445–£485 ($846–$922) suite; £525–£575 ($998–$1,093) master room. Rates include all meals. AE, MC, V. 30km (20 miles) south of Ayr. Free parking. **Amenities:** Restaurant; bar; tennis court; room service; laundry service. *In room:* TV.

Ramada Jarvis Ayr This hotel is a few hundred yards from Ayr's seashore and 455m (1,493 ft.) from the rail station. It offers large, refurbished guest rooms, many with views and all with neat shower-only bathrooms. Bart's Bar and Grill is a lively place to meet and eat, with a selection of freshly roasted joints on the captain's table.

Dalblair Rd., Ayr, Ayrshire KA7 1UG. © 01292/269-331. Fax 01292/610-722. www.ramadajarvis.co.uk. 118 units. £140–£175 ($266–$333) double; £180 ($342) suite. AE, DC, MC, V. Free parking. **Amenities:** Restaurant; bar; health club; room service; laundry service; dry cleaning; nonsmoking rooms; rooms for those w/limited mobility. *In room:* TV, coffeemaker, hair dryer, trouser press.

Savoy Park Hotel ✪ For more than 30 years, the Henderson family has welcomed guests to their classic country hotel, which was designed in the Victorian and Scottish baronial style. The atmosphere is traditional, with paneled walls and ornate ceilings, but modern conveniences have been discreetly added. The pricier bedrooms are larger and more charming. All units include shower-only bathrooms. Evoking a Highland hunting lodge, the Oak Room serves time-tested dishes like baked lemon sole. The Savoy Park is a short drive from 30 first-rate golf courses, and fishing is also possible nearby.

16 Racecourse Rd., Ayr, Ayrshire KA7 2UT. ✆ **01292/266-112.** Fax 01292/611-488. www.savoypark.com. 19 units. £95–£161 ($181–$306) double. Rates include breakfast. AE, MC, V. Free parking. Follow A70 for 3km (2 miles), go through Parkhouse St., turn left into Beresford Terrace, and make 1st right onto Bellevue Rd. **Amenities:** Restaurant; bar. *In room:* TV, coffeemaker, hair dryer, iron.

WHERE TO DINE

Fouter's Bistro MODERN SCOTTISH This restaurant, in the historic heart of Ayr, occupies the cellar of an 18th-century bank, retaining the original sandstone floor and vaulted ceiling covered in terra-cotta tiles. The restaurant's name derives from Scottish argot: *foutering about* is a charming way of saying "bumbling about" (although this place is anything but bumbling). The seamless service focuses on modern Scottish cuisine with a nod to Thailand. You can sample the likes of venison with rowanberry sauce, local Gresshingham duck with black-cherry sauce, and seafood served with saffron cream sauce. In spring, one of the most delicious items is the organically reared lamb from the neighboring Carrick Hills.

2A Academy St. ✆ **01292/261-391.** Reservations recommended. Main courses lunch £10–£15 ($19–$29); main courses dinner £12–£17 ($23–$32); fixed-price lobster lunch (in season only) £18 ($34). AE, DC, MC, V. Tues–Sat noon–2:30pm and 6–10:30pm.

Tudor Restaurant SCOTTISH/INTERNATIONAL This busy family-oriented restaurant has a real Tudor look with dark half-timbering. Most popular here are the fixed-price lunch and the high tea served from 3:15pm to closing. The food includes such rib-sticking specialties as a version of chicken Maryland (breaded and fried breast of chicken with bacon, tomatoes, peaches, and pineapple fritters).

8 Beresford Terrace, on Burns Statue Sq. ✆ **01292/261-404.** Main courses from £6 ($11); fixed-price meal £9.95 ($19) for 2 courses, £12 ($23) for 3 courses; high tea £7–£9 ($13–$17). AE, DC, MC, V. Mon–Sat 9am–8pm; Sun noon–8pm.

AYR AFTER DARK

The famous **Rabbie's Bar** ✪, Burns Statue Square (✆ **01292/262-112**), mixes Scottish poetry with electronic music. The stone walls are highlighted with the pithy verses of Robert Burns, who used to drop in for a pint of ale and conversation. A portrait of Rabbie is painted on the wall. However, don't come here expecting poetry readings in a quiet corner. The crowd, while not particularly literary, is talkative and fun and enjoys live music several nights a week. There's a busy bar, crowded banquettes and copper-topped tables, and a large TV showing videos. It's open Monday through Saturday from 11am to 12:30am and Sunday from noon to midnight.

ALLOWAY ✪: BIRTHPLACE OF RABBIE BURNS

Some 3km (2 miles) south of Ayr, Alloway is where Scotland's national poet was born on January 25, 1759, in the gardener's cottage—the "auld clay biggin"—that his father, William Burns, built in 1757.

SEEING THE SIGHTS

Auld Brig Over the Ayr, mentioned in *Tam o' Shanter,* still spans the river, and **Alloway Auld Kirk,** also mentioned in the poem, stands roofless and haunted not far away. The poet's father is buried in the graveyard of the kirk.

Burns Cottage and Museum 🍴   The cottage still contains some of its original furniture, including the bed in which the poet was born. Chairs displayed here were said to have been used by Tam o' Shanter and Souter Johnnie. Beside the poet's cottage is a museum.

Alloway. 🕿 **01292/441-215.** Admission £4 ($7.60) adults, £2.50 ($4.75) children and seniors, £13 ($25) per family. Apr–Sept daily 10am–5:30pm; Oct–Mar Mon–Sat 10am–5pm. Closed Dec 25–26 and Jan 1–2. Drive 3km (2 miles) south of Ayr on B7024.

Burns Monument and Gardens   This monument, about 1km (½ mile) from the Burns Cottage, is a Grecian-style building erected in 1823; it contains relics, books, and manuscripts associated with Robert Burns. The gardens overlooking the River Doon contain shrubs; some were brought back from the Himalayas and are relatively rare. Everything is small-scale but choice.

Alloway. 🕿 **01292/441-215.** Admission £1 ($1.90). Apr–Sept daily 10am–5pm; Oct–Mar daily 10am–4pm, Sun noon–4pm. Drive 3km (2 miles) south of Ayr on B7024.

Tam o' Shanter Experience   Here, adjacent to the gardens of the Burns Monument, you can watch a film on Burns's life, his friends, and his poetry. There's a well-stocked gift shop and a tearoom. The Russians are particularly fond of Burns and his poetry, and many visit annually to pore over his original manuscripts; the museum has been presented with a translation of the poem *Tam o' Shanter* by Russian enthusiasts.

Murdoch's Lane. 🕿 **01292/443-700.** Admission £1.50 ($2.85) adults, 75p ($1.45) children and seniors. Apr–Oct daily 9:30am–5:30pm, Nov–Mar daily 10am–5pm. Closed Christmas Day, Boxing Day, and New Year's Day. Drive 3km (2 miles) south of Ayr on B7024.

WHERE TO STAY & DINE

Belleisle House Hotel 𝘒𝘪𝘥𝘴   This imposing country house, next to A719, is in a public park noted for its two golf courses. It has a stone exterior and interior paneling with ornate carvings depicting some scenes from Burns's *Tam o' Shanter,* with blazing fireplaces adding to the ambience. The guest rooms range from midsize to spacious; each has traditional furnishings and a small, shower-only bathroom. The place extends a special welcome to children and has a play area set aside for them. The Scottish cooking is excellent.

Belleisle Park, Doonfoot Rd., Alloway, Ayr, Ayrshire KA7 4DU. 🕿 **01292/442-331.** Fax 01292/445-325. www. belleislehotel.co.uk. 14 units. £99 ($188) double; £110 ($209) bridal suite. Rates include Scottish breakfast. AE, MC, V. Free parking. Drive 3km (2 miles) south of Ayr on A719. **Amenities:** Restaurant; bar; 2 golf courses; room service; laundry service; dry cleaning. *In room:* TV, coffeemaker, hair dryer.

Brig o' Doon Hotel 🍴   One of Scotland's most famous footbridges, the Brig o' Doon, is a few steps from this new-style hotel, on the river's east bank. With lovely gardens that are often the backdrop for weddings, this is the choice place to stay. Everything from the plumbing—mainly with both tub and shower—to the stylish guest rooms is state of the art. Reserve early, especially in summer.

Alloway, Ayr, Ayrshire KA7 4PQ. 🕿 **01292/442-466.** Fax 01292/441-999. www.costley-hotels.co.uk. 5 units. £120 ($228) double. Rates include Scottish breakfast. AE, MC, V. Free parking. Drive 3km (2 miles) south of Alloway on B7024. **Amenities:** 2 restaurants; bar; laundry service. *In room:* TV, coffeemaker, hair dryer.

CULZEAN

Some 19km (12 miles) south-southwest of Ayr and 6.5km (4 miles) west of Maybole on A719 is Culzean Castle. Maidens Bus (no. 60) from the Sandgate Bus Station in Ayr runs to Culzean six times per day; a 1-day round-trip ticket is £4.60 ($8.75) for adults and £2.50 ($4.75) for children.

Culzean Castle 🏰🏰   Built by famous Scottish architect Robert Adam in the late 18th century, this cliff-top creation is a fine example of his castellated style; it has a view of Alisa Craig, a 334m-high (1,100-ft.) rounded rock 16km (10 miles) offshore that's a nesting ground and sanctuary for seabirds. Culzean (pronounced "cul-*lane*") replaced an earlier Scots tower house as the family seat of the powerful Kennedy clan. In 1945, the castle and grounds were given to the National Trust for Scotland. It's well worth a visit and is of special interest to Americans because of General Eisenhower's connection—in 1946, the National Guest Flat was given to the general in recognition of his service as supreme commander of the Allied Forces in World War II. An exhibit of Eisenhower memorabilia, including his North African campaign desk, is sponsored by Scottish Heritage U.S.A., Inc. Culzean stands near the famous golf courses of Turnberry and Troon, a fact that particularly pleased the golf-loving Eisenhower. The tour also includes the celebrated round drawing room, delicately painted ceilings, and outstanding Adam oval staircase.

Overlooking the Firth of Clyde. ℂ **01655/884-455**. www.culzeanexperience.org. Admission (including entrance to the Country Park, below) £12 ($23) adults, £8 ($15) seniors and children, £30 ($57) families (2 adults and 2 children). Apr–Oct daily 10:30am–5pm (last admission 30 min. before closing). Closed Nov–Mar.

Culzean Country Park 🏰 (Kids)   Part of the land surrounding the castle includes what in 1969 became the first country park in Scotland. The 228-hectare (565-acre) grounds contain a walled garden, an aviary, a swan pond, a camellia house, an orangery, an adventure playground, and a newly restored 19th-century pagoda, as well as a deer park, kilometers of woodland paths, and beaches. It has gained an international reputation for its visitor center (Adam's home farm) and related visitor and educational services.

On the land surrounding Culzean Castle. ℂ **01655/884-400**. Admission included in admission to Culzean Castle. Daily 9:30am–dusk.

TURNBERRY: WORLD-CLASS GOLF 🏰

South of the castle, on the Firth of Clyde, is the little town of Turnberry—once part of the Culzean Estate and owned by the marquess of Ailsa. It began to flourish early in the 20th century, when the Glasgow and South Western Railway developed rail service, golfing facilities, a recognized golfing center, and a first-class hotel.

From the original two 13-hole golf courses, the complex has developed into the two 18-hole courses, Ailsa and Kintyre, known worldwide as the **Turnberry Hotel Golf Courses.** The Ailsa, one of the most exacting courses yet devised, has been the scene of numerous championship tournaments and PGA events. Come here for the prestige, but prepare yourself for the kind of weather a lobster fisherman in Maine might find daunting. (Its par is 70, its SSS 72, and its yardage 6,976.) Redesigned in 2001, and usually shunted to the role of also-ran, is the Kintyre Course. Call ℂ **01655/334-032** for details. Guests of the hotel get priority on the Ailsa course. The greens fee of £105 ($200) for guests, and £130 ($247) Monday to Friday or £175 ($333) Saturday and Sunday for nonguests, includes 18 holes on the Ailsa course and an 18-hole round on the Kintyre course. Clubs rent for £40 ($76) per round or £55 ($105) per day; caddy service costs £30 ($57) plus tip. If you're not staying here, give them a call in the morning to check on any unclaimed tee times—but it's a long shot.

A short drive east of Turnberry is **Souter Johnnie's Cottage,** Main Road, in Kirkoswald (✆ **01655/760-603**), 6.5km (4 miles) west of Maybole on A77. This was the 18th-century home of the village cobbler, John Davidson (Souter Johnnie), who, with his friend Douglas Graham of Shanter Farm, was immortalized by Burns in *Tam o' Shanter.* The cottage contains Burnsiana—books, letters, and the like—and contemporary cobbler's tools, and in the churchyard are the graves of Tam o' Shanter and Souter Johnnie. From March 30 to September 30, the cottage is open Friday to Tuesday 11:30am to 5pm. Off-season admittance is sometimes available by appointment. Admission is £5 ($9.50) for adults and £4 ($7.60) for seniors.

A final sight is **Carleton Castle,** along A77 some 23km (14 miles) south of Culzean Castle and 5km (3 miles) south (following the coast) from the little seaside town of Girvan. In its heyday it was a watchtower, built to guard the coastline against invaders. A famous ballad grew out of a legend surrounding the castle: It was said to be the headquarters of a baron who married eight times. When this Bluebeard got tired of a wife, he pushed her over the cliff and found himself another. However, he proved no match for his eighth wife, May Cullean. "The Ballad of May Colvin" relates how she's supposed to have tricked and outlived him.

WHERE TO STAY

Malin Court Hotel   On one of the most scenic strips of the Ayrshire coast, this well-run hotel fronts the Firth of Clyde and the Turnberry golf courses. It is not a great country house but rather a serviceable, welcoming retreat offering a blend of informality and comfort. Bedrooms are mostly medium-size. The staff can arrange hunting, fishing, riding, sailing, and golf.

Turnberry, Ayrshire KA26 9PB. ✆ **01655/331-457.** Fax 01655/331-072. www.malincourt.co.uk. 18 units. £104–£124 ($198–$236) double. Rates include breakfast. AE, DC, MC, V. Free parking. Take A74 to Ayr exit, then A719 to Turnberry and Maidens. **Amenities:** Restaurant; bar; room service; laundry service; dry cleaning. *In room:* TV, coffeemaker, hair dryer, iron, trouser press, robes.

Westin Turnberry Resort 🏵🏵🏵   The Turnberry, 81km (50 miles) south of Glasgow on A77, is a remarkable and opulent Edwardian property, built in 1908. From afar, you can see the hotel's white facade, red-tile roof, and dozens of gables. The public rooms contain Waterford crystal chandeliers, Ionic columns, molded ceilings, and oak paneling. Each guest room is furnished in unique early-1900s style and has a marble-sheathed bathroom. The rooms, which vary in size, open onto views of the lawns, forests, and (in some cases) Scottish coastline.

Maidens Rd., Turnberry, Ayrshire KA26 9LT. ✆ **01655/331-000.** Fax 01655/331-706. www.turnberry.co.uk. 221 units. £219–£520 ($416–$988) double; £585 ($1,112) suite. Off-season rates lower. Rates include Scottish breakfast. AE, DC, MC, V. Free parking. **Amenities:** 3 restaurants; 3 bars; indoor pool; tennis courts; exercise room; spa; Jacuzzi; sauna; car-rental desk; salon; room service; babysitting; massage; laundry service; dry cleaning; rooms for those w/limited mobility. *In room:* TV, minibar, coffeemaker, hair dryer, trouser press.

WHERE TO DINE

Cotters Restaurant SCOTTISH   Exemplary service, a scenic location, and the finest local ingredients make a winning combination. The modern, tasteful decor creates a casual, relaxed atmosphere. The lunch menu offers everything from melon slices to pan-fried John Dory. For dinner, you might start with melon and peaches glazed with peach mint yogurt. For a main course, try the baked seared red snapper with chive mash and onion sauce. The tempting desserts include a chocolate and hazelnut tart, warm bread and plum pudding awash in a sea of vanilla sauce, and a fine selection of cheeses.

In the Malin Court Hotel, Turnberry. ℂ **01655/331-457.** Reservations recommended. Main courses £6–£14 ($11–$27); table d'hôte £25 ($48). AE, DC, MC, V. Daily 12:30–2pm and 7:30–9pm.

TROON & THE ROYAL TROON GOLF CLUB 🕭

The resort town of **Troon,** 11km (7 miles) north of Ayr, 50km (31 miles) southwest of Glasgow, and 124km (77 miles) southwest of Edinburgh, looks out across the Firth of Clyde to the Isle of Arran. It's a 20th-century town, its earlier history having gone unrecorded. Troon takes its name from the curiously shaped promontory jutting out into the Clyde estuary, on which the old town and the harbor stand. The promontory was called Trwyn, the Cymric word for "nose." Later this became Trone and then Troon. A massive statue of *Britannia* stands on the seafront as a memorial to the dead of the two world wars.

Troon offers several golf links, including the **Royal Troon Golf Club,** Craigends Road, Troon, Ayrshire KA10 6EP (ℂ **01292/311-555**). This is a 7,079-yard course (one of the longest in Scotland) with an SSS of 74 and a par of 71. Dignified Georgian and Victorian buildings and the faraway Isle of Arran are visible from fairways, which seem designed to steer your golf balls into either the sea or one of dozens of bunkers. The **Old Course** is the more famous, reserved for men. Nonmembers may play only on certain days. A newer addition, the 6,289-yard, par-71 **Portland,** is open to both men and women and is, by some estimates, even more challenging than the Old Course. The British Open has been played here off and on since 1923. The greens fee—£227 ($431) for a day—includes a buffet lunch and two 18-hole sets. For one round of play, a trolley rents for £3 ($5.70) and a caddy £35 ($67); club rental is £25 ($48) per round or £40 ($76) per day.

In summer, visitors find plenty of room on Troon's 3km (2 miles) of **sandy beaches** stretching along both sides of its harbor; the broad sands and shallow waters make it a safe haven. From here you can take steamer trips to Arran and the Kyles of Bute.

Trains from Glasgow's Central Station arrive at the Troon station several times daily (trip time: 40 min.). Call ℂ **08457/484-950** for 24-hour information. Trains also connect Ayr with Troon, a 10-minute ride. Buses and trains from Glasgow cost £5.60 ($11) each way. From the Ayr bus station, you can reach Troon and other parts of the area by bus, costing £2.50 ($4.75) each way. Call ℂ **08706/082-608** for details. From Prestwick, motorists head north along B749.

WHERE TO STAY

You also might want to consider **Highgrove House** (see "Where to Dine," below).

Lochgreen House Hotel 🕭🕭   Adjacent to the fairways of the Royal Troon Golf Course is one of Scotland's loveliest country-house hotels, set on 12 lush hectares (30 acres) of forest and landscaped gardens. The property opens onto views of the Firth of Clyde and Ailsa Craig. The interior evokes a more elegant bygone time, with detailed cornices, antique furnishings, and oak and cherry paneling. Guests meet and mingle in two luxurious sitting rooms with log fires, or take long walks on the well-landscaped grounds. The spacious bedrooms have the finest mattresses.

Monktonhill Rd., Southwood, Troon, Ayrshire KA10 7EN. ℂ **01192/318-343.** Fax 011292/317-661. www.costley-hotels. co.uk. 42 units. £150–£170 ($285–$323) double. Rates include breakfast. AE, MC, V. Free parking. Take B749 to Troon. **Amenities:** 2 restaurants; 2 bars; tennis court; room service; laundry service; dry cleaning. *In room:* TV, coffeemaker, hair dryer, trouser press.

Piersland House Hotel   This hotel was built more than a century ago by Sir Alexander Walker of the Johnnie Walker whisky family. The importation of 17,000 tons of topsoil transformed its marshy surface into a lush 1.6-hectare (4-acre) garden. The moderately sized guest rooms have traditional country-house styling.

15 Craigend Rd., Troon, Ayrshire KA10 6HD. © 01292/314-747. Fax 01292/315-613. www.piersland.co.uk. 30 units. £136 ($258) double; £154 ($293) suite. Rates include Scottish breakfast. AE, DC, MC, V. Free parking. Drive 3 minutes south of the town center on B749. **Amenities:** Restaurant; bar; room service; laundry service; dry cleaning. *In room:* TV, minibar, coffeemaker, hair dryer, trouser press.

WHERE TO DINE

The dining room at the **Piersland House Hotel** (see "Where to Stay," above) is also recommended.

Fairways Restaurant   SCOTTISH/INTERNATIONAL   This landmark 1890s hotel stands on the Ayrshire coast overlooking the Royal Troon Golf Course. The restaurant can satisfy your hunger pangs with some degree of style. Traditional Scottish and French dishes are served. Specialties include such good-tasting dishes as filet of sea bass nestled on sautéed new potatoes and topped with crème fraîche, and roast rump of lamb with couscous.

In the Marine Highland Hotel, 8 Crosbie Rd. © 01292/314-444. Reservations required. Set-price lunch £9–£12 ($17–$23); main courses £12–£22 ($23–$42); Sat dinner/dance 3 courses £24 ($46). AE, DC, MC, V. Daily 12:30–2pm and 7–9:30pm.

Highgrove House   TRADITIONAL SCOTTISH   This charming white-painted, red-roofed brick building is isolated on a hillside known for its scenic view not only of the sea but of the Isle of Arran. The bustling restaurant moves big crowds in and out quickly. Menu items include several varieties of steamed salmon and Scottish venison with rowanberry sauce.

Upstairs are nine simple but comfortable guest rooms with TVs, phones, and hair dryers; breakfast is included. Rooms rent for £110 ($209).

Old Loan's Rd., Troon, Ayrshire KA10 7HL. © 01292/312-511. Reservations recommended. Main courses lunch £6–£18 ($11–$34); main courses dinner £15–£20 ($29–$38); 3-course fixed-price lunch £18 ($34); 3-course fixed-price dinner £28 ($53). AE, MC, V. Daily noon–2:30pm and 6–9:30pm. Drive 3km (2 miles) north of Troon on A78.

Lochgreen House Hotel Restaurant ⊕ SCOTTISH/FRENCH   This is one of the region's most agreeable culinary stopovers, where you'll be tempted by the finest seafood, game, and Scottish beef. The elegant dining room, with its views of woodland and garden, somehow makes the food taste even better. The service is just as flawless. For a main course, sample the poached halibut on a mussel and fennel stew with saffron potatoes and chives, or try steamed Atlantic halibut with slow-cooked onions and a shellfish essence. The wine list roams the world for inspiration, and the desserts often feature the fresh fruit of the season.

Monktonhill Rd., Southwood. © 01292/313-343. Reservations required. Fixed-price menu £25 ($47) for a 3-course lunch, £40 ($75) for a 4-course dinner. AE, MC, V. Daily noon–2pm and 7–9pm. Take B749 to Troon.

8

Argyll & the Southern Hebrides

The old county of Argyll (in Gaelic, *Earraghaidheal,* "coastland of the Gael"), on and off the coast of western Scotland, is a rewarding journey. Summers along the coast are usually cool and damp and winters relatively mild but wet, with little snow.

The major center of Gaelic culture for the district is **Oban** ("small bay"), a great port for the Western Isles and the gateway to the Inner Hebrides (see chapter 12).

There are several island destinations off the Argyll coast that merit your time. The long **peninsula of Kintyre** separates the islands of the Firth of Clyde from the islands of the Inner Hebrides.

From the Isle of Islay to the Mull of Kintyre, the climate is mild. The land is rich and lush, especially on Arran. The peat deposits on Islay lend flavor to the making of such fine malt whiskies as Lagavulin, Bruichladdick, and Laphroaig. There's a diversity of scenic beauty: hills and glens, fast-rushing streams, and little roads that eventually lead to coastal villages displaying B&B signs in summer. The unspoiled and remote island of Jura is easily reached from Islay. And the best news for last: These islands, as well as the Kintyre peninsula, are among the best travel bargains in the British Isles.

1 The Isle of Arran: Scotland in Miniature ★★

Brodick: 119km (74 miles) W of Edinburgh, 47km (29 miles) W of Glasgow

At the mouth of the Firth of Clyde is the Isle of Arran, often described as "Scotland in miniature" because of its wild and varied scenery—the glens, moors, lochs, sandy bays, and rocky coasts that have made the country famous. Once you're on Arran, buses take you to various villages, each with its own character. A coast road, 97km (60 miles) long, runs around the length of the island.

Arran boasts some splendid mountain scenery, notably the conical peak of **Goatfell** in the north (called the "mountain of the winds"), reaching a height of 869m (2,866 ft.). Arran is also filled with beautiful glens, especially **Glen Sannox,** in the northeast, and **Glen Rosa,** north of Brodick. Students of geology flock to Arran to study igneous rocks of the Tertiary period. Cairns and standing stones at Tormore intrigue archaeologists as well. The island is only 40km (25 miles) long and 16km (10 miles) wide and can be seen in a single day.

ESSENTIALS

GETTING THERE   High-speed electric trains operate from Glasgow Central direct to Ardrossan Harbour, taking 1 hour and costing £5.50 ($10) one-way. For 24-hour rail inquiries, call *©* **08475/484-950.** (If you're driving from Glasgow, head southwest along A737 until you reach Ardrossan.) At Ardrossan, you must make a 30-minute ferry crossing to Arran, arriving in Brodick, Arran's main town, on its east coast.

In summer, a small ferry runs between Lochranza, in the north of Arran, across to Claonaig, in Argyll, providing a gateway to the Highlands and a visit to Kintyre. There are six boats daily, and the fare is £21 ($40) for a vehicle, plus £7.85 ($15) per passenger for a return journey. For information about ferry departures (which change seasonally), check with **Caledonian MacBrayne** (© 01457/650-100) at the ferry terminal in Gourock.

VISITOR INFORMATION   The **tourist office** is at The Pier, Brodick (© 01770/302-140; www.ayrshire-arran.com). June to August, it's open Monday to Saturday 9am to 7:30pm and Sunday 10am to 5pm; September to May, hours are Monday to Saturday 9am to 5pm.

EXPLORING THE ISLAND

After the ferry docks at Brodick, you may want to head for Arran's major sights, **Brodick Castle** and the **Isle of Arran Heritage Museum** (see below).

The most intriguing walks on the island are signposted. But if you're really serious about hiking, buy one of two detailed guides at the tourist office—*Seventy Walks in Arran* for £2.50 ($4.75) and *My Walks in Arran* for £2.25 ($4.30). While at the office, ask about any guided walks the Forestry Commission might be conducting. They are scheduled frequently in summer and range from 2 to 5 hours, costing £5 to £8 ($9.50–$15).

If you'd prefer to do your exploring on two wheels, stop by **Mr. Bilsland,** The Gift Shop, Brodick (© 01770/302-272). You'll have to show an ID; rental rates include a helmet and are £9 to £12 ($17–$23) daily £20 to £35 ($38–$67) weekly. It's open daily 9:30am to 6pm. **Brodick Cycles,** Brodick (© 01770/302-460), requires a £9 to £30 ($17–$57) deposit, depending on the type of bike. Daily rentals range from £10 to £12 ($19–$23), with £19 to £36 ($36–$68) for a full week. It's open in summer Monday to Saturday 9am to 6pm and Sunday 10am to 6pm.

South from Brodick is the village/resort of **Lamlash,** on Lamlash Bay. From here, a ferry takes you over to Holy Island with its 303m (1,000-ft.) peak. A disciple of St. Columba founded a church on this island. In the north, **Lochranza** is a village with unique appeal. It opens onto a bay of pebbles and sand, and in the background lie the ruins of a castle that was reputedly the hunting seat of Robert the Bruce.

Brodick Castle ★★   The historic home of the dukes of Hamilton, this red-sandstone castle dates from the 13th century and contains superb silver, antiques, portraits, and objets d'art. Some castle or other has stood on this site since about the 5th century, when the Dalriada Irish, a Celtic tribe, came here and founded their kingdom. The castle is now the property of the National Trust for Scotland and boasts award-winning gardens. Laid out in the 1920s by the duchess of Montrose, they're filled with shrubs, trees, perennials, and herbs from Tasmania, New Zealand, Chile, the Himalayas, and northern Britain. Especially noteworthy are the rhododendrons, which are one of the focal points of the Country Park, a semi-domesticated forest bordering the more formal gardens.

2.5km (1½ miles) north of the Brodick pierhead. © 0844/493-2152. www.nts.org.uk. Admission to both castle and gardens £10 ($19) adults, £7 ($13) seniors and students, free for children under 6. Castle Mar 30–Oct 31 daily 9:30am–4:30pm (to 3:30pm in Oct); Country Park daily 9:30am–sunset; Reception Centre, shop, walled garden Mar 30–Oct 31 daily 10am–4:30pm, Nov 1–Dec 21 Fri–Sun 10am–3:30pm. Bus: Any labeled "Brodick Castle."

Achamore House Gardens **16**
An Tairbeart Heritage Centre **11**
Artic Penguin Heritage Centre **8**
Brodick Castle **19**
Bruce Castle **11**
Castle Lachlan **9**
Crarae Glen Gardens **10**
Dunollie Castle **3**
Dunstaffnage Castle **4**
Dunyvaig Castle **15**
Falls of Cruachan **5**

Gylen Castle **1**
Inverary Castle **7**
Islay Woolen Mill **13**
Isle of Arran Heritage Museum **18**
Jura House Garden and Grounds **12**

Kilchurn Castle **6**
Kildalton Crosses **15**
McCaig's Tower **2**
Museum of Islay Life **14**
Skipness Castle and Chapel **17**

Isle of Arran Heritage Museum   A compound of antique structures once used as outbuildings for the nearby castle, this museum provides the best overview of life on Arran from prehistoric times to the present. The most prominent building is a stone-sided cottage filled with 19th-century memorabilia, costumes, and artifacts, including a working kitchen. Also on site are a blacksmith's shop and forge, geological artifacts, and an archive room housing historic records associated with Arran. Access to the archive room is reserved for scholars pursuing academic research.

Rosaburn, 2.5km (1½ miles) north of the Brodick ferry piers. ☏ **01770/302-636.** www.arranmuseum.co.uk. Admission £3 ($5.70) adults, £2 ($3.80) seniors, £1.50 ($2.85) children, £7 ($13) family. Apr–Oct daily 10:30am–4:30pm. Bus: Any labeled "Brodick Castle."

(Moments **Down a Lovely Glen with a Picnic in Hand**

The best way to discover the island's beauty is to stroll around. Right beyond the Isle of Arran Heritage Museum, at the point where String Road divides the island, you can follow the signs to a beauty spot called **Glen Rosa.** This is the island's loveliest glen, and you might want to pick up the makings of a picnic lunch before setting out. Another great walk is to the village of **Corriegills,** which is signposted along A841 south of Brodick. As you stroll, you'll be treated with the finest views of Brodick Bay.

SHOPPING

Divided into three businesses, the **Duchess Court Shops,** Home Farm, Brodick (© 01770/302-831), comprises the Home Farm Kitchen, selling locally produced chutneys, jams, and marmalades; the Nature Shop, dealing in books, jewelry, wood carvings, T-shirts, and other assorted goods; and an unusual teddy bear shop. Something Special and Inspirations of Arran are other retail outlets associated with the Court shops.

About 10km (6 miles) north of Brodick in Corrie, **Corriecraft & Antiques,** Hotel Square (© 01770/810-661), sells small Arran antiques and pottery. In Lamlash, **Patterson Arran Ltd.,** The Old Mill (© 01770/600-606), offers chutneys, mustards, preserves, and other locally produced condiments.

The **Old Byre Showroom,** Auchencar Farm (© 01770/840-227), 8km (5 miles) north of Blackwaterfoot along the coastal road in Machrie, sells sheepskin, leather, and tweeds, but its biggest draw is the large selection of locally produced wool sweaters.

WHERE TO STAY
IN BRODICK

Auchrannie House Hotel *(Kids)* Acclaimed as the island's finest hotel and restaurant, this Victorian mansion (once the home of the dowager duchess of Hamilton) stands in pristine glory on 2.4 hectares (6 acres) of landscaped gardens and woods, about 1.6km (1 mile) from the Brodick ferry terminal. Guest rooms in the new wing are the most comfortable, but all the rooms are furnished with taste, using select fabrics and decorative accessories. Family suites (two bedrooms) and four-poster rooms are available.

The property's noteworthy leisure center features an indoor pool, a kids' pool, a playroom, a spa, game room, and sauna. You can enjoy drinks in the cocktail bar or the sun lounge before heading for the Garden Restaurant, which offers fixed-price dinners—expensive, but the finest on Arran. The chef is really in his element when preparing West Coast seafood. Nonguests should reserve ahead.

Auchrannie Rd., Brodick, Isle of Arran KA27 8BZ. © 01770/302-234. Fax 01770/302-812. www.auchrannie.co.uk. 28 units. £119–£145 ($226–$276) double with breakfast; £165–£190 ($314–$361) double with half board. AE, MC, V. **Amenities:** 2 restaurants; bar; heated indoor pool; exercise room; spa; sauna; game room; room service; babysitting; laundry service. *In room:* TV, minibar, coffeemaker, hair dryer.

Kilmichael Country House Hotel It was voted Country House Hotel of the Year in a "Taste of Scotland" contest in 1998, and if anything, it's better than ever. Reputedly the island's oldest house, it's certainly the most scenically located. Perhaps

The Isle of Arran & the Kintyre Peninsula

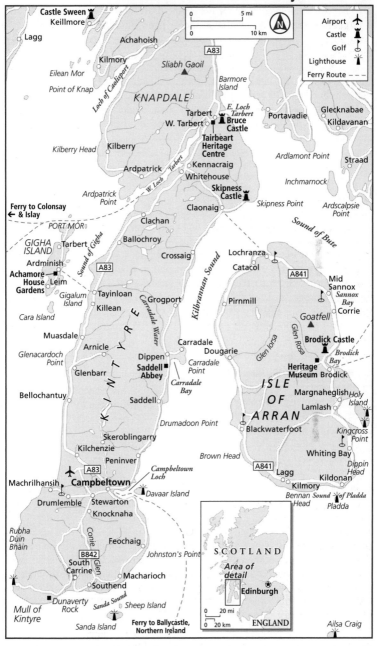

Legend:
- ✈ Airport
- ♜ Castle
- ⚑ Golf
- ✦ Lighthouse
- --- Ferry Route

Castle Sween
Keillmore
Lagg
Achahoish
Kilmory
Eilean Mor
Point of Knap
Sliabh Gaoil
KNAPDALE
Barmore Island
Loch of Caolisport
A83
E. Loch Tarbert
Tarbert
W. Tarbert
Bruce Castle
Portavadie
Glecknabae
Kildavanan
Tairbeart Heritage Centre
Kilberry Head
Kilberry
Kennacraig
Whitehouse
Ardlamont Point
Straad
Ardpatrick
Skipness Castle
Inchmarnock
W. Loch Tarbert
Ardpatrick Point
Claonaig
Skipness Point
Ardscalpsie Point
Ferry to Colonsay & Islay
PORT MÒR
Clachan
Sound of Bute
GIGHA ISLAND
Tarbert
Ballochroy
Lochranza
Catacol
A841
Mid Sannox
Sannox Bay
Ardminish
Crossaig
A83
Sound of Gigha
Achamore House Gardens
Leim
Gigalum Island
Tayinloan
Killean
Grogport
Pirnmill
Goatfell
Corrie
Cara Island
Carradale Water
Glen Iorsa
Brodick Castle
Brodick Bay
Muasdale
Arnicle
Carradale
Dougarie
Glen Rosa
Glenacardoch Point
Dippen
Saddell Abbey
Carradale Point
Heritage Museum Brodick
Glenbarr
Carradale Bay
ISLE OF ARRAN
Bellochantuy
Saddell
Margnaheglish
Holy Island
Lamlash
KINTYRE
Drumadoon Point
Blackwaterfoot
Kingcross Point
Skeroblingarry
Kilchenzie
Peninver
Brown Head
Whiting Bay
Dippin Head
Machrilhansih
A83
Campbeltown Loch
A841
Lagg
Kildonan
Campbeltown
Davaar Island
Kilmory
Drumlemble
Stewarton
Bennan Head
Sound of Pladda
Knocknaha
Pladda
Rubha Dùin Bhàin
Conie Glen
Feochaig
Johnston's Point
B842
South Carrine
Glen
Macharioch
Southend
Dunaverty Rock
Sanda Sound
Sheep Island
Mull of Kintyre
Sanda Island
Ferry to Ballycastle, Northern Ireland
Ailsa Craig

SCOTLAND
Area of detail
★ Edinburgh
ENGLAND

it was once a stamping ground for Robert the Bruce, and reports even exist of a resident ghost. A tasteful combination of the new and antique is used throughout. The guest rooms are beautiful, as are the bathrooms, which offer luxury toiletries. Some rooms have four-poster beds and Jacuzzi tubs. The aura of gentility is reflected in the log fires and the fresh flowers from the garden. A suite and two other rooms, all with private entrances, are located in a converted 18th-century stable a few yards from the main building. The staff is helpful and welcoming.

The food is also noteworthy, made with local produce whenever possible. International dishes are featured, and fine wines and an attention to detail go into the expensive fixed-price menus.

Brodick, Isle of Arran KA27 8BY. ℂ **01770/302-219.** Fax 01770/302-068. www.kilmichael.com. 9 units. £150–£170 ($285–$323) double; £190 ($361) suite. Rates include Scottish breakfast. MC, V. No children under 12. **Amenities:** Restaurant; bar; room service; nonsmoking rooms. *In room:* TV, coffeemaker, hair dryer, iron (in some).

IN LAMLASH

Glenisle Hotel *Finds*   Across the road from the waterfront, Glenisle could be one of the oldest buildings in the village, but no one knows its age or even the century of its construction. The well-kept gardens of this white-sided B&B, with a view across the bay to the Holy Isle, have flowerbeds and tall old trees. Cheerfully decorated are the reception area, the water-view dining room, and the lounge, where drinks are available. Each relatively simple but comfortable guest room has flowered curtains, a small but tidy bathroom, and tasteful decor.

Shore Rd., Lamlash, Isle of Arran KA27 8LY. ℂ **01770/600-559.** Fax 01770/600-966. www.glenislehotel.com. 13 units. £32–£40 ($61–$76) per person with Scottish breakfast. MC, V. Take the Whiting bus from Brodick. **Amenities:** Restaurant; bar; laundry service. *In room:* TV, coffeemaker, hair dryer.

IN WHITING BAY

Grange House Hotel *Kids*   This country-house hotel, operated by Janet and Clive Hughes—who take a personal interest in their guests—has spectacular views of the Firth of Clyde. A gabled stone house standing on landscaped grounds, the Grange offers tastefully furnished, traditional guest rooms. Some units can be arranged to accommodate a family, and one room is suitable for travelers with disabilities. Eight rooms open onto views of the Holy Isle and the Ayrshire coast. Some of the bathrooms are equipped with a tub, others with a shower only. The hosts no longer serve an evening meal, but are happy to make dinner reservations for you in the village.

Whiting Bay, Isle of Arran KA27 8QH. ℂ/fax **01770/700-263.** 9 units, 7 with private bathroom. £65–£80 ($124–$152) double without bathroom; £75–£95 ($143–$181) double with bathroom. Rates include Scottish breakfast. MC, V. Take the Whiting Bay bus from Brodick. **Amenities:** Bar; small exercise room; sauna; room service (8–10am); 1 room for those w/limited mobility. *In room:* TV, coffeemaker, no phone.

Royal Hotel   This granite house, located in the center of the village beside the coastal road, was one of the first hotels ever built on Arran, in 1895. True to its original function as a temperance hotel, it serves no alcohol, but guests can bring their own wine or beer into the dining room, which serves moderately priced dinners nightly at one sitting. Some of the bedrooms enjoy a vista of the bay and its tidal flats. One room contains a four-poster bed and lots of chintz, while another has a small sitting room. Each comes with a neat little shower-only bathroom.

Shore Rd., Whiting Bay, Isle of Arran KA27 8PZ. ℂ/fax **01770/700-286.** www.royalarran.co.uk. 5 units. £84 ($160) double or suite. Rates include Scottish breakfast. No credit cards. Closed Nov–Mar. Take the Whiting Bay bus from Brodick. **Amenities:** Dining room; lounge. *In room:* TV, coffeemaker, hair dryer.

IN KILDONAN

Kildonan Hotel   Built as an inn in 1760, with a section added in 1928, the hotel rises a few steps from the island's best beach. It's in Scottish farmhouse style, with a slate roof, white-painted stone walls, and ample views of seabirds and gray seals basking on the rocks of Pladda Island opposite. Upgraded rooms range from small to midsize. They are traditionally furnished with comfortable beds, and all have private bathrooms with either a tub or shower.

The spacious dining room features moderately priced dinners; less formal lunches and dinners are served in the bar. A specialty available in either setting is crab or lobster salad made from fresh shellfish. A crowd of locals is likely to compete in a friendly fashion over the dartboard and billiards tables in the pub.

Kildonan, Isle of Arran, KA27 8SE. ⓒ **01770/820-207**. Fax 01770/820-320. www.kildonanhotel.com. 22 units. £80 ($152) double; £125 ($238) family suite. Rates include Scottish breakfast. No credit cards. **Amenities:** Restaurant; bar; room service; room for those w/limited mobility. *In room:* Hair dryer, no phone.

Kinloch Hotel   This hotel, made from two joined cream-colored Victorian buildings, appears deceptively small from the road. It's actually the largest building in the village of Blackwaterfoot, with a contemporary wing jutting out along the coast. The midsize guest rooms are modestly comfortable and conservative, each with a small bathroom with shower. Most of the double rooms have sea views, but the singles tend to look out over the back gardens. A few have four-poster beds. The hotel also offers seven self-contained suites with kitchen facilities, plus five two-bedroom suites with a lounge and a small kitchenette.

Blackwaterfoot, Isle of Arran KA27 8ET. ⓒ **01770/860-444**. Fax 01770/860-447. www.bw-kinlochhotel.co.uk. 37 units. £60 ($114) double; £116 ($220) suite. AE, DC, MC, V. Take the Blackwaterfoot bus from Brodick. **Amenities:** Restaurant; 2 bars; indoor heated pool; exercise room; sauna; room service; babysitting; laundry service; nonsmoking rooms. *In room:* TV, coffeemaker, hair dryer.

WHERE TO DINE
IN BRODICK

The hotels reviewed above also have fine restaurants.

Creelers Seafood Restaurant   SCOTTISH   This dining choice lies in a minicompound of gift shops and bistros created from a 1920s-era farm associated with Brodick Castle, and is about 1.6km (1 mile) north of the center of Brodick Village. The most appealing of the places here is Creelers, a family-run enterprise specializing

---

ⓕMoments Seeing the Argyll on Horseback

There's no better way to experience the majestic beauty of the moors, Highlands, and headlands in the Argyll area than on horseback. To arrange an outing, contact the **Ardfern Riding Centre,** Croabh Haven, Loch Gilphead, Argyll (ⓒ **01852/500-632**). A 1-hour ride costs £23 ($43), a 2-hour ride £38 ($71), and a 4-hour ride (with lunch) £70 ($133). In addition to maintaining around 16 horses and a working cattle-and-sheep farm between Oban and Loch Gilphead, the center has a cottage that groups of up to eight equestrians can rent for £220 to £320 ($418–$608) per week. The center is open all year, but the best times to go are from May to early June and from September to October.

in seafood. It includes a "smokery" where salmon, scallops, and duck breast are carefully smoked and served almost immediately. You won't go wrong ordering any of the versions of smoked salmon, presented with capers and horseradish or with mushroom-studded risotto. In a cheerful yellow-and-green dining room, you find some of the freshest seafood in Scotland, much of it pulled in from local fishing boats that day. Especially appealing are seared Arran scallops with monkfish and pesto, baked cod with Arran mustard, black Angus steak with hash brown potatoes, and Scottish lobster with herb-flavored butter sauce.

The Home Farm, Brodick. (*C*) **01770/302-2797.** Reservations recommended. Fixed-price lunch £10–£11 ($19–$21); main courses £10–£16 ($19–$30) at lunch, £14–£33 ($27–$63) at dinner. MC, V. Tues–Sun noon–2:30pm and 6:30–10pm.

ARRAN AFTER DARK

Regulars gather in Brodick's pubs to talk, argue, and drink. The **Brodick Bar,** in the center but without a street address ((*C*) **01770/302-169**), is an old wooden pub open Monday to Saturday 11am to midnight. Drop in for some real Scottish ale and a bar meal of local seafood (meals are served Mon–Sat noon–2:30pm and 5:30–10pm). Featuring wood-and-leather chairs and walls hung with old photographs and riding gear, **Duncan's Bar,** also in the center but with no street address ((*C*) **01770/302-531**), keeps the same hours and serves real cask ales and lagers. Meals, available daily noon to 2pm and 5:30 to 8pm, always include a roast and seafood items.

2 The Kintyre Peninsula

The longest peninsula in Scotland, Kintyre stretches more than 97km (60 miles), with scenery galore, sleepy villages, and miles of sandy beaches. It's one of the country's most unspoiled areas, owing perhaps to its isolation. Kintyre was ancient Dalriada, the first kingdom of the Scots.

If you drive all the way to the tip of Kintyre, you'll be only 19km (12 miles) from Ireland. Kintyre is joined to the mainland of Scotland by a narrow neck of land near the old port of Tarbert. The largest town on the peninsula is the port of Campbeltown, on the southeastern coast.

AREA ESSENTIALS

GETTING THERE   Loganair ((*C*) **0870/011-5795;** www.loganair.co.uk) makes two scheduled 45-minute flights a day from the Glasgow Airport to Campbeltown, the chief town of Kintyre.

From Glasgow, you can take buses to the peninsula (schedules vary seasonally). The trip takes 4 hours one-way and costs £15 ($28) each way. Inquire at the **Scottish Citylink,** Buchanan Street Bus Station, Glasgow ((*C*) **0990/505-050**).

Kintyre is virtually an island unto itself, and the most efficient way to travel is by car. From Glasgow, take A82 up to the Loch Lomond side and cut across to Arrochar and go over the "Rest and Be Thankful" route to Inveraray (A83). Then cut down along Loch Fyne to Lochgilphead and continue on A83 south to Tarbert (see below), which can be your gateway to Kintyre. You can take A83 along the western coast or cut east at the junction of B8001 and follow it across the peninsula to B842. If your target is Campbeltown, you can reach it by either the western shore (much faster and a better road) or the eastern shore.

TARBERT

A sheltered harbor protects the fishing port and yachting center of Tarbert, located on a narrow neck of land at the northern tip of the Kintyre. It's between West Loch Tarbert and the head of herring-filled Loch Fyne and has been called the "world's prettiest fishing port."

Tarbert means "drawboat" in Norse and referred to a place where Vikings dragged their boats across land on rollers from one sea to another. In 1093, King Malcolm of Scotland and King Magnus Barelegs of Norway agreed the Western Isles were to belong to Norway and the mainland to Scotland. An island was defined as anything a Viking ship could sail around, so Magnus proclaimed Kintyre an island by having his dragon ship dragged across the 1.6km (1 mile) of dry land from West Loch Tarbert on the Atlantic to East Loch Tarbert on Loch Fyne. After the Vikings gave way, Kintyre came under the control of the MacDonald lordship of the Isles.

EXPLORING THE AREA

The castle at Tarbert dates from the 13th century and was later extended by Robert the Bruce. The castle ruins, **Bruce Castle,** are on a hillock above the village on the south side of the bay. The oldest part still standing is a keep from the 13th century.

One of the major attractions of the peninsula is the remains of **Skipness Castle and Chapel,** at Skipness along B8001, 16km (10 miles) south of Tarbert, opening onto Loch Fyne. The hamlet was once a Norse village. The ruins of the ancient chapel and castle look out onto the Sounds of Kilbrannan and Bute. In its heyday, it could control shipping along Loch Fyne. A five-story tower remains.

WHERE TO STAY

Stonefield Castle Hotel 🐾🐾   The best hotel choice in the area occupies a commanding position on 24 hectares (60 acres) of wooded grounds and luxurious gardens 3km (2 miles) outside Tarbert. The Stonefield, with turrets and a steeply pitched roof, was built in the 19th century by the Campbells. The well-appointed guest rooms come in a variety of sizes. Some family suites are available as well as some four-poster rooms. The hotel's renowned gardens feature plants from all over the world and are one of the best repositories for more than 20 species of tree-size Himalayan rhododendrons, which in April are a riot of color. Book well in advance because Stonefield has a large repeat crowd.

The kitchen staff does its own baking, and meals feature produce from the hotel's garden.

Tarbert PA29 6YJ. ✆ **01880/820-836.** Fax 01880/820-929. www.stonefieldcastle.co.uk. 33 units. Sun–Thurs £90–£110 ($171–$209) double; Fri–Sat £110–£130 ($209–$247) double. Rates include half board. AE, MC, V. **Amenities:** Restaurant; bar; room service; nonsmoking rooms. *In room:* TV, coffeemaker, hair dryer.

West Loch Hotel   This 18th-century stone inn stands in a rural setting beside A83, 1.6km (1 mile) southwest of town in low-lying flatlands midway between the forest and the loch. Painted white with black trim, it contains two bars and a handful of open fireplaces and wood-burning stoves. The small guest rooms are modestly furnished but comfortable, many with views of the estuary. Each has a small bathroom with either tub or shower. The hotel contains a pub and a restaurant specializing in local seafood and game, using only the best local ingredients.

Tarbert PA29 6YF. ✆ **01880/820-283.** Fax 01880/820-930. www.westlochhotel.co.uk. 8 units. £70 ($133) double. Rates include Scottish breakfast. MC, V. **Amenities:** Restaurant; 2 bars; room service. *In room:* TV, coffeemaker, hair dryer.

Finds **One of Scotland's Great Walks**

The newest long-distance walk in Scotland is now officially open. Called the **Kintyre Way** ✦✦ it stretches for 113km (90 miles), beginning at Tarbert in the north end of the peninsula and rambling all the way to the village of Southend in the south. Hikers traverse the walk in anywhere from 4 to 7 days. Some of the miles are difficult, although nothing to challenge the serious hiker, but miles and miles are filled with gentle rambles along panoramic scenery, rugged coastline, and past much wildlife, especially coastal birds. Pick up a map of the trail at any local tourist office or visit www.kintyreway.com.

WHERE TO DINE

Anchorage Restaurant ✦ *Finds* SCOTTISH/SEAFOOD   The Anchorage remains unpretentious despite its many culinary awards. It is housed in a stone harborfront building that was once a customs house. The daily menu includes such perfectly crafted seafood dishes as king scallops sautéed with lemon-lime butter; halibut with wild mushrooms and a mussel sauce; red mullet with cod frittered king scallops seared with Irish champ and Mornay sauce; and brochette of monkfish with saffron rice. A selection of European wines is available to accompany your fish.

Harbour St., Quayside. © **01880/820-881.** Reservations recommended. Main courses £16–£22 ($30–$42). MC, V. Daily 12:30–2:30pm and 7–10pm. Closed Jan.

CAMPBELTOWN

Campbeltown is a fishing port and resort at the southern tip of the Kintyre Peninsula, 283km (176 miles) northwest of Edinburgh and 217km (135 miles) northwest of Glasgow. Popularly known as the "wee toon," Campbeltown has long been linked with fishing and has a **shingle beach.** For one of the greatest walks on the peninsula, see the box titled "Escape to the Isle That Time Forgot," below.

The **tourist office** is at MacKinnon House, The Pier (© **01586/552-056;** www. scotlandheartland.org). It's open from late June to mid-September, Monday to Saturday 9am to 6:30pm and Sunday 11am to 5pm; mid-September to late October, Monday to Friday 9am to 5pm and Sunday 11am to 4pm; late October to March, Monday to Friday 10am to 4pm; April, Monday to Saturday 9am to 5:30pm; and May to late June, Monday to Saturday 9am to 5:30pm and Sunday noon to 5pm.

EXPLORING THE AREA

On the quayside in the heart of town is the 14th-century **Campbeltown Cross.** This Celtic cross is the finest piece of carving from the Middle Ages left in Kintyre.

One of the area's most famous golf courses, the **Machrilhanish Golf Club,** lies nearby (© **01586/810-213**). It's a 6,225-yard, par-70 course. The daily greens fees are £40 ($76) per round or £60 ($114) per day; on Saturday, the fees are £50 ($95) per round or £75 ($143) per day. No club rentals are available; trolleys cost £4 ($7.60).

Oystercatcher Crafts & Gallery, 10 Hall St. (© **01586/553-334**), sells Campbeltown pottery, wood carvings, and paintings by local artists. If you'd like to take a scenic drive and go shopping at the same time, head for **Ronachan Silks,** Ronachan Farmhouse at Clachan (© **01880/740-242**), 40km (25 miles) north of Campbeltown on

Route 83. In this unusual location, you can buy fashionable clothing and accessories, including kimonos, caftans, women's scarves, men's ties, and cushions. Call ahead to confirm opening times.

WHERE TO STAY & DINE

The Argyll Arms *Kids* The Duke of Argyll no longer calls this his home, although he still maintains a suite on the second floor of this imposing stone building. The public rooms of this converted hotel still possess an aura of Victorian opulence, but the guest rooms are modernized and fairly modest. The rooms come in a variety of sizes, each traditionally furnished and outfitted with a small bathroom. Family rooms are also available. The restaurant specializes in moderately priced fish fresh from the quay.

Main St., Campbeltown PA28 6AB. (© 01586/553-431. Fax 01586/553-594. 25 units. £60–£120 ($114–$228) double. Rates include Scottish breakfast. AE, MC, V. **Amenities:** Restaurant; 2 bars. *In room:* TV, coffeemaker, hair dryer, iron.

Craigard House This inn, built in 1882, is in a neck-and-neck race with Argyll Arms as the best place to stay in the area. The dignified, monastic-looking pile with a bell tower is perched on the northern edge of the loch, about 1.6km (1 mile) from the town center. The guest rooms come with contemporary-looking furniture and some vestiges of the original plasterwork, while the public areas are more traditional and Victorian. Most rooms open onto panoramic views of Campbeltown Loch, and each room comes with a small bathroom—some with tub, some with shower only.

The restaurant's weekly menu may include savory fish crepes, pan-fried duck breast with brandy and pepper-cream sauce, and chicken cacciatore.

Low Askomil, Campbeltown PA28 6EP. (© 01586/554-242. Fax 01586/551-137. 8 units. www.craigard-house.co.uk. £75–£120 ($143–$228) double. Rates include breakfast. AE, MC, V. **Amenities:** Restaurant; bar; room service; laundry. *In room:* TV, coffeemaker, hair dryer.

CAMPBELTOWN AFTER DARK

Pubs, not surprisingly, are the nightlife here, including two that host live music. They're in the center of the village, next door to each other. The **Feathers Cross Street** (© **01586/554-604**), with stone walls, wooden floors, and hanging lamps, hosts bands playing a range of musical styles on Thursday nights. It's open daily from 11am to 1am. The **Commercial Cross Street** (© **01586/553-703**) has a variety of live music on Fridays and alternate Saturdays. A specialty here is real ale. It's open Monday through Saturday from 11am to 1am and Sunday from 12:30pm to 1am. You'll find a quieter evening at the **Burnside Bar,** Burnside Street (© **01586/552-306**), open daily from 11am to 1am. Conversation and local single malts are the preferred distractions here.

Moments **Escape to the Isle That Time Forgot**

Davaar Island, in Campbeltown Loch, is accessible at low tide to those willing to cross the Dhorlin, a 1km (½-mile) run of shingle-paved causeway; boat trips are also possible (ask at the tourist office). Once on the island, you can visit a **crucifixion cave painting,** the work of local Archibald MacKinnon, painted in 1887. It takes about 1½ hours to walk around this tidal island, with its natural rock gardens.

Finds   A Journey to Blood Rock

Dunaverty Rock is a jagged hill marking the extreme southern tip of the Kintyre Peninsula. Located 15km (9 miles) south of Campbeltown and called "Blood Rock" by the locals, it was once the site of a MacDonald stronghold known as Dunaverty Castle, although nothing remains of it today. In 1647, it was the scene of a great massacre, in which some 300 citizens lost their lives. You can reach it by a local bus (marked SOUTH END) traveling from Campbeltown south about six times a day. Nearby, you'll find a series of isolated, unsupervised beaches and the 18-hole **Dunaverty Golf Course** (✆ **01586/830-677**).

SOUTHEND & THE MULL OF KINTYRE

Some 16km (10 miles) south of Campbeltown, the village of Southend stands across from the Mull of Kintyre, and Monday through Saturday three buses a day run here from Campbeltown. It has sandy beaches, a golf course, and views across the sea to the Island of Sanda and to Ireland. Legend has it that footprints on a rock near the ruin of an old chapel mark the spot where St. Columba first set foot on Scottish soil. Other historians suggest that the footprints mark the spot where ancient kings were crowned.

About 18km (11 miles) from Campbeltown is the Mull of Kintyre. Starting at Southend, you can take a narrow road until you reach the "gap," from which you can walk down to the lighthouse, a distance of 2.5km (1½ miles) before you reach the final point. Expect westerly gales as you go along. This is one of the wildest and most remote parts of the peninsula, and it's this desolation that appeals to visitors. The Mull of Kintyre is only 21km (13 miles) from Ireland. When local resident Paul McCartney made it the subject of a song, hundreds of fans flocked to the area.

3 The Isle of Gigha & Scotland's Finest Gardens

5km (3 miles) W of Kintyre's western coast

The 10km-long (6-mile) Isle of Gigha boasts Scotland's finest gardens. Often called sacred and legendary, little has changed on the southern Hebridean isle over the centuries.

ESSENTIALS

GETTING THERE   Take a **ferry** to Gigha from Tayinloan, halfway up the west coast of Kintyre. Sailings are daily and take about 20 minutes, depositing you at **Ardminish,** the main hamlet on Gigha. The round-trip fare is £21 ($39) for an auto plus £5.60 ($11) per passenger. For ferry schedules, call ✆ **08705/650-000** in Kennacraig.

VISITOR INFORMATION   There's no local tourist office, so ask at Campbeltown on the Kintyre Peninsula (see "The Kintyre Peninsula," above).

GETTING AROUND   Because most likely you'll arrive without a car and there's no local bus service, you can either walk or call **Oliver's Taxi** at ✆ **01583/505-251.**

EXPLORING THE ISLAND

Gigha is visited mainly by those wanting to explore its famous gardens. Be prepared to spend your entire day walking. The **Achamore House Gardens** ✮✮✮ (✆ **01583/ 505-267**), 1.6km (1 mile) from the ferry dock at Ardminish, overflow with roses, hydrangeas, camellias, rhododendrons, and azaleas. On a 20-hectare (50-acre) site, they were the creation of the late Sir James Horlick, one of the world's great gardeners. The house isn't open to the public, but the gardens are open year-round, daily from 9am to dusk. Admission is £3 ($5.70). For information about the gardens, call the Gigha Hotel (see below).

The island has a rich Viking past (the Vikings stored their loot here after plundering the west coast of Scotland), and cairns and ruins still remain. **Creag Bhan,** the highest hill, rises more than 100m (330 ft.). From the top you can look out onto the islands of Islay and Jura as well as Kintyre; on a clear day, you can also see Ireland. The **Ogham Stone** is one of only two standing stones in the Hebrides that bears an Ogham inscription, a form of script used in the Scottish kingdom of Dalriada. High on a ridge overlooking the village of Ardminish are the ruins of the **Church of Kilchattan,** dating back to the 13th century.

WHERE TO STAY & DINE

Gigha Hotel ⍓   Standing in a lonely, windswept location, this hotel is a 5-minute walk from the island's ferry landing. Built in the 1700s as a farmhouse, it contains Gigha's only pub, one of its two restaurants, and its only accommodations except for some cottages. Each small but cozy room has a private bathroom. Rather expensive fixed-price dinners are served daily to both guests and nonguests; bar lunches are more affordable.

Ardminish, Isle of Gigha PA41 7AA. ℂ **01583/505-254.** Fax 01583/505-244. www.isle-of-gigha.co.uk/hotel. 13 units. £140 ($266) double. Rates include half board. MC, V. Closed Dec 24–26. **Amenities:** Restaurant; bar. *In room:* TV, coffeemaker, hair dryer.

4 The Isle of Islay: Queen of the Hebrides ⍓⍓

26km (16 miles) W of the Kintyre Peninsula, 1km (¾ mile) SW of Jura

Islay (pronounced "*eye*-lay") is the southernmost island of the Inner Hebrides, separated only by a narrow sound from Jura. At its maximum, Islay is only 32km (20 miles) wide and 40km (25 miles) long. Called the "Queen of the Hebrides," it's a peaceful and unspoiled island of moors, salmon-filled lochs, sandy bays, and wild rocky cliffs—an island of great beauty, ideal for long walks.

ESSENTIALS

GETTING THERE   MacBrayne **steamers** provide daily service to Islay. You leave West Tarbert, on the Kintyre Peninsula, and arrive in Port Askaig, on Islay, in about 2 hours. There's also service to Port Ellen. For information about ferry departures, check with Caledonian MacBrayne (ℂ **08705/650-000**) at the ferry terminal in Gourock.

VISITOR INFORMATION   The **tourist office** is at Bowmore, The Square (ℂ **01496/810-254**). May to September, it's open Monday to Saturday 9:30am to 5pm and Sunday 2 to 5pm; October to April, hours are Monday to Friday noon to 4pm.

EXPLORING THE ISLAND

Near **Port Charlotte** are the graves of the U.S. seamen and army troops who lost their lives in 1918 when their carriers, the *Tuscania* and the *Otranto,* were torpedoed off the shores of Islay. There's a memorial tower on the **Mull of Oa,** 13km (8 miles) from Port

Ellen. For the greatest **walk** on the island, go along Mull of Oa Road toward the sign-posted solar-powered Carraig Fhada lighthouse, some 2.5km (1½ miles) away. The Oa peninsula was once the haunt of illicit whisky distillers and smugglers; the area is filled with sheer cliffs riddled with caves.

The island's capital is **Bowmore,** on the coast across from Port Askaig. Here you can see a fascinating Round Church (no corners for the devil to hide in). But the most important town is **Port Ellen,** on the south coast, a holiday and golfing resort and Islay's principal port. The 18-hole **Machrie golf course** (✆ **01496/302-310**) is 5km (3 miles) from Port Ellen.

You can see the ancient seat of the lords of the Isles, the ruins of two castles, and several Celtic crosses. The ancient **Kildalton Crosses** are in the Kildalton churchyard, about 12km (7½ miles) northeast of Port Ellen—they're two of the finest Celtic crosses in Scotland. The ruins of the 14th-century fortress, **Dunyvaig Castle,** are just south of Kildalton.

In the southwestern part of Islay, in Port Charlotte, the **Museum of Islay Life** (✆ **01496/850-358**) has a wide collection of island artifacts ranging from unrecorded times to the present. Easter to October, the museum is open Monday to Saturday 10am to 4pm. Admission is £3 ($5.70) adults, £2 ($3.80) seniors, and £1 ($1.90) children. The Portnahaven bus from Bowmore stops here.

TOURING THE DISTILLERIES

The island is noted for its distilleries, which still produce single-malt Highland whiskies by the antiquated pot-still method. Of these, **Laphroaig Distillery,** about 1.6km (1 mile) along the road from Ardbeg to Port Ellen (✆ **01496/302-496**), offers guided tours Monday to Friday at 10:15am and 2:15pm. Admission is free and includes a sample dram. **Lagavulin,** Port Ellen (✆ **01496/302-730**), is open Monday to Friday 9:30am to 4:30pm. Tours are by appointment only. Admission is £3 ($5.70) per person and comes with a £3 ($5.70) voucher off the price of a bottle of whisky. A sample is included in the tour. A distillery gift shop is open Monday to Friday 8:30am to noon and 1 to 4:30pm.

Bowmore Distillery, School Street, Bowmore (✆ **01496/810-671**), conducts tours Monday to Friday at 10 and 11am and 2 and 3pm. Admission is £2 ($3.80), which includes a voucher worth £2 ($3.80) off the price of a bottle. Samples are included in the tour. Purchases can be made without taking the tour by stopping at the on-premises gift shop, open Monday to Friday 9am to 5pm and Saturday 10am to noon.

Moments For Birdies & Ramblers

Loch Gruinart cuts into the northern part of Islay, 11km (7 miles) northeast of Port Charlotte and 13km (8 miles) north of Bowmore. As the winter home for wild geese, it has attracted bird-watchers for decades. In 1984, the 1,215 hectares (3,000 acres) of moors and farmland around the loch were turned into the **Loch Gruinart Nature Reserve.**

This is another place for great walks. Beaches rise out of the falling tides, but they're too cold and rocky for serious swimming. This is a lonely and bleak coastline, but because of that it has a certain kind of beauty, especially as you make your way north along its eastern shoreline. On a clear day, you can see the Hebridean islands of Oronsay and Colonsay in the distance.

Port Askaig is home to **Bunnahabhain** (*Ⓒ* **01496/840-646**), which is open year-round Monday to Friday. Call for an appointment. Tours cost £2 ($3.80) and are available at 10:30am and 2 and 3:15pm March to October (call for appointments Oct–Dec). Its gift shop is open to visitors at the end of each tour.

SHOPPING

The **Islay Woollen Mill**, Bridgend (*Ⓒ* **01496/810-563**), has been making a wide range of country tweeds and accessories for more than a century. (It made all the tweeds used in Mel Gibson's *Braveheart*.) The mill shop, open Monday to Saturday from 10am to 5pm, sells items made with the *Braveheart* tweeds as well as tasteful Shetland wool ties, mufflers, Jacob mufflers and ties, flat caps, travel rugs, and scarves.

WHERE TO STAY

Bridgend Hotel *✿*   Victorian spires cap the slate-covered roofs, while roses creep up the walls of this hotel, part of a complex including a roadside barn and one of the most beautiful flower and vegetable gardens on Islay. This is one of the oldest hotels on the island, with somber charm and country pleasures. Guests enjoy drinks beside the open fireplaces in the Victorian cocktail lounge and in the rustic pub, where locals gather at the end of the day. The midsize bedrooms are comfortably and conservatively furnished, each with a small bathroom with either a tub or a shower.

The hotel serves up lots of local produce and many nonguests opt for a moderately priced dinner in the high-ceilinged dining room.

Bridgend, Isle of Islay PA44 7PJ. *Ⓒ* **01496/810-212.** Fax 01496/810-960. www.bridgend-hotel.com. 11 units. £55 ($105) per person; £75 ($143) per person with dinner. Rates include Scottish breakfast. MC, V. **Amenities:** Restaurant; 2 bars; room service; laundry service. *In room:* TV, coffeemaker, hair dryer.

Harbour Inn   Although this establishment is better known for its seafood restaurant (see below), it also offers delightful little bedrooms adjacent to Bowmore Harbour. Family run, the place exudes Hebridean hospitality. Each room is individually decorated in bright colors such as lime or cherry, and the furnishings are mainly wood pieces offset with graceful accessories. All units are equipped with a tidy little bathroom with tub or shower. Every room has a theme for its decor, ranging from a Victorian garden aura to a mahogany "captain's cabin." Two accommodations are suitable for families. The building dates from the 19th century but is completely modernized. The coffee lounge adjacent to the ground-floor dining room features both specialty coffees and fine views of northern Islay and the Paps of Jura.

The Square, Bowmore, Isle of Islay, Argyll PA43 7JR. *Ⓒ* **01496/810-330.** Fax 01496/810-990. www.harbour-inn.com. 7 units. £110–£140 ($209–$266) double. Rates include full breakfast. AE, MC, V. **Amenities:** Restaurant; bar; exercise room; sauna; babysitting; laundry service. *In room:* TV, coffeemaker, hair dryer, iron.

Port Askaig Hotel   Located on the Sound of Islay overlooking the pier, this inn dates from the 18th century but was built on the site of an even older inn. It offers island hospitality and Scottish fare and is a favorite of anglers; the bar is popular with local fisherfolk. Bar meals are available for lunch and dinner. The guest rooms are a bit small, but each is furnished in a comfortable, though not stylish, way; all units have a bathroom, some of which contain a tub/shower combination, the others a shower only.

Hwy. A846 at the ferry crossing to Jura, Port Askaig, Isle of Islay PA46 7RD. *Ⓒ* **01496/840-245.** Fax 01496/840-295. www.portaskaig.co.uk. 8 units. £90–£105 ($171–$200) double. Rates include Scottish breakfast. AE, MC, V. **Amenities:** Restaurant; 2 bars; room service. *In room:* TV, coffeemaker, hair dryer.

Port Charlotte Hotel   This mid-19th-century hotel—actually a trio of cottages joined together—stands next to the small sandy beaches of Port Charlotte with views over Loch Indaal. It has been refurbished and won a four-crown rating from the Scottish Tourist Board in 1998. The guest rooms are beautiful, most with antiques and Oriental rugs. A small bathroom has been installed in each bedroom. The hotel is wheelchair accessible. Features include a large conservatory, a comfortable lounge, and a public bar.

The Port Charlotte is also the best place to dine in the area, with main courses costing £21 to £26 ($40–$49). Typical dishes include sirloin of Islay steak, freshly caught Islay lobster, and grilled filet of Scottish turbot. Packed lunches are available on request.

Main St., Port Charlotte, Isle of Islay PA48 7TU. (*C*) **01496/850-360**. Fax 01496/850-361. www.portcharlottehotel.co.uk. 10 units. £115–£140 ($219–$266) double. Rates include Scottish breakfast. MC, V. **Amenities:** Restaurant; bar; bike rentals; room service; laundry service. *In room:* TV, coffeemaker, hair dryer.

WHERE TO DINE

You can also dine at any of the hotels listed above.

The Croft Kitchen BRITISH   On the main highway running through town is this low-slung, homey, and utterly unpretentious diner/bistro with a friendly staff. Holding no more than 40 customers at a time, it serves wine, beer, and whisky distilled on Islay, along with generous portions of food. The menu includes lots of fresh fish and shellfish, as well as soups, fried scallops, roasted Islay venison with rowanberry jelly, and steamed mussels with white-wine sauce.

Port Charlotte, Isle of Islay. (*C*) **01496/850-230**. Sandwiches £5–£7 ($9.50–$13); main courses £10–£14 ($19–$27) at lunch, £12–£18 ($23–$34) at dinner. MC, V. Daily 10am–8:30pm (last order). Closed mid-Oct to mid-Mar.

Harbour Inn Restaurant ⚘ SEAFOOD/MODERN BRITISH   Back in 2000 this restaurant won the Automobile Association's seafood restaurant of the year award, and the fish is as fresh and as good as ever. High-quality ingredients are used to produce the Scottish bounty served here that includes not only the best of the catch of the day but some outstanding Scottish lamb and beef dishes as well. We've enjoyed some of the best crab, prawns, and lobster in the Hebrides here. Each dish is prepared to order so be prepared to enjoy the wait. You can begin with a selection of smoked Islay seafood with a savory lemon and garlic mayonnaise, or else a terrine of roe deer with a currant and ginger chutney. For a main course opt for stir-fried Lagavulin scallops with fresh lime and sprigs of curry plant, or a bubbling kettle of Islay seafood stew flavored with fennel and served on a bed of linguini with "eggplant spaghetti." The restaurant also offers a selection of locally distilled single-malt whiskies from Islay itself.

The Square, Bowmore, Isle of Islay, Argyll PA43 7JR. (*C*) **01496/810-330**. Reservations recommended on weekends. Lunch main courses £8–£14 ($15–$27); dinner main courses £15–£23 ($29–$44). AE, MC, V. Daily noon–2:30pm and 6–9pm.

ISLAY AFTER DARK

After work, distillery employees gather at the pub at the **Harbour Inn,** Main Street in Bowmore ((*C*) **01496/810-330**), an old pub with stone walls, a fireplace, and wooden floors and furnishings. It's open Monday through Saturday from 11am to 1am and Sunday from noon to 1am. Local seafood is served at lunch and dinner. In summer, reservations are recommended.

5 The Isle of Jura: Deer Island (★)

1km (¾ mile) E of Islay

Jura is the fourth largest of the Inner Hebrides, 43km (27 miles) long and varying from 3 to 13km (2–8 miles) in breadth. It takes its name from the Norse *jura,* meaning "deer island." The red deer on Jura—Scotland's largest animals, at 1.2m (4 ft.) high—outnumber the people by about 20 to 1. The hearty islanders themselves number only about 250, and most of them live along the east coast. Jura is relatively unknown, and its mountains, soaring cliffs, snug coves, and moors make it an inviting place.

ESSENTIALS

GETTING THERE   From Kennacraig (West Loch, Tarbert) you can go to Port Askaig, on Islay (see above), and then take one of the **Caledonian MacBrayne ferries** (② 08705/650-000). The cost is £59 ($112) for a car and £8.30 ($16) per passenger each way (4-day round-trip tickets are more economical). From Port Askaig, you can take a second ferry to Feolin on Jura; call **Western Ferries** at ② 01369/704-452. Car spaces must be booked in advance. The cost for a vehicle is £9.60 ($18), plus £3.40 ($6.45) for a passenger one-way.

VISITOR INFORMATION   The Isle of Islay (see "The Isle of Islay: Queen of the Hebrides," above) has the nearest tourist information office.

EXPLORING THE ISLAND

Since most of the island is accessible only by foot, wear sturdy walking shoes and bring raingear. The best place for walks is the **Jura House Garden and Grounds** at the southern tip. These grounds were laid out by the Victorians to take advantage of the natural beauty of the region, and you can visit the gardens with their sheltered walks and panoramic views daily 9am to 5pm. Admission is £2.50 ($4.75) adults, £1 ($1.90) children 5 to 16. June to August, it's also the best place on the island to have tea, but only Saturday and Sunday. Call ② 01496/820-315 for details.

The capital, **Craighouse,** is hardly more than a hamlet. From Islay, you can take a 5-minute ferry ride to Jura from Port Askaig, docking at the Feolin Ferry berth.

The island's landscape is dominated by the **Paps of Jura,** which reach a peak of 780m (2,571 ft.) at Beinn-an-Oir. An arm of the sea, **Loch Tarbert** nearly divides the island, cutting into it for nearly 10km (6 miles).

The square tower of **Claig Castle,** now in ruins, was the stronghold of the Mac-Donalds until they were subdued by the Campbells in the 17th century.

(Fun Fact The Gloom & Doom of Orwell's *1984*

George Orwell was quite ill when he lived on Jura in the bitter postwar winters of 1946 and 1947, while working on *1984.* After a close call when he and his adopted son ventured too close to the whirlpool in the Gulf of Corryvreckan—they were saved by local fishermen—he went on to publish his masterpiece in 1949, only to die in London of tuberculosis in 1950.

WHERE TO STAY & DINE

Jura Hotel ⚐ *(Finds)*   The island's only hotel is a sprawling gray-walled building near the center of the hamlet. (Craighouse lies east of Feolin along the coast.) Sections date from the 1600s, but what you see today was built in 1956. The midsize guest rooms are high quality, with comfortable mattresses and, in most cases, small bathrooms with a tub/shower combination. In this remote outpost, you'll get a tranquil night's sleep. Kenya-born Fiona Walton and her husband, Steve, are the managing directors. Affordable meals are served daily at lunch and dinner; the dining room's specialty is Jura-bred venison.

Craighouse, Isle of Jura PA60 7XU. ℂ **01496/820-243.** Fax 01496/820-249. www.jurahotel.co.uk. 18 units, 12 with private bathroom. £70 ($133) double without bathroom; £82–£100 ($156–$190) double with bathroom; £110 ($209) suite. Rates include Scottish breakfast. AE, DC, MC, V. Closed 2 weeks at Dec–Jan. **Amenities:** Restaurant; bar; bicycles (a few available for guests); room service. *In room:* Coffeemaker, no phone.

6 Inveraray ⭐⭐

159km (99 miles) NW of Edinburgh, 92km (57 miles) NW of Glasgow, 61km (38 miles) SE of Oban

The small resort and royal burgh of Inveraray occupies a splendid setting on the upper shores of Loch Fyne. It's particularly attractive when you approach from the east on A83. Across a little inlet, you can see the town lying peacefully on a bit of land fronting the loch.

ESSENTIALS

GETTING THERE   The nearest **rail station** is at Dumbarton, 72km (45 miles) southeast, where you can make bus connections to Inveraray. For rail schedules, call ℂ **08457/484-950.**

The Citylink-926 Service operates **buses** out of Glasgow, heading for Dumbarton, before continuing to Inveraray. Transit time is about 2 hours. Monday through Saturday, three buses make this run (only two on Sun). The fare is £7.50 ($14) one-way, £15 ($29) round-trip. For bus schedules, call ℂ **08705/505-050.**

If you're **driving** from Oban, head east along A85 until you reach the junction with A819, at which point you continue south.

VISITOR INFORMATION   The **tourist office** is on Front Street (ℂ **01499/302-063**). It's open from June to mid-September, daily 9am to 6pm; mid-September to October, April, and May, Monday to Saturday 10am to 3pm and Sunday noon to 5pm; and November to March, daily noon to 4pm.

EXPLORING THE ISLAND

At one end of the town's main street is a **Celtic burial cross** from Iona. The parish church is divided by a wall that enables mass to be held simultaneously in Gaelic and English.

Because so many of its attractions and those in its environs involve walking, hope for a sunny day. A local beauty spot is the **Ardkinglas Woodland Garden** (ℂ **01499/600-261**), 6.5km (4 miles) east of Inveraray, at the head of Loch Fyne. People drive from all over Britain to see Scotland's greatest collection of conifers and its masses of rhododendrons bursting into bloom in June. Admission is £3 ($5.70); it's open daily from 9am to 5pm.

If you have a car, you can explore this scenic part of Scotland from Cairndow. Head east along A83 until you reach the junction with A815, at which point proceed south

Hiking in Argyll Forest Park

Argyll Forest Park, in the southern Highlands, stretches almost to Loch Fyne and is made up of Benmore, Ardgartan, and Glenbranter. The park covers an area of 24,000 hectares (60,000 acres), contains some of Scotland's most panoramic scenery, and includes a wide variety of habitats, from lush forests and waterside to bleaker grassy moorlands and mountains. The Clyde sea lochs cut deep into the forested areas, somewhat in the way fjord "fingers" cut into the Norwegian coast; in the northern part are the Arrochar Alps (so called), where **Ben Arthur** reaches a height of 877m (2,891 ft.).

The park attracts not only those interested in natural history and wildlife but also rock climbers, hikers, and hill walkers. There are many recreational activities and dozens of forest walks for trail blazers with all degrees of skill. Trails leading through forests to the loftier peaks are strenuous and meant for skilled hikers; others are easier, including paths from the **Younger Botanic Garden** by Loch Eck leading to Puck's Glen.

There's abundant wildlife in the sea lochs: shark, sea otters, gray seals, sea scorpions, crabs, shrimp, sea lemons, sea anemones, and sea slugs, among other inhabitants. Boats and canoes are available for rent. One of the park's biggest thrills is exploring the underwater caves of Loch Long.

In the early spring and summer, the park trails are at their most beautiful—woodland birds create choruses of song, and the forest is filled with violets, wood anemones, primroses, and bluebells. Sometimes the wildflowers are so thick they're like carpets. In the rainy climate of the southern Highlands, ferns and mosses also grow in abundance.

To reach the park, take A83 to B828 heading for Loch Goll, or follow A815 to Loch Eck and Loch Long. Both Arrochar and Tarbert stops on the Glasgow–Fort William rail line are on the periphery of the park's northeast frontier.

The best place for lodging is **Dunoon,** to the south on the Cowal Penin-sula, an easy gateway to the park. Dunoon has been a holiday resort since 1790, created for the "merchant princes" of Glasgow. Recreational facilities abound, including an indoor pool, tennis courts, and an 18-hole golf course. To pick up information about the park and a trail map, go to the **Dunoon Tourist Center,** 7 Alexandra Parade (ⓒ **01369/703-785**). It's open April to Sep-tember, Monday to Friday 9am to 5:30pm and Saturday and Sunday 10am to 5pm; October to March, Monday to Thursday 9am to 5pm, Friday 10am to 5pm, and Saturday and Sunday 10am to 4pm.

along the western shore of Loch Fyne until you come to the famous inn at Creggans (see below), directly north of **Strachur.** About 8km (5 miles) south from The Creg-gans Inn along the loch is the old **Castle Lachlan** at Strathiachian, the 13th-century castle of the MacLachlan clan. Now in ruins, it was besieged by the English in 1745. The MacLachlans were fervent Jacobites and played a major role in the uprising.

Arctic Penguin Heritage Centre   Built in a former lightship, a three-masted schooner constructed in 1911 called the *Arctic Penguin,* this museum is a mecca for those who love maritime history. You can see handcrafted shell valentines made by a mariner for his love, or depictions of the horrors of traveling on emigrant and slave ships. In stark contrast, there is also the luxurious Lady's Cabin, where the lady of the ship used to spend her time. Visitors can also see the engine room, the Captain's stateroom, and the Grog Barrels. Exhibits detail the history of the Glasgow docks and the launching of the original *Queen Mary* (now in dry dock in California). You can go aboard one of the world's last iron sailing ships, in permanent anchor down by the loch. The cinema, where visitors see a short film on maritime history, and the gift shop are new additions to the still seaworthy *Arctic Penguin.*

The Pier, Inveraray. (C) **01499/302-213.** Admission £3.80 ($7.20) adults, £2.80 ($5.30) seniors, £2.20 ($4.20) children. Daily 10am–5pm.

Crarae Glen Gardens   Lying along Loch Fyne, these are among Scotland's most beautiful gardens, some 20 hectares (50 acres) of rich plantings along with waterfalls and panoramic vistas of the loch. You can enjoy the beauty while hiking one of the many paths.

13km (8 miles) southwest of Inveraray along A83, near the hamlet of Minard. (C) **01546/886-614.** Admission £5 ($9.50) adults, £4 ($7.60) children, £14 ($27) per family. Daily 10am–5pm.

Inveraray Castle   The hereditary seat of the dukes of Argyll, Inveraray Castle has been headquarters of the Clan Campbell since the early 15th century. The gray-green stone castle is among the earliest examples of Gothic Revival in Britain and offers a fine collection of pictures and 18th-century French furniture, old porcelain, and an Armoury Hall, which alone contains 1,300 pieces. On the grounds is a **Combined Operations Museum,** the only one of its kind in the United Kingdom. It illustrates the role No. 1 Combined Training Centre played at Inveraray in World War II. On exhibit are scale models, newspaper reports, campaign maps, photographs, wartime posters and cartoons, training scenes, and other mementos. A shop sells souvenirs, and a tearoom serves homemade cakes and scones.

1km (¾ mile) northeast of Inveraray on Loch Fyne. (C) **01499/302-203.** www.inveraray-castle.com. Admission £6.30 ($12) adults, £5.20 ($9.90) seniors and students, £4.10 ($7.80) children, £17 ($32) per family. Apr–Oct 10am–5:45pm, Sun noon–5:45pm.

WHERE TO STAY & DINE

Argyll Hotel   This waterfront inn, built in 1755, boasts vistas of Loch Fyne and Loch Shira. The comfortable, midsize guest rooms feature decors ranging from flowered chintz to modern, no-nonsense functional, and most open onto panoramic views of Loch Fyne. Four so-called executive rooms have either four-poster or Queen Anne beds. Most rooms come with small, shower-only bathrooms, although some contain bathtubs. On site are a wood-and-gilt public bar, a guests-only cocktail lounge, and a dignified restaurant serving five-course dinners. Even if you're not a guest, consider having a meal here—the chefs feature the best of local produce, especially fish and shellfish from Loch Fyne.

Front St., Inveraray PA32 8XB. (C) **01499/302-466.** Fax 01499/302-389. www.the-argyll-hotel.co.uk. 37 units. £104–£160 ($198–$304) double. Rates include Scottish breakfast. AE, DC, MC, V. **Amenities:** Restaurant; 2 bars; room service; laundry service. *In room:* TV, coffeemaker, hair dryer.

The Creggans Inn ⭐   This inn commemorates the spot where Mary Queen of Scots is said to have disembarked from her ship in 1563 on her way through the Highlands. Painted white and flanked by gardens, the inn rises across A815 from the sea and is owned by Sir Charles MacLean and his mother, Lady MacLean, author of several best-selling cookbooks, most of which are for sale here. The guest rooms are elegant and understated, all traditionally furnished and well-maintained, and each is equipped with a private bathroom. Guests may use the upstairs sitting room and the garden-style lounge. The restaurant has a charcoal grill that produces succulent versions of Aberdeen Angus steaks and lamb kabobs, but you can also enjoy fresh seafood and venison. Reservations are a must. The bar features pub lunches beside an open fire.

Strachur PA27 8BX. ⓒ **01369/860-279.** Fax 01369/860-637. www.creggans-inn.co.uk. 14 units. £130 ($247) double; £170 ($323) suite. Rates include Scottish breakfast. AE, DC, MC, V. **Amenities:** Restaurant; bar; room service; laundry service. *In room:* TV, coffeemaker, hair dryer.

The George Hotel ⭐   One of the most charming hotels in town lies behind a facade built around 1775. Part of the charm derives from the old-fashioned bar, where the Guinness simply seems to taste better than in less evocative settings. The public areas are marked with flagstone floors, beamed ceilings, and blazing fireplaces. The guest rooms are cozy, done in old-fashioned Scottish style. Some have king-size beds (unusual for Scotland) and either claw-foot tubs, full-length Victorian roll-top bathtubs, or Jacuzzis. The restaurant is among the town's most popular, serving moderately priced lunches and dinners daily. Your choices include steaks prepared with pepper or mushroom sauce, grilled halibut, and grilled Loch Fyne salmon with white wine, prawns, and scallops.

Main St. E, Inveraray PA32 8TT. ⓒ **01499/302-111.** Fax 01499/302-098. www.thegeorgehotel.co.uk. 15 units. £110–£130 ($209–$247) double. Rates include breakfast. AE, DC, MC, V. **Amenities:** Restaurant; 2 bars. *In room:* TV, coffeemaker.

7 Loch Awe: Scotland's Longest Loch ⭐⭐

159km (99 miles) NW of Edinburgh, 39km (24 miles) E of Oban, 109km (68 miles) NW of Glasgow

Only 1.6km (1 mile) wide in most places and 36km (22 miles) long, Loch Awe is the longest loch in Scotland and served as a natural freshwater moat protecting the Campbells of Inveraray from their enemies to the north. Along its banks are many reminders of its fortified past. The Forestry Commission has vast forests and signposted trails in this area, and a modern road makes it possible to travel around Loch Awe, so more than ever it's a popular center for angling and walking.

ESSENTIALS

GETTING THERE   The nearest train station is in Oban, where you'd have to take a connecting bus. **Scottish Citylink,** 1 Queens Park Place in Oban (call ⓒ **01631/ 562-856** for schedules), has service to Glasgow with stopovers at Loch Awe.

If you're driving from Oban, head east along A85.

VISITOR INFORMATION   Consult the **tourist office** in Oban (see "Oban: Gateway to Mull & the Inner Hebrides," below).

Moments Castle of the Once Mighty Campbells

The ruins of **Kilchurn Castle** are at the northern tip of Loch Awe, west of Dalmally, and across from the south-bank village of Loch Awe. A stronghold of the Campbells of Glen Orchy in 1440, it's a spectacular ruin with much of the original structure still intact. The ruins have been completely reinforced and balconied so you can now explore them when the weather permits.

Kilchurn Castle is open to the public. The title to the grounds (but not the castle itself—that is part of Historic Scotland) is held by Ian Cleaver, owner of **Highland Heritage Coach Tours** (© **01838/200-444**; www.kilchurncastle.com). The Castle is accessible via an unpaved and rocky road, about a half-mile from the main road, A85. There is no parking area, however.

A simpler alternative is to take a steamboat cruise from Loch Awe. **Ardanaiseig Hotel** (© **01866/833-333**; www.ardanaiseig.com) runs cruises to Kilchurn Castle departing from Loch Awe for £30 ($57) per person, one-way. The trip takes about a half-hour each way.

EXPLORING THE AREA

To the east of the top of Loch Awe is **Dalmally**, a small but historically important town. Its 18th-century church is built in an octagonal shape.

For reminders of the days when the Campbells of Inveraray held supreme power in the Loch Awe region, there's another ruined **castle** at Fincharn, at the southern end of the loch, and another on the island of Fraoch Eilean. The Isle of Inishail has an ancient **chapel and burial ground.**

The bulk of **Ben Cruachan,** rising to 1,119m (3,689 ft.), dominates Loch Awe at its northern end and attracts climbers and hikers. On the Ben is the world's second-largest hydroelectric power station, which pumps water from Loch Awe to a reservoir high up on the mountain.

Below are the **Falls of Cruachan** and the wild **Pass of Brander,** where Robert the Bruce routed the Clan MacDougall in 1308. The Pass of Brander was the scene of many a fierce battle in bygone times, and something of that bloody past seems to brood over the narrow defile. Through it the waters of the Awe flow on their way to Loch Etive. This winding sea loch is 31km (19 miles) long, stretching from Dun Dunstaffnage Bay, at Oban, to Glen Etive, and reaching into the Moor of Rannoch at the foot of the 910m (3,000-ft.) **Buachaille Etive (the Shepherd of Etive).**

WHERE TO STAY & DINE

Hotel Ardanaiseig *★★★* Although this gray-stone manorial seat was built in 1834 by a Campbell patriarch, it's designed along 18th-century lines. Its builder also planted some of the rarest trees in Britain, many of them exotic conifers. Today, clusters of fruit trees stand in a walled garden, and the rhododendrons and azaleas are a joy in May and June. Once a private home, the hotel has formal sitting rooms graced with big chintzy chairs, fresh flowers, and polished tables. The guest rooms are named for various local mountains and lochs, and are uniquely and traditionally furnished with antiques; some have four-poster beds. The price of a room depends on its size, ranging from a small room to a master bedroom with a loch view. The beautifully maintained bathrooms come with either a tub/shower combo or a shower only.

Kilchrenan by Taynuilt PA35 1HE. (℃ **800/548-7790** in the U.S., 800/463-7595 in Canada, or 01866/833-333. Fax 01866/833-222. www.ardanaiseig.com. 16 units. £106–£315 ($201–$599) double. AE, DC, MC, V. Closed Jan to mid-Feb. Drive 34km (21 miles) south of Oban by following the signs to Taynuilt, then turn onto B845 toward Kilchrenan. Turn left at the Kilchrenan Pub and continue on for 6km (3¾ miles), following signs into Ardanaiseig. **Amenities:** Restaurant; tennis court. *In room:* TV, coffeemaker, hair dryer.

8 Oban: Gateway to Mull & the Inner Hebrides ★

137km (85 miles) NW of Glasgow, 81km (50 miles) SW of Fort William

One of Scotland's leading coastal resorts, the bustling port of Oban is in a sheltered bay almost landlocked by the island of Kerrera. A busy fishing port in the 18th century, Oban is now heavily dependent on tourism. Since it lacks major attractions of its own, it's often used as a major refueling stop for those exploring the greater west coast of Scotland.

Oban is the gateway to **Mull,** largest of the Inner Hebrides, and to the island of **Iona.** See chapter 12 for information about these destinations, including ferry service from Oban.

ESSENTIALS

GETTING THERE   From Glasgow, the West Highland lines run directly to Oban, with departures from Glasgow's Queen Street Station (call (℃ **08457/484-950** for 24-hr. info). Three trains per day (only two on Sun) make the 3-hour run to Oban, a one-way fare costing £18 ($34).

Frequent coaches depart from Buchanan Station in Glasgow, taking about the same time as the train, although a one-way fare is only £14 ($27). Call **Scottish Citylink** at (℃ **08705/505-050** in Glasgow or (℃ **01631/563-059** in Oban.

If you're driving from Glasgow, head northwest along A82 until you reach Tyndrum, then go west along A85 until you come to Oban.

VISITOR INFORMATION   The **tourist office** is on Argyll Square (℃ **01631/563-122**). April to mid-June and mid-September to October, it's open Monday to Friday 9:30am to 5pm and Saturday and Sunday 10am to 4pm; mid-June to mid-September, hours are Monday to Saturday 9am to 8pm and Sunday 9am to 7pm; and November to March, it's open Monday to Saturday 9:30am to 5pm and Sunday noon to 4pm.

SPECIAL EVENTS   The **Oban Highland Games** are held in August, with massed pipe bands marching through the streets. Ask at the tourist office for details. The **Oban Pipe Band** regularly parades on the main street throughout summer.

EXPLORING THE AREA

To appreciate the coastal scenery of Oban, consider renting a bike and cycling around. They're available at **Oban Cycles,** Unite 9 Mill Lane. (℃ **01631/564-000**).

Near the little granite **Cathedral of the Isles,** 1.6km (1 mile) north of the end of the bay, is the ruin of the 13th-century **Dunollie Castle,** seat of the lords of Lorn, who once owned a third of Scotland.

On the island of Kerrera stands **Gylen Castle,** home of the MacDougalls, dating back to 1587.

You can visit **Dunstaffnage Castle** ★ (℃ **01631/562-465**), 5.5km (3½ miles) north, believed to have been the royal seat of the Dalriadic monarchy in the 8th century. It was probably the site of the Scots court until Kenneth MacAlpin's unification of Scotland

and the transfer of the seat of government to Scone in the 10th century. The present castle was built around 1263. It's open April to September daily from 9:30am to 5:30pm, and from October to March Saturday to Wednesday from 9:30am to 4:30pm. Admission is £3.50 ($6.65) adults, £2.80 ($5.30) seniors, and £1.75 ($3.35) children. You can take a bus from the Oban rail station to Dunbeg, but it's still a 2.5km (1½-mile) walk to the castle.

SHOPPING

Caithness Glass Oban, Railway Pier (© **01631/563-386**), is the best place for shopping, but you'll find plenty of gift and souvenir shops around town. At this center, locally produced glass items range from functional dinner- and glassware to purely artistic curios. This firm has one of the most prestigious reputations in Scotland.

Many of the crafts items produced in local crofts and private homes eventually end up at gift shops in Oban, where they're proudly displayed among the finest of their kind in the West Country. One of the best outlets is **McCaig's Warehouse,** Argyll Square (© **01631/566-335**), where the tartan patterns of virtually every clan in Scotland are for sale, either by the meter or in the form of kilts, jackets, traditional Highland garb, or more modern interpretation of traditional fashions.

Celtic-patterned jewelry, made from gold, silver, or platinum, and sometimes studded with semiprecious gems, is featured at **The Gem Box,** Esplanade (© **01631/562-180**).

If all other shopping options fail, consider the gift items displayed at the **Oban Tourist Information Office,** Argyll Square (© **01631/563-122**). Inventories include tartans, jewelry, woodwork, and glassware, usually crafted into Celtic designs, and books covering myriad aspects of what to see and do in Scotland.

If you absolutely, positively must have a kilt, a cape, or a full outfit based on your favorite Highland regiment, head for one of the town's two best tailors: **Hector Russell, Kiltmaker,** Argyll Square (© **01631/570-240**), and **Geoffrey Tailors,** Argyll Square (© **01631/570-557**).

WHERE TO STAY

You may also want to check out the rooms offered at the **Balmoral Hotel** or the **Knipoch Hotel Restaurant** (see "Where to Dine," below).

VERY EXPENSIVE

Isle of Eriska Hotel ☆☆☆ The grandest place to stay in the Greater Oban area is this Victorian house that welcomes you at the end of a winding drive. In the Middle Ages, this 121-hectare (300-acre) forested island was a church-protected sanctuary. No more: In the 19th century an industrialist purchased it and planted hundreds of beech trees, building a bridge to the mainland. Today you can savor the splendors of country life in an elegant setting. From the estate you enjoy a panorama of the surrounding waterways and views of a local deer colony. The surrounding forest is a private park.

A magnificent front door leads to the entrance hall where a log burns on chilly nights. A formal sitting room and a library/bar are on the ground floor. A wide staircase leads to the baronial bedrooms. Each of the accommodations is individually furnished, offering both style and comfort with fully tiled and well-lit bathrooms.

Families might consider renting the beautifully and tastefully furnished Lilac Cottage; it lies 100m (328 ft.) from the main building and comes with its own private garden, sitting rooms, and two bedrooms with private bathrooms.

The hotel is known for its refined Scottish cuisine, made primarily from local produce. Adjoining is the Stables Spa with its large heated pool.

A fixed-price dinner at the restaurant is available for £40 ($76) per person; a jacket and tie are required for men.

Ledaig, by Oban, Argyll PA37 1SD. ℭ **01631/720-371.** Fax 01631/720-531. www.eriska-hotel.co.uk. 17 units. £290 ($551) double; £400 ($760) suite; £485 ($922) cottage. Winter rates significantly lower. Rates include breakfast, morning coffee, and afternoon tea. MC, V. Lies 6km (10 miles) north of Oban. **Amenities:** Restaurant; bar; indoor heated pool; 6-hole golf course; tennis court; health club; spa; sauna; room service; babysitting; laundry service; steam room. *In room:* TV, coffeemaker, hair dryer, iron, trouser press.

EXPENSIVE

Manor House Hotel ⦗⦘   This is your best bet for an overnight in Oban. Located on the outskirts of town, and opening onto panoramic views of Oban Bay, this stone house, built in 1780, was once owned by the duke of Argyll. Many antiques grace the public rooms. The good-size guest rooms are filled with tasteful reproductions, and coordinated curtains and bedcovers create a pleasing effect, often in sun-splashed golds and yellows. All have midsize private bathrooms, some with both tub and shower. Children under 12 are not welcome as guests.

The hotel is famous for its restaurant; during the summer, rooms are held for patrons who have dinner reservations. Bookings without dinner reservations are taken only when there are openings. For more on dining here, see "Where to Dine," below.

Gallanach Rd., Oban PA34 4LS. ℭ **01631/562-087.** Fax 01631/563-053. www.manorhouseoban.com. 11 units. £153–£228 ($291–$433) double. Rates include half-board. AE, MC, V. From the south side of Oban, follow the signs for the car ferry but continue past the ferry entrance for about 1km (½ mile). No children under age 12. **Amenities:** Restaurant; bar; room service; laundry service; nonsmoking rooms. *In room:* TV, coffeemaker, hair dryer.

MODERATE

Alexandra Hotel   On the promenade 1.6km (1 mile) from the train station, the late-1860s stone Alexandra boasts gables and turreted towers and a Regency front veranda. From its public room you can look out onto Oban Bay, and two sun lounges overlook the seafront. The midsize guest rooms are modestly furnished but pleasing, with small bathrooms. Some rooms are specially equipped for those with limited mobility. Most units are rented at the lower rate (see below), except for two spacious bedrooms that have dramatic sea views. The restaurant, which serves good food, also opens onto the panorama.

Corran Esplanade, Oban PA34 5AA. ℭ **01631/562-381.** Fax 01631/564-497. 77 units, 2 suites. £90–£250 ($171–$475) double. Rates include Scottish breakfast. AE, MC, V. **Amenities:** Restaurant; bar; indoor pool; small exercise room; room service; laundry service; steam room; rooms for those w/limited mobility. *In room:* TV, coffeemaker, hair dryer.

Columba Hotel   This is one of the most impressive Victorian buildings in Oban. The Columba was built in 1870 by the same McCaig who constructed the hilltop extravaganza known as McCaig's Tower. The location is among the best in town, and the modernized big-windowed dining room offers views of the port. The small guest rooms are unremarkable but well maintained, each with a tiny bathroom with a tub/shower combination, or just a shower. The restaurant offers a mix of seafood and local produce. Live folk music is sometimes performed in the informal Harbour Inn Bar.

The Esplanade, North Pier, Oban PA34 5QD. ℭ **01631/562-183.** Fax 01631/564-683. 50 units. £85–£100 ($162–$190) double. Rates include breakfast. AE, MC, V. Free parking. The Scottish Midland Bus Company's Ganavan bus passes by. **Amenities:** Restaurant; bar; car rental; room service; babysitting; nonsmoking rooms. *In room:* TV, coffeemaker, hair dryer.

Dungallan House Hotel ⟨⋆⟩   One of Oban's more upscale inns, Dungallan House was built for the Campbells around 1870. It was used as a hospital during World War I and as a naval office during World War II, but today it's the artfully furnished domain of Millie and Marion Stevenson-Coates, who maintain the high-ceilinged proportions and antique furniture with devotion. The guest rooms have been refurbished, each with quality furnishings. All but two single rooms have small bathrooms, some of which contain a tub/shower combination. Breakfasts are served in grand style in the formal dining room; dinners can be arranged, and though priority is granted to guests, nonguests can usually have a meal here if they phone ahead. Two hectares (5 acres) of forest and gardens surround the house, and views stretch out over the Bay of Oban and its islands. Children under 12 are not welcome.

Gallanach Rd., Oban PA34 4PD. ⟨ℂ⟩ **01631/563-799**. Fax 01631/566-711. www.dungallanhotel-oban.co.uk. 13 units, 11 with private bathroom. £116–£154 ($220–$293) double with breakfast; £166–£204 ($315–$388) double with full board. MC, V. Closed Nov–Mar. From Oban's center, drive 1km (½ mile), following the signs to Gallanach. **Amenities:** Dining room; lounge; nonsmoking rooms. *In room:* TV, no phone.

Dungrianach ⟨⋆⟩ *(Finds)*   This little B&B is a charmer. In Gaelic, Dungrianach means "the sunny house on the hill," and the description is apt: The hotel sits in the midst of a wooded area, overlooking Oban Bay and some of the islands of the Inner Hebrides. The location is tranquil and seemingly remote, yet it's only a few minutes' walk from the ferry terminal. The house is impressively furnished with both antiques and reproductions. The owners rent a double and a twin-bedded room, each with a little private bathroom with shower. Guests meet fellow guests in the living room, which has a collection of books on Scotland and travel literature in general. Because there are only a handful of rooms, it can be difficult to get a reservation.

Pulpit Hill, Oban, Argyll PA34 4LU. ⟨ℂ⟩/fax **01631/562-840**. www.dungrianach.com. 2 units. £64 ($122) double. Rates include breakfast. No credit cards. Free parking. *In room:* TV, coffeemaker, no phone.

The Oban Caledonian Hotel ⟨⋆⟩   This choice, a favorite of coach tours, makes good on its promise of giving you a "taste of the Highlands." A fine example of Scottish 19th-century architecture, it occupies a landmark position, with a view opening onto the harbor and Oban Bay. This convenient location puts you close to the rail, bus, and ferry terminals, from which you can book passage to the Isles. The guest rooms have up-to-date amenities and small bathrooms, each with a tub/shower combo. The front rooms are the most desirable. Good, reasonably priced Scottish fare is served in the dining room.

Station Sq., Oban PA34 5RT. ⟨ℂ⟩ **01631/563-133**. Fax 01631/562-998. 59 units. £140–£200 ($266–$380) double; £260 ($494) suite. Rates include Scottish breakfast and dinner. AE, MC, V. Free parking. **Amenities:** 2 restaurants; bar; room service; babysitting; laundry service; nonsmoking rooms. *In room:* TV, kitchenette, coffeemaker, hair dryer.

INEXPENSIVE

Foxholes ⟨⋆⟩ *(Finds)*   Far from a foxhole, this is actually a spacious country house set in a tranquil glen to the south of Oban. Operated by Barry and Shirley Dowson-Park, it's for those seeking seclusion. The cozy, tasteful, and comfortable bedrooms are painted in soft pastels and furnished traditionally. All rooms have panoramic views of both the countryside and the hotel's well-maintained gardens. The bathrooms are in excellent condition, and some have a tub/shower combo. A five-course fixed-price meal is available for an additional £21 to £27 ($40–$51) per person.

Cologin, Lerags, Oban. PA34 4SE. ⓒ **0163I/564-982.** Fax 1631/570-890. www.foxholeshotel.co.uk. 7 units. £86–£94 ($163–$179) double. Rates include full Scottish breakfast. MC, V. Closed Dec–Mar. Free parking. Take A816 1.8km (3 miles) south of Oban. **Amenities:** Restaurant; bar; nonsmoking rooms. *In room:* TV, coffeemaker, hair dryer, no phone.

Glenburnie Hotel   One of Oban's genuinely grand houses is on the seafront esplanade and just a 5-minute walk west of the town center. Built in 1897 of granite blocks, with elegant ecclesiastical-looking bay windows, it was designed as the surgical hospital and home of a prominent doctor. Today, it's a guesthouse operated by Graeme and Allyson Strachan, who have outfitted the rooms with comfy furniture, much of it antique. Bathrooms are small but tidy, and most have a tub/shower combination.

The Esplanade, Oban PA34 5AQ. ⓒ/fax **01631/562-089.** www.glenburnie.co.uk. 14 units. £74–£80 ($141–$152) double. Rates include breakfast. MC, V. Closed mid-Nov to Easter. **Amenities:** Nonsmoking rooms. *In room:* TV, coffeemaker.

WHERE TO DINE
EXPENSIVE
Knipoch Hotel Restaurant 👍👍 SCOTTISH   Oban offers a truly fine restaurant 10km (6 miles) south of town on the shores of Loch Feochan. Jenny and Colin Craig, a mother-and-son team, welcome you to their whitewashed Georgian house (the oldest part dates from 1592) and offer a choice of three dining rooms as well as a daily five-course meal. Salmon and halibut are smoked on the premises, and the menu relies heavily on Scottish produce, including fresh fish. Try the cock-a-leekie soup, followed by Sound of Luing scallops. The wine cellar is excellent, especially in its bordeaux.

The hotel rents 21 well-furnished rooms, charging £158 to £170 ($300–$323) per night for a double, with a suite costing £208 to £220 ($395–$418). A full Scottish breakfast is included in the rate.

Hwy. A816, Kilninver, Knipoch, by Oban PA34 4QT. ⓒ **01852/316-251.** Fax 01852/316-249. www.knipochhotel.co.uk. Reservations required. Main courses £15–£20 ($29–$38). AE, DC, MC, V. Daily 7:30–9pm. Closed mid-Dec to mid-Feb. Drive 10km (6 miles) south of Oban on A816.

The Manor House 👍 SCOTTISH   Located in the house built by the duke of Argyll in 1780, this formal, but not stuffy, restaurant overlooks Oban Bay and is one of the finest dining choices along the coast. A traditional Scottish cuisine is served—truly fresh and creative cooking—and the chef uses the highest-quality ingredients. Many visitors to the Highlands opt for venison, which often comes with black pudding, caramelized root vegetables, and rowanberry glaze; and juliennes of veal with mushrooms in a Riesling sauce with potato rosti and salsify. You might want to try the delicious grilled scallops in wilted spinach. There are also some selections for vegetarians. You can order such old-fashioned British desserts as sticky toffee pudding with butterscotch sauce, but for something really Scottish, order marinated brambles with whisky custard.

In the Manor House Hotel, Gallanach Rd. ⓒ **01631/562-087.** Reservations recommended. Main courses £30 ($57); fixed-price 5-course meal £33 ($62). AE, MC, V. Daily noon–2pm and 6:45–9pm.

MODERATE
Balmoral Hotel BRITISH   At the top of a granite staircase whose corkscrew shape is an architectural marvel, this is one of the most popular restaurants in town. Filled with 19th-century charm, it contains Windsor chairs and reproduction Georgian tables. Specialties include sliced chateaubriand with mushrooms; smoked Tobermory trout; haggis with cream and whisky; venison casserole; filet of beef served with a

creamed onion, tomato, and mushroom sauce; and roast pheasant. Less expensive platters are served in the adjacent bar.

The hotel stands on the eastern extension of the town's main commercial street (George St.), a 4-minute walk from the center. It rents 12 well-furnished rooms, with TVs, costing £60 to £75 ($114–$143) double, Scottish breakfast included.

Craigard Rd., Oban PA34 5AQ. © 01631/562-731. Reservations recommended in midsummer. Main courses £8–£20 ($15–$38); bar meals £4.50–£10 ($8.55–$19). AE, DC, MC, V. May to mid-Oct daily noon–2pm and 6–10pm; Mar–Apr and mid-Oct to Dec daily noon–2pm and 6–8pm.

The Gathering BRITISH   Opened in 1882, this imposing building, ringed with verandas, is no longer a private hunting and social club. Today, its ground floor functions as an Irish pub (Mon–Sat 11am–1am, Sun noon–11pm) and its wood-sheathed upper floor as a well-managed restaurant. Dishes are straightforward but tasty. Menu items include lots of local produce, fish, and game dishes, like pheasant, lobster, and lamb. Especially noteworthy are the Highland venison filets with port jelly sauce, loin of saddle of venison with herb-and-port sauce, and local crayfish lightly grilled in garlic butter.

Breadalbane St. © 01631/564-849. Reservations recommended. Bar platters £7–£15 ($13–$29); fixed-price dinners in restaurant £15–£22 ($29–$42). AE, MC, V. June–Sept daily noon–2pm; year-round daily 5–10pm.

McTavish's Kitchens SCOTTISH   Like its cousin in Fort William, this place is overrun with visitors and it's the most popular—though not the best—restaurant in town. Downstairs is a self-service restaurant offering breakfast, lunch, dinner, and tea with shortbread and scones. Upstairs is Lairds Bar, and on the ground floor is McTavish's Bar, where meals are available all day. The licensed second-floor restaurant has a more ambitious Scottish and Continental menu with higher prices. Offerings include haggis, Loch Fyne kippers (oak-smoked herring), prime Scottish steaks, smoked salmon, venison, and local mussels. If you don't expect too much in the way of cuisine here, you won't be disappointed.

34 George St. © 01631/563-064. Main courses £9–£17 ($17–$32); budget 2-course lunch £7 ($13); fixed-price 3-course dinners £8–£18 ($15–$34). MC, V. Self-service restaurant daily 9am–9pm; licensed restaurant daily noon–2pm and 6–10:30pm.

OBAN AFTER DARK

Mid-May to the end of September, entertainment is provided at **McTavish's Kitchens** (see above), with Scottish music and Highland dancing by local artists nightly 8 to 10pm. Admission is £4.50 ($8.55) adults and £2 ($3.80) children. Reduced admission for diners is £2.50 ($4.75) adults and £1 ($1.90) children.

You can while away the evening with the locals at the **Oban Inn,** Stafford Street and the Esplanade (© **01631/562-484**), a popular pub with exposed beams and a flag-covered ceiling. Pints include McEwan's Export, Ale, and Gillespie's Stout. The pub is open daily 11am to 1am.

Another popular hangout is the town's Irish pub, **O'Donnells,** Breadalbane Street (© **01631/566-159**), where you can always expect a warm reception. It serves the ever-popular Guinness and a variety of Irish and Scottish malt whisky. Thursday to Saturday, entertainment is either a live band or a DJ. Over the busy summer, something is scheduled almost every night. Hours are daily 3pm to 1am.

Fife & the Central Highlands

The County of Fife still likes to call itself a kingdom. Even today, its name suggests the romantic episodes and pageantry during the reign of the early Stuart kings, and some 14 of Scotland's 66 royal burghs lie in this shire, which is north of the Firth of Forth from Edinburgh. You can visit many of the former royal palaces and castles, either restored or in colorful ruins.

Legendary **Loch Lomond** is the largest and most beautiful of the Scottish lakes. At Balloch, in the south, it's a Lowland landscape of gentle hills and islands. But as it moves north, the loch narrows and takes on a stark, dramatic Highland character, with moody cloud formations and rugged, steep hillsides.

The **Trossachs** is the collective name given to that wild Highland area east and northeast of Loch Lomond. Here you find Scotland's finest scenery—moor, mountain, and loch—which was immortalized by Sir Walter Scott's vivid passages in *The Lady of the Lake* and *Rob Roy*.

Many sections of this region lie on the doorsteps of Glasgow and Edinburgh; either city can be your gateway to the central Highlands. You can easily reach **Dunfermline** and **St. Andrews** by rail from Edinburgh. (St. Andrews also has good bus connections with Edinburgh.) By car, the main motorway is M9, the express highway that starts on the western outskirts of Edinburgh and is linked to M80 from Glasgow. M9 passes close to Stirling. M90, reached by crossing the Forth Road Bridge, will take you north into the Fife region. **Stirling** is the region's major rail center, with stops at such places as **Dunblane,** and much of Loch Lomond has rail connections. The towns and some villages have bus service, but you'll probably find the connections too limited or infrequent. For bus connections, Stirling is the central point.

Your best bet is to rent a car and discover—at your own pace—hidden towns, scenic loch-side roads, and quiet fishing villages.

1 Dunfermline ⚹ & Its Great Abbey

23km (14 miles) NW of Edinburgh, 63km (39 miles) NE of Glasgow, 84km (52 miles) SW of Dundee

The ancient town of Dunfermline was once the capital of Scotland and is easily reached by the Forth Road Bridge, opened by Elizabeth II in 1964. Scots called their former capital the "auld grey town," and it looms large in their history books. The city is still known for its **Dunfermline Abbey** and former royal palace (now largely gone). When Scotland reunited with England in 1603, the royal court departed to London, leaving Dunfermline to wither with only its memories. The town, however, recovered when it become the center of Scottish linen making, specializing in damask. But by World War I, the market had largely disappeared.

Some of the most interesting sights in Fife are within easy reach of Dunfermline, including the beautiful village of **Culross.** Dunfermline also makes the best base for exploring **Loch Leven** and **Loch Leven Castle.**

ESSENTIALS

GETTING THERE   Dunfermline is a stop along the main rail route from London via Edinburgh to Dundee, which means it has frequent connections to the Scottish capital. For rail schedules and fares, call ✆ **0870/608-2608.**

From its station at St. Andrews Square in Edinburgh, Scottish **Citylink** (✆ **0990/ 505-050**) operates frequent service to Dunfermline.

If you're driving from Edinburgh, take A90 west, cross the Forth Road Bridge, and follow the signs north to the center of Dunfermline.

VISITOR INFORMATION   A **tourist booth** is at 1 High St. (✆ **01383/720-999**). It's open Monday to Saturday 9:30am to 5pm.

EXPLORING THE AREA

Andrew Carnegie Birthplace Museum   In 1835, American industrialist and philanthropist Andrew Carnegie was born at a site about 182m (600 ft.) down the hill from the abbey. The museum comprises the 18th-century weaver's cottage in which he was born and a memorial hall provided by his wife. Displays tell the story of the weaver's son who emigrated to the United States, where he became one of the richest men in the world. From the fortune he made in steel, Carnegie gave away more than £244 million ($464 million) before his death in 1919. Dunfermline received the first of the 2,811 free libraries he provided throughout Britain and the States, and it also received public baths and Pittencrieff Park and Glen, rich in history and natural charm. A statue in the park honors Carnegie, who once worked as a bobbin boy in a cotton factory.

Moodie St. ✆ **01383/724-302.** Free admission. Apr–Oct Mon–Sat 11am–5pm, Sun 2–5pm. Closed Nov–Mar. In the City Centre, at the corner of Moodie St. and Priory Lane (10-min. walk from train station).

Dunfermline Abbey and Palace   The abbey is on the site of two earlier structures, a Celtic church and an 11th-century house of worship, founded by Queen Margaret (later St. Margaret) and dedicated to the Holy Trinity. Culdee Church, from the 5th and 6th centuries, was rebuilt in 1072. Traces of both buildings are visible beneath gratings in the floor of the old nave. In 1150, the church was replaced with a large abbey, the nave of which remains and is an example of Norman architecture. Later, St. Margaret's shrine, the northwest baptismal porch, the spire on the northwest tower, and the flying buttresses were added. While Dunfermline was the capital of Scotland, 22 royal personages were buried in the abbey. However, the only visible memorial or burial places known are those of Queen Margaret and King Robert the Bruce, whose tomb lies beneath the pulpit.

The once-royal palace of Dunfermline stands adjacent to the abbey. The palace witnessed the birth of Charles I and James I. The last king to reside here was Charles II, in 1651. Today, only the southwest wall remains of this formerly gargantuan edifice.

St. Margaret's St. (10-min. walk from train station.) ✆ **01383/739-026.** Admission £3.50 ($6.65) adults, £2.80 ($5.30) seniors, £1.75 ($3.35) children. Apr–Sept daily 9:30am–5:30pm; Oct–Mar daily 9:30am–4:30pm.

WHERE TO STAY

Best Western Keavil House Hotel   This tranquil country hotel, only a 30-minute drive from Edinburgh, is on 4.8 hectares (12 acres) of forested land and gardens

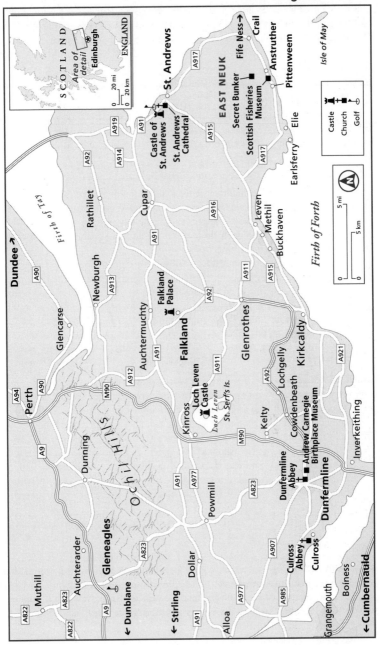

The Kingdom of Fife

and offers lots of leisure facilities. The bedrooms are generous in size and well appointed, each with such amenities as a writing desk and midsize bathrooms (some with tubs). Master bedrooms contain four-poster beds. The hotel offers fine, formal dining in its Cardoon restaurant (see "Where to Dine," below) and less formal food in its Armoury Alehouse & Grill.

Main St., Crossford, Dunfermline, Fife KY12 8QW. © **800/780-7234** or 01383/736-258. Fax 01383/621-600. www. keavilhouse.co.uk. 47 units. £80–£160 ($152–$304) double; £90–£160 ($171–$304) family suite. AE, DC, MC, V. Closed Dec 31–Jan 1. Free parking. Take A994, 3.2km (2 miles) west of Dunfermline; the hotel is off the main street at the west end of village. **Amenities:** 2 restaurants; bar; indoor heated pool; health club; Jacuzzi; sauna; room service; babysitting; laundry service; steam room; nonsmoking rooms; rooms for those w/limited mobility. *In room:* TV, coffeemaker, hair dryer, iron, trouser press, Wi-Fi.

Davaar House Hotel and Restaurant   This large Georgian-style house, in a residential neighborhood a 5-minute walk west of the town center, was built late in the 19th century and boasts distinctive architectural features like a sweeping oak staircase, elaborate moldings, and marble mantelpieces. The largest guest rooms, with the loftiest ceilings, are one floor above street level; slightly less grand rooms are two floors above street level. Each is uniquely decorated in traditional Scottish style. Some of the bathrooms contain a shower only.

The restaurant here is recommended; it's open for dinner Monday through Saturday. Look for moderate prices and home-style cooking from a talented team, with dishes like chicken suprême filled with smoked salmon; lamb, marinated in rosemary and garlic, roasted with red currant sauce; and scallops, prawns, and cod in a phyllo basket with white-wine sauce. Prices range from £9.50 to £18 ($18–$34).

126 Grieve St., Dunfermline, Fife KY12 8DW. © **01383/721-886.** Fax 01383/623-633. www.davaar-house-hotel.com. 10 units. £70–£80 ($133–$152) double. Rates include breakfast. MC, V. Closed Dec 23–Jan 13. Free parking. **Amenities:** Restaurant; bar; room service; laundry service; nonsmoking rooms. *In room:* TV, coffeemaker, hair dryer (in some).

Garvock House ★ *Finds*   Standing in a woodland setting, this was once the private home of a prosperous Victorian family. One family owned the house for a century, but in 1996 it was converted to a small hotel, with many of the original architectural features intact. The public rooms are in the classically decorated main house, with the modish accommodations in a contemporary annex. Each bedroom comes with a sleek modern bathroom with shower. The hotel, even though small, offers a full restaurant menu with sophisticated and good-tasting dishes, including the likes of a filet of sea bass with a crab blini as well as a prawn and mussel ragout. Desserts are exceptional here, including toasted coconut mascarpone cheesecake with caramelized pineapple.

St. John's Dr., Transy, Dunfermline KY12 7TU. © **01383/621-067.** Fax 01383/621-168. www.garvock.co.uk. 26 units. £125 ($238) double; £140 ($266) suite. Rates include breakfast. AE, MC, V. **Amenities:** Restaurant. *In room:* TV, hair dryer, iron, trouser press.

King Malcolm Hotel   A suitable choice for either a meal or a bed is this modern, pastel-colored hotel on a roundabout 1.6km (1 mile) south of Dunfermline (via A823). Named after the medieval king of Fife (and later of Scotland), Malcolm Canmore, it was built in 1972 but has been thoroughly revamped since then. The guest rooms are well furnished though rather standardized.

Richmond's, a glass-sided bar and restaurant, offers Scottish and Continental cuisine at dinner daily.

Queensferry Rd., Dunfermline, Fife KY11 5DS. ℰ **01383/722-611.** Fax 01383/730-865. www.peelhotels.co.uk. 48 units. £120–£135 ($228–$257) double. Children under 14 stay free in parent's room. AE, DC, MC, V. Free parking. Bus: D3 or D4. **Amenities:** Restaurant; 2 bars; room service; laundry service; dry cleaning. *In room:* TV, coffeemaker, hair dryer, trouser press.

WHERE TO DINE

Cardoon MODERN SCOTTISH   Some of the best local produce is used deftly here to create true "taste of Scotland" specialties—and that means the best of Scottish beef, locally caught game, and fish from local rivers. Old-time recipes are given a modern twist by the chef. The imaginative dishes are served with flair and originality, appealing to both traditionalists and those with more adventurous tastes. Try the canon of lamb with Arran mustard, pine-kernel crust, and minted baby-pear soufflé potato; smoked salmon and prawns with salad and Arran mustard dressing; or a real local specialty, a chanterelle and "tattie" scone pocket with a malt vinegar demi-glaze. End with dessert of caramelized heather honey and apple parfait. There's an extensive and well-chosen wine list.

In the Best Western Keavil House Hotel, Main St., Crossford. ℰ **800/780-7234** or 01383/736-258. Reservations recommended. Fixed-price 3-course menu £25 ($48), 2-course menu £20 ($38). AE, DC, MC, V. Daily noon–2pm and 7–9:30pm. Closed Dec 31–Jan 1.

SIDE TRIPS FROM DUNFERMLINE: CULROSS & LOCH LEVEN

Culross 𝕽𝕽𝕽, 10km (6 miles) west of Dunfermline, has been renovated by the Scottish National Trust and is one of the country's most beautiful burghs. As you walk its cobblestone streets—admiring the whitewashed houses with their crow-stepped gables and red pantiled roofs—you feel as if you're taking a stroll back into the 17th century.

Set in tranquil walled gardens in the village center, **Culross Palace** 𝕽𝕽 (ℰ **0844/493-2189**) was built between 1597 and 1611 for prosperous merchant George Bruce. It contains a most beautiful series of paintings portraying moral scenes that illustrate principles like "Honor your parents" and "The spoken word cannot be retracted." During a National Trust restoration, from 1991 to 1994, archaeologists uncovered the remains of a foundation of a long-forgotten building on the east end of the courtyard and the original doorway; there are plans to restore it for use as the public entrance. The palace is open March 31 to May 31 Thursday to Monday from noon to 5pm, June 1 to August 31 daily from noon to 5pm, September Thursday to Monday from noon to 5pm, and October Thursday to Monday from noon to 4pm. The town house and study are open Saturday and Sunday from noon to 4pm. From November to Easter, visits to Culross Palace are by appointment only. Admission is £8 ($15) for adults, £5 ($9.50) for seniors and students, free for those under 19, and £20 ($38) per family.

The other important attraction is 10km (6 miles) southwest of Dunfermline (take A994, following the signs to Culross): **Culross Abbey,** a Cistercian monastery founded by Malcolm, earl of Fife, in 1217. Parts of the nave are still intact, and the choir serves as the Culross parish church. There's also a central tower. From Easter Saturday to the last Saturday in August, the abbey is open daily from 9am to 7pm; at other times, you can visit by prior arrangement with the Church of Scotland (ℰ **01383/880-231**).

Loch Leven 𝕽, 19km (12 miles) north of Dunfermline and 16km (10 miles) south of Falkland via A911, contains seven islands. On **St. Serf's,** the largest of the islands, are the ruins of the Priory of Loch Leven, built on the site of one of the oldest Culdee establishments in Scotland. If you're interested in seeing the ruins, contact the Kinross tourist office at © **01577/863-359.** You'll be put in touch with one of the fishermen who make boat trips to the island.

In **Kinross,** 40km (25 miles) north of Edinburgh, you can take the ferry over to Castle Island to see the ruins of **Loch Leven Castle** (© **07778/040-483**). "Those never got luck who came to Loch Leven"—this saying sums up the history of the Douglas fortress dating from the late 14th century. Among its ill-fated prisoners, none was more notable than Mary Queen of Scots; inside its forbidding walls, she signed her abdication on July 24, 1567, but she escaped from Loch Leven on May 2, 1568. Thomas Percy, seventh earl of Northumberland, supported her cause and "lodged" in the castle for 3 years until he was handed over to the English, who beheaded him at York. Today, you can see a 14th-century tower house and a 16th-century curtain wall, all that remain of a castle that loomed large in Scottish history. The castle is open from March 25 to September 30 daily 9:30am to 5:30pm. Admission is £4.50 ($8.55) for adults, £3.50 ($6.65) for seniors, and £2.25 ($4.30) for children. The admission includes the cost of a round-trip ferry from Kinross to Castle Island.

WHERE TO STAY & DINE
Dunclutha Guest House   A 3-minute walk northeast of the town center is this dignified stone house, which was built around 1890 for the priest at the adjacent Episcopal church. Today, it's the domain of Mrs. Pam McDonald, who infuses lots of personalized hominess into her hotel. The spacious guest rooms are clean, well maintained, and (in most cases) sunny, thanks to big windows with garden views. Breakfast is served in the refulgent breakfast room, which adjoins a lounge containing games and a piano.

16 Victoria Rd., Leven, Fife KY8 4EX. © **01333/425-515.** Fax 01333/422-311. www.dunclutha.mtby.co.uk. 4 units. £50–£60 ($95–$114) double. Rates include breakfast. AE, MC, V. Free parking. **Amenities:** Nonsmoking rooms. *In room:* TV, coffeemaker, no phone.

2 East Neuk's Scenic Fishing Villages ✶✶

Within half an hour's drive south of St. Andrews, on the eastward-facing peninsula incorporating St. Andrews and Anstruther, is the district of East Neuk, dotted with some of eastern Scotland's most scenic and unspoiled fishing villages. You can't reach these villages by rail; the nearest stations are Ladybank, Cupar, and Leuchars, on the main London-Edinburgh-Dundee-Aberdeen line serving northeast Fife. Buses from St. Andrews connect the villages, but you'll really want to have your own car here.

If the weather's right, you can cycle among the villages along some of the most delightful back roads in Fife. Rent a bike at **East Neuk Outdoors,** Cellardyke Park in Anstruther (© **01333/311-929**). This same outfitter can also fix you up for a canoe trip.

PITTENWEEM
If you're at Pittenweem Monday through Saturday morning, try to get caught up in the action at the **fish auction** held under a large shed. The actual time depends on the tides. Afterward, go for a walk through the village and admire the sturdy stone homes, some of which have been preserved by Scotland's National Trust.

The *weem* in the name of the town means "cave," a reference to **St. Fillan's Cave** (© **01333/311-495**), at Cove Wynd in the vicinity of the harbor. This cave is said to contain the shrine of St. Fillan, a hermit who lived in the 6th century. Hours are daily 10am to 5pm; admission is £1 ($1.90), free for children under 15 years old.

The best way to reach **Anstruther** (see below) is to hike the 2.5km (1½ miles) over to it, because the road isn't paved. If the day is clear, this is one of the loveliest walks in eastern Scotland. From Pittenweem, follow a signpost directing you to Anstruther; you cross Scottish meadows and can say hello to a few lambs. You can also take the walk in reverse, as most visitors do. In Anstruther, the path begins at the bottom of West Brases, a small cul-de-sac off the main road in the village.

WHERE TO STAY

The Pittenweem Harbour Guest House   Set directly on the harbor, this charming stone building was erected around 1910 as a private home. The guest rooms contain pinewood furniture and comfortable twin beds, each a cozy, no-frills refuge from the chilly winds and crashing seas. Each unit contains a small, shower-only bathroom. Because it's run by a local company and not by a family, Harbour is a bit more businesslike than a conventional B&B; in fact, it feels like a fishing lodge—if you ask, the staff will direct you to local entrepreneurs who can take you out for a half-day's fishing, or they'll point out spots on the nearby piers and boardwalks where a rod and reel might attract fish.

14 Mid Shore, Pittenweem, Fife KY10 2NL. © **01333/311-273.** Fax 01333/310-014. www.pittenweem.com. 4 units. £42–£60 ($80–$114) double. Rates include breakfast. AE, DC, MC, V. **Amenities:** Nonsmoking rooms. *In room:* TV, coffeemaker, hair dryer.

ANSTRUTHER

Once an important herring-fishing port, Anstruther is now a summer resort, 74km (46 miles) northeast of Edinburgh, 55km (34 miles) east of Dunfermline, 6.5km (4 miles) southwest of Crail, and 37km (23 miles) south of Dundee. The **tourist office** is on High Street (© **01333/311-073**); it's open April to September, Monday, Friday, and Saturday from 10am to 5pm; Tuesday to Thursday 10am to 1pm and 2 to 5pm; and Sunday 11am to 4pm.

The beaches are too chilly for swimming, but they're great for a brisk, scenic walk. The best nearby is **Billow Ness Beach,** a 10-minute walk east of the center.

The **Scottish Fisheries Museum,** St. Ayles, Harbourhead (© **01333/310-628;** bus: 95), is down by the harbor. It was expanded in 1999 to include a building that was a tavern in the 18th century, as well as several re-creations of restored fishing boats. Here you can follow the fisherfolk through every aspect of their industry—from the days of sail to modern times. Associated with the museum, but afloat in the harbor, is an old herring drifter, *The Reaper,* which you can board. April to September, the museum is open Monday to Saturday 10am to 5:30pm and Sunday 11am to 5pm; October to March, hours are Monday to Saturday 10am to 4:30pm and Sunday from noon to 4:30pm. Admission is £5 ($9.50) adults, £4 ($7.60) seniors and children. Last admission one hour before closing time.

From the museum, you can walk to the tiny hamlet of **Cellardyke,** adjoining Anstruther. You'll find many charming stone houses and an ancient harbor where in the year Victoria took the throne (1837), 140 vessels used to put out to sea. You can rent a bike from **East Neuk Outdoors,** Cellardyke Park (© **01333/311-929;** www. eastneukoutdoors.co.uk), where rental rates are £15 ($29) daily and £37 to £54 ($70–$103) weekly, plus a deposit. It's open daily April to September from 9am to 5pm, open by appointment only in winter.

The **Isle of May** , a nature reserve in the Firth of Forth, is accessible by boat from Anstruther. It's a bird observatory and a field station and contains the ruins of a 12th-century chapel as well as an early-19th-century lighthouse.

The **May Princess** (℃ **01333/310-103** or -054; www.isleofmayferry.com) is a 100-passenger boat that departs for the Isle of May from the Lifeboat Station at Anstruther Harbour every day, weather permitting, between April and September. One hour before departure, tickets go on sale from a kiosk beside Anstruther Harbour. The cost is £16 ($30) for adults, £14 ($27) for seniors and students, and £8 ($15) for children 3 to 14. Departure times vary with the season, the day of the week, and the vagaries of the weather, so call in advance before planning for the 4- to 5-hour trip. Between May and July, expect to see hundreds, even thousands, of puffins, which mate on the Isle of May at that time. Credit cards are not accepted.

WHERE TO STAY

Craw's Nest Hotel   This black-and-white step-gabled Scottish manse is a popular hotel, with views over the Firth of Forth and May Island. The midsize guest rooms are handsomely appointed, each with a tub/shower combination. Some of the rooms contain four-posters. The public areas, including both a lounge bar and a bustling public bar, are simply decorated and cozy. The food in the dining room and the wine are reasonably priced.

Bankwell Rd., Anstruther, Fife KY10 3DA. ℃ **01333/310-691.** Fax 01333/312-216. www.crawsnesthotel.co.uk. 50 units. £100–£130 ($190–$247) double; £150 ($285) suite. Rates include Scottish breakfast. AE, DC, MC, V. Bus: 915. **Amenities:** Restaurant; 2 bars; room service; laundry service; dry cleaning; nonsmoking rooms; rooms for those w/limited mobility. *In room:* TV, coffeemaker, hair dryer, trouser press.

Smuggler's Inn   With low ceilings, uneven floors, and winding stairs, this warmly inviting inn evokes memories of smuggling days. An inn has stood on this spot since 1300, and in Queen Anne's time it was a well-known tavern. The guest rooms are comfortably furnished; some bathrooms contain a shower only. The restaurant serves moderately priced regional cuisine at dinner nightly. Try the fish and chips for a real treat. Affordable bar lunches are also available.

High St., East Anstruther, Fife KY10 3DQ. ℃ **01333/310-506.** Fax 01333/312-706. 9 units. £60–£85 ($114–$162) double. Rates include Scottish breakfast. MC, V. Bus: 95. **Amenities:** Restaurant; bar; laundry. *In room:* TV, coffeemaker, hair dryer.

WHERE TO DINE

The Cellar SEAFOOD   This seafood restaurant is the best in town. Its walls were part of a cellar that dates from the 19th century—or possibly earlier. Candles provide the light, and, in winter, so do the fireplaces at opposite ends of the room. The menu offers fresh fish, caught in nearby waters and prepared with light sauces. The best examples are grilled halibut suprême dredged in bread crumbs and citrus juices and served with hollandaise sauce; lobster, monkfish, and scallops roasted with herb-and-garlic butter and served on sweet-pepper risotto; and a limited array of meat dishes.

24 East Green, Anstruther. ℃ **01333/310-378.** Reservations recommended. Fixed-price dinner 2 courses £29 ($54), 3 courses £30 ($56), 4 courses £39 ($73); fixed-price lunch 2 courses £18 ($33), 3 courses £22 ($41). AE, DC, MC, V. Wed–Sun noon–1:30pm; Tues–Sat 7–9:30pm. Bus: 95.

Haven SCOTTISH   Set within a pair of interconnected 300-year-old fishermen's cottages, this is the only restaurant directly on the harbor of Anstruther. Defining itself as a restaurant with a cocktail lounge (not a pub), it serves simple, wholesome food that's flavorful and utterly unpretentious: pan-fried breaded prawns, halibut filets, Angus steaks, local crabmeat salad, and homemade soups and stews. The upper floor contains one of the town's most popular bars, where the same menu is served. The street level, more formal and sedate, is the site of high teas and evening meals.

1 Shore Rd., Cellardyke, Anstruther. © **01333/310-574**. Reservations recommended. Main courses £8–£14 ($15–$27); high teas (tea, toast, and a meal-size platter of food) £6–£9 ($11–$17). MC, V. Mon–Fri noon–2:30pm and 5:30–9pm; Sat noon–3pm and 5:30–9pm; Sun noon–11pm. Bus: 95; a James Anderson & Co. bus runs every hour from St. Andrews, 13km (8 miles) south, to the door of the restaurant.

AFTER DARK

Dreel Tavern ✦, 16 High St. (© **01333/310-727**), was a 16th-century coaching inn and is now a wood-and-stone pub where locals gather to unwind in the evening. Carlsberg-Tetley, Harviestown Bitters Twisted, London Pride, and Speckled Hen are available on hand pump, along with two guest beers that change weekly. The tavern also serves steak pie, roast beef and Yorkshire pudding, smoked fish, and local crab. It's open Monday to Saturday 11am to midnight and Sunday noon to 11pm.

ELIE ✦

With its step-gabled houses and little harbor, Elie, 18km (11 miles) south of Anstruther, is many visitors' favorite village along the coast. Only a 25-minute car ride from Edinburgh, Elie and its close neighbor, Earlsferry, overlook a crescent of gold-sand beach, with more swimming possibilities to be found among sheltered coves. The name Elie is believed to come from the *ailie* (island) of Ardross, which now forms part of the harbor and is joined to the mainland by a road. A large stone building, a former granary, at the harbor is a reminder of the days when Elie was a busy trading port. Of all the villages of East Neuk, this one seems best suited for walks and hikes in all directions.

Earlsferry, to the west, got its name from an ancient ferry crossing, which Macduff, the thane of Fife, is supposed to have used in his escape from Macbeth.

East of the harbor stands a stone structure known as the **Lady's Tower,** used by Lady Janet Anstruther, a noted 18th-century beauty, as a bathing cabana. Another member of the Anstruther family, Sir John, added the interesting **bell tower** to the parish church that stands in the center of the village.

Beyond the lighthouse, on a point of land to the east of the harbor, lies **Ruby Bay,** so named because you can find garnets here. Farther along the coast is **Fossil Bay,** where you can find a variety of fossils.

WHERE TO STAY

The Elms Guest House 𝘝𝘢𝘭𝘶𝘦 𝘒𝘪𝘥𝘴   This 1880 building is on the wide main street behind a conservative stone facade, with a crescent-shaped rose garden in front. The comfortably furnished but small guest rooms contain good beds, washbasins, and showers. There's also a self-catering cottage available for rent that can sleep six comfortably. Home cooking is a specialty of the place, and dishes include Scottish lamb, Pittenweem haddock, haggis, and Arbroath kippers. A simple dinner is available to nonguests. In the walled flower garden behind the house is a large conservatory for guests' use.

14 Park Place, Elie, Fife KY9 1DH. ©/fax **01333/330-404**. www.elms-elie.co.uk. 8 units. £40–£60 ($76–$114) double; cottage £110 ($209). Rates include Scottish breakfast. MC, V. Closed Nov–Mar. **Amenities:** Nonsmoking rooms. *In room:* TV, coffeemaker, hair dryer.

Rockview Guest House *(Kids* Next to the Ship Inn (see below), the Rockview over-looks fine sandy beaches around Elie Bay. The small guest rooms are nicely furnished, each with a good bed and shower-only bathroom. Maintenance is top-notch, and the welcome is warm. A twin-bedded room has a bunk bed for younger children to share with their parents. Food and drink are available at the Ship Inn.

The Toft, Elie, Fife KY9 1DT. ℂ **01333/330-246.** Fax 01333/330-864. www.ship-elie.com. 5 units. £80 ($152) double. Rates include breakfast. MC, V. **Amenities:** Nonsmoking rooms. *In room:* TV, coffeemaker.

WHERE TO DINE

Ship Inn ⋇ SCOTTISH Even if you're not stopping over in Elie, we suggest you drop in at the Ship (from the center, follow the signs marked HARBOUR) and enjoy a pint of lager or real ale or a whisky from the large selection. The building occupied by this pub dates from 1778, and a bar has been in business here since 1830. In summer, you can sit outdoors and look over the water; in colder months, a fireplace burns brightly. On Sundays, May to September, a barbecue operates outside. The set menu with daily specials features such items as steak pie, Angus beefsteaks, and an abundance of fresh seafood.

The Toft. ℂ **01333/330-246.** Main courses £9–£17 ($17–$32). MC, V. Mon–Thurs noon–2pm and 6–9pm; Fri noon–2pm and 6pm–1am; Sat noon–2:30pm and 6pm–1am; Sun 12:30–3pm.

CRAIL ⋇⋇

The pearl of the East Neuk of Fife, Crail is 81km (50 miles) northeast of Edinburgh, 37km (23 miles) south of Dundee, and 15km (9 miles) south of St. Andrews. It's an artists' colony, and many painters live in cottages around the little harbor. Natural bathing facilities are at Roome Bay, and many **beaches** are nearby. The **Balcomie Golf Course** is one of the oldest in the world and is still in good condition.

The old town grew up along the harbor, and you can still see a lot of fishing cottages clustered here. Crab and lobster boats continue to set out hoping for a big catch. **Upper Crail** overlooks the harbor and also merits exploration. The **tollbooth** dates from 1598 and is crowned by a belfry. **Marketgate** is lined with trees and flanked by small two- and three-floor houses. Follow the walkway to **Castle Walk,** which offers the most panoramic view of Crail.

To understand the villages of East Neuk better, visit the **Crail Museum & Heritage Centre,** 62 Marketgate (ℂ **01333/450-869**), which contains artifacts related to fishing and the former trading links of these tiny villages. Admission is free. June to September the center is open Monday to Saturday from 10am to 1pm and 2 to 5pm and Sunday from 2 to 5pm; Easter week Monday to Saturday 10am to 1pm and 2 to 5pm; April 1 to May 2 weekends 2 to 5pm.

WHERE TO STAY

Denburn House *(Kids* Near the town center, in a historic neighborhood known as Marketgate, this guesthouse occupies a 200-year-old stone building that retains many of its interior architectural features, including the paneling in the lounge and an elaborate staircase. All the guest rooms are decorated in a conservative but very pleasing style, each with a shower-only bathroom. A summer only self-catering apartment out back comes complete with three spacious bedrooms (two twins and a king-size) plus a shower-only bathroom, a kitchen, and a combined dining room and lounge. The rear garden offers a scattering of lawn furniture and access to the great Scottish outdoors. Everything is very low-key and unpretentious.

1 Marketgate North, Crail, Fife KY10 3TQ. ⓒ **01333/450-253.** Fax: 01333/312-288. www.denburnhouse.com. 6 units. £50–£60 ($95–$114) double; June–Sept £90 ($171) apt. Rates include breakfast. AE, MC, V. Free parking. **Amenities:** Laundry service; nonsmoking rooms. *In room:* TV, coffeemaker, hair dryer.

3 St. Andrews: The Birthplace of Golf (★(★

23km (14 miles) SE of Dundee, 82km (51 miles) NE of Edinburgh

The medieval royal burgh of St. Andrews was once filled with monasteries and ancient houses that didn't survive the pillages of Henry VIII; regrettably, only a few ruins, rising in ghostly dignity, remain. Most of the town was built of local stone during the 18th, 19th, and early 20th centuries. This is the place where the rules of golf are codified and arbitrated. The sport was played for the first time in the 1400s, probably on the site of St. Andrews's Old Course, and was enjoyed here by Mary Queen of Scots in 1567. Golfers consider this town to be hallowed ground.

ESSENTIALS

GETTING THERE   **BritRail** stops 13km (8 miles) away, at the town of Leuchars (rhymes with "euchres"), on its London-Edinburgh-Dundee-Aberdeen run to the northeast. About 28 trains per day make the trip, which from Edinburgh to Leuchars is about an hour; a one-way fare is £10 ($19). For information, call ⓒ **08457/484-950.**

Once at Leuchars, you can take a bus the rest of the way to St. Andrews. Bus no. 99 departs about every 20 minutes. Fife Scottish bus no. X24 travels from Glasgow to Glenrothes daily, and from there to St. Andrews. Buses operate daily 7am to midnight, and the trip takes between 2½ and 3 hours. Buses arrive at the St. Andrews Bus Station, Station Road, just off City Road (call ⓒ **01334/474-238** for schedules).

By car from Edinburgh, head northwest along A90 and cross the Forth Road Bridge. Take A921 to the junction with A915 and continue northeast until you reach St. Andrews.

VISITOR INFORMATION   The **tourist office** is on 70 Market St. (ⓒ **01334/ 472-021;** www.standrews.com). January to March, as well as November and December, it's open Monday to Saturday 9:30am to 5pm; April hours are Monday to Saturday 9:30am to 5pm and Sunday 11am to 4pm; May, June, September, and October, hours are Monday to Saturday 9:30am to 6pm and Sunday 11am to 4pm; and July and August, hours are Monday to Saturday 9:30am to 7pm and Sunday 10am to 6pm.

HITTING THE LINKS

All six of the St. Andrews courses are fully owned by the municipality and open to the public on a more or less democratic basis—ballots are polled 1 day in advance. This balloting system might be circumvented for players who reserve with the appropriate starters several days or weeks in advance. To play the hallowed Old Course, you must present a current handicap certificate and/or a letter of introduction from a bona fide golf club.

The misty and verdant golf courses are the very symbol of St. Andrews: the famous **Old Course;** the 6,566-yard, par-72 **New Course** (opened in 1896); the 6,805-yard, par-71 **Jubilee Course** (opened in 1897 in honor of Queen Victoria); the 6,112-yard, par-70 **Eden** (opened in 1914); the **Balgove** (a 9-hole course for children's golf training, opened in 1972); and the 5,094-yard, par-67 **Strathtyrum** (the newest and most far-flung, an 8-hole course opened in 1993). Encircled by all of them is the world's most prestigious golf club, the **Royal and Ancient Golf Club** (ⓒ **01334/472-112**), founded in St. Andrews in 1754—it remains more or less rigidly closed as a private-membership men's club. It traditionally opens its doors to the public only on St. Andrews Day so that non-members may view the legendary trophy room. This usually, but not always, falls around November 30.

The **Old Course,** Pilmour Cottage (© **01334/466-666**), is the world's legendary temple of golf, one whose difficulty is shaped by nature and the long-ago paths of grazing sheep. Over the centuries, stately buildings have been erected near its start and finish. Aristocrats from virtually everywhere have lent their names and reputations to enhance the course's glamour, and its nuances have been debated, usually in reverent tones, by golfers in bars and on fairways throughout the world. This fabled par-72 course hosted the 2000 British Open, when golf fans from around the world watched Tiger Woods become the youngest golfer ever to complete a grand slam (and only the fifth golfer ever to perform the feat). Greens fees are £88 to £125 ($167–$238), a caddy costs £50 ($95) plus tip, and clubs rent for £30 to £35 ($57–$67) per round. There are no electric carts allowed, and you can rent a trolley on afternoons only between May and September for £3 ($5.70).

Virtually every hotel in town maintains some kind of facility to assist golfers. The most interesting clubhouse is **The Links Clubhouse,** West Sand Road (© **01334/466-666**). Owned and operated by the St. Andrews Links Trust, and located within 400 yards of the Old Course's 18th hole, it offers, without charge, lockers, showers, and changing facilities. On-site, there's also a bar and restaurant.

Two Californians, Mark Parsinen and Art Dunkley, have invaded the capital of golf and opened a new championship-ready links, **Kingsbarns Golf Links** (© **01334/460-860**). (The land and adjoining North Sea beachfront were utilized as a rehearsal ground during the build-up for the D-day invasion of Normandy in June 1944.) During some of the uprooting of the earth, a 3,000-year-old mummy was discovered. The course is challenging and beautiful, with sometimes blustery winds blowing off the North Sea. "Tighten your kilts, laddies," a woman caddy, Emily Thompson, sometimes tells players facing the course, which plays to a yardage of 7,126.

For more details on golf associations and golf tours, see "Teeing Off: Golfing in Scotland," in chapter 3.

EXPLORING THE AREA

Founded in 1411, the **University of St. Andrews** is the oldest in Scotland and the third oldest in Britain; it's been called the "Oxbridge" of Scotland. At term time, you can see packs of students in their red gowns. The university grounds stretch west of the St. Andrews Castle between North Street and the Scores.

The university's best buildings are the tower and church of St. Salvator's College and the courtyard of St. Mary's College, from 1538. An ancient thorn tree, said to have been planted by Mary Queen of Scots, stands near the college's chapel. St. Leonard's College church is also from medieval days. In 1645, the Scottish Parliament met in what was once the University Library and is now a students' reading room. A modern library, containing many rare volumes, opened in 1976. Its most famous graduate in modern times was Prince William who left with his degree in June of 2005. His graduation was watched by his grandmother, Queen Elizabeth II, and his father, Prince Charles. When William departed, so did the paparazzi who had been hanging out in St. Andrews hoping to get photographs of "Diana's son" and the future heir to the British throne.

Castle of St. Andrews   This ruined 13th-century castle, eerily poised at the edge of the sea, boasts a bottle dungeon and secret passages. Reconstructed several times, it was once a bishop's palace and later a prison for reformers. The bottle dungeon is carved 7m (24 ft.) down into the rock, and both prisoners and food were dropped through it. There's said to be no nastier dungeon in all Scotland.

Much of the eeriness stems from the 1546 arrest of religious reformer George Wishart and the show trial that followed. Convicted by a group of Catholic prelates spearheaded by Cardinal Beaton, Wishart was burned at the stake, reputedly while Beaton and his entourage watched from an upper-floor window. Vowing revenge, a group of reformers waited 3 months before gaining access to the castle while disguised as stonemasons. They overpowered the guards (some they killed, some they threw into the castle moat) and murdered Beaton—although, rather bizarrely, they preserved his corpse in salt so they could eventually give it a proper burial. The reformers retained control of the castle for several months, until the Catholic forces of the earl of Arran laid siege. As part of their efforts, the attackers almost completed a tunnel (they called it "a mine"), dug virtually through rock, beneath the castle walls. The (Protestant) defenders, in response, dug a tunnel ("a countermine") of their own, which intersected the first tunnel at a higher elevation, allowing the defenders to drop rocks, boiling oil, or whatever else on the attackers' heads. The resulting underground battle took on epic proportions during the virtually implacable year-long siege. As part of the tour, you can stumble down the narrow countermine to the place where besieged and besiegers met in this clash.

The Scores (273m/900 ft. northwest of the cathedral). (℃) **01334/477-196.** Combined tickets (castle and cathedral) £7 ($13) adults, £5 ($9.50) seniors, £3.50 ($6.65) children. Apr–Sept daily 9:30am–5:30pm; Oct–Mar daily 9:30am–4:30pm. Last admission 30 min. before closing time.

Holy Trinity Church   Called the Town Kirk, this restored medieval church once stood on the grounds of the now-ruined cathedral (see below). The church was moved to its present site in 1410, considerably altered after the Reformation of 1560, and restored in the early 20th century. Fine stained glass and carvings are inside.

Opposite St. Mary's College, off South St. (℃) **01334/478-817.** Free admission, but call in advance to make sure someone is in attendance. Sat 10am–noon.

St. Andrews Cathedral and Priory   Near the Celtic settlement of St. Mary of the Rock, by the sea at the east end of town, is the semi-ruin of St. Andrews Cathedral and Priory. It was founded in 1160 and begun in the Romanesque style; the construction, however, suffered many setbacks. By the time of its consecration in 1318 in the presence of King Robert the Bruce, it had a Gothic overlay. At the time the largest church in Scotland, the cathedral established St. Andrews as the ecclesiastical capital of the country, but today the ruins only suggest its former beauty and importance. There's a collection of early Christian and medieval monuments, as well as artifacts discovered on the cathedral site.

Off Pends Rd. (℃) **01334/472-563.** Admission museum and St. Rules Tower £4 ($7.60) adults, £3 ($5.70) seniors, £2 ($3.80) children ages 5–15. Combined ticket with St. Andrews Castle £7 ($13) adults, £5 ($9.50) seniors, £3.50 ($6.65) children ages 5–15. Apr–Sept daily 9:30am–5:30pm; Oct–Mar daily 9:30am–4:30pm.

Secret Bunker   Scotland's best-kept secret during 40 years of the Cold War, this amazing labyrinth, built 30m (100 ft.) below ground and encased in 4.5m (15 ft.) of reinforced concrete, is where government and military officials would have run the country if the United Kingdom had been involved in a nuclear conflict. It has a guard-house entrance designed to look like a traditional Scottish farmhouse. You can visit the BBC studio, where emergency broadcasts would have been made, and the switchboard room, set up to handle 2,800 phone lines. The bunker could allow 300 people to live, work, and sleep in safety while coordinating war efforts. It now contains two cinemas showing authentic Cold War films, an audiovisual theater, a cafe, and a gift shop.

You can wander freely through the underground labyrinth, but 30-minute guided tours depart daily at 11am, 1pm, and 3pm. For some amazing reason, since the bunker was decommissioned in 1993, the chapel has been the site of several local weddings.

Underground Nuclear Command Centre, Crown Buildings (near St. Andrews), Fife. © **01333/310-301.** Admission £8 ($15) adults, £6.50 ($12) seniors, £5 ($9.50) children ages 5–16, £23 ($44) families, free for children age 4 and under. Apr–Oct daily 10am–5pm. From St. Andrews, follow the signs to Anstruther, driving 12km (7½ miles) south. At that point, signs show to the bunker.

SHOPPING

Specializing in Scottish art, **St. Andrews Fine Arts,** 84A Market St. (© **01334/474-080**), also sells prints, drawings, and watercolors. All paintings were produced within the national boundaries of Scotland sometime between 1800 and the present. **Renton Oriental Rugs,** 72 South St. (© **01334/476-334**), is one of Scotland's leading dealers of Oriental carpets. Antique rugs or reasonably priced reproductions come in many sizes, prices, and styles. At **St. Andrews Pottery Shop,** 4 Church Sq. (© **01334/850-859**), an array of decorative stoneware, ceramics, and enameled jewelry—most of it produced locally—is for sale. **Bonkers,** 80 Market St. (© **01334/473-919**), is a typical tourist shop, selling T-shirts, regional pottery, and other souvenirs, along with cards and stationery.

WHERE TO STAY
EXPENSIVE

Cambo Estate   In the middle of a 485-hectare (1,200-acre) property sits this Victorian mansion, home of the Erskine family since 1681. The historic building was erected in 1881 and turned into a hotel in the 1990s. The rooms are midsize to spacious, and each has a private bathroom with tub or shower. Depending on which unit you stay in, you can enjoy views of the beautiful property, which includes gardens, a tennis lawn, woods, parkland, and an outdoor playhouse. There is a laundry room, a game room, a sauna, and a barbeque. Be warned, however, that only 7 out of the 11 rooms include heat and electricity. Two of the other four rooms have free electricity, but only include heat out of peak season. The remaining two rooms use a pay-as-you-go meter, called a pound coin meter, to get electricity and heat.

Kingsbarns, St. Andrews, Fife. © **01333/450-054.** Fax 01333/450-987. www.camboestate.com. 11 units. £165–£330 ($314–$627) 1 bedroom; £185–£400 ($352–$760) 2 bedroom; £245–£375 ($466–$713) 3 bedroom. MC, V. **Amenities:** Dining room; sauna; game room; babysitting; laundry services; nonsmoking rooms. *In room:* TV, kitchen (in some), fridge (in some).

Fairmont St. Andrews Bay Golf Resort & Spa ✿✿✿   At last Eastern Scotland has a premier, government-rated five-star hotel. It's perched on a cliff overlooking the North Sea and the River Tay. The hotel and its two championship golf courses sit on 210 hectares (520 acres). The sprawling resort complex, opened by Donald and Nancy Panoz, who run the Château Élan resort and winery in north Georgia, also offers a magnificent spa and a fitness club that counts Prince William among its members.

Bedrooms are the finest in the area, each spacious and equipped with such extras as high-speed Internet links. Style and functionality in the bedrooms combine for grand comfort, ranging from the luxurious bathtubs with separate showers to the soft duvet covers. The best accommodations are the so-called Manor homes next to the 4th fairway of the Torrance Course, each with four large bedrooms and five bathrooms plus a farmhouse-style kitchen. Some of the finest chefs in the U.K. were hired to create an award-winning cuisine whose scope ranges from Mongolian barbecues to Scottish products such as salmon, Ayrshire pork, and Perthshire lamb.

Golf is still the main attraction, however, including the 7,049-yard, par-71 Devlin, designed by Australian pro Bruce Devlin, and the 7,037-yard, par-72 Torrance, designed by Rider Cup captain Sam Torrance. With its treacherous cliff-side green, the most thrilling hole is the 14th.

St. Andrews Bay, St. Andrews, KY16 8PN. © 01334/837-000. Fax 01334/471-115. www.fairmont.com. 209 units. £260–£310 ($494–$589) double; £350–£450 ($665–$855) suite; from £1,000 ($1,900) Manor Home. Rates include breakfast. AE, MC, V. Free valet parking. 5.6km (3½ miles) south of St. Andrews. **Amenities:** 4 restaurants; 3 bars; heated indoor pool; 2 golf courses; health club; spa; Jacuzzi; sauna; children's program on weekends; business center; room service; massage; babysitting; laundry service; dry cleaning; steam room; nonsmoking rooms; rooms for those w/limited mobility . *In room:* TV, minibar, coffeemaker, hair dryer, iron, safe, trouser press, robes, Wi-Fi.

Macdonald Rusacks Hotel   A grand Victorian pile built in 1887 by Josef Rusack, a German from Silesia who recognized St. Andrews's potential as a golf capital, Rusacks sits at the edge of the famous 18th hole of Pilmour Links of the Old Course. The hotel's stone walls are capped with neoclassical gables and slate roofs. Inside, chintz picks up the tones from the flower bouquets, sent in fresh twice a week. Between the panels and Ionic columns of the public rooms, racks of borrowable books re-create the atmosphere of a private country-house library. Upstairs, the spacious guest rooms are themed around some of the world's most famous golfers, tournaments, and course hazards (such as the Valley of Sin room). All contain some carved antiques and modern conveniences, but far less than the St. Andrews Old Course Hotel (see below). Each unit comes with a beautifully maintained private bathroom.

The basement Golf Club has golf-related photos, *trompe-l'oeil* racks of books, Chesterfield sofas, and vested waiters. Light meals and snacks are served here. The Old Course restaurant, overlooking the 18th hole, offers daily specials along with local game, meat, and fish, accompanied by a wine list from a well-stocked cellar.

The hotel has views of the beach that was used in the filming of the movie *Chariots of Fire.*

Pilmour Links, St. Andrews, Fife KY16 9JQ. © 888/892-0038 in the U.S., or 0870/400-8128. www.macdonaldhotels.co.uk. 68 units. £245 ($466) double; from £285 ($542) suite. Rates include breakfast. AE, DC, MC, V. **Amenities:** Restaurant; bar; sauna; room service; laundry service. *In room:* TV, coffeemaker, hair dryer, safe (in some), trouser press.

Peat Inn ⚘⚘   About 11km (7 miles) from St. Andrews, in the village of Cupar, is the Peat, an inn/post office built in 1760. Beautifully furnished guest rooms and spacious suites are offered, and the chef prepares exceptional cuisine in the restaurant. All units are suites that have separate bedrooms and living areas. Most rooms come with shower; some also have a tub. The high-priced restaurant offers dishes made with local ingredients—even the pigeons come from a St. Andrews farm—and serves lunch and dinner Tuesday to Saturday.

Cupar, Fife KY15 5LH. © 01334/840-206. Fax 01334/840-530. www.thepeatinn.co.uk. 8 units. £165 ($314) suite for 2. Rates include continental breakfast. AE, MC, V. From St. Andrews, drive 11km (7 miles) southwest along A915, then branch onto B940. Free parking. **Amenities:** Restaurant; bar; room service. *In room:* TV, hair dryer (in some).

Rufflets Country House Hotel 🏵   The garden-and-golf crowd loves this cozy 1924 country house in a 4.1-hectare (10-acre) garden. Each good-size guest room is furnished in a homelike way (often in Queen Anne style), some with canopied or four-poster beds and all with combination tub/showers. The most modern rooms are in two separate lodges, but traditionalists request space in the handsome main building. Accommodations specially designed for families and for wheelchair-bound guests are available. Special extras in all the rooms include bathrobes, upscale toiletries, and teddy bears on the beds. Reserve well in advance—Rufflets is very popular with British vacationers.

Even if you aren't staying here, you may want to reserve a table at the garden-style Rufflets Hotel Restaurant, overlooking the award-winning garden. Excellent fresh ingredients are used in the Continental and Scottish dishes.

Strathkinness Low Rd., St. Andrews, Fife KY16 9TX. 🕻 **01334/472-594.** Fax 01334/478-703. www.rufflets.co.uk. 24 units. £180–£300 ($342–$570) double; £275–£280 ($523–$532) suite. Rates include Scottish breakfast. AE, DC, MC, V. Take B939 2.5km (1½ miles) from St. Andrews. **Amenities:** Restaurant; bar; room service; babysitting; laundry service; dry cleaning; nonsmoking rooms; rooms for those w/limited mobility. *In room:* TV, minibar (in some), coffeemaker, hair dryer, trouser press.

St. Andrews Golf Hotel 🏵   A combination of greenery, sea mists, and tradition makes this late-Victorian property extremely popular with golfers, despite the fact that many of them confuse it at first glance with the larger and more prestigious St. Andrews Old Course Hotel (see below). Located about 200 yards from the first tee of the famous golf course, it was built as two stately Victorian homes and later expanded and transformed into a hotel. The comfortable but unstylish midsize guest rooms are individually decorated; some have four-poster beds and others boast sea views. The rooms in the front get the view but also the noise.

Bar lunches are served Monday to Saturday, and table d'hôte dinners are presented nightly in an oak-paneled restaurant with a fireplace.

40 The Scores, St. Andrews, Fife KY16 9SP. 🕻 **01334/472-611.** Fax 01334/472-188. www.standrews-golf.co.uk. 22 units. £200–£220 ($380–$418) double; from £250 ($475) suite. Rates include Scottish breakfast. AE, DC, MC, V. Free parking. **Amenities:** Restaurant; 2 bars; room service; laundry service; dry cleaning; nonsmoking rooms. *In room:* TV, coffeemaker, hair dryer, safe (in some), trouser press.

St. Andrews Old Course Hotel 🏵🏵🏵   Many dedicated golfers choose the five-story St. Andrews Old Course Hotel, close to A91 on the outskirts of town, where it overlooks the 17th fairway, the Road Hole of the Old Course. (Don't let the name mislead you: The hotel isn't related to the links of the same name, and guests here find access to the course just as difficult as it is elsewhere.) Fortified by *finnan haddie* (smoked haddock) and porridge, a real old-fashioned Scottish breakfast, you can face that diabolical stretch of greenery where the Scots have been whacking away since the early 15th century. The facade was altered to keep it in line with St. Andrews's more traditional buildings; its balconies afford top-view seats at all golf tournaments. The guest rooms and suites have been remodeled and refurbished, offering traditional wooden furniture and state-of-the-art marble bathrooms.

Well-prepared and high-priced international cuisine is served in the Road Hole Grill. In summer, light meals and afternoon tea are offered in a casual dining room known as Sands. In 2006 the Kohler Company opened its first Waters Spa outside of its flagship spa center in Wisconsin. The revolutionary spa specializes in "remineralizing treatments" that involve freeze-dried seawater among other treatments.

Old Station Rd., St. Andrews, Fife KY16 9SP. ℂ 01334/474-371. Fax 01334/477-668. www.oldcoursehotel.co.uk.
134 units. £214–£264 ($407–$502) double; £314–£364 ($597–$692) junior suite. Rates include Scottish breakfast.
Children under 12 stay free in parent's room. AE, DC, MC, V. **Amenities:** 4 restaurants; 4 bars; indoor pool; health
club; spa; Jacuzzi; children's activities; salon; room service; massage; babysitting; laundry service; steam rooms; nonsmoking rooms; rooms for those w/limited mobility. *In room:* TV, minibar, coffeemaker, hair dryer, safe (in some),
whirlpool bath (in some), iron, trouser press.

MODERATE

Inn at Lathones ✮   Once a coaching inn, this 200-year-old manor has been
thoughtfully restored and provides a reasonable alternative for golfers who can't afford
the grand hotels. All of its midsize guest rooms are nicely furnished, with individually
controlled heating and bathrooms with power showers in the bathtubs. Two units
have log-burning stoves and Jacuzzis with separate showers. The public rooms reflect
Scottish tradition, with open fires and beamed ceilings.

The restaurant is under the guidance of chef Marc Guibert, who has created a
French-inspired Continental cuisine using fresh Scottish produce.

By Largoward, St. Andrews, Fife KY9 1JE. ℂ 01334/840-494. Fax 01334/840-694. www.theinn.co.uk. 14 units.
£180–£245 ($342–$466) double. Rates include Scottish breakfast. Children 12 and under stay free in parent's room.
MC, V. Take A915, 8km (5 miles) southwest of the center of St. Andrews. **Amenities:** Restaurant; bar; laundry service; room service. *In room:* TV, coffeemaker, hair dryer.

Russell Hotel   Once a 19th-century private home, the Russell enjoys an ideal location overlooking St. Andrews Bay, a 2-minute walk from the Old Course's first tee. It's
well run by Gordon and Fiona de Vries and offers fully equipped, though standard,
guest rooms with tub-only bathrooms (showers in some). Some of the rooms offer sea
views. The cozy Victorian pub serves drinks and bar suppers to a loyal local crowd,
while the rather unremarkable restaurant offers moderately priced dinners nightly.

26 The Scores, St. Andrews, Fife KY16 9AS. ℂ 01334/473-447. Fax 01334/478-279. www.russellhotelstandrews.co.uk.
10 units. £85–£140 ($162–$266) double. Children under 13 stay free in parent's room. Rates include Scottish breakfast.
AE, MC, V. Closed Dec 24–Jan 12. **Amenities:** Restaurant; bar; laundry service. *In room:* TV, coffeemaker, hair dryer.

INEXPENSIVE

Ashleigh House Hotel   This B&B near the town center was built in 1883 as a fever
hospital to quarantine patients afflicted with scarlet fever, diphtheria, and other
plagues of the day. After World War I, it was transformed into an orphanage; in the
late 1980s, it was finally converted to a B&B. The trio of thick-walled stone cottages
is connected by means of covered passageways. The guest rooms are outfitted with
good beds and flowered upholstery, and provide tub or shower bathrooms. The bar
offers a wide assortment of single malts and a rough-and-ready kind of charm.

37 St. Mary St., St. Andrews, Fife KY16 8AZ. ℂ 01334/475-429. Fax 01334/474-383. 10 units. £60–£90 ($114–$171)
double. Rates include breakfast. MC, V. **Amenities:** Restaurant; bar; sauna. *In room:* TV, coffeemaker, hair dryer.

Bell Craig Guest House   Occupying a century-old stone-fronted house, this B&B
is in a historic neighborhood, a 3-minute walk from the Old Course. The Bell Craig
has had long practice at housing the parents of students at the nearby university. Sheila
Black, the hardworking owner, runs the place with decency and pride and makes a
point to spruce up each room in a different style at regular intervals. (Our favorite is
the room done in tartan.) Each unit is high-ceilinged, cozy, completely unpretentious,
and well scrubbed. Most units contain a shower and tub; two are fitted with a tub only.

8 Murray Park, St. Andrews, Fife KY16 9AW. ℂ 01334/472-962. www.bellcraig.co.uk. 6 units. £75 ($143) double.
Rates include breakfast. MC, V. **Amenities:** Breakfast room. *In room:* TV, coffeemaker, hair dryer.

WHERE TO DINE

Balaka BANGLADESHI/EUROPEAN/INTERNATIONAL   This Indian and International restaurant, in the heart of St. Andrews, has won a number of local culinary awards for its savory cuisine, which has done much to wake up the taste buds of the local populace. The Balaka is a celeb favorite, drawing such luminaries as Sean Connery (Scotland's favorite son), Arnold Palmer, and even the king and queen of Malaysia. Behind a facade of gray Scottish stone, the restaurant lies in a .4-hectare (1-acre) garden that is planted with vegetables, flowers, and herbs, all of which are used by the kitchen staff. (The flowers, of course, are used only for decoration.) The Rouf family is exceptionally hospitable and will explain menu items as you sit at crisp white tablecloths, smelling the perfumed roses on your table. Homegrown coriander, fresh spinach, spring onions, and mint, among other ingredients, figure into many of the recipes. Start, perhaps, with a *samosa*, a spicy ground beef or vegetable pastry, and follow with such delights as green herb chicken with spring onions, garlic, and freshly chopped coriander with tomato. *Masfbangla* is another justifiably local favorite—Scottish filet of salmon marinated in lime juice and flavored with turmeric, green chile, and other palette-pleasing spices.

Alexandra Place. ☏ 013334/474-825. Reservations recommended. Main courses £8.50–£15 ($16–$29). AE, MC, V. Mon–Sat noon–3pm and 5pm–1am; Sun 5pm–1am.

Grange Inn SCOTTISH/SEAFOOD   An old-fashioned hospitality prevails in this country cottage with its garden, and the Grange offers a good choice of dishes made from fresh produce. Local beef and lamb always appear on the menu, as do fish and shellfish from the fishing villages of East Neuk. Fruits and herbs come from Cupar. Typical of the menu are beef filet with port sauce complemented by wild mushrooms, as well as chicken suprême stuffed with julienne of vegetables and coated with almonds. A classic opener and an old favorite is a stew of mussels and onions.

Grange Rd., at Grange (on B959). ☏ 01334/472-670. Reservations recommended. Fixed-price dinner £26 ($49). DC, MC, V. Daily 12:30–2pm and 7–8:45pm. Drive about 2.5km (1½ miles) from St. Andrews on B959.

Ostlers Close ✦ BRITISH/INTERNATIONAL   Sophisticated and intensely concerned with the quality of its cuisine, this charming restaurant occupies a 17th-century building that functioned in the early 20th century as a temperance hotel. Today, in the heart of the hamlet of Cupar, 11km (7 miles) from St. Andrews, it contains a kitchen in what used to be the hotel's stables, with an elegant set of dining rooms in the hotel's former public areas. Menu items are prepared with seasonal Scottish produce and are likely to include roasted saddle of roe venison with wild-mushroom sauce; roast breast of free-range duck with Bombay potatoes and a plum sauce; and pan-fried scallops with fresh asparagus and butter sauce. Whenever it's available, opt for the confit of duckling with salted pork and lentils.

25 Bonnygate, in the nearby town of Cupar. ☏ 01334/655-574. Reservations recommended. Main courses £12–£16 ($23–$30) at lunch, £18–£21 ($34–$40) at dinner. AE, MC, V. Tues–Sat 7–9:30pm; Sat 12:15–1:30pm. Closed 2 weeks in Apr. From St. Andrews, follow A91 for 11km (7 miles) to the southwest until you reach the village of Cupar.

ST. ANDREWS AFTER DARK

The cultural center of St. Andrews is the **Byre Theatre,** Abbey Street (☏ **01334/ 475-000**), which features drama ranging from Shakespeare plays to musical comedies. Tickets cost £6 to £15 ($11–$29) adults, £5 to £10 ($9.50–$19) children. Pick up a weekly version of *What's on in Fife* from the local tourist office to find out what's featured.

Victoria, 1A St. Mary's Place (© 01334/476-964), is the place to catch a live band in St. Andrews. This student-filled pub features folk, rock, and blues acts occasionally, as well as karaoke every Friday. Because of the absence of students over the summer, there's no live music. John Smiths, Beamish Stout, McEwans Lager, 78 Shilling, and 80 Shilling are available on tap. Open Tuesday to Saturday from 10am to 1am, Sunday 11am to midnight, and Monday 10am to midnight.

A pub since 1904, the **Central Bar,** at the corner of Market and College streets (© 01334/478-296), is an antiquated room with a jukebox, and it can become rowdy during a football or tennis match. The best brews here are Old Peculiar, Theakstons XB, and McEwans Lager. Open Monday to Saturday from 11:30am to 1am.

Chariots, The Scores (© 01334/472-451), in the Scores Hotel, attracts mainly a local crowd, ranging from 30 to 60 years, who gather in the evening for conversation over a pint. Despite a strong regional tradition of beer brewing, two outsiders, Guinness and Millers, are featured on tap. Open daily from 5pm to midnight. Hours can vary, especially on weekends, so please call ahead.

4 Stirling ★★

56km (37 miles) NW of Edinburgh, 45km (28 miles) NE of Glasgow

Stirling is dominated by its impressive castle, perched on a 76m (250-ft.) basalt rock that was formed by the rivers Forth and Clyde and the relatively small parcel of land between them. The ancient town of Stirling, on the main east-west route across Scotland, grew up around the castle. It lies in the heart of an area so turbulent in Scottish history it was called the "cockpit of Scotland." (Here "cockpit" refers to the pit where male chickens would be forced to engage in cockfights.) One memorable battle fought here was the Battle of Bannockburn in 1314, when Robert I (the Bruce) defeated the army of Edward II of England and gained Scotland its independence. Another was the Battle of Stirling Bridge in 1297.

Ever since the release of Mel Gibson's *Braveheart,* world attention has focused on the Scottish national hero William Wallace, a freedom fighter who became known as the "hammer and scourge" of the English. *Braveheart,* however, was filmed mostly in Ireland, and the Battle of Stirling Bridge in the movie was played out on a plane with not a bridge in sight.

Stirling is the central crossroads of Scotland, giving easy access by rail and road to all its major towns and cities.

ESSENTIALS

GETTING THERE   Frequent trains run between Glasgow and Stirling (a 45-min. trip) and between Edinburgh and Stirling (a 60-min. trip). A 1-day round-trip ticket from Edinburgh is £10 ($19) and from Glasgow is £9 ($17). For schedules, call **National Express Enquiries** at © 0345/484-950.

Frequent buses run to Stirling from Glasgow (a 40-min. trip). A 1-day round-trip ticket from Glasgow costs £6.50 ($12). Check with **Scottish Citylink** (© 08705/505-050) for details.

If you're driving from Glasgow, head northeast along A80 to M80, then continue north. From Edinburgh, head northwest along M9.

VISITOR INFORMATION   The **tourist office** is at 41 Dumbarton Rd. (© 01786/475-019; www.visitscotland.com). April to May, it's open Monday to Saturday 9am to 5pm; June to August, hours are Monday to Saturday 9am to 7:30pm and Sunday 9:30am to 6:30pm; September hours are Monday to Saturday 9am to 6pm and Sunday 10am to 5pm; October hours are Monday to Saturday 9:30am to 5pm; and November to March, it's open Monday to Friday 10am to 5pm and Saturday 10am to 4pm.

SEEING THE SIGHTS

To get a real feel for Stirling, stroll the **Back Walk,** beginning near Rob Roy's statue, near the Guildhall in the town center. Following this trail along the outside of the town's once-fortified walls, you'll find good views, see an old watchtower (and a place where prisoners were hanged), and eventually reach Stirling Castle.

Church of the Holy Rude ⟨★   Built in the early 15th century, the Church of the Holy Rude is said to be the only church in the country still in use that has witnessed a coronation. It was 1567 when the 13-month-old James VI—Mary Queen of Scots' son, who was to become James I of England—was crowned here. John Knox preached the sermon. Constructed with the simplest tools more than 600 years ago and built as a reminder of the cross (rude) on which Christ was supposedly crucified, the church is memorable for its rough but evocative stonework and its elaborate 19th-century stained glass—particularly on the south side of the choir. Recent restorations have been done in the most tasteful and unobtrusive styles.

St. John St. ⟨Ⓒ **01786/475-275.** Free admission. Mid-Apr to Sept daily 10am–5pm. Closed Oct to mid-Apr.

Stirling Castle ⟨★★   There are traces of a 7th-century royal habitation of the Stirling area, and on the right bank of the Forth, Stirling Castle dates from the Middle Ages, when its location, on a dividing line between the Lowlands and the Highlands, made it the key to the Highlands. The castle became an important seat of two kings, James IV and James V, both of whom added to it, the latter following classic Renaissance style, then relatively unknown in Britain. Mary Queen of Scots lived here as an infant monarch for the first 4 years of her life. After its final defeat in 1746, Bonnie Prince Charlie's army stopped here. Later, the castle became an army barracks and headquarters of the Argyll and Sutherland Highlanders, one of Britain's most celebrated regiments. An audiovisual presentation explains what you're about to see.

In the castle is the **Museum of the Argyll and Sutherland Highlanders** (Ⓒ **01786/ 475-165**), presenting an excellent exhibit of colors, pipe banners, and regimental silver, along with medals (some of which go back to the Battle of Waterloo) won by Scottish soldiers for valor. Run by Britain's Ministry of Defense, it functions as a showcase for a military unit.

Upper Castle Hill. Ⓒ **01786/450-000.** Admission to castle £8.50 ($16) adults, £6.50 ($12) seniors, £4.25 ($8.10) children 5–15, free for children 4 and under; free admission to museum. Castle Apr–Sept daily 9:30am–6pm; Oct–Mar daily 9:30am–5pm; last entry to castle 45 min. before closing time. Museum Mar–Sept Mon–Sat 10am–5:45pm, Sun 11am–4:45pm; Oct–Feb daily 10am–4:15pm.

EXPLORING NEARBY BANNOCKBURN

You can take an interesting detour to Bannockburn, a name that looms large in Scottish history. It was there that Robert the Bruce, his army of 6,000 outnumbered three to one, defeated the forces of Edward II in 1314. Before nightfall on that day, Robert the Bruce had won back the throne of Scotland. The battlefield, which makes for a peaceful walk today, lies off M80, 3km (2 miles) south of Stirling.

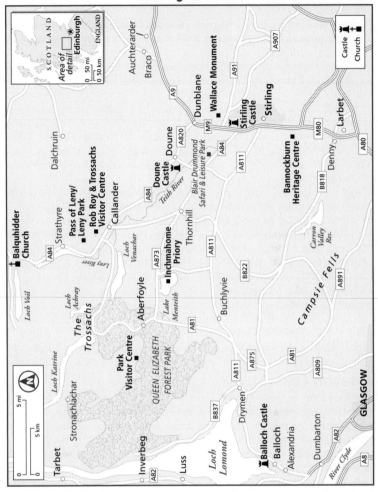

At the **Bannockburn Heritage Centre,** Glasgow Road (✆ **01786/812-664**), an audiovisual presentation tells the story of these events, while *The Kingdom of the Scots* exhibit traces the history of Scotland from William Wallace to the Union of Crowns. The site is open all year, while the Heritage Centre and shop are open April to October, daily 10am to 5:30pm, and in March, November, and December, daily 10:30am to 4pm. The last audiovisual showing is at 5pm. Admission is £3.50 ($6.65) for adults, £2.60 ($4.95) for seniors and children, and £9.50 ($18) per family.

From the **Borestone,** where Robert the Bruce commanded his forces at the start of his battle for Stirling, you can see Stirling Castle and the Forth Valley. He planted his standards (flags) as inspiration for his troops, and today a flagpole capped with the standards of Scotland still flies proudly from atop this low hill. It's located off M80/M9 at Junction 9.

SHOPPING

Stirling's town center has some interesting shopping. One good hunting ground is the **Thistle Centre** indoor shopping plaza, home of about 65 shops at the junction of Port Street and Murray Place.

The best woolen goods are at **R. R. Henderson,** 6–8 Friar St. (© **01786/473-681**), a Highland outfitter selling not only sweaters and scarves but also made-to-order kilts and tartans.

Some of the best shopping is not in Stirling itself but in the outlying area. Take A9 to Larbert and at the roundabout follow A18 west until you see the sign for **Barbara Davidson's Pottery Studio,** Muirhall Farm, Larbert (© **01324/554-430**), 14km (9 miles) south of Stirling. At this 18th-century farmstead, one of Scotland's best-known potters operates her studio and workshop. A large selection of functional wares is exhibited and sold here.

East of Stirling, three towns form the **Mill Trail Country:** Alva, Alloa, and Tillicoultry. Many quality textile mills have factory outlets here, offering bargain prices on cotton, woolens, and even cashmere goods. The best selection of sweaters is available at **Inverallen Handknitters Ltd.,** Alva Industrial Estate, Alva (© **01259/762-292**). The hand-knitted traditional sweaters here are particularly appealing. A good selection of clothing for children and infants supplements the selections for men and women at **Glen Alva Ltd.,** Hallpark, Whine Road, Alloa (© **01259/723-024**). If you're inspired to knit your own creation, head to **Patons & Baldwins,** Kilcraigo Mill, Alloa (© **01325/394-394**), which manufactures quality yarns.

For more complete details, including any directional information or seasonal closings, call or visit the **Mill Trail Visitor Centre,** West Stirling Street at Alva (© **01259/769-696**), 14km (9 miles) east of the center of Stirling. January to June and September to December, it's open daily 10am to 5pm; July to August, it's open daily 9am to 5pm.

WHERE TO STAY
EXPENSIVE

The Stirling Highland Hotel ✹✹   One of Stirling's finer hotels occupies a former high school dating from the early Victorian era. It lies within an easy stroll of the castle. The historic atmosphere was treated with respect, and many of the architectural features were kept. Florals, tartans, and solid-wood furnishings dominate the public rooms and the guest rooms, which are in a three-story annex. Each unit comes with a shower, and a few are also equipped with tubs. From its position close to Stirling Castle, the hotel enjoys views over the town and surrounding region.

Rather high-priced Scottish cuisine is featured in Scholars Restaurant, and Rizzio's Restaurant serves Italian cuisine.

Spittal St., Stirling, Stirlingshire FK8 1DU. © **01786/272-727**. Fax 01786/272-829. www.paramount-hotels.co.uk. 96 units. £135–£170 ($257–$323) double. AE, DC, MC, V. Free parking. **Amenities:** Restaurant; indoor pool; health club; Jacuzzi; secretarial services; salon; room service; babysitting; laundry service; dry cleaning; squash courts; steam room; nonsmoking rooms. *In room:* TV, coffeemaker, hair dryer, trouser press.

MODERATE

Golden Lion Flagship Hotel   About a block downhill from Church of the Holy Rude, the Golden Lion dates from 1786, when it was a coaching inn; but, its sandstone shell was greatly enlarged with the addition of modern wings in 1962. It's now one of the oldest and largest hotels in town and has improved and modernized most of its guest rooms. The rooms are simple and easy on the eye, and bathrooms are equipped with either tub or shower.

8–10 King St., Stirling, Stirlingshire FK8 2ND. ℂ 01786/475-351. Fax 01786/472-755. www.thegoldenlionstirling.com. 67 units. £100–£130 ($190–$247) double. Rates include Scottish breakfast. AE, DC, MC, V. **Amenities:** Restaurant; bar; room service; laundry service; dry cleaning; nonsmoking rooms. *In room:* TV, coffeemaker, hair dryer, trouser press (in some).

The Park Lodge Hotel ⍟ This stylish hotel occupies a 19th-century Italianate mansion, across from a city park in a residential neighborhood. Built of stone blocks and slate, it has a Doric portico, Tudor-style chimney pots, a Georgian-era core from 1825, and climbing roses and wisteria. Anne and Georges Marquetty house guests in 10 upstairs rooms and suggest that they dine at their elegant restaurant, The Heritage. Each room contains antique furnishings (no. 6 has a four-poster bed) as well as tub/shower combination. You might enjoy tea in the walled garden, with its widely spaced iron benches and terra-cotta statues.

32 Park Terrace, Stirling, Stirlingshire FK8 2JS. ℂ 01786/474-862. Fax 01786/449-748. www.parklodge.net. 10 units. £100 ($190) double. Rates include Scottish breakfast. AE, MC, V. Free parking. **Amenities:** Restaurant; bar; nonsmoking rooms. *In room:* TV, coffeemaker, hair dryer, trouser press (in some).

Terraces Hotel ⍥*Value* Built originally as a fine Georgian house of sandstone, this hotel stands on a raised terrace in a quiet residential neighborhood and is now one of the best values in town. Each midsize guest room is furnished in a country-house motif of flowered curtains and solidly traditional furniture, with a shower bathroom (some with tubs). One room has a lovely carved four-poster bed. The half-paneled cocktail bar and velvet-upholstered restaurant are popular settings for local parties and wedding receptions. Melville's Restaurant offers a moderately priced Scottish and Continental menu.

4 Melville Terrace, Stirling, Stirlingshire FK8 2ND. ℂ 01786/472-268. Fax 01786/450-314. www.terraceshotel.co.uk. 17 units. £90–£105 ($171–$200) double; £100–£140 ($190–$266) family room. Rates include Scottish breakfast. AE, DC, MC, V. Free parking. **Amenities:** Restaurant; bar; business facilities; room service; laundry service; nonsmoking rooms. *In room:* TV, coffeemaker, hair dryer, iron, trouser press (in some).

INEXPENSIVE

Allan's Guest House ⍥*Kids* Private and personal, this rambling 1840s stone house is the domain of Mrs. Allan, who rents two of her five bedrooms to guests. The cozy rooms are painted and decorated in shades of pale pink. Mrs. Allan welcomes families with small children.

15 Albert Place (a 10-min. walk north of the town center), Stirling FK8 2RE. ℂ 01786/475-175. 2 units, none with private bathroom. £55 ($105) double. Rates include breakfast. No credit cards. Closed Nov–Feb. *In room:* Coffeemaker, no phone.

West Plean House ⍟*Value* This working farm is a delight. It has a lovely walled garden and is a great base for taking walks into the surrounding woodland. Your hosts are welcoming and helpful, and they offer extremely good value. Their guest rooms are spacious and well furnished, with an eye to comfort and conveniences, and each is equipped with a shower-only bathroom. Their home-cooked breakfast makes this place a winner.

Denny Rd. (6km/3½ miles from Stirling on A872), Stirling FK7 8HA. ℂ 01786/812-208. Fax 01786/480-550. www.westpleanhouse.com. 3 units. £60–£64 ($114–$122) double. Rates include breakfast. No credit cards. Closed 2 weeks in late Dec. *In room:* TV, coffeemaker, no phone.

WHERE TO DINE

The Heritage 🞋 FRENCH/SCOTTISH   Culinary sophistication and beautiful decor make this one of the best restaurants in the district. It's in the stylish Park Lodge Hotel (see above), on a quiet residential street near the center of town, a 5-minute walk east of the rail station. You can enjoy a drink in the gentlemen's parlor, with somber walls and enviable antiques, before descending to the low-ceilinged basement. Amid a French-inspired decor, you'll taste some of the best cuisine in Stirling, prepared with finesse by Georges Marquetty. In his youth, he worked as an executive chef in Paris and later spent 12 years in Cincinnati (where he was voted one of the leading chefs of America). His specialties include scallops, scampi, and prawns in Pernod sauce; filet of Dover sole with shallots, cream, brandy and a lobster sauce; and foie gras with truffles.

At The Park Lodge Hotel. 32 Park Terrace, Stirling, Stirlingshire FK8 2QC. 🞋 01786/473-660. Fax 01786/449-748. Reservations recommended. Main courses £15–£21 ($29–$40); fixed-price 2-course lunch £14 ($27); fixed-price 3-course dinner £28 ($53). MC, V. Daily noon–2pm and 6:30–9:30pm. Closed Sun in winter.

Hermann's Brasserie AUSTRIAN/SCOTTISH   This reliable favorite is housed in an old, traditional town house with high beamed ceilings and features pine tables and chairs and tartan carpeting. Part of the restaurant opens onto a conservatory. You get tried-and-true platters of Scottish food here, as well as a touch of Vienna, especially in the golden-brown Wiener schnitzel that's served with a salad and sautéed potatoes. Scottish Highland venison is a regular feature; the plate here is attractively adorned with a whisky cream sauce. You might start your meal with the most typical of Scottish soups: *Cullen skink,* made with smoked fish and potatoes. Our forever favorite is the fast-seared filet of salmon, served with a savory sauce laced with pink peppercorns.

58 Broad St., Mar Place House. 🞋 01786/450-632. Reservations recommended. Main courses £14–£17 ($27–$32). AE, MC, V. Daily noon–2:30pm and 6–9:30pm.

STIRLING AFTER DARK

On the campus of Stirling University, the **Macrobert Arts Centre** (🞋 01786/466-666) features plays, music, films, and art exhibits. The 497-seat main theater often presents dramas and symphony concerts, and the 140-seat studio theater is used mainly for films. Cinema tickets cost £4 ($7.60) for adults and £3 ($5.70) for seniors and children; theater tickets generally run £8 to £11 ($15–$21). Admission to most concerts is £10 to £15 ($19–$29). Call for current listings.

   All that Jazz, 9 Upper Craigs (🞋 01786/451-130), is a lively bar popular with students. Music is usually provided via the stereo, but bands also appear infrequently. The bar serves a good range of single malts and pints of Kronenberg, Beamish Red, and McEwans. The adjoining restaurant serves a mix of Cajun and traditional Scottish fare, including haggis, between 5 and 10pm every evening. The same menu is available throughout the day in the bar, which is open Monday to Friday from 11am to midnight, Friday and Saturday 11am to 1am.

   O'Neill's, 11 Maxwell Place (🞋 01786/459-901), is a traditional Irish pub popular with Scottish students, who come to hear the Irish and Scottish folk bands play. To find out who's performing, check the flyers posted in the pub. There's never a cover. Open Sunday to Thursday noon to midnight and Friday and Saturday 11am to 1am.

5 Dunblane & Its Grand Cathedral

11km (7 miles) N of Stirling, 68km (42 miles) NW of Edinburgh, 47km (29 miles) SW of Perth, 53km (33 miles) NE of Glasgow

A small cathedral city on the banks of the Allan Water, Dunblane takes its name from the Celtic church of St. Blane, which once stood on the site now occupied by the fine 13th-century Gothic cathedral. The cathedral is the main reason to visit; if that doesn't interest you, you'll find more romantic and lovelier places from which to explore the nearby Trossachs and Loch Lomond (say, Callander or Aberfoyle).

ESSENTIALS
GETTING THERE   Trains run between Glasgow and Dunblane with a stopover at Stirling, a one-way fare costing £6 to £8 ($11–$15). Rail connections are also possible through Edinburgh via Stirling for £6.30 ($12) one-way. For 24-hour information, call ℭ **08457/484-950.**

Buses travel from the Goosecroft Bus Station in Stirling to Dunblane, costing £2 to £3 ($3.80–$5.70) each way. Call **First Edinburgh Busline** at ℭ **08708/727-271** for information.

If you're driving from Stirling, continue north along M9 to Dunblane.

VISITOR INFORMATION   A year-round **tourist office** is on Stirling Road (ℭ **01786/824-428**). April 1 to June 1, it's open Monday to Saturday 9am to 5pm; June 2 to June 29 Monday to Saturday from 9am to 6pm, Sunday 10am to 4pm; June 30 to August 31 Monday to Saturday 9am to 7:30pm, Sunday 9:30am to 6:30pm; September 1 to September 7 Monday to Saturday 9am to 7pm and Sunday 10am to 5pm; September 8 to September 21 Monday to Saturday 9am to 6pm, Sunday 10am to 4pm; September 22 to October 19 Monday to Saturday 9:30am to 5pm; October 20 to March 31 Monday to Friday 10am to 5pm, Saturday 10am to 4pm.

SEEING THE SIGHTS
After you visit the cathedral, you can wander and discover the streets around it. They're narrow and twisting and flanked by mellow old town houses, many from the 18th century.

Cathedral Museum   In the 1624 Dean's House, the Cathedral Museum contains articles and papers displaying the story of Dunblane and its ancient cathedral; you can also visit an enclosed garden with a very old, though now restored, well. A 1687 structure on the grounds contains the library of Bishop Robert Leighton, an outstanding 17th-century churchman; of interest to scholars is material about the troubled times in Scotland, primarily from before the Industrial Revolution. It's open the same hours as the Cathedral Museum.

On Cathedral Square in the Dean's House. ℭ **01786/823-440**. www.dunblanemuseum.org.uk. Free admission. May–Oct Mon–Sat 10:30am–4:30pm.

Dunblane Cathedral 𝕽𝕽   An excellent example of 13th-century Gothic ecclesiastic architecture, this cathedral was spared the ravages of attackers who destroyed other Scottish worship centers. Altered in the 15th century and restored several times in the 19th and 20th centuries, it may have suffered most from neglect subsequent to the Reformation. A Jesse Tree window is in the west end of the building; and of interest are the stalls, the misericords, the pulpit with carved figures of early ecclesiastical figures, and the wooden barrel-vaulted roof with colorful armorials. A Celtic stone from about A.D. 900 is in the north aisle.

Cathedral Close. © **01786/823-388.** www.dunblanecathedral.org.uk. Free admission. Apr–Sept Mon–Sat 9:30am–6pm, Sun 1:30–6pm; Oct–Mar Mon–Sat 9:30am–4:30pm, Sun 1:30–4pm.

WHERE TO STAY

Cromlix House *★★★*   This manor house, built in 1880 as the seat of a family that has owned the surrounding 1,215 hectares (3,000 acres) for the past 500 years, is now the area's most elegant hotel. The owners still live on the estate and derive part of their income from organizing hunting and fishing expeditions in the nearby moors and forests and on the River Allan. Fishing in three private lakes and hunting is available, as is tennis, and you can walk through the forests and farmland. It's also a popular spot for weddings.

The manor has an elegant drawing room with big bow windows, and antiques are scattered about both the public and guest rooms. Bouquets of fresh flowers and open fires in cool weather add to the overall charm and comfort of the place. The individually decorated guest rooms (including eight suites with sitting rooms) are carpeted, and most have Queen Anne furnishings.

Kinbuck, Dunblane FK15 9JT. © **01786/822-125.** Fax 01786/825-450. www.cromlixhouse.com. 14 units. £175–£195 ($333–$371) double; £215–£275 ($409–$523) suite. AE, DC, MC, V. Closed Jan. Take A9 to B8033; the hotel is 5km (3¼ miles) north of Dunblane just beyond the village of Kinbuck. **Amenities:** Restaurant; bar; room service; laundry service; nonsmoking rooms. *In room:* TV, coffeemaker, hair dryer, trouser press (in some).

Kippenross *★* *(Finds)*   This country manor boasts a richer and more unusual history than many of the region's B&Bs. It was built in 1750 according to the Palladian-neoclassical lines of William Adam, father of Britain's most celebrated neoclassical architect, Robert Adam. Surrounded by 81 hectares (200 acres) of parks, lawns, and gardens, and artfully landscaped with exotic plantings, it's a perfect example of Scottish country-house living, supervised by the Stirling-Aird family. Two of the guest rooms overlook the sprawling front lawns; the other overlooks the forests at the back. Each unit comes with a tub or shower. Guests are welcomed into the family's drawing room and to formal breakfasts in the dining room. If any guest wants to stay for dinner and reserves in advance, Susan Stirling-Aird prepares elegant dinners for an extra £28 ($53) per person. The Stirling-Airds invite guests to bring their own liquor or wine, because the place doesn't have a liquor license. ***Note:*** Susan's husband, Patrick, is a devoted ornithologist and bird-watcher.

Dunblane FK15 0LQ. © **01786/824-482.** Fax 01786/823-124 3 units. £76–£87 ($144–$165) double. Rates include breakfast. MC, V. From Stirling, drive 8km (5 miles) north, then take A9 toward Perth and exit onto B8033, following the signs to Dunblane. **Amenities:** Dining room; nonsmoking rooms. *In room:* Hair dryer (at front desk), no phone.

6 Callander & a Trio of Lochs *★*

26km (16 miles) NW of Stirling, 69km (43 miles) N of Glasgow, 84km (52 miles) NW of Edinburgh, 68km (42 miles) W of Perth

In Gaelic, the Trossachs means the "bristled country," an allusion to its luxuriant vegetation. The thickly wooded valley contains three lochs: Venachar, Achray, and Katrine. In summer, the steamer on Loch Katrine offers a fine view of the splendid wooded scenery.

The Trossachs: Scotland's Fabled Scenic Trail

In 1691, the Rev. Robert Kirk called the Trossachs a commonwealth of "elfs, fawns, and fairies." Known for its idyllic landscapes, the Trossachs is certainly one of Scotland's most fabled and beautiful regions.

Callander is ideal for exploring the Trossachs, which lie to the immediate west of town. The **Trossachs Trail** extends west from Callander to Loch Lomond, and the area stretches south to Aberfoyle, with the Crianlarich Hills and Balquhidder forming its northern boundary.

You probably won't have time to see all the Trossachs. Our suggestion is to drive 11km (6¾ miles) from Callander to the village of Brig o'Turk, which lies between lochs Achray and Venachar, at the foot of Glen Finglas. Here you should get out of your car for a walk. In almost any direction you head, the forested landscape is scenic, with many lochs or lakes. Our favorite walk is the one signposted toward the Archray Forest. Allow at least 2 or 3 hours for exploring this area. You will also see a signpost to the Glen Finglas circular walk. Many hikers set out from Brig o'Turk via Glen Finglas to Balquhidder.

For many, the small town of Callander makes the best base for exploring the Trossachs and Loch Katrine, Loch Achray, and Loch Venachar. (The town of Aberfoyle, discussed below, is another excellent choice.) For years, motorists—and before them, passengers traveling by bumpy coach—stopped here to rest up on the once-difficult journey between Edinburgh and Oban.

Callander stands at the entrance to the Pass of Leny in the shadow of the Callander Crags. The rivers Teith and Leny meet to the west of the town.

ESSENTIALS

GETTING THERE   Stirling (see "Stirling," earlier in this chapter) is the nearest rail link. Once at Stirling, continue the rest of the way to Callander on a First Edinburgh Bus from the Stirling station on Goosecroft Road. Contact **First Edinburgh Buses** at © **08708/727-271.** A one-way fare is £2.90 ($5.50).

Driving from Stirling, head north along M9, cutting northwest at the junction of A84 to Callander, bypassing Doune.

EXPLORING THE AREA

In the scenic Leny Hills, to the west of Callander beyond the Pass of Leny, lie **Leny Park** and **Leny Falls.** At one time all the lands in Leny Park were part of the Leny estate, home of the Buchanan clan for more than 1,000 years. In the wild Leny Glen, a naturalist's paradise, you can see deer grazing. Leny Falls is an impressive sight, near the confluence of the River Leny and the River Teith. In this area you see the remains of an abandoned railway, now a wonderful footpath or cycling path for exploring this scenic area. Rent a bike at **Wheels/Trossachs Backpackers,** on Invertrossachs Road in Callander (© **01877/331-100;** daily 10am–6pm), which charges £15 to £25 ($29–$48) for a full day, £8 to £16 ($15–$30) for a half-day, and from £50 to £110 ($95–$209) for a week. It also provides bikers with sleeping rooms from about

£16 ($30) per night, including continental breakfast, conducts organized walks, and, on request, arranges canoe trips. You must make reservations in advance.

About 6.5km (4 miles) beyond the Pass of Leny is **Loch Lubnaig** (crooked lake), divided into two reaches by a rock and considered fine fishing waters. Nearby is **Little Leny,** the ancestral burial ground of the Buchanans.

You'll find more falls at **Bracklinn,** 2.5km (1½ miles) northeast of Callander. Bracklinn, in a gorge above the town, is one of the most scenic of the local beauty spots.

One of the most interesting sites around Callander is **Balquhidder Church** ⚑, 21km (13 miles) northwest off A84. This is the burial place of Rob Roy MacGregor. The church also has the St. Angus Stone from the 8th century, a 17th-century bell, and some Gaelic Bibles.

A good selection of woolens is at **Callander Woollen Mill,** 12–18 Main St. (© **01877/330-273**)—everything from scarves, skirts, and jackets to kilts, trousers, and knitwear. Another outlet for woolen goods, tartans, and woven rugs is the **Trossachs Woollen Mill** (© **01877/330-178**), 1.6km (1 mile) north of Callander on A84 in the hamlet of Kilmahog.

The town has an excellent golf course, the wooded and scenic **Callander Golf Course,** Aveland Road (© **01877/330-090**). At this 5,125-yard par-66 course, greens fees are £22 ($42) per round or £30 ($57) per day on weekdays, £30 ($57) per round or £40 ($76) per day on Saturdays and Sundays. The trolley charge is included in club rental, which runs £10 to £15 ($19–$29) for 18 holes. No caddy service is available. The hilly fairways offer fine views, and the tricky moorland layout demands accurate tee shots.

WHERE TO STAY

Rooms are also available at **Dalgair House Hotel** (see "Where to Dine," below).

Arden House ⚑   This stone-sided Victorian B&B is instantly recognizable to several generations of British TV viewers because of its 1970s role as the setting for a BBC series, *Dr. Finlay's Casebook.* (Its plot involved two bachelor doctors and their interactions with their attractive housekeeper and the fictional town of Tannochbrae, which was modeled after Callander.) Built in 1870 as a vacation home for Lady Willoughby and still maintained by two attractive bachelors, William Jackson and Ian Mitchell, it offers a soothing rest amid gardens at the base of a rocky outcropping known as the Callander Crags. The well-known Bracklinn Falls are within a 5-minute walk. The public areas boast Victorian antiques, while the high-ceilinged guest rooms are tasteful and comfortable (the most appealing is the plush Tannochbrae Suite). Each guest room comes with a shower; only the suite has a tub bath. Children under 14 are not accepted as guests.

Bracklinn Rd., Callander FK17 8EQ. © 01877/330-235. Fax 01877/330-235. www.ardenhouse.org.uk. 5 units. £65 ($124) double; £75 ($143) suite. Rates include breakfast. MC, V. Free parking. From Callander, walk 5 min. north, following the signs to Bracklinn Falls. No children under age 14. **Amenities:** Nonsmoking rooms. *In room:* TV, coffeemaker, no phone.

Highland House Hotel   In the center of Callander, this Georgian town house from 1790 has been successfully turned into a small hotel lying off the main street of town, a short walk form the Teith River. Bedrooms are cozy and traditionally furnished, including one family room, and each has a small bathroom with shower. An intimate bar on the ground floor offers many fine brands of malt whisky, and a tea room opened in the spring of 2007, featuring soups, sandwiches, cakes, coffee, and tea, of course. A very generous Scottish breakfast is served, including sausages, bacon, black pudding, a fried egg, and other adornments such as mushrooms and a selection of juices.

S. Church St. (just off A84, near Ancaster Square), Callander FK17 8BN. © **01877/330-269.** Fax 01877/339-004. www.highlandhouseincallander.co.uk. 9 units. £50 ($95) double. Rates include Scottish breakfast. MC, V. Free parking. **Amenities:** Bar; room service; nonsmoking rooms. *In room:* TV, coffeemaker, trouser press.

Lubnaig House   It's not the Roman Camp (see below), but other than that competition this 1864 Victorian house, full of character, is the best place in town to lay your head. On the outskirts of town, it stands in landscaped gardens. It's a B&B—no restaurant—and it's small and family run, just the way we like them. The rooms in the main house are attractively furnished and comfortable, each a double or twin, and there are some smaller rooms in the coach house which was converted from stables. No family units are available, and children accepted must be 7 or older. The gabled house was constructed in 1864 by a Glasgow merchant, but it became a hotel about 30 years ago.

Leny Feus, Callander, FK17 8AS. © **01877/330-376.** www.lubnaighouse.co.uk. 8 units. £78–£100 ($148–$190) double. Rates include breakfast. No children under 7. MC, V. Closed mid-Oct to Apr. *In room:* TV, hair dryer, iron, trouser press.

Roman Camp Country House Hotel ★★★   This is the leading hotel in town. Once a 17th-century hunting lodge with pink walls and small gray-roofed towers, it was built on the site of a Roman camp. Today you drive up a 182m (197-ft.) driveway, with shaggy Highland cattle and sheep grazing on either side. Inside, owners Eric and Marion Brown welcome you into a gracious country house. The dining room was converted from the old kitchen in the 1930s. The ceiling design is based on Scottish painted ceilings of the 16th and 17th centuries. The library, with its ornate plasterwork and richly grained paneling, is an elegant holdover from yesteryear.

Seven of the comfortable guest rooms are on the ground floor; all have shower-equipped bathrooms (two with tub). Some rooms are furnished with bedhead crowns, gilt-framed mirrors, and stenciled furnishings; a few have four-posters, and others are contemporary with blond-wood pieces. Suites have separate sitting areas.

Main St., Callander FK17 8BG. © **01877/330-003.** Fax 01877/331-533. www.roman-camp-hotel.co.uk. 14 units. £135–£175 ($257–$333) double; from £205 ($390) suite. Rates include Scottish breakfast. AE, DC, MC, V. As you approach Callander on A84, the entrance to the hotel is signposted between 2 pink cottages on Callander's Main St. **Amenities:** Restaurant; bar; room service; nonsmoking rooms; 1 room for those w/limited mobility. *In room:* TV, coffeemaker, hair dryer, trouser press.

WHERE TO DINE

Dalgair House Hotel SCOTTISH   This place is best known for its food and wine cellar. The bar, lined in gray bricks, boasts rustic accessories and flickering candles. Australian, German, and Austrian wines, sold by the glass, give the place the aura of a wine bar. The menu choices include haddock and mince and tatties. More formal meals are served after dark in the restaurant, where menu items might include pasta Neapolitan or Sicilian chicken; Cajun salmon filet and wildberry coulis; and Scottish filet steak garni.

The hotel's eight rooms contain hair dryers, TVs, and tub/shower combos. Rooms rent for £65 to £90 ($124–$171) double, Scottish breakfast included.

113–115 Main St., Callander FK17 8BQ. © **01877/330-283.** Fax 01877/331-114. www.dalgair-house-hotel.co.uk. Reservations recommended in restaurant, not necessary in bar. Main courses £5.50–£15 ($10–$29) in restaurant, £3.50–£8 ($6.65–$15) in bar. AE, DC, MC, V. Restaurant daily noon–8:30pm; bar food service daily 11am–8:30pm.

Finds A Side Trip to Loch Voil

This was an area known to Rob Roy MacGregor, who died in 1734 but lives on in legend as the Robin Hood of Scotland and in the Liam Neeson film. If you visit Rob Roy's grave at Balquhidder, you may find this remote part of Scotland so enchanting you'll want to continue to drive west and explore the **Braes o' Balquhidder** and the banks of **Loch Voil,** where you can enjoy some of the loveliest countryside walks in the Trossachs. You can go through the churchyard where the Scottish hero is buried up to Kirkton Glen, continuing along through grasslands to a little lake. This signposted footpath leads to the next valley, called Glen Dochart, before it links up once again with A84, on which Callander lies.

Lade Inn INTERNATIONAL/SCOTTISH   Surrounded by fields and within earshot of the Leny River, the Lade was built as a teahouse, then converted after World War II to a pub and restaurant. The local favorite attracts residents from the surrounding farmlands, as well as visitors from afar, to enjoy the Highland scenery (which includes Ben Ledi, one of the region's most prominent peaks) and to sample the wide range of cask-conditioned ales and cider. If you're hungry, meals of such Scottish standards as rack of lamb, chicken, pork, venison, steaks, salmon, and trout are prepared with the finest local ingredients.

Trossachs Rd. at Kilmahog, Callander. (C) **01877/330-152.** Main courses £10–£20 ($19–$38). MC, V. Mon–Fri noon–2:30pm and 5:30–9pm; Sat noon–9pm; Sun 12:30–8pm. 1.6km (1 mile) north of Callander on A84.

CALLANDER AFTER DARK

The **Bridgend Hotel Pub,** Bridgend ((C) **01877/330-130**), is an old watering hole that has been done up in matching dusky-red wood paneling and carpeting. Tennant brews are available on tap. They have karaoke on some nights and live Scottish music, mainly on the weekend. Open Monday to Wednesday 11:30am to 2:30pm and 5:30pm to midnight; Thursday and Sunday 12:30pm to midnight; and Friday and Saturday 11:30am to 12:45am.

Another old-fashioned bar that's a local favorite is the **Crown Hotel Pub,** 13 Main St. ((C) **01877/330-040**); it sometimes features live folk music. Otherwise it's a mellow old place for a pint of lager. Open Sunday to Thursday from noon to 11pm and Friday and Saturday 11am to 12:30am.

7 Aberfoyle: Gateway to the Trossachs ★

90km (56 miles) NW of Edinburgh, 44km (27 miles) N of Glasgow

Looking like an alpine village in the heart of Rob Roy country, the small resort of Aberfoyle, near Loch Ard, is the gateway to the Trossachs, one of the most beautiful and bucolic regions of Scotland. As one poet wrote: "So wondrous and wild, the whole might seem the scenery of a fair dream."

This was the land of Rob Roy (1671–1734), the outlaw and leader of the MacGregors. Sir Walter Scott recounted the outlaw's exploits in _Rob Roy,_ first published in 1818. Scott's romantic poem _The Lady of the Lake_ greatly increased tourism to the area, eventually attracting Queen Victoria, who was enchanted by its beauty. Wordsworth and Coleridge were eventually lured here away from England's Lake District. Wordsworth was so inspired, he wrote "To a Highland Girl."

ESSENTIALS

GETTING THERE   It's tough to get here by public transportation; you'll really need to drive. From Stirling, take A84 west until you reach the junction of A873 and continue west to Aberfoyle.

VISITOR INFORMATION   The **Trossachs Discovery Centre** is on Main Street (© 01877/382-352). It's open April to June daily 10am to 5pm; July to August daily 9:30am to 6pm; September to October daily 10am to 5pm; November to March Saturday and Sunday 10am to 4pm.

EXPLORING THE AREA

About 6.5km (4 miles) east of Aberfoyle on A81 is **Inchmahome Priory,** on an island in Lake Menteith. From the Port of Menteith, you can take a ferry to the island (weather permitting). The fare is £4.50 ($8.55) for adults, £3.50 ($6.65) for seniors and students, and £2.25 ($4.30) for children. Once here, you'll find the ruins of a 13th-century Augustinian house where Mary Queen of Scots was sent as a baby in 1547. For information, call © **01877/385-294.**

A nature lover's delight, the **Queen Elizabeth Forest Park** ⊕ lies between the eastern shore of Loch Lomond and the Trossachs. Some 18,225 hectares (45,000 acres) of moor, woodland, and mountain have been set aside as a preserve for walking and exploring. From mid-March to mid-September, it's open daily from 10am to 6pm. Admission is free. From the lodge, you enjoy views of Ben Lomond, the Menteith Hills, and the Campsie Fells. For walking maps and information, stop at the **Queen Elizabeth Forest Park Visitor Centre** (© **01877/382-258**), in the David Marshall Lodge, off A821, 1.6km (1 mile) north of Aberfoyle.

Another great walk in the area is the **Highland Boundary Fault Walk,** which follows the Highland boundary fault edge. Here you can see panoramic views of the Highlands to the north and the Lowlands to the south. It begins 10km (6 miles) south of the Trossachs on A821. Detailed information is provided by the Forestry Commission in Aberfoyle (© **01877/382-383**).

North of Aberfoyle, **Dukes Pass** (A821) climbs through Achray Forest past the Queen Elizabeth Forest Park Visitor Centre (see above), where you can stop for snacks and a panoramic view of the Forth Valley. Information on numerous walks, cycling routes, the Achray scenic forest drive, picnic sites, parking areas, and many other activities is available at the center. The road runs to the Trossachs between lochs Achray and Katrine.

Loch Katrine ⊕⊕, where Rob Roy MacGregor was born, owes its fame to Sir Walter Scott's poem *The Lady of the Lake.* The loch is the principal reservoir of the city of Glasgow. A small steamer, the **SS *Sir Walter Scott,*** plies the waters of the loch, which has submerged the romantic poet's "silver strand." Sailings are twice a day from Easter to late October, between Trossachs Pier and Stronachlachar, at a round-trip fare of about £8 ($15) for adults, £7 ($13) for seniors and students, £6 ($11) for those under 16, or £15 ($29) per family. Prices vary depending on time of day. (Morning sailings are more expensive.) Complete information on sailing schedules is available from the **Trossachs' Discovery Center** (© **0141/355-5333**). Light refreshments are available at Trossachs Pier.

If you'd like to explore the countryside on two wheels, head for **Trossachs' Cycle Hire,** Trossachs Holiday Park, Aberfoyle (© **01877/382-614**). The rental rates are £14 ($27) per day. Open daily from 8:30am to 6pm.

Shoppers will want to check out the **Scottish Wool Centre,** Main Street (© **01877/382-850**), which sells a big selection of knitwear and woolens from surrounding mills, including jackets, hats, rugs, sweaters, and cashmere items. It also houses an amphitheater that holds a textile display area, along with live specimens of different breeds of Scottish sheep (but no clones yet). Spinning and weaving demonstrations are presented, and baby lambs fill a children's petting zoo. Admission to the shop is free, but the exhibition costs £4 ($7.60) for adults or £9 ($17) per family. The whole complex is open daily from 10am to 6pm, with exhibitions at 11am, noon, 2pm, and 3pm.

WHERE TO STAY

Creag-Ard House 🎔   This Victorian villa is one of the stateliest houses in the region. Its steep rooflines and stone-ringed bay windows give it an appealingly quirky, even Gothic-looking, allure. Built in 1885 on 1.2 hectares (3 acres) of forested parkland with spectacular stands of azaleas and rhododendrons (blooming in late May), it's a stone's throw from the shores of Loch Ard, the inn's private lake. Guests are welcome to fish from the water's edge, and rowboats are available for rent. The inn offers cozy, well-upholstered rooms with attractive furniture, lots of sun, and private bathrooms.

Milton, Aberfoyle FK8 3TQ. ©/fax **01877/382-297**. www.creag-ard.co.uk. 6 units. £70–£90 ($133–$171) double. Rates include breakfast. MC, V. Free parking. Open Easter–Oct. From Aberfoyle, drive 1.6km (1 mile) west, following B829 toward Kinlochard. **Amenities:** Bar; breakfast room; boat rental; nonsmoking rooms. *In room:* Coffeemaker, no phone.

Forest Hills 🎔🎔 *Kids*   This country house overlooking Loch Ard is the choice address in the area. It was the winner of "The Scottish Family Hotel of the Year" award in 2007. In the foothills of the Trossachs, the resort stands in 10 hectares (25 acres) of private lands which are riddled with trails running alongside tumbling burns (creeks). A haven of tranquillity, the house with its open fires and panoramic views also has the best leisure facilities in the area, with a good gym and an indoor pool plus a steam room and spa bath.

Families often prefer the lodges facing toward the loch, as each unit comes with one to three bedrooms, each with private balcony or patio plus a fully equipped kitchen. In addition, there are 17 family units. Even the standard bedrooms are comfortably sized and well laid out, each attractively furnished in modern styling. All units come with private bathroom with shower units. The cuisine in the Garden Restaurant is excellent, relying on Scottish regional products such as fresh Tay salmon, Perthshire lamb, wild venison, or west coast seafood. Less formal dining is in the Rafters steakhouse with its menu of steaks, pizzas, burgers, and pasta.

Kinlochard, Aberfoyle, FK8 3TL. © **0870/194-2105**. Fax 0870/738-7307. www.macdonaldhotels.co.uk. 115 units. Summer £150 ($285) double (rate includes breakfast), £160 ($304) double (rate includes breakfast and dinner); off season £100 ($190) double (rate includes breakfast); £140 ($266) double (rate includes breakfast and dinner).

Inchrie Castle The Covenanters Inn   Overlooking the waters of the River Forth, this pleasing inn was built in the 1800s as a private home with architecture inspired by Scottish castles. It was enlarged in the 1960s and 1980s and transformed into a hotel. Part of its name comes from the famous convention held here in 1949, when a group of church and political leaders issued a then famous Second Covenant promoting the separation of Scotland from England. On Christmas Eve of 1952, the hotel again became famous (or notorious) after the theft from Westminster Abbey of the Stone of Scone. The Stone was recovered after having spent a night here, it's claimed. (A controversy continues as to the authenticity of the recovered artifact.)

Cozy public areas have oak-beam ceilings and stone fireplaces. The dignified yet comfortable guest rooms are furnished in Scottish country-house style, and many offer splendid views of the Trossachs.

The bar serves drinks from a wide selection of single-malt whiskies, as well as affordable meals. The more formal restaurant offers moderately priced dinners.

Duchray Rd. (about 1km/½ mile southwest of Aberfoyle), Aberfoyle FK8 3XD. © 01877/382-347. Fax 01877/ 382-785. 45 units. £110 ($209) double. Rates include breakfast. 25% discount to children under 14. AE, DC, MC, V. Free parking. From Aberfoyle take A81 south. Turn right on Duchray Rd. **Amenities:** Restaurant; lounge; bar; access to indoor swimming pool and health club (a 20-min. drive away); nonsmoking rooms. *In room:* TV, coffeemaker, hair dryer.

WHERE TO DINE

Braeval Restaurant ♠ SCOTTISH   Overlooking a golf course, this restaurant is housed in a former stone mill, and the owners have kept an antique waterwheel to remind diners of the building's former function. The chefs here display inventiveness and solid technique. We especially like how the kitchen takes full advantage of the region's riches, including game in season. The repertoire embraces both traditional and modern British dishes on a changing fixed-price menu. You might begin with game terrine with pear chutney; for main dishes, sample such delights as seared bass bream with salad Niçoise, a lasagna of chicken livers flavored with lemon and thyme, or filet of salmon with mussel-and-basil butter sauce.

Callander Rd. (A81). © 01877/382-711. Reservations required. Main courses £12–£16 ($23–$30); Sat night fixed-price menu £25–£36 ($48–$68). MC, V. Tues–Sun 10am–5pm; Sat 7:30–9pm by reservation only. Closed 1 week in Feb, 1 week in June, and 2 weeks in Oct. Drive 1.6km (1 mile) east of Aberfoyle on A81 (Callander Rd.).

8 On the Bonnie, Bonnie Banks of Loch Lomond ♠♠♠

Loch Lomond is the largest of Scotland's lochs. The center of the ancient district of Lennox, it was possessed by the Stewart (Stuart) family, to which Lord Darnley (second husband of Mary Queen of Scots) belonged. The ruins of **Lennox Castle** are on Inchmurrin, one of the loch's 30 islands; Inchmurrin has ecclesiastical ruins and is noted for its yew trees, planted by King Robert the Bruce to ensure a suitable supply of wood for the bows of his archers. The loch is fed by at least 10 rivers from west, east, and north and is about 39km (24 miles) long; it stretches 8km (5 miles) at its widest point. On the eastern side is Ben Lomond, which rises to a height of 968m (3,192 ft.).

The song "Loch Lomond" was supposedly composed by one of Bonnie Prince Charlie's captured followers on the eve of his execution in Carlisle Jail. The "low road" of the song is the path through the underworld that his spirit will follow to his native land after death, more quickly than his friends can travel to Scotland by the ordinary high road.

If you're going to Loch Lomond by train, call **08457/484-950** for rail information. Glasgow is the best rail center for trips to the loch. Trains depart Monday to Saturday from the Glasgow Queen Street Station or from Glasgow Central on Sunday at the rate of two per hour. The trip takes 45 minutes and costs £4 ($7.60) for a one-way ticket. Arrivals are at the town of Balloch.

Scottish Citylink (© **08705/505-050**) runs seven buses a day to Balloch, costing £4 ($7.60) for a one-way ticket; the trip takes 45 minutes. These buses also continue along the western shoreline to other centers such as Luss and Tarbet, which also open onto Lomond. If you wish to explore the eastern side of the loch, take bus no. 309 from Balloch.

The easiest way to see the famous loch is not by car but by one of the local ships owned by **Sweeney's Cruisers Ltd.,** and based at Sweeney's Shipyard, 26 Balloch Rd., Balloch G83 8LQ (© **01389/752-376;** www.sweeney.uk.com). Cruises on various boats last for about an hour and in summer depart every hour 10:30am to 7:30pm (departures in other months are based on demand). At £4 to £6.50 ($7.60–$12) per person round-trip, cruises sail from Balloch toward a wooded island, Inchmurrin, year-round home to five families, several vacation chalets, and a summer-only nudist colony. The ship doesn't dock at the island, however.

BALLOCH

At the southern end of Loch Lomond is Balloch, the most touristy of the towns and villages around the lake. It grew up on the River Leven, where the water leaves Loch Lomond and flows south to the Clyde. Today, Balloch is visited chiefly by those wanting to take boat trips on Loch Lomond; these sail in season from Balloch Pier.

EXPLORING THE AREA

The best place to go for information about the area is **Loch Lomond Shores,** standing side-by-side with the **National Park Gateway Centre,** Ben Lomond Way (© **01389/722-600**). Staffed by park rangers, the center contains information about Scotland's first national park—which extends into both Loch Lomond and the Trossachs—as well as local wildlife and flora, organized talks, and recommended ways to explore the area. There's a rooftop viewing gallery for panoramic vistas of both the loch and the national park, which opened in 2002. The center also features a 40-minute film, *Legend of Loch Lomond.* On-site are restaurants, cafes, and shops. Hours are daily: April 1 to May 29 10am to 6pm; May 30 to June 26 9:30am to 6pm; June 27 to September 4 9:30am to 6:30pm; September 5 to October 2 9:30am to 6pm; October 3 to October 30 10am to 6pm; October 31 to March 31 10am to 5pm. Entrance is free.

The 81-hectare (200-acre) **Balloch Castle Country Park** is on the bonnie banks of Loch Lomond, 1.2km (¾ mile) north of Balloch Station. The present **Balloch Castle** (© **01389/722-600**), replacing one that dated from 1238, was constructed in 1808 for John Buchanan of Ardoch in the castle-Gothic style. Its visitor center explains the history of the property. The site has a walled garden, and the trees and shrubs, especially the rhododendrons and azaleas, reach the zenith of their beauty in late May and early June. You can also visit a Fairy Glen. The park is open all year, daily 8am to dusk,

---

Moments **You Take the High Road & I'll Take the Low Road**

One of the great marked footpaths of Scotland, the **West Highland Way** goes along the complete eastern sector of lovely Loch Lomond. The footpath actually begins at Milngavie, outside Glasgow. Serious backpackers often do the entire 153km (95-mile) trail, but you can tackle just sections of it for marvelous day hikes that will allow you to enjoy the scenery.

with free admission. Easter to the end of October, the visitor center is open daily 10am to 6pm.

Dumbarton District's Countryside Ranger Service is based at Balloch Castle and conducts **guided walks** at various locations around Loch Lomond throughout the summer.

A fascinating side trip is possible to the village of **Drymen** which lies 8km (5 miles) northeast of Balloch along A811. At the edge of the village stands the palatial ruin of **Buchanan Castle** ⟨★★⟩, the ancient fortress of the Duke of Montrose. Hitler's deputy, Rudolf Hess, was imprisoned here in 1941 after he flew to Britain in hopes of ending the war between his country and the Allies. Other illustrious guests have included the Shah of Iran, King George V and Queen Mary, and King Victor Emmanuel of Italy. The roof was removed in 1955 to avoid paying tax, and the castle fell into ruin. But what magnificent ruins. The original Buchanan Castle was destroyed in 1852 but the 4th Duke of Montrose commissioned the famous architect, William Burn, to design what in Victoria's day became one of the most spectacular castles in Scotland. Wandering around the ruins is both a ghostly and a sightseeing thrill.

WHERE TO STAY & DINE

Balloch House Hotel   Called Balloch's grande dame, this was the first hotel built in town. In 1860, the Balloch welcomed the Empress Eugénie, wife of Napoleon III, when she toured Scotland. (She slept in the Inchmoan Room.) It stands beside the river in the center of the village, offering basic, functionally furnished rooms, each with a shower (some with a tub as well).

Balloch Rd., Balloch G83 8LQ. Ⓒ **01389/710-344.** Fax 01389/755-604. 10 units. £65 ($124) double. Rates include Scottish breakfast. AE, DC, MC, V. **Amenities:** Restaurant; bar; room service; nonsmoking rooms. *In room:* TV, coffeemaker, hair dryer, trouser press.

Cameron House ⟨★★★⟩ *Kids*   This is one of the great country houses of Scotland, the ancestral home of the Smolletts. Its most distinguished son was Tobias Smollet, the 18th-century novelist whose humorous works have been read around the world. Over the years the house has been visited by such illustrious guests as the emperor of Brazil, Sir Winston Churchill, Princess Margaret, and Earl Mountbatten. Literary celebrities have also shown up at the doorstep, none more famous than Dr. Samuel Johnson and his indefatigable biographer, James Boswell. Dr. Johnson later wrote, "We have had more solid talk in this house than in any other place where we have been."

Today this house has been converted into top-rated accommodations, with one of the best spas in this part of Scotland. The resort also contains some of the finest indoor leisure facilities in the area. The smallest rooms are called "house rooms," with standard rooms being slightly larger and better. Best of all are the spacious suites, furnished with four-poster beds. All rooms are nonsmoking. Many of the furnishings are in the traditional Georgian style, with dark mahogany pieces set against floral bathrooms, some of which have tub/shower combinations, others either a tub or a shower.

Children are warmly welcomed and the hotel has a supervised playroom where parents can leave kids for a couple of hours while they relax in the gorgeous lagoon pool or the spa. The Scottish and French cuisine served in the Georgian Room is among the most refined in this part of Scotland. You can also dine informally in two other restaurants. Many sporting adventures, ranging from golf to fishing to private yacht parties, can be arranged.

Alexandria, Loch Lomond, G83 8QZ. ℭ **01389/755-565.** Fax 01389/759-522. www.cameronhouse.co.uk. 96 units. £179–£289 ($340–$549) double; £349–£469 ($663–$891) suite. Children £20 ($38) extra. Rates include full breakfast. AE, DC, MC, V. Take M8 to A82 to Loch Lomond; follow signs to hotel. **Amenities:** 3 restaurants; bar; indoor heated pool; golf course; health club; spa; marina; watersports equipment/rentals; children's center; room service; babysitting; laundry service; dry cleaning; steam room; Turkish bath; nonsmoking rooms. *In room:* TV, minibar, coffeemaker, hair dryer.

LUSS

The village of Luss, 14km (9 miles) north of Balloch on A82 on the western side of Loch Lomond, is the traditional home of the Colquhouns. Among its stone cottages, on the water's edge, is a branch of the Highland Arts Studios of Seil. Cruises on the loch and boat rentals may be arranged at a nearby jetty.

If your travels in Scotland inspire you to put on a kilt and blow your own set of bagpipes, stop by **Thistle Bagpipe Works** (ℭ **01436/860-250;** www.kiltsandbagpipes.co.uk), in the center of Luss. Here, not only can you order custom-made bagpipes but you can also purchase a clan kilt to go with the instrument. Your neighbors back home will be thrilled.

WHERE TO STAY & DINE

The Lodge on Loch Lomond Hotel   Surrounded by mountain, loch, and woodland, you can live in Scottish country-house style and take in panoramic views of legendary Loch Lomond. The hotel, in fact, was designed for this very purpose. But that's not the only reason to stay here. This lodging, much improved in recent years, offers tasteful bedrooms and numerous comforts. The executive rooms are set up for wheelchair access, and each contains a two-person sauna. The hotel will also arrange local activities, including salmon fishing and private charter cruises, as well as horseback riding.

The fine restaurant is yet another excellent reason to stay here, or at least to drop in for an evening. It uses only the finest and freshest local ingredients, serving individually prepared meals that are the best in the area. The accommodating staff makes this a relaxed, comfortable place. Although the menu changes, main courses might include pan-fried venison loin with haggis skirlie, or speared tiger prawns with chile and garlic nut-brown butter. There is a wide selection of Aberdeen Angus beef priced according to weight, and lobster is served in a multitude of ways. For something really Scottish, try roast pheasant with bacon-braised barley and a whisky cream sauce. Those who want a lighter meal can opt for a burger, fish and chips, pasta, or pizza. The quality of the food is excellent, matched by panoramic views of the loch. Reservations are recommended and can be made by calling ℭ **01436/860-201.** Main courses are £11 to £25 ($21–$48). American Express, MasterCard, and Visa are accepted. The restaurant is open daily noon to 2:30pm and 6 to 9:30pm.

Luss, Argyll G83 8PA. ℭ **01436/860-201.** Fax 01436/860-203. www.loch-lomond.co.uk. 46 units. £90–£169 ($171–$321); £159–£279 ($302–$530) suite. Rates include full Scottish breakfast. AE, MC, V. Free parking. Take A82 from Glasgow. **Amenities:** Restaurant; bar; indoor heated pool; gym; spa; room service; laundry service; steam room; nonsmoking rooms; rooms for those w/limited mobility. *In room:* TV, coffeemaker, hair dryer, iron.

10

Aberdeen & the Tayside & Grampian Regions

The two historic regions of Tayside and Grampian offer a vast array of sightseeing, even though they're relatively small. Tayside, for example, is about 137km (85 miles) east to west and 97km (60 miles) south to north. The regions share the North Sea coast between the Firth of Tay in the south and the Firth of Moray farther north, and the so-called Highland Line separating the Lowlands in the south from the Highlands in the north crosses both. The Grampians, Scotland's highest mountain range, are to the west of this line.

Carved out of the old counties of Perth and Angus, **Tayside** is named for its major river, the 192km-long (119-mile) Tay. The region is easy to explore, and its waters offer some of Europe's best salmon and trout fishing. Tayside abounds with heather-clad Highland hills, long blue lochs under forested banks, and miles of walking trails. Perth and Dundee are among Scotland's largest cities. Tayside provided the backdrop for many novels by Sir Walter Scott, including *The Fair Maid of Perth, Waverley,* and *The Abbot.* And its golf courses are world famous, ranging from the trio of 18-hole courses at Gleneagles to the Open Championships links at Carnoustie.

Grampian boasts Aberdeen, Scotland's third-largest city, and Braemar, site of the most famous of Highland Gatherings. The queen herself comes here for holidays, to stay at Balmoral Castle, her private residence, a tradition dating back to the days of Queen Victoria and her consort, Prince Albert. As you journey on the scenic roads of Scotland's northeast, you pass moorland and peaty lochs, wood glens and rushing rivers, granite-stone villages and ancient castles, and fishing harbors and North Sea beach resorts.

1 Aberdeen: The Castle Country ★ ★

209km (130 miles) NE of Edinburgh, 108km (67 miles) N of Dundee

Bordered by fine sandy beaches (delightful if you're a polar bear), Scotland's third city, Aberdeen, is often called the "Granite City" because its buildings are constructed largely of pink or gray granite, hewn from the Rubislaw quarries. The harbor is one of the country's largest fishing ports, filled with kipper and deep-sea trawlers, and Aberdeen lies on the banks of the salmon- and trout-filled Don and Dee rivers. Spanning the Don is the **Brig o' Balgownie,** a steep Gothic arch begun in 1285.

Although it hardly compares with Glasgow and Edinburgh, Aberdeen is the center of a vibrant university; it boasts a few marvelous museums and galleries; and it's known for great nightlife and shopping, the best in the northeast. Old Aberdeen is the seat of one of Scotland's major cathedrals, St. Machars. It's also a good base for exploring the greatest castles of Grampian and the towns and villages along the splendid salmon river, Deeside.

ESSENTIALS

GETTING THERE Aberdeen is served by a number of airlines, including British Airways, British Midland, Easy Jet, and KLM. For flight information, phone the Aberdeen Airport at ✆ **01224/722-331.** The airport is about 11km (7 miles) away from the heart of town and is connected to it by a bus service costing £1.50 ($2.85) one-way. Taxis cost about £13 ($25).

Aberdeen has direct rail links to the major cities of Britain. SuperSaver fares, available by avoiding travel on Friday and Saturday, make the price difference between a one-way fare and a round-trip ticket negligible. Another efficient way of saving on fares by another £10 ($19) is reserving through the booking agency, Apex. For fares in Scotland, call ✆ **0845/755-0033** with at least 48 hours' notice. For fares from London, call ✆ **0845/722-5225** with a minimum of 1 week's notice. The prices here are for tickets bought on the day of departure, excluding Friday, when prices are higher. Nineteen trains per normal weekday arrive from Edinburgh; a regular one-way ticket costs £18 to £21 ($34–$40). Trip time is about 3½ hours. Another 19 trains per day arrive from Glasgow, costing £34 ($65) one-way or £48 ($91) round-trip. Some 12 trains per day arrive from London as well, with a one-way fare of £72 ($137) and a round-trip fare of only £98 ($186). For rail schedules, call ✆ **0345/484-950.**

Several bus companies have express routes serving Aberdeen, and many offer special round-trip fares to passengers avoiding travel on Friday or Saturday. Frequent buses arrive from both Glasgow and Edinburgh, costing £25 to £31 ($48–$59). There are also frequent arrivals from Inverness. For bus schedules in Aberdeen, call ✆ **01224/212-266.**

It's also easy to drive to the northeast. From the south, drive via Edinburgh over the Forth and Tay Road bridges and take the coastal road. From the north and west, approach the area from the much-improved A9, which links Perth, Inverness, and Wick.

VISITOR INFORMATION The **Aberdeen Tourist Information Centre** is in St. Nicholas House, Broad Street, Aberdeen, Aberdeenshire AB10 1DE (✆ **01224/632-727**). July and August, it's open Monday to Friday from 9am to 7pm, Saturday from 9am to 5pm, and Sunday from 10am to 4pm. All other months, it's open Monday to Friday from 9am to 5pm and Saturday from 10am to 2pm.

EXPLORING ABERDEEN

In old Aberdeen is the **University of Aberdeen,** a fusion of two colleges. Reached along University Road, **King's College** (✆ **01224/272-137;** bus: 6 or 20) is Great Britain's oldest school of medicine. The college is known for its chapel (ca. 1500) with pre-Reformation carved woodwork, the finest of its kind in Scotland; it's open daily 9am to 4:30pm, charging no admission. On Broad Street is **Marischal College** (✆ **01224/273-131**), founded in 1593 by Earl Marischal—it's the world's second-biggest granite structure (El Escorial, outside Madrid, is much larger). The main structure is no longer in use, but on-site is the Marischal Museum displaying exhibits and photos of the university and the Scottish culture of the northeast in general; admission is free, and the museum is open Monday to Friday from 10am to 5pm and Sunday from 2 to 5pm. In 1860, the colleges joined together to form the nucleus of the University of Aberdeen.

The Tayside & Grampian Regions

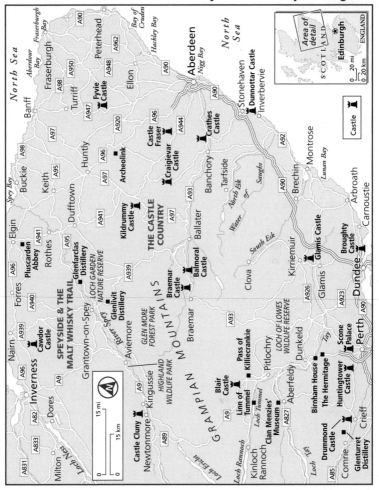

Also at the University of Aberdeen, the **Cruickshank Botanic Garden,** St. Machar Drive (© **01224/272-704; bus: 6 or 20**), displays alpines, shrubs, and many herbaceous plants, along with rock and water gardens. It's open Monday to Friday from 9am to 5pm; in summer, it's also open Saturday and Sunday from 2 to 5pm. Admission is free.

The **Cathedral of St. Machar,** Chanonry (© **01224/485-988** in the morning or 01224/317-424 in the afternoon; bus: 1, 2, 3, 4, 5, 6, 7, or 26), was founded in 1131, but the present structure dates from the 15th century. Its splendid heraldic ceiling contains three rows of shields. Be sure to note the magnificent modern stained-glass windows by Douglas Strachan and the pre-Reformation woodwork. The cathedral is open daily 9am to 5pm.

At **Alpine Bikes,** 66–70 Holburn St. (② **01224/211-455**), you can rent a bike so that you can go exploring on two wheels. Rates are £15 ($29) daily or £27 ($51) for weekends, with weekly rates at £60 ($114). It's open Sunday from 11am to 5pm, Monday to Wednesday and Friday from 9am to 6pm, and Thursday from 9am to 8pm.

Aberdeen Art Gallery ⭐ Built in 1884 in a neoclassical design by A. Marshall MacKenzie, this building houses one of the most important art collections in Great Britain. It contains 18th-century portraits by Raeburn, Hogarth, Ramsay, and Reynolds, as well as acclaimed 20th-century works by Paul Nash, Ben Nicholson, and Francis Bacon. The exhibits also include excellent pieces by Monet, Pissarro, Sisley, and Bonnard as well as a collection of Scottish domestic silver. Special exhibits and events are frequently offered.

Schoolhill. ② **01224/523-700**. www.aagm.co.uk. Free admission. Mon–Sat 10am–5pm; Sun 2–5pm. Bus: 20.

Aberdeen Maritime Museum Using a unique collection of ship models, paintings, artifacts, computer interaction, and exhibits, this museum tells the story of the city's long and fascinating relationship with the sea. A major display on the offshore oil industry features a model of the Murchison oil platform. The complex is on four floors, incorporating the 1593 Provost Ross House linked by a modern glass structure to the granite Trinity Church. Windows open onto panoramic views of the harbor.

Shiprow. ② **01224/337-700**. www.aagm.co.uk. Free admission. Mon–Sat 10am–5pm; Sun noon–3pm. Bus: 20.

Dunnottar Castle The well-preserved ruins of Dunnottar are on a rocky promontory towering 49m (160 ft.) above the surging sea, and the best way to get here is by a dramatic 30-minute walk from Stonehaven along the cliffs. The ruins include a great square tower and a chapel built in 1292. William Wallace stormed it in 1297, but failed to take it. In 1991, it was the setting for Zeffirelli's film of *Hamlet,* starring Mel Gibson. You can reach Stonehaven from Aberdeen by taking Bluebird Northern bus no. 107, which costs £5.70 ($11) round-trip, and then walking for 5 minutes. Trains run about every half-hour from Aberdeen to Stonehaven, costing £6 to £7.50 ($11–$14) round-trip. Departures are every 30 minutes during the day; the trip takes 30 minutes.

3km (2 miles) south of Stonehaven off A92. ② **01569/762-173**. Admission £5 ($9.50) adults, £1 ($1.90) children under 16. Easter–Oct Mon–Sat 9am–6pm, Sun 2–5pm; Nov–Easter Fri–Mon 9am–dusk.

Provost Skene's House This attraction is named for a rich merchant who was Lord Provost of Aberdeen from 1676 to 1685. It's a museum, off Broad Street, with period rooms and artifacts of domestic life. Provost Skene's kitchen has been converted into a cafe.

5 Guestrow, off Broad St. ② **01224/641-086**. Free admission. Mon–Fri 10am–5pm; Sat 10am–4pm; Sun 1–3pm. Bus: 20.

SHOPPING

The main shopping districts center on specialty shops on **Chapel** and **Thistle streets** and on the well-known chains on **George** and **Union streets.** Of interest to collectors, **Colin Wood,** 25 Rose St. (② **01224/643-019**), stocks furniture, wall clocks, and grandfather clocks from the 17th to the early 20th centuries. Its specialty, however, is maps from the Elizabethan through the Victorian eras. The shop also sells 17th- to early-20th-century prints of northern Scotland. You may also want to browse through

Aberdeen

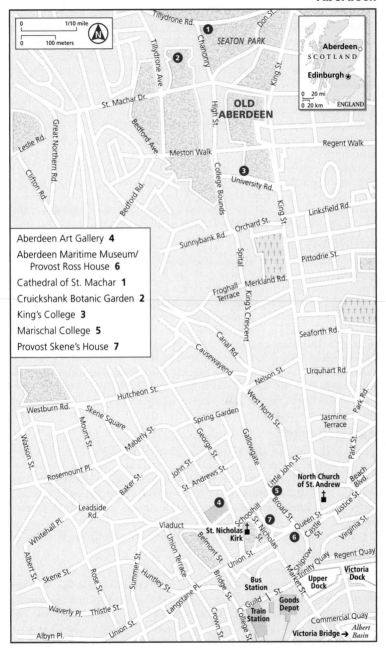

Aberdeen Art Gallery **4**

Aberdeen Maritime Museum/
  Provost Ross House **6**

Cathedral of St. Machar **1**

Cruickshank Botanic Garden **2**

King's College **3**

Marischal College **5**

Provost Skene's House **7**

the eclectic mix of bric-a-brac antiques at **Elizabeth Watts Studio,** 69 Thistle St. (© **01224/647-232**), where items include glass, brass, antique jewelry, china, silver, and a few small furniture pieces. The shop is actually best known for its china and glass restoration studio. For one-stop gift shopping, drop in at **Nova,** 20 Chapel St. (© **01224/643-607**), which stocks china, silver jewelry, rugs, clothing, toys, cards, and gift paper.

To trace your Scottish ancestry, go to the **Aberdeen Family History Shop,** 164 King St. (© **01224/646-323**), where membership to the Aberdeen and North East Family History Society costs £15 ($29) cash, check, or credit card. Once you join, you can go through a vast range of publications kept on hand to help members trace their family histories.

Other noteworthy shops are **Grandad's Attic,** 12 Marischal St. (© **01224/213-699**), which specializes in Art Deco ceramics and antique pine furniture; **Just Scottish,** 4 Upperkirkgate (© **01224/621-755**), retailers of quality items—all made in Scotland, including ceramics, knitwear, textiles, silver, and jewelry; and **Alex Scott & Co.,** 43 Schoolhill (© **01224/643-924**), the town's finest kiltmakers.

HITTING THE LINKS

Aberdeen has a good range of golf courses in and around the city, with several other notable courses within an easy drive. As always, reservations are essential at any course. If the two below don't suit you, ask the tourist office for details on other options.

Among the top courses is **Balgownie, the Royal Aberdeen Golf Club** (© **01224/702-571**), created in 1780 in classic links style. An uneven layout, sea breezes, and grassy sand dunes add to the challenge of this 6,415-yard, par-70 course. Greens fees are £100 ($190) per round, or £150 ($285) per day, Monday to Friday, and after 3pm on weekends. A letter of introduction is required to play here.

About 11km (7 miles) west of Aberdeen, the par-69 **West Hills Golf Course,** West Hill Heights, West Hill Skene (©/fax **01224/740-159**), features 5,849 yards of playing area. Greens fees are £20 ($38) Monday through Friday, or £25 ($48) Saturday and Sunday.

WHERE TO STAY

Because of increasing numbers of tourists and business travelers to the Granite City—Europe's offshore oil capital—hotels are likely to be heavily booked any time of year. If you haven't reserved ahead, stop by the **Aberdeen Tourist Information Centre,** Alford Street (© **01224/288-828**), where the staff can usually find just the right lodging for you—a family-run B&B, a guesthouse, or a hotel. A £2.50 ($4.75) service fee is charged.

Rooms are also available at **Ferryhill House** (see "Where to Dine," below).

EXPENSIVE

Hilton Aberdeen Treetops 🐾 *Kids* A 10-minute drive west of the center of Aberdeen off A93, this comfortable hotel, built in the 1960s and renovated in 1991, offers a sweeping white facade of traditional design. The windows of its contemporary guest rooms look over landscaped grounds; some units have balconies with lake views, and all have well-maintained bathrooms with combo tub/shower. Some 30 accommodations are large enough to house families, and a playground is available for children.

161 Springfield Rd., Aberdeen AB15 7AQ. © **01224/313-377.** Fax 01224/028-504. www.aberdeen.hilton.com. 120 units. £124–£155 ($236–$295) double; £144–£195 ($274–$371) suite. AE, DC, MC, V. Free parking. Bus: 11. **Amenities:**

Restaurant; bar; health club; children's programs; business center; room service; babysitting; laundry service; dry cleaning; nonsmoking rooms; rooms for those w/limited mobility. *In room:* TV, coffeemaker, hair dryer.

Marcliffe at Pitfodels ✸✸✸ On the city's western edge, less than a half-hour from the airport, is this deluxe hotel—superior to all others in the area. The traditional three-story manor house was constructed around a courtyard and stands on 3.2 hectares (8 acres) of landscaped grounds. The Oriental rugs, placed on stone floors, and the tartan sofas set the tone in the public rooms; a scattering of antiques add a grace note. The rather spacious guest rooms are furnished in Chippendale and reproduction pieces, with armchairs and desks, plus a host of extras such as fresh milk in the minibar.

At breakfast you can sample Aberdeen *rowies,* a local specialty, made with butter, that's like a flattened croissant. The conservatory restaurant offers regional dishes like Highland lamb and fresh Scottish salmon. In the library lounge, you can choose from more than 130 scotches, 500 wines, and 70 cognacs.

N. Deeside Rd., Aberdeen AB1 9YA. ✆ **01224/861-000.** Fax 01224/868-860. www.marcliffe.com. 42 units. £185–£205 ($352–$390) double; £245–£295 ($466–$561) suite. Rates include breakfast. AE, DC, MC, V. Free parking. Lies on the Deeside Rd. out of Aberdeen (well signposted). **Amenities:** Restaurant; bar; room service; laundry service; dry cleaning; nonsmoking rooms. *In room:* TV, minibar, coffeemaker, hair dryer, iron.

Simpson's Hotel ✸ This hotel, which opened in 1998, enjoys great popularity. Two traditional granite town houses were joined to offer comfortable accommodations. Rooms are decorated with furniture from Spain and painted in rich, bold colors that create a cool, Mediterranean ambience. Amenities include complimentary use of the health spa.

The hotel bar and brasserie offers a range of moderately priced Scottish and international dishes prepared with the finest of local ingredients.

59 Queens Rd., Aberdeen AB15 4YP. ✆ **01224/327-777.** Fax 01224/327-700. www.simpsonshotel.co.uk. 50 units. £130–£140 ($247–$266) double; suites from £170 ($323). Rates include breakfast. AE, MC, V. Follow signs for A96 North, and turn right at Queens Rd. Roundabout. **Amenities:** Restaurant; bar; spa; room service; babysitting; laundry service; dry cleaning; nonsmoking rooms. *In room:* A/C, TV, minibar, coffeemaker, hair dryer, iron, trouser press.

Thistle Aberdeen Caledonian ✸ The Thistle occupies a grand stone-fronted Victorian that's in the center of Aberdeen and a 2-minute walk form the rail station. Restorations have added a veneer of Georgian gloss to one of the most elegant series of public rooms in town. The guest rooms are at the top of a 19th-century stairwell, with Corinthian columns and a freestanding atrium. They vary a good deal in size, but all contain double-glazed windows and bathrooms with tub/shower combinations. Each of the accommodations is comfortably furnished with taste.

10–14 Union Terrace (off Union St.), Aberdeen AB10 1WE. ✆/fax **0870/333-9131.** www.thistlehotels.com/aberdeen caledonian. 77 units. £115–£130 ($219–$247) double; from £235 ($447) suite. Children age 11 and under stay free in parent's room. AE, DC, MC, V. Limited free parking. Bus: 17. Pets allowed. **Amenities:** Restaurant; bar; secretarial services; room service; laundry service; dry cleaning; nonsmoking rooms. *In room:* TV, minibar, coffeemaker, hair dryer, iron.

MODERATE

The Jays Guest House *Value* This is one of the nicest guesthouses in Aberdeen, located near the university and the Offshore Survival Centre. Alice and George Jennings are welcoming hosts, and many repeat visitors consider Alice their candidate for "landlady of the year." Everything runs smoothly, and the guest rooms are bright and airy, each newly renovated.

422 King St., Aberdeen AB24 3BR. ✆ **01224/638-295.** Fax 0122/638-360. www.jaysguesthouse.co.uk. 10 units. £80–£90 ($152–$171) double. Rates include Scottish breakfast. MC, V. Free parking. Lies 3 blocks north of the Civic Centre. Bus: 1, 2, 3, 4, or 7. **Amenities:** Nonsmoking rooms; Wi-Fi. *In room:* TV, coffeemaker, no phone.

Mannofield Hotel Built of silver granite around 1880, this hotel is a Victorian fantasy of step gables, turrets, spires, bay windows, and a sweeping mahogany-and-teakwood staircase. Owners Bruce and Dorothy Cryle offer a warm Scottish welcome. The guest rooms, with paisley curtains and quilts, are equipped with well-maintained shower-only bathrooms.

447 Great Western Rd., Aberdeen AB10 6NL. ✆ **01224/315-888.** Fax 01224/208-971. 9 units. £70 ($133) double. Rates include Scottish breakfast. AE, DC, MC, V. Free parking. Bus: 18 or 19. **Amenities:** Restaurant; room service; babysitting; laundry service; dry cleaning. *In room:* TV, coffeemaker, hair dryer.

The Palm Court Hotel Aberdeen (Value) Set a bit away from central Aberdeen, this is a highly praised, well-run hotel that locals recommend to visitors. The hotel is tranquil and known for its good value and fine bedrooms, which are comfortably furnished and well decorated (though not overly spacious). Each comes with a small but tidily kept bathroom with tub or shower. If you don't want to wander the streets of Aberdeen at night, seeking a restaurant, you'll find a good dining room on site at Hickory's Restaurant, specializing in fine Scottish food such as salmon.

81 Seafield Rd., Aberdeen AB15 7YX. ✆ **01224/310-351.** Fax 01224/312-707. 24 units. £85–£100 ($162–$190) double. AE, MC, V. Rates include full breakfast. Free parking. Bus: 11. **Amenities:** Restaurant; bar; business services; room service; laundry service; nonsmoking rooms; rooms for those w/limited mobility. *In room:* TV, coffeemaker, hair dryer, trouser press.

LUXURY ACCOMMODATIONS ON THE OUTSKIRTS OF ABERDEEN

Aberdeen Mercure Ardoe House (Finds) This turreted baronial mansion, built in 1878, sits in the midst of lush gardens and manicured grounds, offering panoramic views of the River Dee. Though it's close to Aberdeen, it's a world apart. Its old-fashioned interior, with wood paneling, carved fireplaces, and stained-glass windows, reflects the best in traditional Victorian style. The mansion was recently expanded, but even so, each room is individually decorated and well appointed with many extras, including immaculate bathrooms. In the formal dining room, you can order a blend of traditional and modern Scottish cuisine made from fresh local ingredients.

S. Deeside Rd. (3km/5 miles south of Aberdeen on B9077), Blairs, Aberdeen AB12 5YP. ✆ **01224/867-355.** Fax 01224/861-283. www.mmercure-co.uk. £120–£160 ($228–$304) double. AE, DC, MC, V. Pets welcome. **Amenities:** 2 restaurants; 2 bars; health club; spa; Jacuzzi; sauna; business center; room service; babysitting; laundry service; dry cleaning; steam room; nonsmoking rooms; rooms for those w/limited mobility. *In room:* TV, coffeemaker, minibar, hair dryer, iron.

Kildrummy Castle Hotel This 19th-century gray-stone mansion, on acres of landscaped gardens, overlooks the ruined castle of Kildrummy. Its guest rooms, many furnished with antiques, vary in size; some of the master rooms feature four-poster beds and fireplaces. The dignified public rooms have oak-paneled walls and ceilings, mullioned windows, and window seats. The drawing room and bar open onto a flagstone terrace.

Traditional Scottish food, including *Cullen skink* (smoked haddock soup) and filet of sole stuffed with smoked Scottish salmon, is served in the dining room.

Kildrummy by Alford AB33 8RA. ✆ **01975/571-288.** Fax 01975/571-345. www.kildrummycastlehotel.co.uk. 16 units. £165–£195 ($314–$371) double. Rates include Scottish breakfast. AE, MC, V. Closed Jan. From Aberdeen, take A944 and follow signs to Alford; then take A97, following signs to Kildrummy. **Amenities:** Restaurant; bar; room service; babysitting; laundry service; nonsmoking rooms. *In room:* TV, coffeemaker, hair dryer, trouser press.

Macdonald Pittodrie House ✶✶   Dating from 1490, the castle here was burned down and then rebuilt in 1675 as a family home—and that in turn became a country-house hotel when Royal Deeside became prominent through Queen Victoria's adoption of Balmoral as her holiday retreat. The guest rooms are divided between those in the old house (with good views and antique furniture) and the smaller rooms in the recent extension (decorated in keeping with the style of the house but with less atmosphere). Most of the bathrooms have combination tub/showers. The public rooms boast antiques, oil paintings, and open fires. The elegant restaurant serves venison, grouse, partridge, pheasant, and fresh fish.

Chapel of Garioch, Pitcaple AB5 5HS. ✆ **0870/194-2111.** Fax 01467/681-648. www.macdonald-hotels.co.uk/pittodrie. 27 units. £130–£170 ($247–$323) double. Rates include Scottish breakfast. AE, DC, MC, V. From Aberdeen, take A96, following signs to Inverness; remain on A96, bypassing Inverurie, then follow signs to Chapel of Garioch. **Amenities:** 2 restaurants; bar; room service; laundry service; nonsmoking rooms. *In room:* TV, coffeemaker, hair dryer, iron.

Thainstone House Hotel ✶✶✶   One of northeast Scotland's most elegant country hotels, set on 16 hectares (40 acres), the Thainstone House is a Palladian-style mansion whose adornments give it the air of a country club. It can serve as both a retreat and a center for exploring this historic part of Scotland, including the Malt Whisky Trail (see "Speyside & the Malt Whisky Trail," later in this chapter). Guests enter the mansion, which was designed by Archibald Simpson (the famed architect of many of Aberdeen's public buildings), through a grand portal up an elegant stairway. The high ceilings, columns, neoclassical plaster reliefs, and cornices evoke Simpson's trip to Italy. A modern section of the house skillfully blends the old with the new. The elegantly furnished guest rooms vary in size and offer extra touches such as sherry and shortbread.

The chef at Simpson's Restaurant turns out a Continental and Scottish menu with a light, inventive touch.

Inverurie AB51 5NT. ✆ **01467/621-643.** Fax 01467/625-084. www.swallow-hotels.com/thainstone-house. 48 units. £83–£185 ($158–$352) double; £275 ($523) suite. Rates include Scottish breakfast. AE, DC, MC, V. From Aberdeen, take A96, following signs to Inverness; just before Inverurie, turn left and follow signs to the hotel. **Amenities:** Restaurant; bar; indoor pool; health club; spa; Jacuzzi; room service; massage; babysitting; laundry service; steam room; nonsmoking rooms. *In room:* TV, coffeemaker, hair dryer, iron.

WHERE TO DINE

Ferryhill House INTERNATIONAL   Located in its own park and garden on the city's southern outskirts, Ferryhill House dates back 250 years. It has Georgian detailing, but refurbishment has removed many of the original panels and all the ceiling beams. The restaurant boasts one of the region's largest collections of single-malt whiskies—more than 140 brands. There's a fireplace for chilly afternoons and a beer garden for midsummer, as well as a conservatory. Though unexceptional, the food is prepared with market-fresh ingredients. It's more wholesome, hearty, and filling than gourmet. Menu items include steak or vegetable tempura, chicken dishes like chicken fajita, fried haddock filet, pastas, and chili.

Ferryhill House also rents nine standard guest rooms, with TVs, phones, and hair dryers. The rate for a double is £65 to £100 ($124–$190), breakfast included.

Bon Accord St., Aberdeen AB11 6UA. ✆ **01224/590-867.** Fax 01224/586-947. Reservations recommended Sat–Sun. Main courses £12–£15 ($23–$29). AE, DC, MC, V. Free parking. Bus: 16.

Howies Aberdeen ✦ SCOTTISH/INTERNATIONAL   This is the latest—and even better—reincarnation of the locally famous Gerard's, which stood here for many years. Modern Scottish cookery with international influences is presented exceedingly well. The medallions of Aberdeen Angus filet are always reliable, as are the fresh fish and chicken dishes, each prepared with flair. The bar stocks a wide range of single malts and ports in addition to some wines unavailable elsewhere in the region.

50 Chapel St. ✆ **01224/639-500.** Reservations recommended. Fixed-price lunch £9–£13 ($17–$25); fixed-price dinner £18–£22 ($34–$42). AE, MC, V. Daily noon–2:30pm and 6–10pm. Lies a 15-min. walk southwest of train station.

Martha's Vineyard Bistro/The Courtyard Restaurant SCOTTISH/CONTINENTAL   One of the most appealing restaurant complexes in Aberdeen occupies two floors of what was built around 1900 as an extension of the local hospital. Today, a robust and rustic-looking bistro (Martha's Vineyard) is on the street level, with a more formal restaurant (The Courtyard) upstairs. The bistro menu ranges from smoked salmon and asparagus salad to gigot of lamb with a compote of leeks in mustard sauce. Upstairs, you'll find dishes like local brie wrapped in smoked salmon or rosemary-flavored loin of Highland venison with wild mushrooms. Dessert in either place might be warm orange pudding with Grand Marnier sauce served with vanilla-ginger ice cream.

Alford Lane. ✆ **01224/213-795.** Reservations recommended in The Courtyard, not necessary in Martha's Vineyard. Main courses bistro £9–£14 ($17–$27); main courses restaurant £13–£19 ($25–$36). AE, DC, MC, V. Mon–Sat noon–2:15pm; Tues–Sat 6–10pm. Bus: 1, 2, 3, or 4.

Silver Darling ✦✦ FRENCH/SEAFOOD   Silver Darling (a local nickname for herring) is a definite asset to the dining scene in Aberdeen. Occupying a former customhouse at the mouth of the harbor, it spins a culinary fantasy around the freshest catch of the day. You might begin with a savory fish soup, almost Mediterranean in flavor, then go on to one of the barbecued fish dishes or pan-fried tuna rolled in crushed peppercorns. Salmon is the invariable favorite of the more discriminating diners.

Pocra Quay, Footdee. ✆ **01224/576-229.** Reservations recommended. Main courses £20–£27 ($38–$51); lunch main courses £10–£16 ($19–$30). AE, DC, MC, V. Mon–Fri noon–2pm and 7–10pm; Sat 7–10pm; Sun 6–9pm summer only. Closed Dec 23–Jan 8. Bus: 14 or 15.

ABERDEEN AFTER DARK

Tickets to events at most venues are available by calling the **Aberdeen Box Office** at ✆ **01224/641-122.** Open Monday to Saturday 9am to 6:30pm.

THE PERFORMING ARTS   The **Aberdeen Arts Centre,** King Street (✆ **01224/635-208**), has a 350-seat theater that is rented to professional and amateur groups hosting everything from poetry readings and plays to musical concerts in various styles. Ticket prices and performance times vary; call for information. Also on the premises is a 60-seat video projection theater that screens world cinema offerings, and ticket prices vary depending on what is showing but start at £6 ($11). A large gallery room holds month-long visual-art exhibitions. A cafe/bar, offering light meals and drinks, is open during performance times.

Near Tarves, about 32km (20 miles) from Aberdeen, you'll find **Haddo House** (✆ **01651/851-440**), which hosts operas, ballets, and plays from Easter to October. An early-20th-century hall built of pitch pine, Haddo House is based on the Canadian town halls that Lord Aberdeen saw in his travels abroad. The hall was built for the people of the surrounding area on Aberdeen family land, and the present Lady

Aberdeen still lives in a house on this property. Follow B9005, 29km (18 miles) north to Tarves, then follow the National Trust and Haddo House signs 3km (2 miles) east to arrive here. Admittance to the house is £8 ($15) for adults, £5 ($9.50) for seniors and children, and £20 ($38) for a family ticket. The house is open March 31 to June 30 Friday to Monday from 11am to 5pm, July to August daily 11am to 5pm, September to November 7 Friday to Monday 11am to 5pm, the shop from 11am to 5pm, and the gardens from 9:30am to sunset. A stylish cafe offers light meals, tea, and other beverages daily, Easter to October, from 11am to 6pm.

The 19th-century **Music Hall,** Union Street (© **01224/641-122**), is an ornately gilded 1,282-seat theater that stages concerts by the Scottish National Orchestra, the Scottish Chamber Orchestra, visiting international orchestras, and pop bands; it also hosts ceilidhs, crafts fairs, and book sales. Tickets for year-round musical performances average £14 to £32 ($27–$61). The **Aberdeen International Youth Festival** is held annually in this hall in August, and features youth orchestras, choirs, and dance and theater ensembles. Daytime and evening performances are held, and tickets range from £7.50 to £15 ($14–$29). Contact the Music Hall or the Aberdeen Box Office (above) for more information.

His Majesty's Theatre, Rosemount Viaduct (© **01224/641-122**), was designed by Frank Matcham in 1906 and is the only theater in the world build entirely of granite. The interior is late Victorian, and the 1,445-seat theater stages operas, dance performances, dramas, classical concerts, musicals, and comedy shows year-round. Tickets range from £10 to £30 ($19–$57).

A mixed venue is the **Lemon Tree,** 5 W. North St. (© **01224/642-230**). Its 150-seat theater stages dance recitals, theatrical productions, and stand-up comedy, with tickets generally priced between £8 to £24 ($15–$46). On Saturday, there's often a matinee at 2 or 3pm, and evening performances are at 7pm. Downstairs, the 500-seat cafe/theater hosts folk, rock, blues, jazz, and comedy acts, with shows starting between 8 and 10pm. On Sunday afternoon there's free live jazz.

DANCE CLUBS   **DeNiro's,** 120 Union St. (© **01224/640-641**), has dancing to house music from 10pm until 2am on Friday and Saturday only. The cover charge is £10 ($19), but may vary depending on the guest DJ.

Scotland's Castle Trail

Scotland's Castle Trail takes visitors on a tour of fairy-tale castles, imposing stately homes, magnificent ruins, and splendid public gardens. The only sign-posted route of its kind in Scotland, it guides motorists around rural Aberdeenshire. An accompanying leaflet highlights 11 of the finest properties, from the ruins of the 13th-century Kildrummy Castle and the elegant five-towered Fyvie Castle to two grand examples of the work of the 18th-century architect William Adam—Duff House and Haddo House.

The leaflet also details other noteworthy sites, including Balmoral Castle, a royal home since Queen Victoria's day, and Pitmedden Garden, where the centerpiece Great Garden was laid out in 1675. The leaflet, *Scotland's Castle Trail,* is available at local tourist offices or by calling © **0845/225-5121.** Information can also be found on the Aberdeen and Grampian Tourist Board website (**www.agtb.org**).

The Pelican, housed in the Hotel Metro, 17 Market St. (© **01224/583-275**), offers dancing Thursday to Saturday 10pm to 2am. The cover charge on Thursday is £5 ($9.50) and Friday and Saturday £6 ($11). There's a live band every second Thursday of the month.

A PUB   The **Prince of Wales** ✪, 7 St. Nicholas Lane (© **01224/640-597**), in the heart of the shopping district, is the best place in the old city center to go for a pint. Furnished with pews in screened booths, it boasts Aberdeen's longest bar counter. At lunch, it's bustling with regulars who devour chicken in cider sauce or Guinness pie. On tap are such beers as Buchan Gold and Courage Directors. Orkney Dark Island is also sold here.

SIDE TRIPS FROM ABERDEEN: CASTLE COUNTRY

Aberdeen is the center of "castle country"—40 inhabited castles lie within a 65km (40-mile) radius. Here is a selection of the best of them.

Castle Fraser ✪   One of the most impressive of the fortress-like castles of Mar, Castle Fraser stands on 10 hectares (25 acres) of parkland. The sixth laird, Michael Fraser, began the structure in 1575, and his son finished it in 1636. Visitors can tour the spectacular Great Hall and wander around the grounds, which include an 18th-century walled garden.

Sauchen, Inverurie. © **01330/833-463**. Admission £8 ($15) adults, £5 ($9.50) seniors, £2 ($3.80) children, free for children under 5. Mar 31–June 30 Wed–Sun 11am–5pm; July–Aug 31 daily 11am–5pm; Sept–Oct Wed–Sun noon–5pm. Closed Nov–Mar. Head 5km (3 miles) south of Kemnay, 26km (16 miles) west of Aberdeen, off A944.

Craigievar Castle ✪   Structurally unchanged since its completion in 1626, Craigievar Castle is an exceptional tower-house where Scottish baronial architecture reached its pinnacle of achievement. It has contemporary plaster ceilings in nearly all its rooms. The castle was continuously inhabited by the descendants of the builder, William Forbes, until it came under the care of the National Trust for Scotland in 1963. The family collection of furnishings is complete.

Some 6km (4 miles) south of the castle, clearly signposted on a small road leading off A980, near Lumphanan, is **Macbeth's Cairn,** where the historical Macbeth is believed to have fought his last battle. Built of timber in a rounded format known by historians as "motte and bailey," it's now nothing more than a steep-sided hillock marked with a sign and a flag.

This castle started renovations in August of 2007. Please call ahead to make sure the property will be open.

Hwy. A980, 10km (6 miles) south of Alford. © **01339/883-635**. Admission £10 ($19) adults, £7 ($13) seniors and children. Castle Mar 31–June 30 Fri–Tues noon–5:30pm, July 1–Aug daily noon–5:30pm; grounds year-round Fri–Tues 9:30am–sunset. Head west on A96 to Alford, then south on A980.

Crathes Castle & Gardens ✪✪   This castle, 3km (2 miles) east of Banchory, has royal historical associations from 1323, when the lands of Leys were granted to the Burnett family by King Robert the Bruce. The castle's features include remarkable late-16th-century painted ceilings and a garden that's a composite of eight separate gardens, giving a display all year. The great yew hedges date from 1702. The grounds are ideal for nature study, and there are five trails, including a long-distance layout with ranger service. The complex has a licensed restaurant, a visitor center, a souvenir shop, a plant sales area, a wayfaring course, and picnic areas.

Banchory. ℂ 01330/844-525. Admission £10 ($19) adults, £7 ($13) children and seniors, £25 ($48) per family. Grounds, adventure area, and park daily 9am–sunset; visitor center, shop, and restaurant Good Friday to Oct daily 10:30am–5:30pm; Nov 1–Mar 31 daily 10am–4:30pm; castle Apr 1–Sept 30 daily 10:30am–5:30pm, Oct daily 10am–4:30; Nov–Mar Wed–Sun 10:30am–3:45pm. From Aberdeen, take A93 24km (15 miles) west.

Fyvie Castle ✮   The National Trust for Scotland opened this castle to the public in 1986. The oldest part, dating from the 13th century, has been called the grandest existing example of Scottish baronial architecture. There are five towers, named after the families who lived here over 5 centuries. Originally built in a royal hunting forest, Fyvie means "deer hill" in Gaelic. The interior, created by the first Lord Leith of Fyvie, reflects the opulence of the Edwardian era. His collections contain arms and armor, 16th-century tapestries, and important artworks by Raeburn, Gainsborough, and Romney. The castle is rich in ghosts, curses, and legends.

Turriff, on the Aberdeen-Banff road. ℂ 01651/891-266. Admission £8 ($15) adults, £5 ($9.50) seniors and children, £20 ($38) family. Mar 31–June and Sept–Oct Sat–Wed noon–5pm; July–Aug Sat–Wed 11am–5pm. Closed Nov–Mar. Take A947 for 37km (23 miles) northwest of Aberdeen.

2 Perth ✮: Gateway to the Highlands & Scone Palace

71km (44 miles) N of Edinburgh, 35km (22 miles) SW of Dundee, 103km (64 miles) NE of Glasgow

From its majestic position on the Tay, the ancient city of Perth was the capital of Scotland until the mid–15th century. It's here that the Highlands meet the Lowlands. Perth makes a good stop if you're heading north to the Highlands. Perth itself has few historic buildings, but it does offer some good shopping. The main attraction, Scone Palace, lies on the outskirts, and the surrounding countryside is wonderful for strolling and hiking.

ESSENTIALS

GETTING THERE   By Train   ScotRail provides service between Edinburgh and Perth (trip time: 90 min.), with continuing service to Dundee. The trip to Perth costs £9.75 ($19) from Edinburgh; phone ℂ 08457/484-950 for 24-hour information.

By Bus   Edinburgh and Perth are connected by frequent bus service (trip time: 1½ hr.). The fare is £8 ($15). For more information and schedules, check with Citylink (ℂ 0990/505-050).

By Car   To reach Perth from Edinburgh, take A90 northwest and go across the Forth Road Bridge, continuing north along M90 (trip time: 1½ hr.).

VISITOR INFORMATION   The **tourist information center** is at Lower City Mills, West Mill St. (ℂ 01738/450-600), and is open April to June daily 9am to 6pm, July to September daily from 9am to 7pm, October daily from 9am to 6pm, and November to March, Monday to Saturday from 10am to 5pm.

EXPLORING THE AREA

For the best view of this scenic part of Scotland, take Bowerswell Road 1.6km (1 mile) to the east of Perth center to visit **Kinnoull Hill,** rising 240m (792 ft.). After an easy climb, you get a bird's-eye view of the geological Highland Line dividing the Highlands from the Lowlands. A marked nature trail beginning at the Braes Road car park leads, after a 25-minute walk, to the panoramic view from the top. Here you can see a folly, the **Kinnoull Watch Tower,** and its counterpart, 1.6km (1 mile) to the east, **Binn Hill.** Both structures are imitations of castles along the Rhine.

Tips **Calling All Artists**

In May, the 10-day **Perth Festival of the Arts** attracts international orchestras and chamber music societies. There are some dance recitals as well, and a recent trend is to celebrate some aspects of pop culture. Concerts are held in churches, auditoriums, and even Scone Palace.

Balhousie Castle   In the 16th century, this was the home of the earls of Kinnoull, but today it houses the Black Watch Regimental Museum, with hundreds of weapons, medals, and documents of the Black Watch Regiment from the 18th century on. The regiment was recruited in 1739 by Gen. George Wade to help the government pacify rebellious Highlanders and became famous all over the United Kingdom for its black tartans in contrast to the red of government troops.

After visiting the castle, you can explore **North Inch,** a 41-hectare (100-acre) parkland extending north along the west bank of the Tay. This is the best place for a long walk in the Perth area. The grounds are given over mainly to sports facilities, particularly the domed Bells Sports Centre. North Inch, as depicted in Sir Walter Scott's *The Fair Maid of Perth,* was the site of the great 1396 Clan Combat between 30 champions from the clans Kay and Chattan, attended by Robert III and his queen.

Hay St., right beyond Rose Terrace on the west side of North Inch. ℂ 0131/310-8530. Free admission. May–Sept Mon–Sat 10am–4:30pm; Oct–Apr Mon–Fri 10am–3:30pm.

Branklyn Garden 🌰   Once the finest private garden in Scotland, the Branklyn now belongs to the National Trust for Scotland. It has a superb collection of rhododendrons, alpines, and herbaceous and peat-garden plants from all over the world.

116 Dundee Rd. (A85), in Branklyn. ℂ 01738/625-535. Admission £5 ($9.50) adults, £4 ($7.60) children, students, and seniors, £14 ($27) family ticket. Mar–Oct daily 9:30am–sunset. Closed in winter.

Kirk of St. John the Baptist   This is the main sightseeing attraction in "the fair city." It's believed that the original foundation is from Pictish times. The present choir dates from 1440 and the nave from 1490. In 1559, John Knox preached his famous sermon attacking idolatry, which caused a turbulent wave of iconoclasm to sweep across the land. In its wake, religious artifacts, stained glass, and organs were destroyed all over Scotland. The church was restored as a World War I memorial in the mid-1920s.

31 St. John Place. ℂ 01738/622-241. Free admission (donations suggested). Mon–Fri 10am–noon and 2–4pm.

Perth Art Gallery and Museum   This museum has paintings that illustrate the town's history, as well as archaeological artifacts. The growth of the whisky industry and its major role in the area's economy is particularly emphasized. You find everything from grandfather clocks to Georgian silver to an effigy of a 29kg (65-lb.) salmon caught by some proud fisherman back in 1922. The most notable artworks are large Scottish landscapes by John Millais (1829–96). Horatio McCulloch (1805–67) was known as a specialist of Highland scenes, and his *Loch Katrine* (1866) is one of his finest works.

78 George St., at the intersection of Tay St. and Perth Bridge. ℂ 01738/632-488. Free admission. Mon–Sat 10am–5pm.

Round House and Fergusson Gallery   If you're interested in Scottish art, head for the Fergusson Gallery, which displays some 6,000 works by Scottish artist J. D. Fergusson (1874–1961). He is acclaimed as one of the best watercolorists in the country, and his Scottish scenes are widely produced on postcards and calendars. In the paintings *Princess Street Gardens* and *The White Dress,* you see the muted colors of his early portraits and landscapes. Later, as he was more inspired by Fauvism, his work became more vibrant and luminous, evidenced by *Cassis from the West* and *Sails at Royan.* His female nudes, however, always generate the most excitement, especially *Danu Mother of the Gods, The Parasol,* and *Bathers in Green. The Red Dress* (1950) is very evocative of Glasgow scenes.

Marshall Place. (℃ **01738/441-944.** Free admission. Mon–Sat 10am–5pm.

SHOPPING

Cairncross Ltd., 18–20 St. John's St. (℃ **01738/624-367**), sells jewelry, both custom-made and from other manufacturers. The specialty is Scottish freshwater pearls. **Timothy Hardie,** 25 St. John's St. (℃ **01738/633-127**), deals in antique jewelry and has a large selection of Victorian pieces. It also sells antique silver tea services. **Whispers of the Past,** 15 George St. (℃ **01738/635-472**), offers an odd mix of items: jewelry, both new and antique, ranging from costume baubles to quality gold and silver pieces; china; pine furniture; and some linens.

   C & C Proudfoot, 112 South St. (℃ **01738/632-483**), is an eclectic shop whose merchandise includes leather jackets, hand-knitted Arran sweaters, Barbour waxed-cotton jackets, sheepskin jackets and rugs, and wool rugs, as well as a range of handbags, briefcases, scarves, and gloves.

   Watson of Perth, 163–167 High St. (℃ **01738/639-861**), has been in business since 1900. It specializes in bone china produced by Royal Doulton, Wedgwood, and others; it also offers cut crystal from Edinburgh, Stuart, and Waterford.

   Caithness Glass, Inveralmond Industrial Estate, on A9 (℃ **01738/637-373**), is a glass factory on the edge of Perth. Follow A9, going through the roundabout marked A9 NORTH to Inverness; the factory is in the industrial complex a short way past the roundabout. Its outlet sells paperweights, vases, and bowls, balanced with a range of Royal Doulton items. While here, you can watch the glassblowers at work.

   Perthshire Shop, Lower City Mills, Mill Street (℃ **01738/627-958**), sells jams, mustards, and oatmeal along with items produced in the neighboring mills. On the shelves are wooden bowls, *spirtles* (wooden stirrers often used in making porridge), and Perthshire tartan scarves and ties, along with a large selection of cookbooks.

HITTING THE LINKS NEARBY

North of Perth is one of Scotland's acclaimed golf links, the 18-hole **Blairgowrie,** Golf Course Road, Rosemont, Blairgowrie (℃ **01250/872-622**), which includes 6,229 yards of playing area with a par of 72. This is a challenging course, which has a rolling, wild layout of pine, birch, and fir; you might even spot a deer or two grazing on the course. The greens fees are £25 to £65 ($48–$124) for one round, £60 to £80 ($114–$152) for the day, with even higher rates on weekends. There's a pro shop where you can rent clubs and trolleys; caddy service is £24 ($46), plus tip.

WHERE TO STAY

Huntingtower Hotel (℞   This late-Victorian country house is set on 1.4 hectares (3½ acres) of well-manicured gardens, with a modern wing of rooms added in 1998.

Taste and care went into the interior decoration. Rooms vary in size, and each has a specific charm. Seven offer spa baths. The cottage suites are in a renovated bungalow and have twin beds and a sitting room.

The fine Scottish and Continental cuisine is reason enough to stay here. The elegant main restaurant serves nightly table d'hôte dinners.

Crieff Rd., Perth PH1 3JT. © 800/780-7234 in the U.S and Canada or 01738/583-771. Fax 01738/583-777. www.huntingtowerhotel.co.uk. 34 units. £132–£159 ($251–$302) double; from £125 ($238) cottage suite. Rates include Scottish breakfast. AE, DC, MC, V. Drive 6km (3½ miles) west on A85. Free parking. **Amenities:** Restaurant; bar; room service; laundry service; dry cleaning; nonsmoking rooms. *In room:* TV, dataport (in some), minibar, coffeemaker, hair dryer.

The New County Hotel   The best feature about this family-run hotel is the warm, congenial staff. And the location, in the city center of Perth, isn't bad either. It's a 5-minute walk from bus and train stations, movie theaters, and other entertainment. The rooms are well kept and comfortable, each with a tidy bathroom with tub or shower. Adjacent to the reception area is Café 22, the hotel's contemporary coffee and tea bar. The Place Bar and Bistro is an elegant restaurant serving market-fresh ingredients. Smoking is discouraged in the hotel, but none of the rooms is specifically designated nonsmoking.

26 County Place, Perth. © 01738/623-355. Fax 0173/628-969. www.newcountyhotel.com. 23 units. £99–£140 ($188–$266) double. Rates include breakfast. Free parking. MC, V. **Amenities:** Restaurant; bar; business services; room service; laundry service; nonsmoking rooms. *In room:* TV, beverage maker.

Parklands Hotel ⚘   This hotel near the rail station opened in 1991 and immediately became Perth's most fashionable lodging. The classic Georgian town house was the home of the city's Lord Provost from 1867 to 1873. The spacious and beautifully decorated guest rooms, filled with wood paneling and cornices, overlook the South Inch Park. The beautiful Victorian conservatory is ideal for afternoon tea.

2 St. Leonard's Bank, Perth PH2 8EB. © 01738/622-451. Fax 01738/622-046. www.theparklands.com. 14 units. £99–£119 ($188–$226) double. Rates include breakfast. AE, DC, MC, V. From the M90 (Edinburgh or Dundee) take junction 10. Take the right-hand fork signed for Perth. At the end of the road turn left at the traffic lights and follow the edge of South Inch Park. Parklands is the first building on the left-hand side. **Amenities:** 2 restaurants; bar; room service; laundry service; dry cleaning; nonsmoking rooms. *In room:* TV, dataport, coffeemaker, hair dryer.

WHERE TO DINE

Keracher's Restaurant and Oyster Bar ⚘ SCOTTISH/SEAFOOD   For five generations, the Kerachers have been serving some of the finest seafood in Perth. Chef Andrew Keracher carries on the family tradition by using the freshest ingredients, which are cooked to order. Food is prepared with imagination and panache, but also with a healthy respect for the natural tastes and textures of the produce. Among the main courses on the extensive menu are a filet of Scottish salmon glazed with honey-mustard and served with a leek and vermouth cream sauce; a filet of wild sea trout with garlic cream and seafood sauce; and a filet of lemon sole on a bed of Continental vegetables with a tomato basil dressing. For dessert, try the steamed ginger pudding with vanilla ice cream and vanilla anglais. The Oyster Bar has a retail counter where you can grab a quick, tasty range of Keracher products.

168 South St. (45 min. from Edinburgh on the A90) © 01738/449-777. Reservations recommended. Main courses £10–£18 ($19–$34); set menus £12 ($23) for 2 courses, £15 ($29) for 3 courses. MC, V. Tues–Sat noon–2:30pm; Mon–Sat 6–10pm. Closed 2 weeks in Jan.

Let's Eat ✦ BRITISH/INTERNATIONAL   The most visually striking—and, indeed, most appealing—restaurant in Perth occupies a theater built in 1822. There's a particularly cozy lounge, site of a log-burning stove and comfy sofas. Menu items, which change frequently, are sophisticated. They might include a gratin of goat cheese studded with roasted peppers and served with rocket salad, new potatoes, and chutney; grilled brochettes of monkfish with king prawns, rice, and salad; handmade black puddings served with "smash" (mashed potatoes), applesauce, and onion gravy; lightly blackened filet of salmon with herb-crushed potatoes, olive oil, and saffron sauce; roast Scottish lamb Moroccan-style with minted couscous and spiced red-wine gravy; and risotto studded with wild mushrooms. Be careful not to confuse this restaurant with its less grand, less expensive sibling, Let's Eat Again.

77–79 Kinnoull St. (3 blocks north of High St.). ℭ 01738/643-377. Reservations recommended. Lunch main courses £9.50–£11 ($18–$21); dinner main courses £10–£19 ($19–$36). AE, MC, V. Tues–Sat noon–2pm and 6:30–9:45pm.

The Library Restaurant ✦✦ SCOTTISH   If you're in the mood to dine in a grand castle with equally grand food and service, head here. Using the costliest of Scottish ingredients, all deftly handled, chef Jeremy Brazelle has established a reputation for excellence. The best venison, Angus beef, and salmon are offered along with area fine choice of wines. A sample meal might include pumpkin-and-leek soup followed by filet of halibut with buttered noodles, stir-fried vegetables, and chili and soy dressing. You might also try roast rump of black-faced lamb with fresh vegetables cooked in the Provençal style with virgin olive oil and garlic.

In Kinfauns Castle. ℭ 01738/620-777. Reservations required. Jacket and tie required for men. Fixed-price 3-course lunch £22–£24 ($42–$46); fixed-price dinner £38 ($72) for 3 courses, £40 ($76) for 5 courses. AE, MC, V. Daily noon–1:30pm and 7–8:30pm. Closed 3 weeks in Jan.

PERTH AFTER DARK

The Victorian **Perth Repertory Theatre,** 185 High St. (ℭ **01738/621-031**), hosts performances of plays and musicals between mid-September and May. From the end of May to early June, it's also a venue for some of the events of the Perth Festival of the Arts. The box office is open Monday to Saturday from 10am to 7:30pm. Tickets cost £7 to £27 ($13–$51).

Perth City Hall, King Edward Street (ℭ **01738/624-055**), is a year-round venue for musical performances and dances; many local organizations (including the Freemasons, the Royal Geographical Society, churches, and various amateur societies) book events here year after year. Entertainment is usually along the lines of a classical concert or a Highland ball.

A SIDE TRIP TO SCONE

Old Scone, 3km (2 miles) from Perth on the River Tay, was the ancient capital of the Picts. The early Scottish monarchs were enthroned here on a lump of sandstone called the "Stone of Destiny." In 1296, Edward I, the "Hammer of the Scots," moved the stone to Westminster Abbey, and for hundreds of years it rested under the chair on which British monarchs were crowned. The Scots have always bitterly resented this theft, and at last, it has been returned to Scotland, to find a permanent home in Edinburgh Castle, where it can be viewed by the public.

The seat of the earls of Mansfield and birthplace of David Douglas (of fir-tree fame), **Scone Palace** ✦✦, along A93 (ℭ **01738/552-300**), was largely rebuilt in

1802, incorporating the old palace of 1580. Inside is an impressive collection of French furniture, china, ivories, and 16th-century needlework, including bed hangings made by Mary Queen of Scots. A fine collection of rare conifers is found on the grounds in the Pinetum. Rhododendrons and azaleas grow profusely in the gardens and woodlands around the palace. To reach the palace, head northeast of Perth on A93. The site is open April 1 to October 31 only, daily from 9:30am to 5:30pm. Admission is £7.50 ($14) for adults, £6.50 ($12) for seniors, and £4.50 ($8.55) for children under 17. Admission to the grounds only is £4 ($7.60) for adults, £3.65 ($6.95) seniors, and £2.75 ($5.25) for children. Family admission to both the house and grounds is £25 ($48).

WHERE TO STAY & DINE

Murrayshall House Hotel & Golf Courses ✿✿✿   This elegant country-house hotel, set on 122 hectares (300 acres) of parkland, is one of the showpieces of Perthshire. Golfers and their families flock here for the excellent, challenging courses. The hotel's public rooms and guest rooms are all traditionally styled, but bedrooms vary in size and comfort. The superior accommodations are the suites and executive rooms, which have the best amenities and views. The standard rooms are also comfortable but lack the character of the others. *Note:* On a windy night in Scotland there is no better place to be than the well-stocked bar with its log fire.

New Scone, Perthshire PH2 7PH. ✆ **01738/551-171.** Fax 01738/552-595. www.murrayshall.com. 41 units. £150–£170 ($285–$323) double; £160–£210 ($304–$399) suite; lodge £150–£170 ($285–$323). Rates include Scottish breakfast. AE, DC, MC, V. Take A94 2.5km (1½ miles) east of New Scone. **Amenities:** Restaurant; 2 bars; 2 golf courses; tennis courts; exercise room; Jacuzzi; room service; babysitting; laundry service; dry cleaning; steam room; nonsmoking rooms. *In room:* TV, hair dryer.

3 Gleneagles: Hitting the Links

90km (56 miles) NE of the Glasgow Airport, 81km (50 miles) NW of the Edinburgh Airport

This famous golfing center and sports complex is on a moor between Strathearn and Strath Allan. Gleneagles has four **18-hole golf courses:** King's Course, the longest; Queen's Course, next in length; Prince's Course, the shortest; and Glendevon—the newest of the quartet—which was built in 1980. They're among the best courses in Scotland, and the sports complex ranks among Europe's finest. The center gets its name from the Gaelic *Gleann-an-Eaglias,* meaning "glen of the church."

ESSENTIALS

GETTING THERE   By Train   The 15-minute ride from Perth costs £5 ($9.50). The trip takes 1 hour and 25 minutes from Edinburgh and costs £11 ($21). For information, call ✆ **08457/484-950.**

By Bus   The only service departs from Glasgow. The trip takes slightly more than an hour and costs £6.50 ($12). For information and schedules, call ✆ **08705/808-080.**

By Car   Gleneagles is on A9, about halfway between Perth and Stirling, a short distance from the village of Auchterarder. It lies 88km (55 miles) from Edinburgh and 72km (45 miles) from Glasgow.

VISITOR INFORMATION   The year-round **tourist center** is at 90 High St., Auchterarder (✆ **01764/663-450**). It's open November to March, Monday to Friday 10am to 2pm, Saturday 11am to 3pm; April to June, Monday to Saturday 9:30am to 5:30pm, Sunday 11am to 4pm; July and August, Monday to Saturday 9am to 7pm,

Sunday 11am to 6pm, and September and October, Monday to Saturday 9:30am to 5:30pm, Sunday 11am to 4pm.

WHERE TO STAY & DINE

The Gleneagles Hotel 🏨🏨🏨   Britain's greatest golf hotel stands on its own 336-hectare (830-acre) estate. When it was built in isolated grandeur in 1924, it was Scotland's only government-rated five-star hotel. It is a true resort and has kept up with the times by offering spa treatments as well as many other activities. Public rooms are classical, with pilasters and pillars. The guest rooms vary greatly in size. The best and most spacious choices are in the 60-to-90-block series; they have recently been refurbished. The less desirable rooms are called courtyard units; these are a bit small and equipped with shower-only bathrooms. Linked to the rest of the hotel through a glass walkway, Braid House, which opened in 2002, added another 59 deluxe rooms to the existing property. Braid House guests have separate check-in facilities and private access.

At the on-site and Michelin-starred restaurant, Andrew Fairlie is perhaps the country's most outstanding chef. He orders his food from the Rungis Market, outside Paris, or from local Scottish suppliers. Signature dishes include his smoked lobster. The unique flavor comes from smoking lobster shells over old whisky barrels for 12 hours. The chef deserves heaps of praise for taking some of Europe's prime raw materials—Aberdeen Angus beef, pheasant, and salmon—and fashioning them into superb dishes.

Auchterarder PH3 1NF. ℂ 866/881-9525 in the U.S., or 01764/662-231. Fax 01764/662-134. www.gleneagles.com. 232 units. £280–£500 ($532–$950) double; £625–£1,600 ($1,188–$3,040) suite. Rates include Scottish breakfast. AE, DC, MC, V. Free parking. Take A9 2.5km (1½ miles) southwest of Auchterarder. **Amenities:** 4 restaurants; 4 bars; indoor heated pool; outdoor hot pool; lap pool; 3 golf courses; tennis court; health club; spa; Jacuzzi; sauna; complimentary bike use; salon; room service; massage; babysitting; laundry service; dry cleaning; equestrian center; falconry school; hunting and fishing excursions; squash court; Turkish bath; nonsmoking rooms, rooms for those w/limited mobility. *In room:* TV, minibar, coffeemaker, hair dryer, iron, safe, trouser press.

4 Crieff 🟉 & Drummond Castle Gardens 🟉

29km (18 miles) W of Perth, 97km (60 miles) NW of Edinburgh, 81km (50 miles) NE of Glasgow

From Perth, head west on A85 for 29km (18 miles) to Crieff. At the edge of the Perthshire Highlands, Crieff makes a pleasant stopover, with good fishing and golf. This small burgh was the seat of the court of the earls of Strathearn until 1747, and the gallows in its marketplace were once used to execute Highland cattle rustlers.

You can take a "day trail" into **Strathearn,** the valley of the River Earn, the very center of Scotland. Here Highland mountains meet gentle Lowland slopes, and moorland mingles with rich green pastures. North of Crieff, the road to Aberfeldy passes through the narrow pass of the **Sma' Glen,** a famous spot of beauty, with hills rising on either side to 600m (2,000 ft.).

ESSENTIALS

GETTING THERE   By Train   There's no direct service. The nearest rail stations are at Gleneagles, 14km (9 miles) away, and at Perth, 29km (18 miles) away. Call ℂ 08457/484-950 for information and schedules.

By Bus   Once you arrive in Perth, you'll find regular connecting bus service hourly during the day. For information and schedules, call **Stagecoach** at ℂ 01738/629-339. The bus service from Gleneagles is too poor to recommend.

By Taxi   A taxi from Gleneagles will cost from £16 to £20 ($30–$38).

VISITOR INFORMATION The year-round **tourist information office** is in the Town Hall on High Street (© **01764/652-578**). It's open November to March, Monday to Friday 9:30am to 5pm, Saturday 10am to 2pm; April to June, Monday to Saturday 9:30am to 5:30pm, Sunday 11am to 4pm; July and August, Monday to Saturday 9am to 7pm, Sunday 11am to 6pm; and September and October, Monday to Saturday 9:30am to 5:30pm, Sunday 11am to 4pm.

EXPLORING THE AREA

Drummond Castle Gardens ⋘ The gardens of Drummond Castle, first laid out in the early 17th century by John Drummond, second earl of Perth, are among the finest formal gardens in Europe. There's a panoramic view from the upper terrace, overlooking an example of an early Victorian parterre in the form of St. Andrew's Cross. The multifaceted sundial by John Mylne, master mason to Charles I, has been the centerpiece since 1630.

Grimsthorpe, Crieff. © **01764/681-433.** Admission £4 ($7.60) adults, £3 ($5.70) seniors, £1.50 ($2.85) children. May–Oct daily 2–6pm; Easter weekend 2–6pm. Closed Nov–Apr. Take A822 for 5km (3 miles) south of Crieff.

The Glenturret Distillery Ltd. Scotland's oldest distillery, Glenturret was established in 1775 on the banks of the River Turret. Visitors can see the milling of malt, mashing, fermentation, distillation, and cask filling, followed by a free "wee dram" dispensed at the end of the tour. Guided tours take about 25 minutes and leave at frequent intervals—sometimes as often as every 10 minutes when there's a demand. This can be followed or preceded by a 20-minute video, *The Water of Life,* which is presented adjacent to a small museum devoted to the implements of the whisky trade.

The Hosh, Hwy. A85, Glenturret. © **01764/656-565.** Guided tours £4.50 ($8.55) adults, £3.50 ($6.65) seniors and children ages 10–17, free for children under 10. Jan Mon–Fri 11:30am–4pm; Feb Mon–Sat 11:30am–4pm, Sun noon–4pm; Mar–Dec Mon–Sat 9:30am–6pm, Sun noon–6pm. Take A85 toward Comrie; 1.2km (¾ mile) from Crieff, turn right at the crossroads; the distillery is .5km (¼ mile) up the road.

WHERE TO STAY

Murraypark Hotel This 19th-century stone-fronted house lies in a residential neighborhood about a 10-minute walk from Crieff's center and close to a golf course. In 1993, a new wing was opened, enlarging the public areas and the number of well-furnished rooms. Bedrooms in this former sea captain's house vary in size and shape, but most open onto views. Although rooms in the new wing are more comfortable, they are hardly as evocative; we still prefer the older wing's traditional Victorian aura.

The hotel's excellent restaurant serves traditional Scottish cuisine in a candle-lit dining room.

Connaught Terrace, Crieff PH7 3DJ. © **01764/653-731.** Fax 01764/655-311. www.murraypark.com. 19 units. £119–£185 ($226–$352) double or suite. Rates include Scottish breakfast. AE, DC, MC, V. Free parking. A 10-min. walk from the center of Crieff; the hotel lies northwest of Perth St. **Amenities:** Restaurant; bar; babysitting; nonsmoking rooms. *In room:* TV, coffeemaker, hair dryer, iron, trouser press.

WHERE TO DINE

The Bank MODERN SCOTTISH This dignified red-sandstone building was constructed in 1901 as a branch of the British Linen Bank, now part of the Bank of Scotland. Today it contains one of the most appealing restaurants in town, thanks to the superb cuisine, a hardworking staff, and a decor of mostly original paneling, an ornate plaster ceiling, and a huge arched window. Menu items may include wild-mushroom risotto with truffle oil and cheddar cheese from the Isle of Mull; saddle of venison with spiced red cabbage, turnip gratin, and a game and juniper sauce; or roasted East Coast Halibut with red chard, shellfish risotto, and a curry and parsley dressing.

32 High St. (lies right on the main street in the center of town). ✆ 01764/656-575. Reservations recommended. Main courses £16–£18 ($30–$34). AE, DC, MC, V. Tues–Sat noon–1:30pm and 7–9:30pm (Aug also Sun 7–10pm).

5 Dunkeld ⭐

93km (58 miles) N of Edinburgh, 23km (14 miles) N of Perth, 158km (98 miles) SW of Aberdeen

Dunkeld lies in a thickly wooded valley of the Tay River at the edge of the Perthshire Highlands. Once a major ecclesiastical center, it's one of the seats of ancient Scottish history and was an important center of the Celtic church. It's an attractively restored town that invites exploration on foot.

The surrounding countryside is beautiful, and you can take great walks and day hikes on both sides of the River Tay going from Dunkeld to Birnam. In all, there are 58km (36 miles) of paths that have been joined to create a network of circular routes. Pick up maps and detailed descriptions from the tourist office and set out on a day's adventure, armed with the makings of a picnic, of course.

ESSENTIALS
GETTING THERE **By Train** Trains from Perth arrive every 2 hours and cost £7 ($13). Travel time is 1½ hours. Call ✆ 0345/484-950 for information and schedules.

By Bus Pitlochry-bound buses leaving from Perth make a stopover in Dunkeld, letting you off at the Dunkeld Car Park, which is at the train station (trip time: 50 min.). The cost is £5 ($9.50). Contact **Stagecoach** at ✆ 01738/629-339.

By Car From Aberfeldy, take A827 east until you reach the junction of A9 heading south to Dunkeld.

VISITOR INFORMATION A **tourist information office** is at The Cross (✆ 01350/727-688). It's open April to June, Monday to Saturday 9:30am to 5:30pm and Sunday 11am to 4pm; July 1 to September 8, Monday to Saturday 9:30am to 6:30pm and Sunday 11am to 5pm; September 9 to October 27, Monday to Saturday 9:30am to 5:30pm and Sunday 11am to 4pm; October 28 to December, Monday to Saturday 9:30am to 5:30pm (closed Jan–Mar).

EXPLORING THE AREA
Founded in A.D. 815, **Dunkeld Cathedral** ⭐ was converted from a church to a cathedral in 1127 by David I. It stands on Cathedral Street in a scenic setting along the River Tay. The cathedral was first restored in 1815, and traces of the 12th-century structure remain today. Admission is free, and the cathedral is open May to September, Monday to Saturday 9:30am to 6:30pm, Sunday 2 to 6:30pm; October to April, Monday to Saturday 9:30am to 4pm. There is no parking at the site.

The National Trust for Scotland has restored many of the old houses and shops around the marketplace and cathedral. The trust owns 20 houses on **High Street** and **Cathedral Street** as well. Many of them were constructed in the late 17th century after the rebuilding of the town following the Battle of Dunkeld. The Trust runs the **Ell Shop,** The Cross (✆ 01350/727-460), which specializes in Scottish handicrafts. Easter weekend to December 24, it's open Monday through Saturday from 10am to 5:30pm.

Shakespeare fans may want to seek out the oak and sycamore in front of the destroyed **Birnam House,** 1.6km (1 mile) south. This was believed to be a remnant of the Birnam Wood in *Macbeth;* you may recall, "Macbeth shall never vanquished be until great Birnam Wood to high Dunsinane Hill shall come against him."

The **Hermitage,** off A9 about 3km (2 miles) west of Dunkeld, was called a folly when it was built in 1758 above the wooded gorge of the River Braan. Today, it makes for one of the most scenic woodland walks in the area.

Our favorite spot in the area is the **Loch of Lowes Wildlife Reserve** (© 01350/727-337), 3km (2 miles) from the center of town, along A923 heading northeast. It can be accessed from the south shore, where there's an observation lookout and a visitor center. Filled with rich flora and fauna, the 99-hectare (245-acre) reserve takes in the freshwater lake that's home to rare ospreys. Although common in the United States, these large brown-and-white sea eagles are on the endangered-species list in Britain, and bird-watchers from all over the country come here to observe them.

PLAYING GOLF

Dunkeld & Birnam, at Dunkeld (© **01350/727-524**), is touted as the best in the area, and offers sweeping views of the surrounding environs. Greens fees: Monday to Friday £25 ($48) for 18 holes; Saturday and Sunday £30 ($57) for 18 holes. There are no electric carts; pull carts are available for £5 ($9.50) per round. Hours are daily 7am to 11pm April to September. October to March, greens fees are reduced and hours are daily from 8am to 4pm. There's no official dress code, although if the starter feels you are not dressed "appropriately" you will be asked to "smarten up" the next time you play the course. Jeans and collarless shirts are not acceptable.

WHERE TO STAY & DINE

Dunkeld offers some very good, but rather pricey, accommodations, unless you avail yourself of dozens of B&Bs, some of which go in and out of business. However, the tourist office (see above) keeps an up-to-date list. Prices start around £21 ($40) per person for an overnight stay and breakfast the following morning.

Hilton Dunkeld House Hotel   This hotel offers the quiet dignity of a Scottish country house and is ranked as one of the leading leisure and sports hotels in the area. The surrounding grounds—113 hectares (280 acres) make for a parklike setting on the banks of the Tay. The house is beautifully kept, and rooms come in a wide range of sizes, styles, and furnishings. In 1999, an annex was converted into an extra wing offering another nine rooms. Guests fish for salmon and trout right on the grounds, and participate in other outdoor activities as well.

Dunkeld PH8 0HX. © **01350/727-771**. Fax 01350/728-924. www.hilton.co.uk/dunkeld. 96 units. £107–£270 ($203–$513) double; £265–£295 ($504–$561) suite. Rates include Scottish breakfast. AE, DC, MC, V. Free parking. Follow Atholl St. out of town; the hotel is signposted. **Amenities:** Restaurant; bar; indoor heated pool; putting green; tennis courts; health club; sauna; business center; salon; room service; massage; babysitting; laundry service; dry cleaning; fishing; skeet/trapshooting; steam room; nonsmoking rooms. *In room:* TV, minibar, hair dryer, trouser press.

Kinnaird Estate   This is, quite simply, Scotland's finest hotel. All the pursuits that intrigued Edwardian gentlemen—Edward VII among them—can be pursued on this mansion's 3,600-hectare (9,000-acre) estate, including fishing on the River Tay, shooting clays, and walking through gorse-covered moors. This place is so special that you'll find a bedside decanter of "Highland Heater," a wonderful elixir of whisky (of course), fresh herbs, and spices. There's a house-party feeling here, and, indeed, Kinnaird looks and feels like a perfectly restored private mansion. All the beautifully furnished rooms have king-size beds, full private bathrooms, and views.

Some overlook the valley of the River Tay; others open onto gardens and woodlands. There are eight cottages on the estate, two of which sleep eight and the others four.

Kinnaird, Kinnaird Estate, Dunkeld PH8 0LB. © **01796/482-440.** Fax 01796/482-289. www.kinnairdestate.com. 9 units and 8 estate cottages. £275–£475 ($523–$903) double; £200–£550 ($380–$1,045) estate cottages. Double and suite rates include dinner and Scottish breakfast; meals are not included in the cottage rates. AE, MC, V. Free parking. No children under 12 accepted in the hotel, but they may stay in the cottages. From Perth take the A9 north (signposted Inverness) and travel for 24km (15 miles) to Dunkeld. Do not exit Dunkeld; continue on for another 3.2km (2 miles). Turn left on to the B898, which is signposted for Dalguise, Kinnaird, and Balnagard. Follow this road for 7.2km (4½ miles) and the main gates of Kinnaird will be on your right-hand side. **Amenities:** Restaurant; bar; tennis court; salon; room service; laundry service; dry cleaning; nonsmoking rooms. *In room:* TV, hair dryer.

6 Pitlochry ✦

114km (71 miles) NW of Edinburgh, 44km (27 miles) NW of Perth, 24km (15 miles) N of Dunkeld

A popular resort, Pitlochry is a good base for touring the Valley of the Tummel. Ever since Queen Victoria declared it one of the finest resorts in Europe, it has drawn the hordes. It's also home to the renowned **Pitlochry Festival Theatre,** Scotland's theater in the hills.

Pitlochry doesn't exist just to entertain visitors, although it would appear that way in summer—it also produces Scotch whisky. And it's a good overnight stop between Edinburgh and Inverness, 137km (85 miles) north. You can spend a very busy day in town, visiting its famous distilleries, seeing its dam and fish ladder, and budgeting some time for the beauty spots in the environs, especially **Loch Rannoch** and the **Pass of Killiecrankie,** both ideal for walks. At Blair Atholl stands one of the most highly visited and intriguing castles in the country, **Blair Castle.**

ESSENTIALS

GETTING THERE   Five **trains** (© **08457/484-950**) per day arrive from Edinburgh, and an additional three from Glasgow (trip time from each: 2 hr.). A one-way fare is £25 ($48) from either city. **Buses** arrive hourly from Perth. The one-way fare is £4.80 ($9.10). Contact **Stagecoach** (© **01738/629-339**) for schedules. If you're **driving** from Perth, continue northwest along A9.

VISITOR INFORMATION   The **tourist office** is at 22 Atholl Rd. (© **01796/ 472-215**). From June to September, it's open daily 9am to 8pm; May and October, hours are daily 9am to 6pm; and November to April, hours are Monday to Friday 9am to 5pm and Saturday 10am to 3pm.

EXPLORING THE AREA

Pitlochry Dam was created because a power station was needed, but in effect the engineers created a new loch. The famous **salmon ladder** was built to help the struggling salmon upstream. An underwater portion of the ladder has been enclosed in glass to give sightseers a fascinating look. An exhibition (© **01796/473-152**) is open from April to the last Sunday in October, daily from 10am to 5:30pm; it costs £2 ($3.80) for adults and seniors and £1 ($1.90) for children.

There are terrific scenic hikes along the **Linn of Tummel,** with several signposted trails going along the river and into the forest directly to the north of the center. Just north of here you come to the stunning **Pass of Killiecrankie** ✦. If you're driving, follow A9 north. The National Trust has established the **Killiecrankie Visitor Centre** (© **01796/473-233**) here, open April to October daily from 10am to 5:30pm. You

---

Fun Fact   **The Wee-est of Wee Drams**

Stop in at **Edradour Distillery** (© **01796/472-095**), Scotland's smallest distillery, for a complimentary "wee dram" and a tour of this picturesque facility. The gift shop sells Edradour single malts, as well as various blends that contain the whisky. January 3 through February, tours are available 10am to 4pm Monday to Saturday and noon to 4pm Sunday; March 1 to October 31, tours are available Monday to Saturday 9:30am to 6pm and Sunday 11:30am to 5pm; November 1 to December 31, tours are Monday to Saturday 9:30am to 5pm and Sunday 11:30am to 5pm. It is closed December 25 and 26 and January 1 and 2. Take A924 3km (2 miles) east toward Braemar.

---

can learn about a famous battle that occurred here during the 1689 Jacobite rebellion. John Graham of Cleverhouse (1649–89) rallied the mainly Highlander Jacobite army to meet government troops. Graham was killed, and the quest for Scottish independence soon fizzled.

B8019 leads to **Loch Rannoch,** almost 16km (10 miles) long and 1.2km (¾ mile) wide. Many consider this to be the most beautiful lake in the Highlands. The setting so impressed Robert Louis Stevenson, he wrote about it in *Kidnapped* (1886): "Much of it was red with heather, much of the rest broken up with bogs and hags and peaty pools." To see this desolate but awesomely beautiful spot, follow B8019 to the Linn of Tummel north of Pitlochry, venturing onto B846 at the Bridge of Tummel.

Blair Castle 🏰   Home of the dukes of Atholl, this is one of the great historic castles of Scotland. Dating from 1269, it saw many alterations before it was finally turned into a Georgian mansion. Plan to spend about 2 hours viewing the palace's antiques, 18th-century interiors, and paintings, along with an outstanding arms, armor, and porcelain collection. After viewing the castle, you can stroll through the Victorian walled garden and take a long walk in the parklands.

Blair Atholl. © **01796/481-207**. Admission £6.90 ($13) adults, £5.90 ($11) seniors, £5.60 ($11) children. Apr to late Oct daily 9:30am–4:30pm; Oct 31–Mar 27 Tues–Sat 9:30am–12:30pm. Closed Dec 22–Jan 4. From the town center, follow A9 to Blair Atholl, where you'll see signs.

WHERE TO STAY

East Haugh House (see "Where to Dine," below) also rents rooms.

Acarsaid Hotel   This graceful but solid-looking stone house dates from 1880, when it was the home of the countess of Kilbride. Greatly expanded, the hotel contains cozy guest rooms with contemporary furnishings and immaculately kept shower-only bathrooms. The bar serves snacks at lunch (for guests only), while the more elaborate restaurant offers fixed-price dinners. Menu items focus on fresh ingredients, most of them Scottish.

8 Atholl Rd., Pitlochry PH16 5BX. © **01796/472-389**. Fax 01796/473-952. www.acarsaidhotel.co.uk. 20 units. £68–£92 ($129–$175) double. Rates include breakfast. MC, V. Free parking. **Amenities:** Restaurant; bar; access to nearby health club; business services; laundry service; nonsmoking rooms. *In room:* TV, coffeemaker, hair dryer.

Balrobin   This traditional Scottish country house opens onto views of the Perthshire Hills and the Tummel Valley. Built in 1889 as a cottage for fishing and shooting holidays, it's now a government-rated two-star hotel with average-size guest rooms furnished in simple provincial style (with shower-only bathrooms). Added to the "auld hoose" were a west and an east wing that kept with the stone construction. Affordable dinners are served nightly, and there's a guests-only bar and country lounge.

Higher Oakfield, Pitlochry PH16 5HT. ℂ 01796/472-901. Fax 01796/474-200. www.balrobin.co.uk. 14 units. £66–£90 ($125–$171) double. Rates include Scottish breakfast. MC, V. Closed mid-Oct to Apr 1. **Amenities:** Restaurant; bar; nonsmoking rooms. *In room:* TV, coffeemaker, hair dryer, no phone.

The Green Park Hotel

This white-painted mansion, with carved eaves and a backdrop of woodland, is about 1km (½ mile) from Pitlochry's center. Guest rooms vary in style and size; the half-dozen or so rooms in the garden wing enjoy a view of nearby Loch Faskally. Some rooms contain showers only.

Drinks are available in a lounge overlooking the water. Popular during festival season, the dining room serves dinner nightly, with many traditional Scottish dishes. *Note:* Smoking is prohibited throughout the premises.

Clunie Bridge Rd., Pitlochry PH16 5JY. ℂ 01796/473-248. Fax 01796/473-520. www.thegreenpark.co.uk. 39 units. £66–£87 ($125–$165) double. Rates include half-board. MC, V. Signposted from A9 north of Pitlochry. **Amenities:** Restaurant; bar; nonsmoking rooms. *In room:* TV, coffeemaker, hair dryer, trouser press.

Killiecrankie Hotel 🐟

This typically Scottish country house, built in 1840 for the local church minister, is surrounded by lawns and woodlands, including a herbaceous border garden. The guest rooms are individually decorated in subtle tones, and most of the bathrooms contain combination tub/shower. The walls are a foot thick, so light sleepers can rest in peace. The restaurant serves high-priced dinners that feature fresh produce and seasonal meat, fish, and game.

A924, Killiecrankie PH16 5LG. ℂ 01796/473-220. Fax 01796/472-451. www.killiecrankiehotel.co.uk. 10 units. £178–£198 ($338–$376) double. Rates include half-board. MC, V. Free parking. Signposted from A9 north of Pitlochry. **Amenities:** Restaurant; bar; room service. *In room:* TV, coffeemaker, hair dryer.

Knockendarroch House 🐟 *(Finds*

Built in 1880, this award-winning Victorian mansion opens onto panoramic views of the Tummel Valley, and is set amid lovely gardens. The bedrooms, which vary in size and style, are attractively decorated in cool colors. The cozy attic units have balconies overlooking the rooftops of Pitlochry. All rooms are nonsmoking. Guests are offered a free glass of sherry before dinner, which might be wild venison chops in red-wine and juniper-berry *jus;* mushroom and nut roast on the chiffonade of cabbage in rich tomato and sherry sauce; or baked filet of halibut served on a bed of braised cabbage and smoked bacon wrapped in dill sauce. The food is first-rate, and prices are more moderate than might be expected. Overall, the warmth of the staff and the evocative atmosphere of the mansion make it a place worth visiting.

Higher Oakfield, Pitlochry PH16 5HT. ℂ 01796/473-473. Fax 01796/474-068. www.knockendarroch.co.uk. 12 units. £112–£124 ($213–$236) double. Rates include breakfast and dinner. MC, V. Closed Nov–Mar. Turn off A9 going north at PITLOCHRY sign. After rail bridge, take 1st right, then 2nd left. **Amenities:** Restaurant; bar; laundry service. *In room:* TV, coffeemaker, hair dryer.

Pine Trees Hotel 🐟

This 19th-century country house is a 15-minute walk from the town center and 5 minutes from the golf course that hosts the Highland Open Championships. The family-run Pine Trees has spacious public rooms, an atmosphere of warmth, and a reputation for good food and wine. The guest rooms are in either the main house or a 1970s annex designed to blend into the period of the central structure. All units are nonsmoking. Bar lunches and full lunch and dinner menus are offered, with fresh and smoked salmon always featured. Trout and salmon fishing can usually be arranged.

Strathview Terrace, Pitlochry PH16 5QR. ☏ **01796/472-121.** Fax 01796/472-460. www.pinetreeshotel.co.uk. 20 units. £74–£100 ($141–$190) double. Rates include Scottish breakfast. AE, MC, V. Turn right up Larchwood Rd., below the golf course on the north side of Pitlochry. **Amenities:** Restaurant; bar; dry cleaning; nonsmoking rooms. *In room:* TV, coffeemaker, hair dryer.

WHERE TO DINE

East Haugh House ✦ MODERN BRITISH   Although it contains 13 comfortable guest rooms, East Haugh House is best known for its well-prepared cuisine. Located in a Teutonic-looking granite house, which was commissioned in the 1600s by the duke of Atholl for one of his tenant farmers, the restaurant offers a menu that relies exclusively on fresh Scottish ingredients. Meals in the cozy bar may include mixed grills, steaks, and haggis. The cuisine in the elegant restaurant is more adventurous, featuring such dishes as zucchini flowers stuffed with wild-mushroom duxelles, terrine of local pigeon with orange salad and *mange tout* (a kind of bean), and roast rack of lamb served on a potato roshtie.

The spacious guest rooms make guests think they're staying in a country mansion. Including a Scottish breakfast and dinner, doubles run £99 to £119 ($188–$226).

Old Perth Rd., East Haugh, Pitlochry PH16 5JS. ☏ **01796/473-121.** Fax 01796/472-473. www.easthaugh.co.uk. Reservations recommended. Table d'hôte dinner £35 ($66); bar platters £4.50–£19 ($8.55–$36). MC, V. Restaurant daily 7–9pm; bar daily noon–2:30pm and 6–9pm. Drive 1.6km (1 mile) south of Pitlochry on A9 toward Inverness; it's across the road from the Tummel River.

PITLOCHRY AFTER DARK

The town is famous for its **Pitlochry Festival Theatre** (☏ **01796/484-626**). Founded in 1951, it draws people from all over the world to its repertory of plays, concerts, and varying art exhibits, presented from April 30 to October 9. The theater complex opened in 1981 on the banks of the River Tummel, near the dam and fish ladder; it has a restaurant serving coffee, lunch, and dinner, along with other facilities for visitors. Tickets for plays and concerts are £12 to £25 ($23–$48).

For the area's best pub, head to the peaceful grounds of the **Killiecrankie Hotel,** signposted from A9 north of Pitlochry (☏ **01796/473-220**). It serves 20 malt whiskies as well as great food that's reasonably priced. Upholstered chairs, wildlife paintings, and plants and flowers make for an inviting atmosphere.

7 Dundee & Glamis Castle

102km (63 miles) N of Edinburgh, 108km (67 miles) SW of Aberdeen, 36km (22 miles) NE of Perth, 134km (83 miles) NE of Glasgow

The old seaport of Dundee, on the north shore of the Firth of Tay, the fourth-largest city in Scotland, is now an industrial city. When steamers took over the whaling industry from sailing vessels, Dundee became the home port for ships from the 1860s until World War I. Long known for its jute and flax operations, Dundee is linked with the production of rich Dundee fruitcakes and Dundee marmalades and jams.

Spanning the Firth of Tay is the **Tay Railway Bridge,** opened in 1888. Constructed over the tidal estuary, the bridge is 3km (2 miles) long, one of the longest in Europe. There's also a road bridge 2km (1¼ miles) long, with four traffic lanes and a walkway in the center.

Dundee has only minor attractions itself, but it's a base for exploring Glamis Castle (one of the most famous in Scotland) and the little town of Kirriemuir, which Sir James M. Barrie, author of *Peter Pan,* disguised in fiction as the Thrums. Dundee also makes a good base for those who want to play at one of Scotland's most famous golf courses, Carnoustie.

ESSENTIALS
GETTING THERE   By Train   ScotRail offers frequent service between Perth, Dundee, and Aberdeen. One-way fare from Perth to Dundee is £6 ($11); from Aberdeen, £21 ($40). Phone *C* **08457/484-950** for schedules and departure times.

By Bus   Citylink buses offer frequent bus service from Edinburgh and Glasgow. Call *C* **0990/505-050** for information.

By Car   The fastest way to reach Dundee is to cut south back to Perth along A9 and link up with A972 going east.

VISITOR INFORMATION   The **tourist information office** is at 21 Castle St. (*C* **01382/527-527**). April to September, hours are Monday to Saturday 9am to 6pm, Sunday 10am to 4pm; October to March, Monday to Saturday 9am to 5pm.

EXPLORING THE AREA
For a panoramic view of Dundee, the Tay Bridge across to Fife, and the mountains to the north, go to **Dundee Law,** a 174m (572-ft.) hill, 1.6km (1 mile) north of the city. The hill is an ancient volcanic plug.

Broughty Castle   This 15th-century estuary fort is 6.5km (4 miles) east of the city center at Broughty Ferry, a fishing village that was the terminus for ferries crossing the Firth of Tay until the bridges were built. Besieged by the English in the 16th century and attacked by Cromwell's army under General Monk in the 17th, it was restored in 1861 as part of Britain's coastal defenses. The museum has displays on local history, arms and armor, seashore life, and Dundee's whaling story. The observation area at the top of the castle provides fine views of the Tay estuary and northeast Fife.

Castle Green, Broughty Ferry. *C* **01382/436-916**. Free admission. Apr–Sept Mon–Sat 10am–4pm, Sun 12:30–4pm; Oct–Mar Tues–Sat 10am–4pm, Sun 12:30–4pm. Bus: 75 or 76.

HMS *Unicorn* *★*   This 46-gun ship of war, commissioned in 1824 by the Royal Navy, is now the oldest British-built ship afloat. It has been restored and visitors can explore all four decks: the quarter-deck, with its 14.5-kilogram (32-lb.) carronades; the gun deck, with its battery of 8-kilogram (18-lb.) cannons and captain's quarters; the berth deck, with its officers' cabins and crew's hammocks; and the orlop deck and hold. Various displays portraying life in the navy and the history of the *Unicorn* make this a rewarding visit.

Victoria Dock. *C* **01382/200-900**. Admission £3.50 ($6.65) adults, £2.50 ($4.75) seniors and children, £7.50–£9.50 ($14–$18) family ticket. Easter–Oct daily 10am–5pm; Nov–Easter Wed–Sun 10am–4pm. Bus: 6, 23, or 78.

Verdant Works   This refurbished ex-mill, known as the Jute House, is dedicated to the history of an industry that sustained Dundee throughout most of the 19th and 20th centuries. The first floor shows how raw jute from Bangladesh was processed, and includes a display on a weaver's loom. On the second floor is a section about the socio-historical aspect of the city and how the different social classes lived in 19th-century

Dundee. In the courtyard are 18th- and 19th-century street games, such as stilts, whips, and tops.

West Henderson's Wind. © 01382/225-282. Admission £5.95 ($11) adults, £4.45 ($8.45) seniors, £3.85 ($7.30) children. Apr–Oct Mon–Sat 10am–6pm, Sun 11am–6pm; Nov–Mar Wed–Sat 10:30am–4:30pm, Sun 11am–4:30pm. Lies a 15-min. walk north of train station (it's well signposted).

WHERE TO STAY

Craigtay Hotel   Although this hotel was constructed around the core of an 18th-century farm building, few if any hints of its age are visible. In the 1960s, it was Dundee's first disco, before a local entrepreneur transformed it into a tearoom. Much enlarged and modernized, it's now a small hotel lying 1.6km (1 mile) from the center; its functional guest rooms have small shower-only bathrooms. The pub and restaurant serve moderately priced dinners nightly.

101 Broughty Ferry Rd., Tayside, Dundee DD4 6JE. © 01382/451-142. Fax 01382/452-940. www.craigtay.co.uk. 18 units. £60–£65 ($114–$124) double. Rates include breakfast. AE, MC, V. From Dundee, drive 1.6km (1 mile) east of town, following signs to Broughty Ferry. Free parking. Courtesy pickup from train or airport. **Amenities:** Restaurant; bar; laundry service; nonsmoking rooms. *In room:* TV, coffeemaker, hair dryer (on request), iron, trouser press.

Hilton Dundee ✦   This chain hotel helps to rejuvenate the once-seedy waterfront of Dundee. Although built in a severe modern style, the five-story block contains well-furnished guest rooms, some of which overlook the Firth, the river, or the Tay Bridge. Both business and leisure travelers will find solace here in rooms with bright floral upholstery and draperies, blond wood furnishings, and small bathrooms with shower or tub.

Earl Grey Place, Dundee DD1 4DE. © 01382/229-271. Fax 01382/200-072. www.dundee.hilton.com. 129 units. £108–£141 ($205–$268) double; from £185 ($352) suite. AE, DC, MC, V. Free parking. Bus: 1A, 1B, or 20. From the south, the hotel is on the left side as you come over the Tay Rd. Bridge into town. **Amenities:** Restaurant; bar; indoor pool; health club; sauna; business center; 24-hr. room service; laundry service; dry cleaning; steam room; nonsmoking rooms; rooms for those w/limited mobility. *In room:* TV, coffeemaker, hair dryer, trouser press.

Invercarse Hotel   This Best Western hotel, 5km (3 miles) west of the heart of Dundee, has landscaped gardens that overlook the River Tay. Many prefer it for its fresh air, tranquil location, and Victorian country-house aura. Well-maintained rooms come in a variety of sizes and open onto views across the Tay to the hills of the kingdom of Fife.

371 Perth Rd., Dundee DD2 1PG. © 800/780-7234 in the U.S. and Canada, or 01382/669-231. Fax 01382/644-112. www.redwoodleisure.co.uk/invercarse. 44 units. £89–£100 ($169–$190) double. Rates include Scottish breakfast. AE, DC, MC, V. Free parking. Drive 5km (3 miles) west of Dundee on the Perth Rd. The hotel is clearly signposted. **Amenities:** Restaurant; bar; access to nearby health club; business center; limited room service; laundry service; dry cleaning; nonsmoking rooms. *In room:* TV, coffeemaker, hair dryer, iron, trouser press.

Queen's Hotel ✦   For the past century and a quarter, the Queen's has been a venue for that special occasion in town, be it a wedding or a school reunion. This historical hotel has stayed abreast of the times in terms of services and amenities, but it has retained much of its Victorian charm. Bedrooms come in a variety of sizes, though most are quite large, each with a well-kept bathroom. Rooms are decorated in rich colors, such as classic shades of amber gold or red-wine burgundy. One room is suitable for guests with limited mobility. Nosey Parkers, a favorite local bistro and restaurant, has a Scottish and Continental menu that's supplemented by blackboard specials.

160 Nethergate, Dundee DD1 4DU. © 800/780-7234 in the U.S. and Canada, or 01382/322-515. Fax 01382/202-668. www.queenshotel-dundee.com. 52 units. £60–£90 ($114–$171). Rates include breakfast. AE, DC, MC, V. Free parking.

Lies a 4-min. walk west of the Dundee Train Station. **Amenities:** Restaurant; bar; room service; laundry service; dry cleaning; nonsmoking rooms; 1 room for those w/limited mobility. *In room:* TV, coffeemaker, hair dryer, iron.

Swallow Hotel *(Kids)*   This restored Victorian mansion sits on 2.2 hectares (5 acres) of well-landscaped gardens on the outskirts of Dundee. It comes complete with a nature trail and an adventure playground for the kids. It's also one of the best-equipped hotels in the area, with a leisure club, an outdoor heated pool, and a spa. Bedrooms are well laid out, tastefully furnished, and comfortable, each with a carefully maintained bathroom. The so-called executive rooms are more modern than the traditional doubles. Most of the rooms are tartan-themed, though others are aflame in floral colors.

Kingsway West, Invergowrie, DD2 5JT. © **01382/641-122.** Fax 01382/631-201. www.swallowhotels.com/dundee. 103 units. £60–£100 ($114–$190) double; £140 ($266) suite. AE, MC, V. Free parking. Signposted on the Dundee Kingsway, on the western outskirts of Dundee. **Amenities:** Restaurant; bar; indoor heated pool; health club; spa; room service; babysitting; laundry service; dry cleaning; steam room. *In room:* TV, coffeemaker, hair dryer, iron.

WHERE TO DINE

Other dining options include the restaurants in the hotels listed above.

Het Theatercafe INTERNATIONAL   Located in the Dundee Repertory Theatre, this is both an upstairs cafe-bar and an excellent restaurant on the ground floor. It's become one of the most fashionable dining places in Dundee. Naturally, it's ideal for pre-theater meals. Freshly prepared, good-tasting food, combined with reasonable prices, makes the restaurant a success. The most popular item on the menu is steak frites—an 8-ounce rib-eye steak with chips. You can also order tasty fish cakes with deep-fried potatoes and an herb-laced salad, or a hot-and-spicy blackened chicken breast. If you like your chicken even more exotic, opt for the marinated grilled chicken served with a spicy peanut sauce.

Tay Square. © **01382/206-699.** Reservations recommended. Main courses £8–£12 ($15–$23). MC, V. Mon–Sat noon–3pm and 5–9pm.

Jahangir Tandoori INDIAN   Built around an indoor fish pond in a dining room draped with the soft folds of an embroidered tent, this is the best Indian restaurant in Dundee—and one of the most exotic in the region. Meals are prepared with fresh ingredients and run the gamut of recipes from both north and south India. The food is sometimes slow-cooked in clay pots (tandoori) and is seasoned to the degree of spiciness you prefer. Both meat and vegetarian dishes are available.

1 Sessions St. (at the corner of Hawk Hill). © **01382/202-022.** Reservations recommended. Main courses £10–£15 ($19–$29). AE, MC, V. Daily 5pm–midnight.

DUNDEE AFTER DARK

The **Dundee Rep Theatre,** Tay Square (© **01382/223-530**), is likely to stage anything from *Peter Pan* to an opera, from plays to Scottish ballet or even flamenco. You can purchase tickets Monday to Saturday 10am to 7:30pm (to 6pm on performance days). Tickets generally cost £8 to £20 ($15–$38). The theater provides audio descriptions for those with visual impairments, and, for the hearing impaired, sign language is available. On-site is the **Het Theatercafe** (see above).

A SIDE TRIP TO GLAMIS CASTLE

The little village of Glamis (pronounced *glams*) grew up around **Glamis Castle** *★★*, Castle Office, Glamis (© **01307/840-393;** www.glamis-castle.co.uk). Visitors to Scotland most want to see Glamis Castle for its link with the crown. For 6 centuries, the

In Search of Peter Pan

The little town of **Kirriemuir** is reached by heading north of Glamis Castle for 6.5km (4 miles) or by traveling 26km (16 miles) north of Dundee via A929 and A928. Thousands of visitors per year come here to pay their respects to Sir James M. Barrie (1860–1937), author of *Peter Pan*.

The little town of red-sandstone houses and narrow crooked streets, located in the heart of Scotland's raspberry country, saw the birth of Barrie in 1860. His father was employed as a hand-loom weaver of linen. **Barrie's birthplace** still stands at 9 Brechin Rd. (© **01575/572-646**), now a property of the National Trust for Scotland. The small house contains some of the writer's manuscripts and mementos. From March through June, the house is open Saturday through Wednesday from noon to 5pm and Sunday from 1 to 5pm; July through August Monday to Saturday 11am to 5pm and Sunday 1pm to 5pm; September through October, hours are Saturday to Wednesday from noon to 5pm and Sunday from 1 to 5pm. Admission is £5 ($9.50) for adults, £4 ($7.60) for seniors, students, and children; £14 ($27) family.

Barrie first became known for his sometimes-cynical tales of Kirriemuir, disguised as Thrums, in such works as *Auld Licht Idylls* (1888) and *A Window in Thrums* (1889). He then turned to the theater and in time became known for bringing supernatural and sentimental ideas to the stage. It's said that talking to a group of children while walking his dog gave him the idea for the stories about Peter Pan, which were first presented to the public in 1904. It wasn't until 1957 that *When Wendy Grew Up: An Afterthought* was published.

He went on to write more dramas, including *Alice Sit-by-the-Fire* (1905), *What Every Woman Knows* (1908), *The Will* (1913), and *Mary Rose* (1920), the latter a very popular play in its day. But, besides Barrie scholars, who remembers these works now? On the other hand, Peter Pan has become a legendary figure, known by almost every child in the Western world through films, plays, musicals, and the original book.

Although he spent most of his working life in London, Barrie is buried in Kirriemuir Cemetery. To reach **Barrie's grave,** turn left off Brechin Road and follow the cemetery road upward. The path is clearly marked, taking you to the grave pavilion. A camera obscura in the **Barrie Pavilion** on Kirriemuir Hill gives views over Strathmore to Dundee and north to the Highlands.

castle has been connected to members of the British royal family: The Queen Mother was brought up here; and Princess Margaret was born here, making her the first royal princess born in Scotland in 3 centuries. The current owner is the queen's great-nephew. The castle contains Duncan's Hall—the Victorians claimed this was where Macbeth murdered King Duncan, but in the play, the murder takes place at Macbeth's castle (Cawdor), near Inverness. (Incidentally, Shakespeare was wrong in naming Macbeth Thane of Glamis; Glamis wasn't made a thaneship—a sphere of influence in medieval Scotland—until years after the play takes place.)

The present Glamis Castle dates from the early 15th century, but there are records of a hunting lodge having been here in the 11th century. The Lyon family has owned Glamis Castle since 1372, and it contains some fine plaster ceilings, furniture, and paintings.

A self-service restaurant has been installed in the old kitchens, with a chalkboard featuring daily specials and excellent home-cooked and baked dishes.

The castle is open to the public, with access to the Royal Apartments and many other rooms, as well as the fine gardens, from the end of March to October, Monday to Saturday 10am to 6pm; November and December, Monday to Saturday 11am to 5pm. Admission to the castle and gardens is £7.50 ($14) adults, £6.30 ($12) seniors, £4.30 ($8.15) children, family ticket £22 ($41). The charge to visit only the grounds is £3.70 ($7.05) adults, £2.70 ($5.15) seniors and children. Buses run between Dundee and Glamis. The 35-minute ride costs £4 ($7.60) one-way. *Note:* Buses don't stop in front of the castle, which is 1km (1½ mile) from the bus stop.

WHERE TO STAY

Castleton House ★★ (Finds   This country-house hotel is run with love and care by owners David Webster and Verity Nicholson, who acquired it in 2000. In cool weather you're greeted by welcoming coal fires in the public lounge; the youthful staff is the most considerate we've encountered in the area. Rooms of various sizes are furnished with reproductions of antiques; the suite features a genuine Regency four-poster bed. Chef Andrew Wilkie presides over the award-winning restaurant, where most of the fruits and vegetables served are grown on the hotel's grounds.

Eassie by Glamis, Forfar, Tayside DD8 1SJ. (℃) **01307/840-340.** Fax 01307/840-506. www.castletonglamis.co.uk. 6 units. £200–£220 ($380–$418) double. Rates include Scottish breakfast. AE, MC, V. Drive 5km (3 miles) west of Glamis on A94. **Amenities:** Restaurant; bar; 9-hole putting green; room service; laundry service; dry cleaning; non-smoking rooms. *In room:* TV, coffeemaker, hair dryer.

WHERE TO DINE

Strathmore Arms CONTINENTAL/SCOTTISH   Try this place near the castle for one of the best lunches in the area. You might begin with the freshly made soup of the day or the fresh prawns. Dishes regularly featured include steak pie and venison. For something a little more exotic, go for the Indian chicken breast marinated in yogurt and spices; for vegetarians try phyllo parcels stuffed with asparagus and cauliflower.

The Square Glamis. (℃) **01307/840-248.** Reservations recommended. Main courses £9–£19 ($17–$36). AE, MC, V. Daily noon–2pm and 6:30–9pm.

8 Ballater & Balmoral Castle ★

179km (111 miles) N of Edinburgh, 66km (41 miles) W of Aberdeen, 108km (67 miles) NE of Perth, 113km (70 miles) SE of Inverness

Located on the Dee River, with the Grampian Mountains in the background, Ballater is a resort center, but most visitors come here with only one goal in mind—to walk the grounds of Balmoral Castle, the far northern home of the Windsors. The town still centers on its Station Square, where the royal family used to be photographed as they arrived to spend holidays. (The railway is now closed.) From Ballater, you can drive west to view the scenery of Glen Muick and Lochnagar, where you'll see herds of deer. Incidentally, the drive between Ballater and Braemar (see "Braemar," below) is very scenic.

ESSENTIALS

GETTING THERE   **By Train**   Go to Aberdeen and continue the rest of the way by connecting bus. For rail schedules and information, call ℂ 08457/484-950.

By Bus   Buses run hourly from Aberdeen to Ballater. The bus and train stations in Aberdeen are next to each other on Guild Street (ℂ 01224/212-266 for information). Bus no. 201 from Braemar runs to Ballater (trip time: 1¼ hr.). The fare is £6 ($11).

By Car   From Braemar, go east along A93.

VISITOR INFORMATION   The **tourist information office** is at Station Square (ℂ 01339/755-306). July and August, hours are daily 10am to 1pm and 2 to 6pm; September, October, May, and June, Monday to Saturday 10am to 1pm and 2 to 5pm, Sunday 1 to 5pm. Closed November to April.

THE CASTLE

Balmoral Castle ✸   "This dear paradise" is how Queen Victoria described Balmoral Castle, rebuilt in the Scottish baronial style by her beloved Albert. And Balmoral was the setting for the story of Victoria and her faithful servant, John Brown, as shown in the film *Mrs. Brown.* Today, Balmoral is still a private residence of the British sovereign. Albert, Victoria's prince consort, leased the property in 1848 and bought it in 1852. As the original castle of the Farquharsons proved too small, the present edifice was built, completed in 1855. Its principal feature is a 30m (100-ft.) tower. Of the actual castle, only the ballroom is open to the public; it houses an exhibit of pictures, porcelain, and works of art. On the grounds are many memorials to the royal family, along with gardens, country walks, souvenir shops, a refreshment room, and pony trekking for £30 ($57) for a 2-hour ride (available to adults and children over 12 10am–noon and 2–4pm).

Balmoral, Ballater. ℂ 01339/742-534. www.balmoralcastle.com. Admission £7 ($13) adults, £6 ($11) seniors, £3 ($5.70) for children ages 5–16, free for children under 5. Mar–July 30 daily 10am–5pm. Closed Aug–Feb. Crathie bus from Aberdeen to the Crathie station; Balmoral Castle is signposted from there (a short walk).

WHERE TO STAY

You can also stay at the **Green Inn** (see "Where to Dine," below).

Balgonie Country House ✸ *Finds*   In the heart of Royal Deeside, to the west of town, this Edwardian country house is set amid 1.6 hectares (4 acres) of gardens, overlooking the Ballater Golf Course and providing panoramic views of the hills of Glen Muick. It offers a peaceful haven of beautifully furnished rooms (some with shower only) and fine Scottish food. The owners can advise on golfing, salmon fishing, and hiking in the area.

Braemar Place, Ballater AB35 5NQ. ℂ/fax 01339/755-482. www.royaldeesidehotels.com. 9 units. £130 ($247) double. Rates include breakfast. AE, MC, V. Closed Jan. Free parking. Signposted off A93, Ballater-Perth, on the western outskirts. **Amenities:** Restaurant; bar; nonsmoking rooms. *In room:* TV, hair dryer.

Darroch Learg Hotel ✸ *Finds*   Built in 1888 as an elegant country home, this pink-granite hotel stands in 2 hectares (5 acres) of lush woodlands opening onto views of the Dee Valley toward the Grampian Mountains. Constructed at the peak of the golden age of Victorian Royal Deeside, the hotel is imbued with a relaxing charm. The individually decorated bedrooms are divided between the main house and Oakhall, a baronial mansion on the same grounds. Some units have four-poster beds and private terraces; and all have well-maintained bathrooms with showers. The hotel's main attraction is its Conservatory Restaurant, which is open to nonguests (see "Where to Dine," below). The chef will accommodate special diets by arrangement.

Darroch Learg, Braemar Rd. (on A93 at the west end of Ballater), Ballater AB35 5UX. (C) **01339/755-443.** Fax 01339/755-252. www.darrochlearg.co.uk. 17 units. £130–£160 ($247–$304) double in main house; £85 ($162) double in Oakhall. Rates include breakfast. AE, DC, MC, V. Closed Christmas and last 3 weeks in Jan. Free parking. **Amenities:** Restaurant; room service; laundry service; rooms for those w/limited mobility. *In room:* TV, coffeemaker, hair dryer, trouser press.

Deeside Hotel
This well-managed guesthouse occupies an 1890 pink-granite house surrounded by late-Victorian gardens, and is a 3-minute walk west of the town center. The small guest rooms are simple, with white walls, wood furniture, and bathrooms with showers. Upscale dinners are prepared nightly. Good-tasting offerings include grilled oatmeal-dredged herring with Dijon mustard sauce; venison filet with hawthorn jelly; and lamb shank braised in red wine, orange, and rosemary.

45 Braemar Rd., Ballater AB35 5RQ. (C) **01339/755-420.** Fax 01339/755-357. www.deesidehotel.co.uk. 9 units. £45 ($86) double. Rates include breakfast. Pets welcome. MC, V. Closed Jan. **Amenities:** Restaurant; bar; nonsmoking rooms. *In room:* TV, coffeemaker, no phone.

Hilton Craigendarroch Hotel *Kids*
This hotel, built in the Scottish baronial style, is set amid old trees on an 11-hectare (28-acre) estate. Modern comforts have been added, but a 19th-century aura remains. Public areas are luxurious, especially the study with oak paneling, a log fire, and book-lined shelves. The fair-size guest rooms open onto views of Ballater and the River Dee. Each is furnished in individual style, with shower-only bathroom. For longer stays, you can inquire about renting one of the one-, two-, or three-bedroom villas, each with a private terrace.

Braemar Rd., Ballater AB35 5XA. (C) **01339/755-858.** Fax 01339/755-447. www.hilton.com. 45 units. £70–£125 ($133–$238) double; £175 ($333) suite. Rates include Scottish breakfast and dinner. AE, DC, MC, V. Free parking. Signposted directly west of town on the road to Braemar. **Amenities:** 3 restaurants; 2 bars; indoor pool; tennis court; health club; Jacuzzi; sauna; children's playground; business center; salon; room service; babysitting; laundry service; dry cleaning; coin-operated laundry; squash court; steam room; nonsmoking rooms; rooms for those w/limited mobility. *In room:* TV, coffeemaker, hair dryer, trouser press.

WHERE TO DINE
Other dining options include the restaurants in the hotels listed above.

Balgonie Country House Restaurant SCOTTISH/FRENCH For Scottish salmon, local game, or Aberdeen Angus beef, this restaurant is among the finest in the Royal Deeside. John and Priscilla Finnie welcome hotel guests and nonguests to their dining room, where the kitchen makes a major effort to secure some of the finest Scottish products. The menu changes daily, but you're likely to find tender filet of beef served with layered potato cake and truffles with wild mushrooms and spinach in a foie gras *jus,* or loin of lamb with a red-currant *jus.* While enjoying views of the Glenmuick Hills, you can delight in any number of French-inspired dishes, such as halibut with asparagus and a tomato confit.

In the Balgonie Country House (see "Where to Stay," above), Braemar Place. (C) **01339/755-482.** Reservations recommended. Fixed-price 4-course menu £36 ($68). AE, MC, V. Daily 12:30–2pm and 7–9pm. Closed Jan.

The Conservatory Restaurant *SCOTTISH*
Head here for innovative, imaginative cuisine. This award-winning dining room has views over the River Dee. The chef uses only the freshest ingredients, like lamb, venison, and Aberdeen Angus beef. Seafood options include filet of halibut with basil and olive-oil crust combined with fried squid and avocado salsa; and pan-fried sea trout with pomme puree.

In the Darroch Learg Hotel (see "Where to Stay," above), Darroch Learg, Braemar Rd. ℭ **01339/755-443**. Reservations required. Fixed-price 3-course menu £40 ($76). AE, DC, MC, V. Daily 12:30–2pm and 7–9pm. Closed Christmas and last 3 weeks in Jan.

Green Inn ✿✿ SCOTTISH/FRENCH This hotel restaurant is now the premier choice for dining. Trevor and Evelyn O'Halloran, along with head chef, son Chris, have improved the cuisine to such an extent that locals drive for miles around just to dine here. A large and welcoming conservatory, with a wood-burning stove for nippy nights, allows you to relax with an aperitif while you make your selection from the imaginative menu prepared with market-fresh ingredients. Chris trained with chef Raymond Blanc at Le Manoir aux Quat' Saisons, which is acclaimed as the premier restaurant of the Midlands in England.

The menu varies nightly. We salute such appetizers as a terrine of filets of roe deer, teal, lamb, and pheasant wrapped in a mousse of their own livers or a rabbit lasagna flavored with truffles. For a main dish, you can taste such exciting offerings as roasted organic pork tenderloin with braised cheek and wild rice, with fresh morels and a truffle cream sauce, or oven-roasted estate partridge with caramelized apples and pears. For dessert, such lovely concoctions await as a warm chocolate tart with chestnut cream and orange sauce.

Three simply furnished double rooms, with shower-only bathroom, TV, and half-board, go for £60 ($114) per person.

9 Victoria Rd., Ballater AB35 5QQ. ℭ/fax **01339/755-701**. Reservations required. Fixed-price menu £32 ($61) for 2 courses, £37 ($70) for 3 courses. AE, DC, MC, V. Mar–Oct daily 7–9pm; Nov–Feb Tues–Sat 7–9pm.

La Mangiatoia ITALIAN In a converted early-18th-century stable beside the River Dee in the heart of Ballater, this is one of the most architecturally unusual restaurants in the region. Amid a deliberately rustic decor that includes artfully placed bales of hay, lots of equine accessories, and a high wooden ceiling, you order from a menu that features a savory array of barbecue dishes. Choices include chicken, salmon, pastas, and baguette sandwiches. Everybody's favorite dessert seems to be sticky toffee pudding.

Bridge Sq. ℭ **01339/755-999**. Main courses lunch £6–£10 ($11–$19); main courses dinner £10–£17 ($19–$32). MC, V. Mon–Fri 5–10pm; Sat–Sun noon–10pm.

Oaks Restaurant ✿ BRITISH The most glamorous restaurant in the region, the Oaks is in a century-old mansion that was originally built by the marmalade kings of Britain, the Keiller family. This is the most upscale restaurant in a resort complex that includes hotel rooms, time-share villas, and access to a nearby golf course. To start, try the venison and duck terrine flavored with orange and brandy and served with a warm black conch vinaigrette. Main courses include roast rack of lamb, breast of Grampian chicken, and loin of venison.

In the Hilton Craigendarroch Hotel (see "Where to Stay," above), Braemar Rd. ℭ **01339/755-858**. Reservations strongly recommended. Fixed-price 4-course dinner £36 ($68). AE, DC, MC, V. Daily 7–10:30pm.

9 Braemar

137km (85 miles) N of Edinburgh, 93km (58 miles) W of Aberdeen, 82km (51 miles) N of Perth

In the heart of some of Grampian's most beautiful scenery is Braemar, known for its romantic castle. It's also a good center for exploring the area that includes Balmoral Castle (see above) and is home to the most famous of the Highland Gatherings. The village is set against a massive backdrop of hills, covered with heather in summer, where Clunie Water joins the River Dee. The massive **Cairn Toul** towers over Braemar, reaching a height of 1,287m (4,241 ft.).

ESSENTIALS

GETTING THERE   By Train   Take the train to Aberdeen, then continue the rest of the way by bus. For information and schedules, call © **08457/484-950.**

By Bus   Buses run six times a day from Aberdeen to Braemar (trip time: 2 hr.). One-way fare is £9 ($17). The bus and train stations in Aberdeen are next to each other on Guild Street (© **01224/212-266** for information about schedules).

By Car   To reach Braemar from Dundee, return west toward Perth, then head north along A93, following the signs into Braemar. The 113km (70-mile) drive will take 70 to 90 minutes.

VISITOR INFORMATION   The year-round **Braemar Tourist Office** is in The Mews, Mar Road (© **01339/741-600**). In June, hours are daily 10am to 6pm; July and August, daily 9am to 7pm; and in September, daily 10am to 1pm and 2 to 6pm. In off season, hours are Monday to Saturday 10am to 1pm and 2 to 5pm, Sunday noon to 5pm.

SPECIAL EVENTS   The spectacular **Royal Highland Gathering** takes place annually in late August or early September in the Princess Royal and Duke of Fife Memorial Park. The queen herself often attends the gathering. These ancient games are thought to have been conceived by King Malcolm Canmore, a chieftain who ruled much of Scotland at the time of the Norman conquest of England. He selected his hardiest warriors from all the clans for a "keen and fair contest."

Call the tourist office (see "Visitor Information," above) for more information. Braemar is overrun with visitors during the gathering—anyone thinking of attending would be wise to reserve accommodations anywhere within a 32km (20-mile) radius of Braemar no later than early April.

EXPLORING THE AREA

You might spot members of the royal family, even the queen herself, at **Crathie Church,** 14km (9 miles) east of Braemar on A93 (© **01339/742-208**), where they attend Sunday services when in residence. Services are at 11:30am; otherwise the church is open April to October, Monday to Saturday 9:30am to 5:30pm and on Sunday 2 to 5:30pm.

Nature lovers may want to drive to the **Linn of Dee,** 10km (6 miles) west of Braemar, a narrow chasm on the River Dee, which is a local beauty spot. Other nature sites include Glen Muick, Loch Muick, and Lochnagar. A **Scottish Wildlife Trust Visitor Centre,** reached by a minor road, is located in this Highland glen, off the South Deeside road. An access road joins B976 at a point 26km (16 miles) east of Braemar. The tourist office (see above) provides maps.

Braemar Castle ♤   This romantic 17th-century castle is a fully furnished private residence with architectural grace and scenic charm. The castle has barrel-vaulted ceilings and an underground prison and is known for its remarkable star-shaped defensive curtain wall. Under renovation at press time, the castle has not announced its opening date; check locally before heading here.

On the Aberdeen-Ballater-Perth Rd. (A93). © **01339/741-219.** www.braemarcastle.co.uk. Admission £4 ($7.60) adults, £3.50 ($6.65) seniors and students, £1.50 ($2.85) children ages 5–15, free for children under 5. Apr–Oct Sat–Thurs 10am–6pm (July–Aug also open Fri). Closed Nov–Easter. Take A93 .8km (½ mile) northeast of Braemar.

PLAYING GOLF

Braemar Golf Course, at Braemar (ⓒ **01339/741-618**), is the highest golf course in the country. The 2nd-hole green is 380m (1,250 ft.) above sea level—this is the trickiest hole on the course. Pro golf commentator Peter Alliss has deemed it "the hardest par 4 in all of Scotland." Set on a plateau, the hole is bordered on the right by the River Clunie and on the left by rough. Greens fees are: Monday to Friday £20 ($38) for 18 holes and £25 ($48) for a day ticket; Saturday and Sunday £25 ($48) for 18 holes and £30 ($57) for a day ticket. Pull carts can be rented for £5 ($9.50) per day, and sets of clubs can be borrowed for £9 ($17) per day. The only dress code is "be reasonable." The course is open only April to October daily (call in advance as hours can vary).

WHERE TO STAY & DINE

Braemar Lodge Hotel   This hotel, popular with skiers who frequent the nearby Glenshee slopes, is set on extensive grounds at the head of Glen Clunie. Bedrooms vary in shape and size, but each is comfortable and well equipped, containing well-maintained bathrooms. Rooms are bright and airy, with soothing color schemes. Two rooms are large enough for families. On cool evenings, guests are greeted with log fires. The hotel is on the road to the Glenshee ski slopes, near the cottage where Robert Louis Stevenson wrote *Treasure Island.* Three log cabins have been built on the grounds. Fully equipped with all modern conveniences, they sleep up to six persons.

6 Glenshee Rd., Braemar AB35 5YQ. ⓒ/fax **01339/741-627.** www.braemarlodge.co.uk. 7 units. £70 ($133) double; £450–£500 ($855–$950) log cabin. Rates include Scottish breakfast. MC, V. Free parking. Closed Nov. Lies a 2-min. walk south from the bus station. **Amenities:** Restaurant; bar; laundry service; dry cleaning; nonsmoking rooms; 1 cabin for those w/limited mobility. *In room:* TV, hair dryer.

Callater Lodge Hotel *(Finds*   Full of rural charm, this 1861 granite house is about .5km (¼ mile) south of the center of Braemar, off the side of A93 in a spacious garden. Built around 1865, with a small-scale enlargement completed during the 1970s, Callater Lodge bristles with bay and dormer windows and offers a different decor in each of its cozy guest rooms. Each room has a bathroom with shower; two rooms have bathtubs as well. On request, the owners prepare picnics and offer advice on great scenic places to hike. Evening meals can be arranged.

9 Glenshee Rd., Braemar AB35 5YQ. ⓒ **01339/741-275.** Fax 01339/741-345. www.hotel-braemar.co.uk. 6 units. £56–£60 ($106–$114) double. Rates include breakfast. MC, V. Closed Nov–Dec. Free parking. From the center of Braemar, drive south on Glenshee Rd. *In room:* TV, coffeemaker, hair dryer, no phone.

Invercauld Arms Thistle Hotel *⊛*   This is the town's leading inn, with more amenities and greater comfort than Braemar Lodge. The oldest part of the Invercauld Arms, an old granite building, dates from the 18th century. In cool weather there's a roaring log fire on the hearth. You can go hill walking and see deer, golden eagles, and other wildlife. Fishing and, in winter, skiing are also available to guests. Rooms are comfortably furnished. Although they lack distinct style or glamour, they serve their purpose well and come in a wide range of sizes. In the pub close by, you meet the "ghillies" and "stalkers" (hunting and fishing guides), then return to the hotel for its Scottish and international fare.

Invercauld Rd., Braemar AB35 5YR. ⓒ **01339/741-605.** Fax 01339/741-428. 68 units. £115 ($219) double. Rates include Scottish breakfast. AE, DC, MC, V. Free parking. Bus: 201. **Amenities:** Restaurant; bar; laundry service; dry cleaning; nonsmoking rooms. *In room:* TV, coffeemaker, hair dryer.

10 Speyside ✶ & the Malt Whisky Trail ✶

Much of the Speyside region covered in this section is in the Moray district, on the southern shore of the Moray Firth, a great inlet cutting into the northeastern coast of Scotland. The district stretches in a triangular shape south from the coast to the wild heart of the Cairngorm Mountains near Aviemore. It's a land steeped in history, as its many castles, battle sites, and ancient monuments testify. It's also a good place to fish and, of course, play golf. Golfers can purchase a 5-day ticket from tourist information centers that gives them access to more than 11 courses in the area.

One of the best of these courses is **Boat of Garten,** Speyside (ⓒ **01479/831-282**). Relatively difficult, the almost 6,000-yard course is dotted with many bunkers and wooded areas. April to October, greens fees are £32 ($61) Monday to Friday and hours are from 7:30am to 11pm. Saturday greens fees are £37 ($70), and hours are from 10am to 4pm. In winter, call to see if the course is open. Greens fees are then reduced to £18 ($34). Pull-carts rent for £2.50 ($4.75), electric carts for £10 ($19). Dress reasonably; blue jeans are not acceptable.

The valley of the second-largest river in Scotland, the Spey, is north and south of Aviemore and a land of great natural beauty. The Spey is born in the Highlands above Loch Laggan, which lies 65km (40 miles) south of Inverness. Little more than a creek at its inception, it gains in force, fed by the many "burns" that drain water from the surrounding hills. It's one of Scotland's great rivers for salmon fishing, and it runs between the towering Cairngorms on the east and the Monadhliath Mountains on the west. Its major center is Grantown-on-Spey.

The primary tourist attraction in the area is the **Malt Whisky Trail,** 113km (70 miles) long, running through the glens of Speyside. Here distilleries, many of which can be visited, are known for their production of *uisge beatha,* or "water of life." "Whisky" is its more familiar name.

Half the malt distilleries in the country lie along the River Spey and its tributaries. Here peat smoke and Highland water are used to turn out single-malt (unblended) whisky. There are five malt distilleries in the area: **Glenlivet, Glenfiddich, Glenfarclas, Strathisla,** and **Tamdhu.** Allow about an hour each to visit them.

The best way to reach Speyside from Aberdeen is to take A96 northwest, signposted Elgin. If you're traveling north on the A9 road from Perth and Pitlochry, your first stop might be at Dalwhinnie, which, at 575m (1,888 ft.), has the highest whisky distillery in the world. It's not in the Spey Valley but is at the northeastern end of Loch Ericht, with views of lochs and forests.

KEITH

Keith, 18km (11 miles) northwest of Huntly, grew because of its strategic location, where the main road and rail routes between Inverness and Aberdeen cross the River Isla. It has an ancient history, but owes its present look to the town planning of the late 18th and early 19th centuries. Today it's a major stopover along the Malt Whisky Trail.

The oldest operating distillery in the Scottish Highlands, the **Strathisla Distillery,** on Seafield Avenue (ⓒ **01542/783-044**), was established in 1786. Hours are March to October, Monday to Friday 10am to 4pm, Sunday 12:30 to 4pm. Admission is £5 ($9.50) for adults, and free for children ages 8 to 18; children under 8 are not admitted. The admission fee includes a £3 ($5.70) voucher redeemable in the distillery shop against a 70-cubic-liter bottle of whisky. Be warned that tours of this distillery are self-guided.

WHERE TO STAY

Grange House ✸ *(Finds)*   This dignified-looking stone house dates from 1815, when it was the manse for the nearby Church of Scotland, which is still the most prominent building in this tiny hamlet. Doreen Blanche and her husband, Bill, rent two well-decorated and comfortable rooms within their private home. The venue is upscale, charming, and comfortable, with a tranquillity that's enhanced by the 3.2 hectares (8 acres) of parks and gardens that surround this isolated place. Ask the owners to point out the late-Victorian addition, completed in 1898, which greatly enlarged the size of the original house.

Grange, near Keith AB55 6RY. ✆/fax **01542/870-206**. www.aboutscotland.com/banff/grangehouse.html. 2 units. £75 ($143) double. Rates include breakfast. No credit cards. From Keith, drive 5km (3 miles) east of town, following the signs to Banff, into the hamlet of Grange. Free parking. **Amenities:** Babysitting; laundry service; nonsmoking rooms. *In room:* Coffeemaker, hair dryer.

DUFFTOWN

James Duff, the fourth earl of Fife, founded Dufftown in 1817. The four main streets of town converge at the **clock tower,** which is also the **tourist office** (✆ **01340/ 820-501**). April to June, September, and October, the office is open Monday through Saturday from 10am to 1pm and 2 to 5:30pm and Sunday from 1 to 5pm; July and August, hours are Monday to Saturday 10am to 7pm and Sunday from 1 to 7pm.

A center of the whisky-distilling industry, Dufftown is surrounded by seven malt distilleries. The family-owned **Glenfiddich Distillery** is on A941, 1km (½ mile) north (✆ **01340/820-373**). It's open Monday through Friday from 9:30am to 4:30pm (Easter to mid-Oct, also Sat 9:30am–4:30pm and Sun noon–4:30pm). Guides in kilts show you around the plant and explain the process of distilling. A film on the history of distilling is also shown. At the end of the tour, which is free, you're given a dram of malt whisky to sample. There's also a souvenir shop.

Other sights include **Balvenie Castle,** along A941 (✆ **01340/820-121**), the ruins of a moated 14th-century stronghold that lie on the south side of the Glenfiddich Distillery. During her northern campaign against the earl of Huntly, Mary Queen of Scots spent 2 nights here. April to September, it's open daily from 9:30am to 6:30pm. Admission is £3.50 ($6.65) for adults, £2.80 ($5.30) for seniors, and £1.75 ($3.35) for children.

DINING

Taste of Speyside ✸ SCOTTISH   True to its name, this restaurant in the town center, just off the main square, avidly promotes Speyside cuisine as well as the product of Speyside's 46 distilleries. A platter including a slice of smoked salmon, smoked venison, smoked trout, pâté flavored with malt whisky, locally made cheese (cow or goat), salads, and homemade oat cakes is offered at noon and at night. Nourishing soup is made fresh daily and is served with homemade bread. There's also a choice of meat pies, including rabbit or venison with red wine and herbs. For dessert, try Scotch Mist, which contains fresh cream, malt whisky, and crumbled meringue.

10 Balvenie St. ✆ **01340/820-860**. Reservations recommended for dinner. Main courses £15–£17 ($29–$32); Speyside platter £14 ($27) lunch, £17 ($32) dinner. AE, MC, V. Mon–Sat noon–9pm. Closed Nov–Feb.

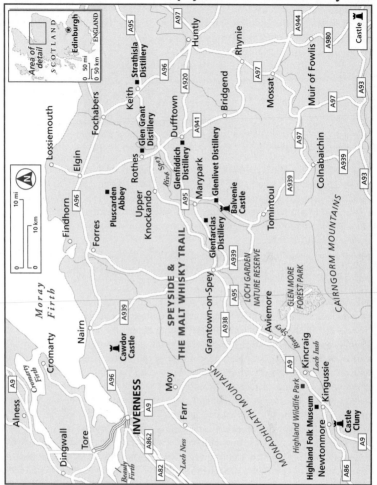

Speyside & the Malt Whisky Trail

GRANTOWN-ON-SPEY

This vacation resort, with its gray-granite buildings, is 55km (34 miles) southeast of Inverness in a wooded valley with views of the Cairngorm Mountains. It's a center for winter sports, and salmon fishing on the Spey is first-rate. Founded on a heather-covered moor in 1765 by Sir James Grant, Grantown-on-Spey became the seat of Grant's ancient family. The town was famous in the 19th century as a Highland tourist center.

From here, you can explore the valleys of the Don and Dee, the Cairngorms, and Culloden Moor, scene of the historic battle in 1746, when Bonnie Prince Charlie and his army were defeated.

A year-round **tourist information office** is on High Street (© **01479/872-773**). April to October, hours are daily 9am to 5pm, Sunday 10am to 4pm; November to March, Monday to Friday 9am to 4pm, Saturday 10am to 4pm.

WHERE TO STAY

Garth Hotel   The elegant, comfortable Garth stands on 1.6 hectares (4 acres) beside the town square. Guests enjoy sitting in the spacious lounge, whose high ceilings, wood-burning stove, and vine-covered veranda make it an attractive place for morning coffee or afternoon tea. The handsomely furnished guest rooms have all the necessary amenities, including well-maintained bathrooms with shower units. Extensive and selective meals favor Scottish dishes—with a bit of French influence—made from fresh local produce.

The Square, Castle Rd., Grantown-on-Spey, Morayshire PH26 3HN. ℂ 01479/872-836. Fax 01479/872-116. www.garthhotel.com. 18 units. £76 ($144) double. Rates include Scottish breakfast. MC, V. Free parking. **Amenities:** Restaurant; bar; room service; nonsmoking rooms. *In room:* TV, coffeemaker, hair dryer.

Tigh na Sgiath Country House Hotel ✿ (Finds)   A splendid country home set amid private grounds and woods, this is a welcoming place for an extended stay. Built in 1902 as a Victorian hunting lodge for the Lipton tea family, the hotel overlooks the Cairngorm Mountains and retains many of its original Victorian features, including open fireplaces and wood paneling. Bedrooms are well appointed, with immaculate, shower-only bathrooms.

4.8km (3 miles) south of Grantown-on-Spey by A95 on A938, Dulnain Bridge, PH26 3PA. ℂ 01479/851-345. Fax 01479/821-173. www.tigh-na-sgaith.co.uk. 9 units. £110–£173 ($209–$329) double with breakfast and dinner. MC, V. **Amenities:** Restaurant; 2 bars; lounge; nonsmoking rooms. *In room:* TV, hair dryer, coffeemaker, no phone.

Tulchan Lodge ✿✿   This place offers elegant accommodations and a vivid glimpse into the grandeur of country living during the height of the British Imperial Age. Indeed, the Tulchan has been the subject of numerous PBS programs. It was built in 1906 by the founder of the McCorquodale publishing empire, who conceived it as a symbol of the power of the British press. If you stay in the main house, expect relatively formal evenings with a daytime emphasis on the sporting life. Guests eat at a communal dining table. Scattered across the undulating grounds, you find seven houses (the staff members refer to them as "cottages" even though some contain five bedrooms), suitable for between four and nine occupants. The cottages each have fully equipped kitchens and a decor that reflects the elegance of the main house. Favored mostly by fishermen, they do not include meal service, and are rented exclusively by the week.

Advie, near Grantown-on-Spey PH26 3PW. ℂ 01807/510-200. Fax 01807/510-234. www.tulchan.com. 13 bedrooms in the main house, 7 outlying cottages. £377–£538 ($716–$1,022) double. Rates include full board. Cottages £650–£3,250 ($1,235–$6,175) for 4–12 occupants, without meals. MC, V. Closed Feb–Mar. Drive 14km (8½ miles) northeast of Grantown on B9102, following the signs to Elgin. **Amenities:** 2 dining areas; bar; tennis court; limited room service; babysitting; laundry service; dry cleaning; nonsmoking rooms. *In room:* TV, hair dryer.

WHERE TO DINE

Craggan Mill BRITISH/ITALIAN   This licensed restaurant and lounge-bar, a 10-minute walk south of the town center, occupies a restored granite mill whose waterwheel is still visible. The owners offer British and Italian cuisine at attractive prices. Your appetizer might be smoked trout in deference to Scotland, or ravioli inspired by Italy. Main courses might be breast of chicken with cream or chicken cacciatore, followed by a dessert of rum-raisin ice cream or peach Melba. You've probably had better versions of all the dishes offered here, but what you get isn't bad. A good selection of Italian wines is also offered.

Hwy. A95, 1.2km (¾ mile) south of Grantown-on-Spey. ℂ 01479/872-288. Reservations recommended. Main courses £14–£20 ($27–$38). MC, V. May–Sept daily noon–2pm and 6–11pm; Oct–Apr Tues–Sun 7–10pm. Closed 1st 2 weeks in Nov.

GLENLIVET

As you leave Grantown-on-Spey and head east along A95, drive to the junction with B9008; go south and you won't miss the **Glenlivet Distillery.** The **Glenlivet Reception Centre** (© **01340/821-720**) is 16km (10 miles) north of the nearest town, Tomintoul. Near the River Livet, a Spey tributary, this distillery is one of the most famous in Scotland. It's open mid-March to October, Monday to Saturday 10am to 4pm and Sunday 12:30 to 4pm. Admission is free.

Back on A95, you can visit the **Glenfarclas Distillery** at Ballindalloch (© **01807/500-209**), one of the few malt whisky distilleries that's still independent of the giants. Founded in 1836, Glenfarclas is managed by the fifth generation of the Grant family. There's a small craft shop, and each visitor is offered a dram of Glenfarclas Malt Whisky. The admission of £3.50 ($6.65) is for visitors over age 18, and there's a discount of £1 ($1.90) on any purchase of £10 ($19) or more. It's open all year, Monday to Friday 10am to 5pm; June to September, it's also open Saturday 10am to 5pm and Sunday 10am to 4pm.

WHERE TO STAY

Minmore House Hotel 𝄞   This impressive country house stands on 2 hectares (5 acres) of private grounds adjacent to the Glenlivet Distillery. It was the home of the distillery owners before becoming a hotel. The proprietors have elegantly furnished their drawing room, which opens onto views of the plush Ladder Hills. The well-furnished bedrooms, some with four-poster beds, have all the vital amenities, and the oak-paneled lounge-bar has an open log fire on chilly nights.

Glenlivet, Banffshire AB37 9DB. © 01807/590-378. Fax 01807/590-472. www.minmorehousehotel.com. 10 units. £116–£144 ($220–$274) double; £192 ($365) suite. Rates include breakfast. AE, MC, V. **Amenities:** Restaurant; bar; outdoor pool; tennis court; hunting and fishing outings. *In room:* Coffeemaker, hair dryer.

KINCRAIG

Kincraig enjoys a scenic location at the northern end of Loch Insh, overlooking the Spey Valley to the west and the Cairngorm Mountains to the east. Near Kincraig, the most notable sight is the **Highland Wildlife Park** 𝄞 (© **01540/651-270**), a natural area of parkland with a collection of wildlife, some of which is extinct elsewhere in Scotland. Herds of European bison, red deer, shaggy Highland cattle, wild horses, St. Kilda Soay sheep, and roe deer roam the park. In enclosures are wolves, polecats, wildcats, beavers, badgers, and pine martens. You can observe protected birds, such as golden eagles and several species of grouse—of special interest is the capercaillie ("horse of the woods"), a large Eurasian grouse that is native to Scotland's pine forests. There's a visitor center with a gift shop, cafe, and exhibition areas. Ample parking and a picnic site are also available.

You need a car to go through the park; walkers are discouraged and are picked up by park rangers. The park is open every day at 10am. April and October, the last entrance is at 4pm, except during July and August, when the last entrance is at 5pm. November to March, the last entrance is at 2pm. All people and vehicles are expected to vacate the park within 2 hours of the day's last admission. The entrance fee is £10 ($19) for adults, seniors, and students, and £8 ($15) for children. A family ticket costs £29 ($55).

KINGUSSIE

Your next stop along the Spey might be at the little summer vacation resort and winter ski center of Kingussie (pronounced "king-*you*-see"), just off A9, the capital of

Badenoch, a district known as "the drowned land" because the Spey can flood the valley when the snows of a severe winter melt in the spring.

Kingussie, 188km (117 miles) northwest of Edinburgh, 66km (41 miles) south of Inverness, and 18km (11 miles) southwest of Aviemore, practically adjoins Newtonmore directly northeast along A86.

The **Highland Folk Museum** ☆, Duke St. (© **01540/661-307**), was the first folk museum established in Scotland (1934), and its collections are based on the life of the Highlanders. You'll see domestic, agricultural, and industrial items. Open-air exhibits include a turf kailyard (kitchen garden), a Lewis "black house," and old vehicles and carts. Traditional events, such as spinning, music making, and handicraft fairs, are held throughout the summer. Admission is free. April to August, hours are Monday to Saturday 10am to 5pm, September and October, Monday to Friday 10am to 4pm.

A summer-only **tourist center** is on King Street (© **01540/661-297**). It's open only April to October, Monday to Saturday 10am to 1pm and 2 to 6pm, and on Sunday 10am to 1pm and 2 to 5pm.

WHERE TO STAY

Homewood Lodge ☆ *Kids*   One of the best B&Bs in the area, this small Highland house in a garden and woodland setting offers large, simply furnished rooms, each with a shower-only bathroom. The sitting room has an open fireplace. Good traditional fare is served in the evening (reservations recommended). Summer barbecues are also offered, and children are welcome. Picnic lunches can be arranged.

Newtonmore Rd., Kingussie PH21 1HD. © **01540/661-507**. www.homewood-lodge-kingussie.co.uk. 4 units. £50–£60 ($95–$114) double. Rates include Scottish breakfast. No credit cards. Free parking. **Amenities:** Restaurant; laundry service; dry cleaning; nonsmoking rooms. *In room:* TV, coffeemaker, hair dryer.

Osprey Hotel   This 1895 Victorian structure, 275m (902 ft.) from the rail station, is a convenient place to stay, with comfortable (though plain) bedrooms, all with shower-only bathrooms, electric blankets, and electric fires. The place is known for its fresh, homemade food. Prime Scottish meats are served; in summer, salmon and trout from local rivers are offered either fresh or peat-smoked.

Ruthven Rd. (at High St.), Kingussie PH21 1EN. ©/fax **01540/661-510**. www.ospreyhotel.co.uk. 8 units. £60–£70 ($114–$133) double. Rates include breakfast. MC, V. Free parking. **Amenities:** Restaurant; bar; babysitting. *In room:* TV, coffeemaker, hair dryer, no phone.

WHERE TO DINE

The Cross ☆☆ SCOTTISH   This chic restaurant, in a remote Highland village, serves superlative meals that involve theater as much as fine food (though the food itself has put The Cross on Scotland's gastronomic map). The restaurant stands on 1.6 hectares (4 acres), with the Gynack Burn running through the grounds. The main building is an old tweed mill. It has an open-beam ceiling and French doors leading to a terrace, over the water's edge, where alfresco dinners are served. Specialties depend on the availability of produce in the local markets and might include wild Scrabster seabass or breast of Gressingham duck.

Eight rooms are rented in a new building. Each room is different—for example, two rooms have canopied beds, and another has a balcony overlooking the mill pond. Doubles, including half board, cost from £200–£240 ($380–$456). Rooms don't have televisions.

Tweed Mill Brae, off the Ardbroilach road, Kingussie PH21 1TC. ℂ **01540/661-166**. Fax 01540/661-080. www.the cross.co.uk. Reservations recommended. Fixed-price 3-course dinner £41–£45 ($78–$86). MC, V. Tues–Sat 7–9pm. Closed Dec–Feb.

ROTHES

A Speyside town with five distilleries, Rothes is just to the south of the Glen of Rothes, 79km (49 miles) east of Inverness and 100km (62 miles) northwest of Aberdeen. Founded in 1766, the town is between Ben Aigan and Conerock Hill. A little settlement, the basis of the town today, grew up around **Rothes Castle,** ancient stronghold of the Leslie family, who lived here until 1622. Only a single massive wall of the castle remains.

The region's best distillery tours are offered by the **Glen Grant Distillery** (ℂ **01542/ 783-318**). Opened in 1840 by a hardworking and hard-drinking pair of brothers, James and John Grant, and now administered by the Chivas & Glenlivet Group (a division of Seagram's), it's 1km (½ mile) north of Rothes, beside the Elgin-Perth (A941) highway. It's open March 21 to October, Monday to Saturday 10am to 4pm and Sunday from 12:30 to 4pm. Admission is free; children under 8 aren't allowed. Visits include the opportunity to buy the brand's whisky at a discount.

ELGIN ⭐

The center of local government in the Moray district and an ancient royal burgh, the cathedral city of Elgin is on the Lossie River, 61km (38 miles) east of Inverness and 110km (68 miles) northwest of Aberdeen. The city's medieval plan has been retained, with "wynds" and "pends" connecting the main artery with other streets. The castle, as was customary in medieval town layouts, stood at one end of the main thoroughfare, with the cathedral—now a magnificent ruin—at the other. Nothing remains of the castle, but the site is a great place for a scenic walk. Samuel Johnson and James Boswell came this way on their Highland tour and reported a "vile dinner" at the Red Lion Inn in 1773.

Lady Hill stands on High Street, opposite the post office. This is the hilltop location of what was once the royal castle of Elgin. **Birnie Kirk,** at Birnie, 5km (3 miles) south of Elgin and west of A941 to Rothes, was for a time the seat of a bishopric. It dates from about 1140, when it was constructed on the site of a much earlier church founded by St. Brendan. One of the few Norman churches in Scotland still in regular use, it's open daily from 10am to 4pm.

On King Street are the ruins of the **Elgin Cathedral** ⭐ (ℂ **01343/547-171**), off North College Street near A96. It was founded in 1224 but destroyed in 1390 by the "wolf of Badenoch," the natural son of Robert II. After its destruction, the citizens of Elgin rebuilt their beloved cathedral and turned it into one of the most attractive and graceful buildings in Scotland. However, when the central tower collapsed in 1711, the cathedral was allowed to fall into decay. It's open April to September, daily 9:30am to 5:30pm; and October to March, Saturday to Wednesday 9:30am to 4:30pm. Admission is £4.50 ($8.55) for adults, £3.50 ($6.65) for seniors, and £2.25 ($4.30) for children.

After exploring Elgin, you can drive 10km (6 miles) southwest to **Pluscarden Abbey,** off B9010. This is one of the most beautiful drives in the area, through the bucolic Black Burn Valley, where a priory was founded in 1230 by Alexander II. After centuries of decline, a new order of Benedictines arrived in 1974 and re-established monastic life. You can visit restored transepts, monastic buildings, and the church choir. Admission is free to this active religious community, which is open daily from 9am to 5pm.

If you're a fan of Scottish ruins, head for **Spynie Palace** (© **01343/546-358**), reached along A941. The former 15th-century headquarters of the bishops of Moray was used until 1573, when it was allowed to fall into ruins; for safety reasons, you can view them only from the outside. This is another great place for country walks, and from the top of a tower are magnificent vistas over the Laigh of Moray. It's open April to September, Monday through Saturday from 9:30am to 5:30pm; and October to March, Saturday and Sunday 9:30am to 4:30pm. Admission is £3.50 ($6.65) for adults, £2.80 ($5.30) for students and seniors, and £1.75 ($3.35) for children.

WHERE TO STAY

Many B&Bs lie two blocks north of the rail station between Moray Street and Moss Street. Our favorite is **Richmond Bed & Breakfast,** 48 Moss St. (© **01343/542-5611;** www.milford.co.uk/go/richmondelgin.html). It offers handsomely furnished, comfortable double rooms, all with private bathrooms with tub or shower, costing only £40 to £50 ($76–$95) per night. No credit cards are accepted.

Mansion House Hotel 𝒜𝒜   This elegantly appointed hotel, with the baronial proportions of the original design intact, is at the edge of the River Lossie, about .5km (¼ mile) from the center of Elgin. The guest rooms are standard; most have four-poster beds.

The Haugh, Elgin IV30 1AW. © **01343/548-811.** Fax 01343/547-916. www.mansionhousehotel.co.uk. 23 units. £155–£200 ($295–$380) double. Rates include Scottish breakfast. AE, DC, MC, V. Follow A96 onto Alexandra Rd. to the turnoff onto Haugh Rd. Free parking. **Amenities:** 2 restaurants; bar; heated indoor pool; health club; Jacuzzi; sauna; salon; room service; massage; babysitting; laundry service; nonsmoking rooms. *In room:* TV, coffeemaker, hair dryer, trouser press.

WHERE TO DINE

Abbey Court Restaurant SCOTTISH/ITALIAN   Abbey Court, in the center of town behind the county building, is an excellent restaurant decorated with stone- and earth-colored quarry tile, along with an artificial pergola, a separate bistro corner, and a more formal dining area in the rear. The fresh pasta is homemade, and fish is delivered daily. The cooking is straightforward and unpretentious.

15 Greyfriars St. © **01343/542-849.** Reservations recommended. Main courses £10–£19 ($19–$36). AE, DC, MC, V. Mon–Sat noon–2pm; Mon–Thurs 6:30–9:30pm; Fri–Sat 6:30–10pm.

11

Inverness & the West Highlands

The romantic glens and rugged mountain landscapes of the West Highlands are timeless and pristine. Deer graze only yards from the highway, and, at a secluded loch, you can enjoy a picnic or fish for trout and salmon. The shadow of Macbeth still stalks the land. (Locals will tell you that this 11th-c. king was much maligned by Shakespeare.) The area's most famous resident, however, is said to live in mysterious Loch Ness: First sighted by St. Columba in the 6th century, "Nessie" has cleverly evaded searchers ever since.

Centuries of Highland invasions, rebellions, and clan feuds are now distant memories. Indeed, the region isn't as remote as it once was, when many Londoners believed that the men of the Highlands had tails.

Fort William is a major center for the West Highlands, surrounded by wildly beautiful **Lochaber,** the "land of bens, glens, and heroes." Dominating the area is **Ben Nevis,** Britain's highest mountain. This district is the western end of what is known as the **Glen Mor**—the Great Glen, geologically a fissure dividing the northwest of Scotland from the southeast and containing Loch Lochy, Loch Oich, and Loch Ness. The Caledonian Canal, opened in 1847, linked these lochs, the River Ness, and Moray Firth, providing boats a safe alternative to the stormy route around the north of Scotland. Eventually, larger steamships made the canal out of date commercially, but fishing boats and pleasure craft still use it. Good roads run the length of the Great Glen, partly following the line of Gen. George Wade's military road. The English general became famous for his road and bridge building in Scotland, which did much to open the Highlands to greater access from the south. From Fort William, you can take steamer trips to Staffa and Iona (see chapter 12 for more information).

Aviemore and the villages and towns of the Spey Valley offer visitors many activities. In the Spey Valley you're at the doorway to the Malt Whisky Trail (see chapter 10 for more information). Aviemore is the **winter-sports capital of Britain,** and Aviemore Centre offers a multitude of outdoor pursuits: golfing, angling, skiing, and ice skating.

Inverness and legendary **Loch Ness,** the most popular West Highlands attractions, are overcrowded in summer but surrounded by villages and towns that make good stop-offs—especially if you're driving. If you're dependent on public transportation, make Inverness your base; it has good rail and bus connections to the rest of Scotland and also to England.

Finally, if you have time, visit the loneliest part of Scotland, the far north. This section of the Highlands, **Sutherland** and **Caithness,** isn't for everyone. Crumbling watchtowers no longer stand guard over anything except sheep-cropped wilderness. Moss-green glens give way to inland lochs and sea fords. Summer, of course, is the best time to view these deep-blue lochs, towering cliffs, and gentle glens. Many relics of Scotland's turbulent past dot the landscape, with castles left in ruins. Today, visitors come to get away from it all and enjoy outdoor activities in a wild, pristine setting. Craft centers have also sprung up, with silversmiths, glassmakers, and weavers deriving inspiration from their surroundings.

1 Around Loch Linnhe & Loch Leven

South of Fort William is one of the most historic sections of Scotland, a group of settlements around Loch Linnhe and Loch Leven (not the also-famous Loch Leven near Dunfermline). The best-known village is **Glencoe,** site of the famous 1692 massacre when the Campbells slaughtered the MacDonalds. Glencoe is the most dramatic glen in Scotland, austere in its beauty. Around both lochs are impressive landscapes and moorland, with flora and fauna unique to the West Highlands. Robert Louis Stevenson captured much of the essence of this moorland and wilderness in his novel *Kidnapped.*

ONICH

On the shores of Loch Linnhe is the charming little village of Onich, which lies to the north of Ballachulish Bridge, 14km (9 miles) southwest of Fort William. It's a good center if you're taking the western route to Inverness or going to Skye and Fort William.

WHERE TO STAY & DINE

Allt-nan-Ros Hotel ✿   This inn lies across the highway from the edge of the loch and boasts dozens of elaborate gables and interesting architectural touches. Allt-nan-Ros was built around 1885 as a hunting lodge and weekend getaway for an industrialist. Today, this much-enlarged place with relatively recent additions offers comfortable guest rooms and a well-managed dining room, which is open to the public. The rooms have dark mahogany furniture and floral-patterned upholsteries in an Edwardian country-house style, and most offer views of the loch or the stream running through the garden. Some bathrooms contain showers only. In "The Stables" are found two spacious country cottage-like bedrooms, with four-poster beds.

Onich, Fort William PH33 6RY. ✆ **01855/821-210.** Fax 01855/821-462. www.allt-nan-ros.co.uk. 20 units. £85–£120 ($162–$228) double. Rates include breakfast. AE, DC, MC, V. From Fort William, drive 18km (11 miles) south along A82. **Amenities:** Restaurant; bar; nonsmoking rooms; rooms for those w/limited mobility. *In room:* TV, coffeemaker, hair dryer.

The Lodge on the Loch Hotel ✿   Between the edge of the loch and a semi-forested rocky ridge, this granite hotel dates from the 19th century. Only a handful of the high-ceilinged guest rooms are in the mansion's core; most are in a bulky-looking 1960s extension but are just as comfortable, with a mix of conservative and traditional furnishings. Some units even have an Eastern or Art Deco influence. The most expensive rooms contain plush extras like CD players, bathrobes, and Jacuzzi baths. If the hotel is full, there are two other choices (under the same management) within a short drive.

The restaurant is one of the big draws, serving an expensive fixed-price dinner that features Scottish produce and many variations of salmon, trout, and pheasant dishes. There's also a cocktail bar with a log fire and a fine selection of whiskies.

Onich, near Fort William PH33 6RY. ✆ **01855/821-238.** Fax 01855/821-190. www.lodgeontheloch.com. 16 units. £75–£115 ($143–$219) double. Rates include breakfast and dinner. MC, V. Closed Nov–Mar. From Fort William, drive 16km (10 miles) south of town, following A82 and the signs to Glasgow. Children under 16 discouraged. **Amenities:** Restaurant; bar; access to nearby health club; limited room service; massage. *In room:* TV, coffeemaker, hair dryer, iron.

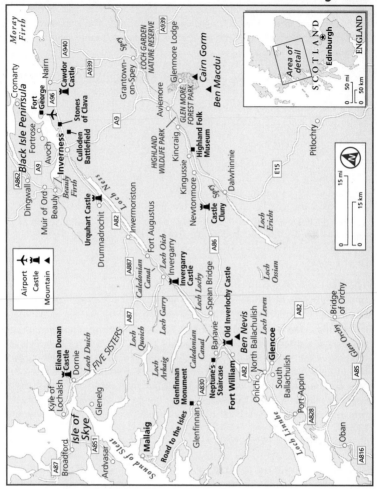

GLENCOE: SCENERY & SORROW ★★

Near the spot where Loch Leven joins Loch Linnhe, **Ballachulish Bridge** links the villages of North and South Ballachulish at the entrance to Glencoe. The bridge saves a long drive to the head of the loch if you're coming from the north, but the scenic drive to Kinlochleven lets you come on the celebrated wild Glencoe from the east. Glencoe runs from Rannoch Moor to Loch Leven between majestic mountains, including 1,147m (3,766-ft.) **Bidean nam Bian.** In this resplendent area, with its towering peaks and mysterious glens, you can well imagine a fierce battle between kilted Highlanders.

Known as the "Glen of Weeping," Glencoe is the place where, on February 11, 1692, the Campbells massacred the MacDonalds—men, women, and children—who'd been their hosts for 12 days. Although mass killings weren't uncommon in those times, this one shocked even the Highlanders because it was a breach of hospitality. The **Monument to the Massacre of Glencoe,** at Carnoch, was erected by the chief of the MacDonald clan. After the incident, the crime of "murder under trust" was introduced into Scottish law as an aggravated form of murder that carried the same penalty as treason.

The **Glencoe Visitor Centre** at Glencoe (© **01855/811-507**) is built on the site of the massacre of the Clan Maclains. The center tells the story of the massacre and offers a fine exhibition on mountaineering. Visitors can also see an audiovisual presentation. The center is open March daily 10am to 4pm, April to May daily 9:30am to 5:30pm, September to October daily 10am to 5pm, and November to February Thursday to Sunday 10am to 4pm, charging £5 ($9.50) adults, £4 ($7.60) seniors, students, and children, for admission.

Glen Orchy, to the south, is well worth a visit for its wild river and photogenic mountain scenery. It was the birthplace of Gaelic bard Duncan Ban MacIntyre, whose masterpiece is the song "In Praise of Ben Doran."

This is great country for hiking and bike rides. In Glencoe village, go to the **Mountain Bike Hire** at The Clachaig Inn (© **01855/811-252**), where you not only can rent a bike but can also get advice about scenic routes. The cost is £12 ($23) per half-day or £30 ($57) per week.

WHERE TO STAY & DINE

Some visitors base themselves in Fort William (see "Fort William: Gateway to Ben Nevis," below) and explore the Glencoe area on day trips.

Ballachulish House ✸✸   This charming country inn, with its lime-washed stone, dates back to the 1640s, though it was tastefully expanded in 1997. The owners spent enormous sums renovating the place, and since then have hosted the occasional celebrity. The guest rooms have flowered wallpaper and a mix of old and new furniture; each has a view of the loch or forest. The more luxurious units have bathrooms with both tub and shower. There's ample opportunity for long walks beside the loch. (Sometimes one of the owners' dogs will join you.) Dinner is a treat, making use of fresh ingredients.

Ballachulish, near Fort William PH49 4JX. © **01855/811-266**. Fax 01855/811-498. www.ballachulishhouse.com. 54 units. £125–£210 ($238–$399) double. Rates include breakfast. MC, V. Closed Jan. Drive west of Ballachulish for 4km (2½ miles), following A82 until it intersects with A828. Follow the signs to Ballachulish House. **Amenities:** Restaurant; bar; access to nearby health club; nonsmoking rooms. *In room:* TV, coffeemaker.

The Clachaig Inn   After the bleakness of Glencoe, the trees ringing this place make it seem like an oasis. It's the only hotel in the glen, on the site where the massacre took place. The Daynes family offers Highland hospitality, good food, and an excellent selection of British ales. They rent some contemporary chalets in the back garden, plus several small to midsize guest rooms—all of which are nonsmoking—in the main house. The furnishings are basic, and each of the rooms comes with a small, shower-only bathroom. Live folk music brings the place to life on Wednesday and Saturday nights.

Glencoe, Ballachulish PH49 4HX. © **01855/811-252**. Fax 01855/812-030. www.clachaig.com. 23 units. £74–£84 ($141–$160) double. Rates include Scottish breakfast. MC, V. Take A82 south for 15km (9½ miles) from Fort William; the inn is signposted. **Amenities:** Restaurant; 3 bars. *In room:* TV, coffeemaker, hair dryer.

King's House Hotel   The solid walls of this historic inn were built in the 1600s on a windswept plateau. It lies beside A82, 19km (12 miles) southeast of Glencoe village, at the strategic point where Glencoe joins the Glen Etive, near the jagged mountain

Buachaille Etive Mor. Most of the modestly furnished guest rooms offer sweeping views but lack certain amenities (air-conditioning and televisions, for example); about half are equipped with small tub-only bathrooms. Simple meals are served in the bar; the dining room boasts a selection of fine wines and freshly prepared meals. The hotel is a 30-minute walk from a ski center with a chairlift.

Glencoe PA39 4HZ. ✆ **01855/851-259.** Fax 01855/851-216. www.kingy.com. 22 units, 12 with private bathroom. £60 ($114) double without bathroom; £70 ($133) double with bathroom. MC, V. You can arrange to be met at the Bridge of Orchy rail station. **Amenities:** Restaurant; bar; laundry service. *In room:* Coffeemaker, hair dryer.

2 Fort William ★: Gateway to Ben Nevis ★★

214km (133 miles) NW of Edinburgh, 109km (68 miles) S of Inverness, 167km (104 miles) N of Glasgow

Fort William, on the shores of Loch Linnhe, is the best place for an overnight stop between here and Inverness, in the northeast. It's a good base for exploring **Ben Nevis,** Scotland's highest mountain, and also for a day trip to Glencoe (see above).

Fort William stands on the site of a fort built by General Monk in 1655 to help crush any rebellion that Highlanders might have been plotting. After several reconstructions, it was finally torn down in 1864 to make way for the railroad. During the notorious Highland Clearances, a few wealthy landowners evicted many starving tenants or squatters, who were shipped to the United States. Today, Fort William is a bustling town, thriving on the summer tourist trade and filled with shops, hotels, and cafes.

ESSENTIALS

GETTING THERE   Fort William is a major stop on the scenic West Highland rail line that begins at the Queen Street Station in Glasgow and ends at Mallaig, on the west coast. Three trains a day run this route at a one-way cost of £25 ($48). For schedules, contact the tourist office (see below) or call ✆ **01463/239-026** in Inverness.

Four buses per day run from Glasgow to Fort William, taking 3 hours and costing £14 ($27) one-way. Call the Citylink Bus Station at ✆ **0870/550-5050** in Glasgow for schedules. If you're driving from Glasgow, head north along A82.

VISITOR INFORMATION   The **tourist office** is at Cameron Centre, Cameron Square (✆ **01397/703-781**). April and May, it's open Monday to Saturday 9am to 5pm and Sunday 10am to 4pm; June 1 to June 28, hours are Monday to Saturday 9am to 5:30pm and Sunday 10am to 4pm; June 29 to July 26, hours are Monday to Saturday 9am to 7pm and Sunday 10am to 6pm; July 27 to August 16, it's open Monday to Saturday 9am to 8pm and Sunday 10am to 6pm; and August 17 to August 30, hours are Monday to Saturday 9am to 7pm and Sunday 10am to 6pm. August 31 to September 20, hours are Monday to Saturday 9am to 6pm and Sunday 10am to 5pm; September 21 to November 1, hours are Monday to Saturday 9am to 4pm and Sunday 10am to 3pm; and November 2 to March, Monday to Saturday 9am to 5:30pm and Sunday 10am to 4pm.

EXPLORING THE AREA

You can reach the ruins of **Old Inverlochy Castle,** scene of a famous battle, by driving 3km (2 miles) north of Fort William on A82. Built in the 13th century, the ruined castle still has round corner towers and a walled courtyard. One of the towers was the keep, the other a water gate. The castle looms in the pages of Scottish history—here in 1645 a small army of Scots defeated government forces, although 1,500 men were lost that day. The former castle was once the stronghold of a clan known as the Comyns, and Inverlochy was the scene of many battles.

Neptune's Staircase, 5km (3 miles) northwest of Fort William, off A830 at Banavie, is a series of nine locks that were constructed at the same time as the Caledonian Canal, raising Telford's canal 19m (64 ft.). This "staircase" is one of Scotland's most prominent engineering triumphs of the mid–19th century, when the eastern seacoast at Inverness was connected, via the canal, to the western seacoast at Fort William. This greatly shortened the distance required for goods moving from the North Sea to the Atlantic Ocean, and bypassed the treacherous storms that often rage around Scotland's northern tier.

Since much of Fort William is relatively flat, consider biking. The best rentals are at **Off Beat Bikes,** 117 High St. (© **01397/704-008**), costing £10 ($19) for a half-day, £15 ($29) for a full day. You need only your ID for the deposit. It's open Monday to Saturday from 9am to 5:30pm and Sunday from 9:30am to 5pm.

In the north end of town, the **Ben Nevis Woollen Mill,** Belford Road (© **01397/704-244**), is a shop (not a functioning mill) where you find a large selection of clothing and accessories: wools, tweeds, tartans, and handknit Arran sweaters, as well as gifts and souvenir items. An on-premises restaurant features regional fare.

Shoppers might also want to check out the **Granite House,** High Street (© **01397/703-651**), a family-run business that has been around for a quarter-century. The owners call themselves "giftmongers" and see their shop as a mini–department store. There's a large selection of Scottish jewelry, with silver pieces in both traditional and contemporary designs and numerous watches. Collectibles like Lilliput Lane china and crystal by Edinburgh, Wedgwood, and Border Fine Arts are found here, and the traditional music department offers more than 1,000 Irish and Scottish music CDs and an array of traditional instruments, including pennywhistles and the *bhodrain* (a large drum struck with a single stick using both ends). The store also carries traditional toys for all ages.

Scottish Crafts & Whisky Centre, 135–139 High St. (© **01397/704-406**), is another place with a good mix of the best of all things Scottish: regionally produced jewelry, garden fountains, rugs, and clothing. Whisky connoisseurs will find some limited-edition and very rare bottles stocked, including a 1958 Ben Nevis. Handmade chocolates by Fergusons are also available. **Treasures of the Earth,** Main Street, Corpach (© **01397/772-283**), 6.5km (4 miles) west of Fort William along A830, sells crystals, minerals, and polished stones from around the world. They are available loose or set in jewelry, watches, and clocks.

Glenfinnan Monument Located at the head of Loch Shiel, at Glenfinnan, this eponymous monument marks the spot where Bonnie Prince Charlie unfurled his proud red-and-white silk banner on August 19, 1745, in his ill-fated attempt to restore the Stuarts to the British throne. The figure of a kilted Highlander tops the monument. At the visitor center, you learn of the prince's campaign from Glenfinnan to Derby, which ended in his defeat at Culloden.

About 23km (14 miles) west of Fort William, on A830 toward Mallaig. © 01397/722-250 for visitor center. Free admission. Visitor center Mar 31–June 30 daily 10am–5pm, July–Aug 31 daily 9:30am–5:30pm, Sept 1–Oct 31, daily 10am–5pm.

West Highland Museum The collection in this museum sheds light on all aspects of local history, especially the 1745 Jacobite Rising; it also has sections on tartans and folk life. Among the Jacobite collections and Highland weaponry is a facsimile for the order of the Massacre of Glencoe (see above).

Cameron Sq. ⓒ **01397/702-169**. www.fort-william.net/museum. Admission £2 ($3.80) adults, £1.50 ($2.85) seniors, 50p (95¢) children. June–Sept Mon–Sat 10am–5pm (July–Aug also Sun 2–5pm); Oct–May Mon–Sat 10am–4pm.

WHERE TO STAY

There's no shortage of B&Bs in Fort William; the tourist office can supply you with a list if the selections below are full.

VERY EXPENSIVE

Inverlochy Castle ✦✦✦   Inverlochy Castle, set against the scenic backdrop of Ben Nevis, has hosted Queen Victoria and remains the premier address in this part of Scotland. Back then (1870), it was a newly built Scottish mansion; the monarch claimed in her diary, "I never saw a lovelier or more romantic spot." Now a Relais & Châteaux property, the Inverlochy has undergone a major refurbishment but has retained its charm. Luxurious appointments, antiques, artwork, and crystal, plus a profusion of flowers, create a mood of elegance and refinement. The prices certainly reflect this opulence.

The cuisine here is some of the finest in Scotland, with food cooked to order and served on silver platters. See "Where to Dine," below, for details. Nonguests can dine here if there's room, but reservations are mandatory.

Torlundy, Fort William PH33 6SN. ⓒ **888/424-0106** in the U.S., or 01397/702-177. Fax 01397/702-953. www.inverlochycastlehotel.com. 17 units. £300–£510 ($570–$969) double; £450–£600 ($855–$1140) suite. Rates include Scottish breakfast. AE, MC, V. Closed early Jan to late Feb. Free valet parking. Take A82 for 5km (3 miles) northeast of town. **Amenities:** Restaurant; tennis court; room service; babysitting; laundry service; nonsmoking rooms. *In room:* TV, hair dryer, iron, safe.

MODERATE

Alexandra Milton Hotel   Across from the rail terminal, the Alexandra boasts the tall gables and formidable granite walls so common in this part of the Highlands. It has been completely modernized, offering pleasant and comfortably furnished guest rooms with shower-only bathrooms. More than 40 rooms were upgraded and renovated in 2007. The chef makes excellent use of fresh fish, and the wine cellar is amply endowed. Guests have free use of the facilities at the nearby Milton Hotel and Leisure Club.

The Parade, Fort William PH33 6AZ. ⓒ **01397/702-241**. Fax 01397/705-554. www.strathmorehotels.com. 97 units. £60–£135 ($114–$257) double. Rates include breakfast. AE, DC, MC, V. Free parking. From the north, take A82 into Fort William following signs for the town center. At the roundabout, turn right and drive through the next roundabout. The Alexandra is on the left–hand side. **Amenities:** 2 restaurants; bar; access to nearby health club; room service; laundry service; nonsmoking rooms. *In room:* TV, coffeemaker.

The Moorings Hotel   One of the most up-to-date hotels in the region, the Moorings was designed in a traditional style in the mid-1970s, with bay and dormer windows and a black-and-white facade. The interior is richly paneled in the Jacobean style. The guest rooms are attractive and modern, each with a shower-only bathroom. Bar lunches and suppers are offered in the Mariner Wine Bar, while formal meals are served in the Moorings Restaurant, where an even greater selection of wine (more than 200 vintages) accompanies dishes like smoked venison, Scottish oysters, homemade terrines, and wild salmon in lemon-butter sauce.

Banavie, Fort William PH33 7LY. ⓒ **01397/772-797**. Fax 01397/772-441. www.moorings-fortwilliam.co.uk. 28 units. £94–£122 ($179–$232) double. Rates include Scottish breakfast. AE, DC, MC, V. Drive 5km (3 miles) north of Fort

William to the hamlet of Banavie, beside B8004. **Amenities:** Restaurant; bar; room service; laundry service; nonsmoking rooms. *In room:* TV, coffeemaker, hair dryer, iron.

INEXPENSIVE

Croit Anna Hotel   Overlooking Loch Linnhe, the Croit Anna Hotel opens onto fine views of the Ardgour Hills. It's owned and managed by the same family who built it on a traditional Highland croft that has been in their possession for more than 250 years. All the midsize guest rooms have tidily kept but small shower-only bathrooms. During July and August, entertainment is provided on most evenings.

Achintore Rd., Druimarbin, Fort William PH33 6RR. ℂ 01397/702-268. Fax 01397/704-099. www.visit-fortwilliam. coluk/croitanna. 92 units. £52–£72 ($99–$137) double. Rates include Scottish breakfast. MC, V. Take A82 4km (2½ miles) south of town. **Amenities:** Restaurant; 2 bars; laundry service; nonsmoking rooms; rooms for those w/limited mobility. *In room:* TV, coffeemaker, hair dryer, iron.

The Lime Tree   This well-kept B&B in the center of town is housed in what is reputed to be the oldest fully surviving building in Fort William. It was built in the early 1800s as the manse for the nearby Church of Scotland. Today, it offers pastel guest rooms (with small, shower-only bathrooms) and exhibition space for local painters, including respected artist David Wilson.

The Old Manse, Achintore Rd., Fort William. ℂ 01397/701-806. www.limetreefortwilliam.co.uk. 5 units, 3 with private bathroom. £54–£74 ($103–$141) double without bathroom; £90–£110 ($171–$209) double with bathroom. DC, MC, V. Free parking. Follow A82 into Fort William. **Amenities:** Nonsmoking rooms. *In room:* TV, coffeemaker, no phone.

Lochview Guest House *Value*   South of Fort William's center, and about a 15-minute walk uphill, is this nonsmoking guesthouse, designed around 1950. The guest rooms are outfitted with comfortable furnishings by Denise and Alan Kirk, who maintain the .4 hectare (1 acre) of lawn surrounding their building, and protect the view of the loch and the rest of the town. Each unit comes with a small shower-only bathroom. Other guesthouses in town might be more historic—but for the price, Lochview represents good value, and the Kirk family is unfailingly generous.

Heathercroft, Argyll Rd., Fort William PH33 6RE. ℂ/fax 01397/703-149. www.lochview.co.uk. 6 units. £56 ($106) double. Rates include breakfast. MC, V. Closed Oct–Easter. **Amenities:** Nonsmoking rooms. *In room:* TV, coffeemaker, Wi-Fi, no phone.

Tornevis   The goal of owners Allan and Sandra Henderson was to create a peaceful retreat away from the noise of city life, while still keeping their guests within walking distance of civilization. After running the extremely successful Asburn House, the Hendersons embarked on a new challenge: having an architect design a house that faces east to Ben Nevis and south to Loch Linnhe, two of the area's geographical wonders. The bed-and-breakfast's three nonsmoking rooms are midsize and comfortable, two with "Super King-size beds" and one with two twin beds. The bathrooms are spacious, with both a shower and a tub. In order to "keep the peace," management does not allow children under 12 to stay here.

Banavie, Fort William PH33 7LX. ℂ 01397/777-2868. Fax 01397/777-2868. www.scotland2000.com/tornevis. 3 units. £70–£80 ($133–$152) double. Rates include Scottish breakfast. Free parking. MC, V. Follow A830 out of town center for 4.8km (3 miles). **Amenities:** Dining room; nonsmoking rooms. *In room:* TV, beverage maker, hair dryer.

WHERE TO DINE

Crannog Seafood Restaurant   SEAFOOD   Occupying a converted ticket office and bait store in a quayside setting overlooking Loch Linnhe, this restaurant serves seafood so fresh that locals claim "it fairly leaps at you." Much of the fish comes from the owners' own fishing vessels or from their smokehouse. Bouillabaisse is a specialty, as are king prawns and langoustines. A vegetarian dish of the day is invariably featured.

Town Pier. ✆ **01397/705-589**. Reservations recommended. Main courses £10–£20 ($19–$38). MC, V. Daily noon–2:30pm and 6–9pm. Closed Jan 1–2 and Dec 25–26.

Inverlochy Castle ✩✩✩ BRITISH   This is one of the grandest restaurants in Britain (as it should be, at these prices!). The cuisine here has been celebrated ever since Queen Victoria got a sudden attack of the munchies and stopped in "for a good tuck-in." The kitchen uses carefully selected local ingredients, including salmon from Spean, crabs from Isle of Skye, crayfish from Loch Linnhe, and produce from the hotel's own gardens such as chervil, basil, chives, and tarragon. Ever had bubble-gum tuna? It may not be what you think. This is the British term for tuna with pink flesh. Partridge and grouse are offered in season, and roast filet of Aberdeen Angus beef is a classic. Other menu items include gin-poached loin of venison with braised little gem and caramelized figs; and crispy sea bass with Jerusalem artichoke ravioli. The caramel poached pear with toffee mousse, may be the best we've ever tasted. Dinner is served in rooms decorated with period and elaborate furniture presented as gifts to Inverlochy Castle from the king of Norway. The formal service is the finest in the Highlands.

Torlundy, Fort William PH33 6SN. ✆ **01397/702-177**. Reservations required. Fixed-price lunch £30 ($57); set-price dinner £55 ($105). AE, MC, V. Daily 12:30–1:30pm and 7–9pm. Closed Jan–Feb.

FORT WILLIAM AFTER DARK

Ben Nevis Bar, 103–109 High St. (✆ **01397/702-295**), offers free entertainment by rock, blues, jazz, and folk bands on Thursday and Friday. On tap are McEwan's, Foster's, and Kronenberg lagers, McEwan's 70 Shilling, and Guinness and Gillespie's stouts.

McTavish's Kitchens, High Street (✆ **01397/702-406**), presents a Scottish show just for tourists. It's fun but corny, featuring tartan-clad dancers, bagpipes, and other traditional instruments every night May to September from 8 to 10pm. You can see the show with or without dinner. A three-course "Taste of Scotland" meal costs £22 ($41). On tap is Tennant's Special and Lager, available for £2.95 ($5.60) per pint. Admission to the show is £4.50 ($8.55) adults and £2 ($3.80) children if you're eating; the show only costs £2.50 ($4.75) adults and £1 ($1.90) children.

Grog & Gruel, 66 High St. (✆ **01397/705-078**), serves up regional cask-conditioned ales. There's an occasional live band, ranging from rock and pop to folk and Scottish music.

3 Invergarry

40km (25 miles) NE of Fort William, 254km (158 miles) NW of Edinburgh

A Highland center for fishing and for exploring Glen Mor and Loch Ness, Invergarry is noted for its fine scenery. At Invergarry, the road through the western Highland glens and mountains begins, forming one part of the famous "Road to the Isles" that terminates at Kyle of Lochalsh. If you're short on time, you can easily skip this place. Most people stop off here to stay at the Glengarry Castle Hotel, which looks haunted and even has the ruins of a long-abandoned castle on its grounds.

ESSENTIALS

GETTING THERE   The nearest **rail service** runs to Fort William, where you take a connecting bus to get to Invergarry, a half-hour ride away. **Highland Omnibuses**

offers this service. The tourist office in Fort William can provide schedules. If you're **driving** from Fort William, proceed north on the Inverness road (A82) to Invergarry.

VISITOR INFORMATION The nearest **tourist office** is in Fort William (see "Fort William: Gateway to Ben Nevis," earlier in this chapter).

SEEING THE SIGHTS

From Invergarry, drive 5.5km (3½ miles) south, following A82 toward Fort William if you want to visit the 1812 monument **Well of the Heads** (*Tobar nan Ceann* in Gaelic). The only sign indicating the well's position is a grocery store (Well of the Seven Heads Grocery & Convenience Mart). At the store, a staff member will direct you down a short forest path to the well itself. The well was erected by MacDonnell of Glengarry to commemorate the decapitation of seven brothers who had murdered the two sons of a 17th-century chief of Clan Keppoch, a branch of the MacDonnells, at Glengarry. An obelisk supports the bronzed heads of the seven victims. The legend of the well, alas, is more exciting than the actual site.

On the grounds of Glengarry Castle Hotel (see below), you can see the meager ruins of **Invergarry Castle,** the stronghold of the MacDonnells of Glengarry. A few grim walls remain. The site of the castle on Raven's Rock, overlooking Loch Oich in the Great Glen, was a strategic one in the days of clan feuds and Jacobite risings. Because the castle ruins aren't safe, you can view them only from outside. From Invergarry, drive 2.5km (1½ miles) south, following A82 toward Fort William, then turn off to follow the signs pointing to the hotel. The ruins lie beside the hotel's very long main driveway, surrounded by trees.

WHERE TO STAY & DINE

Glengarry Castle Hotel This mid-19th-century mansion, with gables and chimneys, is an impressive sight. On its vast grounds are the ruins of Invergarry Castle (see above). The hotel makes a pleasant base for fishing, tennis, walking, and rowing. The midsize to spacious guest rooms are comfortably old-fashioned, reminiscent of the 1950s, and each comes with a small bathroom with tub. The dining room offers good home-cooked (but rather basic) meals. Nightly fixed-price dinners are expensive. Affordable light lunches are served, but the special Sunday version is more elaborate and pricier.

Invergarry PH35 4HW. ✆ **01809/501-254.** Fax 01809/501-207. www.glengarry.net. 26 units. £86–£160 ($163–$304) double. Rates include Scottish breakfast. MC, V. Closed mid-Nov to late Mar. From Invergarry, drive 2.5km (1½ miles) south, following A82 toward Fort William; turn off to follow signs pointing to the hotel. **Amenities:** Restaurant; lounge; tennis court; nonsmoking rooms. *In room:* TV, coffeemaker, hair dryer.

4 Aviemore 🏕

208km (129 miles) N of Edinburgh, 47km (29 miles) SE of Inverness, 137km (85 miles) N of Perth

A bit tacky for our tastes, Aviemore, a year-round resort on the Spey, was opened in 1966 in the heart of the Highlands, at the foot of the historic rock of **Craigellachie.** The center of Aviemore itself, with ugly concrete structures, has little of the flavor of Scotland. But visitors flock here for its accessibility to some of the most beautiful scenery in the Highlands, especially the Cairngorm Mountains, known for their skiing in winter and hiking in summer.

A vast 3,800-sq.-km (1,467-sq.-mile) area of the Scottish Highlands has been designated as the largest national park in Britain. An area of outstanding natural beauty, containing some of Scotland's highest peaks, **Cairngorms National Park** 🏕🏕 is sparsely populated at 11.7 persons per square mile but contains 52 mountain summits, including four of Scotland's highest peaks. Rivers, lochs, and forests are interspersed with farms and small hamlets. The park also embraces a number of old castles, a few rural museums, and some Scotch whisky distilleries.

With its cycling and walking trails, the park's most interesting stretch is the Victorian Heritage Trail that includes the royal family's Balmoral Castle. For more information, check out www.castlesandwhisky.com. For maps, advice on walks or hikes, and complete information, you can write, phone, or fax: **Cairngorms National Park Authority,** 14 The Square, Grantown-on-Spey PH26 3HG (© **01479/873-535;** fax 01479/873-527).

ESSENTIALS

GETTING THERE Aviemore, on the main Inverness-Edinburgh rail line, is the area's major transportation hub. For rail schedules in Aviemore, call © **01479/810-221.** Some eight trains a day from Inverness pass through (trip time: 30–45 min.), at £9 ($17) one-way. Twelve trains per day also arrive from Glasgow or Edinburgh. Trip time from each city is 3 hours, and a one-way ticket from either is £30 ($57).

Aviemore is on the main Inverness-Edinburgh bus line, with frequent service. The trip from Edinburgh takes about 3 hours (call © **0990/808-080** in Edinburgh for schedules) and costs £5 ($9.50). Frequent buses throughout the day also arrive from Inverness (trip time: 40 min.).

If you're driving from Edinburgh, after crossing the Forth Bridge Road, take M90 to Perth, then continue the rest of the way along A9 into Aviemore.

VISITOR INFORMATION The **Highlands of Scotland Tourist Office** (Aviemore branch) is on Grampian Road (© **01479/810-363**). June to August, it's open Monday to Friday 9am to 7pm, Saturday 9am to 6pm, and Sunday 10am to 5pm; September to May, hours are Monday to Friday 9am to 5pm and Saturday and Sunday 10am to 5pm.

EXPLORING THE AREA

North of Aviemore, the **Strathspey Railway,** Dalfaber Road (© **01479/810-725;** www.strathspeyrailway.co.uk), is your best bet in Scotland to learn firsthand what it was like to ride the rails in the 19th century. The railway follows the valley of the River Spey between Boat of Garten and Aviemore, a distance of 8km (5 miles). The train is drawn by a coal-burning steam locomotive. The newest locomotive used was made nearly 4 decades ago, the oldest being of 1899 vintage. The trip is meant to re-create the experience of travel on a Scottish steam railway that once carried wealthy Victorians toward their hunting lodges in North Britain. The round-trip takes about an hour. The rail station at Boat of Garten, where you can board the train, has also been restored.

Round-trip passage costs £15 ($29) first class or £9.50 ($18) third class. Schedules change frequently, but from July to the end of August, trains make four round-trips daily. From May to June and September, they run three times daily, and from March to April and October, they run Sunday, Wednesday, and Thursday. There's no regular service in winter but special Christmas-season trips are made with Santa Claus aboard. To complete the experience, you can wine and dine onboard on Sunday and Friday in July and August, when a single-seating casual lunch is served; the cost for the fare and meal is £19 ($36). Reservations must be made for the meals. The dining car is a replica of a Pullman parlor car, the Amethyst. For reservations and hours of departure, call © **01479/831-692.**

Skiers are attracted to the area any time after October, when snow can be expected. You can rent ski equipment and clothing at the Day Lodge at the main Cairngorm parking area. Weather patterns can change quickly in the Cairngorm massif. Call the number above for a report on the latest weather conditions. To reach the area, take A951, branching off from A9 at Aviemore, then head for the parking area at the Day Lodge.

There are several places to rent bikes in the area. **Speyside Sports,** Grant Road (© **01479/810-656**), rents bikes at £10 ($19) for a half-day, £13 ($25) for a full day, and £40 ($76) for 6 days. **Bothy Bikes,** 81 Grampian Rd. (© **01479/810-111**), charges £10 ($19) for a half-day, £15 ($29) for a full day, and £160 ($304) for 6 days. Discounts apply when you rent for 2 days or more.

The tourist office can give you hiking maps and offer advice, especially about weather conditions. One of the best trails is reached by following B9760 to the signposted **Glenmore Forest Park,** in the vicinity of Loch Morlich.

For the grandest view of the Cairngorm peaks, you can take the **Cairngorm Mountain Railway** (© **01479/861-261;** www.cairngormmountain.com), to the top. The best views of the Valley of the Spey can be seen from the point where the funicular railway lets you off. At the peak is a visitor center and restaurant. Wear warm gear because it gets mighty cold at the top, some 900m (3,000 ft.) above sea level. The railway is signposted off B9152. If weather permits, the train runs daily from 10am to 4:20pm, costing £8.95 ($17) for adults, £7.75 ($15) for seniors, £5.65 ($11) students and children. From late June to the end of August, the last train is at 5:15pm.

WHERE TO STAY

Corrour House Hotel ⭐ *(Finds)*   This isolated granite house is an oasis of personality. Built around 1880 on 1.6 hectares (4 acres) of forest and garden, it contains simple but comfortable rooms that are attractively decorated, each with a shower-only bathroom. Your hosts are the Catto family, who will prepare dinner if arranged in advance. Many of their dishes have a true "taste of Scotland" flavor, including Ballindalloch pheasant with a sauce made from red wine, oranges, red currants, and fresh herbs.

Rothiemurchus, by Aviemore PH22 1QH. © **01479/810-220.** Fax 01479/811-500. www.corrourhousehotel.co.uk. 8 units. £70–£110 ($133–$209) double. Rates include breakfast. AE, MC, V. Closed mid-Nov to Christmas. From Aviemore, drive 1km (½ mile) east on B970, following the signs to Glenmore. **Amenities:** Restaurant; bar; nonsmoking rooms. *In room:* TV, coffeemaker, hair dryer.

Hilton Coylumbridge Aviemore ⭐ *(Kids)*   This is the resort area's best hotel because of its extensive sports and leisure facilities, which are spread across 26 hectares (65 acres) of tree-studded grounds. The midsize guest rooms are spacious and well appointed, with comfortable furnishings and average-size bathrooms, some with both tub and shower. You have a choice of two dining rooms, although the food in both is fairly standard. There's often evening entertainment, particularly on weekends. In winter, downhill and cross-country ski equipment can be rented, and lessons are available. The sports and leisure hall's Fun House caters to children.

Center of Aviemore PH22 12N. © **01479/810-661.** Fax 01479/810-534. www.hiltonhotels.com. 88 units. £135–£170 ($257–$323) double; £200 ($380) suite. AE, DC, MC, V. In Aviemore, turn into the junction immediately opposite the railway station at the south end of the village. Follow the roundabout; the hotel is signposted. **Amenities:** 3 restaurants; bar; 2 indoor heated pools; exercise room; sauna; business center; room service; babysitting; laundry service; nonsmoking rooms; rooms for those w/limited mobility. *In room:* TV, coffeemaker, hair dryer, iron.

Lynwilg House ⭐ The Victorian solidity of this house is particularly noteworthy in Aviemore, considering the relative modernity of the other resort hotels. It was built by the duke of Richmond in the 1880s. Today, it retains 1.6 hectares (4 acres) of its original park and gardens overlooking the mountains, with high-ceilinged guest rooms containing comfortable furnishings and shower-only bathrooms. In front of the house is a croquet lawn, and at the bottom of the well-tended garden is a stream where guests like to relax.

Lynwilg by Aviemore PH22 1PZ. ©/fax **01479/811-685.** www.lynwilg.co.uk. 2 units. £275–£650 ($523–$1,235) double per week. Rates include breakfast. MC, V. Take A9 for 2.5km (1½ miles) south of Aviemore's center, following the signs to Perth. *In room:* TV, coffeemaker, hair dryer.

WHERE TO DINE

The Bar/The Restaurant SCOTTISH   Although the golf course, health club, and leisure facilities of this country club are open only to members, visitors are welcome in the cozy bar and restaurant, which is outfitted in tartan carpets and heavy brocade curtains. In the bar, where live entertainment is featured nightly, the fare includes venison cutlets, burgers, sandwiches, steak pies, and a variety of malt whiskies. The restaurant serves seafood, such as skewered tiger prawns soaked with butter, as well as grilled Angus steaks, main-course salads, and a limited number of vegetarian dishes. Several nights per week, the restaurant hosts theme nights with entertainment.

In the Dalfaber Golf and Country Club, about 1.5km (1 mile) north of the center of Aviemore. © **01479/811-244.** Reservations required in the restaurant. Main courses dinner £7–£20 ($13–$38); lunch main courses £4–£9 ($7.60–$17). MC, V. Restaurant daily 10am–9:30pm. Bar daily 11am–11pm.

AVIEMORE AFTER DARK

The main hot spot at night is **Cafe Mambo,** 12–13 Grampian Rd. (© **01479/ 811-670**), which is both a restaurant and bar. The specialty is "fetish" cocktail pitchers, costing £13 ($25). On Friday and Saturday night from 10pm to 1am there is dancing to the latest recorded music. Otherwise, the restaurant and bar are open Sunday to Wednesday 11am to 11pm, Thursday to Saturday noon to 1am. Food, however, is served on until 8:30pm.

5 Along Loch Ness ⭐⭐

Sir Peter Scott's *Nessitera rhombopteryx,* one of the world's great mysteries, continues to elude her pursuers. The Loch Ness monster, or "Nessie" as she's more familiarly known, has captured the imagination of the world, drawing thousands of visitors yearly to Loch Ness. Half a century ago, A82 was built alongside the banks of the loch's western shores, and since then many more sightings have been claimed.

All types of high-tech underwater contraptions have gone in after the Loch Ness monster, but no one can find her in spite of the photographs and film footage you might have seen in magazines or on TV. Dr. Robert Rines and his associates at the Academy of Applied Science in Massachusetts maintain an all-year watch with sonar-triggered cameras and strobe lights suspended from a raft in Urquhart Bay. However, some people in Inverness aren't keen on collaring the monster, and you can't blame them: An old prophecy predicts a violent end for Inverness if the monster is ever captured.

The loch is 39km (24 miles) long, 1.6km (1 mile) wide, and some 229m (755 ft.) deep. If you'd like to stay along the loch and monster-watch instead of basing yourself at Inverness, see our recommendations below. Even if the monster doesn't put in an

Spotting Nessie

She's affectionately known as Nessie, but her more formal name is *Nessitera rhombopteryx,* and she has the unflattering appellation of the Loch Ness monster. Is she the beast that never was, or the world's most famous living animal? You decide. Real or imagined, she's Scotland's virtual mascot, and even if she doesn't exist, she's one of the major attractions of the country. Who can drive along the dark waters of Loch Ness without staring at the murky depths and expecting a head or a couple of humps to appear above the water's surface at any minute?

The latest evidence that made world headlines in June 2007 was a photograph of Nessie taken by an amateur scientist. "I couldn't believe my eyes when I saw this jet black thing, about 45 feet long, moving fairly fast in the water," said Gordon Holmes, a lab technician from Yorkshire who shot footage of Nessie on May 26, 2007. The Loch Ness center at Drumnadrochit proclaimed this "as some of the best footage we've seen yet." Marine biologist Adrian Shine told news media that Holmes "panned back to get the background shore into the shot, so it's far less likely to be a fake and allows scientists to calculate the size of the creature and how fast it is going." Holmes estimated the monster's speed at about 6 mph.

If Nessie does exist, exactly who is she? A sole survivor from prehistoric times? A gigantic sea snake? It has even been suggested she's a cosmic wanderer through time. Chances are you won't see her on your visit, but you can see a fantasy replica of the sea beast at the official Loch Ness Monster Exhibition at Drumnadrochit (p. 337).

---

appearance, you'll enjoy the scenery. In summer, you can take boat cruises across Loch Ness from both Fort Augustus and Inverness.

If you're driving, take A82 between Fort Augustus and Inverness running along Loch Ness. Buses from either Fort Augustus or Inverness also traverse A82, taking you to Drumnadrochit.

DRUMNADROCHIT

The bucolic village of Drumnadrochit is about 1.6km (1 mile) from Loch Ness, at the entrance to Glen Urquhart. It's the nearest village to the part of the loch in which sightings of the monster have most frequently been reported.

Although most visitors arrive at Drumnadrochit to see the Loch Ness monster exhibit (see "Seeing the Sights," below), you can also take an offbeat adventure in the great outdoors at the **Highland Riding Centre,** Borlum Farm, Drumnadrochit (© **01456/450-220**). This is a 343-hectare (850-acre) sheep farm on moorlands overlooking Loch Ness; follow A82 for about 23km (14 miles) west of Inverness and make a reservation in advance. In summer, the stable's 45 horses are booked throughout the day. Depending on demand, tours depart almost every day; they leave between 9:30am and 4:30pm, last 60 to 120 minutes, and start at £21 ($40). **Wilderness Cycles,** The Cottage (© **01456/450-223**), will rent you a bike so you can go exploring on your own. Rentals costs £8 ($15) for a half-day, £12 ($23) daily, and £35 to £50 ($67–$95) weekly. It's open daily 9am to 6pm.

Loch Ness Monster Exhibition   This is Drumnadrochit's big attraction, featuring a scale replica of Nessie. It opened in 1980 and has been packing 'em in ever since. Follow Nessie's story from A.D. 565 to the present in photographs, audio, and video, and then climb aboard the sonar research vessel *John Murray*. This is the most visited place in the Highlands of Scotland, with more than 200,000 visitors annually.

Drumnadrochit. ✆ **01456/450-573.** Admission £5.95 ($11) adults, £4.50 ($8.55) students, £5 ($9.50) seniors, £3.50 ($6.65) children ages 7–16, £15 ($29) families, free for children under 8. Easter–May daily 9:30am–5pm; June and Sept daily 9am–6pm; July–Aug daily 9am–8pm; Oct daily 9:30am–5:30pm; Nov–Easter daily 10am–3:30pm. Follow the main A82 trunk road between Inverness and Fort William to the north shore of Loch Ness.

Urquhart Castle   This ruined castle, one of Scotland's largest, is on a promontory overlooking Loch Ness. The chief of Clan Grant owned the castle in 1509, and most of the extensive ruins date from that period. In 1692, the castle was blown up by the Grants to prevent it from becoming a Jacobite stronghold. Rising from crumbling walls, the jagged keep still remains. It's at Urquhart Castle that sightings of the Loch Ness monster are most often reported.

Loch Ness along A82. ✆ **01456/450-551.** Admission £6.50 ($12) adults, £5 ($9.50) seniors, £3.25 ($6.20) children. Apr–Sept daily 9:30am–6pm; Oct–Mar daily 9:30am–4:30pm. Drive 2.5km (1½ miles) southeast of Drumnadrochit on A82.

FORT AUGUSTUS

Fort Augustus, 58km (36 miles) south of Inverness along A82 and 267km (166 miles) northwest of Edinburgh, stands at the head (the southernmost end) of Loch Ness. The town became fortified after the 1715 Jacobite rising. Gen. George Wade, of road- and bridge-building fame, headquartered here in 1724, and in 1729, the government constructed a fort along the banks of the loch, naming it Augustus after William Augustus, duke of Cumberland, son of George II. Jacobites seized the fort in 1745 and controlled it until the Scottish defeat at Culloden. Now gone, Wade's fort was turned into the Fort Augustus Abbey at the south end of Loch Ness. A Benedictine order was installed in 1867, and the monks today run a Catholic secondary school on the site.

Fort Augustus is mainly a refueling stop for those who want to stay on Loch Ness itself—perhaps in hopes of seeing the monster—instead of dropping anchor in a larger town like Fort William to the south or Inverness to the north. The only other reason to stop by is that it's the most panoramic place to see the locks of the Caledonian Canal in action.

Bisecting the actual village of Fort Augustus, the locks of the **Caledonian Canal** are a popular attraction when boats are passing through. Running across the loftiest sections of Scotland, the canal was constructed between 1803 and 1822. Almost in a straight line, it makes its way from Inverness, in the north, to Corpach, in the vicinity of Fort William. The canal is 97km (60 miles) long: 35 man-made kilometers (22 miles), and the rest are natural lochs.

Caley Cruisers, Canal Road, Inverness (✆ **01463/236-328;** fax 01463/714-879; www.caleycruisers.co.uk), maintains a fleet of 50 cruisers (with skippers) that groups of two to six people can rent from March to October—even if their marine experience is relatively limited. Rentals last for 1 week, long enough to negotiate the 97km (60 miles) of the Caledonian Canal in both directions between Inverness and Fort William. (There are about 15 locks en route; tolls are included in the rental fee). Depending on the craft's size and the season, a week's rental ranges from £457 to £2,144 ($868–$4,074); the cost of fuel and taxes for a week is £85 to £130 ($162–$247), plus another £35 to £55 ($67–$105) for a reasonably priced insurance policy. Except for the waters of Loch Ness, which can be rough, the canal is calm enough and doesn't pose the dangers of cruising on the open sea.

WHERE TO STAY & DINE

Inchnacardoch Lodge   Inchnacardoch Lodge is a family-run hotel in a panoramic setting overlooking Loch Ness, 1km (½ mile) north of the town center. In 1878 a country residence of the Fraser clan's chief, Lord Lovat, the hotel offers comfortable guest rooms along with efficiently organized bathrooms, most with combination tub/showers. The common areas have recently been refurbished, but the traditional ambience remains. You can relax in the bar while watching the waters for the mysterious monster; have a few wee drams of malt and you may just find her. If you can tear yourself away from the view, the hotel restaurant offers moderately priced main courses.

Hwy. A82, Fort Augustus PH32 4BL. (℧ **01456/450-900**. Fax 01320/366-248. www.inchnacardoch.co.uk. 15 units. £75–£110 ($143–$209) double. Rates include Scottish breakfast. AE, MC, V. Parking. Drive 1km (½ mile) north of Fort Augustus on A82. **Amenities:** Restaurant; bar; nonsmoking rooms. *In room:* TV, coffeemaker.

6 Inverness ⟨★⟩: Capital of the Highlands

251km (156 miles) NW of Edinburgh, 216km (134 miles) NW of Dundee, 216km (134 miles) W of Aberdeen

The capital of the Highlands, Inverness is a royal burgh and seaport at the north end of Great Glen on both sides of the Ness River. For such a historic town, the sights are rather meager, but Inverness makes a good base for touring. If your time is limited, confine your visits to Culloden Battlefield, Cawdor Castle of *Macbeth* fame (see "Nairn & Cawdor Castle," later in this chapter), and Black Isle (see "The Black Isle Peninsula," later in this chapter), the most enchanting and scenic peninsula in Scotland.

ESSENTIALS

GETTING THERE   Domestic flights from various parts of Britain arrive at the Inverness Airport. Flight time from London's Gatwick to the Inverness/Dalcross Airport is 1¾ hours. Call (℧ **01667/464-000** in Inverness for flight information.

Some five to seven trains per day arrive from Glasgow and Edinburgh (on Sun, two or three trains). The train takes 3½ hours from either city, and a one-way fare from either is £33 ($63). Trains pull into Station Square, off Academy Street in Inverness (℧ **08457/484-950** for schedules).

Scottish Citylink coaches provide service for the area (℧ **08705/505-050** for schedules). Frequent service through the day is possible from either Edinburgh or Glasgow (a 4-hr. trip each way), at a one-way fare of £16 ($30). The bus station is at Farraline Park, off Academy Street (℧ **01463/233-371**).

Driving from Edinburgh, take M9 north to Perth, then follow along the Great North Road (A9) until you reach Inverness.

VISITOR INFORMATION   The Inverness branch of the **Highlands of Scotland Tourist Board** is at Castle Wynd, off Bridge Street (℧ **01463/234-353**). October to mid-April, it's open Monday to Friday 9am to 5pm and Saturday 10am to 4pm; mid-April to May, hours are Monday to Friday 9am to 5pm, Saturday 9:30am to 5pm, and Sunday 9:30am to 4pm; June hours are Monday to Friday 9am to 6pm, Saturday 9am to 5pm, and Sunday 9:30am to 5pm; July and August, it's open Monday to Saturday 9am to 6pm and Sunday 9:30am to 5pm; September hours are Monday to Saturday 9am to 6pm and Sunday 9:30am to 5pm.

Inverness

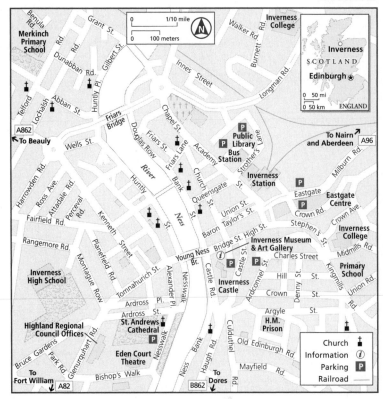

SPECIAL EVENTS At the **Highland Games** in July, with its sporting competitions and festive balls, the season in Inverness reaches its social peak. For more information and exact dates, consult the tourist office (see above).

SEEING THE SIGHTS

Inverness is one of the oldest inhabited sites in Scotland. On **Craig Phadrig** are the remains of a vitrified fort, believed to date from the 4th century B.C. One of the most important prehistoric monuments in the north, the **Stones of Clava** are about 10km (6 miles) east of Inverness on the road to Nairn. These cairns and standing stones are from the Bronze Age.

The old castle of Inverness stood to the east of the present street Castlehill, and the site still retains the name "Auld Castlehill." David I built the first stone castle in Inverness around 1141, and the **Clock Tower** is all that remains of a fort erected by Cromwell's army between 1652 and 1657. The rebellious Scots blew up the old castle in 1746 to keep it from falling to government troops, and the present **castle** was constructed by the Victorians in the 19th century. Today, this landmark houses the law courts of Inverness and local government offices.

The 16th-century **Abertarff House,** Church Street, is now the headquarters of An Comunn Gaidhealach, the Highland association that preserves the Gaelic language

---

Moments **The Hill of the Fairies**

West of the river rises the wooded hill of **Tomnahurich,** known as the "hill of the fairies." Now a cemetery, it's the best place to go for a country walk, with panoramic views. The boat-shaped hillock is immediately to the southwest of the center. In the Ness are wooded islands, linked to Inverness by suspension bridges, that have been turned into parks.

---

and culture. Opposite the town hall is the **Old Mercat Cross,** with its Stone of the Tubs, said to be the stone on which women rested their washtubs as they ascended from the river. Known as "Clachnacudainn," the lozenge-shaped stone was the spot where local early kings were crowned.

St. Andrew's Cathedral (1866–69), Ardross Street, is the northernmost diocese of the Scottish Episcopal church and a fine example of Victorian architecture, both imposing and richly decorated. Be sure to check out the icons given to Bishop Eden by the czar of Russia. The cathedral is open daily from 9:30am to 6pm. For information, get in touch with the Provost, 15 Ardross St. (© **01463/225-553**).

If you're interested in bus tours of the Highlands and cruises on Loch Ness, go to **Inverness Traction,** 6 Burnett Rd. (© **01463/239-292**). In summer, there are also cruises along the Caledonian Canal from Inverness into Loch Ness.

Shoppers might want to check out a family-owned shrine to Scottish kiltmaking, **Duncan Chisholm & Sons,** 47–51 Castle St. (© **01463/234-599**). The tartans of at least 50 of Scotland's largest clans are available in the form of kilts and kilt jackets for men and women. If your heart is set on something more esoteric, the staff can acquire whatever fabric your ancestors would have worn to make up your garment. A section is devoted to Scottish gifts (ties, scarves, yard goods, kilt pins in thistle patterns) and memorabilia. You can visit the on-premises workshop. The town's best jewelry store, with an unusual collection of bangles and bracelets inspired by the decorative traditions of Celtic Scotland, is **D&H Norval,** 88 Church St. (© **01463/232-739**). At **Celtic Spirit,** 14 Church St. (© **01463/714-796**), the focus is on New Age books and an unusual collection of wind chimes.

Golfers can head about 64km (40 miles) north to hit the links at the renowned **Royal Dornoch Golf Club.** Closer is the 5,288-yard **Torvean Golf Course,** Glen Q Road (© **01463/225-651**), an 18-hole, par-69 course with greens fees of £16 ($30) Monday to Friday, and £19 ($36) Saturday and Sunday.

Culloden Battlefield ☆   At Culloden Battlefield, Bonnie Prince Charlie and the Jacobite army were finally crushed on April 16, 1746. A path leads from the visitor center through the Field of the English, where 52 men of the duke of Cumberland's forces who died during the battle are said to be buried. Features of interest include the **Graves of the Clans,** communal burial places with simple stones bearing individual clan names; the great **memorial cairn,** erected in 1881; the **Well of the Dead;** and the huge **Cumberland Stone,** from which the victorious "Butcher" Cumberland is said to have reviewed the scene. The battle lasted only 40 minutes; the prince's army lost some 1,200 men out of 5,000, and the king's army 300 of 9,000. In the visitor center is an audiovisual presentation on the background and history of the famous battle. Also on the premises are a restaurant and bookshop.

Culloden Moor, 10km (6 miles) southeast of Inverness. (☎ **01463/790-607** for visitor center. Admission to visitor center £5 ($9.50) adults, £4 ($7.60) seniors and children, £14 ($27) families. Visitor center Mar 31–June and Sept–Oct daily 9am–6pm; Nov–Dec and Feb–Mar 30 daily 11am–4pm. Closed in Jan.

Fort George/Queen's Own Highlanders Regimental Museum   Fort George was called the "most considerable fortress and best situated in Great Britain" in 1748 by Lt. Col. James Wolfe, who went on to fame as Wolfe of Quebec. Built after the Battle of Culloden, the fort was occupied by the Hanoverian army of George II and is still an active army barracks. The rampart, almost 1.6km (1 mile) around, encloses some 17 hectares (42 acres). Dr. Samuel Johnson and James Boswell visited here in 1773 on their Highland trek. The fort contains the admission-free **Queen's Own Highlanders Regimental Museum,** with regimental exhibits from 1778 to today, representing a number of Highland regiments as well as its namesake. A new exhibit about the 1990s Gulf War has been recently added.

On Moray Firth by the village of Ardersier, 18km (11 miles) northeast of Inverness, 13km (8 miles) northwest of Cawdor along B9006. (☎ **0131/310-8701**. Admission £6.50 ($12) adults, £5 ($9.50) seniors, £3.25 ($6.20) children ages 5–15, free for children under 5. Apr–Sept daily 10am–5:30pm; Oct–Mar daily 9:30am–4:30pm.

Inverness Museum and Art Gallery   This museum in the town center is a top attraction, its displays representing the social and natural history, archaeology, art, and culture of the Scottish Highlands, with special emphasis on the Inverness district. Don't miss the important collection of Highland silver and reconstructed silversmith's workshop, displays on the life of the clans, a reconstruction of a local taxidermist's workshop, and a reconstructed 1920s Inverness kitchen.

Castle Wynd, off Bridge St. (☎ **01463/237-114**. Free admission. Mon–Sat 9am–5pm.

SHOPPING

There are two major shopping areas in the center of Inverness: the **Eastgate Inverness Shopping Centre,** Millburn Road (www.inverness-eastgate.com) and **Victorian Market,** Academy Street, which is the more traditional of the two. The building itself was constructed in 1870 and the market's history is reflected in the wide range of its shops, which are generally open Monday to Saturday.

   Silvercraft, 5–7 Market Arcade (☎ **01463/232-686**), is a family-run jewelry store that opened in the Victorian Market in 1960. The friendly atmosphere and wide selection of diamond, gold, and silver jewelry make for a lovely shopping experience.

   Heraldic Art Design, 6 Victorian Market Arcade (☎ **01463/714-605**), specializes in hand-embroidered coats of arms made in the United Kingdom with gold and silver threads. These aren't cheap, but they are lasting. Also available are the crests of military branches or your favorite football (soccer) team.

   Boarstone Tartans, 14–16 New Market (☎ **01463/239-793**), is one of the primary kiltmakers in Inverness. Every traditional Scottish clothes item—from kilt jackets to tartan trousers to Highland dress outfits—can be purchased here. Shooting coats, tweed caps, deerstalker hats, tweed rugs, scarves, ties, Celtic jewelry, and pewter flasks are also for sale.

WHERE TO STAY
EXPENSIVE
Bunchrew House Hotel and Restaurant ⭐   This fine Scottish mansion on the shores of Beauly Firth is the ancestral home of both the Fraser and the McKenzie clans. The house dates from 1621 and is set on 8 hectares (20 acres) of landscaped gardens.

You get a glimpse of a bygone era while relaxing in the paneled drawing room with roaring log fires. The guest rooms are individually decorated; the Lovat Suite, for example, has a canopied four-poster bed. Some bathrooms contain showers only. Guests can dine in the candlelit restaurant on prime Scottish beef, fresh lobster and crayfish, local game, and fresh vegetables.

Bunchrew, Inverness, Inverness-shire IV3 8TA. ⒸⒸ 01463/234-917. Fax 01463/710-620. www.bunchrew-inverness.co.uk. 16 units. £150–£220 ($285–$418) double. Rates include Scottish breakfast. AE, MC, V. Drive 5km (3 miles) west of Inverness on A862. **Amenities:** Restaurant; bar; room service; laundry service; nonsmoking rooms. *In room:* TV, fridge, coffeemaker, hair dryer.

Culloden House *Ⓐ Ⓐ* This is the most elegant country retreat in the area. Culloden House, a Georgian mansion with a much-photographed Adam facade, includes part of the Renaissance castle in which Bonnie Prince Charlie slept the night before Culloden, the last great battle on British soil. Superbly isolated, with extensive gardens and parkland, it's perfect for a relaxed Highland holiday. At the iron gates to the broad front lawn, a piper in full Highland garb often plays at sundown, the skirl of the bagpipe accompanied by the barking of house dogs. Cozy yet spacious guest rooms have sylvan views and a history-laden atmosphere. The Prince of Wales and the crown prince of Japan have stayed here.

Culloden, Inverness IV2 7BZ. Ⓒ **01463/790-461.** Fax 01463/792-181. www.cullodenhouse.co.uk. 28 units. £150–£210 ($285–$399) double; £180–£240 ($342–$456) suite. Rates include Scottish breakfast. AE, DC, MC, V. Drive 5km (3 miles) east of Inverness on A96. **Amenities:** Restaurant; bar; tennis court; sauna; room service; laundry service; croquet lawn; nonsmoking rooms. *In room:* TV, hair dryer, trouser press.

Dunain Park Hotel *Ⓐ Ⓐ* The Dunain Park stands in 2.4 hectares (6 acres) of garden and woods between Loch Ness and Inverness. This 18th-century Georgian house is furnished with fine antiques, allowing it to retain an atmosphere of a private country house. Although Dunain Park has won its fame mainly as a restaurant (see "Where to Dine," below), it does offer guest rooms with a host of thoughtful details and pretty furnishings. Each unit has a shower or tub bathroom.

Dunain Park, Inverness IV3 8JN. Ⓒ **01463/230-512.** Fax 01463/224-532. www.dunainparkhotel.co.uk. 11 units. £128–£198 ($243–$376) double; from £200 ($380) suite. Rates include Scottish breakfast. AE, MC, V. Drive 1.6km (1 mile) southwest of Inverness on A82. **Amenities:** Restaurant; bar; indoor pool; room service; laundry service; nonsmoking rooms. *In room:* TV, fridge (in suite), coffeemaker, hair dryer, trouser press.

MODERATE

Glen Mhor Hotel On the River Ness, this house of gables and bay windows is a hospitable family-run hotel. From many of the individually styled guest rooms you have views of the river, castle, and cathedral; some are suitable for families. Ten rooms are in an annex called the Cottage. Each unit has a well-maintained bathroom, all with showers, some with tub/shower combinations. In the Riverview Restaurant, which overlooks the river and specializes in seafood and Scottish dishes, you can enjoy salmon caught in the Ness. The wine list is one of the best in the country. There's also a European bistro bar called Nico's.

9–12 Ness Bank, Inverness IV2 4SG. Ⓒ **01463/234-308.** Fax 01463/713-170. www.glen-mhor.com. 43 units. £80–£110 ($152–$209) double; £110–£150 ($209–$285) junior suite. Rates include Scottish breakfast. AE, DC, MC, V. From Inverness, follow signs to Dores (B862); hotel is on the south bank. **Amenities:** 2 restaurants; bar; room service; nonsmoking rooms. *In room:* TV, coffeemaker, hair dryer.

Glenmoriston Town House Hotel *Ⓐ (Kids)* This hotel, on the River Ness, is a short walk from the town center, and it's the finest town-house hotel in Inverness. Rooms have been stylishly refurbished, are well maintained and individually designed, and come with spacious private bathrooms. Some accommodations are suitable for use as family units. Guests can enjoy temporary membership at a nearby Squash and Tennis Club. Of the two hotel restaurants, La Terrazza is open daily for lunch, whereas La Riviera is more formal, specializing in a fine Italian cuisine, with many Tuscan dishes.

20 Ness Bank, Inverness IV2 4SF. ℂ **01463/223-777.** Fax 01463/712-378. 15 units. www.glenmoriston.com. £130–£170 ($247–$323) double. Rates include full Scottish breakfast. AE, MC, V. Free parking. Lies a 5-min. walk south of the train station. **Amenities:** 2 restaurants; bar; access to nearby health club; room service; nonsmoking rooms. *In room:* TV, fax, coffeemaker, hair dryer.

Inverness Marriott Hotel ⓡ   Once a private mansion, this hotel is a charming 18th-century country house set amid a woodland garden that's adjacent to an 18-hole golf course. Over the years it has attracted royals, high-ranking government officials, film stars, and even Robert Burns himself. The staff maintains the country-house atmosphere with an informal and hospitable style. The furnishings throughout are high quality, and all the guest rooms are attractively furnished, each with tub/shower combo.

The restaurant's fish dishes are exceptional at dinner. Bar lunches and snack meals include mostly Scottish fare. A notice in the lobby tells you Robert Burns dined here in 1787, and the "Charles" who signed the guest register in 1982 was (you guessed it) the Prince of Wales. His sister, Princess Anne, has also stayed here.

Culcabock Rd., Inverness IV2 3LP. ℂ **01463/237-166.** Fax 0870/400-7392. www.marriott.com. 82 units. £150–£174 ($285–$331) double; £180–£210 ($342–$399) suite. Rates include Scottish breakfast. AE, DC, MC, V. Take Kingsmill Rd. 1.6km (1 mile) east of the center of Inverness. **Amenities:** Restaurant; bar; indoor pool; health club; sauna; room service; laundry service; 3-hole mini-golf course; nonsmoking rooms. *In room:* TV, minibar, coffeemaker, hair dryer, iron, trouser press.

The Royal Highland Hotel   It's like Inverness of yesterday at this somber gray-stone hotel, built in 1859 across from the train station to celebrate the arrival of rail lines connecting the Highlands, via Inverness, to the rest of Britain. Today, it's an antiques-strewn, slightly faded hotel, despite the gradual modernizations and the contemporary decor in half of the guest rooms. (The other half are charmingly dowdy.) Each unit is equipped with a shower or tub bathroom. The massive lobby contains the showiest staircase in Inverness. The dining room retains its elaborate high ceiling and a sense of the Victorian age. Seafood and shellfish are house specialties.

18 Academy St., Inverness IV1 1LG. ℂ **01463/231-926.** Fax 01463/710-705. www.royalhighlandhotel.co.uk. 75 units. £149–£189 ($283–$359) double. Rates include breakfast. DC, MC, V. **Amenities:** Restaurant; 2 bars; nonsmoking rooms. *In room:* TV, coffeemaker, hair dryer, iron, trouser press.

INEXPENSIVE

Ballifeary House Hotel ⓡ *Value*   This well-maintained 1876 Victorian stone villa, with a pleasant garden, is one of the area's finest B&Bs. Mr. and Mrs. Luscombe, the owners, offer their guests individual attention. The rooms, although a bit small, are comfortably furnished, with shower-only bathrooms. This nonsmoking hotel discourages families with children under 15.

10 Ballifeary Rd., Inverness IV3 5PJ. ℂ **01463/235-572.** Fax 01463/717-583. www.ballifearyhousehotel.co.uk. 6 units. £60–£76 ($114–$144) double. Rates include Scottish breakfast. MC, V. From Fort William on A82 as you're approaching Inverness, turn right on Ballifeary Rd. **Amenities:** Bar; nonsmoking rooms. *In room:* TV, coffeemaker, hair dryer, no phone.

Ivybank Guest House *Value*   This is one of the best B&Bs in Inverness. Located off Castle Road about a 10-minute walk north of the town center, Ivybank was built in

1836 and retains its original fireplaces and an oak-paneled and beamed hall with a rosewood staircase. It features a walled garden and comfortably furnished guest rooms, all nonsmoking and each with hot and cold running water. Three units contain shower-only bathrooms. Mrs. Catherine Cameron is the gracious hostess, making guests feel at ease. Breakfast is the only meal served.

28 Old Edinburgh Rd., Inverness IV2 3HJ. ©/fax **01463/232-796.** www.ivybankguesthouse.com. 6 units, 3 with private bathroom. £56 ($106) double without bathroom; £64 ($122) double with bathroom. Rates include Scottish breakfast. AE, MC, V. **Amenities:** Nonsmoking rooms. *In room:* TV, coffeemaker, hair dryer.

The Lodge at Daviot Mains This refurbished, cozy country home has become one of the most welcoming spots to stay in Inverness. Highland charm amid 32 hectares (80 acres) of farmland makes this place relaxing and traditionally Scottish. The rooms, each named after local rivers, have their own personalities. However, the one trait they all have in common is cleanliness. Each unit is nonsmoking and comes with a private bathroom (with shower). Out of your room's window, you can see cows, sheep, and a pony named Seamus grazing. The comfort of the rooms isn't the only reason to stay here, though. Ms. Hutchinson lights up the kitchen with her Scottish treats, using local produce and fish whenever she can.

Daviot Mains Farm, Inverness IV2 53R. © **01463/772-215.** Fax 01463/772-099. www.thelodgeatdaviotmains.co.uk. 7 units. £70–£95 ($133–$181) double. MC, V. Lies 8km (5 miles) off Inverness on A9. **Amenities:** Dining room. *In room:* TV, beverage maker, hair dryer.

WHERE TO DINE

Abstract ⭐⭐⭐ FRENCH/SCOTTISH   Using Scottish produce but French cooking techniques, this restaurant has moved near the top of the finest dining experiences in Inverness. It employs top chefs from many of Europe's major restaurants. They show great skill in razor-sharp techniques utilizing high quality, market-fresh ingredients.

The starters, prepared fresh nightly, are stunning with their unusual ingredients and harmonious flavors—take for example, Scottish scallops with a hazelnut crust served with braised pork belly and white asparagus, or lightly smoked local roe deer filet with a poached quail egg. Main dishes are to be savored, especially the assiette of Ross-shire lamb with a rhubarb couscous or the Scottish brown hare filets with a passion fruit compote. Fish is fresh from the sea, including Scottish red mullet in a Japanese bouillon and a wasabi emulsion or the wild halibut with braised fennel and an eggplant purée. The dessert menu nightly is the most tempting in town, featuring the likes of a raspberry soufflé with a hot pepper sauce or dark chocolate mousse with pistachio ice cream.

64–66 Academy St. © **01463/237-755.** Reservations recommended. Main courses £14–£18 ($27–$34); tasting menu £50 ($95) per person. AE, MC, V. Mon–Sat noon–2pm; daily 5:30–11pm.

Chez Christophe ⭐⭐ FRENCH   If you're looking for French food in Inverness, this is one of the finest choices. Husband and wife team Christophe and Carol Magie have created a place where modern and traditional recipes are blended together. This 16-seat restaurant is plainly decorated, letting the food speak for itself. We recommend starting with the *mille-feuille* of apple and fresh duck foie gras roasted in Pineau des Charentes. After that, move on to the roasted cannon of Scottish lamb served with a casserole of white coco beans, lardoons, and onions, and dressed with its own lamb and pink garlic roasting *jus*. Finish off with a warm dark chocolate *coulant gateaux* (purposefully moist cake) served with a vanilla and mascarpone ice cream. A selection of French cheeses and wines is also available.

16 Ardross St. ✆ **01463/717-126.** Reservations required. Fixed-price menus £24–£29 ($46–$55). DC, MC, V. Mon–Sat 7–10pm. Closed last 2 weeks of Feb and first 2 weeks of July.

Dunain Park Restaurant ✦ SCOTTISH   Ann Nicoll presides over the kitchen here, offering Scottish food with French flair. A game terrine of chicken and guinea fowl is layered with venison and pigeon, and meats are wrapped in bacon and served with a delicious onion confit. Other dishes that may appear on the menu are hare-and-pigeon casserole with roasted shallots and wild mushrooms; medallions of venison rolled in oatmeal and served with a Claret and crème de Cassis sauce; and Shetland salmon baked in sea salt, served with a white-port, lime, and ginger sauce. The restaurant also specializes in Aberdeen Angus steaks. Try one of the desserts from the buffet: crème brûlée, chocolate roulade, or marshmallow pudding.

In the Dunain Park Hotel, Dunain Park. ✆ **01463/230-512.** Reservations recommended. Main courses £17–£21 ($32–$40). AE, DC, MC, V. Daily 7–9pm.

MODERATE

Café 1 INTERNATIONAL/SCOTTISH FUSION   One of the most pleasant restaurants in town is in a century-old stone-fronted building on a street dotted with shops. Inside, you find varnished paneling, wooden tables, potted plants, and a soothing New Age atmosphere. Dine on generous portions of Angus rump steak with rocket and parmesan salad; penne pasta with fresh tomatoes, spinach, garlic, and chili Buffalo mozzarella; tenderloins of Highland lamb wrapped in Parma ham; or halibut filet with fondant potatoes, ratatouille and crispy leeks. For dessert, try the dark-chocolate tart with white-chocolate shavings or a crepe filled with homemade Maltese ice cream with butterscotch sauce.

75 Castle St. ✆ **01463/226-200.** Reservations recommended. Main courses lunch £7.50–£12 ($14–$23), dinner £8.50–£18 ($16–$33). MC, V. Mon–Sat noon–2pm and 6–9:30pm.

INEXPENSIVE

Dickens International Restaurant INTERNATIONAL   On a downtown street next to the oldest house in Inverness, Aberton House, this restaurant boasts a decor that has been revamped and updated with furnishings in the style created by Charles Rennie Mackintosh (1868–1928), Scotland's most famous designer. A wide selection of European, Chinese, and international dishes is offered, including seafood and vegetarian options, Dickens's own steak, aromatic duck, and chateaubriand. The wide choice of side dishes ranges from fried rice to bean sprouts to cauliflower with cheese.

77–79 Church St. ✆ **01463/713-111.** Reservations required on weekends. Main courses £10–£14 ($19–$27). AE, DC, MC, V. Mon–Sat noon–2pm and 5:30–11pm.

Riva ITALIAN/INTERNATIONAL   One of Inverness's best restaurants occupies a site on the opposite *riva* (riverbank) from the rest of the town. Deliberately unpretentious, it has only 18 tables. At least a dozen kinds of pastas are offered as either starters or main courses. Entrees include tagliatelle with prosciutto, monkfish with caramelized cauliflower, roast breast of Barbary duck with orange sauce, and chicken with crispy Parma ham and risotto. Between mealtimes, the place functions as a simple cafe serving sandwiches.

4–6 Ness Walk. ✆ **01463/237-377.** Reservations required. Main courses £8.95–£19 ($17–$35) in restaurant; 2-course lunch £11 ($20); 3-course lunch £14 ($27). MC, V. Restaurant Mon–Sat noon–2:30pm and 5–10pm (last order), Sun 5–10pm; cafe Mon–Sat 10am–9:30pm, except during above-mentioned meal hours.

INVERNESS AFTER DARK

One of the most happening places in town is **Hootananny,** Church St. (© **01463/233-651**), a Scottish Ceilidh Cafe Bar with three venues. On the ground floor is the **Ceilidh Cafe Bar** itself, the most popular place. On the next floor is the **Mad Hatters Bar** serving locally produced real ales, and on the top floor is the **Bothy Sofa Bar,** for a more intimate rendezvous. The best time to show up is on a Friday night at 10:30pm when local singers and songwriters showcase their talents. Traditional music is featured on many a night, interspersed with video tracks. Every Saturday afternoon there is a ceilidh from 2:30 to 6pm. Hours vary here, and on weekends it often opens in the afternoon. Most nights it closes at 1am, and, depending on the venue and entertainment, a £5 ($9.50) cover charge might be imposed.

Johnny Foxes, 26 Bank St. (© **01463/236-577**), is an Irish bar that draws the largest number of backpackers. Food is served and live music is presented Monday to Saturday, with Sunday nights devoted to karaoke. A range of popular and traditional music is offered, along with Scottish and Irish tunes. Open Monday to Tuesday 11am to 1am, Wednesday to Saturday 11am to 2am, and Sunday 12:30pm to 2am. Food is served daily from noon to 3pm.

G's Nightclub, 21 Castle St. (© **01463/233-322**), has some of the best live music in town. A sing-along boogie is presented here long after the pubs have shut down for the night. For the best dancing, show up on Friday and Saturday night to join a crowd in their 20s and 30s. A cover is imposed Thursday to Saturday nights, ranging from £3 to £6 ($5.70–$11). Open Wednesday to Thursday 9:30pm to 2am, Friday and Saturday 9:30pm to 3am.

Barbazza, 5–9 Young St. (© **01463/242-342**), provides live entertainment Thursday to Sunday until 2am. It's also a casual place to dine during the day, opening at 11am Monday to Saturday or noon on Sunday. Everything from rock and karaoke is presented here, including punk and indie. Depending on the night, a £5 ($9.50) cover might be imposed.

You can also spend an evening in the town's pubs sampling single-malt whiskies or beers on tap. Although the pubs here may not have the authentic charm of the isolated pubs in more rural areas, you'll still find a lot of Highlander flavor. Try the pub in the **Loch Ness House Hotel,** Glenurquhart Road (© **01463/231-248**), on the western periphery of town; **Gellions Pub,** 8–14 Bridge St. (© **01463/233-648**); or **Gunsmith's Pub,** 30 Union St. (© **01463/710-519**).

SIDE TRIPS FROM INVERNESS

MUIR OF ORD

This small town, 16km (10 miles) west of Inverness, makes a good touring center for a history-rich part of Scotland. If you stay at the hotel recommended below, you can take day trips around Black Isle, which boasts beautiful scenery (see "The Black Isle Peninsula," later in this chapter). Outdoorsy types are drawn here for fishing, golf, and shooting.

WHERE TO STAY & DINE

Dower House 𝕘 *(Finds* *(Kids*   This charming 18th-century guesthouse is a perfect base for exploring the area. The rooms are decorated in the fine tradition of a Scottish country house, with flowers cut from the garden. A small three-bedroom cottage is perfect for families. Be sure to make reservations for the Dower House well in advance; the comfortable atmosphere is very much in demand.

Even if you don't stay here, you might want to call for a dinner reservation. After a cocktail in the lounge, you proceed to the dining room for a three-course meal (£38/$72) of modern British cuisine made from produce grown on the grounds; expensive fixed-price menus are served nightly.

Highfield, Muir of Ord IV6 7XN. ℂ/fax **01463/870-090**. www.thedowerhouse.co.uk. 5 units. £120–£140 ($228–$266) double; £130–£160 ($247–$304) cottage. Rates include Scottish breakfast. MC, V. Drive 1.6km (1 mile) north of A862. **Amenities:** Restaurant; bar; room service; babysitting; nonsmoking rooms. *In room:* TV, coffeemaker, hair dryer, iron.

BEAULY ✶

The French monks who settled here in the 13th century named it literally "beautiful place"—and it still is. You see the **Highland Craftpoint** on your left as you come from Inverness. In summer, there's an interesting exhibit of Scottish handicrafts. Beauly is 19km (12 miles) west of Inverness on A862, and Inverness Traction, a local bus company, has hourly service from Inverness.

Dating from 1230, the **Beauly Priory** (℗ **01463/782-309**), now a roofless shell, is the only remaining one of three priories built for the Valliscaulian order, an austere body drawing its main components from the Cistercians and the Carthusians. Some notable windows and window arcading are still left among the ruins. Hugh Fraser of Lovat erected the Chapel of the Holy Cross on the nave's north side in the early 15th century. You can tour the priory at any time; if it's locked, ask for a key from the Priory Hotel across the way.

If you're interested in tweeds, don't miss **Campbells of Beauly,** Highland Tweed House (℗ **01463/782-239**), operated by the same family since 1858. An excellent selection of fine tweeds and tartans is offered, and you can have your material tailored. Blankets, travel rugs, tweed hats, and kilts are sold, as well as cashmere and lambswool sweaters. It's on the main street at the south end of the village square, next to the Royal Bank of Scotland.

WHERE TO STAY & DINE

Priory Hotel ✶ The Priory Hotel is on the historic main square of town, a short walk from the ruins of the priory. The hotel has recently expanded into an adjacent building, adding four rooms to its well-furnished offerings. A frequently changing dinner menu features a variety of fish and local game as well as a good selection of steaks; bar meals are similar dishes served in smaller portions. In addition, high tea is served daily.

The Square, Beauly IV4 7BX. ℗ **01463/782-309**. Fax 01463/782-531. www.priory-hotel.com. 36 units. £90 ($171) double. Rates include Scottish breakfast. AE, DC, MC, V. **Amenities:** Restaurant; bar; room service; laundry service; dry cleaning; nonsmoking rooms. *In room:* TV, coffeemaker, hair dryer, iron.

7 Nairn & Cawdor Castle ✶

277km (172 miles) N of Edinburgh, 147km (91 miles) NW of Aberdeen, 26km (16 miles) E of Inverness

A favorite family seaside resort on the sheltered Moray Firth, Nairn (from the Gaelic for "Water of Alders") is a royal burgh at the mouth of the Nairn River. Its fishing harbor was constructed in 1820, and golf has been played here since 1672—as it still is today.

ESSENTIALS

GETTING THERE Nairn can be reached by train from the south, with a change at either Aberdeen or Inverness. The service between Inverness and Nairn is frequent;

Moments **In the Footsteps of Macbeth**

A **large beach** draws crowds in summer. Anglers also find the area is a good spot. Nairn is great walking country, and the tourist office will give you a map and details about the various possibilities, including hikes along the banks of the River Nairn. The best walks are five signposted nature trails, called the **Cawdor Castle Nature Trails.** They're signposted from Cawdor Castle, of Macbeth fame, and they take you along some of the loveliest and most varied forests and wooded areas in the Highlands.

---

this is the most popular route. For information, check with the Inverness train station at Station Square (© **08457/484-950**).

From Inverness, Inverness Traction runs daily buses to Nairn. Call © **0870/ 608-2608** for schedules.

If you're driving from Inverness, take A96 east to Nairn.

VISITOR INFORMATION The **tourist office** is at 62 King St. (© **01667/ 452-753**). April to mid-May, it's open Monday to Saturday 10am to 5pm; mid-May to June, hours are Monday to Saturday 10am to 5pm and Sunday 11am to 4pm; July and August, hours are Monday to Saturday 9am to 6pm and Sunday 10am to 5pm; and September and October, hours are Monday to Saturday 10am to 5pm.

SEEING THE SIGHTS

Brodie Country Faire, on A96, 5km (3 miles) east of Nairn in Brodie (© **01309/ 641-555**), is a family-owned shopping complex with vendors carrying a variety of merchandise. Of greatest interest are the regionally produced knitwear, gift items, and foodstuff; the latter includes smoked meats, jams, mustards, and other condiments. Also on the premises is a fully licensed restaurant serving Scottish cuisine daily from 9:30am to 5pm (to 7pm Thurs), with main courses averaging about £6 ($11).

Nairn Antiques, St. Ninian Place (© **01667/453-303**), carries a broad range of antiques and a section of upscale crafts and reproductions. Scottish pottery, silver, and fine porcelains are the main draw, but there's also furniture and bric-a-brac from around the world. This is the only shop in the entire north country to stock high-quality Lalique crystal from France.

The Taste of Moray, on the Nairn-Inverness Road, 10km (6 miles) north of Nairn (© **01463/237-776;** www.tasteofmoray.co.uk), is all about the pleasures of preparing and consuming Scottish cuisine, with products ranging from quality cookware to regional domestic stoneware. The food hall offers an array of Scottish condiments and smoked meats, and if shopping here makes you hungry, you can step into the adjacent restaurant that serves seafood dishes and steaks, with main courses averaging £8–£25 ($15–$48). Food service is daily from 10am to 9pm.

The 18-hole **Nairn Dunbar Golf Club,** Loch Loy Road (© **01667/452-741**), is a 6,700-yard course with a par of 72. Monday to Friday, greens fees are £60 to £84 ($114– $160) per round and Saturday and Sunday £70–£100 ($133–$190) per round.

Cawdor Castle 🞰 To the south of Nairn, you encounter 600 years of Highland history at Cawdor Castle, the home of the thanes of Cawdor since the early 14th century. Although the castle was constructed 2 centuries after his time, it has nevertheless been romantically linked to Shakespeare's *Macbeth,* once the thane of Cawdor. The castle has all the architectural ingredients you'd associate with the Middle Ages: a drawbridge, an ancient tower, and fortified walls. Its severity is softened by the handsome gardens and rolling lawns. On the grounds are five nature trails through beautiful woodland, a 9-hole golf course, a putting green, a snack bar, a picnic area, shops, and a licensed restaurant serving hot meals, teas, and coffees all day.

Between Inverness and Nairn on B9090 off A96, Cawdor. © **01667/404-675**. Admission £7.30 ($14) adults, £6.30 ($12) seniors and students, £4.50 ($8.55) children ages 5–15, free for children under 5. May–2nd Sun in Oct daily 10am–5:30pm.

WHERE TO STAY

Boath House 🎇🎇 This Georgian mansion is set amid 8 hectares (20 acres) of lush greenery. Built in 1825, the house has been restored to its original elegance. In spite of its classic look, the atmosphere is relaxed and informal. There are two lounges and a library where you can enjoy a dram of whisky. Bedrooms are splendidly decorated with antiques and period furniture. An on-site salon is open to both guests and nonguests, offering everything from aromatherapy to galvanic slimming treatments. The salon uses only products with natural ingredients from pure plant and flower essences. The hotel is also home to an award-winning restaurant (see "Where to Dine," below).

Auldearn, Nairn IV12 5TE. © **01667/454-896**. Fax 01667/455-469. www.boath-house.com. 6 units. £190–£330 ($361–$627) double. Rates include breakfast. AE, DC, MC, V. Free parking. 3.2km (2 miles) east of Nairn on A96. **Amenities:** Restaurant; exercise room; spa; nonsmoking rooms. *In room:* TV, coffeemaker, hair dryer.

Clifton House 🎇🎇 *(Finds* This intimate hotel reflects the dynamic personality of J. Gordon Macintyre, owner of the vine-covered, honey-sandstone Victorian mansion. His home for more than 60 years, it stands on the seafront, 3 minutes from the beach and equidistant to both golf links. Mr. Macintyre has spent a great deal of time and care decorating and refurbishing the house. Most of the furniture is antique; the collection of paintings, engravings, and drawings is unusual and extensive. Each guest room is pleasantly appointed, with complete tub/shower bathroom. Mr. Macintyre organizes a series of concerts, plays, and recitals to entertain his guests.

In 2003, Mr. Macintyre closed down the on-site restaurant (which till then had been open to nonresidents of his hotel), and began insisting that all overnight guests (and *only* his overnight guests) participate in the evening dinner ritual. This is conducted family-style, with a predetermined (and predefined) dinner menu that's shared, by all parties, as part of the general house-party atmosphere.

The hotel is a licensed theater, and performances are presented September to March.

1–3 Viewfield St., Nairn, Nairnshire IV4 4HW. © **01667/453-119**. Fax 01667/452-836. www.cliftonhousenairn.co.uk. 8 units. £220 ($418) double. Rates include Scottish breakfast and dinner. AE, DC, MC, V. Turn east of the town roundabout on A96. **Amenities:** Restaurant for guests; nonsmoking rooms. *In room:* Coffeemaker, hair dryer, no phone.

Greenlawns *(Value* This Victorian house, within easy reach of the beaches and golf courses, is a pleasant base for touring the Loch Ness region. The owners have completely refurbished Greenlawns while retaining its traditional charm. All the good-size guest rooms are nonsmoking and come with showers or large tubs.

13 Seafield St., Nairn IV12 4HG. © **01667/452-738**. Fax 01667/452-738. www.greenlawns.uk.com. 7 units. £41–£70 ($78–$133) double. Rates include Scottish breakfast. AE, MC, V. Turn down Albert St. from A96. **Amenities:** Restaurant; bar; nonsmoking rooms. *In room:* TV, coffeemaker, safe (in some), no phone.

WHERE TO DINE

The Boath House Restaurant ✦✦ SCOTTISH/CONTINENTAL   Located in a Georgian mansion, this restaurant has won numerous awards. Traditional Scottish fare is given a Continental twist to create a well-balanced menu that changes daily. The atmosphere is romantic with antique decor, and in the evening, the room is bathed in candlelight. Menu items might include seared filet of sea bass on a citrus couscous, tapenade, and a basil-infused oil; or roasted gray-legged partridge with a ragout of red cabbage and onion. There is also a good selection of wines.

In the Boath House, Auldearn. ℂ **01667/454-896.** Reservations recommended. Fixed-price 5-course dinner £45 ($86). AE, DC, MC, V. Daily 7–8:30pm. Closed Mon–Tues to nonguests. On A96, 3.2km (2 miles) east of Nairn.

Cawdor Tavern MODERN SCOTTISH   This atmospheric restaurant occupies what was built as a stone-sided carpenter shop for Cawdor Castle, fewer than 150m (500 ft.) away. Many visitors opt for just a drink, choosing any of the single-malt whiskies that adorn the bar. Others come for the food, served in generous portions with a focus on local produce and regional fish and meats. Examples include breast of guinea fowl on a bed of noodles or seared scallops on black pudding with apple jelly and chile oil.

The Lane, Cawdor. ℂ **01667/404-777.** Reservations recommended for dinner. Main courses lunch £7–£12 ($13–$23), dinner £10–£18 ($19–$34). AE, DC, MC, V. Daily noon–2:30pm and 5:30–9pm.

NAIRN AFTER DARK

Locals gather to drink and talk at the **Claymore House Hotel Bar,** Seabank Road (ℂ **01667/453-731**). During cold weather, an open fireplace takes the chill out of the air, as does the selection of malt whiskies. The **Millford Hotel Pub,** Mill Road (ℂ **01667/453-854**), features free live music on Saturday, mainly middle-of-the-road country, pop, blues, or folk bands. Once a month, there's a country-western night with dancing.

   Clifton House, 1–3 Viewfield St. (ℂ **01667/453-119**), offers classical concerts by solo artists and small ensembles about once every 3 weeks between September and March.

8 The Black Isle Peninsula ✦

Cromarty: 37km (23 miles) NW of Inverness (via Kessock Bridge)

The Black Isle is one of Scotland's most enchanting peninsulas, a land rich in history, beauty, and mystery. Part of Ross and Cromarty County, it's northwest of Inverness, a 20-minute drive or bus ride away. A car tour would be about 60km (37 miles), but allow plenty of time for stops and country walks along the way.

   There's much confusion about the name of the peninsula, because it's neither black nor an island. In summer, the land is green and fertile, with tropical plants flourishing. It has forests, fields of broom and whin, and scattered coastal villages. The peninsula has been inhabited for 7,000 years, as 60-odd prehistoric sites testify. Pictish kings, whose thrones passed down through the female line, once ruled this land. Then the Vikings held sway, and the evidence of many gallows hills testifies to their harsh justice.

ESSENTIALS

GETTING THERE   The nearest **rail service** goes to Inverness. From there, the High-land Bus and Coach Company serves the peninsula (nos. 26, 26A, and 126), making stops at North Kessock, Munlochy, Avoch, Fortrose, Rosemarkie, and Cromarty. **Buses** depart from Farraline Park in Inverness (ℂ **01463/233-371** for schedules).

If you're **driving,** head to Fortrose as your first stop (see below), taking A9 north from Inverness. (Follow the signs toward Wick.) Stay on A9 for 6.5km (4 miles), until you see the Kessock Bridge. Go over the bridge and take the second road to the right, toward Munlochy. (Fortrose is 13km/8 miles from this turnoff.) Follow A832 through Munlochy, and at the junction take the road right, signposted Fortrose. Continue straight through Avoch to Fortrose.

VISITOR INFORMATION   Ask at the **Inverness tourist office** (see "Inverness: Capital of the Highlands," earlier in this chapter) for details on Black Isle, because the peninsula is often included on a day tour from that city.

NORTH KESSOCK

Your gateway to the Black Isle, the village of North Kessock lies 7.8km (5 miles) from Inverness on the south coast at the narrows where the Beauly Firth becomes the Moray Firth. The village is directly opposite Inverness. North Kessock is bypassed by the A9 which crosses the Kessock Bridge, which means it's rather peaceful and spared heavy traffic.

The village is a well-known spot for watching bottlenose dolphins, which live in the Moray Firth—and are, in fact, the most northerly group of bottlenose dolphins in the world.

Most of the village lies along its Main Street, which could be a base for food and lodging if you're touring Black Isle.

WHERE TO STAY & DINE

North Kessock Hotel *Value*   This is a family-run hotel, overlooking Beauly Firth, the Kessock Bridge, and Ben Wyvis mountain. Established back in the early 1980s, it offers good value and is a suitable choice for comfortable accommodations, or else good food and drink. The hotel provides binoculars for dolphin spotting, and there is also a well-kept garden and terrace.

Each accommodation is furnished in a modern style with a choice of sea or garden views. Even if you're not staying here, consider stopping for a meal as the hotel kitchen serves the best food in the area, the menu based on fresh local produce. Many of its dishes are international, although some are pure Scottish such as breast of chicken stuffed with haggis and served with a whisky and mushroom cream sauce. An average meal here costs £20 ($38).

Main St., North Kessock IV1 3XN. *©* **01463/731-208.** www.north-kessock-hotel.com. 5 units. £75 ($143) double; £90 ($171) triple. Rates include breakfast. DC, MC, V. **Amenities:** Restaurant; bar. *In room:* Coffeemaker, hair dryer, iron, no phone.

FORTROSE *&* & ROSEMARKIE

Fortrose is a good place to start. Along the way, you'll pass a celebrated wishing well, or **clootie well,** festooned with rags. Dedicated to St. Boniface, the well dates back to pagan times. It's said that anyone removing a rag will inherit the misfortunes of the person who placed it there.

The ruins of **Fortrose Cathedral** stand in this sleepy village. Founded in the 13th century, the cathedral was dedicated to St. Peter and St. Boniface. You can still see fine detailing from the 14th century. If the stones scattered about don't seem adequate enough to fill in the gaps, it's because Cromwell's men removed many of them to help build a fort in Inverness. There are no formal hours; you can wander through the ruins at any time.

Fortrose adjoins **Rosemarkie,** up the road. The site has been inhabited since the Bronze Age. A center of Pictish culture, the town saw the arrival of the first Christian missionaries. It's reported that St. Moluag founded a monastery here in the 6th century. Rosemarkie became a royal burgh in 1216. The twin hamlets share a golf course today, and they're the site of the Chanonry Sailing Club, whose annual regatta brings entries from all over Scotland. Right beyond Rosemarkie is the mysterious **Fairy Glen,** signposted at the end of the village. It's one of the loveliest places in the Black Isle for a long walk.

Also at Rosemarkie is the **Groam House Museum,** High Street (© 01381/620-961), which tells the story of the region from prehistoric times. The museum's main exhibit is 15 carved Pictish stones, some dating back to the 8th century A.D. when the area was a major center of early Christianity. The pride of the collection is the **Rosemarkie cross-slab** 🌟🌟, decorated with enigmatic Pictish symbols. Visitors can also learn about the legendary prophet, Brahan Seer, who was buried alive at Chanonry Point. The admission-free museum is open daily May to October Monday to Saturday 10am to 5pm, Sunday 2 to 4:30pm. Off season it is open Monday to Friday 2 to 4pm.

CROMARTY

Cromarty stands at the tip of the peninsula, where the North and South Sutors guard the entrance to the Cromarty Firth, the second-deepest inland-waterway estuary in Europe. Much of the Black Isle invites country walks, but in Cromarty you may want to stay in the village itself, exploring each street, with its rows of terraced cottages that seem to hunch against the prevailing north winds. The town has been handsomely restored, and the old merchants' houses are superb examples of domestic 18th-century architecture.

Once a flourishing port and a former royal burgh, the town gave the world a famous son: Hugh Miller. Born here in 1802, Miller was a stonemason as a young man, but in time he became a recognized expert in the field of geology, as well as a powerful man of letters in Scotland. **Hugh Miller's Cottage,** Church Street (© 01381/600-245), contains many of his personal belongings and collections of geological specimens. The thatched cottage was built in 1698. From Easter to September, it's open Monday through Saturday from noon to 1pm and 2 to 5pm and Sunday from 2 to 5pm; October, Sunday to Wednesday noon to 5pm. Admission is £5 ($9.50) for adults, £4 ($7.60) for students and seniors, and £8 ($15) per family.

WHERE TO STAY & DINE

Royal Hotel Cromarty   The only hotel in town sits on an embankment near one of the deepest estuaries in Europe. Around 1940, the British navy combined a series of waterfront buildings into living quarters for sailors. Today, the hotel is a cozy enclave with wood-burning stoves and open fireplaces. The guest rooms are traditionally furnished. The dining room, which spills onto a glassed-in extension overlooking the harbor, features specialties like steaks and stroganoff. You can also enjoy a good bar menu, with a tempting list of burgers, crepes, and salads. The hotel will prepare picnic or packed lunches for guests on request.

Marine Terrace, Cromarty IV11 8YN. © 01381/600-217. Fax 01381/600-813 www.royalcromartyhotel.co.uk. 10 units. £70–£80 ($133–$152) double. Rates include Scottish breakfast. AE, DC, MC, V. Bus: 26, 26A, or 126 from Inverness. **Amenities:** Restaurant; 2 bars; laundry service; nonsmoking rooms. *In room:* TV, coffeemaker, hair dryer, no phone.

9 Sutherland: The Gem of Scotland

Sutherland has more sheep than people (a 20-to-1 ratio). It's genuinely off the beaten track, but if you have time to travel this far, you'll find it perhaps the most beautiful county in Scotland. Adding to the haunting beauty are lochs and rivers, heather-covered moors and mountains—in all, 5,200 sq. km (2,000 sq. miles) of territory. It may not offer many "attractions," but it's a wonderful setting for outdoor pursuits like golf and fishing.

Sutherland, which is northwest of Inverness, has three coastlines—on the north and west, the Atlantic, and on the east, the North Sea. Most villages have only 100 or so hearty inhabitants. Sutherland was the scene of the notorious 19th-century Highland Clearances, when many residents were driven out of their ancestral crofts. Some made their way to the New World. In certain deserted glens, you still see traces of former crofting villages.

DORNOCH ✦

The ancient cathedral city of Dornoch, 101km (63 miles) northwest of Inverness and 353km (219 miles) northwest of Edinburgh, is Sutherland's major town and the area's most interesting stop. The major sightseeing attraction nearby is **Dornoch Cathedral** (see below). Dornoch is also known for its sandy beaches, which do make for lovely walks, but we find that the swimming is best left to polar bears.

A **tourist office** is at the Square (© **01862/810-400**). It's open November to March daily 10am to 1:30pm; April to May, Monday to Saturday 10am to 5pm and Sunday 10am to 4pm; June to July, Monday to Saturday 10am to 4:30pm and Sunday 10am to 4pm; August, Monday to Saturday 10am to 6pm and Sunday 10am to 4pm; September, Monday to Saturday 10am to 5pm and Sunday 10am to 4pm; and October, Monday to Saturday 10am to 5pm. From the Inverness bus station at Farraline Park, off Academy Street (call © **01463/233-371** for schedules), three local companies run daily **buses** to Dornoch: Stagecoach, Scottish Citylink, and Highland Country Buses. The trip takes between 60 and 90 minutes and costs £8 ($15) one-way.

EXPLORING THE AREA

The village of Dornoch has long been known for its golf club on the sheltered shores of Dornoch Firth, the northernmost first-class course in the world. The turf of the **Royal Dornoch Golf Club,** Golf Road (© **01862/810-219**), is considered sacred by aficionados. Golf was first played here by monks in 1614. A curious meander of the Gulf Stream as it bypasses northern Scotland keeps the climate balmier than you'd expect. The club itself was founded in 1877, and a royal charter was granted by Edward VII in 1906. Prince Andrew and the duchess of Sutherland are both members. Its SSS is 73; its par is 70 for an 18-hole yardage of 6,185. Greens fees are from £52 to £88 ($99–$167). Golf club and trolley rentals are £20 to £25 ($38–$48) and £3 ($5.70), respectively. Caddy service is available for £35 ($67) plus tip.

Dornoch Cathedral, Castle Street, was built in the 13th century and partially destroyed by fire in 1570. It has undergone many restorations, but you can still see its fine 13th-century stonework. The cathedral is famous for its modern stained-glass windows—three are in memory of Andrew Carnegie, the American steel king. The cathedral is open daily from 9am to dusk. The **Plaiden Ell,** found in the cathedral's cemetery where a marketplace used to be, was a medieval method for measuring cloth. (An *ell* was a unit of measure equaling about 96cm/38 in.) The Ell is carved in stone in a flat shape similar to a tombstone's, but with two pieces of metal rising about 5 centimeters (2 in.) above the level of the stone. The distance between those two pieces of metal is an ell. In one of the gardens is the 1722 **witch's stone** marking the spot where the last burning of a so-called witch took place in Scotland.

If the weather is fair, Dornoch is great for country strolls—the town is flanked by miles of clean sand opening onto chilly waters. You often see migrant birds on these beaches. At **Embo,** some 5km (3 miles) north of the beaches of Dornoch, are the remains of two funereal vaults believed to date from around 2000 B.C.

Three kilometers (2 miles) north of Embo are the shores of lovely **Loch Fleet,** where there's a meager ruin of **Skelbo Castle.** It's now on a lonely grassy mound, but in the 14th century Skelbo was a powerful fortification.

Shoppers should check out the **Dornoch Craft Centre,** Town Jail, Castle Street (© **01862/810-555**), in the center of town opposite the cathedral. You can wander through the selection of crafts, jewelry, and pottery, and then visit the Textile Hall and browse through the range of knitwear, tartans, mohair goods, and tweeds.

WHERE TO STAY

Carnegie Club at Skibo Castle ⭐⭐⭐   Skibo Castle is as massive a baronial house as you're likely to find in Scotland, an Edwardian pile created from a unique combination of Scottish heritage and one of the most potent fortunes of the Industrial Revolution. Steel magnate Andrew Carnegie, who emigrated from Scotland's textile mills to America in the mid–19th century, yearned for a return to the land of his birth after he acquired his fortune. In 1898, after he bought the historic but dilapidated Skibo, 8km (5 miles) east of Dornoch, Carnegie and his second wife, Louise, massively enlarged the place, pouring £2 million ($3.8 million) into its refurbishment. Here they welcomed a stream of distinguished visitors, including Edward VII, during the months they spent in Scotland in their final years.

In 1990, Peter de Savary, the force behind posh semiprivate clubs in London and Antigua, acquired the property and its 2,835 hectares (7,000 acres), installed an 18-hole golf course designed by Donald Steel, and created a resort that's a combination golf mecca and semiprivate club for the celebs, CEOs, and aristocrats who can afford the sky-high rates. You may visit only once as a guest, then you must be a guest of a member. Meals are served at a long table in the style of an Edwardian house party. Evenings of Scottish dance are featured every Saturday; other nights, there are dinner performances of Scottish flute, Celtic harp, or piano. Sports opportunities include trap and skeet shooting, falconry, trout and salmon fishing, and golf (on the resort's course or at the nearby Royal Dornoch Course). *Note:* All rooms at Skibo are now nonsmoking.

Skibo Castle, Dornoch IV25 3RQ. © **01862/894-600.** Fax 01862/894-601. www.carnegieclub.co.uk. 21 units. £710 ($1,349) double members; £1,115 ($2,119) double nonmembers. Rates include meals, drinks, and sporting activities (including greens fees at the resort's golf course). Membership is currently closed but interested parties can place their names on waiting list. AE, DC, MC, V. The club will send a car to Dornoch or anywhere in Inverness to meet new arrivals. **Amenities:** Restaurant (guests only); indoor pool; golf course; tennis court; spa; children's activities; room service (7am–10:30pm); babysitting. *In room:* TV, hair dryer.

Dornoch Castle Hotel   This unusual hotel, close to the Royal Dornoch Golf Course, occupies what was once the residence of the bishops of Caithness, built of stone in the center of town in the late 15th or early 16th century. Today, its winding stairs, labyrinthine corridors, and impenetrable cellars have been converted into a well-directed hotel and restaurant. The guest rooms are in the original building and an extension overlooking the garden; all tend to be dowdy, however. Most bathrooms contain a combination tub/shower. Restaurant specialties include leg of Sutherland lamb with onion marmalade and Highland Estate venison with black currants. Reservations are suggested.

Castle St., Dornoch IV25 3SD. © **01862/810-216.** Fax 01862/810-981. www.dornochcastlehotel.com. 18 units. £82–£165 ($156–$314) double. Rates include Scottish breakfast. AE, MC, V. **Amenities:** Restaurant; bar; nonsmoking rooms. *In room:* TV.

The Far North

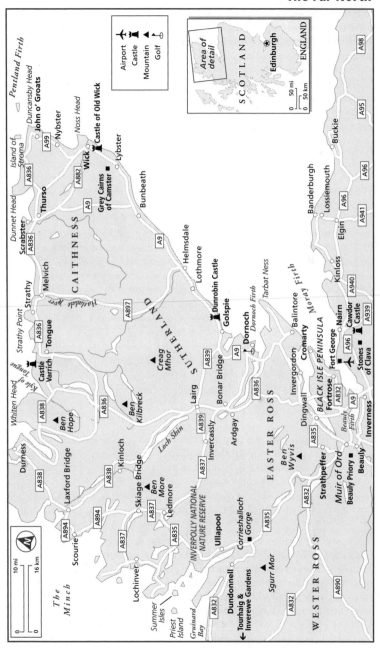

WHERE TO DINE

Sutherland House SCOTTISH   Although hardly in the gourmet range of 2 Quail (see below), this long-established restaurant is the best choice for a traditional "taste of Scotland," menu, including the inevitable haggis and the freshest of seafood. A wide range of dishes, including the best of Scottish beefsteak, is offered, and there is also an extensive vegetarian menu. The fresh mussels are always superb, as is the supreme of chicken Glenmorangie. The saddle of venison is a winner, and it's followed with one of the homemade desserts which are made fresh daily.

Argyle Street. ✆ **01862/811-023.** Main courses £8.50–£15 ($16–$29). MC, V. Daily noon–2:30pm and 5:30–9:30pm.

2 Quail ★★★ *Finds* SCOTTISH/CONTINENTAL   At this renovated Victorian Highland town house, you may be served your greatest meal north of Inverness. In an elegant, book-lined setting, with only a dozen covers, the restaurant is self-billed as "The Smallest Golf Hotel & Restaurant in Scotland." It also rents three rooms if you'd like to overnight here. Michael and Kerensa Carr—he trained at London's Ritz Hotel—preside over a restaurant that serves intriguing dishes with a high level of skill and sensitivity, creating tasty fare using market-fresh, quality ingredients.

The four-course set menu changes nightly but might begin delectably with smoked pheasant salad with a blueberry and walnut dressing, and then follow with West Coast scallops in a Thai broth. For a main course, a faultlessly prepared roast best end of Ross-shire lamb might arrive at table with Provençal style vegetables and a thyme gravy. Dessert might be a vanilla bavarois with a raspberry coulis, followed with selected cheese with crackers and oatcakes. The homemade ice creams here have been called "seriously classy—far too good for children."

The trio of nonsmoking bedrooms is tastefully furnished with feather duvet-covered beds, power showers, and comfortable, wooden natural grain furnishings. Rates range from £80 to £100 ($152–$190) in a double.

Castle St. ✆ **01862/811-811.** Reservations required. Fixed-price 4-course menu £39 ($74). AE, MC, V. Apr–Oct 7:30– 9:30pm. Off season Fri–Sat 7:30–9:30pm.

GOLSPIE

This family resort town with a golf course sits on A9 and looks out across the water to the Dornoch Firth, with a crescent of sandy beach. Golspie, 367km (228 miles) northwest of Edinburgh and 116km (72 miles) northwest of Inverness, is visited chiefly because of its towering Dunrobin Castle.

Dunrobin Castle ★   Home of the earls and dukes of Sutherland, Dunrobin is not only the most northerly of Scotland's great houses but also the biggest in the northern Highlands, dating in part from the early 13th century. Its formal gardens are laid out in the manner of Versailles. On the grounds is a museum containing many relics from the Sutherland family. Some of the castle's 180 rooms are open to the public—the ornately furnished dining room, a billiard room, and the room and gilded four-poster bed where Queen Victoria slept when she visited in 1872.

Golspie, Sutherland KW10 6SF. 1km (½ mile) northeast of Golspie on A9. ✆ **01408/633-177.** Admission £7 ($13) adults, £6 ($11) students and seniors, and £5 ($9.50) children 5–16. Apr–May and Oct Mon–Sat 10:30am–4:30pm, Sun noon–4:30pm; June–Sept Mon–Sat 10:30am–5:30pm. Last entrance 30 min. before closing.

WHERE TO STAY & DINE

Golf Links Hotel   The best place to stay in Golspie dates from the early 1900s, when it was built as the stone rectory for the local minister. Many of the guests are golfers drawn to the nearby Golspie, Royal Dornoch, and Brora courses. The rooms in the main building are well furnished, each with a midsize bathroom. Scottish and Continental cuisine are served in a dining room with a view of Ben Bhraggie.

Church St., Golspie KW10 6TT. (✆ 01408/633-408. Fax 01408/634-184. www.golflinkshotel.co.uk. 9 units. £65 ($124) double. Rates include Scottish breakfast. MC, V. **Amenities:** Restaurant; 2 bars; tour desk; laundry service; nonsmoking rooms. *In room:* TV, coffeemaker, hair dryer, iron, Wi-Fi, no phone.

TONGUE

Heading north along A836, you cross high moors and brooding peaks to Tongue, 414km (257 miles) northwest of Edinburgh and 163km (101 miles) northwest of Inverness. For the nature lover and hiker, there's a lot to see, from the mighty cliffs of **Clo Mor,** near Cape Wrath (known for its large colonies of puffins), to waterfalls like **Eas-Coul-Aulin** (the highest in Britain) and the **Falls of Shin,** where you can see salmon leap. Masses of land, like **Ben Loyal** (known as the queen of Scottish mountains), suddenly rise from a barren landscape. Any of the district's tourist offices, including the one in Dornoch, can provide a map of the local hills, valleys, and trails. The one closest to the above-mentioned trekking sites is the office on Main Street in Bettyhill (✆ **01641/521-342**), a coastal village about 24km (15 miles) from Tongue.

West of Tongue, on a promontory, stand the ruins of **Castle Varrich,** said to have been built by the Vikings. Possibly dating from the 14th century, this castle was the Mackay stronghold. This is a great place for a walk.

A rather dramatic hike from the center is to the **Kyle of Tongue,** crossed by a narrow causeway. Protected from the wild and raging sea nearby, this is a long, shallow inlet. At low tide, wearing a pair of boots, you can wade out to Rabbit Island, lying at the mouth of Kyle of Tongue. You pass towering cliffs, sandy bays, odd rock formations, and deserted rocky islets that time has seemingly forgotten.

WHERE TO STAY & DINE

Ben Loyal Hotel   This is a good choice, with everything under the careful attention of Paul and Elaine Lewis. The guest rooms are a bit plain but comfortably furnished in traditional style, with shower-only bathrooms and electric blankets. Several superior rooms have four-poster beds and views over the castle ruins and loch. Home-cooked meals feature local beef and produce grown on the grounds. A fine wine list and an assortment of malt whiskies complement the cuisine. The Ben Loyal incorporates 19th-century stables, a former post office, a shop, and a village bakery.

Main St., Tongue IV27 4XE. (✆ **01847/611-216**. Fax 01847/611-336. www.benloyal.co.uk. 11 units. £70–£80 ($133–$152) double. Rates include breakfast. MC, V. **Amenities:** Restaurant; bar; nonsmoking rooms. *In room:* TV, coffeemaker, hair dryer.

Tongue Hotel 🐾   Since Queen Victoria's day, the best place to stay in town has been the Tongue Hotel, 1.6km (1 mile) north of the village center beside the road leading to Durness. Built of gray stone in the baronial style in 1850, it began as a hunting lodge for the duke of Sutherland. The hotel opens onto the Kyle of Tongue and still possesses much of its original character. Both the public rooms and the guest rooms are decorated in Victorian style, with flowered curtains and well-upholstered furniture. Most of the bathrooms are equipped with tub/shower combinations.

The quality of the food is well known locally. A hearty, moderately priced dinner usually includes a choice of game or fresh fish caught in the region. Affordable bar meals are served in the popular pub, with an open fireplace and impressive collection of whiskies, and in the more sedate cocktail lounge.

Tongue, Sutherland IV27 4XD. (*C*) **01847/611-206.** Fax 01847/611-345. www.scottish-selection.co.uk. 19 units. £90–£120 ($171–$228) double. Rates include Scottish breakfast. MC, V. **Amenities:** Restaurant; 2 bars; laundry service; nonsmoking rooms. *In room:* TV, coffeemaker, hair dryer.

10 Caithness: Unspoiled Country

It doesn't look like the Highlands at all, but Caithness is the northernmost county of mainland Scotland, where the ancient landscape is gentle and rolling. Within its 1,820 sq. km (700 sq. miles) you find traces of the Stone Age—the enigmatic **Grey Cairns of Camster** date from 4000 B.C. The county is filled with cairns, mysterious stone rows and circles, and standing stones. The Vikings once occupied this place, with its rock stacks, old harbors, craggy cliffs, and quiet coves, and many place names are in Old Norse. It has churches from the Middle Ages, as well as towering castles on cliff tops. The Queen Mother's home, the **Castle of Mey,** dating from 1570, is between John o' Groats and Thurso.

Rich in bird and animal life, Caithness is unspoiled country. Fishing draws people to the area: Wild brown trout are found in some 100 lochs, along with salmon in the Thurso and Wick rivers. Most people head for Caithness with **John o' Groats** as their final destination. John o' Groats is popularly called the extreme northern tip of the British mainland. Actually, Dunnet Head is farther north by a few kilometers.

Scrabster, a ferry harbor, is the main car-and-passenger service that operates all year to the Orkney Islands (see chapter 13 for more information). There are day trips in summer.

WICK

The famous old herring port of Wick, on the eastern coastline of Caithness, 462km (287 miles) northwest of Edinburgh and 203km (126 miles) northwest of Inverness, is a popular stop for those heading north to explore what's often called the John o' Groats Peninsula. The town has some claim as a holiday resort as well: Robert Louis Stevenson spent part of his boyhood in Wick when his father worked here on an engineering project. Today, a sleepy nostalgia hangs over the town. There's daily bus and rail service from Inverness, from which train connections are possible via Edinburgh, Glasgow, or Stirling.

At **Caithness Glass,** Airport Industrial Estates (*C* **01955/602-286**), you can watch glassblowing and tour the factory Monday to Friday 9am to 5pm. The shop and restaurant are open Monday to Saturday 9am to 5pm (Sat to 5pm June–Sept). The **Wick Heritage Centre,** 20 Bank Row (*C* **01955/605-393**), has many exhibits pertaining to Wick's herring-fishing industry in days of yore. From Easter to October, it's open Monday to Saturday 10am to 5pm; last entrance is at 3:45pm. Admission is £3 ($5.70) for adults and 50p (95¢) for children 5 to 16.

Visitors are welcome at **Pulteney Distillery,** Huddart Street (*C* **01955/602-371;** www.oldpulteney.com). A tour will take you on a journey back to discover the history and "art" of whisky making. A wide range of products, including single malts produced on site, are for sale in the distillery shop. Costing £3.50 ($6.65), tours are offered Monday to Friday at 11am and again at 2pm.

The most visited sites in the area are the two megalithic **Grey Cairns of Camster,** 10km (6 miles) north of Lybster on the Watten Road off A9. The ruins of the **Castle of Old Wick** are also worth exploring, and they're always accessible. The location is off A9, 2.5km (1½ miles) south of Wick. Once known as Castle Olipant, the ruined structure dates back to the 14th century. You can still see three floors of the old castle rising on a rocky promontory.

WHERE TO STAY & DINE

Breadalbane House Hotel   This 1891 building on the southern outskirts of town, a 5-minute walk from the center, was once the home of a furniture maker. It's now an unpretentious guesthouse with traditionally decorated rooms. You can dine in the restaurant or in the cozy bar. Food offerings vary from curries and steaks to a traditional roast dinner served on weekends.

20 Breadalbane Crescent, Wick KW1 5AQ. © **01955/603-911.** Fax 01955/603-911. www.breadalbanehouse.com. 10 units, 7 with private bathroom. £50–£60 ($95–$114) double. Rates include Scottish breakfast. AE, MC, V. **Amenities:** Restaurant; 2 bars; babysitting; nonsmoking rooms. *In room:* TV, coffeemaker, no phone.

Mackay's   This refurbished hotel on the south shore of the River Wick is the home of the Lamont family, who have welcomed guests for more than 40 years. All bedrooms are tastefully decorated and provide well-maintained shower-only bathrooms. Located in the heart of Wick, the hotel is a short walk to the Heritage Center as well as the swimming pool and leisure center. The restaurant, specializing in traditional Scottish fare, offers fixed-price five-course meals.

Union St. (opposite Caithness General Hospital), Wick KW1 5ED. © **800/528-1234** or 01955/602-323. Fax 01955/605-930. www.mackayshotel.co.uk. £90 ($171) double; £125 ($238) family room. Rates include breakfast. AE, MC, V. Closed Jan 1–2. **Amenities:** Restaurant; 2 bars; nonsmoking rooms. *In room:* TV, coffeemaker, hair dryer.

JOHN O' GROATS

John o' Groats, 27km (17 miles) north of Wick, is the northern equivalent of Land's End, at the tip of the Cornish peninsula in England. The southern tip of England is 1,414km (878 miles) south of John o' Groats. From here, there are views north to the Orkney Islands and the Pentland Firth.

John o' Groats was named after a Dutch ferryman, Jan de Groot. His tombstone can still be seen at Cabisbay Church. The town abounds with souvenir shops, some selling small Arctic cowrie shells once used as decoration by the first settlers in Caithness. You can take interesting walks along the coast to **Duncansby Head,** 3km (2 miles) east—one of the most dramatic coastlines in this part of Scotland. Many species of sea birds, especially puffins, live among the jagged cliffs. A road leads out to a lighthouse suspended on the cliffs; from here you get a panoramic view over Pentland Firth. These turbulent waters have been a nightmare to mariners, with some 400 wrecks reported in the past century and a half.

The late Queen Mother's legacy to Scotland is the restored **Castle of Mey** ⭐⭐, lying 9.6km (6 miles) west of John o'Groats on A836 (© **01847/851-473**). Her Majesty first saw the castle in 1952 when she was mourning the death of her husband, King George VI; hearing that it was to be abandoned, she set out to restore both the castle and its gardens. She returned every summer for the rest of her life, and one of her heirs, Prince Charles, now follows in her footsteps.

Overlooking Pentland Firth and the Orkney Islands, the castle was constructed on a Z-plan between 1566 and 1572, with jutting towers and corbelled turrets. It was built by the 4th Earl of Caithness and remained the seat of this royal family for a century. The castle is furnished just as it was when the Queen Mother departed it. You can even see her gumboots beside the dog bowl and her blue coat hanging on the back of a chair. The walled kitchen garden in July is one of the most beautiful private gardens in Scotland.

The castle and gardens are open from May 1 to July 26 and August 8 to September 30 from 10:30am to 4pm daily. Admission is £7.50 ($14) for adults, £6.50 ($12) for students, and £3 ($5.70) for children 12 and under, with a family ticket costing £19 ($36). Allow 1½ hours for a visit.

In summer, there's daily passenger-only ferry service to Orkney. Bus tours of the island are included. The Orkney Islands are just a 45-minute sail from John o' Groats across the Pentland Firth (see chapter 13).

WHERE TO STAY & DINE

Seaview Hotel   The Seaview is a family-run hotel whose severe and streamlined sides rise abruptly from a flat, windswept landscape beside the town's only highway. Built in the 1950s, it's covered with roughly textured white stucco that locals refer to as pebble dash. Each guest room is rather austere but comfortable, with a shower-only bathroom and electric blanket. Bar lunches and dinners draw an appreciative crowd to the pub. Main courses in the restaurant are moderately priced.

John o' Groats KW1 4YR. (℃)/fax **01955/611-220**. www.seaviewhoteljohnogroats.com. 9 units, 5 with private bathroom. £40–£50 ($76–$95) double. Rates include Scottish breakfast. MC, V. **Amenities:** Restaurant; bar. *In room:* TV, coffeemaker, no phone.

THURSO

Many visitors drive through the northern port of Thurso as they're heading for Scrabster, where ferries leave for the Orkney Islands (see chapter 13). The town, located on the River Thurso, is only mildly interesting; it is used mainly as a refueling stop for those who have made it this far north. It remains a big, bustling holiday resort with a still-active fishing fleet. In the center, many restored sandstone town houses date from the 1700s.

Once an important Viking stronghold, Thurso—meaning "river of the god Thor"—had its greatest power and prestige in the 11th century, when it was ruled by Thorfinn, who had defeated King Duncan's nephew in 1040. In medieval times, Thurso became the major trading town between Scotland and the Norse countries.

To the west are the cliffs of Holborn Head and Dunnet Head, which boast a lighthouse. Many visitors walk out to the northern point of mainland Britain for its panoramic views of the Orkneys. Thurso is 214km (133 miles) northwest of Inverness, 34km (21 miles) northwest of Wick, and 32km (20 miles) west of John o Groats.

If you'd like to explore by bike, head for **Sandra's Back Packer Hostel,** 24 Princes St. (℃ **01847/894-575**). Open daily 9am to midnight. Rental rates are from £9 ($17) per bed, per night.

For information on Thurso, visit the **tourist office** at Riverside (℃ **01847/892-371**), open April to October, Monday to Saturday 10am to 5pm and Sunday 10am to 4pm.

The Arts in John O' Groats

In an old converted country school, the **Lyth Arts Centre** (℃ **01955/641-270**) stages year-round performances of innovative and experimental works by small touring companies, from drama and dance to jazz, folk, and new music. There's also a permanent collection of art related to northern Scotland, and July and August bring touring exhibits of contemporary art, photography, and some crafts. Exhibits are open daily from 10am to 6pm; admission is £2 ($3.80) for adults, £1 ($1.90) seniors, and 50p (95¢) for students and children. Performances usually start at 8pm. Advance booking is necessary for all shows, so call ahead. Tickets cost £10 ($19) for adults, £8 ($15) for seniors, and £6 ($11) for students and children. Coffee, tea, and light snacks are available on performance evenings. The arts center is signposted, 6.5km (4 miles) off A99 between Wick and John o' Groats.

WHERE TO STAY & DINE

The Park Hotel   With an almost Scandinavian style, this hotel offers comfortable, adequately furnished rooms with small shower-only bathrooms; eight units can accommodate families. Guests receive a warm reception and friendly service. Both the lounge and restaurant offer reasonably priced meals accompanied by a fine selection of wines, beers, and malt whiskies. High tea is served as well.

Thurso KW14 8RE. ℂ **01847/893-251.** Fax 01847/804-044. www.parkhotelthurso.co.uk. 21 units. £80 ($152) double. Rates include full Scottish breakfast. AE, DC, MC, V. Closed Jan 1–3. Located on the right-hand side of the A9 on approach to the Thurso town center. **Amenities:** Restaurant; 2 bars; nonsmoking rooms. *In room:* TV, coffeemaker, hair dryer, iron.

The Weigh Inn & Lodges ⍟   This is the most modern hotel in the far north of Scotland, overlooking the Pentland Firth with panoramic views that extend (on a clear day) to the Orkney Islands. It's on the outskirts of Thurso, at the junction of the A9 to Scrabster Harbour and the main artery leading to the western coast of the Highlands. Many travelers planning to take the morning car ferry to the Orkney Islands stay overnight here. The wide variety of accommodations includes doubles, twins, singles, and even family rooms. Some bathrooms contain showers only.

Burnside, Thurso KW14 TUG. ℂ **01847/893-722.** Fax 01847/892-112. www.weighinn.co.uk. 16 units. £50–£85 ($95–$162) double. MC, V. **Amenities:** Restaurant; bar; nonsmoking rooms. *In room:* TV, coffeemaker, iron.

ULLAPOOL ⍟

Ullapool is an interesting village, the largest in Wester Ross, 95km (59 miles) northwest of Inverness and 383km (238 miles) north of Glasgow. It was built by the British Fishery Society in 1788 as a port for herring fishers and is still a busy harbor. The original town plan hasn't been changed, and many of the buildings look much as they did at the time of their construction. Ullapool has long been an embarkation point for travelers crossing the Minch, a section of the North Atlantic separating Scotland from the Outer Hebrides.

EXPLORING THE AREA

One of our favorite towns in this region of Scotland, Ullapool was founded on the lovely shores of the salt water **Loch Broom.** The site of the ferry docks for the island of Lewis, Ullapool remains a bustling fishing station. It's also the best embarkation point for trips to the Summer Isles (see below).

One of the most dramatic and scenic drives in this part of Scotland is from Ullapool to the village of Lochiner (a 64km/40-mile run north following the signposts). Take A835 north from Ullapool, enjoying the views of Loch Broom as you go along. You'll pass the hamlet of Armair on Loch Kanaird, then come to the **Inverpolly National Nature Reserve** of some 10,935 hectares (27,000 acres), including lochs and lochans along with the peaks of Cul Mor at 849m (2,786 ft.), Cul Beag at 769m (2,523 ft.), and Stac Pollaidth at 612m (2,010 ft.).

At **Knockan,** 24km (15 miles) north of Ullapool, a signposted nature trail along the cliff offers the most dramatic views in the area and is the best place to observe the regional flora, fauna, and geology.

At the Ledmore junction, take A837 to the left, passing along **Loch Awe,** with the mountain peaks of Canisp at 847m (2,779 ft.) and Ben More Assynt at 984m (3,230 ft.) forming a backdrop. You'll reach the lovely 10km-long (6-mile) **Loch Assynt.** The road along this lake-dotted landscape eventually carries you to **Lochiner,** a hamlet with fewer than 300 souls. It's known for its scenery, sandy coves, and crofting communities. For tourist information, call ℂ **01854/612-135.**

There are a number of day trips you can take from Ullapool, including a jaunt to the **Corrieshalloch Gorge,** 19km (12 miles) southeast, a nature reserve along A835 at Braemore. From this point, the Falls of Measach plunge 45m (150 ft.) into a 1.6km-long (1-mile) wooded gorge. A bridge over the chasm and a viewing platform offer a panoramic way to enjoy this spectacular scenery.

Another interesting excursion is to the **Inverewe Gardens** (✆ 01445/781-200). An exotic mix of plants from the South Pacific, the Himalayas, and South America gives the gardens year-round color. They can be reached along A832, 10km (6 miles) northeast of Gairloch. Open March 31 to October, daily from 9:30am to 9pm; January to March, daily from 9:30am to 4pm. Admission is £8 ($15) for adults, £5.25 ($10) for seniors and children, £16 ($30) per family.

From either Ullapool or Achiltibuie, you can take excursions in season to the **Summer Isles** 🌟🌟, a beautiful group of almost uninhabited islands off the coast. They get their name because sheep are transported here in summer for grazing; the islands are a mecca for bird-watchers. Boat schedules vary, depending on weather conditions. Information is available from the **tourist office** on Argyle Street (✆ **01854/612-135**).

WHERE TO STAY

Dromnan Guest House (Value) Mrs. MacDonald is your host at this 1970s stone guesthouse on the southern outskirts of town, a 10-minute walk from the center. The place is very well maintained, and the guest rooms are described by the kindly owner as being decorated in a combination of Marks & Spencer department-store goods and Shand-Kydd wallpapers and fabrics designed by the mother of the late Princess Diana. Each unit is equipped with a small bathroom with shower.

Garve Rd., Ullapool IV26 2SX. ✆ 01854/612-333. Fax 01854/613-364. www.dromnan.co.uk. 7 units. £54–£60 ($103–$114) double. Rates include breakfast. MC, V. **Amenities:** Access to nearby pool, tennis courts, and sauna; laundry service; nonsmoking rooms; rooms for those w/limited mobility. *In room:* TV, coffeemaker, hair dryer, Wi-Fi, no phone.

Royal Hotel The Royal sits on a knoll on the Inverness side of town, overlooking the harborfront. Graced with curved walls and large sheets of glass, it was reconstructed in 1961 from an older building, with an added east wing. It offers well-furnished guest rooms, half with balconies opening onto views of Loch Broom. All are equipped with shower-only bathrooms. Live entertainment is offered in season. Scottish fare is served in the dining area; afterward, guests sit around a log fire in the well-appointed lounge.

Garve Rd., Ullapool IV26 2SY. ✆ **01854/612-181** Fax 01854/612-951. www.royalhotel-ullapool.com. 52 units. £70–£85 ($133–$162) double. Rates include Scottish breakfast. MC, V. Closed Nov to early Mar. **Amenities:** Restaurant; 2 bars; access to nearby pool; 2 tennis courts; sauna; room service; nonsmoking rooms. *In room:* TV, coffeemaker, hair dryer (on request).

WHERE TO DINE

Mariner's Restaurant SCOTTISH/INTERNATIONAL Within the simple confines of a somewhat battered building, this restaurant serves food that is both upscale and elegant. Lunches are deceptively promoted as bar snacks, even though they include full-fledged waitress service and elaborate versions of lobster, oak-roasted smoked salmon, and haggis with black pudding. Dinners are in the same price range as lunch, but are served in a separate dining room.

On the premises are 12 motel rooms, clean and unassuming but not particularly distinctive. Doubles go for £50 to £55 ($95–$105) and come with TV and phone.

North Rd. ✆ 01854/612-161. Reservations recommended. Main courses £10–£28 ($19–$53). DC, MC, V. Daily noon–2pm and 5:30–9:30pm.

12

The Hebridean Islands

Once, the Hebridean islands were visited only by geologists, bird-watchers, and the occasional fisher or mountain climber. Today, this island chain, which makes up the Inner Hebrides, is becoming more and more accessible to the general visitor. But what about the Outer Hebrides? One of the lesser-known parts of western Europe, these are splintered, windswept islands stretching for some 209km (130 miles) from the Butt of Lewis, in the north, all the way to Barra Head, in the south. With rugged cliffs, clean beaches, archaeological treasures, and tiny bays, the Outer Hebrides lure an increasing number of visitors every year.

1 The Inner & Outer Hebrides: An Overview

THE INNER HEBRIDES If you travel to the Inner Hebrides, the chain of islands just off the west coast of the Scottish mainland, you'll be following in the footsteps of Samuel Johnson and his faithful Boswell. The **Isle of Skye** is the largest. **Mull** has wild scenery and golf courses, and just off its shores is the important **Iona,** the isle that played a major part not only in the spread of Christianity in Britain, but also in the preservation of the culture and learning of the ancient world (when it was being forgotten throughout Europe). Adventurous travelers also regularly seek out **Coll, Tyree,** and the **Isle of Colonsay,** as well as **Rhum (Rum), Eigg,** and the tiny island of **Raasay,** off Skye.

If your time is limited, we suggest you concentrate on Skye. It offers your best chance for getting the flavor of the Hebrides, all in a 2-day trip. The island's natural beauty ranges from the rugged Trotternish Peninsula to the jagged peaks of the Cuillin Hills. The Cuillins are called both Black Cuillins (the hills encircling the glacial trough of Loch Coruisk) and Red Cuillins (based on the pink granite found in the hills). A favorite of hill climbers, these often harsh mountains make for some of the grandest walks in Skye.

Our favorite drive in all the Hebrides is to the Trotternish Peninsula and northeast Skye, which you can easily tour in a day from Portree. This is only a 32km (20-mile) peninsula but is so fascinating you can easily spend a day enjoying it. The highlight of the drive is 13km (8 miles) north of Portree: the **Old Man of Storr,** a stone pinnacle standing 48m (160 ft.) high. Once at the top, you are rewarded with great views of the island.

If you have time for one more Hebridean island, make it **Mull.** From Mull you can also spend an afternoon visiting the ancient ecclesiastical center off the coast at **Iona.** Spend the morning exploring parts of Mull, including a visit to Torosay Castle and Gardens. Have lunch on Mull, and then hop over to the little island of Iona.

THE OUTER HEBRIDES At first you may feel you've come to a lunar landscape where there's a sense of timelessness. The character of the Outer Hebrides is quite different from that of the Inner Hebrides. This string of islands, stretching for 209km (130 miles), is about 64km (40 miles) off the northwest coast of Scotland, and the main islands to visit are **Lewis** and **Harris** (parts of the same island despite the different names), **North Uist, Benbecula, South Uist,** and **Barra.** The archipelago also includes some minor offshore islands. Gaelic is spoken here; its gentle cadence is said to have been the language spoken in the Garden of Eden. Presbyterianism is still very strong (in one B&B, watching TV on Sun is forbidden). Before you go, we suggest reading *Whisky Galore,* Compton Mackenzie's novel set in the Hebrides.

The islands knew 2 centuries of Viking invasions, but today are the retreat of many a disenchanted artist from the mainland. They come here, take over old crofter's cottages, and devote their days to such pursuits as pottery making and weaving. Birdwatchers flock here to see the habitats of the red-necked phalarope, corncrake, golden eagle, Arctic skua, and grayleg goose. Golfers come to play on these far-northern courses, including one at Stornoway (Lewis) and another at Askernish (South Uist). Anglers come to fish for salmon, brown trout, and sea trout.

You can see much of the dim past on these islands, including a version of Stonehenge. A good time to visit is June and July, when adults' and children's choirs compete for honors at festivals celebrating Gaelic music and poetry. All the main islands have accommodations, most of which are small, family-run guesthouses and hotels. Many are crofter's cottages that take in B&B guests, mainly in summer. Advance reservations are important.

ESSENTIALS

GETTING THERE **By Ferry** From Gourock, the ferry terminal near Glasgow, **Caledonian MacBrayne** (© **01475/650-100** for information, or 0990/650-000 for reservations) sails to 23 Scottish islands in the Firth of Clyde and the Western Isles, including Skye and Mull, as well as the Outer Hebrides. The company also offers inclusive tours ideal for visiting places well off the beaten track.

For Mull and Iona, Oban is your port. These islands are part of the Inner Hebrides and enjoy fairly good connections with the mainland. From Oban, the ferries to the offshore islands run only twice a day until summer; then there are cruises to Iona from early June to late September. For details about ferry services to Mull, Iona, and the Outer Hebrides, get in touch with Caledonian MacBrayne's Oban office (© **08705/ 650-000**). It sails to 24 islands, with fares ranging from £35 ($67) per car and £3.25 ($6.20) per adult passenger for travel to Mull up to £65 ($124) per car plus £18 ($34) per adult passenger for travel to Barra. Book in advance, particularly in summer, as the ferries often sell out.

By Car If you're driving from the mainland, you can take the "Road to the Isles," heading for the Kyle of Lochalsh if your destination is Skye. The more remote Outer Hebrides are linked by car ferries from mainland ports like Ullapool (© **01854/ 612-358** in Stornoway for schedules). The main islands to visit here are Lewis and Harris.

By Air Glasgow has **air service** to the airport at Stornoway on Lewis; call British Airways (© **0845/773-3377** in Glasgow) for details.

The Hebrides

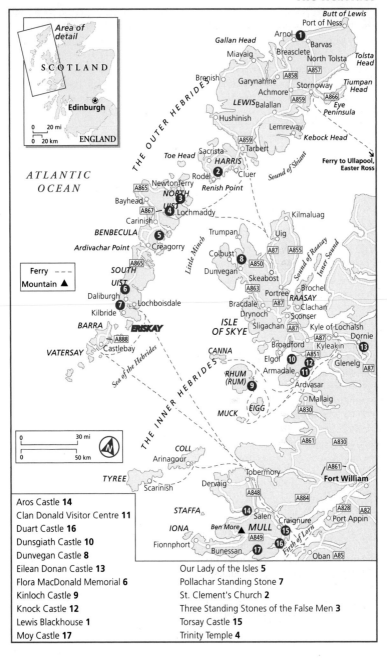

2 Kyle of Lochalsh: Gateway to the Isle of Skye

329km (204 miles) NW of Edinburgh, 132km (82 miles) SW of Inverness, 201km (125 miles) N of Oban

The popular Kyle of Lochalsh is the gateway to the island of Skye (reached by bridge). You can drive the length of Skye in a day, returning to the mainland by night if you want.

ESSENTIALS

GETTING THERE   Three **trains** per day (one on Sun) arrive from Inverness, taking about 2½ hours and costing £16 ($30) each way and £28 ($53) round-trip. Call © 08457/484-950 for schedules.

Both **Scottish Citylink** and **Skye-Ways** coaches arrive daily from Glasgow at the Kyle of Lochalsh (trip time: 5 hr.), costing £24 ($46) each way. Skye-Ways also operates three buses a day from Inverness (trip time: 2 hr.), costing £12 ($23) one-way. Call © 08705/808-080 for schedules.

If you're **driving** from Fort William, head north along A82 to Invergarry, where you cut west onto A87 to the Kyle of Lochalsh.

VISITOR INFORMATION   The **tourist office** is at the Kyle of Lochalsh Car Park (© 01599/534-276; www.highlandfreedom.com). It's open April to June, Monday to Saturday 9am to 5:30pm; July and August, Monday to Saturday 9am to 7pm and Sunday 10am to 4pm; September and October, Monday to Friday 9am to 5pm; and November to March, Monday to Friday 9am to 5pm and Saturday 10am to 4pm.

A NEARBY ATTRACTION

Eilean Donan Castle   This romantic castle was built in 1214 as a defense against the Danes. In ruins for 200 years, it was restored by Colonel MacRae, of Clan MacRae, in 1932 and is now a clan war memorial and museum, containing Jacobite relics, mostly with clan connections. A shop here sells kilts, woolens, and souvenirs.

Dornie. © 01599/555-202. Admission £4.95 ($9.40) adults, £3.95 ($7.50) seniors, students, and children, £11 ($20) per family. Apr–Oct daily 10am–5:30pm; Mar and Nov daily 10am–3:30pm. Drive 13km (8 miles) east of the Kyle of Lochalsh on A87.

WHERE TO STAY

The lodgings here are limited, just barely adequate to meet the demand for rooms.

Kyle Hotel   This modernized stone hotel in the center of town, a 5-minute walk from the train station, is your best all-around bet in the moderate category. The mid-size guest rooms are furnished in a functional style, with neatly kept bathrooms (some with shower only). The hotel serves reasonably priced dinners in the lounge nightly.

Main St., Kyle of Lochalsh IV40 8AB. © 01599/534-204. Fax 01599/534-932. www.kylehotel.co.uk. 31 units. £90–£130 ($171–$247) double. Rates include Scottish breakfast. MC, V. **Amenities:** Restaurant; 2 bars; laundry service; nonsmoking rooms. In room: TV, coffeemaker, hair dryer.

Lochalsh Hotel ⚘   This landmark hotel is the most refined nesting ground in the area. It was built as a luxury oasis when the British Railway finally extended its tracks in this direction. The hotel's crafted small-paned windows with hardwood and brass fittings will remind you of those on an oceangoing yacht. The comfortable guest rooms have been stylishly overhauled and include state-of-the-art bathrooms. Upscale dinners in the restaurant include the best Scottish cuisine and ingredients, accompanied by a panoramic view.

Ferry Rd., Kyle of Lochalsh IV40 8AF. ℂ **01599/534-202.** Fax 01599/534-881. www.lochalshhotel.com. 38 units. £70–£90 ($133–$171) double. Rates include Scottish breakfast. AE, MC, V. **Amenities:** Restaurant; bar; room service; nonsmoking rooms. *In room:* TV, coffeemaker, hair dryer.

WHERE TO DINE

The Seafood Restaurant ⭐ SEAFOOD   This blue-and-white clapboard building, from 1880, was originally a waiting room for rail passengers en route to other destinations; now it's one of the most frequented restaurants in town. The menu items are flavorful but unfussy, prepared with attention to detail. The best examples are Lochalsh langoustines in herb-flavored butter sauce and local queen scallops in white-wine sauce.

In the Railway Station. ℂ **01599/534-813.** Main courses lunch £8–£14 ($15–$27), dinner £10–£18 ($19–$34). MC, V. Mon–Fri 10am–3pm; daily 6–9pm. Closed Oct–Easter.

3 The Isle of Skye: Star of the Hebrides ⭐⭐

134km (83 miles) W of Inverness, 283km (176 miles) NW of Edinburgh, 235km (146 miles) NW of Glasgow

Off the northwest coast of Scotland, the mystical Isle of Skye, largest of the Inner Hebrides, is 77km (48 miles) long and varies between 5 and 40km (3–25 miles) wide. It's separated from the mainland by the Sound of Sleat (pronounced Slate). At Kyleakin, on the eastern end, the channel is only .5km (¼ mile) wide.

Dominating the land of summer seas, streams, woodland glens, mountain passes, cliffs, and waterfalls are the **Cuillin Hills** ⭐⭐⭐, a range of jagged black mountains that are a mecca for rock climbers. The Sleat Peninsula, the island's southernmost arm, is known as the "Garden of Skye." There are many stories about the origin of the name *Skye.* Some believe it's from the Norse *ski,* meaning "cloud," and others say it's from the Gaelic word for "winged." There are Norse names on the island, however, as the Norsemen held sway for 4 centuries before 1263. Overlooking the Kyle is the ruined **Castle Maol,** once the home of a Norwegian princess.

On the island you can explore castle ruins, *duns* (hill forts), and *brochs* (prehistoric round stone towers). For the Scots, the island will forever evoke images of Flora MacDonald, who conducted the disguised Bonnie Prince Charlie to Skye after the Culloden defeat.

ESSENTIALS

GETTING THERE   From the Kyle of Lochalsh, drive west along the bridge over the strait to Kyleakin.

VISITOR INFORMATION   The **tourist office** is at Bayfield House in Portree (ℂ **01478/612-137;** www.highlandfreedom.com). It's open April to June, Monday to Saturday 9am to 5:30pm; July to mid-August, Monday to Saturday 9am to 8pm and Sunday 10am to 4pm; mid-August to October, Monday to Saturday 9am to 5:30pm; and November to March, Monday to Friday 9am to 5pm and Saturday 10am to 4pm.

OUTDOOR PURSUITS AROUND THE ISLAND

BIKING   Gently undulating hills, coupled with good roads and a dearth of traffic, make the Isle of Skye appealing to cyclists. The island's premier rental outfits are **Island Cycles,** The Green, in the coastal city of Portree (ℂ **01478/613-121**), and **Fairwinds Bicycle Hire,** Elgol Road, Broadford (ℂ **01471/822-270**), farther inland, near the center of the island. Both charge £8 to £15 ($15–$29) a day. Island Cycles is open Monday to Saturday from 9:30am to 5pm; Fairwinds is open daily from 9am to 7pm.

BOATING   The coast of Skye is the most ruggedly beautiful this side of the Norwegian fjords, and several entrepreneurs offer boat trips letting you drink in the scenery. Foremost is **Bella Jane Boat Trips,** The Harbourfront, Elgol (© **0800/731-3089** in Britain, or 01471/866-244). From the piers in the village of Elgol, you'll board a sturdy vessel that sails daily (if there's enough business) between Easter and October into the rock-ringed borders of Loch Coruisk, at the foot of the Cuillin Hills, which are rich in bird life. Most visitors opt for the standard return trip; you're carried to the base of the hills, deposited for 90 minutes of wandering, and then returned over water to Elgol. It lasts 3 hours and costs £18 ($34) per person, £6 ($11) for children 4 to 12. If you're hardy and really interested in hiking, you can extend this experience to a full day.

GOLF   Golfing on Skye means an almost total absence supervision, weather that can rain out or dry out a game with almost no notice, and, often, a lack of players. Whether you find this charming depends on your expectations, but overall, the island's best course is the 9-hole **Isle of Skye Golf Club** (© **01478/650-414**), adjacent to the hamlet of Sconser, on the southeast coast. Maintained by the local municipality, it has a simple snack bar and pub, and an on-again–off-again employee who cuts the grass whenever necessary. Less desirable, but still prized for its convenience to residents of the **Skeabost House Hotel** (see "Skeabost Bridge," later in this chapter), is the 9-hole course associated with the hotel. Nonguests can play if they phone ahead. Greens fees at both courses are £27 ($51) for a full day's play.

HIKING   Any branch of Skye's tourist office will offer advice on the many hikes available through the heather and glens of the island. If you enjoy walking, and you're stout-hearted and fit, consider extending a boat trip on the Bella Jane (see above) with an additional 23km (14-mile) overland hike from the Cuillin Hills back to more heavily populated regions of the island. To do this, take the boat trip (one-way only) from Elgol to the Cuillin Hills. From here, brown-and-white signs direct you across an undulating, rock-strewn landscape to the Sligachan Hotel (see below), the premier hotel for trekkers. You can overnight at the hotel or take a bus or taxi the remaining 11km (7 miles) back to Portree.

KYLEAKIN

The seaport community of Kyleakin is the site of the old ferry terminal where the boats from the Scottish mainland used to arrive before Skye became linked by a bridge. Many visitors still prefer to stay here rather than on more remote, less convenient parts of the island.

Kyleakin opens onto a small bay and is dominated by a ruin, **Castle Maol,** on a jagged knoll. For a lovely walk, go from the town center up to this ruin, which dates from the 12th century, when it was a fortified stronghold of the Mackinnon clan.

WHERE TO STAY & DINE
The White Heather Hotel   These two connected buildings provide good accommodations with up-to-date amenities. For more than half a century, this family-run guesthouse, with its panoramic views of the Torridon mountains to the north, has provided accommodations to wayfarers. The small, nonsmoking guest rooms are well maintained (some with shower only) and comfortably furnished. The laundry service uses only environmentally friendly products, and, in consideration of people with allergies, no feathers are used in pillows or duvets. Moderately priced dinners are served nightly in the dining room. The lounge, licensed only to serve guests, has a pleasant view of the Castle Maol. The hotel is convenient to both the ferry dock and the bus terminals.

The Isle of Skye

The Pier, Kyleakin, Isle of Skye IV41 8PL. ☎ **01599/534-577**. Fax 01599/534-427. www.whiteheatherhotel.co.uk. 9 units. £60–£66 ($114–$125) double. Rates include Scottish breakfast. MC, V. Closed Oct–Feb. **Amenities:** Nonsmoking rooms. *In room:* TV, coffeemaker, hair dryer, no phone.

SLIGACHAN

The village of Sligachan sits at the head of a sea loch in a setting of scenic beauty with views of the Cuillin Hills (pronounced "*coo*-lin"). It's one of the best bases for exploring Skye because of its central location. Visitors enjoy sea-trout fishing, with an occasional salmon caught on the Sligachan River. It's also possible to rent a boat from the hotel below to explore the Storr Lochs, 24km (15 miles) from Sligachan, known for good brown-trout fishing from May to September.

A 10-minute drive directly west of Sligachan leads to the village of Carbost and the **Talisker Distillery,** along B8009 (☎ **01478/640-203**), opening onto the shore of Loch Harport. A distillery since 1843, the plant was mentioned by Robert Louis Stevenson in his 1880 poem *Scotsman's Return from Abroad.* Today it offers a 40-minute tour that includes a wee dram and a discount voucher to purchase a bottle of single malt. Whisky lovers from all over the world flock here, meeting members of the MacLeod clan, who make up more than half of the factory's 14 employees. The center is open Monday to Friday 9am to 5pm (off season by appointment only). Admission is £5 ($9.50). For more information, search www.scotchwhisky.com/focus/talisker.htm.

Crafts on Skye

Edinbane Pottery, on A850, 13km (8 miles) east of Dunvegan (© **01470/ 582-234**), celebrated its 30th anniversary in 2002. The three artists working in this studio produce wood-fired stoneware and salt-glazed pottery, and they can fill custom orders in a wide range of finishes.

Artist Tom Mackenzie's etchings, prints, aquatints, and greeting cards are all inspired by the scenery and day-to-day life of the island. You can find his work at **Skye Original Prints at Portree,** 1 Wentworth St. (© **01478/612-544**).

Since 1974, Stewart John Wilson has been designing and producing silver and gold jewelry, ceramic tiles, chessboards, platters, and clocks, all featuring intricate Celtic patterns. You can see his work at **Skye Silver,** in the Old School, on Glendale Road (B884), 11km (7 miles) west of Dunvegan (© **01470/ 511-263**). The selection of tiles is especially vast.

Craft Encounters, in the Post Office building in Broadford (© **01471/ 822-754**), showcases many of Skye's talented artists. You'll find pewter jewelry, stained-glass light catchers, salt-dough bric-a-brac, folk and landscape paintings, tartan ties, and handmade jumpers (sweaters). Celtic patterns show up on glassware, tableware, linens, and pieces of marquetry. The island's musical talent is represented in a selection of traditional Scottish music CDs.

Skye Batik, The Green (© **01478/613-331**), is one of the best crafts shops in Scotland. It sells wall hangings and cotton, tweed, wool, and linen clothing handprinted with Celtic designs from the 6th to the 8th centuries.

In **Harlequin Knitwear,** next to the Duisdale Hotel on Sleat (© **01471/ 833-321**), local knitter Chryssy Gibbs designs men's and women's machine-knit Shetland wool sweaters. Her work is bright and colorful.

For more knitwear, go to **Ragamuffin,** on the pier in Armadale (© **01471/ 844-217**), featuring quality Scottish, Irish, and British handknits for the whole family, as well as accessories like hats, gloves, and scarves.

WHERE TO STAY & DINE

Sligachan Hotel *Kids*   This family-run hotel is nestled at the foot of the Cuillins on the main road between Portree and Kyleakin, and is an ideal center from which to explore Skye. It's one of Skye's oldest coaching inns, built sometime in the 1830s. The guest rooms are old and a bit outdated, but still reasonably comfortable, each with a tub and shower. And the food is good, consisting of freshly caught seafood and at least one vegetarian selection served at dinner nightly. The bar also serves simple meals in front of an open fireplace, and live music is often presented. Children are welcome and there's a separate menu for them, as well as toys to keep them amused. In fact, the hotel is the most kid-friendly place on the island.

Sligachan, Isle of Skye IV47 8SW. © **01478/650-204.** Fax 01478/650-207. www.sligachan.co.uk. 21 units. £70–£100 ($133–$190) double. Rates include Scottish breakfast. MC, V. **Amenities:** Restaurant; 2 bars; room service; laundry service; nonsmoking rooms. *In room:* TV, coffeemaker, hair dryer, no phone.

PORTREE 🎖🎖

Skye's capital, Portree, is the port for steamers making trips around the island and linking Skye with the 24km-long (15-mile) island of Raasay. Sligachan, 14km (9 miles) south, and Glenbrittle, 11km (7 miles) farther southwest, are centers for climbing the Cuillin Hills.

WHERE TO STAY

Bosville Hotel   This well-established hotel stands in the center of Portree and commands panoramic views of the harbor and the Cuillin Hills. It's a bright, welcoming inn known equally for its cuisine (see The Chandlery Restaurant, below) and for its well-decorated and generally spacious bedrooms.

Bosville Terrace, Portree, Isle of Skye IV51 9DG. ✆ 01478/612-846. Fax 01478/613-434. www.bosvillehotel.co.uk. 15 units. £86–£106 ($163–$201) double; £105–£125 ($200–$238) family room; £154 ($293) suite. Rates include Scottish breakfast. AE, MC, V. **Amenities:** Restaurant; bar; room service; laundry service; dry cleaning; nonsmoking rooms. *In room:* TV, coffeemaker, hair dryer, trouser press.

The Cuillin Hills Hotel 🎖   This stone-sided manor was built in the 1820s as a hunting lodge for the MacDonald clan. Located almost 1km (½ mile) north of Portree's center, the comfortable hotel appeals to hikers and bird-watchers. Views from the guest rooms encompass the unspoiled Cuillin Hills, Portree's harbor, or the sea. Each unit is outfitted with reproductions of old-fashioned furniture against a backdrop of flowered wallpaper. Rather expensive dinners are available to both guests and nonguests who phone in advance.

Portree, Isle of Skye IV51 9LU. ✆ 01478/612-003. Fax 01478/613-092. www.cuillinhills.demon.co.uk. 27 units. Winter £120–£140 ($228–$266) double; summer £170 ($323) double. Rates include full Scottish breakfast. AE, MC, V. **Amenities:** Restaurant; bar; room service; laundry service; nonsmoking rooms. *In room:* TV, coffeemaker, hair dryer, iron, trouser press.

The Rosedale Hotel   Located in one of the more secluded parts of Portree, on the harbor and 91m (299 ft.) from the village square, The Rosedale opens directly onto the sea. It was created from a row of fishermen's dwellings dating from the reign of William IV. The midsize guest rooms in this warm and welcoming place are decorated in modern style. The dining room serves expensive Scottish fare with the requisite seafood.

The Harbour, Portree, Isle of Skye IV51 9DF. ✆ 01478/613-131. Fax 01478/612-531. www.rosedalehotelskye.co.uk. 19 units. £85–£115 ($162–$219) double. Rates include Scottish breakfast. MC, V. **Amenities:** Restaurant; bar. *In room:* TV, coffeemaker.

The Royal Hotel   The Royal stands on a hill facing the water and is said to have extended hospitality to Bonnie Prince Charlie during his 1746 flight. Back in those faraway days, the building that stood here was the old MacNab Tavern. In less dramatic circumstances, you can book one of its comfortable, small to midsize guest rooms; the preferred ones open onto the sea. Formal meals and bar snacks are offered.

Bank St., Portree, Isle of Skye IV51 9BU. ✆ 01478/612-525. Fax 01478/613-198. www.royal-hotel.demon.co.uk. 21 units. £91–£99 ($173–$188) double. Rates include Scottish breakfast. MC, V. **Amenities:** 2 restaurants; 3 bars; exercise room; spa; sauna; room service; nonsmoking rooms. *In room:* TV, coffeemaker, hair dryer.

Viewfield House 🎖 *(Finds)*   For lovers of Victoriana, this is an idyllic choice, a grand extravaganza with an equally grand portico from 200 years ago. Exotic objects from over the former British Empire adorn this house which lies in 20 acres of woodland garden. Its original charm and interior have also been preserved intact. A stay here is like a Scottish house party where guests get to know each other. Rooms are spacious and traditionally furnished. Viewfield lies only a 10-minute walk from the center of Portree.

Portree, Isle of Skye IV51 9EU. © **01478/612-217.** Fax 01478/613-517. www.skye.uk.com/viewfield. 12 units, 10 with bathroom. £80–£110 ($152–$209) double. MC, V. **Amenities:** Laundry service; communal TV; Wi-Fi. *In room:* Coffeemaker, hair dryer.

WHERE TO DINE
The Chandlery Restaurant SCOTTISH/SEAFOOD
This restaurant attracts visitors and locals alike. The highly skilled chef creates delicious, innovative dishes such as king scallops with green garlic butter and crispy bacon, rosemary roast loin of venison with fondant potatoes, puy lentils and beans with light port sauce, and a dessert of ripe pear poached in port and flavored with cinnamon, served with a tartlet of whisky, honey, and oatmeal ice cream.

In the Bosville Hotel, Bosville Terrace. © **01478/612-846.** Reservations recommended. Main courses £17–£19 ($32–$36). AE, MC, V. Daily 6–10pm.

UIG 🏵
The village of Uig is on Trotternish, the largest Skye peninsula. The ferry port for Harris and Uist in the Outer Hebrides, it's 24km (15 miles) north of Portree and 79km (49 miles) from the Kyle of Lochalsh. Many people like to anchor here because it's convenient for early departures. Uig is also one of the most beautiful places in Skye to spend the night, as it opens onto Uig Bay and is known for its **sunrises and sunsets.**

Once a virtual ruin and only of passing interest, the recently renovated **Monkstadt House,** 2.5km (1½ miles) north, is where Flora MacDonald brought Bonnie Prince Charlie after their escape from Benbecula. This famous Scottish heroine was buried in **Kilmuir churchyard,** 8km (5 miles) north.

While on the Trotternish peninsula, you can also visit the **Skye Museum of Island Life** (© 01470/552-206), at Kilmuir. The old way of island life is preserved here, along with artifacts based on farming on the crofts. Some interiors from the 18th and 19th centuries have been reconstructed. Admission is £2.50 ($4.75) for adults, £2 ($3.80) for seniors and students, and 50p (95¢) for children. From Easter to October, the museum is open Monday through Saturday from 9:30am to 5pm.

WHERE TO STAY & DINE
Ferry Inn This building was first a bank and later a post office, but today this hotel's main focus is its popular pub serving affordable meals. There are a handful of cozy guest rooms upstairs, each comfortably furnished. You'll recognize this place in the town center by its roadside design of late-Victorian gables.

Uig, Isle of Skye IV51 9XP. © **01478/611-216.** Fax 01478/611-224. www.ferryinn.co.uk. 6 units. £60 ($114) double. Rates include Scottish breakfast. MC, V. **Amenities:** Restaurant; 2 bars. *In room:* TV, coffeemaker.

DUNVEGAN
The village of Dunvegan, northwest of Portree, grew up around Skye's principal sight: **Dunvegan Castle** 🏵 (© **01470/521-206**), the seat of the chiefs of Clan MacLeod, who have lived here for 800 years. Standing on a rocky promontory and said to be Britain's oldest inhabited castle, it was once accessible only by boat, but now the moat is bridged and the castle open to the public. It contains many relics, like a "fairy flag" believed to have been given to the MacLeods by woodland spirits and reputed to have brought good luck in battle. The castle is open daily: Mid-March to October, from

10am to 5pm and November to mid-March, from 11am to 4pm. Admission to the castle and gardens is £6.80 ($13) for adults, £5.80 ($11) for seniors, and £3.80 ($7.20) for children. Admission to the gardens only is £4.80 ($9.10) for adults and seniors and £2.80 ($5.30) for children.

WHERE TO STAY

Atholl House Hotel *Kids*   Opposite the post office and near Dunvegan Castle, this hotel was once the home of a local priest. It stands at the heart of the village, .6km (1 mile) from Dunvegan Castle. This well-run little hotel rents nicely furnished rooms with tub or shower bathrooms (eight with shower only and one with a tub/shower combo). The hotel was completely refurbished in 2007. Two units have four-poster beds along with the best views of the mountain moorland and Loch Dunvegan. The chef prepares quality cuisine using an abundance of locally caught seafood.

Dunvegan, Isle of Skye IV55 8WA. **(** **01470/521-219.** Fax 01470/521-481. www.athollhotel.co.uk. 9 units. £80 ($152) double. Rates include Scottish breakfast. AE, MC, V. **Amenities:** Restaurant; bar; laundry service; nonsmoking rooms. *In room:* TV, coffeemaker, hair dryer.

WHERE TO DINE

Three Chimneys Restaurant *★★★* SCOTTISH   The Three Chimneys, located in a stone crofter's house, is the winner of multiple awards. In 2003, *Restaurant Magazine* proclaimed Chimneys as one of the world's top 50 restaurants. And the same high standards prevail today. Specialties are fresh seafood and Highland game, with examples like Aberdeen Angus beef with potatoes Dauphinoise; seared loin of lamb with fruity couscous; and pan-fried Scottish salmon with asparagus, and lemon sauce. The dessert menu includes scrumptious treats like marmalade pudding and Drambuie custard. More than 100 vintages from the wine list are available to accompany your meal.

Six luxurious suites are located a few steps away from the restaurant. The House Over-By boasts a panoramic view of the sea, and each suite is fully equipped with amenities such as a TV, VCR, CD player, phone, minibar, and hair dryer. The cost is a very pricey £250 ($475) for a double; £510 ($969) for a family room. Rates include breakfast. Both the restaurant and the suites have been given a five-star rating by the Scottish Tourist Board.

Hwy. B884, Colbost, Isle of Skye, IV55 8ZT. **(** **01470/511-258.** Fax 01470/511-358. www.threechimneys.co.uk. Reservations required for dinner, recommended for lunch. Fixed-price dinner £50 ($95) for 3 courses. AE, MC, V. Mon–Sat 12:30–2pm (last order); daily 6:30–9:30pm (last order). Drive 6.5km (4 miles) west of Dunvegan on B884.

SKEABOST BRIDGE

Eastward from Dunvegan, Skeabost Bridge has an island cemetery of great antiquity. The graves of four Crusaders are here.

WHERE TO STAY & DINE

Skeabost Country House Hotel *★*   This is one of the most inviting country homes on Skye. Built in 1851 as a private estate, it has been converted into a lochside hotel boasting dormers, chimneys, tower, and gables. The Skeabost owns 13km (8 miles) of the bank of the River Snizort, so it attracts many folks who come to fish. In addition, guests can play the hotel's par-3 golf course. The comfortable bedrooms come in a variety of shapes and sizes. The main dining room offers expensive table d'hôte menus focusing on seafood.

Skeabost Bridge, Isle of Skye IV51 9NP. **(** **01470/532-202.** Fax 01470/532-454. www.oxfordhotelsandinns.com. 26 units. £80 ($152) double; £149 ($283) suite. Rates include Scottish breakfast. MC, V. Closed Dec–Mar. **Amenities:** 2

restaurants; 2 bars; 18-hole golf course; game room; room service (8am–10:30pm); babysitting; laundry service; non-smoking rooms. *In room:* TV, coffeemaker, hair dryer.

SLEAT PENINSULA

A lot of Skye can look melancholy and forlorn, especially in misty weather. For a change of landscape head for the **Sleat Peninsula,** the southeastern section of the island. Because of the lushness of its vegetation (the shores are washed by the warmer waters of the Gulf Stream), it has long been known as the "Garden of Skye." As you drive along, you notice the intense green of the landscape and the well-kept grounds of locals' homes.

A ruined stronghold of the MacDonalds, **Knock Castle** is off A851 some 19km (12 miles) south of Broadford. Another MacDonald stronghold, **Dunsgiath Castle,** has some well-preserved ruins open to view. They're found at Tokavaig on an unclassified road (watch for a sign) at a point 32km (20 miles) south and southwest of Broadford. You can visit both these evocative ruins for free, day or night. Inquire at the number given below for the Armadale Castle Gardens & Museum of the Isles.

Armadale Castle Gardens & Museum of the Isles   You don't have to have Mac-Donald as your last name to enjoy a stop at Skye's award-winning Clan Donald Visitor Centre. From Broadford, travel along a winding seaside road to the ruins of Armadale Castle and the rebuilt baronial stables. A multimedia exhibit tells of the lost culture of the ancient Gaelic world under the MacDonalds as lords of the Isles. The countryside ranger service offers a full summer program of guided walks and talks that introduce you to several kilometers of trails and to the history of the Highland estate. A licensed restaurant in the stables offers good local food, from tea to a full meal. The drive from the ferry at Kyleakin is about 30 minutes, and the center is along A851 (follow the signs) near the Armadale-Mallaig ferry.

Armadale. ⓒ **01471/844-305.** Admission £5 ($9.50) adults, £3.90 ($7.40) seniors and children 5–15, £14 ($27) per family. Apr 2–Oct 26 daily 9:30am–5:30pm (last entry at 5pm); Nov to mid-Mar Mon–Wed 11am–3pm.

WHERE TO STAY & DINE

Ardvasar Hotel ⚹ *Kids*   The oldest part of this 1800s coaching inn is a stone-trimmed pub in what was once a stable. In 1990, a major renovation added bathrooms with tub and shower to each of the guest rooms and a cottage-cozy decor that includes pastels and chintz. Virtually everyone in the area comes to the restaurant for a mug of lager and a taste of the fine cuisine. Menu items include starters like peppered mushrooms with hot brandy sauce, followed by smoked chicken with cranberry sauce, although seafood is the specialty.

Ardvasar, Isle of Skye IV45 8RS. ⓒ **01471/844-223.** Fax 01471/844-495. www.ardvasarhotel.com. 10 units. £85 ($162) double. Rates include Scottish breakfast. MC, V. **Amenities:** Restaurant; 2 bars; room service; laundry service; nonsmoking rooms. *In room:* TV, coffeemaker, hair dryer.

ISLE ORNSAY

Adjacent to Sleat Peninsula is the Isle of Ornsay, also called Eilean Iarmain in Gaelic. It is a lovely, remote islet in a small, rocky bay with mountains of Knoydart in the background. Its heyday as Skye's main fishing port is long gone. Today you'll find little whitewashed cottages around the small harbor. The island's landlord is Sir Iain Noble, who also owns the hotel below.

WHERE TO STAY

Hotel Eilean Iarmain ⚹⚹ *Finds*   Most often called "Isle Ornsay Hotel," this elegant harbor-side retreat is one of the most award-winning hotels in Britain. Sir Iain and

Lady Noble welcome guests to the century-old Eilean Iarmain, where original antiques, wood paneling, and chintz fabrics create an aura of a tasteful country house. In winter, the charming atmosphere is enhanced by log fires and the performances by guest musicians. All the accommodations are individually styled, with the suites housed in a former stable block dating back to the 1870s. Of particular note is the Tower Room, with its pine-paneled walls, a great mahogany double bed, and views toward the sea. All the rooms contain tastefully furnished bathrooms.

Isle of Ornsay, Sleat, Isle of Skye, 1V43 8QR. (C) 01471/833-332. Fax 01471/833-275. www.eilean-iarmain.co.uk. 16 units. £80–£140 ($152–$266) double; £140–£250 ($266–$475) suite. Rates include breakfast. AE, MC, V. **Amenities:** Restaurant; bar; room service; babysitting; laundry service; dry cleaning. *In room:* TV, minibar (in suites), coffeemaker, hair dryer.

Kinloch Lodge (★★)   The white-stone walls of this manor are visible from across the scrub- and pine-covered hillsides bordering the property. Built in 1680 as a hunting lodge, it's now the elegant residence of Lord and Lady MacDonald. Portraits of the family's 18th-century forebears are a striking feature of the reception rooms, as are the open fireplaces and the scores of antiques. The guest rooms come in various shapes and sizes (some with shower only); from the windows of some, you can occasionally glimpse the sea. In 1998, a new house, also impressive architecturally, was completed 50m (164 ft.) from the main lodge; it contains an additional five handsomely furnished bedrooms. Every evening, you can enjoy drinks in the drawing room before dining on one of the upscale meals for which Lady MacDonald is famous. The author of 13 cookbooks, she applies her imaginative recipes to ingredients shot, trapped, netted, or grown on Skye.

Isle of Ornsay, Sleat, Isle of Skye IV43 8QY. (C) **01471/833-333.** Fax 01471/833-277. www.kinloch-lodge.co.uk. 15 units. £175–£275 ($333–$523) double. Rates include dinner and Scottish breakfast. AE, MC, V. **Amenities:** Restaurant; bar; nonsmoking rooms. *In room:* TV, coffeemaker, trouser press.

4 Rhum (Rum)

14km (9 miles) SW of the Isle of Skye

The enticingly named island of Rhum is only about 13km (8 miles) wide and 13km (8 miles) long. There are those who advise against visiting: "If you like a barren desert where it rains all the time, you'll love Rhum," a skipper in Mallaig once told us, and his comment remains true today. It's stark, all right. And very wet. In fact, with more than 229 centimeters (90 in.) of rainfall recorded annually, it's said to be the wettest island of the Inner Hebrides.

Since the mid-1950s, Rhum has been owned by the Edinburgh-based Nature Conservancy Council, an ecological conservation group. Attempts are being made to bring back the sea eagle, which inhabited the island in Queen Victoria's day. On this storm-tossed outpost in summer, mountain climbers meet challenging peaks and anglers come for good trout fishing. Bird-lovers seek out the Manx shearwaters that live on the island in great numbers. Red deer and ponies, along with the wildflowers of summer, add color to an otherwise bleak landscape.

ESSENTIALS

GETTING THERE   A passenger **ferry** from Mallaig, on the western coast of Scotland, leaves about five times a week. No cars are allowed on the island. For information, contact **Caledonian MacBrayne** ((C) **01687/462-403** in Mallaig). Sailings are from April to October only, on Monday to Wednesday at 10:30am, Friday at

---

Tips Before You Go

Before traveling to Rhum, you must contact **Denise Reed,** the reserve manager at the Scottish Natural Heritage Nature Reserve, by calling ℂ **01687/462-026.** The office will help you organize accommodations on the island.

12:30pm, and Saturday at 6:20am and 12:30pm. A round-trip is £15 ($28) for adults. **Arisaig Marine** (ℂ **01687/450-224**) sails from Arisaig to Rhum on Tuesday, Thursday, Saturday, and Sunday at 11am. A round-trip ticket is £20 ($38) for adults, £10 ($19) for children 12 to 16, and £6 ($11) for those under 12. Schedules can vary, so it's best to call for confirmations. It takes about 2 hours to reach Rhum from one of these ports.

WHERE TO STAY & DINE

Kinloch Castle ★ *Finds*   You'll be astonished that in such a forbidding place, you can find a hotel that has been called "Britain's most intact example of an Edwardian country house." Of course, it's sadly run down and the bedrooms are a bit musty. But you get the feeling you're living life as experienced back in 1901, maybe something from the pages of an Agatha Christie novel. Located on the seafront in the center of Rhum's biggest hamlet, Kinloch, this mansion was completed for Sir George Boullough, a wealthy Lancashire textile magnate. The castle still contains a ballroom, a massive Adam-style fireplace, and monumental paintings and stuffed animals. (This section is now part of an exhibit; to visit these areas, enter the front of the castle for a tour.) The former servants' quarters are now a simple and functional hostel, while the private rooms are furnished with four-poster beds (these share spacious bathrooms with tubs). Because guests spend their days trekking around the island, all lunches are packed picnics at £5 ($9.50) per person. The restaurant serves breakfasts at reasonable prices.

Kinloch, Isle of Rhum PH43 4RR. ℂ/fax **01687/462-037.** kinloch@highland-hostels.co.uk. 27 units, none with private bathroom; 52 hostel beds. Rooms £60 ($114) double; hostel £13 ($25) per person in rooms with 2–5 beds. No credit cards. **Amenities:** Restaurant; nonsmoking rooms. *In room:* No phone.

5 Eigg & Muck

Eigg: 6.5km (4 miles) SE of Rhum; Muck: 11km (7 miles) SW of Eigg

The tiny islands of Eigg and Muck lie in the Sea of the Hebrides, which separates the Inner from the Outer Hebrides. If you're doing the whirlwind tour of Europe, Eigg and Muck will hardly top your agenda. They appeal only to nature lovers seeking a variety of Hebridean scenery and a chance to look at life of long ago. If your time is limited and you can visit only one isle, make it Eigg, which has the most dramatic scenery.

ESSENTIALS

GETTING THERE   Before venturing to either Eigg or Muck, confirm the schedule of the ferry's return. Because service isn't every day, you may find yourself staying at least 2 nights on either island. **Caledonian MacBrayne** (ℂ **01687/462-403** in Mallaig) sails from Mallaig to Eigg on Monday and Thursday at 10:30am and Saturday at 1:40pm. The round-trip ticket is £15 ($29). From Arisaig, **Arisaig Marine** (ℂ **01687/450-224**) sails to Muck on Monday, Wednesday, and Friday (but departure days and times can vary). Sailings to Eigg are Friday through Wednesday. Most departures are at either 11 or 11:30am (subject to change, based on weather conditions). The round-trip fare for either is £16 ($30).

VISITOR INFORMATION   For assistance in finding accommodations on Eigg or Muck, and for general information, contact **Mrs. Mairi Kirk,** 7 Cleadane, Isle of Eigg (© **01687/482-416**).

EIGG

Eigg, about 7 by 5km (4½ by 3 miles), is some 19km (12 miles) out in the Atlantic. The island is owned by the Isle of Eigg Heritage Trust, which consists of about 70 island residents and the Highland Council and Scottish Wildlife Trust. The farmers, shepherds, fishermen, and innkeepers who live here raised the $2.4 million to buy their island through a worldwide public appeal over the Internet.

The **Sgurr of Eigg,** a tall column of lava, is thought to be the biggest such pitchstone (volcanic rock) mass in the United Kingdom. Climbers on its north side try to reach the 394m (1,300 ft.) summit. It's said that the last of the pterodactyls roosted here.

After your arrival at **Galmisdale,** the principal hamlet and pier, you can take an antique bus to Cleadale. Once there, walk across moors to **Camas Sgiotaig,** with its well-known **beach of the Singing Sands.** Since the island is crisscrossed with paths and tracks, and access isn't restricted, you can walk in any direction that captures your fancy.

Visitors come to Eigg for the remoteness and the sense of living in the 19th century. The island is known for its plant, animal, and bird life, including golden eagles and seals. In summer, you can sometimes see minke whales and porpoises in the offshore waters. The island's resident warden leads guided walks of Eigg once a week in summer; call © **01687/482-477** for details.

MUCK

Lying 11km (7 miles) southwest of Eigg, Muck has such an unappetizing name that visitors may turn away. However, the name of this 6.5-sq.-km (2½-sq.-mile) island was originally a Gaelic word, *muic,* meaning "island of the sow." Naturalists come here to see everything from rare butterflies to otters. Large colonies of nesting seabirds can be viewed in May and June.

Muck is actually a farm, and the entire island is owned by two brothers: the Laird of Muck, Lawrence MacEwan, and his younger brother, Ewen MacEwan. There are hardly more than 30 residents, and all are concerned with the running of the farm. There are no vehicles on the island except for bicycles and tractors.

What's the real reason to come? To see and explore a tiny, fragile Hebridean community that has survived, sometimes against great odds. The scenery and the solitude are wonderful, as are the cattle, sheep, hens, house cats, and ducks roaming with relative freedom. If you walk to the top of the highest hill, **Ben Airean,** at 137m (451 ft.), you'll have a panoramic view of Muck and its neighbor islands of Rhum and Eigg.

6 Coll & Tyree

145km (90 miles) NW of Glasgow, 77km (48 miles) W of Fort William

If you like your scenery stark and tranquil, try tiny Coll and Tyree. The outermost of the Inner Hebrides, they're exposed to the open Atlantic and said to get the most sunshine in Britain. On Tyree (also spelled Tiree), the shell-sand *machair* (sand dunes) increase the arable area, differentiating it from the other inner isles.

Trees are scarce on both islands, but that doesn't mean they're bleak. Both are rich in flora, with some 500 species. The islands' roughly 150 bird species, including Arctic skuas and razorbills, make them a bird lover's paradise. Both common and gray seals have breeding colonies on the islands. There are few cars for rent here, but visitors don't seem to mind biking around the islands or catching a ride on Tyree's least expensive method of transport: a mail bus serves most of the island. Boat rentals and sea angling can also be arranged.

GETTING TO THE ISLANDS

British Airways (© **0845/733-3377** in Glasgow) flies directly to Tyree from Glasgow, with about six 90-minute flights per week (none on Sun). A **car ferry** sails from Oban to Coll (a 3-hr. trip, costing £20/$38 round-trip) and Tyree (an extra 45 min.), but in very rare instances gales may force cancellation of the trip. If the gale is very strong, you might be stranded on an island for a while, waiting for the next departure. Details and bookings, essential for cars, are available from **Caledonian MacBrayne** (© **08705/650-000**).

COLL

Lying in the seemingly timeless world of the Celtic west, the island of Coll, with a population of some 130 hearty souls, is rich in history. Distances from one place to another are small, since the island averages about 5km (3 miles) in breadth; at its longest point, it stretches for some 21km (13 miles).

Coll has a partially restored castle, **Breacachadh,** rising majestically from its southeastern side. A stronghold of the Macleans in the 15th century, it is now a private residence, although on some occasions it's open to the public. Immediately adjacent is the so-called **New Castle,** built for Hector Maclean in 1750. It provided shelter for Samuel Johnson and James Boswell when they were stranded on the island for 10 days because of storms at sea. The castle, still a private home, was altered considerably in the 19th century and embellished with pepper-pot turrets and parapets.

In the western part of the island at Totronald are two standing stones called **Na Sgeulachan ("Teller of Tales").** The stones pre-date the Druids and are thought to have been the site of a temple. The highest point on Coll is **Ben Hogh** (103m/340 ft.), which you can climb for a panoramic view.

On the road to Sorisdale, at **Killunaig,** stand the ruins of a church, from the late Middle Ages, and a burial ground. Going on to **Sorisdale,** you see the ruins of houses occupied by crofters earlier in the last century. Hundreds of families once lived here. Some were chased away in the wake of the potato famine, and many were forced out in Land Clearance programs.

WHERE TO STAY & DINE

Isle of Coll Hotel   This hotel enjoys the dubious honor of having been immediately rejected by Samuel Johnson and James Boswell as an inappropriate place to spend the night during their 18th-century tour of Scotland. (They eventually succeeded in securing lodgings with the laird of Coll.) Today, the small to midsize guest rooms are far more comfortable, with electric blankets, either shower-only or combination tub/shower bathrooms, and simple but functional furniture. The dining room serves good but rather expensive dinners. The hotel contains the town's only pub, in which you're likely to meet locals over a pint of ale and a platter of affordable bar food. The hotel sits on a hilltop at the end of the Arinagour estuary, about a 10-minute walk north of town, beside B8071.

Arinagour, Isle of Coll PA78 6SA. ℭ **01879/230-334**. Fax 01879/230-317. www.collhotel.com. 6 units. £70–£180 ($133–$342) double. Rates include Scottish breakfast. MC, V. **Amenities:** Restaurant; bar; children's play area. *In room:* TV, coffeemaker, hair dryer, no phone.

TYREE (TIREE)

A fertile island, flat Tyree has a population of some 800 residents, mostly in farming communities, who enjoy its gentle landscape, **sandy beaches,** and rolling hills. As you travel about the island, you see many 1800s crofter's houses with thatched roofs. In 1886, the duke of Argyll caused a scandal when he ordered marines and police to clear the crofters off the land. Many were sent, destitute, to Canada.

Most of the population is centered around **Scarinish,** with its little stone harbor where lobster boats put in. Fishing isn't what it used to be; the appearance of fast and dangerous squalls and storms are said to scatter the fleet as far as the shores of North America.

Bird-watchers are drawn to the shores of **Loch Bhasapoll,** a favorite gathering place of wild geese and ducks, and to a cave on the coast at **Kenavara,** where many seabirds can be observed.

Ancient duns and forts are scattered around Tyree. The best of these is a broch at **Vaul Bay,** with walls more than 3.5m (12 ft.) thick. At **Balephetrish,** on the northern rim of the island, stands a huge granite boulder. Locals call it the Ringing Stone, because when struck it gives off a metallic sound. In the western part of the island, at Kilkenneth, are the ruins of the **Chapel of St. Kenneth,** dedicated to a comrade of St. Columba.

WHERE TO STAY & DINE

Scarinish Hotel ★ *Finds*   Serving the best food in the area, this hotel also offers well-maintained and comfortable bedrooms in a superb location right on the sea. The Hebridean hospitality and service is another good reason for staying here, that and the succulent lobster served at the Old Harbour Restaurant, which also offers the best of local lamb and Scottish beefsteaks.

Bedrooms are done in a simple but comfortable style, and each has been refurbished with crisp, white linen. Guests meet each other in the Upper Deck Lounge with its views over the harbor, or else in the Lean to Bar, which is a friendly place where islanders gather at night in front of the fire. The full Scottish breakfast served here will fortify you for most of the day.

Scarnish, Isle of Tyree PA77 6UH. ℭ **01879/220-308**. Fax 01879/220-410. www.tireescarinishhotel.com. 5 units. £70–£80 ($133–$152) double; £75 ($143) 2 adults (children half price) in family suite. Rates include breakfast. DC, MC, V. **Amenities:** Restaurant; bar. *In room:* TV, no phone.

Tiree Lodge Hotel   This is the nerve center of the island. Built as a simple hunting lodge around 1790, it was greatly enlarged in the 1970s with a modern addition. About 1.6km (1 mile) east of the island's only ferry landing, the hotel contains one of Tyree's two pubs and attracts a crowd of locals and visitors. The small guest rooms are well maintained and comfortable; most units contain a small, shower-only bathroom (some have tub/shower combinations).

Kirkatol, Isle of Tyree PA77 6TW. ℭ **01879/220-368**. Fax 01879/220-884. 12 units, 9 with private bathroom. £50 ($95) double without bathroom; £54 ($103) double with bathroom. Rates include Scottish breakfast. MC, V. **Amenities:** Restaurant; bar; nonsmoking rooms. *In room:* TV, coffeemaker, no phone.

7 Mull (★)

195km (121 miles) NW of Edinburgh, 145km (90 miles) NW of Glasgow

The third-largest island in the Hebrides, Mull is rich in legend and folklore, a land of ghosts, monsters, and the wee folk. The island is wild and mountainous, characterized by sea lochs and sandy bars. Mull was known to the classical Greeks, and its prehistoric past is recalled in forts, duns, and stone circles. Be sure to bring a raincoat: the island is one of the wettest in the Hebrides, a fact that upset Dr. Johnson, who visited in 1773.

Many visitors consider Mull more beautiful than Skye, a controversy we stay out of because we love them both. Mull has varied scenery with many waterfalls, and the wild countryside was the scene of many of David Balfour's adventures in *Kidnapped,* by Robert Louis Stevenson. Its highest peak is **Ben More,** at 961m (3,169 ft.), but it also has many flat areas. The island's wildlife includes roe deer, golden eagles, polecats, seabirds, and feral goats. Mull is also a jumping-off point to visit Iona and Staffa (see "Iona & Staffa: An Abbey & a Musical Cave," later in this chapter).

Guarding the bay (you'll see it as you cross on the ferry) is **Duart Castle,** restored just before World War I. In the bay—somewhere—lies the *Florencia,* a Spanish galleon that went down laden with treasure. Many attempts have been made to find it and bring it up, but so far all have failed. To the southeast, near Salen, are the 14th-century ruins of **Aros Castle,** once a stronghold of the MacDonalds, lords of the Isles. On the far south coast at Lochbuie, **Moy Castle** has a water-filled dungeon.

At the end of the day, you might enjoy a dram from the **Tobermory Malt Whisky Distillery,** in Tobermory (℗ **01688/302-647**), which opened in 1823. Tours are given Monday through Friday from 10am to 5pm; the cost is £3 ($5.70) for adults, £1.50 ($2.85) for seniors, and free for children. Be sure to call in advance—the distillery seems to shut down from time to time.

ESSENTIALS

GETTING THERE   It's a 45-minute trip by **car ferry** from Oban to Craignure, on Mull. For departure times, contact **Caledonian MacBrayne** (℗ **08705/650-000**). From Oban, there are about five or six sailings per day at a round-trip cost of £7.10 ($13) for adults. The cost for a car is £50 ($94) for a 5-day round-trip ticket.

GETTING AROUND   Use **Bowmans Coaches Mull** (℗ **01680/812-313**) to go around the island. Coaches connect with the ferry at least three times per day and will take you to Fionnphort or Tobermory for £12 to £17 ($23–$32) round-trip. Another option is to buy a ticket combining the cost of the ferry with a guided bus tour to Fionnphort and Iona. The tour begins when you board the 10am ferry and ends at about 5:40pm, back at Oban. The cost is £44 ($84) for adults and £22 ($42) for children.

VISITOR INFORMATION   The **tourist office** is on Main Street in Tobermory (℗ **01688/302-182**). From Easter to October, it's open Monday to Friday 9am to 5pm (to 6pm July–Aug).

(Tips) A Word on Driving

If you're driving along any of Mull's single-track roads, remember to take your time and yield to the sheep and cattle. Also, a car coming downhill toward you has the right of way, so look for a spot to pull off.

Moments **Close Encounters with Nature**

Several operators will take you out to see whales, dolphins, and seals. Two of the best are **Sea Life Surveys,** Beadoun, Breidwood, Tobermory (© **01688/400-223**), and a hardworking entrepreneur named **Mr. Liverty,** High Street (© **01688/302-048**), who maintains midsize boats for 6 to 12 passengers each. An all-day whale watch costs £70 ($133) for adults and children. A half-day whale watch is £40 ($76) for adults, £35 ($67) for children. A 2-hour seal watch cruise is £12 ($23) for adults; £6 ($11) for children.

Visitors can also experience the wildlife-rich natural habitat with **Island Encounters** (© **01680/300-441**). Guided by a local expert, you can spend the day on a safari, exploring the most remote and scenic areas of the island in a comfortable eight-seat vehicle. The cost for the day is £34 ($65). Binoculars and lunch are included in the price, and pick-up can be arranged at all ferry terminals on Mull.

SPECIAL EVENTS   In July, the **Mull Highland Games** feature traditional events such as bagpipes, caber tossing, and dancing. The **Tour of Mull Rally** is held in early October. Ask at the tourist office for exact dates.

OUTDOOR PURSUITS AROUND THE ISLAND

BIKING   Its combinations of heather-clad, rock-strewn moors and sylvan forests make Mull especially appropriate for cycling. To rent a bike, try **On Yer Bike,** The Pierhead, in Craignure (© **01680/300-501**), 35km (22 miles) from Tobermory. In Tobermory itself, consider **Brown's,** High Street (© **01688/302-020**). Both charge £15 to £18 ($29–$34) per day and are open daily from 8:45am to around 5:30pm.

GOLF   Just over 35km (22 miles) west of Tobermory is the isolated 9-hole **Craignure Golf Course,** with an honesty box into which you deposit the greens fees of £15 ($29) per day. For information about this course, contact its secretary, D. Howitt, at © **01680/300-402.**

HIKING   Mull is wonderful for hiking. You'll probably drive off to a trail head, park your car beside the road (most residents boast that they haven't locked their car in decades), and then set off on foot in total isolation. The tourist office sells two books, each costing £3.95 ($7.50): *Walks in North Mull* and *Walks in South Mull.* They provide detailed options for specific routes with historic, ethnographical, scenic, or geological interest. Dress in layers, and wear something waterproof.

CRAIGNURE

Even passengers who arrive with a car might want to take a 20-minute excursion on the **Mull Railway,** Old Pier Station, Craignure (© **01680/812-494**), the only passenger rail in the Hebrides. It was inaugurated in 1983, but its puffing engine and narrow-gauge tracks are thoroughly old-fashioned. The tracks begin at the Old Pier in Craignure, running 2.5km (1½ miles) to Torosay Castle and its famous gardens. The view is one of unspoiled mountains, glens, and seaside; you can sometimes see otters, eagles, and deer. The trains operate from late March to mid-October; the most frequent service is from June to mid-September, when daily trips begin around 11am. One-way fares are £3 ($5.70) for adults, £2 ($3.80) for children, and £7.50 ($14) for families. For details, call the Mull & West Highland Railway Company at © **01680/300-389.**

A good way to see the sights of Mull is to book a ticket for "The Mull Experience," a tour offered by **Caledonian MacBrayne.** For information, call **Torosay Castle** (© **01680/812-421**). The tour begins in Oban, where you board a ferry for Craignure. Once in Craignure, you catch the train to Torosay Castle, where you'll spend a few hours exploring. The next stop is the castle of Duart. You then return to Oban by ferry. The tour is offered from May to September at a cost of £25 ($48) for adults and £15 ($29) for children.

Duart Castle 🏰   You can visit both Torosay Castle (see below) and Duart Castle on the same day. Located 5km (3 miles) west of Torosay, this castle dates from the 13th century and was the home of the fiery Maclean clan. A majestic structure, it was sacked in 1791 by the dukes of Argyll in retaliation for the Macleans' support of the Stuarts in 1715 and 1745. It was allowed to fall into ruins until Sir Fitzroy Maclean, the 26th chief of the clan and grandfather of the present occupant, began a restoration in 1911 at the age of 76. It had been his ambition since he was a boy to see his ancestral home restored (he lived until he was 102).

Off A849, on the eastern point of Mull. © **01680/812-309.** Admission £5 ($9.50) adults, £4.50 ($8.55) seniors and students, £2.50 ($4.75) children 3–15, £13 ($24) per family. Late Mar to mid-Oct daily 11am–4pm.

Torosay Castle and Gardens   This is the only private castle and garden in the western Highlands that is open daily to visitors. The Victorian mansion was built in the mid–19th century by David Bryce, a famous Scottish architect. In his early years, Winston Churchill was a frequent visitor. One writer said a visit here is like returning to the Edwardian age of leisure, and so it is. To the surprise of visitors, the armchairs are labeled PLEASE SIT DOWN instead of PLEASE KEEP OFF. The portraits are by such famous artists as Sargent. You can wander through 4.9 hectares (12 acres) of Italian-style terraced gardens, and enjoy extensive views of the Appin coastline from Ben Nevis to Ben Cruachan.

2.5km (1½ miles) south of Craignure on A849. © **01680/812-421.** Admission to castle and gardens £5.50 ($10) adults, £3 ($5.70) seniors and students, £1.50 ($2.90) children 6–16, £15 ($29) per family. Admission to gardens and tearoom only £4.75 ($9.05) adults, £4 ($7.60) seniors and students, £2.50 ($4.75) children. Easter to mid-Oct daily 10:30am–5:30pm.

WHERE TO STAY & DINE
Isle of Mull Hotel   This inn stands near the ferry and the meeting point of the Sound of Mull and Loch Linnhe. From the picture windows of its public rooms, you have panoramic vistas of mountains and the island of Lismore. The guest rooms are

---

Moments A Stunning View

Even locals sometimes drive out of their way to catch the sunset over the **Gribun Rock,** a large peninsula, midway along the island's western coast, whose centerpiece is the windy uplands of Ben More. The entire stretch of single-lane highway on the western flank of Ben More is a particularly spectacular highlight. To reach it from Tobermory or Craignure, follow the signs to the hamlet of Salen, then drive west to Gribun. En route, you pass through the hamlets of Knock, Balnahard, and Balevuin. From dozens of points along the way, views stretch over the cliff tops, encompassing the setting sun (if your timing is right) as well as the isles of Staffa, Coll, and Tyree.

small but handsomely furnished. The chef serves British and Continental food in the attractive dining room.

Craignure, Isle of Mull PA65 6BB. © 01680/812-351. Fax 01680/812-462. www.crerarhotels.com. 65 units. £110–£190 ($209–$361) double. Rates include Scottish breakfast. MC, V. **Amenities:** Restaurant; bar; room service; nonsmoking rooms. *In room:* TV, coffeemaker, hair dryer.

SALEN

Near Salen are the ruins of **Aros Castle,** once a stronghold of the lords of the Isles, the MacDonalds. It dates from the 14th century and was last occupied in the 17th century. Most of the former castle has been carted off, but the site is still visible 18km (11 miles) southeast of Tobermory.

WHERE TO STAY & DINE

Glenforsa Hotel   This secluded seaside hotel was built in 1968 of Norwegian pine logs. It's near the Sound of Mull and the River Forsa, 18km (11 miles) southeast of Tobermory, and visitors like to come here in late summer to fish for salmon. The guest rooms are well appointed. The bar serves an array of tempting food, with venison, trout, and salmon offered in season for guests and nonguests alike. The hotel has an adjacent grass airstrip, at which private and charter planes can land from dawn to dusk.

Salen, by Aros, Isle of Mull PA72 6JW. © 01680/300-517. Fax 01680/300-535. www.glenforsa.co.uk. 14 units, 13 with private bathroom. £82 ($156) double. Rates include Scottish breakfast. MC, V. **Amenities:** Restaurant; bar; limited room service; nonsmoking rooms. *In room:* Coffeemaker, hair dryer, no phone.

TOBERMORY

Founded as a fishing village in 1789, Tobermory, one of the most sheltered harbors in Scotland, is the unofficial capital of Mull. Its little bright-pastel buildings open onto a boat-filled harbor, and the village is set against a backdrop of wooded hills. Great photo ops abound. Yachts and ferry boats to and from Kilchoan arrive here in the summer, and Tobermory is a busy little bustling village with its shops, hotels, and pubs.

Mull Museum (© 01688/302-208) exhibits material relating to the island in an old bakery building on Main Street. From Easter to mid-October, it's open Monday to Friday from 10am to 4pm and Saturday 10am to 1pm. Admission is £1 ($1.90) for adults and 20p (40¢) for children.

Isle of Mull Silver, Main Street (© 01688/302-345), stocks jewelry made by a number of Scottish designers. Among the unique items made on the premises are traditional Scottish silver *quaich* (drinking vessels) and christening spoons. **Mull Pottery,** Main Street (© 01688/302-057), features tableware, ovenware, and lamps in seashore, seagull, and turquoise patterns. **Tackle & Books,** Main Street (© 01688/302-336), carries fishing gear, bait, and an impressive array of reading materials—especially works by local authors and anything in print about Mull.

The **Western Isle Golf Course** dates from the 1930s and is said to have possibly the best views of any course in the world.

WHERE TO STAY

Glengorm Castle ★★★ *Finds*   This is the premier place to stay on the island, certainly the most elegant B&B, and the address is imbued with the most character. Built in 1860 and much restored, the castle today is owned by Tom and Marjorie Nelson. On the northern tip of Mull, near Tobermory, the castle, overlooking the Atlantic, is surrounded by green hills, forests, and lakes, with views of the Outer Hebrides from the rooms. At night a roaring fire blazes while guests enjoy fine vintages of Scotch from the well-stocked bar.

The bedrooms are furnished in a luxurious way, with both taste and style, and each room comes with a private bathroom with tub (one unit has a private bathroom outside the door). Each accommodation has been individually decorated. Guests meet fellow guests in the dining room the following morning, enjoying local produce for breakfast. Later in the day guests either go sightseeing or else enjoy bird-watching, hiking, or fishing. The hotel has a Victorian stone bathing pool constructed in the early 1900s at water's edge. On the grounds is a stone-built structure that is home to the Glengorm Coffee Shop, selling freshly baked goods and excellent lunches often made with produce from the castle farm. It adjoins an art gallery displaying the works of local artists.

Route B8073, Tobermory, Isle of Mull PA75 6QE. © **01688/302-321**. Fax 01688/302-738. www.glengormcastle.co.uk. 5 units. £120–£160 ($228–$304) double. Rates include breakfast. DC, MC, V. **Amenities:** Coffee shop; bar; outdoor pool; farm shop; art gallery; laundry service. *In room:* TV, hair dryer, no phone.

Tobermory Hotel   Even though it's located on the upper end of the town's main street, this hotel offers guests a sense of privacy, having been converted from a row of fishermen's cottages that stood here in the late 18th century. Most guest rooms look out onto the harbor, often dotted with fishing boats; the others have views of the tree-lined cliff, which rises abruptly behind the hotel. The bathrooms are small but neat (some with shower only). The dining room serves dinner nightly. Children are welcome here—a toy chest is ready for small visitors.

53 Main St., Tobermory, Isle of Mull PA75 6NT. © **01688/302-091**. Fax 01688/302-254. www.thetobermoryhotel.com. 16 units. £70–£114 ($133–$217) double. Rates include Scottish breakfast. MC, V. Parking available on nearby streets. **Amenities:** Restaurant; room service; laundry service; nonsmoking rooms. *In room:* TV, coffeemaker, hair dryer, no phone.

Western Isles Hotel   In a scenic location on a bluff above the harbor, the Western Isles is a large, gray-stone country inn. It was constructed by the Sandeman sherry company in 1883 as a hunting and fishing lodge for top-level staff and customers. The current owners welcome guests to homey rooms decorated in a mix of styles, with small bathrooms. The hotel has a conservatory bar as well as an upscale restaurant.

Tobermory, Isle of Mull PA75 6PR. © **01688/302-012**. Fax 01688/302-297. www.mullhotel.com. 28 units. £98–£196 ($186–$372) double; £164–£234 ($312–$445) suite. Rates include Scottish breakfast. AE, MC, V. Closed Dec 18–28. **Amenities:** Restaurant; bar; room service; nonsmoking rooms. *In room:* TV, coffeemaker, hair dryer.

WHERE TO DINE

Gannet's Restaurant SCOTTISH   This place enjoys a quayside setting in one of the stone-fronted 200-year-old buildings along Main Street. It's one of the best independent restaurants here. You get fresh seafood, much of it caught locally, along with salads, juicy steaks, and some fine vegetable dishes, finished off by creamy desserts. During the day, you might stop in for sandwiches and fresh coffee.

25 Main St. © **01688/302-203**. Main courses £8–£14 ($15–$27). MC, V. Easter–Oct daily 10am–9pm; Nov–Easter daily 10am–3pm.

TOBERMORY AFTER DARK

Macgochan's Pub, Ledaig (© **01688/302-350**), is an old traditional pub that has free Scottish music most nights from 9pm to 1:30am. There's also a game room with a pool table. The **Mishnish Hotel,** Main Street (© **01688/302-009**), is a faux-traditional pub featuring Scottish music nightly. In pleasant weather, you can step into the beer garden for a breath of fresh air.

DERVAIG ⌖

The loveliest village on Mull, Dervaig (Little Grove) is a 13km (8-mile) drive west from Tobermory. The **Old Byre Heritage Centre** (✆ **01688/400-229**) houses one of the most charming museums you could hope to find. The main exhibit features 25 scale models, painstakingly made by a local historian, showing the history of Mull from the first settlers to the Highland Clearances. A fully licensed tearoom serves light meals. Admission is £3 ($5.70) for adults, £2 ($3.80) for seniors and students, and £1.50 ($2.85) for children 5 to 12. From Easter to October, it's open daily from 10:30am to 6:30pm. Take the twice-daily bus from Tobermory.

Just outside Dervaig is the 43-seat **Mull Little Theater,** founded in 1966. According to the *Guinness Book of World Records,* this makes it the smallest professional theater in Great Britain. See "Dervaig After Dark," below, for details.

From Dervaig, you can cruise to the lonely **Treshnish Isles,** a sanctuary for seabirds and seals. From April to September, a local entrepreneur operates the *Turus Mara* (✆ **01688/400-297**), carrying up to 60 passengers on half-day visits at £42 ($80) or full-day visits at £46 ($87). The boat departs from the Ulva Ferry Piers, on the west side of Mull. The Treshnish Isles are murky, muddy, and boggy, so bring dry clothes, boots, and a sense of humor.

WHERE TO STAY

Druimard Country House   This restored Victorian country house, in the northwestern part of Mull, has views of an idyllic glen and of the River Bellart, where it flows into Loch Cuin and out to sea. For old-fashioned Scottish comfort and a tranquil atmosphere, the Druimard is the place to be. The bedrooms are tastefully furnished and contain small bathrooms. Your hosts, Haydn and Wendy Hubbard, are a fountain of information about Mull. They'll arrange cruises to remote isles, wildlife expeditions, and whale-watching jaunts. Even if you don't stay here, consider a visit to their award-winning restaurant (see below).

Dervaig, Isle of Mull PA75 6QW. ✆ 01688/400-345. Fax 01688/400-291. www.druimard.co.uk. 7 units. £90 ($171). Rates include breakfast. MC, V. Closed Nov–Mar. Follow signs to Mull Little Theatre. **Amenities:** Restaurant; bar; nonsmoking rooms. *In room:* TV, coffeemaker, hair dryer.

Druimnacroish Hotel   Visitors come here to leave modern life behind. Even though the owners have recently refurbished and upgraded the place, they purposefully left TVs and phones out of the guest rooms, but they're available upon request. Families might be interested in the self-catering apartment, available for weekly stays. In summer, guests can enjoy a drink and views of the glen in the comfortable conservatory. The moderately priced meals feature simple modern Scottish cuisine, taking full advantage of fresh local produce.

Dervaig, Isle of Mull PA75 6QW. ✆/fax 01688/400-274. www.druimnacroish.co.uk. 6 units. £64–£76 ($122–$144) double. Room rates include Scottish breakfast. MC, V. Closed Nov–Mar. **Amenities:** Restaurant; bar; nonsmoking rooms. *In room:* Coffeemaker, hair dryer, iron, no phone.

WHERE TO DINE

Druimard Hotel Restaurant ⌖ SCOTTISH   This acclaimed restaurant offers a varied menu based on local produce and supplies, ranging from the freshest fish to tender Scottish beef. The cuisine is skillfully prepared, often with unusual sauces. You might begin with a wild mushroom soup served with cream and sautéed mushrooms. The potato pancake topped with spring onion crème fraîche and a basil oil dressing will win you over. Meat-eaters dig into the filet of Aberdeen Angus topped with caramelized shallots and red-wine sauce.

In the Druimard Hotel, Dervaig. ℭ **01688/400-345.** Reservations recommended. Fixed-price 5-course dinner £42 ($80). MC, V. Daily 7–8:30pm. Closed Nov–Mar.

DERVAIG AFTER DARK

Located 14km (8½ miles) west of Tobermory, the **Mull Little Theatre,** Tobermory-Dervaig Road (ℭ **01688/302-828**), is indeed quite small, with an audience capacity of 43 people for the dramas staged inside a former byre (stable). The season runs from Easter to September, with visiting companies as well as the small-but-capable Mull Theater Company filling the bill. Adult tickets run £8 ($15); seniors, students, and children pay £6 ($11). Tickets should be reserved in advance. There's no seat allocation, so arrive early.

FIONNPHORT

At the western tip of the Ross of Mull is Fionnphort, a tiny port that sees a lot of traffic. This is where the road ends, and regular ferry passage is available across the 1.6km (1 mile) Sound of Iona to the Isle of Iona, one of the most visited attractions in Scotland. Less than 3km (2 miles) to the south is the tidal island of Erraid, where David Balfour had adventures in Stevenson's *Kidnapped.*

WHERE TO STAY

Achaban House *Kids* Its almost indestructible walls (1m/3 ft. thick in places) were built in 1820 of pink granite for the supervisor of the local quarry. Shortly after, the building was converted into the manse for the local church. Today, it sits beside the town's only highway, a 10-minute walk east of the ferry landing. All rooms have private bathrooms (some with shower only), though some are across the hall. One family room is available. Fixed-price dinners are prepared on request and might include excellent poached local salmon wrapped in a sheath of herbs. No smoking is permitted.

Fionnphort, Isle of Mull PA66 6BL. ℭ **01681/700-205.** Fax 01681/700-649. www.achabanhouse.co.uk. 6 units. £32 ($60) double; £95 ($181) family room. Rates include Scottish breakfast. MC, V. *In room:* Coffeemaker, hair dryer, no phone.

WHERE TO DINE

Keel Row SCOTTISH   The undisputed leader in providing food and drink to passengers waiting for a ferry to Iona, this friendly place is in two connected buildings near the pier. Food is served in a cedar-sided building overlooking the waterfront, while drinks are offered in a 19th-century stone cottage whose blazing fireplace adds cheer to many a gray day. Meal options include spicy fried crab with coriander, onions, tomatoes, and spices served with turmeric rice and salad, or the national dish of haggis with *neeps and tatties* (turnips and mashed potatoes).

At the harborfront, at the end of A849. ℭ **01681/700-458.** Main courses £9–£14 ($17–$27); sandwiches and burgers £3.50–£7 ($6.65–$13). MC, V. Restaurant summer only, daily noon–3pm and 6–9pm; snacks and drinks year-round, daily noon–11pm; meals served in the bar during winter, daily 6–8pm; drinks year-round, daily noon–11pm.

TIRORAN

Close to Ben More, Mull's highest mountain, Tiroran is isolated in the countryside. It's on the north shore of Loch Scridain, on the southern part of the island, and is reached along B8035.

WHERE TO STAY

Tiroran House *⭐ Finds*   Located on the north shore of Loch Scridain, standing on its own bucolic grounds, Tiroran House is ideal for a romantic getaway; it's surrounded by gardens and spacious lawns that open onto the wild sea. A stay here is like being lodged in an elegant Scottish manor. All the bedrooms have distinct character, with touches of elegance, and each is equipped with a luxurious bathroom (with tub or shower). To supplement its regular bedrooms, the owners also rent out two beautiful cottages, ideal for a family vacation. These cottages usually require at least a week's rental.

Tiroran, PA69 6ES Isle of Mull. ⓒ **01681/705-232.** Fax 01681/705-240. www.tiroran.com. 6 units. £100–£140 ($190–$266) double. Rates include breakfast. MC, V. **Amenities:** Dining room. *In room:* Kitchen in cottages only.

8 Iona ⭐ & Staffa ⭐: An Abbey & a Musical Cave

Iona: 209m (⅛ mile) W of Mull; Staffa: 10km (6 miles) NE of Iona

A remote, low-lying, and treeless green island with high cliffs and rolling meadows, Iona is off the southwestern coast of Mull across the Sound of Iona. It's only 1.5 by 5.5km (1 by 3½ miles). Staffa, with its famous **musical cave,** is a 30-hectare (75-acre) island in the Inner Hebrides, lying to the west of Mull.

Staying at Iona Abbey

Some people consider a visit to Iona the highlight of their trip to Scotland. Besides being impressed by the unusual historical and archaeological site, many gain a renewed interest in the power of religion. If that's what you're seeking, you can contact the **Iona Community** (ⓒ **01681/700-404**), an ecumenical group that maintains a communal lifestyle in the ancient abbey and offers full board and accommodations to visitors who want to share in the community's daily life. The only ordained members of the group are its two wardens, one of whom belongs to the Presbyterian Church of Scotland, the other to the Scottish Episcopal Church.

From March to October, the community leads a series of discussion seminars, each lasting from Saturday to Saturday. A recent seminar focused on the role of the Christian Church in the united Europe of the 21st century. The cost of a week's full board during one of these seminars is £290 ($551) per person. The abbey also opens to guests from late November to mid-December, although no seminars are offered then. The per-week price is the same as in summer. Guests are expected to contribute about 30 minutes per day to the execution of some kind of household chore. The daily schedule involves a wake-up call at 8am, communal breakfast at 8:20am, a morning religious service, and plenty of unscheduled time for conversation, study, and contemplation. Up to 44 guests can be accommodated at one time in bunk-bedded twin rooms without private bathrooms. In addition to the abbey, there's the Iona Community's center for reconciliation, the **MacLeod Centre,** built for youth, people with disabilities, and families. It accommodates up to 50 guests, during summer only. For further details, phone ⓒ **01681/700-404.**

IONA

Iona has been known as a place of spiritual power and pilgrimage for centuries and was the site of the first Christian settlement in Scotland, preserving the learning that was nearly lost in the Dark Ages.

The island was owned by the dukes of Argyll from 1695, but to pay £1 million ($1.9 million) in real-estate taxes, the 12th duke was forced to sell it to Sir Hugh Fraser, former owner of Harrods. Fraser secured Iona's future and made it possible for money raised by the National Trust for Scotland to be turned over to the trustees of the restored abbey. The only village on Iona, **Baille Mor,** sits in the most sheltered spot, allowing some trees and garden plots to be cultivated. The best way to get around is to walk.

Iona is accessible only by passenger ferry from the Island of Mull. (Cars must remain on Mull.) Service is informal but fairly frequent in summer. In the off season, transport depends entirely on the weather. The round-trip fare is £4 ($7.60). Call **Caledonian MacBrayne** (© **01688/302-017** in Tobermory) for exact times.

Today, the island attracts nearly 1,000 visitors a week in high season. Most come to see the Benedictine **Iona Abbey** ⊛, part of which dates from the 13th century. People also come to visit relics of the settlement founded here by St. Columba in A.D. 563, from which Celtic Christianity spread through Scotland and beyond to Europe. The abbey has been restored by the Iona Community, and is run by Historic Scotland, which leads tours and runs a coffee shop daily from 10am to 4:30pm. Admission is £4.50 ($8.55) adults, £3.50 ($6.65) students and seniors, £2.25 ($4.30) children. The community also offers room and board to interested visitors, conducts workshops on Christianity, sponsors a youth camp, and each Wednesday leads a 11km (7-mile) hike to the island's holy and historic spots.

Despite the many visitors, the atmosphere on the island remains peaceful and spiritual. You can walk off among the sheep and cows that wander freely everywhere to the top of **Dun-I,** a small mountain, and contemplate the ocean and the landscape as though you were the only person on earth.

WHERE TO STAY & DINE

Most of the islanders live by crofting and fishing and supplement their income by taking in paying guests in season, usually charging very low or at least fair prices. You can, of course, check into the hotels below, but a stay in a private home may be an altogether rewarding adventure.

Argyll Hotel ⊛ *(Finds* Housed in an 1868 Victorian, this hotel stands 600 yards from the ferry dock and overlooks the Sound of Iona and Mull. The small guest rooms are comfortably furnished. The good home cooking includes very fresh fish and baked goods; vegetarian meals are available, too. The hotel is licensed to serve alcohol to guests.

Isle of Iona PA76 6SJ. © **01681/700-334.** Fax 01681/700-510. www.argyllhoteliona.co.uk. 16 units, 15 with private bathroom. £64–£116 ($122–$220) double. Rates include Scottish breakfast. MC, V. **Amenities:** Restaurant; non-smoking rooms. *In room:* Coffeemaker, hair dryer, no phone.

Martyr's Bay Restaurant ⊛ *(Finds* SCOTTISH/SEAFOOD Down by the docks, this is the best place on Iona for pub grub. One local said that it looks like a village hall from a 1970s British suburb, and so it does; but it warms considerably once you go inside, especially after you've had a pint or two of Guinness. The seafood, best showcased in the cold shellfish platter, is the best on island. The Grant family, the owners, not only secure the finest catch of the day, but they also prepare dishes made from fresh local meat, especially lamb. Portions are huge, so come here with a large appetite.

Isle of Iona. ⓒ **01681/700-382.** Reservations recommended on weekends. Main courses £7–£18 ($13–$34). DC, MC, V. Bar daily 11:30am–11:30pm; restaurant 9:30am–5pm and 6–8:30pm.

St. Columba Hotel This hotel, built of clapboard and white stone, is just uphill from the village and about .5km (¼ mile) from the jetty. Built as a manse for Presbyterian clergy in 1846, its guest rooms are rather monastic but clean and reasonably comfortable for the price. Bathrooms are small and equipped with either a tub or a shower. Try to get a room overlooking the sea, and reserve well in advance in summer. A set dinner is served nightly at 7pm, with hearty and wholesome food. Vegetarian meals are available on request.

Isle of Iona PA76 6SL. ⓒ **01681/700-304.** Fax 01681/700-688. www.stcolumba-hotel.co.uk. 18 units. £122–£178 ($232–$338) double. Rates include half-board. MC, V. Closed Oct 18 to mid-Mar. **Amenities:** Restaurant; bar. *In room:* Coffeemaker, hair dryer, no phone.

STAFFA

The attraction of the island of Staffa, 10km (6 miles) north of Iona, is **Fingal's Cave** ⊛, a lure to visitors for more than 200 years and the inspiration for music, poetry, paintings, and prose. Its Gaelic name, *An Uamh Ehinn,* means "musical cave." It's the only such formation known in the world that has basalt columns; over the centuries, the sea has carved a huge cavern in the basalt, leaving massive hexagonal columns. The sound of the crashing waves and swirling waters (the music) inspired Mendelssohn to write the *Fingal's Cave Overture.* Turner painted the cave on canvas, and Keats, Wordsworth, and Tennyson all praised it in their poetry.

Staffa has been uninhabited for more than 170 years, but you can still explore the cave, which is protected from development by the National Trust. Entrance is free, requiring only payment for boat passage from Mull or Iona at £18 ($34) for adults and £7.50 ($14) for children under 14. The boat runs twice daily from Iona and Mull between March and October. Rubber-soled shoes and warm clothing are recommended. Reservations are important; call **Mrs. Carol Kirkpatrick,** whose husband, David, operates the boat, at *Tigh-na-Traigh* (House by the Shore), Isle of Iona (ⓒ **01681/700-358**).

9 Colonsay

24km (15 miles) S of the Isle of Mull

The most remote of the islands of Argyll, Colonsay shares some of the same characteristics as Iona, Tyree, and Coll. To the west, it faces nothing but the open Atlantic—only a lighthouse stands between Colonsay and Canada. The island encompasses 52 sq. km (20 sq. miles). It's more tranquil than Mull and Skye because it doesn't accommodate day-trippers.

A ferry, operated by **Caledonian MacBrayne** (ⓒ **08705/650-000** for schedules), sails between Oban and Colonsay three times a week. The 60km (37-mile) crossing takes 2½ hours.

You can explore all parts of the island along its one-lane roads. Many visitors prefer renting a bike rather than driving. You can also rent sailing dinghies and rowboats and sail around the island, following in the grand tradition of the Vikings. Go to the **Isle of Colonsay Hotel** (see below), whose staff rent out bikes (£5/$9.50 per day or

£15/$29 per week) or put you in touch with local fishermen and entrepreneurs; a boat should cost around £15 ($29) per hour.

Wildlife abounds: golden eagles, falcons, gray seals, otters, and wild goats with elegant horns and long shaggy hair. Prehistoric forts, stone circles, and single standing stones attest to the antiquity of Colonsay, which has been occupied since the Stone Age.

It's estimated that there are some 500 species of flora on the island. The gardens of the 1722 **Colonsay House** (not open to the public) are filled with rare rhododendrons, magnolias, eucalyptus, and even palm trees; from April to October, Wednesday noon to 5pm and Friday 2 to 5pm, you can visit the gardens for £3 ($5.70). There's also an 18-hole golf course.

The little island of **Oransay** was named for Oran, a disciple of St. Columba. It's joined at low tide by the Strand, and you can wade across the sands during a 2-hour period. The ancient monastic ruins here date from the 6th century.

WHERE TO STAY & DINE
Isle of Colonsay Hotel 🐦 *Finds*   This is Great Britain's most isolated hotel and Colonsay's social center. Its mid-18th-century gables and chimneys rise above surrounding herb and vegetable gardens. The bedrooms are small and decidedly informal, with basic but comfortable furnishings. Guests who want to get close-up views of the island's abundant flora and fauna can ask to be dropped off by courtesy car to go on rambles. A meal in the tongue-and-groove-paneled dining room is an event for locals, who appreciate the ambience of the cocktail lounge and bar. The inn serves lunch and rather expensive fixed-price dinners daily, with selections like homemade soup, fresh mussels, and vegetables from the garden.

Isle of Colonsay PA61 7YP. ⓒ 01951/200-316. Fax 01951/200-353. www.colonsay.org.uk/hotel.html. 12 units, 9 with private bathroom. £85–£140 ($162–$266) double. Rates include half-board. MC, V. **Amenities:** Restaurant; bar; bike and scooter rental; laundry service. *In room:* TV, coffeemaker, hair dryer, iron, no phone.

10 Lewis 🐦: Island of Heather
336km (209 miles) NW of Edinburgh, 343km (213 miles) NW of Glasgow

The most northerly of the Outer Hebrides—and also the largest, at 100km (60 miles) long and 29 to 45km (18–28 miles) across—Lewis is easily reached by ferry from Ullapool (see chapter 11 for more information). The island was once known as Lews, or, more poetically, the "island of heather"—the sweetness of the lamb raised here is said to come from their heather diet. Lewis and Harris (see "Harris," below) form part of the same island, stretching for a total of 153km (95 miles). Filled with marshy peat bogs, Lewis's landscape is relatively treeless, thanks in part to Norse raider Magnus Barelegs. He and his Viking warriors burned most of the trees, leaving Lewis as bare as his shanks.

Even though the whole world has heard of Harris tweed, it might as well be called Lewis tweed, because Stornoway, with a population of 5,000, has taken over the industry. Located on the eastern side of the island, **Stornoway** is the only real town in the Outer Hebrides; it's a landlocked harbor where you can see gray seals along with fishing boats. There are some 600 weavers on the island, and one of the attractions of this rather bleak port is visiting a mill shop or a weaver's cottage.

ESSENTIALS
GETTING THERE   An **airport,** which doubles as an RAF base, is 5.5km (3½ miles) from the center of Stornoway. Stornoway receives flights from Glasgow and

Inverness Monday to Saturday, as well as frequent service from Benbecula. Phone **British Airways** (© **0845/733-3377** in Glasgow) to make reservations.

Monday through Saturday, **Caledonian MacBrayne** (© **08705/650-000** at the ferry terminal in Gourock) operates two or three ferries from Ullapool to Stornoway. One-way passage costs £16 ($30). Cars can be transported as well. Trip time is 3½ hours.

VISITOR INFORMATION   The **Western Isles Tourist Board,** which has information about all the Outer Hebrides, is at 26 Cromwell St., Stornoway (© **01851/703-088**). It's open April to October, Monday to Friday 9am to 6pm and Saturday 9am to 5pm and 8 to 9pm; and October to April, Monday to Friday 9am to 5pm.

EXPLORING THE ISLAND

The island's major attraction is the Neolithic temple of **Callandish** ★★, 26km (16 miles) west of Stornoway, off A858. Only Stonehenge, in the West Country of Britain, equals these 13 standing stones as a site of prehistoric archaeological splendor. The stones are laid out to depict a Celtic cross with a burial cairn at the center. They are approached from either north or south by a road lined with erect stone pillars. The site dates from about 1800 B.C. An old Gaelic legend claims that when the alleged giants of old, who were said to inhabit the island, refused to convert to Christianity, St. Kieran turned them to stone. You can wander among the ruins for free, day or night. The "visitor center" provides historical background and charges £1.75 ($3.35) if you want to see videos on the site. It's open Monday to Saturday from 10am to 6pm (9am–6:30pm July–Aug). Also here are a gift shop and cafe.

Just west of the harbor at Stornoway, you can visit the grounds of **Lews Castle** (which uses the old spelling), built in 1818. The castle itself is closed to the public, but you can wander through the garden, which is at its flowery best in May.

At Arnol, 24km (15 miles) northwest of Stornoway, off A858, is the thatched **Lewis Blackhouse** (© **01851/710-395**), constructed without mortar and preserved to show what a typical Hebridean dwelling once looked like. It's called a "black house" because it was believed the smoke from the open peat fires was good for the thatched roof— the Leodhasach (as the islanders are called) built their houses with no chimneys so the smoke could pass through the thatch. From April to September, it's open Monday to Saturday 9:30am to 6:30pm (to 4pm Oct–Mar). Admission is £4 ($7.60) for adults, £3 ($5.70) for seniors, and £1.60 ($3.05) for children 5 to 15.

At 6m (19 ft.) tall and 2m (6 ft.) wide, the **Clach an Trushal** at Balanthrushal, Barvas, is the largest single monolith in northern Scotland. It's signposted beside the main highway leading north from Stornoway. Along A858, 32km (20 miles) northwest of Stornoway, stands **Dun Carloway Broch,** a 9m (30-ft.) broch (round-sided stone tower) left over from the Iron Age. You can visit at any time for free.

At Dun Borranish, near the village of Ardroil, the famous **Lewis Chessmen** were dug up in 1831 outside Uig Sands. Made of walrus tusks and reputed to have been carved around A.D. 500, they now form an outstanding exhibit in the British Museum in London. If you're a chess player, you may want to purchase a reproduction set in Lewis.

At Ness, toward that northerly outpost, the Butt of Lewis, is **St. Moluag's Church,** a Scottish Episcopal church that still holds occasional services. The chapel, known in Gaelic as *Teampull Mhor* ("big temple"), is from about the 12th century, founded by Olav the Black during the Norse occupation.

Tips Watersports in the Outer Hebrides

If you prefer the quiet and calm paddling of a sea kayak, contact **Hebridean Explorations,** 19 West View Terrace, Stornoway, Isle of Lewis (© **01851/705-655**), which offers rentals, guided tours, and advice about how best to view the flora and fauna.

And if you'd rather just be a passenger, you might take a day cruise with **Sea Trek,** 16 Uigen, Miavaig, Isle of Lewis (© **01851/672-464**); **Island Cruising,** 1 Erista, Uig, Isle of Lewis (© **01851/672-381**); or **Strond Wildlife Charters,** 1 Strond, Isle of Harris (© **01859/520-204**). All specialize in full- and half-day (or any amount of time you want) cruises that focus on the wildlife, bird life, and ecology of the Hebridean archipelago, usually with special emphasis on the seal colonies that thrive offshore.

Borge Pottery, on A857 at Borve, 27km (17 miles) from Stornoway on the road to Ness (© **01851/850-345**), has been in business for more than 20 years, producing hand-thrown stoneware in pink, blue, red, green, black, and cream. Its name is spelled with a *g,* the Gaelic spelling of Borve.

The Isle of Lewis's contribution to the world of golf is the 18-hole **Golf Club,** Willow Glen Road, about 1.6km (1 mile) from Stornoway (© **01851/702-240**). It's a windswept, isolated course carved out of the moors. Greens fees are £20 ($38) per round or per day.

If you'd like to rent a bike, head for **Alex Dan's Cycle Centre,** 67 Kenneth St., Stornoway (© **01851/704-025**).

WHERE TO STAY

Cabarfeidh Hotel *Finds* Cabarfeidh is one of the best hotels on Lewis. It stands about 1.6km (1 mile) north of Stornoway, midway between Laxdale and Newmarket, in a 3.2-hectare (8-acre) garden. Designed as a contemporary arrangement of cubes, it was built by a Mackenzie, who named it after the battle cry of his fighting clan, "stag antlers," and the decor includes a collection of just that. The pleasant guest rooms have small, attached bathrooms. The dining room offers the best local produce, fresh fish, and local beef and lamb. The convivial bar is shaped like a Viking longship.

Manor Park, Stornoway, Lewis, Outer Hebrides H51 2EU. © **01851/702-604.** Fax 01851/705-572. www.cacabarfeidh-hotel.co.uk. 46 units. £125 ($238) double. Rates include Scottish breakfast. AE, DC, MC, V. Free parking. **Amenities:** Restaurant; bar; room service; babysitting; laundry service; nonsmoking rooms. *In room:* TV, coffeemaker, hair dryer, trouser press, Wi-Fi.

Caladh Inn A 5-minute walk from the town center, the Caladh is one of the most modern hotels—and the largest—in the Outer Hebrides. The public rooms have several full-size snooker tables; there's a bar as well as a basement nightclub open Friday and Saturday. The guest rooms don't have a lot of charm but are well-equipped. The restaurant offers a reasonably priced three-course dinner menu. The fare is rather plain but hearty, a combination of Scottish and Italian dishes.

9 James St., Stornoway, Lewis, Outer Hebrides HS1 2QN. © **01851/702-740.** Fax 01851/703-900. www.caladhinn.co.uk. 69 units. £170 ($323) double. Rates include Scottish breakfast. AE, MC, V. Free parking. Closed Jan. **Amenities:** Restaurant; bar; babysitting; laundry service; nonsmoking rooms. *In room:* TV, coffeemaker, hair dryer, trouser press.

WHERE TO DINE

Park Guest House SCOTTISH/FRENCH   Located in a century-old stone house about a 10-minute walk north of the ferry terminal, this is the best dining room in town. It has a country-house decor and a fireplace in the style of Charles Rennie Mackintosh. Menu items feature seasonal game, such as venison in port-wine sauce, and seafood choices like oysters raw or au gratin, pan-fried scallops in lemon butter and herbs, and turbot filet grilled with herb butter. The restaurant is fully licensed and at its most elegant between 7 and 9pm.

Nine simple guest rooms cost £46 to £90 ($87–$171) each for a double, including breakfast. Units come with TV, hair dryer, and coffeemaker.

30 James St., Stornoway, Lewis, Outer Hebrides H51 2QN. ⓒ **01851/702-485.** Reservations required. Main courses £14–£22 ($27–$42); fixed-price 2-course early-bird dinner (5:30–6:45pm) £15 ($29). MC, V. Tues–Sat 5–8:45pm.

STORNOWAY AFTER DARK

Most of the pubs lining the waterfront have live music on weekends, usually traditional Celtic or Scottish performers. There's generally no cover. **Clachan Bar,** North Beach Street (ⓒ **01851/703-653**), boasts none of the quaintness of a traditional pub, but locals and visitors alike come on Friday and Saturday for live bands downstairs or for the disco upstairs. Another updated bar with live music is **Lewis Bar,** South Beach Street (ⓒ **01851/704-567**). On Saturday, the stage might hold anything from a rock band to a traditional Scottish group.

An Lanntair Gallery, Town Hall, South Beach Street (ⓒ **01851/703-307**), stages musical and theatrical events with a strong emphasis on Gaelic culture. The center also has jazz, folk, and traditional music concerts, plus classic and contemporary drama, comedy, and children's shows. Tickets are £8 to £12 ($15–$23) for adults and £3 to £5 ($5.70–$9.50) for children under 16. Productions take place in either the gallery space, which seats 55, or the town hall, which holds 350.

11 Harris ⓐ

351km (218 miles) NW of Glasgow, 90km (56 miles) NW of Mallaig, 396km (246 miles) NW of Edinburgh, 55km (34 miles) S of Stornoway

Harris, south of Lewis but really part of the same island, has a different geography. North Harris is full of mountains, dominated by the **Clisham,** which at 789m (2,600 ft.) is the highest peak in the Outer Hebrides. Harris may not have as many ancient relics as Lewis, but most visitors agree that the mountains, beaches, and scenic vistas make up for it. The **beaches** in the west are good for strolling, swimming (if you're hardy), or camping; the bays in the east are ideal for fishing and sailing.

The locals, some 3,000 in all, are called Hearach, and they're different from the people of Lewis, even speaking with a different accent. If you arrive in Lewis, you can drive to Harris on a single-lane road that connects the two areas. As you go along the rugged terrain, you might meet another car, in which case use one of the "passing places." No matter what, drive slowly because sheep might suddenly scamper in front of your wheels. The distance from Stornoway, the capital of Lewis, to Tarbert, the capital of Harris, is 55km (34 miles).

Many visitors prefer to take the ferry from the little port of Uig on the Isle of Skye; it heads for Harris Monday through Saturday, and transports both cars and passengers. Even in the busiest season, Harris isn't overrun. From Harris you can also make connections to Lochmaddy on North Uist (see "North & South Uist," below).

Harris has long been known for its hand-weaving and tweed. Although that industry has now passed to Stornoway (see "Lewis: Island of Heather," above), you can still buy Harris tweed jackets in Harris. In summer, you see them displayed on the walls of roadside sheds, selling for very good prices.

The island is bisected by two long sea lochs that meet at Tarbert, the single-street main village. Whatever you need in the way of supplies, you should pick up here—otherwise you'll be out of luck. If you're touring by car, also fill up with petrol (gas) here. Ask at the tourist center about the island bus tours conducted in summer. For an adventure, take the car ferry, which runs regularly across the sound, to the little fishing community of **Scalpay,** an offshore island.

ESSENTIALS

GETTING THERE You can take a **car/passenger ferry** to Tarbert, capital of Harris, from Uig on the Isle of Skye, Monday to Saturday. There are one or two ferries per day; a one-way ticket for the 1¾-hour trip costs £9.80 ($19) Call **Caledonian MacBrayne** (© 08705/650-000; www.calmac.co.uk) for schedules.

Buses run from Stornoway to Tarbert daily (a 70-min. trip). Call **Harris Coaches** (© 01859/502-441) for schedules. At least five buses per day make the run Monday to Saturday.

If you're **driving** from Stornoway on Lewis in the north, head south along A859 to reach Tarbert.

VISITOR INFORMATION A **tourist office** operates from the port at Tarbert (© 01859/502-011). April to October, it's open Monday to Saturday 9am to 5pm; November to March, it's open Monday and Friday 11am to 1pm; Tuesday, Thursday, and Saturday 11am to 2pm.

EXPLORING THE ISLAND

The lack of roads makes it impossible to take a circular tour of the island. However, using Tarbert as your base, you can set out northwest along the coast of **West Loch Tarbert,** with the Forest of Harris to your north. Or you can go south from Tarbert, hugging the western coast road along the Sound of Taransay, with Rodel as your final destination.

Taking the northwesterly route first, you come to an **Old Whaling Station** at Bunavoneadar. In the early 20th century, Norwegians set up the station, but because of dwindling profits it was abandoned in 1930. If you continue north along B887, you'll arrive at the **Amhuinnsuidhe Estate,** a Scottish baronial castle built in 1868. The river to the left has one of the most beautiful salmon leaps in Scotland. The road beyond the castle continues to **Hushinish Point,** where you can see the little island of Scarp, which was once inhabited.

Returning to Tarbert, you can take A859 south. Some of the South Harris coastline will remind you of Norway, with its sea lochs and fjord fingers. The main road to Rodel is mostly two lanes and well surfaced; the east-coast road, however, is a winding single lane. Along the way you pass the **Clach Mhicleoid** ("standing stone"). Locals call it MacLeod's Stone.

From here you can look out across the Sound of Taransay, to the **Island of Taransay,** named after St. Tarran. It has several ancient sites, including the remains of St. Tarran's Chapel. Like Scarp, it was once populated, but now its grazing fields have been turned over to sheep. Continuing on the coastal road along the wild Atlantic—actually the Sound of Taransay—you see another ancient stone, the **Scarista Standing Stone.**

Before reaching it, you pass **Borve Lodge,** the former home of Lord Leverhulme, the soap tycoon.

The road south passes the little promontory of Toe Head, which juts into the Atlantic. An ancient chapel, **Rudhan Teampull,** stands about 1.2km (¾ mile) west of Northton and is reached by a sand track. Many prehistoric sites were uncovered and excavated on the tiny machair-studded peninsula of Toe Head.

The next village is **Leverburgh,** named after Lord Leverhulme. He's credited with trying to bring the people of the area into the 20th century, but his efforts to rejuvenate the economy largely failed. From here you can take a small passenger ferry to North Uist and Berneray.

Finally, drive east to Rodel, where **St. Clement's Church** 🏆 stands high in the village. Overlooking Loch Rodel, this church is one of the most important monuments in the Western Isles. Cruciform in plan, it has a western tower, a nave, and two cross aisles. Some of the masonry work in freestone is similar to that used at Iona Abbey. The church is believed to have been built in the late 15th century or very early 16th century.

In the Sound of Harris, separating Harris from North Uist, lie the islands of **Ensay, Killegray,** and **Pabbay.** They were once populated, but now are the domain of grazing sheep.

The island has a 9-hole **Golf Club,** Sgarasta (🕿 **01859/502-214**), an isolated, windswept course carved into the Hebridean moors. This course is being renovated into an 18-hole golf course. Completion of the course is estimated sometime in 2008.

WHERE TO STAY & DINE

Harris Hotel 🏆   This hotel, a landmark since it was built in 1865, remains one of the most popular places in the Outer Hebrides. In the 1920s, the novelist J. M. Barrie visited and found inspiration for his story *Mary Rose.* His initials, which he etched, can still be seen on the dining room window. Each guest room has hot and cold running water and lots of old-fashioned comfort. Some family rooms are available, many overlooking the garden. The pub is the social center for locals. You can order pub grub throughout the day; a more formal restaurant offers moderately priced dinners.

Tarbert, Harris, Outer Hebrides HS3 3DL. 🕿 01859/502-154. Fax 01859/502-281. www.harrishotel.com. 24 units, 20 with private bathroom. £60 ($114) double without bathroom; £80–£120 ($152–$228) double with bathroom. Rates include Scottish breakfast. MC, V. **Amenities:** Restaurant; bar. *In room:* TV, coffeemaker, hair dryer, no phone.

Leachin House 🏆 *(Finds*   Located on the north shore of the loch, this house was built of Berneray granite (a form of gneiss) with Victorian gingerbread trim. Its original owner was Norman McLeod, the fisherman and entrepreneur credited as being the father of the Harris tweed industry. The house is now loaded with antiques and paintings. The comfortable, high-ceilinged guest rooms make you think you're staying in a friend's home, while the rather pricey dinners have the feel of a private dinner party. The food is based on modern Scottish cuisine. Children under 10 are not welcome.

Tarbert, Isle of Harris HS3 3AH. 🕿/fax 01859/502-157. 3 units, 1 with private bathroom. £100 ($190) double with or without bathroom. Rates include breakfast. MC, V. Closed Dec–Jan. From Tarbert, follow A859 for 1.6km (1 mile), signposted to Stornoway. **Amenities:** Restaurant; laundry service; nonsmoking rooms. *In room:* TV, coffeemaker, hair dryer, iron, no phone.

Rodel Hotel 🏆 *(Finds*   Built at land's end in the shadows of the 500-year-old St. Clement's Church, this hotel is at the southernmost tip of Harris. Because it fronts a harbor with an anchorage, the Rodel is a favorite retreat for anglers seeking trout and salmon. The exterior dates to the 18th century but its interior has been comfortably and somewhat luxuriously modernized. Bedrooms are all nonsmoking and elegantly furnished, each decorated with a charming character and ambience. A bathtub and power shower are found in every room. Harris tweed bed covers and matching curtains are placed throughout. In the restaurant, the best local produce is used, including island lamb and beef and, when available, rabbit and geese. Freshwater fish comes from the local fisheries, including sea trout, crab, and monkfish. A wide selection of Highland malts and Island scotch, along with good local ales, is available in the bar, where you can join the locals.

Rodel, HS5 3TW Isle of Harris. © **01859/520-210.** Fax 01859/520-219. www.rodelhotel.co.uk. £90–£120 ($171–$228) double. MC, V. From Tarbert head south for 3.2km (2 miles). **Amenities:** Restaurant; bar. *In room:* Beverage maker, hair dryer.

Scarista House ★★   Built long ago as a Georgian vicarage, this is now a lovely hotel with handsome guest rooms and two self-catering cottages. Some summer guests enjoy a bracing dip in the icy water of Scarista Beach, while others prefer to read in the well-stocked library. Here you get the best breakfast around: freshly squeezed orange juice, compote of fresh and dried fruits, organic oatmeal porridge with cream, Lewis kippers, Stornoway black pudding, bacon, sausage, fresh eggs, fresh herring rolled in oatmeal, and a variety of baked goods. If you plan to burn off this morning feast on a hike, a packed lunch will be provided. Most guests return for a drink by the fireplace, and then, at 8pm, they enjoy an upscale four-course dinner featuring local shellfish and heather-fed lamb.

Scarista, Harris, Outer Hebrides HS3 3HX. © **01859/550-238.** Fax 01859/550-277. www.scaristahouse.com. 5 units. £170–£189 ($323–$359) double. Room rates include Scottish breakfast. £315–£575 ($599–$1093) per week, cottage. MC, V. 24km (15 miles) SW of Tarbert on A859. **Amenities:** Restaurant; lounge; babysitting; laundry service. *In room:* Coffeemaker, hair dryer.

12 North & South Uist

145–161km (90–100 miles) NW of Glasgow

Standing stones, chambered cairns, ruins, and fortresses indicate a history-rich past on North Uist and South Uist, connected by the smaller island of Benbecula.

ESSENTIALS

GETTING THERE   British Airways flies Monday through Saturday to **Benbecula Airport** (the nearest connection for North Uist) from Glasgow, a 1-hour trip. Phone © **0141/887-1111** at the Glasgow Airport for flight information.

Lochboisdale is the site of the ferry terminal providing a link between South Uist and the mainland at Oban, taking 5½ hours. Monday through Saturday, one ferry per day runs from Oban to Lochboisdale, costing £20 ($38) one-way. Some of these ferries stop at Castlebay, on Barra. Other ferries run from Uig, on the Isle of Skye, to Lochmaddy, North Uist, once or twice daily. The most popular connection, this car/passenger ferry trip takes anywhere from 2 to 4 hours and costs £9.80 ($19) one-way. For information, consult **Caledonian MacBrayne** (© **08705/650-000** in Lochmaddy).

North Uist is linked to Benbecula and South Uist by causeways and bridges, so you can **drive** to or from either of these islands along A867, which becomes A865.

VISITOR INFORMATION   Consult the **Western Isles Tourist Board** in Stornoway (see "Lewis: Island of Heather," earlier in this chapter). There's also a **tourist office** at the pier in Lochmaddy, on North Uist (© **01876/500-321**), open Monday to Friday 9am to 5pm; Saturday 9:30am to 1pm and 2 to 5:30pm; and Monday, Wednesday, and Friday 7:30 to 8:30pm. The staff can arrange accommodations if you've arrived without a reservation. On South Uist, the **tourist office** at the pier at Lochboisdale (© **01878/700-286**) is open Easter to October only, Monday to Saturday 9am to 5pm. It's also open for late ferry arrivals, usually Monday to Thursday and Saturday 9 to 10pm and Friday 7:30 to 8:30pm. Accommodations can be arranged through this office as well.

NORTH UIST

A real bogland where hardy crofters try to wrestle a living from a turbulent sea and stubborn ground, North Uist is one of the lesser-known islands in the Outer Hebrides, but it's beautiful nonetheless. Its antiquity is reflected in the brochs, duns, wheelhouses, and stark monoliths, all left by the island's prehistoric dwellers.

The population of North Uist is about 2,000, and the island is about 20km (12 miles) wide by 56km (35 miles) at its longest point. North Uist is served by a circular road, usually a single lane with passing places, and several feeder routes that branch east and west.

The main village is **Lochmaddy,** on the eastern shore. Whatever you need, you're likely to find it here (if it's available on North Uist at all), from a post office to a petrol station. Lochmaddy is also the site of a ferry terminal. In addition to the ferries from Oban and Uig, a small private ferry runs from Newton Ferry, north of Lochmaddy, to Leverburgh, on Harris. This isn't a car ferry, but it does allow small motorcycles and bikes. A small vehicular ferry will take you to the island of Berneray. In keeping with the strict religious tradition of these islands, the ferry doesn't operate on Sunday—and neither, seemingly, does anything else.

EXPLORING THE ISLAND

North Uist may be small, but its scenery is extremely varied. The eastern shores possess an untamed beauty. The coastline is dotted with trout-filled lochs, and everything is set against a backdrop of rolling heather-clad hills. Nights come on fast in winter; sunsets linger in summer. The western side of North Uist is a land of rich meadows filled with wildflowers. Here you find **long white beaches,** where Atlantic rollers attract hardy surfers.

Heading northwest from Lochmaddy for 4km (2½ miles), you come to the hamlet of **Blashaval,** where you find the **Three Standing Stones of the False Men.** Local tradition has it that this trio of stones, known in Gaelic as *Na Fir Bhreige,* were actual men, wife deserters from Skye turned into stone by a witch.

Continuing along the road for 6.5km (4 miles), you approach uninhabited **Dun Torcuill Island,** rising above the west side of **Loch an Duin.** Access to the island is possible on foot only during low tide; exercise caution. On the island is a broch; it's a ruined, though still fine, example of the circular fortified towers that provided defense during the Middle Ages. Most visitors prefer to admire it from across the water.

Turning north on B893, you come to **Newton Ferry.** A 15-minute crossing takes you to the little offshore island of **Berneray,** which has some ancient sites, including the mysterious-looking **Borve Standing Stone.** There's a privately run hostel here. The 140 or so people who live on the island are mainly engaged in crofting and fishing and may regard *you* as a sightseeing attraction.

After you return to Newton Ferry, head south on the same road. A left-hand fork takes you to **Trumisgarry** to see the ruins of an old chapel where an early Christian settlement was founded. **St. Columba's Well** (*Tobar Chaluim Chille* in Gaelic) is named after the saint.

Return to the main road and head west toward Sollas. On both sides of the road are cairns and standing stones, many from 2000 B.C. Pass through **Hosta,** a site of the Highland Games, heading for the **Balranald Nature Reserve,** 5km (3 miles) northwest of Bayhead. At a reception cottage at **Goulat,** near Hougharty, you can learn more about the birds inhabiting the Outer Hebrides. You can walk through the reserve at any time at no charge, but guided tours (£3/$5.70) are given at 2pm Tuesday and Friday.

Back on the main road, heading southeast, you pass through **Bayhead.** Again, the area is filled with an astonishing number of ancient monuments. At the junction, take A867 back toward Lochmaddy. You'll see a sign pointing to **Ben Langass.** On the mountain slopes is a chambered cairn thought to be at least 3,000 years old, one of the best preserved on the island. Some historians believe a warrior chieftain was buried here, but others suggest it was a communal burial ground. Bones and pottery fragments removed from excavations were sent to the National Museum in Edinburgh.

Returning to the main road again, retrace your trail and head south for Carinish, a hamlet known for the **Carinish Stone Circle** and the **Barpa Carinish,** the site of the major attraction on the island, **Trinity Temple** (*Teampull na Trionad* in Gaelic), off A865 some 13km (8 miles) southwest of Lochmaddy. Admission is free and it's open at all times. The monastery is said to have been founded in the 13th century by Beathag, the first prioress of Iona, daughter of Somerland, an Irish mercenary and the founding father of the MacDonalds.

WHERE TO STAY & DINE

Langass Lodge ⋆ *(Finds)*   This hotel's spaciousness and comfort come as a welcome surprise after the miles of windswept, barren countryside you traverse before reaching it. The nearby sycamores are cited by the staff as among the few trees on all North Uist. Built as a hunting lodge in 1876, the hotel today attracts hunters, anglers, and nature lovers. The guest rooms were completely refurbished in 1997, with solid furnishings and pleasant decor. Each has a small, shower-only bathroom (some have tubs) and views of the nearby loch.

Locheport, North Uist, Outer Hebrides HS6 5HA. ℂ **01876/580-285.** Fax 01876/580-385. www.langasslodge.co.uk. 6 units. £90–£110 ($171–$209) double. Rates include Scottish breakfast. MC, V. Closed Feb. **Amenities:** Restaurant; bar; laundry service; nonsmoking rooms. *In room:* TV, coffeemaker, hair dryer.

Lochmaddy Hotel   You can't miss the peaked gables of this white-walled hotel, a few steps from the ferry terminal. Those who come to fish for the area's brown trout, sea trout, and salmon often stay here. (Guests are welcome to use the hotel's scales to weigh the catch of the day.) This is one of the few places on the island where you can buy fishing permits; prices are £6–£40 ($11–$76) a day, depending on what kind of fish you're seeking and on the season. The guest rooms are tasteful, each with a small, shower-only bathroom. The bar offers about the best collection of single-malt whiskies in the Outer Hebrides. The dining room serves fresh local produce, lobster, king prawns, venison, and salmon.

Lochmaddy, North Uist, Outer Hebrides HS6 5AA. ℂ **01876/500-331.** Fax 01876/500-210. www.lochmaddyhotel. co.uk. 15 units. £75–£90 ($143–$171) double. Rates include Scottish breakfast. AE, MC, V. **Amenities:** Restaurant; 2 bars; watersports; nonsmoking rooms. *In room:* TV, coffeemaker, hair dryer.

SOUTH UIST

South Uist holds a rich treasure trove of antiquity. A number of ecclesiastical remains are scattered along its shores, and Clan Ranald left many ruins and fortresses known as *duns*. Ornithologists and anglers alike are attracted to this island. Part bogland, it's 32km (20 miles) long and 10km (6 miles) wide at its broadest. A main road, A865, bisects the island, with feeder roads branching off east and west.

EXPLORING THE ISLAND

The biggest village in South Uist is **Lochboisdale,** at the head of a deep-sea loch on the southeastern part of the island. It was settled in the 19th century by crofters who had been forced off their land in the notorious Land Clearances. The ruins of a small medieval castle are at the head of the loch, on the island of Calvay, one of the many places where Bonnie Prince Charlie hid out.

Leaving Lochboisdale, A865 goes west for 5km (3 miles) to Daliburgh, where you can pick up B888 south to Pollachar, on the southern shore, a distance of 10km (6 miles). The village is named for the **Pollachar Standing Stone,** a jagged dolmen rising a few paces from the hamlet's center. Continue east along a minor road for 4km (2½ miles) to the Ludag jetty, where a private ferry goes to Eriskay and Barra.

The next stop is the **Klipheder Wheelhouse,** 3km (2 miles) west of A865, the meager ruins of a circular building from A.D. 200. Back on the main road again, you come to Askernish, site of a 9-hole **golf course.**

About 5km (3 miles) north from Daliburgh, at Airidh Mhuilinn, is a **Flora Mac-Donald memorial.** West of A865, 182m (600 ft.) up a little farm track about 1km (½ mile) north of Milton, a cairn atop a little hill marks the spot where this woman was born in 1722. She is revered for helping Bonnie Prince Charlie escape from George II and his supporters.

If you stay on the minor roads, you'll see the dramatic machair-fringed shoreline and pass through the hamlets of Bornish, Ormiclete, and Stoneybridge. At Ormiclete are the ruins of **Ormiclete Castle,** constructed by the Clan Ranald chieftains in the early 18th century.

Rejoin the main road at Howbeg. The part of the island directly north of Howbeg is rich in archaeological remains. Ruins of several **medieval chapels** are all that's left of a major South Uist ecclesiastical center.

Farther north, A865 passes the **Loch Druidibeg National Nature Reserve,** the most significant breeding ground in the country for the native grayleg goose. Attracting the dedicated bird-watcher, it's a setting of machair and brackish lochs. At Drimsdale lie the ruins of a big dun, a fortification in a loch where the villagers retreated when under attack. It continued as a stronghold for the Clan Ranald until the early 1500s.

The road continues past the Royal Artillery Rocket Range. On the flank of Reuval Hill stands **Our Lady of the Isles,** a 9m (30-ft.) statue of the Virgin and Child. Erected in 1957, it's the largest religious statue in Britain. **Loch Bee,** inhabited by mute swans, nearly bisects the northern part of South Uist.

You'll find **Hebridean Jewelry,** Garrieganichy, Iochdar (© **01870/610-288**), signposted on the north end of the Iochdar Road. The shop produces silver and gold pendants and brooches featuring Celtic patterns. The artists here create custom pieces on request.

If you'd like to explore the island by bike, head for **Rothan Cycles,** 9 Howmore (© **01870/620-283**).

WHERE TO STAY & DINE

Borrodale Hotel   Located near the center of the island, 4km (2½ miles) west of Loch Boisdale along A865, this gabled hotel stands in a landscape of freshwater lakes, heather, and gorse. The hotel underwent extensive renovations in 1997, and the guest rooms, common areas, and upscale restaurant were all updated. The owners can assist in arranging fishing and golf expeditions.

Daliburgh, South Uist, Outer Hebrides HS8 5SS. ℃ 01878/700-444. Fax 01878/700-446. www.uistonline.com/borrodalehotel.htm. 14 units, 12 with private bathroom. £100 ($190) double. Rates include Scottish breakfast. MC, V. **Amenities:** Restaurant; 2 bars; babysitting; nonsmoking rooms; 1 room for those w/limited mobility. *In room:* TV, coffeemaker, hair dryer, iron.

13 Barra ⭐: Garden of the Hebrides

190km (118 miles) NW of Edinburgh, 142km (88 miles) NW of Glasgow

Barra lies at the southern end of the Outer Hebrides. Locals claim it has some 1,000 varieties of wildflowers. The island is one of the most beautiful in the Hebridean chain, with heather-clad meadows, beaches, sandy grasslands, peaks, rocky bays, and lofty headlands. Since the days of the conquering Vikings, it has been associated with the Clan MacNeil.

Most of the 200 inhabitants of Barra are centered at **Castlebay,** its capital, a 19th-century herring port and the best place to stock up on supplies. In the background of the port is **Ben Heaval,** Barra's highest mountain (379m/1,250 ft.). A circular road of 16km (10 miles) will take you around the island, which is about 6.5 by 13km (4 by 8 miles).

ESSENTIALS

GETTING THERE   At the northern end of Barra is **Cockle Strand,** the airport. A long and wide beach of white sand, it's the only runway in Britain that's washed twice daily by sea tides. The Scottish airline **Loganair** (call British Airways at ℃ 0845/777-3377 in Glasgow for flight information) flies here from Glasgow or from Benbecula, on Lewis.

From the mainland at Oban, Barra can be reached by **Caledonian MacBrayne** car ferry (℃ 08705/650-000 for information), which docks at Castlebay. Subject to weather conditions, departures from Oban are on Monday, Wednesday, Thursday, and Saturday, with a return on Tuesday, Thursday, Friday, and Sunday. Sailing time is 5 hours, and a one-way ticket is £22 ($41).

VISITOR INFORMATION   The **Castlebay Tourist Information Centre** (℃ 01871/810-336) is near the pier where the ferry docks. From Easter to mid-October, it's open Monday to Saturday 9am to 5pm. The staff will help you locate a room should you arrive on Barra without a reservation.

EXPLORING THE ISLAND

The most important attraction sits on a rocky islet in the bay: **Kisimul Castle** (℃ 01871/810-313), built for strategic purposes, was the longtime stronghold of the notorious MacNeils of Barra, a clan known for piracy and lawlessness. The oldest part of the castle is a tower dating from 1120. In 1938, the 45th chieftain, the late Robert Lister MacNeil of Barra, began restoration work on his ancestral home. From April to October, you can visit on Monday, Wednesday, and Saturday afternoons. A boatman can take you over and back from 9:30am to 6:30pm. Entrance is £4.50 ($8.55) for adults, £3.50 ($6.65) for seniors, and £2.25 ($4.30) for children, including the boat ride.

To drive around the island, head west from Castlebay until you reach Kinloch. On the left is **Loch St. Clair,** reached by a tiny track road. In the loch, on an islet, stand the ruins of St. Clair Castle, called **MacLeod's Fort.**

Continuing north toward Borve, you see the **Borve Standing Stones** on your left. At Borve, the north fork leads to a chambered cairn and the hamlet of **Craigston,** which has a church dedicated to St. Brendan, the Irish navigator who many cite as the discoverer of America. In the area are two interesting ruins: **Dun Bharpa,** a collection of stones encircled by standing stones, and **Tigh Talamhanta,** a ruined wheelhouse.

Continue north to Allasdale. **Dun Cuier** is one of the few excavated Hebridean Iron Age forts, better preserved than most. Opposite Allasdale is **Seal Bay,** a beautiful spot where the seals do as much inspection of you as you of them.

At **Northbay,** at Loch an Duin, the remains of an old dun protrude from the water. Continue north to Eoligarry, site of a small ferry terminal taking passengers to Ludag on South Uist. Eoligarry's proud possession is **St. Barr's Church,** named after St. Findbarr of Cork (A.D. 550–623), who's said to have converted the islanders to Christianity after finding many of them practicing cannibalism when he arrived. The original 12th-century chapel was restored by Fr. Callum MacNeil.

For bike rentals and advice on scenic routes, head for **Barra Cycle Hire,** 29 St. Brendans Rd. (© **01871/810-284**).

WHERE TO STAY & DINE

Castlebay Hotel   Built around 1890, this gabled hotel overlooks the bay and the ferry terminal where most of the island's visitors disembark. The small guest rooms are simply but comfortably furnished, each with a neat, shower-only bathroom. Its cocktail bar has a quiet corner reserved for dining. Adjacent to the hotel and under the same management is the Castlebay Bar, the island's most popular gathering place.

Castlebay, Barra, Outer Hebrides HS9 5XD. © **01871/810-223**. Fax 01871/810-455. www.castlebay-hotel.co.uk. 14 units. £89–£95 ($169–$181) double. Rates include Scottish breakfast. MC, V. Closed Dec 22–Jan 5. **Amenities:** Restaurant; 2 bars; nonsmoking rooms. *In room:* TV, coffeemaker, hair dryer.

Isle of Barra Hotel ✴ *(Finds)*   The best food on Barra is served at this low-slung seashore hotel—architecturally striking, and for the Outer Hebrides, it's a luxury choice. Its brick walls are adorned with nautical paraphernalia, and the hotel is a favorite with the yachting crowd. It commands a view of the tranquil, less-populated western shore of the island, and its pub, the most westerly in Scotland, is widely touted as the "last dram before America." From the dining room and many of the well-furnished guest rooms (most equipped with a combination tub/shower), you can see everything that's coming and going at sea.

Tangusdale, Castlebay, Barra, Outer Hebrides HS9 5XW. © **01871/810-383**. Fax 01871/810-385. www.isleofbarra hotel.co.uk. 30 units. £60–£90 ($114–$171) double with breakfast; £109–£121 ($207–$230) double with half-board. MC, V. Closed Oct 18–Mar 20. **Amenities:** Restaurant; bar; nonsmoking rooms. *In room:* TV, coffeemaker, no phone.

13

The Orkney & Shetland Islands

Northern outposts of civilization, the Orkney and Shetland archipelagos consist of around 200 islands, about 40 of which are inhabited. "Go to Shetland for scenery, Orkney for antiquities"—that's the saying, anyway. That doesn't mean the Orkneys don't have scenery, too. They do, in abundance.

These far-flung and scattered islands are rich in a great Viking heritage. Ceded to Scotland by Norway as part of the 1472 dowry of Princess Margaret, when she married James III, the islands were part of the great Norse earldoms. They were a gathering place for Norse fleets and celebrated in the Orkneyinga Saga, which detailed the exploits of the Viking warriors.

Before the Vikings, however, tribes of Stone Age people occupied both the Shetlands and the Orkneys. The Picts came

later, and you can still see ruins of their round forts dotting the coastlines. The island chains aren't part of the Highlands and are entirely different from both the Inner and the Outer Hebrides. Clans, Gaelic, and kilts were unfamiliar to the Orcadians and the Shetlanders—until the Scots arrived. At first these merchants and newcomer landlords were bitterly resented. Even today, the islanders are fiercely independent. They refer to themselves as Orcadians and Shetlanders rather than as Scots. And Orkney and Shetland not only are different from the Highlands, but they're different from each other.

Inevitably, change has come to the Orkneys and Shetlands by way of oil and modern conveniences. But tradition remains strong, which has a lot to do with climate and ancestry.

1 The Orkney Islands: An Archaeological Garden ★★

10km (6 miles) N of John o' Groats (mainland Scotland) across Pentland Firth, 451km (280 miles) N of Edinburgh

To visit the Orkney Islands, an archipelago measuring about 81km (50 miles) from northeast to southwest, is to look at 1,000 years of history. Orkney is a virtual archaeological garden. Some 100 of the 500 known brochs—often called the "castles of the Picts"—are found here. Built by Orkney chiefs, they were fortified structures where islanders could find refuge from invaders, and wells inside provided water. The Orkneyinga Saga, written in the 9th or 10th century, is the record of the pomp and heraldry of Orkney's "golden age."

Covering a land area of 978 sq. km (376 sq. miles), the islands lie 10km (6 miles) north of the Scottish mainland. The terrain has lots of rich and fertile farmland but also dramatic scenery: Britain's highest perpendicular cliffs rise to 346m (1,140 ft.). The population of the entire chain is less than 20,000, spread sparsely across about 29 inhabited islands. The people are somewhat suspicious of strangers, and if you meet an Orcadian in a local pub, you'll have to break the ice. The climate is far milder than the location would suggest because of the warming currents of the Gulf Stream. Indeed, there are few extremes in temperature. From May to July, the sunsets are

The Orkney Islands

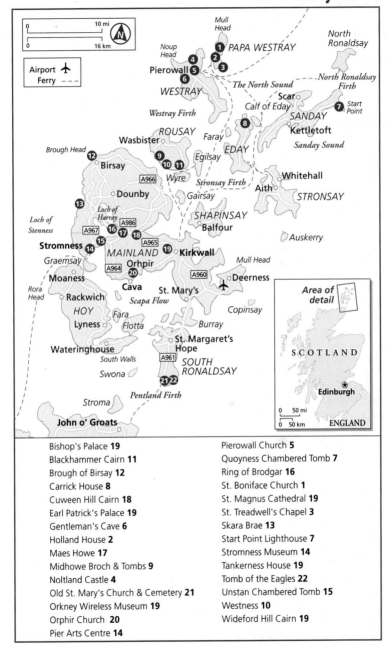

Bishop's Palace **19**
Blackhammer Cairn **11**
Brough of Birsay **12**
Carrick House **8**
Cuween Hill Cairn **18**
Earl Patrick's Palace **19**
Gentleman's Cave **6**
Holland House **2**
Maes Howe **17**
Midhowe Broch & Tombs **9**
Noltland Castle **4**
Old St. Mary's Church & Cemetery **21**
Orkney Wireless Museum **19**
Orphir Church **20**
Pier Arts Centre **14**

Pierowall Church **5**
Quoyness Chambered Tomb **7**
Ring of Brodgar **16**
St. Boniface Church **1**
St. Magnus Cathedral **19**
St. Treadwell's Chapel **3**
Skara Brae **13**
Start Point Lighthouse **7**
Stromness Museum **14**
Tankerness House **19**
Tomb of the Eagles **22**
Unstan Chambered Tomb **15**
Westness **10**
Wideford Hill Cairn **19**

astonishing, with the midsummer sun remaining above the horizon for 18¼ hours a day. The Orcadians call their midsummer sky "Grimlins," from the Old Norse word *grimla,* which means to twinkle or glimmer. There's enough light for golfers to play at midnight.

The Orkneys are also known for their flora, including the Scottish primrose, which is no more than 5 centimeters (2 in.) in height and is believed to have survived the Ice Age by growing in small ice-free areas. The amethyst, with a pale-yellow eye, is found only in the Orkneys and parts of northern Scotland.

ORKNEY ESSENTIALS

GETTING THERE   Monday to Saturday, **British Airways** (© 08870/850-9850; www.britishairways.com) offers service to Kirkwall Airport, on Mainland Orkney (the largest Orkney island), from Glasgow, Inverness, and Aberdeen, with connections from London and Birmingham.

Motorists can visit Orkney with their cars by booking passage on one of the **North-Link Ferries** (© 0845/600-0449). The line offers service from Scrabster (near Thurso), on Scotland's north coast, to the Orkneys. It's a 2-hour trip made 2 to 3 times Monday to Saturday or twice a day on Sunday. A round-trip ticket, valid for 5 days, is £20 ($38) per person or £118 ($224) per car and driver. If you don't have to transport a car, you can take one of the **John O' Groats Ferries** (© 01955/611-353), which operates May to December only 2 to 4 times a day, depending on demand (trip time: 40 min.). Round trip fares are £24 ($46) per passenger.

GETTING AROUND   Island-hopping is common in the north of Scotland. **Loganair** (call British Airways at © 01856/873-434 for reservations) operates flights from Kirkwall Airport on Mainland to the isles of Sanday, Stronsay, Westray, Eday, North Ronaldsay, and Papa Westray.

Orkney Ferries Ltd. (© 01856/872-044 in Kirkwall; www.orkneyferries.co.uk) operates scheduled service from Kirkwall to Orkney's north and south islands: Eday, Papa Westray, Sanday, Stronsay, Westray, North Ronaldsay, and Shapinsay. From Houton, there's service to the south isles: Flotta, Hoy at Longhope, and Lyness, and from Tingwall to Rousay, Egilsay, and Wyre. There's also a private ferry service to take you to Hoy, departing from Stromness. The tourist office has details on departures.

The Churchill barriers, erected to impede enemy shipping in World War II, have been turned into a road link between the islands of Mainland and South Ronaldsay.

VISITOR INFORMATION   To find out what's going on during your visit, consult the *Orcadian,* a weekly published since 1854. There are **tourist offices** in Kirkwall and in Stromness (see below). You can also get information at **www.visitorkney.com**.

SPECIAL EVENTS   These sparsely populated islands generate quite a bit of cultural activity, especially in celebrating the region's music. A number of festivals draw both curious visitors and fans of Scottish and, more specifically, Orcadian music. Information is available through the Kirkwall tourist office (see below), which publishes the yearly *Orkney Diary,* listing events and dates.

The season kicks off in February with the **Drama Festival,** which hosts traveling companies presenting an array of productions in venues spread across the islands. Ticket prices hover around £7 to £10 ($13–$19). May finds the **Orkney Traditional Folk Festival** in full swing. Both feature ceilidhs and concerts of traditional music; tickets to most events are £6 to £8 ($11–$15). June brings a change of pace in the form of the **St. Magnus Festival,** which celebrates classical music and the dramatic arts, as well as music and drama workshops. Tickets average £6 to £20 ($11–$38).

TOURS   Bus tours operate throughout the year, but with limited schedules in winter. One reliable choice is **Wildabout Tours,** 5 Clouston Corner, Stenness (© **01856/ 851-011**). Its full- and half-day minibus tours (of no more than 15 passengers) take in prehistoric and Neolithic monuments and local wildlife. Prices range from £30 to £45 ($57–$86). The tours are popular, particularly in summer, so it's wise to book seats in advance.

KIRKWALL

Kirkwall, established by Norse invaders on the island called Mainland, has been the capital of the Orkney Islands for at least 900 years. Formerly known as Kirkjuvagr ("church bay"), it was named after a church built around 1040 to honor the memory of King Olaf Harraldsson, who was later the patron saint of Norway. That church no longer stands.

The Old Norse streets of Kirkwall are very narrow, to protect the buildings from galelike winds. But don't get the idea that they're pedestrian walkways: That myth is dispelled when a car comes roaring down the street.

The **tourist office** is at 6 Broad St. (© **01856/872-856;** www.visitorkney.com). It's open in April, Monday to Saturday 9am to 5pm; May to September, daily 8:30am to 8pm; and October to March, Monday to Saturday 9:30am to 6pm.

SEEING THE SIGHTS

For the most scenic walk in town, providing views of Kirkwall and the North Isles, head up **Wideford Hill,** about 3km (2 miles) west of town. On the western slope of this hill, 4km (2½ miles) west of Kirkwall, is the **Wideford Hill Cairn,** a trio of concentric walls built around a passage and a megalithic chamber.

The "Pride of Orkney" is **St. Magnus Cathedral** ⚘⚘, on Broad Street (© **01856/ 874-894**). Jarl Rognvald, nephew of the martyred St. Magnus, the island chain's patron saint, founded the cathedral to honor him in 1137, and the remains of the saint and Rognvald were interred between the two large East Choir piers. The cathedral is a "Norman" building, constructed of gray and pinkish rose sandstone. Work went on over centuries, and additions were made in the transitional and very early Gothic styles. It's still in regular use as a church. You can visit from April to September, Monday to Saturday 9am to 6pm and Sunday 2 to 6pm; and October to March, Monday to Saturday 9am to 1pm and 2 to 5pm.

Across from the cathedral are the ruins of a 12th-century **Bishop's Palace,** Broad Street (© **01856/875-461**), with a round tower from the 16th century. King Haakon came here to die in 1263, following the Battle of Largs and his attempt to invade Scotland. The palace was originally constructed for William the Old, a bishop who died in 1168. An easy scenic walk will take you to the impressive ruins of **Earl Patrick's Palace** ⚘, on Watergate (© **01856/721-205**). Built in 1607, it has been called the most mature and accomplished piece of Renaissance architecture left in Scotland. Earl Patrick Stewart was the son of the illegitimate brother of Mary Queen of Scots, and the palace figured in Sir Walter Scott's *The Pirate.* Both the Bishop's Palace and Earl Patrick's Palace are open April through September, daily from 9:30am to 6:30pm. Admission covering both palaces is £2 ($3.80) for adults, £1.50 ($2.85) for seniors and students, and 75p ($1.45) for children 5 to 16.

Nearby is the 1574 **Tankerness House** (also known as the **Orkney Museum**), on Broad Street (✆ **01856/873-191**), an example of a merchant laird's mansion, with crow-stepped gables, a courtyard, and gardens. The museum depicts life in the Orkneys over the past 5,000 years. Exhibits range from the bones of the earliest prehistoric inhabitants and Neolithic pottery to Pictish stone symbols and domestic utensils. It's open Monday to Saturday 10:30am to 5pm. Admission is free, though donations are welcome.

Orkney Wireless Museum, Kiln Corner, Junction Road (✆ **01856/873-191**), is a museum of wartime communications used at Scapa Flow, which was a major naval anchorage in both world wars. Today, this sea area, enclosed by Mainland and several other islands, has developed as a pipeline landfall and tanker terminal for North Sea oil. You can also see a large collection of early domestic radios. It's open from April to September, Monday to Saturday 10am to 4:30pm and Sunday 2 to 4:30pm. Admission is £2 ($3.80) for adults and £1 ($1.90) for children.

In the environs are the **Grain Earth Houses** at Hatson, near Kirkwall. This is an Iron Age souterrain (underground cellar), with stairs leading down to the chamber. Another Iron Age souterrain, **Rennibister Earth House,** is about 7km (4½ miles) northwest of Kirkwall. This excavation also has an underground chamber with supporting roof pillars.

SHOPPING

The **Longship,** 7–15 Broad St. (✆ **01856/888-790**), is the retail outlet of Ola Gorie for Orkney jewelry in Kirkwall. This family business has a wide range of high-quality pieces, including some inspired by stone carvings found at archaeological digs and others by the rich flora and fauna of the islands. A collection based on Charles Rennie Mackintosh designs has proved popular. The Longship also offers a variety of gifts, including fashion and furnishing accessories by Orkney-based Tait & Style.

Sheila Fleet, 30 Bridge St. (✆ **01856/876-900;** www.sheila-fleet.co.uk), is the leading competitor to Ola Gorie, and is also acclaimed as one of the best jewelry designers in Scotland. Her designs reflect the sea, the sky, and landscape colors of the Orkneys. Some of her designs show a Scandinavian influence.

Ortak Jewelry, 10 Albert St. (✆ **01856/873-536**), is the main shop of the famous jewelry studio that produces a wide range of silver and gold pieces featuring Celtic, traditional Orcadian, Victorian, and Art Nouveau designs. The shop also sells items like pottery, barometers, and crystal made by other local artists. The **Ortak Factory Shop,** Hatson Industrial Estate (✆ **01856/872-224**), is adjacent to the Ortak factory, and is the only shop that carries the complete Ortak line. A visitor center shows videos on jewelry making, and free factory tours are offered Monday to Friday in July and August. In winter, the shop and visitor center are open by appointment only.

Judith Glue, 25 Broad St. (✆ **01856/874-225**), produces hand- and machine-made knitwear for the entire family. The artisans tend to favor old-fashioned island patterns, handed down over the generations. Also available are wares of other local artists, along with an interesting selection of handmade pottery, jewelry, greeting cards, soaps, and island music.

WHERE TO STAY

You can also rent rooms at the **Foveran Hotel** (see "Where to Dine," below).

Ayre Hotel   Located midway between the town's copper-spired church and the harbor front, the Ayre consists of a 1792 stone core and a sprawling, uninspired 1970s addition. When it was first built, it was a social center for the town, hosting dances and bridge parties. Today, guests congregate in the popular bar. The small bedrooms are functionally modern and well appointed, each with a shower. The restaurant and bar serve moderately priced meals.

Ayre Rd., Kirkwall, Orkney KW15 1QX. © **01856/873-001.** Fax 01856/876-289. www.ayrehotel.co.uk. 33 units. £100 ($190) double with breakfast. £148 ($281) double with Scottish breakfast and dinner. AE, MC, V. **Amenities:** Restaurant; bar; rooms for those w/limited mobility. *In room:* TV, coffeemaker, hair dryer.

Berstane House *(Finds)*   This isolated manse was once the home of Dr. John Rae, the famous explorer and unsung Orkney hero. Set on 3.2 hectares (8 acres) of woodland, it lies just outside Kirkwall on Mainland Orkney. Its spacious, well-furnished bedrooms open onto views of Berstance Bay, Inganess Bay, and Shapinsay Sound. No place even in Kirkwall captures the authentic Orkney experience as much as this family run B&B where the hospitality is the best in the area. If you don't mind a slight commute, we'd recommend staying here instead of in Kirkwall.

St. Ola (outside Kirkwall), Orkney KW15 1SZ. ©/fax **01856/876-277.** www.berstane.co.uk. 3 units. £40–£50 ($76–$95) double. Rates include breakfast. No credit cards. **Amenities:** Breakfast room; laundry service. *In room:* TV, beverage maker, hair dryer.

Orkney Hotel   Although this hotel has been fully refurbished and the guest rooms modernized (with shower-only bathrooms), the overall style is traditional. The restaurant offers a moderately priced table d'hôte menu nightly as well as an extensive a la carte selection. There are also two well-stocked bars, both offering affordable food.

40 Victoria St., Kirkwall, Orkney KW15 1DN. © **01856/873-477.** Fax 01856/872-767. www.orkneyhotel.co.uk. 30 units. £110 ($209) double; £129 ($245) suite. Rates include Scottish breakfast. MC, V. **Amenities:** Restaurant; 2 bars; nearby golf; business center; room service. *In room:* TV, coffeemaker, hair dryer.

West End Hotel   This hotel offers simple comforts but is still among the top three or four places to stay in town. In 1824, it was built just outside of Kirkwall by a retired sea captain, and became Orkney's first hospital in 1845. Today, owners Jimmy and Isabelle Currie provide a warm welcome and comfortable guest rooms, each with shower-only bathroom. The property has been refurbished in the past few years and is now fresh and inviting. Cost-conscious meals are served in a small restaurant and bar. Fully licensed to sell alcohol, the hotel attracts both locals and visitors.

14 Main St., Kirkwall, Orkney KW15 1BU. © **01856/872-368.** Fax 01856/876-181. www.westendhotel.org.uk. 16 units. £74–£90 ($141–$171) double. Rates include Scottish breakfast. AE, DC, MC, V. Free parking. **Amenities:** Restaurant; bar. *In room:* TV, coffeemaker, hair dryer.

WHERE TO DINE

Dil Se *(*NORTH INDIAN/BANGLADESHI   This newcomer provides the spiciest cuisine in the Orkney Islands. It makes a marvelous change of pace for your palate while traveling in these northern climes. In the town center, the kitchen takes care with its ingredients, spices, and flavors, everything tasting harmoniously blended as in a good curry house. Our favorite is the garlic chicken, but you can also order several tandoori delicacies, piping hot from a clay oven, including tasty skewered vegetables, a mixed grill, king prawn, and several other chicken dishes. The head chef prepares a number of signature dishes, especially a fiery chili *balti* with green chili, a special sauce, and fresh garlic. This chili dish can be ordered with chicken, lamb, vegetables, or prawns—your choice. The chef's vegetarian selections, such as spicy spinach laced with garlic, are the finest in town.

7 Bridge St. ℂ **01856/875-242**. Reservations recommended on weekends. Main courses £7.45–£13 ($14–$25). MC, V. Daily 4–11pm.

Foveran Hotel ☆ SCOTTISH   Located on 14 hectares (34 acres) overlooking the Scapa Flow, where the German Imperial Fleet was sunk in 1919, the Foveran resembles a modern hotel of Scandinavian design. Licensed to sell alcohol, its restaurant offers the best cuisine in the area, and emphasizes "taste of Scotland" menus. The catch of the day might turn out to be lobster, grilled salmon, deep-fried squid, giant crab claws (known locally as "partan toes"), or brown trout. Vegetarian meals are also served, as well as succulent portions of Orkney Island beef, lamb, and farm-made cheeses.

The hotel rents eight pleasant guest rooms; doubles go for £95 to £99 ($181–$188), which includes breakfast.

St. Ola (3km/2 miles west of Kirkwall), Kirkwall, Orkney KW15 1SF. ℂ **01856/872-389**. Fax 01856/876-430. Reservations recommended. Main courses £12–£22 ($23–$42). MC, V. Daily 7–9pm.

KIRKWALL AFTER DARK

The most action spins around **Fusion,** Ayres Road (ℂ **0856/873-359;** www.fusion club.co.uk), which lies in a restored waterfront warehouse. It was the creation of Neil Stevenson, a Kirkwall native, who is credited with bringing a renaissance to Kirkwall, which is keeping many young people at home. In the past many of them headed for Glasgow, Edinburgh, or even London. Although Stevenson has moved on, his creation remains, booking well-known local bands. It also has a DJ booth. A Glasgow design firm restored the main floor creating the biggest dance floor in the Orkneys holding as much as 500 revelers. It's more intimate upstairs at the Firelounge. The doors open Thursday to Saturday (last entry at 11:45pm), shutting down anywhere from 1am to 2:30am. A cover might be assessed depending on the night's entertainment.

EXPLORING MAINLAND FROM KIRKWALL TO STROMNESS

Heading south from Kirkwall along the southern coastal road toward Stromness, you come first to the hamlet of Orphir. **Orphir Church,** along A964, is 10km (6 miles) southwest of Kirkwall. These ruins are of the country's only circular medieval church, built in the first part of the 1100s and dedicated to St. Nicholas. At Orphir, you can see vast tracts of land set aside for bird-watching. This area is also ideal for scenic walks, even if you aren't a "birdie." If you're an angler, take advantage of the free fishing on Kirbister Loch. Ferries leave the Houton Terminal for Hoy and Flotta five or six times a day.

In the area is the **Cuween Hill Cairn,** along A965, 1km (½ mile) south of Finstown and 10km (6 miles) northwest of Kirkwall. The owner of a nearby farmhouse (look for the signs) has the key that opens a door to reveal a low mound over a megalithic passage tomb, probably dating from the 3rd millennium B.C. Ancient human bones, along with those of their oxen and dogs, were excavated here.

Bypassing Stromness for the moment, you can continue on a circular tour of the island. Near Stromness, lying off A965, is **Maes Howe,** 16km (10 miles) west of Kirkwall. Dating from 2700 B.C., this is a superb achievement of prehistoric architecture, constructed from single slabs more than 5.5m (18 ft.) long and some 1.2m (4 ft.) wide. There's a passageway that the sun shines through only at the winter solstice. It also contains the world's largest collection of Viking rune inscriptions, the work of marauding Norsemen who broke into the chambered cairn in search of buried treasure.

The **Ring of Brodgar** ⟡, between Lochend Stenness and Loch of Harray, is 8km (5 miles) northwest of Stromness. Dated to 1560 B.C., a circle of some 36 stones is surrounded by a deep ditch carved out of solid bedrock. Its purpose remains a mystery, though some believe that it was a lunar observatory. In the vicinity are the **Stenness Standing Stones,** a quartet of upright stones from 3000 B.C.

Unstan Chambered Tomb ⟡, 3km (2 miles) northeast of Stromness along A965, and 16km (10 miles) west of Kirkwall, is a big (35m/115 ft. in diameter) burial mound dating from 2500 B.C. For its type, it's unsurpassed in western Europe. There's a chambered tomb more than 2m (6 ft.) high. It's open throughout the day, and admission is free. For information, call the **Tankerness House** (✆ **01856/873-191**). Unstan Ware is the name given to pottery discovered in the tomb.

Last occupied about 2500 B.C., **Skara Brae** ⟡⟡ (✆ **01856/841-815**), 12km (7½ miles) north of Stromness, was a collection of Neolithic village houses joined by covered passages. This colony, which was believed to have sheltered farmers and herders, remained buried in the sands for 4,500 years, until a storm in 1850 revealed the ruins. You can see the remains of six houses and a workshop. The walls were made from flagstone rock and the roofs were skins laid on wooden or whalebone rafters. A fireplace was in the center; beds were placed against the side walls. The bed "linen" was bracken or heather, and the "quilts" were animal skins. This prehistoric village is the best preserved of its type in Europe. It's open from April to September, daily 9:30am to 6:30pm; and October to March, daily 9:30am to 5pm. Admission is £6.50 ($12) adults, £5 ($9.50) for seniors, and £3.25 ($6.20) for children.

Brough of Birsay, in Birsay at the northern end of Mainland, about 18km (11 miles) north of Stromness, is the ruin of a Norse settlement and Romanesque church on an islet that you can reach only at low tide. You can see a replica of a Pictish sculptured stone. (The original was removed to a museum for safekeeping.) The site is open daily year-round; admission is free. Nearby are the ruins of the **Earls' Palace** at Birsay, a mansion constructed in the 16th century for the earls of Orkney.

Click Mill, off B9057, 3km (2 miles) northeast of Dounby, is the only still-functioning example of an old horizontal water mill on the island.

If you'd like to explore the region described above on two wheels, stop by **Bobby's Cycle Centre,** Kirkwall (✆ **01856/875-777**), whose rates are £8 ($15) daily or £50 ($95) weekly. It's open Monday to Saturday 9am to 5:30pm.

Every Wednesday night, the **Ayre Hotel,** in Kirkwall (✆ **01856/873-001;** www. ayrehotel.co.uk), hosts the **Accordion and Fiddle Club.** On Thursday nights in winter, locals gather at the Town Hall to enjoy the music of the **Reel and Strathspey Society.** Admission to these events is about £5 to £8 ($9.50–$15). Parish halls in the different communities host an erratic schedule of ceilidhs and concerts throughout the year. Check with the Kirkwall tourist office (see above) for details.

WHERE TO STAY

Barony Hotel   Sitting on the shores of the Boardhouse Loch, this family-run hotel is a primary location for adventure trips in Orkney. In close vicinity to the hotel are three bird reserves, four trout fishing lochs, and numerous archaeological sites. The Broch of Gurness, a fortress built in the Iron Age, is a short drive away, as is the Earl's Palace, built in the 16th century. The midsize rooms—all nonsmoking—are well maintained, but in this part of Scotland you won't spend much time in them. Owners Anne and Dave Davidson are masters at helping visitors find things to do. They know all the best spots for bird-watchers to see red-throated divers and for nature lovers to see aerial views of Brough. Breakfast is good, made from fresh, local produce. The Davidsons have boats available to rent and a private harbor for them to be used in.

Birsay, KW17 2LS Orkney. © **01856/721-327.** Fax 01856/721-302. www.baronyhotel.com. 11 units. £70 ($133) double. Rates include breakfast. MC, V. **Amenities:** Dining room; room service; laundry service. *In room:* TV, beverage maker, hair dryer.

WHERE TO DINE

Scorrabrae Inn BRITISH   Located in an extension attached to a 19th-century grocer's shop, this simple but convenient restaurant also contains Orphir's only pub. The bar features whiskies distilled in the Orkneys. The menu offers a wide variety of choices, including several fish and chicken dishes, lasagna, salads, and vegetarian meals.

Orphir. © **01856/811-262.** Reservations recommended. Main courses £9–£16 ($17–$30). No credit cards. May–Aug Mon–Thurs 6–11pm, Fri 5pm–1am, Sat noon–2pm and 5pm–1am, Sun 12:30–10pm; Sept–Apr Mon–Sat 6–10pm, Sat noon–2pm, Sun noon–10pm. Bar open year-round to at least 11:30pm.

STROMNESS

Set on the west coast of Mainland against a hill called Brinkie's Brae, Stromness was once known as Hamnavoe ("haven bay") in Old Norse. With its sheltered anchorage, it's the main port of Orkney, and the stone-flagged main street is said to "uncoil like a sailor's rope." Fishing boats find shelter here from storms in the North Atlantic.

With its waterfront gables, nousts (slipways), and jetties, Stromness strikes many visitors as more interesting than Kirkwall. It's an ideal place to walk about, exploring whatever captures your fancy. In the old days, you could see whaling ships in port, along with vessels belonging to the Hudson's Bay Company, for which some young Orcadians went to Canada to man fur stations. For many transatlantic vessels, Stromness was the last port of call before the New World. At Login's Well, many ships were outfitted for Arctic expeditions.

Stromness has a **tourist office** in the ferry terminal building (© **01856/850-716**), open from April to October, Monday to Friday 8am to 5pm, Saturday and Sunday 10am to 3pm (it also opens to greet all incoming ferries, as late as 9pm; July–Aug, Sun hours are 9am–4pm); and November to March, Monday to Friday 8am to 5pm and Saturday 9am to 4pm.

A small but well-planned bookshop, **Stromness Books and Prints,** 1 Graham Place (© **01856/850-565**), specializes in books about Orkney and has in-stock copies of the *Orkneyinga Saga.* It's open Monday through Saturday from 10am to 6pm and sometimes during ferry arrival times in the evening.

The **Pier Arts Centre,** Victoria Street (© **01856/850-209**), has dazzled Orcadians with its "St. Ives school" of art, which includes works by Barbara Hepworth and Ben Nicholson. Admission is free; it's open Tuesday to Saturday 10:30am to 5pm (closed 12:30–1:30pm in winter).

At the **Stromness Museum,** 52 Alfred St. (© **01856/850-025**), you can see a collection of artifacts relating to the history of the Orkneys, especially a gallery devoted to maritime subjects, such as the Hudson's Bay Company and the sinking of the German Imperial Fleet. The section on natural history has excellent collections of local birds and their eggs, fossils, shells, and butterflies. It's open from April to September, daily from 10am to 5pm; and October to March, Monday to Saturday 11am to 3:30pm. Admission is £8 ($15) for adults, £5 ($9.50) seniors, £6 ($11) children under 16, and £12 ($23) per family.

If you want to rent a bike, head for **Orkney Cycle Hire,** 52 Dundas St. (**©** **01856/ 850-255**), which charges £6 to £10 ($11–$19) daily and £40 to £50 ($76–$95) weekly. Summer hours are daily from 8:30am to dusk.

WHERE TO STAY & DINE

Ferry Inn   As its name implies, this modernized hotel is near the ferry. The small guest rooms are simple and utilitarian. Affordable meals are served at lunch and dinner; look for typical Scottish fare like haggis, smoked salmon, and steak pie. To finish, try a clootie dumpling with cream.

John St., Stromness, Orkney KW16 3AA. **©** 01856/850-280. Fax 01856/851-332. www.ferryinn.com. 12 units, 8 with private bathroom. £45 ($86) double without bathroom; £65 ($124) double with bathroom. V. **Amenities:** Restaurant; bar. *In room:* TV, coffeemaker, hair dryer, no phone.

Mill of Eyrland 🌟 *Finds*   A water mill from 1861 has been successfully converted into an upmarket B&B. And a stay here is like a nostalgic journey into the past—you can hear the rippling sound of the mill stream from your open bedroom window. Island antiques abound throughout the property, which lies behind white stone walls. Located 4.8km (3 miles) from Stromness, the property also contains some of the mill's old machinery. But it's hardly an industrial site, as beautiful and well-tended gardens surround the building. Ian and Margo Heddle took over the abandoned mill and spent 20 years restoring it and bringing it back into shape. All the bedrooms are modernized and comfortably furnished. Packed lunches are made for those setting out for a day's exploration of Orkney's archaeological attractions. Good-tasting Scottish dinners can be prepared on request.

Stenness, Orkeny, KW16 3HA. **©** 01856/850-136. Fax 01856/851-633. www.millofeyrland.com. 5 units, 2 with bathroom. £60 ($114) double without bathroom. £80 ($152) double with bathroom. Rates include breakfast. No credit cards. Free parking. **Amenities:** Laundry service. *In room:* TV, coffeemaker, hair dryer, no phone.

Stromness Hotel   Behind an elaborate Victorian facade of symmetrical bay windows and beige sandstone blocks sits the most important hotel in the Orkneys' second-most important community. Once a bit dowdy, the Stromness has been extensively renovated. Small guest rooms are outfitted with old-fashioned furniture and shower-only bathrooms; many offer views of the harbor. Lunch and dinner, simple but hearty, are served in the lounge; the moderately priced restaurant focuses on seafood and steaks from Orkney.

Victoria St., Stromness, Orkney KW16 3AA. **©** 01856/850-298. Fax 01856/850-610. www.stromnesshotel.com. 42 units. £58–£96 ($110–$182) double. Rates include Scottish breakfast. MC, V. Free parking. **Amenities:** Restaurant; 2 bars; bike rental; laundry service. *In room:* TV, coffeemaker.

BURRAY

Burray and South Ronaldsay (see below) are two of the most visited of the southeastern isles, lying within an easy drive of Kirkwall on Mainland. Both are connected to Mainland by the Churchill Barriers causeway, which links the islands of Glims Holm, Burray, and South Ronaldsay. The Vikings called the island Borgarey ("broch island").

Come to Burray for scenic drives, coastal views, lush pastures, and rugged grandeur. A center for watersports in summer, it also boasts several sandy beaches. You can inquire locally about the possibilities, as everything is casually run. But many Scots come here for canoeing, diving, sailing, swimming, and water-skiing.

The island is an ornithologist's delight, with a **bird sanctuary** filled with a wide range of species, including grouse, lapwing, curlew, and the Arctic tern. Look also for the puffin, the cormorant, and the oystercatcher. You see gray seals along various shorelines. Their breeding ground is Hesta Head.

Burray is one of the major dive centers of the Orkneys. **Scapa Flow** is the best dive site in the northern hemisphere, for here lay the remnants of the German High Seas fleet scuttled on June 21, 1919. Seven warships range from light cruisers to battleships. Many block ships were sunk before the building of the Churchill Barriers, constructed to prevent enemy ships from coming into British waters. Marine life, including some rare sponges, enhances the variety of the dives. If you'd like a diving adventure, call the **Scapa Scuba,** Stromness (© **01856/851-218**).

WHERE TO STAY & DINE

Sands Hotel Bar & Restaurant　One of the island's most prominent structures, this building was originally a fish-processing plant. The hostelry sits in the center of Burray Village, 13km (8 miles) north of the passenger ferry at Burwick, on South Ronaldsay. There are four upper-story flats, each containing three rooms and a kitchenette. These can be rented for less than a week (if they're not fully booked, most likely in low season).

The reputable restaurant contains the island's only pub. Lunch and dinner choices may include preparations of local trout as well as other Orkney products.

Burray Village, Burray, Orkney KW17 2SS. © **01856/731-298**. www.thesandshotel.co.uk. 6 units. £80 ($152) double, £95 ($181) family room. MC, V. **Amenities:** Restaurant; bar. *In room:* TV, kitchenette, fridge, coffeemaker, iron.

SOUTH RONALDSAY

Also joined by the Churchill Barriers, the island of South Ronaldsay is unspoiled, fertile countryside. The hamlet St. Margaret's Hope was named after the young Norwegian princess, the "Maid of Norway," who was Edward II's child bride. She was slated to become queen of England, which at the time laid claim to Scotland. South Ronaldsay is the nearest Orkney island to mainland Scotland, 10km (6½ miles) north of the port of John o' Groats. It's separated from the British mainland by the waters of Pentland Firth.

The island offers some of the best **sea angling** waters in the world. Record-breaking catches, particularly in halibut and skate, have been recorded, and you can hire local boats on a daily basis. There's also excellent fishing from local shores and rocks.

Tomb of the Eagles, south of Windwick Bay at the southern tip of the island, is a fine chambered tomb dating from 3000 B.C. Nearby is a recently excavated mound dating from 1500 B.C. Mr. R. Simison of Liddle Farm, who has excavated the area, will be happy to explain the mound and tomb. Please call at the farm before visiting the tomb and mound (© **01856/831-339**). Admission is £5.50 ($10) for adults, £4.50 ($8.55) for seniors, £3 ($5.70) students, and £2 ($3.80) for children 5 to 12. Open March daily 10am to noon, April to October 9:30am to 6pm.

In the southwest corner of the island, on the opposite side from the Tomb of Eagles, stands **Old St. Mary's Church and Cemetery.** This ancient church is stone-carved with the shape of two feet. Other similar stones have been found, and they're thought to be coronation stones for tribal chiefs or petty kings.

The Workshop, Front Road (© **01856/831-587**), is a craft producers' cooperative in the center of the village of St. Margaret's Hope. It sells a wide range of locally produced crafts, including pottery, jewelry, baskets, rugs, and fine-quality handknits.

WHERE TO DINE

Creel Restaurant 🐾 SCOTTISH   This cozy restaurant overlooking the bay has won the "Taste of Scotland" award. The kitchen uses a large variety of local products. Specialties include smoked haddock and roasted monkfish tails with ratatouille and a chervil sauce. The strawberry shortcake, made with homemade shortbread, cream, and fresh Orkney strawberries in season, is also a treat.

The restaurant rents three guest rooms that cost £105 ($200) for a double, which includes a Scottish breakfast.

Front Rd., St. Margaret's Hope, Orkney KW17 2SL. © **01856/831-311**. Reservations recommended. All main dishes £19 ($35). MC, V. Apr–Oct daily 7–9pm; open some weekends in winter (call first).

SHAPINSAY

Visitors come here mainly for the **secluded beaches,** the many walking trails, and the wildlife, including seals. Getting here is fairly easy if you're based on Kirkwall; the **Orkney Ferries Ltd.,** Shore Street (© **01856/872-044;** www.orkneyferries.co.uk), comes here six times a day. The round-trip passage is £21 ($39) for vehicles, £6.60 ($13) for adults, and £3.30 ($6.25) for children.

The island was the seat of the Balfours of Trenabie. John Balfour was a nabob, making his fortune in India before becoming the member of Parliament for Orkney and Shetland in 1790. He launched the Scottish baronial castle Balfour. Several Neolithic sites—most unexcavated—are on the island.

WHERE TO STAY & DINE

Balfour Castle 🐾🐾 *Finds*   There are no more unusual accommodations in all the Orkney Islands, an unexpected discovery billed as "the most northerly castle hotel in the world." The region's most important benefactors were the Balfour family, worldwide shipping magnates. John Balfour began work on this castle in the southwest corner of Shapinsay, but it was completed by his heir in 1847. In the 1950s, when the last Balfour died without an heir, the castle and estate were bought by a former Polish cavalry officer, Tadeusz Zawadski, and his Scottish wife, Catherine. Today, the place is run by the widow Catherine and her family. It accepts no more than 12 guests at a time, and the family treats them to conversation and entertainment. The guest rooms boast antique or semi-antique furniture and lots of character.

The estate shelters the only forest in the Orkney Islands, planted in the 19th century by the Balfours and composed chiefly of sycamores. In its center, a 3.5m (12-ft.) stone wall surrounds the kitchen gardens, where greenhouses produce peaches, figs, and grapes; and strawberries, cabbages, and salad greens grow well within the shelter of the wall. The estate is still a working farm, involved with beef cattle, sheep, and grain production. The hosts will take the time to give guests a tour of the property and also to arrange fishing trips or bird-watching expeditions, as well as photographic and ornithological trips with guide and boat. Between May and July, the bird life is unbelievably profuse. Guests may also be taken to the family's 40-hectare (100-acre) uninhabited island, where colonies of gray seals and puffins like to say hello.

The kitchen relies on such tempting ingredients as local wild duck and fresh scallops, crabmeat, and lobster. Guests who catch their own dinner will have it cheerfully prepared for them.

Balfour Village, Shapinsay, Orkney KW17 2DY. © **01856/711-282**. Fax 01856/711-283. www.balfourcastle.com. 6 units. £100–£125 ($190–$238) per person. Rates include 2 meals. Discount of 30% for children under 12. There is a discount of 10% for a 3 or more day stay. MC, V. **Amenities:** Restaurant; bar. *In room:* Coffeemaker, hair dryer, iron, no phone.

ROUSAY

Called the "Egypt of the North," the island of Rousay lies off the northwest coast of Mainland. Almost moon-shaped and measuring about 10km (6 miles) across, the island is known for its trout lochs, which draw anglers from all over Europe. Much of the land is heather-covered moors. Part of the island has hills, including **Ward Hill,** which many people walk up for a panoramic sweep of Orcadian seascape. In the northwestern part of the island is **Hellia Spur,** one of Europe's most important seabird colonies. As you walk about, you can see the much-photographed puffin.

But where does the bit about Egypt come in? Rousay boasts nearly 200 prehistoric monuments. The most significant site, the Iron Age **Midhowe Broch and Tombs** ⍟, is located in the west of the island and was excavated in the 1930s. The walled enclosure on a promontory is cut off by a deep rock-cut ditch. The cairn is more than 23m (75 ft.) long and was split among a dozen stalls or compartments. The graves of some two dozen settlers, along with their cattle, were found inside. One writer called the cairn the "great ship of death." The other major sight, the **Blackhammer Cairn,** lies north of B9064 on the southern coast. This megalithic burial chamber is believed to date from the 3rd millennium B.C. It was separated into about half a dozen compartments for the dead.

In 1978, excavation began on a Viking site at **Westness,** which figured in the Orkneyinga Saga. A farmer digging a hole to bury a dead cow came across an Old Norse grave site. Three silver brooches, shipped to the National Museum of Scotland at Edinburgh, were discovered among the ruins; the earliest one dated from the 9th century. Die-hard archaeology buffs might like to know that a 1.6km (1-mile) archaeological trail begins here; a mimeographed map (not very precise) is sometimes available from the tourist office. The trail is clearly marked with placards and signs describing the dusty-looking excavations that crop up on either side.

To reach Rousay, you can rely on the service provided by the **Orkney Ferries Ltd.,** in Kirkwall (© **01856/872-044;** www.orkneyferries.co.uk). The trip is made six times daily; round-trip passage is £20 ($37) for vehicles, £6.60 ($13) for adults, and £3.30 ($6.25) for children.

EDAY

Called the "Isthmus Isle of the Norsemen," Eday is the center of a hardworking and traditional crofting community that ekes out a living among the heather and peat bogs of this isolated island.

Life isn't easy here, for most of this north isle is barren, with heather-clad and hilly moorlands that often lead to sheer cliffs or give way to sand dunes with long sweeping beaches. Chambered cairns and standing stones bespeak ancient settlements. In the 18th and 19th centuries, the island was a major supplier of peat.

Today, most of the population derives its income from cattle and dairy farming, although other products include hand-knit sweaters, cheese, and a highly rated beer brewed in individual crofts by local farmers and their families.

People come to this almost-forgotten oasis today for bird-watching, beachcombing, and sea angling. Others prefer the peaceful scenic walks to the **Red Head cliffs,** likely to be filled with guillemots and kittiwakes. The cliffs rise to a height of 61m (200 ft.), and on a clear day you can see Fair Isle.

On its eastern coastline, Eday opens onto Eday Sound, where pirate John Gow was captured. After a trial in London, he was hanged in 1725; his exploits are detailed in

Sir Walter Scott's *The Pirate*. Following his capture, Gow was held prisoner at **Carrick House,** discreetly signposted on the northern part of the island. Carrick House was built in 1633 by James Stewart, the second son of Robert Stewart, who had been named earl of Carrick. It's now the home of **Mrs. Joy** (*C* **01857/622-260**), but if you're polite and have a flexible schedule, she might open her house to a visit. There may or may not be a fee—about £2.50 ($4.75) per person "feels right." She's most amenable to visitors between late June and mid-September, and Sundays are an especially good time to test your luck. Despite the sale of various parcels of land to the island's 130 to 140 inhabitants, most of the island is owned by the laird of Eday, Mrs. Rosemary Hebdon Joy, whose link to the island dates to around 1900, when her grandfather bought it from his London club. The circumstances surrounding the island's inheritance have made it one of the few matriarchal lairdships in Scotland— its ownership has passed from mother to daughter for several generations.

Because of limited accommodations, Eday is most often visited on a day trip. **Loganair,** in Kirkwall (call British Airways at *C* **0845/722-2277** for reservations), offers service to Eday every Wednesday. **Orkney Ferries Ltd.,** Shore Street in Kirkwall (*C* **01856/872-044;** www.orkneyferries.co.uk), crosses to Eday about twice daily. The round-trip fare is £31 ($57) for vehicles and £13 ($25) for adults.

WHERE TO STAY

There's no formal tourist office in Eday. However, **Mrs. Popplewell** (*C* **01857/ 622-248**) from Little Croft House (see "Where to Dine," below) provides an information service and can assist you with finding accommodations or organizing any activities.

Skaill Farm *(Finds)* Operated by a pair of English expatriates fleeing the congestion of the London suburbs, Skaill is the centerpiece for the island's third-largest farm. It's set on 324 hectares (800 acres) of windswept grazing land, midway along the length of the island (near its narrowest point), and 8km (5 miles) from both Calfsound and Backaland. Skaill is in a stone building whose 18th-century core was constructed on the foundations of Orkney's medieval skaill. (A skaill is the honorific home of an earl, designed to shelter him during his visits from other parts of his realm.) Michael and Dee Cockram welcome you to their home, providing well-prepared dinners and simple but comfortable guest rooms. Meals might include fresh vegetables from the family garden, lobsters, scallops, lamb, and beef.

Skaill, Eday, Orkney KW17 2AA. *C*/fax 01857/622-271. 2 units, none with private bathroom. £75 ($143) double. Rates include half-board. No credit cards. Closed Apr–May. *In room:* No phone.

WHERE TO DINE

Little Croft House *(Value)* SCOTTISH One of the most charming possibilities for a meal on Eday is provided by Emma Popplewell, who, if notified in advance, will prepare fixed-price lunches and dinners. Meals are often served to a loyal following of "off-island" yacht owners enjoying the nautical challenges of the local waters. The setting is a croft cottage whose 76-centimeter-thick (30-in.) stone walls were built around 1900. Its flower and vegetable gardens slope down to the edge of the sea, source of some of the kelp and seaweed Mrs. Popplewell uses to flavor her succulent versions of Orkney lamb. Depending on what's available, menu items may include grilled halibut with scallops and local dill and fennel, salads made with wild greens gathered from the hills, homemade raspberry bramble sorbet, locally made cheeses and beers, and aromatic crusty bread that's freshly baked every morning.

In one of the croft's outbuildings (a former boathouse), Mrs. Popplewell sells sweaters, accessories, and caftans that are handknit on Eday by local women. Also for sale are paintings and sculptures by island artists.

Mrs. Popplewell also rents four comfortably furnished rooms containing TVs; the two doubles are £65 ($124), including half-board.

Isle of Eday, Orkney KW17 2AB. (01857/622-248. Reservations required as far in advance as possible. About £10 ($19) per person. No credit cards. Time to be arranged when making reservations.

SANDAY

Sanday means "sand island," which is fitting: The island's long white beaches have grown as tides have changed over the last century. With few residents or visitors, the stretches of seashore are often deserted—perfect for long, solitary walks. One of the largest of the North Isles, some 26km (16 miles) in length, Sanday is part of the eastern archipelago.

On the Elsness Peninsula, jutting southeast from the bulk of Sanday Island, you find one of the most spectacular chambered cairns in the Orkneys: the **Quoyness Chambered Tomb** . The tomb and its principal chamber, which reaches a height of some 4m (13 ft.), date from around 2900 B.C. Access is by key, which is available at the local post office in Lady Village. Other ancient monuments, including Viking burial grounds and broch sites, have been found on Sanday.

You can see rare migrant birds and terns at the **Start Point Lighthouse,** near the extreme tip of Start Point, a tidal peninsula jutting northward from the rest of Sanday. The early-19th-century lighthouse is one of the oldest in the country, but since the 1960s has been on "automatic pilot," without a permanent resident to tend the machinery except for a part-time warden ((01857/600-385) who may or may not be here at the time of your visit. The number of ships wrecked off Sanday's shore is topped only by North Ronaldsay; you can see the wreck of a German destroyer on the Sand of Langamay. If you want to see this monument, know that only specialized vehicles can drive across the tidal flats, and only at low tide. Locals, however, are aware of the times when a trekker can safely walk across the kelp-strewn sandy flats. If you feel adventurous, ask a local how to get here or phone the warden for advice.

Loganair flies in from the Kirkwall Airport ((01856/872-494) twice a day Monday to Friday and once on Saturday at a cost of £31 ($59). **Orkney Ferries Ltd.,** Shore Street, Kirkwall ((01856/872-044; www.orkneyferries.co.uk), crosses to the island about two times daily. Round-trip fares are £13 ($25) for adults and £30 ($57) for vehicles.

WHERE TO STAY & DINE

Accommodations are extremely limited, so book your room in advance.

Belsair Hotel   This stone and clapboard inn is located in the village of Kettletoft, about 13km (8 miles) northeast of Sanday's roll-on/roll-off ferry pier. Kettletoft consists of about 15 buildings and is the most central of the island's four communities. The Belsair's functionally furnished guest rooms were upgraded and renovated in 1992, but the original building dates back to 1879, when it was built by ancestors of the hotel's present owners.

The Belsair is the site of the island's only restaurant. Gardens across the road produce many of the vegetables served in the dining room, where moderately priced dishes include straightforward but flavorful preparations of fish, beef, and lamb.

Kettletoft, Sanday, Orkney KW17 2BJ. ℭ **01857/600-206.** 3 units. £35 ($67) double without bathroom; £60 ($114) double with bathroom. Rates include full Scottish breakfast. No credit cards. **Amenities:** Restaurant. *In room:* TV, coffeemaker, no phone.

WESTRAY

One of the biggest of the North Isles, Westray is fertile and has a closely knit community; many of its inhabitants are believed to have Spanish blood, owing to shipwrecks of the Armada off the island's stormy shores. The western coastline is the steepest, rising in parts to some 61m (200 ft.), from which you can enjoy panoramic vistas. The island is a bird-watcher's paradise—you can see seabirds like guillemots around Noup Head, with its red-sandstone cliffs. Along the lochs are many **sandy beaches.**

Below the cliffs is the so-called **Gentleman's Cave.** A Balfour of Trenabie is said to have found refuge in this cave, along with his comrades, after the defeat at Culloden in 1746. As winter winds howled outside, they drank to the welfare of the "king over the water," Bonnie Prince Charlie. A hike to the remote cave is recommended only for the hardy, and only after you've talked to locals first about how to access it.

At **Pierowall,** the major hamlet, you can see **Pierowall Church,** a ruin with a chancel and a nave. There are also some finely lettered grave slabs.

The most famous attraction is **Noltland Castle,** a former fortress overlooking Pierowall. A governor of the island, Thomas de Tulloch, had this castle built in 1420. Eventually it was occupied by Gilbert Balfour of Westray, who had it redesigned as a fortress in a "three-stepped" or Z plan. This would have provided complete all-around visibility against attack—but it was never finished. The castle's present ruins date from around the mid-1500s. It was destroyed in part by a fire in 1746. A kitchen, a stately hall, and a winding staircase are still standing.

Orkney Ferries Ltd. (ℭ **01856/872-044** in Kirkwall; www.orkneyferries.co.uk) sails to Pierowall, Westray, two to three times daily. Bookings are required for cars; the cost is £30 ($57) round-trip. Adult passengers pay £13 ($25). **Loganair** flies to Westray one to two times Monday through Saturday at a cost of £35 ($67). Phone ℭ **01856/872-494** in Kirkwall for information; for reservations, call British Airways at ℭ **0845/722-2277.**

WHERE TO STAY & DINE

Because accommodations are very limited, make reservations in advance.

Pierowall Hotel Built a century ago as a manse for a nearby Presbyterian church, this cozy hotel, 12km (7½ miles) north of the roll-on/roll-off ferry terminal, is the domain of Mrs. Jean Fergus and John James. The pub offers affordable food and drink.

Pierowall Village, Westray, Orkney KW17 2BZ. ℭ **01857/677-472.** Fax 01857/677-707. www.orknet.co.uk/pierowall. 5 units, 2 with private bathroom. £44 ($84) double without bathroom; £56 ($106) double with bathroom. Rates include Scottish breakfast. MC, V. **Amenities:** Restaurant; 2 bars. *In room:* TV, coffeemaker, hair dryer, no phone.

PAPA WESTRAY

Both bird-watchers and students of history are drawn to Papa Westray, which was believed to have been settled by 3500 B.C. One of the most northerly isles in the Orkneys, it's rich in archaeological sites. In the fertile farmland around Holland, the **Knap of Howar** was discovered; it's the earliest standing house in northwestern Europe, dating from before 3000 B.C.

On the eastern shore of Loch Treadwell, on a peninsula jutting southeast from the bulk of Papa Westray, you can visit the ruins of **St. Treadwell's Chapel,** believed to have marked the arrival of Christianity in the Orkney Islands. The chapel, now in ruins, was dedicated to Triduana, a Celtic saint. When a Pictish king, Nechtan, admired her lovely eyes, she is said to have plucked them out and sent them by messenger to the king—she hoped he'd learn it was foolish to admire physical beauty. For many decades, the chapel was a place of pilgrimage for those suffering from eye problems.

On the island's western edge, about 3km (2 miles) from St. Treadwell's Chapel, north of the airport, is **St. Boniface Church,** also a Celtic site. Stone Celtic crosses were found here, as well as a series of much-eroded grave slabs carved from red sandstone. This is believed to have been a Christian Viking burial ground, now exposed to the howling winds and bleak sunlight of this rocky peat-clad island.

A major attraction here is **Holland House,** formerly the home of the Traills of Holland. Dating from the 17th century, the house is a fine example of a circular "Horse Engine House," which was driven by 11 horses and a dovecote. The house is now owned by farmer John Rendall (© **01857/644-251**); you might be able to see inside if you're polite and Mr. Rendall is feeling sociable.

The northern end of the island has been turned into a **nature reserve,** which is the best place to go for scenic walks. Along with colonies of guillemots and kittiwakes, **North Hill** is the site of one of the largest breeding colonies of the Arctic tern.

Twice-daily flights to Papa Westray from Kirkwall on Mainland are offered by **Loganair** (© **01856/872-494,** or call British Airways at © **0845/772-2277** for reservations). **Orkney Ferries Ltd.,** Shore Street, Kirkwall (© **01856/872-044;** www. orkneyferries.co.uk), sails to Papa Westray direct on Tuesdays and Fridays; on other days, the ferry stops at Westray, where you catch a smaller ferry service to Papa Westray. Round-trip fares are £30 ($57) for vehicles and £13 ($25) for adult passengers.

Check locally to see if any accommodations are open at the time of your visit. If nothing is operating, you'll have to view Papa Westray as only a day trip.

2 Fair Isle ⍟

43km (27 miles) S of Lerwick, Shetland Islands

Called the "most isolated inhabited part of Britain," Fair Isle lies on the same latitude as Bergen, Norway. It measures only about 1.6 by 6km (1 by 3½ miles) and sits about midway between the Orkneys and the Shetlands, administered by the latter. Relentless seas pound its 32km (20-mile) coast in winter and powerful westerly winds fling Atlantic spray from one side of the island to the other. It's home to fewer than 100 rugged, self-reliant souls.

An important staging point for migrating birds, Fair Isle is even better known for its patterned pullovers, which greatly aid the island's economy. In stores around the world, you see these intricately patterned garments retailing at high prices. The homegrown product is sold on Fair Isle at half the price. Fair Isle knitting is even a part of the curriculum at all primary schools, and many jobless men have turned to knitting.

Originally the fame of the sweaters was spread in the 1920s by the prince of Wales. The pattern is of mysterious origin. Some suggest that it was derived from Celtic sources, others that it came from the island's Viking heritage. A more daring theory maintains the themes were Moorish, learned from Spanish sailors shipwrecked off Fair Isle in 1588.

In 1954, the island was acquired by the National Trust for Scotland. The **bird observatory** installed here is the most remarkable in the country. Since work began in

1948, some 200 species have been ringed. Fair Isle is an important breeding ground for everything from the puffin and the Arctic skua to the razorbill and the storm petrel.

GETTING THERE

Loganair operates scheduled service in a seven-seat "Islander"; flight time is 25 minutes. From Sumburgh Airport, there's a flight on Saturday only, which links with incoming Loganair flights from both Glasgow and Edinburgh. From Lerwick Airport, flights are once or twice a day from Monday to Saturday. Call Loganair at ℂ **01856/ 873-434** or British Airways at ℂ **0845/722-2277** for more information.

The mailboat *Good Shepherd* sails on Tuesday, Thursday, and Saturday from Grutness Pier, Sumburgh Head, on Shetland. It's advisable to check sailing times from Grutness by phoning before 9:30am on the day of the scheduled departure for Fair Isle, in case of weather delay. Bookings for the trips to Fair Isle can be made through **J. W. Stout,** Skerryholm, Fair Isle (ℂ **01595/760-222**). A one-way fare is £2.60 ($4.95); the trip takes 2½ hours.

WHERE TO STAY & DINE

Fair Isle Lodge and Bird Observatory ⚘ *Finds*   Even if you're not a bird-watcher, you might want to stay at this low-slung, big-windowed building in the shelter of treeless hillsides. Located near the sea at the northern end of the island, the lodge was the dream of a well-respected ornithologist, George Waterston, who bought it in 1948 and created the observatory. It's now administered by the Fair Isle Bird Observatory Trust. Adjacent accommodations were constructed to provide housing for visitors. There are 33 beds for rent. It's also possible to stay in a dorm room, with four to six beds.

The place is most popular during the spring and autumn bird migrations. It's always wise to reserve well in advance, especially during those seasons. Sometimes the wardens will take guests on before-breakfast tours of bird traps, which, for tagging purposes, are placed in strategic points along the stone dikes surrounding the island.

Fair Isle, Shetland ZE2 9JU. ℂ/fax **01595/760-258**. www.fairislebirdobs.co.uk. 14 units, none with private bathroom. £78 ($148) double; £30 ($57) dorm bed. Rates include full board. MC, V. Closed Nov to late Apr. **Amenities:** Bar; nonsmoking rooms. *In room:* No phone.

3 The Shetland Islands: A Land of Stark Beauty ⍟

97km (60 miles) N and NE of the Orkneys

The northernmost part of the British Isles, the archipelago of the Shetland Islands comprises some 100 islands that make up 130 sq. km (50 sq. miles) of land. Many are merely islets or rocks, but 17 are inhabited. The major island is called Mainland, as in the Orkneys. This island, on which the capital, Lerwick, is located, is about 89km (55 miles) long and 32km (20 miles) wide. It has been turned into what some critics have called "a gargantuan oil terminal." The Shetlands handle about half of Britain's oil.

The islands also have been called "that long string of peat and gneiss that stands precariously where three seas—the Atlantic Ocean, the North Sea, and the Arctic Ocean—meet." Shetland's fjordlike voes (sheer rock cliffs) make the islands beautiful in both seascape and landscape. But it's a stark beauty, wild and rugged, with windswept moors. Because there are few trees, the landscape at first looks barren. After a while, though, it begins to seem fascinating, especially when you come upon a typical Shetlander, in his sturdy Wellington boots and thick woolen sweater, cutting peat along a bog as his ancestors did before him. Shetlanders are proud, warm, and often eager to share the treasures of their island chain with you. At no point in Shetland are you more than 5km (3 miles) from the sea—the coastline stretches for some 4,830km (3,000 miles).

The major airport is at **Sumburgh,** on the southern tip of the southernmost island of Mainland. The far-northern outpost is **Muckle Flugga Lighthouse,** an advanced achievement of engineering. Standing poised on near-vertical rock, it's the "last window on the world" through which Great Britain looks out to the north. It's not as cold here as you might think: The Shetland archipelago benefits from the warming influence of the Gulf Stream, but even in summer the weather tends to be chilly. Shetland has less than half the annual rainfall recorded in the western Highlands. In summer, there's almost continuous daylight. The Shetlanders call it "Simmer Dim." In midwinter, there are no more than 5 hours of daylight.

Civilization here dates back some 5,000 years. The Shetlands were inhabited more than 2,000 years before the arrival of the Romans, who called them "Ultima Thule." The Neolithic people arrived first, followed by the people of the Iron and Bronze Ages, who gave way to the Picts and the Celts. But the most enduring influence came from the Vikings, who ruled the Shetlands until some 500 years ago. The Norse established an influence that lasted for centuries and is still evident today in language, culture, and customs.

The Vikings held the islands from A.D. 800 until they were given to Scotland in 1469 as part of the wedding dowry of Princess Margaret of Norway when she married James III. Scotland's takeover of the Shetlands marked a sad period in the life of the islanders, who found themselves under the sway of often cruel and unreasonable feudal barons. One of the most hated of rulers was Earl Patrick Stewart, who was assigned the dubious task of imposing Scottish customs on a people who had known only Viking law. His son matched him in cruelty, and eventually both earls were executed in Edinburgh for their crimes. Shetlanders still think of themselves as separate from Scots.

The impact of the North Sea oilmen on this traditionally straitlaced community is noticeable, in overcrowding and other ways. However, away from all the oil activity, life in the Shetlands goes on much as it always did, except for the profusion of modern conveniences and imported foodstuffs. Speaking of food, you'll notice that food on Shetland tastes better when it's from Shetland—try the distinctive salted and smoked Reestit mutton to see what we mean.

The islands are famous for their ponies and wool. **Shetland ponies** roam freely among the hills and common grazing lands in the island chain. Some are shipped south to England, where they're popular as children's mounts. The Shetlands also have 10% of all the seabirds in the British Isles, and several of the smaller islands or islets have nature reserves. Seals are protected and welcomed here—you can see them drifting among the waves, sliding down in pursuit of a fish dinner, or lounging about on the rocks and beaches. Most of them are Atlantic gray seals, with their big angular heads. The common seal, with a dog-shaped head, is most often found on the islet of Mousa. And if you want to see otters, you have a better chance in Shetland than anywhere else in Britain.

Anglers find some 200 freshwater lochs in Shetland, and deep-sea angling makes for a memorable sport. Many world fishing records have been set in Shetland. "Ton-up" fish are common.

The Shetland Islands

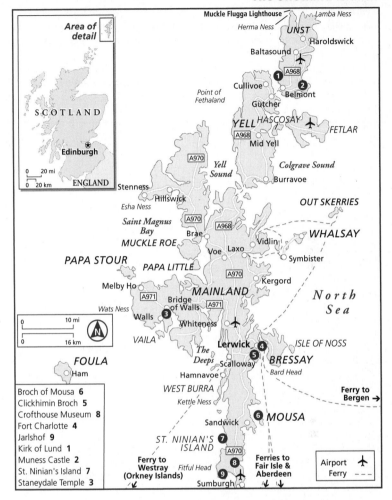

Broch of Mousa **6**
Clickhimin Broch **5**
Crofthouse Museum **8**
Fort Charlotte **4**
Jarlshof **9**
Kirk of Lund **1**
Muness Castle **2**
St. Ninian's Island **7**
Staneydale Temple **3**

The island craftspeople are noted for their creativity, reflected in their handicrafts, jewelry, and knitware. In some places, you can watch these items being made in the workshops of the artists. **Hand-knitted sweaters** are still produced in great numbers, and anyone contemplating a visit might want to return with at least one.

Note: It's imperative to have advance reservations if you're considering a trip to the Shetlands, especially in midsummer.

SHETLAND ESSENTIALS

GETTING THERE   Shetland is a 2½-hour flight from London. By air or sea, Aberdeen is the major departure point from Scotland. **British Airways (© 800/247-9297** in the U.S., or 0845/772-2277) flies from Aberdeen four times per day Monday to Friday, with reduced service on Saturday and Sunday. The flight takes less than an hour.

Roll-on/roll-off car ferries operate from Aberdeen to Shetland Monday through Friday, carrying up to 600 passengers and 240 cars. For information, contact **NorthLink** (© **0845/600-0449**). The trip takes about 14 hours and costs £63 to £87 ($120–$165) per person. On-board facilities include restaurants, cafeterias, bars, lounges, and gift shops.

NorthLink offers year-round ferry service once a week, departing on Sunday at noon and Tuesday at 10pm from Stromness, Orkney, heading for Lerwick, in the Shetlands.

GETTING AROUND If you have a problem with transportation either to or around the islands, you can always check with the tourist office in Lerwick (see below).

Loganair (© **01856/873-434**) provides daily and weekly service to the islands of Whalsay, Fetlar, Foula, and Out Skerries. Although flying is a bit more expensive than taking a ferry, the bonus is that you can go and return on the same day as opposed to spending 2 or possibly 3 days on a rather small island.

Most of the inhabited islands are reached from the Shetland Mainland, and passenger fares are nominal because they're heavily subsidized by the government. Service is 13 to 16 times a day to the islands of Unst, Yell, Whalsay, Fetlar, and Bressay. Passenger and cargo vessels service the islands of Fair Isle, Foula, the Skerries, and Papa Stour. Scheduled services to the little-visited places operate only once or twice a week, however. Boat trips to the islands of Mousa and Noss can be arranged in summer. Call the **Shetland Islands Tourism office** (© **01595/693-434**) for more information.

In summer, buses travel around Mainland to all the major places of interest. Call the leading bus company, **John Leask & Son** (© **01595/693-162**), or pick up a copy of the *Inter-Shetland Transport Timetable*, costing £1 ($1.90) at the Shetland Islands Tourism office (see below).

It's easier to drive around the Shetlands than you'd think, as there are some 805km (500 miles) of passable roads—no traffic jams, no traffic lights. Many of the islands are connected by road bridges, and for those that aren't, car ferries provide service. Renting a car might be the best solution if you want to cover a lot of ground in the shortest time. You can either bring a car from mainland Scotland or pick one up in Lerwick. As yet, no major international car rental firm maintains an office in the Shetlands. However, Avis and Europcar have as their on-island agents **Bolts Car Hire,** 26 North Rd., Lerwick (© **01595/693-636**); a competitor is **Grantsfield Garage,** North Road, Lerwick (© **01595/692-709**).

If you want to pedal your way around, **Grantsfield Garage,** North Road (© **01595/692-709**), rents bikes for £9 ($17) per day and £35 ($67) per week. If you're planning on renting a bike for several days, reserve at least a day in advance.

VISITOR INFORMATION The **Shetland Islands Tourism office** is at the Market Cross in Lerwick (© **01595/693-434;** www.visitshetland.com). The helpful staff does many things, such as arranging rooms and providing information on ferries, boat trips, car rentals, and local events—they even rent fishing tackle. It's open from April to September, Monday to Friday 8am to 6pm and Saturday 8am to 4pm (May–Aug also Sun 10am–1pm); and October to March, Monday to Friday 9am to 5pm.

SPECIAL EVENTS Festivals and a festive atmosphere surround the communities of these remote islands, where the slightest excuse will kick off music and revelry. Pubs and community centers regularly schedule music and dancing, and on most weekend nights, all you have to do is go in search of a pint of beer to find live traditional music.

The **Shetland Folk Festival** (© **01595/694-757** for information; www.shetland folkfestival.com) takes place at Lerwick around the end of April and the beginning of May. Young fiddlers on the island take part, and international artists fly in for 4 days of concerts, workshops, and informal jam sessions, climaxed by what is called the "Final Foy." Concerts, usually incorporating dinner and dancing, take place in local halls throughout the islands, with most events costing about £20 to £30 ($38–$57). Often festival entertainers will convene at the pubs and join local performers.

January also finds Lerwick hosting **Up Helly Aa,** its famous **Fire Festival,** on the last Tuesday of the month, when a thousand locals, torches held high, are cheered on as they storm an effigy of a Viking longboat and set it aflame. These heroes and their witnesses follow this with a long night of eating, drinking, playing music, and dancing. The celebrations spread out from here, and more remote communities hold their local versions of the event over the next 3 months.

Summer weekends bring regularly scheduled local **regattas,** in which different communities compete in sailing and rowing competitions. Afterward, there are celebratory dinners, music, and dancing in local venues.

LERWICK

The capital of the Shetlands since the 17th century, Lerwick, on the eastern coast of Mainland, is sheltered by the little offshore island of Bressay. In the 19th century, it was the herring capital of northern Europe, and, before that, a haven for smugglers. The fishing fleet of the Netherlands puts in here after combing the North Sea. Even before Victoria came to the throne in 1837, Lerwick had a bustling, cosmopolitan atmosphere. And, with the influx of foreign visitors, it's even livelier.

Believe it or not, Lerwick is sometimes the sunniest place in Britain, experiencing some 12 hours of sunshine a day in early summer. Commercial Street is the town's principal artery, and it's said that beneath the steep and narrow lanes runs a network of passages used by smugglers. Lerwick today is the main port and shopping center of Shetland.

EXPLORING THE TOWN

Your first stop should be at the Shetland Islands Tourism office (see above). The helpful staff members are used to unusual requests: Sometimes visitors from Canada or the United States drop in here wanting their ancestors traced.

Shetland Library and Museum, Lower Hillhead Road, a 5-minute walk west of Lerwick's center (© **01595/695-057;** www.shetland-museum.org.uk), has, in addition to a reading room, four galleries devoted to exhibits covering art and textiles, shipping, archaeological digs, and oil exploration. Admission is free. It's open Monday, Wednesday, and Friday 10am to 7pm and Tuesday, Thursday, and Saturday 10am to 5pm.

Entered via both Market Street and Charlotte Street, pentagonal **Fort Charlotte** (© **01595/841-815**), built in 1665, contains high walls with gun slits pointing, naturally, at the sea. Eight years after it was constructed, it was burned by the Dutch. Restoration came in 1781. It's open daily from 9:30am to sunset; admission is free.

Clickhimin Broch, about .4km (¼ mile) southwest of Lerwick, beside A970, was fortified at the beginning of the Iron Age. Excavated in the 1950s, the site revealed 1,000 years of history. It was at one time turned into a broch, rising 5m (17 ft.) and built inside the fort. Admission is free; it's open daily with no set hours. It's a great place to go for a scenic walk.

A 12m (40-ft.) replica of a Viking longboat, *Dim Riv* (**"Morning Light"**), is available for a tour of the harbor on summer evenings. The boat was constructed by Lerwick craftsmen in 1980. Ask at the tourism office (see above).

Of the many shops in Lerwick, you may want to drop in at **Anderson & Co.,** Shetland Warehouse, Commercial Street (✆ **01595/693-714**), which sells handmade crofter and designer sweaters as well as other cottage-industry goods. **G. Rae,** 92 Commercial St. (✆ **01595/693-686**), sells silver and gold jewelry featuring Celtic motifs and images based on Norse mythology and Shetland legends. Gold- and silversmith Rosalyn Thompson produces the jewelry sold at **Hjaltasteyn,** 161 Commercial St. (✆ **01595/696-224**), where you find a selection of sterling silver and gold items, some of which are set with garnets and amethysts.

WHERE TO STAY

Glen Orchy House   Near the top of a brae (gently sloping hill) and not far from a 9-hole golf course that's free to the public, Glen Orchy House is a 4-minute walk from the center of town. The building was constructed in 1904 as an Episcopalian convent; the most recent modifications to it were in 1997, when a new wing was added. Besides singles and doubles, there are now four family rooms. The hosts will provide an affordable evening meal to those who request it.

20 Knab Rd., Lerwick, Shetland ZE1 0AX. ✆/fax **01595/692-031**. www.guesthouselerwick.com. 22 units. £75 ($143) double. Rates include Scottish breakfast. MC, V. Pets accepted. **Amenities:** Bar. *In room:* A/C (some rooms), TV, coffeemaker, hair dryer.

Grand Hotel ✦   A grander hotel would be hard to find anywhere in Shetland. With pointed turrets, weather vanes, crow's-step gables, and solid stone walls, it lies a block from the waterfront, in the town center. The guest rooms are conservative yet comfortable, each with a shower-only bathroom. The extensively modernized hotel has two lounge bars, a dining room, and a nightclub open Wednesday, Friday, and Sunday. The Grand shares its reservations facilities and some of its staff with the Queens Hotel (see below).

149 Commercial St., Lerwick, Shetland ZE1 0AB. ✆ **01595/692-826**. Fax 01595/694-048. www.kgqhotels.co.uk. 24 units. £100 ($190) double; £135 ($257) family room. Rates include Scottish breakfast. AE, DC, MC, V. Free parking in nearby public lot. **Amenities:** Restaurant; 2 bars; room service. *In room:* TV, coffeemaker, hair dryer.

Lerwick Hotel ✦   This is one of the biggest and most up-to-date hotels in the Shetlands, sprawling beside a gravel- and kelp-covered beach. Its simply furnished guest rooms offer various amenities and small, shower-only bathrooms; half have views over the water toward Bressay. The upscale restaurant offers at least one seafood and one vegetarian choice as well as chicken or wild game. In summer, dinner dances that combine hearty meals with traditional Scottish fun are frequently held.

15 South Rd., Shetland ZE1 0RB. ✆ **01595/692-166**. Fax 01595/694-419. www.shetlandhotels.com. 35 units. £100 ($190) double; £130 ($247) suite. Rates include Scottish breakfast. AE, DC, MC, V. Take Scalloway Rd. west from the center for 5 min. **Amenities:** 2 restaurants; bar; room service; laundry service. *In room:* TV, coffeemaker, hair dryer, trouser press.

Queens Hotel ✦   Its foundations rise directly from the sea at the harborfront, so on blustery nights, fine sprays of saltwater sometimes coat the windowpanes of the lower floors. Built of natural stone around 1860, the Queens rivals the nearby Grand Hotel (see above) as the most prestigious hotel in Lerwick. They share the same reservations staff. The small guest rooms are conservatively and comfortably furnished, each with shower. Inexpensive bar lunches are offered in the cocktail lounge, and more formal dinners with Shetland cuisine are served in the dining room (see "Where to Dine" below).

24 Commercial St., Lerwick, Shetland ZE1 0AB. ℂ 01595/692-826. Fax 01595/694-048. www.kgqhotels.co.uk. 26 units. £100 ($190) double; £130 ($247) family room. Rates include Scottish breakfast. AE, DC, MC, V. **Amenities:** Restaurant; bar; room service. *In room:* TV, coffeemaker, hair dryer.

Shetland Hotel Built in 1984, this four-story brick, stone, and concrete structure is one of the most modern hotels in the Shetlands. It's opposite the ferry terminal and has a nice view of the harbor. The good-size guest rooms are well furnished. The two on-site restaurants offer local fish and vegetarian items. It has been upgraded and much improved in the wake of the Shetland oil boom, when oil executives often filled up its rooms.

Holmsgarth Rd., Lerwick, Shetland ZE1 0PW. ℂ 01595/695-515. Fax 01595/695-828. www.shetlandhotels.com. 65 units. £95 ($181) double; £105 ($200) suite. Rates include Scottish breakfast. AE, DC, MC, V. **Amenities:** 2 restaurants (see Oasis Bistro, below); 2 bars; room service; laundry service; rooms for those w/limited mobility. *In room:* TV, coffeemaker, hair dryer, trouser press.

WHERE TO DINE

Golden Coach CHINESE   One of the two Chinese restaurants in the Shetlands, this intimate place is softly lit and contemporary in decor. Try the barbecued Peking duck or deep-fried shredded beef in sweet-and-sour sauce. Malaysian chicken comes in a peanut sauce, or you can order king prawns Peking with garlic sauce. No MSG is used in food preparation.

17 Hillhead. ℂ 01595/693-848. Reservations required Sat–Sun. Main courses £9–£11 ($17–$21); fixed-price lunch £9 ($17); fixed-price dinner menu £22 ($42). MC, V. Mon–Fri noon–2pm and 5:30–11pm; Sat–Sun noon–11pm.

Oasis Bistro SCOTTISH   This eatery is a good choice for a light snack at odd hours; salads and sandwiches are served all day. The restaurant also offers hot meals at lunch and dinner. Emphasis is on fresh fish and vegetarian fare straight from Shetland gardens.

In the Shetland Hotel, Holmsgarth Rd. ℂ 01595/695-515. Main courses £10–£13 ($19–$25). AE, DC, MC, V. Daily 11am–9:30pm; hot meals noon–2pm and 5–9:30pm.

Queens Hotel (Kids) BRITISH   On the lobby level of this previously recommended hotel (see above) is a pink-and-white dining room that overlooks the sea, the wharves, and the many fishing boats bobbing at anchor. It caters to families, many of whom seem to arrive in groups as part of reunions. Many locals consider it the best restaurant in Lerwick, a staple on the island's culinary scene. Specialties include goujons of haddock with tartar sauce, roast beef sirloin with Yorkshire pudding, chicken Caribbean with pineapple sauce, braised lamb cutlets, and conservative preparations of fish dishes.

24 Commercial St. ℂ 01595/692-826. Reservations recommended. Main courses £13–£19 ($25–$36); fixed-price 3-course dinner £22 ($42). AE, DC, MC, V. Daily noon–2pm and 6–9:30pm.

LERWICK AFTER DARK

From May to September, the **Islesburgh Community Centre,** King Harold Street (ℂ 01595/692-114), hosts dancing to Shetland fiddle music called the Summer Exhibition on Wednesdays and Fridays from 7 to 9:30pm. Admission is £4 ($7.60). The **Lounge Bar,** Mounthooly Street (ℂ 01595/692-231), hosts an informal evening of traditional fiddle music on Wednesdays, usually starting around 9:30pm. There's also live music on Friday nights and often on Saturday afternoons. There's no cover.

SOUTH MAINLAND

This part of Shetland, reached by heading south from Lerwick along A970, is both ancient and modern. On the one hand, there's the gleaming **Sumburgh Airport,** which has played a major role in the North Sea oilfields development and services many of the offshore rigs today. On the other hand, you'll stumble on the ruins of **Jarlshof** (see below), which may have been inhabited for some 3,000 years.

EXPLORING THE AREA

As you go down Shetland's "long leg," as it's called, heading due south, passing a peaty moorland and fresh meadows, the first attraction is not on Mainland but on an off-shore island called Mousa: the famous **Broch of Mousa** *★★*, a Pictish defense tower that guarded the islet for some 2,000 years. It reached the then-incredible height of some 12m (40 ft.) and was constructed of local stones, with two circular walls, one within the other. They enclosed a staircase leading to sleeping quarters. It's the best-preserved example of an Iron Age broch in Britain. The village of **Sandwick,** 11km (7 miles) south of Lerwick, is the ferry point for reaching Mousa. There's daily bus service between Lerwick and Sandwick. A local boatman, Mr. Jamieson, will take you across to Mousa, a 15-minute trip. From April to September only, you can visit Mousa Monday to Saturday. The cost is £10 ($19) for adults and £5 ($9.50) for children 5 to 16. For boat schedules, call the tourist office in Lerwick at ℂ **01595/693-434.**

South of Sandwick, you reach the parish of Dunrossness. At Boddam is the **Croft-house Museum** (ℂ **01595/695-057**), east of A970 on an unmarked road 40km (25 miles) south of Lerwick. Rural Shetland life comes alive here in this thatched croft house from the mid-1800s. The museum also has some outbuildings and a functioning water mill. It's open from May to September. Admission is free.

Continuing south, you reach Shetland's outstanding man-made attraction, **Jarlshof** *★*, Sumburgh (ℂ **01950/460-112**), near the Sumburgh Airport. It has been called the most remarkable archaeological discovery in Britain. In 1897, a violent storm performed the first archaeological "dig," washing away sections of the large mound; huge stone walls were revealed. Excavations that followed turned up an astonishing array of seven distinct civilizations. The earliest was from the Bronze Age, but habitation continued at the site through the 1500s, from wheelhouse people to Vikings, from broch builders to medieval settlers. A manor house was built here in the 16th century by the treacherous Earl Patrick Stewart, but it was sacked in 1609. The site is open April to September, daily from 9:30am to 6:30pm. Admission is £4.50 ($8.55) for adults, £3.50 ($6.65) for seniors, and £2.25 ($4.30) for children.

Also nearby is the **Sumburgh Lighthouse,** one of many Scottish lighthouses constructed by the grandfather of Robert Louis Stevenson. The lighthouse is now fully automated. The property offers a self-catering four-bedroom cottage, costing £50 ($95) per day. Built in 1821, it can be visited by the public, but you must phone the Lerwick tourist office (ℂ **01595/693-434**) for an appointment; reservations for the cottage can also be made with the owner, Catrina Canter, at ℂ **01595/694-688.** Reserve at least 3 months in advance.

On the coast at the tip of Scatness, about 1.6km (1 mile) southwest of Jarlshof at the end of the Mainland, is the **Ness of Burgi,** which was a defensive Iron Age structure related to a broch.

Heading back north toward Lerwick, you can veer west for a trip to **St. Ninians Island,** which is in the southwestern corner of Shetland. It's reached by going along B9122. The island is approached by what's called a *tombolo* (bridging sandbar). An early monastery once stood on this island, but it wasn't uncovered until 1958. Puffins often favor the islet, which has a pure white sandy beach on each side. The island became famous in 1958 when a group of students from Aberdeen came upon a rich cache of Celtic artifacts, mainly silverware, including brooches and other valuable pieces. Monks are believed to have hidden the treasure trove, fearing a Viking attack. The St. Ninian treasure is in the National Museum of Scotland at Edinburgh.

WHERE TO STAY & DINE

Sumburgh Hotel   This is an old favorite. Its turrets and towers were built in 1857 for the laird of Virkie, the Victorian descendant of Robert the Bruce. Set on 4.9 barren hectares (12 acres) of land jutting dramatically out to sea, it lies at the southernmost end of the Shetland Islands, at the end of A970. A modern addition completed in the 1960s doubled the size of the place, which contains the Voe Room restaurant (offering affordable dinners nightly) and two popular bars. Recent refurbishments have made the bedrooms more inviting.

Sumburgh Head, Virkie, Shetland ZE3 9JN. (C) 01950/460-201. Fax 01950/460-394. www.sumburgh-hotel.zetnet.co.uk. 32 units. £65–£85 ($124–$162) double. Rates include Scottish breakfast. AE, MC, V. **Amenities:** Restaurant; 2 bars; room service; laundry service. *In room:* TV, coffeemaker, hair dryer, trouser press.

SCALLOWAY

On the western coast, 10km (6 miles) west of Lerwick, Scalloway was once the capital of Shetland. This town was the base for rescue operations in Norway during the darkest days of World War II. Still an important fishing port, Scalloway has been changed by the oil boom. New businesses have opened, attracting more and more people to the area, which has emerged after a long slumber into a prosperous and lively place in this remote corner of the world.

Dominating the town are the ruins of corbel-turreted medieval **Scalloway Castle** ((C) **01856/841-815**), commissioned by the dreaded Earl Patrick Stewart at the beginning of the 17th century and built with forced (slave) labor culled from the island's residents. After it was built, he imposed exorbitant taxes and fines on the islanders. In 1615, the Earl and all his sons were executed in Edinburgh, partly as a means of placating the islanders, partly because he rebelled against the powers of the central Scottish-British government. Admission is free; hours are those of the Shetland Woollen Company (see below), from which you must get the key to enter.

The **Shetland Woollen Company** ((C) **01595/880-243**) is open Monday to Friday 9am to 5pm (in summer, also Sat 9am–5pm). You can see the processing and finishing of Shetland knitware, and then visit the showroom where a selection of garments is sold.

To escape to a beautiful area, ideal for long walks or drives, follow B9075 east off A970 to the top of a small sea inlet that will lead you to the surprisingly lush **Kergord.** This green valley contains forests ideal for long strolls.

WEST MAINLAND

It's said you can see more of Shetland from the **Scord of Weisdale** than from any other vantage point in the archipelago. This is a hill or plateau lying west of Weisdale that offers a dramatic and panoramic view of the Shetland. This vista changes constantly, depending on the time of the day, the weather, and, of course, the season.

Shetland's only stone-polishing business operates at **Hjaltasteyn,** Whiteness, 14km (9 miles) west of Lerwick. You can visit the showroom at 161 Commercial St., Lerwick ((C) **01595/696-224**). It's open in summer only, Thursday to Saturday, Monday, and Tuesday 9:15am to 4:45pm, and Wednesday 10am to 4pm (closed daily 1–2pm for lunch).

Continuing north, you can watch high-quality jewelry being made at **Shetland Jewelry,** Soundside, Weisdale (© **01595/830-275**), where the artisans base many of their designs on ancient Celtic and Viking patterns. It's open Monday to Friday 9am to 1pm and 2 to 5pm.

You can continue your tour of West Mainland by heading west along A971 toward Walls. You come first to **Staneydale Temple,** 4.5km (2¾ miles) outside Walls. This early Bronze Age (perhaps Neolithic) hall once had a timber roof. It's called a temple because it bears a remarkable resemblance to similar sites on Malta, lending support to the theory that the early settlers of Shetland came from the Mediterranean.

Continuing past several lochs and sea inlets, you come to **Walls,** a hamlet built on the periphery of two voes (a local term for inlet). Its natural harbor is sheltered by the offshore islet of Vaila.

WHERE TO STAY & DINE

Burrastow House (★★ (Finds)   This is the most tranquil, idyllic retreat in the Shetlands. Located about 5km (3 miles) southwest of Walls, a 40-minute drive northwest of Lerwick, this simple but comfortable building was constructed in 1759 as a *haa* (home of the farm manager of a laird's estate) and has been a guesthouse since 1980. Set amid lands still used for grazing sheep, it lies at the widest section of a windswept peninsula, with views of a cluster of rocky and sparsely inhabited islands. The well-furnished guest rooms evoke country-house living. There's one family suite, consisting of a double room and a twin room connected by a bathroom. The establishment is now licensed for civil marriages.

The food is the best on the island. The daily menu in the oak-paneled dining room is likely to include nettle-and-oatmeal fritters, mussel brose (a stew of mussels thickened with oatmeal), and monkfish with anchovy stuffing, lamb, and Scottish beef. Lunch, high tea, and upscale dinners are served daily. The proprietors ask that you call ahead if you want a hot meal. The restaurant is closed Sunday and Monday to nonguests.

Walls, West Mainland, Shetland ZE2 9PD. © **01595/809-307.** Fax 01595/809-213. www.users.zetnet.co.uk/burrastow-house-hotel. 6 units. £150 ($285) double; £86 ($163) per person in family room. Rates include half-board. AE, DC, MC, V. Closed Nov. **Amenities:** Restaurant. *In room:* TV (on request), coffeemaker, no phone.

SIDE TRIP TO PAPA STOUR

Papa Stour, the "great island of priests," is shaped like a large starfish and lies off the west coast of Mainland, 40km (25 miles) northwest of Lerwick. As its name indicates, it was an early base for monks. Two centuries ago there was a leper colony here on the little offshore islet of Brei Holm.

Legend has it that its profusion of wildflowers had such a strong scent that old fishermen could use the perfume—borne far out on the wind—to fix their positions. Papa Stour is very isolated, and once it was feared the island might be depopulated, but about 26 settlers live here now.

In the darkest days of winter, bad weather can cut it off for days. But if you see it on a sunny day, it's striking. Encircled by pillars of rock and reefs, its sea caves, sculpted by turbulent winds and raging seas, are among the most impressive in Britain. The largest of these is **Kirstan's Hole,** extending some 73m (240 ft.).

Boats go to Papa Stour about seven times per day, 5 days a week, from West Burra-firth on Mainland, at a cost of £3 ($5.70) each way. Call **Mr. Clark** at © **01595/810-460** for information on these constantly changing details.

WHERE TO STAY & DINE

Northhouse *Finds*   Within walking distance of the island's only pier, just outside Housa Voe (the only hamlet, with seven buildings), this stone croft is an unusual building. The foundations are Viking, and Dutch coins from the 1620s have been unearthed here. It's the domain of Andrew and Sabina Holt-Brook, who moved from mainland Scotland more than 20 years ago. Now owners of 12 hectares (30 acres) of windswept peninsula, they offer the only accommodations and meals on the island. The rooms are comfortable and inviting, and the "garden room" has its own entrance. Meals are served to both guests and nonguests, but for just a meal, call in advance. The working farm supplies the Holt-Brooks with free-range eggs and fresh vegetables. The inexpensive lunches are brown-bag affairs (homemade sandwiches and cakes) to be taken along while you enjoy the island's wild landscapes.

North-house, Papa Stour, Shetland ZE2 9PW. *C* **01595/873-238.** 4 units, 1 with private bathroom. £40–£44 ($76–$84) double. Rates include breakfast. No credit cards. **Amenities:** Dining room; lounge; nonsmoking rooms. *In room:* Coffeemaker, hair dryer, no phone.

SIDE TRIP TO FOULA

This tiny, remote island is only 5km (3 miles) wide by 8km (5 miles) long, with five high peaks. Called the "Island West of the Sun," Foula may have been the Romans' legendary Thule. In local dialect, *foula* means "bird island"—and the name fits. Uncountable numbers of birds haunt the isle. Its towering sea cliffs include the second-highest cliff face in Britain, the **Kame,** at 370m (1,220 ft.). About 3,000 pairs of the world's great skuas, known as "bonxie," live here. You'll hear many stories about the rock-climbing prowess of locals who go in search of gulls' eggs.

The island lies 43km (27 miles) west of Scalloway, on the west coast of Mainland, and the locals are vastly outnumbered by sheep. Until the beginning of the 19th century, Old Norse was the language spoken. Its 400 people remain very traditional. If you're lucky, you might see them dance the Foula reel, a classic dance in Shetland.

If the weather's right, a weekly mailboat sails to Foula from Walls on Mainland. Even in summer, the seas are likely to be turbulent, and in winter, Foula has been known to be cut off from the rest of Britain for weeks. The trip takes 2½ hours. **Loganair** also operates a summer service from Tingwall on Monday, Wednesday, and Friday; trip time is 15 minutes.

WHERE TO STAY & DINE

Because of the interest by visitors in recent years, some islanders have taken to offering accommodations that include half-board.

Mrs. Marion Taylor   Owners Bryan and Marion run this cozy modern farmhouse near the geographical center of the island, within walking distance of everything. The comfortable rooms in the main house have easy access to the large kitchen, whose brick hearth is the focal point of the farm. The cottage has two bedrooms, a sitting room, and a kitchen. There are no food shops on the island, so you have to bring your own supplies, as the rates for the cottage don't include meals. The Taylor's 2.8 hectares (7 acres) are a sheep farm, and they augment their income by knitting and spinning— you can order a custom-made, handknit sweater.

Leraback, Isle of Foula, Shetland ZE2 9PN. *C* **01595/753-226.** 3 units, none with private bathroom; 1 cottage. £55 ($105) double; £30 ($57) per day in cottage (sleeps up to 4). Free pickup from airstrip or pier. No credit cards. *In room:* TV, fridge, microwave, no phone.

NORTH MAINLAND

The Shetlands' most rugged scenery is in the northern part of Mainland. Some visitors have found that the area reminds them of Norway, and we agree. That's especially true in the tiny village of **Voe,** with its little wooden houses.

Heading north from Voe along A970, you reach the eastern junction of B9071, which takes you to **Vidlin,** where the **Lunna Kirk,** one of the oldest churches in the archipelago, still holds services. Construction began in 1753. The church has a "leper hole," from which the poor victims could listen to the sermon without being seen.

Heading west back to A970, continue north to **Mavis Grind,** a narrow isthmus marking the point where the North Mainland is at its most narrow. The touristy thing to do in North Mainland is to pause at Mavis Grind, take a couple of stones, and throw one to your right into the North Sea and the other to your left into the Atlantic Ocean.

Near the villages of **Brae** and **Busta,** you find some of the best food and hotels in Shetland. Oil contractors, helicopter pilots, and shipping executives sent by mainland companies to service the nearby Sullom Voe, site of the largest oil terminal in Europe, often stay in this area.

If you head north along A970, we suggest you take the secondary road going west to **Esha Ness** 🏕🏕, where you'll come upon the most dramatic cliff scenery not only in Shetland but in all of Britain. This is simply a gorgeous area for **hiking.**

WHERE TO STAY & DINE

Brae Hotel   Built in 1979, this modern building lies in the center of Brae, 45km (28 miles) north of Lerwick; it's beside A970, about 1.6km (1 mile) south of the narrow isthmus that separates North from South Mainland. The small, pastel-toned guest rooms are reassuringly warm. Each comes with a small, shower-only bathroom. The restaurant serves affordable meals.

Brae, North Mainland, Shetland ZE2 9QJ. ✆ **01806/522-456.** Fax 01806/522-026. www.braehotel.co.uk. 36 units. £80 ($152) double with Scottish breakfast, £100 ($190) with Scottish breakfast and dinner. Discounts offered for stays of 4 or more days. AE, MC, V. **Amenities:** Restaurant; bar; billiard room. *In room:* TV, coffeemaker.

Busta House 🏕🏕   Busta House is the oldest continuously inhabited house in the Shetlands. Built in 1580, it was the original *busta* (homestead) of the medieval Norwegian rulers of the island. Rising above its own small harbor a short drive from A970, a 10-minute drive south of the village of Sullom, and 2.5km (1½ miles) from Brae, the hotel has crow's-foot gables, stone walls measuring 2m (6 ft.) thick, and an appearance of a fortified manor house. The proprietors maintain the antique charm of the public rooms and the chintz-filled guest rooms, and prepare upscale dinners as well.

Busta, near Brae, North Mainland, Shetland ZE2 9QN. ✆ **01806/522-506.** Fax 01806/522-588. www.bustahouse. com. 20 units. £100–£140 ($190–$266) double. Rates include Scottish breakfast. Discounts offered for stays of 4 or more days. AE, DC, MC, V. **Amenities:** Restaurant; bar; business center; room service; laundry service; nonsmoking rooms. *In room:* TV, coffeemaker, hair dryer.

SIDE TRIP TO YELL & UNST

The second-largest island in the Shetlands, Yell measures 9.6km (6 miles) north to south, with a population that has shrunk to 1,000, down from its high of 2,600 in 1841. This is the least cultivated Scottish Island because the majority of it lies under a peat blanket 3m (10 ft.) deep. The Yell Ferry is one of the "roll-on/roll-off" ferries sailing between Toft, near Mossbank on the mainland, to Ulstra at the southwesterly corner of Yell. The crossing from Toft to Ulstra takes about 25 minutes, with ferries generally leaving throughout the day at half-hour intervals. A car, driver, and adult passenger pays £5 ($9.50) one-way, and booking for the ferry is possible Monday to Saturday 8:30am to 5pm by calling © **01957/722-259.**

From Yell, remote and beautiful Unst is easy to reach. Drive along A968 to the little harbor at Gutcher, northeast of Yell. The **Shetland Island's Council** (© **01595/ 743-980** for schedules) operates a ferry crossing from here fairly frequently each day. The cost is £7 ($13) for a car and driver, £3 ($5.70) for each extra adult, and 40p (75¢) per child. **Loganair** (© **01595/840-246**) flies to Unst from both Lerwick and Sumburgh, once a day from Monday to Friday.

An **Old Norse longhouse,** believed to date from the 9th century, was excavated at Underhoull. The best beach is at **Skaw,** set against the backdrop of **Saxa Vord,** legendary home of the giant Saxi. A drive to the top will reward you with a view of the Burra Firth. Visitors go to Haroldswick to mail their cards and letters in the northernmost post office in the British Isles.

The roll-on/roll-off car ferry from Yell comes into Belmont. Nearby is **Muness Castle,** constructed in 1598 by Laurence Bruce, a relative of the notorious Earl Patrick Stewart, who ruled Shetland so harshly. Built with rubble and known for its fine architectural detail, the castle was inhabited for less than a century. Normally it's open April to September, daily 9am to 7pm. If it's closed, ask for the key at Mrs. Peterson's cottage across the way. For information, call © **01856/841-815.**

The ruins of the **Kirk of Lund,** dating from the Middle Ages, can be seen on Unst, which is also home to the **Hermaness Bird Reserve** ⓕ, one of the most important ornithological sites in Britain. Ideal for scenic walks, its 182m (600-ft.) cliffs are filled with kittiwakes, razorbills, guillemots, and the inevitable puffins.

WHERE TO STAY & DINE

Baltasound Hotel *(Finds)*   Built 150 years ago for the local laird and converted into a hotel in 1939, this granite house sits in isolation, beside the sea, about .5km (¼ mile) from the hamlet of Baltasound. The simple, uncluttered bedrooms are in what locals call a "Scandinavian extension" jutting out to the building's side, sheathed with blackened wood siding. In 1992, the hotel was enlarged with a series of motel-like "chalet" rooms attached to the main building. The bar serves lunch and inexpensive dinners; the restaurant offers moderately priced dinners, which you should book in advance.

Baltasound, Unst, Shetland ZE2 9DS. © **01957/711-334.** Fax 01957/711-358. www.baltasound-hotel.shetland. co.uk. 25 units. £78 ($148) double. Rates include Scottish breakfast. MC, V. **Amenities:** Restaurant; bar. *In room:* TV, coffeemaker, hair dryer (on request).

Appendix:
Scotland in Depth

A small nation ('Tis a wee country, aye—but a bonnie one), Scotland is only 443km (275 miles) long and some 242km (150 miles) wide at its broadest. No Scot lives more than 65km (40 miles) from saltwater. But despite the small size of their country, the Scots have extended their influence around the world. And in this land of bagpipes, clans, and kilts, you'll find some of Europe's grandest scenery.

Inventor Alexander Graham Bell and explorers Mungo Park and David Livingstone came from Scotland. This country gave the world entrepreneur Andrew Carnegie, poet Robert Burns, novelist Sir Walter Scott, actor Sean Connery, singer Sheena Easton, and comedian/actor Billy Connolly. But, curiously, for a long time its most famous resident has been neither man nor woman but Nessie, the Loch Ness Monster.

The border is just a line on a map; you're hardly aware of crossing out of England into Scotland. Yet even though the two countries have been joined constitutionally since 1707, Scotland is quite different from England and is very much its own country. (In fact, on July 1, 1999, Scotland was granted greater independence when a reform instituted by Prime Minister Tony Blair brought back regional government, and a new Scottish Parliament was opened by Queen Elizabeth in Edinburgh.)

In Scotland, you'll discover mountains and glens, lochs and heather-covered moors, skirling bagpipes and twirling kilts, and rivers and streams filled with trout and salmon. Lush meadowlands are dotted with sheep, and rocky coves and secret harbors await the adventurous. You can hear the sounds of Gaelic, admire the misty blue hills, and attend a Highland Gathering. You can schedule quiet contemplation or an activity-filled calendar. And in Scotland, you'll find one of Europe's biggest welcomes.

1 History 101

Much of Scottish history has been shaped by the country's location in a remote corner of northwestern Europe. Amazingly, Scotland encompasses 787 islands (although only about a fourth are inhabited). Its 10,004km (6,214 miles) of coastline are deeply penetrated by the Atlantic Ocean on the west and the often turbulent North Sea on the east. Most places lie no more than 97km (60 miles) inland. In fact, the sea has shaped Scotland's destiny more than any other element and bred a nation of seafarers, many of whom still earn their living on the water.

Scotland is a world apart, a distinctly unique nation within the United Kingdom. Just more than half the size of England, with only a tenth of England's population, it boasts more open spaces and natural splendor than England ever did. The Scots are hard to classify: They're generous yet have a reputation for stinginess, eloquent yet dour at times, and romantic at heart yet brutally realistic in their appraisals (especially of the English). Even the Romans couldn't subdue these Caledonians, and they remain Braveheart proud and fiercely independent.

But how did it all begin?

EARLY HISTORY Scotland was a melting pot from its earliest days. Standing stones, *brochs* (circular stone towers), cromlechs, cairns, and burial chambers attest to its earliest inhabitants, but we know little about these first tribes and invaders. When the Roman armies decided to invade in A.D. 82, the land was occupied by a people the Romans called the Picts (Painted Ones). Despite spectacular bloodletting, the Romans were unsuccessful, and the building of Hadrian's Wall effectively marked the northern limits of their influence.

Parts of Hadrian's Wall still stand, but in England, not Scotland. The wall extends for 118km (73 miles) across the north of England, from the North Sea to the Irish Sea, its most interesting stretch consisting of 16km (10 miles) west of the town of Housesteads. If you're driving north from England into Scotland, you might want to stop and see the remains of this wall before penetrating the Border Country of Scotland.

By A.D. 500, the Picts were again attacked, this time by the Dalriada Irish called Scots, who were successful. They established themselves on the Argyll Peninsula and battled and intermarried with the Picts. Britons emigrated from the south and Norsemen from the east, creating new bloodlines and migratory patterns. Druidism, a little-understood mystical form of nature worship whose most visible monuments are runic etchings and stone circles, flourished at this time. Languages of the era included a diverse array of Celtic and Norse dialects with scatterings of Low German and Saxon English.

The power of the Scotians, entrenched in western Scotland, was cemented when a missionary named Columba (later canonized) arrived from Ireland in 563. The rocky Hebridean island of Iona became the base for his Christian mission. Christianity, already introduced by Sts. Ninian and Mungo to Strathclyde and Galloway, became widespread.

If you have an interest in this early part of Scottish history, visit remote Iona, part of the Hebrides (see chapter 12 for more information). More than any dull recitation of history, a visit here, especially to Iona Abbey, can recapture some of this land's dim, often unrecorded history.

THE MIDDLE AGES The Scots and the Picts were united in 843 under the kingship of an early chieftain named Kenneth MacAlpin, but it was the invasionary pressures from England and Scandinavia and the unifying force of Christianity that molded Scotland into a relatively coherent unit. Under Malcolm II (1005–34), the British and the Angles, who occupied the southwest and southeast of the Scottish

Dateline

- **6000 B.C.** The earliest known residents of Scotland establish settlements on the Argyll Peninsula.
- **3000 B.C.** Celtic tribes invade, making the use of Gaelic widespread.
- **A.D. 82** Roman armies directed by Agricola push into southern Scotland; the Roman victories, however, are short-lived.
- **A.D. 90** Romans abandon the hope of conquering Scotland, retreating to England and the relative safety of Hadrian's Wall.
- **500** Newcomers from Ireland, identified as Scots, invade from the west, mingling their bloodlines with Norse, Pictish, Celtic, and Teutonic tribes.
- **563** St. Columba establishes a mission on Iona, accelerating the movement established by earlier ecclesiastics to Christianize Scotland.
- **843** Kenneth MacAlpin unifies the Picts and the Scots.
- **1005–34** Malcolm II unites the four major tribes of Scotland into one roughly cohesive unit.
- **1124–53** David I builds monasteries, consolidates royal power and prestige,

continues

mainland, merged with the Scots and the Picts. Malcolm's son and heir, Duncan, was murdered by Macbeth of Moray, and this event fueled the plotline of Shakespeare's famous "Scottish play." Glamis Castle, outside Dundee, contains Duncan's Hall, where the Victorians imagined Macbeth killed Duncan. See chapter 10 for details on Glamis.

Malcolm III's marriage to an English princess, Margaret, furthered the Anglicization of the Scottish Lowlands. A determined woman of strong ideas, she imported English priests into Scotland and carried out church reforms that soon replaced St. Columba's Gaelic form of Christianity. Her Anglicization efforts and introduction of the English language as a teaching tool laid important groundwork for making Scotland into a potential English kingdom. She led a life of great piety and was canonized as St. Margaret in 1251.

While Europe's feudal system was coming to full flower, Scotland was preoccupied with the territorial battles of clan allegiances and the attempt to define its borders with England. Cultural assimilation with England continued under David I (1081–1153), who made land grants to many Anglo-Norman families, providing Scotland with a feudal aristocracy and bringing in ancient names like Fraser, Seton, and Lindsay. He also

embarked on one of the most lavish building sprees in Scottish history, erecting many abbeys, including Jedburgh, Kelso, Melrose, and Dryburgh. You can still see these abbeys or their ruins.

In 1266, after about a century of Norse control, the foggy and windswept Western Isles were returned to Scotland following the Battle of Largs. Despite nominal allegiance to the Scottish monarch, this region's inhabitants quickly organized themselves around the Donald (or Mac-Donald) clan, which for nearly 100 years was one of the most powerful, ruling its territory almost as an independent state. The honorary title of their patriarch, Lord of the Isles, is still one of the formal titles used on state occasions by Britain's Prince of Wales. To learn more about what may be the most important clan in Scottish history, you can visit the Clan Donald Visitor Centre at Armadale on the Isle of Skye (see chapter 12).

In the meantime, real trouble was brewing in the south. Edward I, ambitious Plantagenet king of England, yearned to rule over an undivided nation incorporating England, Scotland, and Wales. Successful at first, he set up John de Balliol as a vassal king to do homage to him for Scotland. Many of Scotland's legendary heroes lived during this period: Sir William Wallace (1270–1305), who drove the English out of Perth and Stirling; Sir

---

and imports clearly defined Norman values.

- **1266** The Hebrides and the coast of western Scotland are released from Norse control; the Donald clan consolidates power here into a semi-autonomous state within Scotland.

- **1272** Edward I of England embarks on an aggressive campaign to conquer both Wales and Scotland but is

deflected by Robert the Bruce, among others.

- **1314** The victory of the Scots over the English armies at Bannockburn leads to the Treaty of Northampton (1328), formally recognizing Scotland's independence from England.

- **1468** The Orkney and the Shetland Islands are given to Scotland as part of the marriage dowry of a Norse princess to a Scottish king.

- **Late 1400s** The Auld Alliance with France, a cynical arrangement based mostly on mutual distrust of England, is born.

- **1535** At the urging of Henry VIII of England, Parliament officially severs all ties with the Catholic Church, legally sanctioning the Reformation.

- **1559–64** John Knox lays out the rough outline of the Scottish Presbyterian Church.

James Douglas, the Black Douglas (1286–1330), who terrorized the English borders; and Robert the Bruce (1274–1329), who finally succeeded in freeing Scotland from England. Crowned Robert I at Scone in 1306 in defiance of the English, Robert the Bruce decisively defeated Edward II of England at the 1314 Battle of Bannockburn. Scotland's independence was formally recognized in the 1328 Treaty of Northampton, inaugurating a heady but short-lived separation from England.

For more legend and lore about those towering Scottish heroes William Wallace and Robert the Bruce, see chapter 9. You can also visit Stirling Castle, which loomed so large in Scottish history. If you'd rather see where the crucial Battle of Bannockburn took place, visit the Bannockburn Heritage Centre outside Stirling (see chapter 9).

In 1468, the Orkneys and the Shetlands, Norse to the core, were brought into the Scottish web of power as part of the marriage dowry of the Norse princess Margaret to James III. This acquisition was the last successful expansion of Scottish sovereignty during the period when Scottish power and independence were at their zenith. It was at this time the Scots entered with the French into an alliance that was to have far-reaching effects. The line of Stuart (or Stewart) kings, so named because the family had become powerful as stewards of the English king, were generally accepted as the least troublesome of a series of potential evils. Real power, however, lay with Scotland's great lords, patriarchs of the famous clans. Jealous of both their bloodlines and their territories, they could rarely agree on anything other than their common distrust of England.

THE REFORMATION The passions of the Reformation burst on an already turbulent Scottish scene in the person of John Knox, a devoted disciple of the Geneva Protestant John Calvin and a bitter enemy of both the Catholic Church and the Anglican Church. Knox became famous for the screaming insults he heaped on ardently Catholic Queen Mary and for his absolute lack of a sense of humor. His polemics were famous—in his struggle against Queen Mary, he wrote his *First Blast of the Trumpet Against the Monstrous Regiment of Women.* His was a peculiar mixture of piety, conservatism, strict morality, and intellectual independence that's still a pronounced feature of the Scottish character.

Knox's teachings helped shape the democratic form of Scottish government and set the Scottish Church's austere moral tone for generations to come. He focused on practical considerations as well as religious ones: church administration and

- **1561** Queen Mary returns to Scotland from France.
- **1568** Mary is defeated and flees to England.
- **1572** John Knox dies; his work is continued by Andrew Melville.
- **1587** Mary Queen of Scots is executed.
- **1603** Mary's son, James VI of Scotland, accedes to the throne of England as James I and unifies the two countries.

- **1689** Parliament strips the uncompromising Catholic James II of his crown and imports the Protestant William and Mary from Holland to replace him.
- **1746** Bonnie Prince Charlie's attempt to reclaim his grandfather's throne ends in defeat at the Battle of Culloden, destroying any hope of a Stuart revival.

- **1750–1850** England and Scotland experience rapid industrialization; the Clearances strip many crofters of their farms, creating epic bitterness and forcing new patterns of Scottish migrations.
- **1789** The French Revolution begins; British monarchists tighten their grip on civil unrest in Scotland.

continues

funding, and the relationship between church and state. Foremost among the tenets were provisions for a self-governing congregation and pure allegiance to the Word of God as contained in meticulous translations of the Old and New Testaments. In Edinburgh, you can still visit the John Knox House, where the reformer lived (see chapter 5 for more information).

On Knox's death, in 1562, his work was continued by Scots-born, Geneva-trained Andrew Melville, who may have hated ecclesiastical tyranny even more than Knox himself. Melville reorganized the Scottish universities and emphasized classical studies and the study of the Bible in its original Hebrew and Greek. Under his leadership emerged a clearly defined Scottish Presbyterian Church whose elected leaders were responsible for practical as well as spiritual matters.

Later, the Church of Scotland's almost obsessive insistence on self-government led to endless conflicts, first with the Scottish and then, after unification, with the British monarchs.

MARY QUEEN OF SCOTS When Mary Stuart, Queen of Scots (1542–87), took up her rule, she was a Roman Catholic of French upbringing trying to govern an unruly land to which she was a relative newcomer. Daughter of Scotland's James V and France's Mary of Guise, she became queen at only 6 days old. She was sent to be educated in France and at age 15 married the heir to the French throne; she returned to Scotland only after his death. Mary then set out on two roads that were anathema to the Scots—to make herself absolute monarch in the French style and to impose Roman Catholicism. The first alienated the lords who held the real power, and the second made her the enemy of John Knox and the Calvinists. After a series of disastrous political and romantic alliances and endless abortive episodes of often indiscreet intrigue, her life was ended by the headsman's ax in England. The execution order was reluctantly issued by her cousin Elizabeth I, who considered Mary's presence an incitement to civil unrest and a threat to the stability of the English throne.

Of all the towering figures in Scottish history, only Mary Queen of Scots left an extensive trail of palaces and castles that you can still visit. Begin in the Borders at Mary Queen of Scots House (see chapter 6 for more information) and go on to the Palace of Holyroodhouse in Edinburgh (see chapter 5), where her Italian secretary, David Rizzio, was stabbed 56 times in front of her. The queen used to come to Falkland Palace for hunting and hawking and lived at Stirling Castle as an infant monarch for the first 4 years of her life (see chapter 9).

- **Late 19th century** An astonishing success in the sciences propels Scotland into the role of arbiter of industrial know-how around the globe.
- **Mid–20th century** The decline of traditional industries, especially shipbuilding, painfully redefines the nature of Scottish industry.
- **1970** The discovery of North Sea oil deposits brings new vitality to Scotland.
- **1973** Scotland, as part of the United Kingdom, becomes a member of the Common Market.
- **1974** The old counties or shires are reorganized; many regions are renamed.
- **1979** Scots vote on devolution (separation from England): 33% vote yes, 31% vote no, and 36% don't vote at all.
- **1981** The largest oil terminal in Europe is launched at Sullom Voe in the Shetland Islands.
- **1988** Scottish nationalism revives under the marching cry of "Scotland in Europe"; Pan Am Flight 103 from London crashes at Lockerbie, killing all passengers, including some locals.
- **1992** The Scots continue to express dissatisfaction with English rule: Polls show one out of two favor independence.

⟋Tips A Scot Is Not a Scotch

Remember one thing: Scotch is a whisky and not the name of the proud people who inhabit the country. They're called **Scots,** and the adjective is **Scottish.** Don't worry—if you forget and call them Scotch, they'll forgive you. What they won't forgive is your calling them English.

The power of the great lords of Scotland was broken only in 1603, when Mary's son, James VI of Scotland, assumed the throne of England as James I, Elizabeth's heir. James succeeded where his doomed mother had failed. He was the first of the Stuarts to occupy the English throne, and his coronation effectively united England and Scotland.

UNION WITH ENGLAND Despite hopes for peace that accompanied the union, religion almost immediately became a prime source of discontent. From their base in England, the two Stuart kings attempted to promote a Church of Scotland governed by bishops, in opposition to the Presbyterian Church's self-ruling organization. So incensed were the Scots that in 1638 they signed the National Covenant, which not only reasserted the Reformation's principles but also questioned the king's right to make laws, a role the Covenanters believed should be filled by Parliament. However, the monarch was still allowed a

role, unlike the position the Puritans took in England.

Charles I, king of England from 1625 to 1649, believed strongly in the divine right of kings. When Parliament stripped away much of his authority in 1642, Charles went north to organize an army against the Parliamentary forces centered in London. A civil war ensued, and the forces of Parliament were led to victory by Oliver Cromwell (1599–1658). Charles fled to Scotland, but the Scots turned him over to Parliament, and in 1649 he was convicted of treason and beheaded. Under the Commonwealth setup, Cromwell assumed a dominant political role and became Lord Protector in 1653. King in all but name, he ruled England until his death.

But trouble brewed in Scotland. The death of Charles I led to deep divisions in the country, which finally openly defied Cromwell, proclaiming Charles II king. The Scots even launched abortive invasions of England. Cromwell's forces

---

- **1996** A psychopath guns down 16 schoolchildren and a teacher in one of Britain's greatest mass-murder sprees.
- **1997** A sheep is cloned for the first time; Scotland votes to establish a legislature of its own for the first time since 1707.
- **1999** British Prime Minister Tony Blair holds off threats from the Nationalist Party as his own Labour Party triumphs in national elections; on

July 1, Queen Elizabeth opens a new Scottish Parliament for the first time in 300 years.
- **2001** Scottish Parliament opens to bad press—it's called the "silly season" and "the totally absurd."
- **2003** Scotland joins England in sending troops to Iraq.
- **2004–05** Scotland grapples with long-overdue land reform.
- **2007** Scotland marks 300 years with England.

The Stone of Destiny, Home at Last

After a rocky journey, the Stone of Scone, or Stone of Destiny, has finally been returned to Scotland. The stone is physically only a block of sandstone, measuring 26 inches long and 16 inches wide and weighing 336 pounds. But it's not just a stone: Revered for centuries as a holy relic, it allegedly came from the Middle East, and in biblical times Jacob is said to have used the stone as a pillow.

The stone was used at Dunadd, Iona, and Dunstaffnage for enthroning the Dalriada Irish Monarchs called Scots. Later it was moved to Scone, and in 1292 John Balliol became the last king to be crowned on the stone in Scotland. So powerful was its legend that Edward I took it to England in 1296, believing possession of the stone gave him sovereignty over Scotland. There it stayed, under the coronation chair in Westminster Abbey. In 1328, the Treaty of Northampton, recognizing Scotland's independence, returned the stone to Scotland, but the English reneged on the promise and the stone never moved from Westminster Abbey.

On Christmas Day 1950, the stone was taken from the abbey by a group of Scottish Nationalists. No one knows where it went then, but it was found about 4 months later in Arbroath Abbey and returned to Westminster. A rumor went around that the found stone was actually a replica and that the replica was carted back to London, but this has never been proved.

In 1996, the Stone of Destiny left Westminster Abbey by Land Rover, crossing from England into Scotland at the border town of Coldstream, where a small but moving ceremony was held. On November 30 of that year, the stone proceeded with pomp and circumstance up the Royal Mile in Edinburgh to its permanent home beside the Scottish Crown Jewels in Edinburgh Castle, where you can see it today (see chapter 5).

Scots hailed the return of the stone after 700 years in English captivity. Yet not all are pleased with the return of the stone. Some have denounced it as a "cheap political ploy," especially as the queen claims she's "lending" it to her Scottish subjects—the idea is that after 7 centuries, possession is nine-tenths of the law, and it can be called back to London for a future coronation.

Some Scots want to see the stone returned to Scone. "Edinburgh has no claim, legally, morally, or whatever, to the Stone of Scone," said Andrew R. Robinson, administrator of Scone Castle. "It's not called the Stone of Edinburgh, is it?"

finally defeated the Scots at Dunbar in 1650. For nearly 9 years (1651–60), Scotland was under Commonwealth military occupation, although the result of that invasion had virtually nothing to do with what you'll see as a visitor today. Religious friction continued, however, after the restoration of Charles II to the English throne.

THE JACOBITES   In 1689, when the English Parliament stripped Catholic James II of his crown and imported Protestant monarchs William and Mary from

Holland, the exiled ex-king and then his son James Edward (the Old Pretender) became focal points for Scottish unrest. The Jacobites (the name comes from *Jacobus,* the Latin form of James) attempted unsuccessfully in 1715 to place the Old Pretender on the English throne and restore the Stuart line. Although James died in exile, his son Charles Edward (the Young Pretender), better known as Bonnie Prince Charlie, carried on his father's dream. Charismatic but with an alcohol-induced instability, he was the central figure of the 1745 Jacobite uprising. For more legend and lore about Bonnie Prince Charlie, see chapter 12.

Although the revolt was initially promising because of the many Scottish adherents who crossed religious lines to rally to the cause, the Jacobite forces were crushed at the Battle of Culloden, near Inverness, by a larger English army led by the duke of Cumberland. Many supporters of the Pretender's cause were killed in battle, some were executed, and others fled to safe havens such as the United States. Fearing a rebirth of similar types of Scottish nationalism, the clan system was rigorously suppressed; clans that supported the Jacobite cause lost their lands, and, until 1782, the wearing of Highland dress was made illegal. Ten kilometers (6 miles) southeast of Inverness, you can still visit the historic battlefield at Culloden (see chapter 11 for more information).

The Young Pretender himself was smuggled unglamorously out of Scotland, assisted by Flora MacDonald, a resident of the obscure Hebridean island of South Uist. One of the era's most visible Scottish heroines, she has ever since provided fodder for the Scottish sense of romance. The Bonnie Prince dissipated himself in Paris and Rome, and the hopes of an independent Scotland were buried forever.

ECONOMIC GROWTH & THE INDUSTRIAL REVOLUTION During the 18th century, the Scottish economy underwent a radical transformation of growth and diversification. The British government, fearing civil unrest, commissioned one of its most capable generals to build roads and bridges throughout the country, presumably to increase military access from London in the event of a revolt—however, they actually encouraged business and commerce.

As trade with British overseas colonies, England, and Europe increased, the great ports of Aberdeen, Glasgow, and Leith (near Edinburgh) flourished. The merchants of Glasgow grew rich on a nearly monopolistic tobacco trade with Virginia and the Carolinas, until the outbreak of the Revolution sent American tobacco elsewhere. Other forms of commerce continued to enrich a battalion of shrewd Scots.

The 1789 outbreak of the French Revolution engendered so much Scottish sympathy for the cause that a panicked government in London became more autocratic than ever in its attempts to suppress antimonarchical feelings.

The infamous Clearances (1750–1850) changed forever Scotland's demographics. Small farmers, or crofters, were expelled from their ancestral lands to make way for sheep grazing. Increased industrialization, continued civil unrest, migration into urban centers, and a massive wave of emigration to the United States, Canada, Australia, South Africa, and New Zealand all contributed to a changing national demographic and a dispersal of the Scottish ethic throughout the world.

Meanwhile, rapid progress in the arts, sciences, and education, coupled with the arrival of the Industrial Age, meshed neatly with the Scottish genius for thrift, hard work, shrewdness, and conservatism. The 19th century produced vast numbers of prominent Scots who made broad and sweeping contributions to nearly all fields of endeavor.

THE 20TH CENTURY & BEYOND

Scotland endured bitter privations during the Great Depression and the two world wars. In the 1960s and 1970s, Scotland found that, like the rest of Britain, its aging industrial plants couldn't compete with more modern commercial competition from abroad. The most visible decline occurred in the shipbuilding industries. The vast Glasgow shipyards that had once produced some of the world's great ocean liners went bankrupt. The companies that produced automobiles were wiped out during the 1930s. Many commercial enterprises once controlled by Scots had been merged into English or multinational conglomerates.

However, all wasn't bleak on the Scottish horizon. The 1970 discovery of North Sea oil by British Petroleum boosted the economy considerably and provided jobs for thousands of workers. Oil has continued to play a prominent role in the Scottish economy. In 1981, the largest oil terminal in Europe opened at Sullom Voe in the remote Shetland Islands.

As part of the United Kingdom, Scotland became a member of the European Common Market in 1973, although many Scots—perhaps owing to their longtime isolationism—opposed entry. Some voters expressed a fear that membership would take away some of their rights of self-government and determination. In 1974, Scotland underwent a drastic revision of its counties, and many regions were renamed. Tayside, for example, was carved out of the old counties of Perth and Angus.

A landmark scientific breakthrough occurred in 1997. The Scots had always contributed almost disproportionately to the world's sciences and technology. Now the land that gave us Sir Alexander Fleming, a Nobel Prize winner who discovered penicillin, cloned a sheep. The issue of *Nature* for February 27, 1997, reported the event, the work of scientists in Roslin. Dolly was the first lamb to be produced by cloning the udder cells of an adult sheep. In the summer of 1997, another major step was taken, and Polly was created, a lamb that has a human gene in every cell of its body. The work was hailed as a milestone. Animals with human genes (at least in theory) could be used to produce hormones or other biological products to treat human diseases or even to produce organs for human transplant.

In 1999, under Prime Minister Tony Blair's reforms, Scotland was allowed to elect its own legislature for the first time since its 1707 union with England. A total of 129 Scots were elected to this newly formed Parliament. Unlike the Welsh Parliament, the Scottish version, centered at Edinburgh, has the power to tax and make laws, as well as to pursue such matters as health care, education, public transportation, and public housing. Scotland is still represented in the main British Parliament in London. Scotland, however, must bow to the greater will of Britain in matters of foreign policy.

The Scottish Parliament got off to a bad start in 2000, with Scotland's 21 robustly competitive newspapers writing of "the silly season" or the "totally absurd." The press noted that members of Parliament awarded lawmakers with commemorative medals before they had done anything, granted bonuses, and fretted about parking spaces and vacation grants instead of tackling some of the country's serious problems, such as a feudal landowning system. Some lawmakers found themselves heckled in the streets, and they had to endure the bite of such popular comics as Billy Connolly, who dismissed the body "as a wee pretendy Parliament." This characterization was most dramatically illustrated in 2003, when Scotland, despite widespread opposition on the homefront, along with England and Wales, sent soldiers and equipment to do battle in Iraq, toppling the dictator Saddam Hussein.

In 2004 and 2005, the Scottish Parliament came face to face with one of its biggest challenges. Half of the country belongs to just 350 people, the "lairds" as they are called in Scotland, including English aristocrats, reclusive foreign investors, pop stars, desert shieks, offshore companies, and rich people from London's financial sector. Dating from the 12th century and reinforced by the infamous Highland Clearances of the early 1800s, the ancient system is coming under review. And the battle rages on—for example, the islanders of Gigha won the fight to own their own land even though they were not the top bidder for its sale. The 1,375-hectare (3,400-acre) island has been handed over to a community trust. Developments on the island are being closely watched. Indeed, Gigha could be a test case for Scottish land ownership in the 21st century.

On a more optimistic front, Scotland is turning a strong face to the world, with its abundant natural resources: oil, water, gas, and coal. Its high-tech industries have played an important role in the technological revolution, and today the country produces 13% of Europe's personal computers, 45% of Europe's workstations, and 50% of Europe's automated banking machines. Everything in the country is loosening up—blue laws are disappearing, later hours are being kept, nightlife is looking up, and ecotourism is being developed. Scotland's time-tested crafts (woolen tweeds and knitwear) are thriving, the market for Scotch whisky has burgeoned all around the world, and tourists are visiting in record numbers.

In 2007 Scotland marked its 300-year anniversary with England by focusing attention more on the perennial discord than the ties that bind their two members of Great Britain. "This treaty [a reference to the Treaty of Union] can and will be undone, and at the moment there is a wellspring of Scottish nationalism," said Murray Ritchie, convener of the Scottish Independence convention, an advocacy group. "What we need is a referendum to settle the issue of independence." The union has been contested since 1707. The Scottish poet, Robert Burns, labeled those who voted for union as a "parcel of rogues."

As Scotland goes deeper into the 21st century, there's a new esprit in the land. Scots are on a roll, declaring that their country is not a mere tartan theme park.

And speaking of tartans, nothing has shaken up the identity of Scotland more than the kilts designed by Howie Nicholsby of Edinburgh. To model his kilt design, Howie secured tough rugby star Chris Capaldi. The kilt is transparent—and in pink, no less. Is nothing sacred?

In July 2007 extremists with ties to the foiled car-bomb plot in London rammed a flaming jeep into the main terminal at Glasgow Airport, one of the largest in the United Kingdom, sending shock waves throughout the country. The nation was even more shocked to find that some of the perpetrators were young doctors who came to Britain from the Middle East. In the wake of the attacks, all of Britain went on a terror alert, as the press called these plotters "Doctors of Doom."

2 A Portrait of the Scots

LANGUAGE   In Scotland's earliest history, its prevailing language was Gaelic, along with a smattering of Norse dialects. When English was introduced and Scottish English developed, it borrowed heavily not only from Gaelic but also from Scandinavian, Dutch, and French. In the 15th and 16th centuries, when Scotland had close ties to France, French was a literary language of precision and grace, and it was the language of Mary Queen of Scots, who spoke no Gaelic at all. After

How the Scots Say It

aber   river mouth
ach   field
aird   promontory
alt   stream
auch   field
auld   old
baillie   magistrate
bal   hamlet or tiny village
ben   peak, often rugged
birk   birch tree
brae   hillside, especially along a river
brig   bridge
broch   circular stone tower
burn   stream
cairn   heap of stone piled up as memorial or landmark
ceilidh   Scottish hoedown with singing, music, and tall tales
clach   stone
clachan   hamlet
close   narrow passage leading from the street to a court or tenement
craig   rock
creel   basket
croft   small farm worked by a tenant, often with hereditary rights
cromlech, dolmen   prehistoric tomb or monument consisting of a large flat stone laid across upright stones
dram   ⅛ fluid ounce
drum   ridge
dun   fortress, often in a lake, for refuge in times of trouble
eas   waterfall
eilean   island
factor   manager of an estate
fell   hill
firth   arm of the sea reaching inland

the Scottish court moved to England in 1603, Scottish English was looked on as a rather awkward dialect.

As the centuries progressed, the ancient and complex Gaelic diminished in importance, partly because the British government's deliberate policy was to make English the language of all Britain. By the 1980s, less than 2% of the Scottish population understood Gaelic. Most of those who still speak it live in the northwestern Highlands and in the Hebridean Islands—especially the Isle of Skye, where about 60% of the population still use Gaelic.

Scottish English never developed the linguistic class divisions that exist so strongly in England among upper-, middle-, and lower-class speech patterns. Throughout most of its English-speaking

gait   street (in proper names)
gil   ravine
glen   a small valley
haugh   water meadow
how   burial mound
howff   small, cozy room or meeting place
inver   mouth of a river
kil, kin, kirk   church
kyle   narrows of ancient or unknown origin
land   house built on a piece of ground considered as property
larig   mountain pass
links   dunes
loch   lake
machair   sand dune, sometimes covered with sea grass
mon   hill
muir   moor
mull   cape or promontory
ness   headland
neuk   nose
pend   vaulted passage
provost   mayor
reek   smoke
ross   cape
schist   highly compact crystalline rock formation
strath   broad valley
tarbert   isthmus
tolbooth   old town hall (often with prison)
uig   sheltered bay
uisge   water
uisge beatha   water of life, whisky
way   bay
wynd   alley

history, the hardships of Scotland were suffered in common by a society that had few barriers between the classes. Social snobbery was relatively unknown and the laird (estate owner) and his man conversed as equals.

At the end of the 20th century, the great leveling effects of TV and radio had begun to even out some of the more pronounced burrs and lilts of the Scottish tongue. However, the dialect and speech patterns of the Scots are still rich and evocative. Today, after years of struggle, Scottish students are rewarded with approval by pro-Scots educators when they say, "Whos all comin tae the jiggin?" ("Who's coming to the dance?"). This increasing pride in the Scottish language is in direct contrast to what happened in classrooms back in, say, the 1950s. At

Garb o' the Gods

A memorable photograph from the handover of Hong Kong may spare the First Battalion of the Black Watch from having to answer the question most frequently put to men in kilts. As the flags were being lowered at the Cenotaph, a rush of wind lifted the tartan fabrics from the backside of Lance Cpl. Lee Wotherspoon and revealed nothing at all but his backside. He received a lot of mail and an admiring review from a gay publication in France.

—Warren Hoge, *New York Times* (1998)

Although not every visitor to Scotland is descended from a clan, almost all are familiar with plaids and the traditions associated with them. Over the centuries, each clan developed a distinctive pattern to be worn by its members, presumably to better identify its soldiers in the heat of battle. (Today, *tartan* is used interchangeably with *plaid,* but the word *tartan* originally referred specifically to a mantle of cloth draped over the back and shoulders.)

Kilts enjoy an ancient history. Checkered tartans were first mentioned in a 1471 English inventory. The clans developed special dyeing and weaving techniques, with colors and patterns reflecting their flair and imagination. The craft of dyeing was raised to an art that was a point of pride for the clan: Alder bark, steeped in hot water, produces a black dye; gorse, broom, and knapweed produce shades of green; cup moss produces purple; dandelion leaves produce magenta; bracken and heather produce yellow; white lichens produce red; and indigo had to be imported for blue.

When Bonnie Prince Charlie launched his rebellion in 1745, he used tartans as a symbol of his army, and this threatened the English enemy so much that public display of tartans was banned for a period after his defeat. Tartans came into high fashion in Queen Victoria's day, when she and her kilt-wearing German consort, Albert, made all things Scottish popular.

that time, students were under a constant threat of a whack from a tawse (leather strap) if they blurted out a single *aye.*

HIGHLAND GAMES & GATHERINGS Highland Gatherings or Games have their origins in the fairs organized by the tribes or clans for the exchange of goods. At these gatherings, there were often trials of strength among the men, and the strongest were selected for the chief's army.

The earliest games were held more than 1,000 years ago. The same tradition continues today: throwing hammers, putting rounded stones found in the rivers, tossing tree trunks, and running in flat races and up steep hillsides. Playing the bagpipes and performing dances have always been part of the gatherings. The Heavies, a breed of gigantic men, draw the most attention with their prowess. Of all the events, the most popular and most spectacular is the tossing of the caber (the throwing of a great tree trunk).

Queen Victoria, who had a deep love for Scotland (which was dramatized in the film *Mrs. Brown*), popularized the Highland Games, which for many decades had been suppressed after the failure of the 1745 rebellion. In 1848, the queen and her consort, Prince Albert, attended the Braemar Gathering and saw Duncan, her *ghillie,* win the race up the

Today, there are at least 300 tartans, each subtly distinct from the others, and all are available for sale in Scotland's shops and markets. If you're not fortunate enough to be of Scottish extraction, Queen Victoria long ago authorized two Lowland designs as suitable garb for Sassenachs (the English and, more remotely, the Americans).

Few people realize that from 6.3 to 9m (21–30 ft.) of tartan wool cloth goes into the average kilt. Even fewer non-Scots know what's actually worn beneath those folds strapped over the muscular thighs of a parading Scotsman. For a Highlander, the answer to that question is nothing, an answer that goes along with such defenders of ancient tradition who hold that only a Stewart can wear a Stewart tartan, only a Scotsman looks good in a kilt, and only a foreigner would stoop to wearing anything under it.

Alas, commercialism has reared its head with the introduction of undershorts to match the material making up bagpipe players' kilts. A story is told of a colonel who heard a rumor that the soldiers of his elite Highland Light Infantry regiment were mollycoddling themselves with undershorts. The next day, his eyebrows bristling, he ordered the entire regiment to undress in front of him. To his horror, half a dozen of his soldiers had disgraced the regiment by putting on what only an Englishman would wear. He publicly ordered the offending garments removed, and when he gave the order the next day to drop your kilts, not a soldier in the regiment had on the trews (close-cut tartan shorts).

Even in today's general decline of standards, the mark of a man in the Highlands is still whether he can abide the drafts up his thighs and the feel of wool cloth against his tender flesh.

hill of Craig Choinnich, as she recorded in her journal. (*Ghillie* originally meant a male attendant or Scottish Highland chief, though today it's used to refer to a hunting or fishing guide; incidentally, Duncan was reputedly the queen's lover.)

The most famous gathering nowadays is at Braemar, held in late August or early September and patronized by the royal family. When that chief of chiefs takes the salute, Queen Elizabeth is fulfilling a role assumed by a predecessor of hers in the 11th century.

Other major games are held at Ballater (Grampian), Aberdeen, Elgin, and Newtonmore.

CLANS, TARTANS & KILTS   To the outsider, Scotland's deepest traditions appear to be based on the clan system of old with all the familiar paraphernalia of tartans and bagpipes. However, this is a romantic memory, and in any case, a good part of the Scots—the 75% of the population who live in the central Lowlands, for example—have little or no connection with the clansmen of earlier times.

The clan tradition dates from the tribal units of the country's earliest Celtic history. Power was organized around a series of chieftains who exacted loyalties from the inhabitants of a particular region in exchange for protection against exterior invasions. The position of chieftain wasn't hereditary, and land was owned by the clan, not by the chieftain. Clan members had both rights and duties. Rigidly militaristic and paternalistic—the stuff with which Scottish legend is imbued—the clan tradition is still emphasized today, albeit in a much friendlier fashion than when claymores and crossbows threatened a bloody death or dismemberment for alleged slights on a clan's honor.

Chieftains were absolute potentates, with life and death power over members and interlopers, although they were usually viewed as patriarchs actively engaged in the perpetuation of the clan's bloodlines, traditions, and honor. The entourage of a chieftain always included bodyguards, musicians (harpers and pipers), a spokesman (known as a tatler), and—perhaps most important to latter-day students of clan traditions—a bard. The bard's role was to sing, to exalt the role of the clan and its heroes, to keep a genealogical record of births and deaths, and to compose or recite epic poems relating to the clan's history.

Most of the clans were organized during two distinctly different eras of Scottish history. One of the country's oldest and largest is Clan Donald, whose original organization occurred during the Christianization of Scotland, and whose headquarters has traditionally been Scotland's northwestern coast and western islands. The fragmentation of Clan Donald into subdivisions (which include the Sleat, the Dunyveg, the Clanranald, and the Keppoch clans) happened after the violent battles of succession over control of the clan in the 1400s. These feuds so weakened the once powerful unity of the MacDonalds that a new crop of former vassal tribes in northwestern Scotland declared their independence and established new clans of their own. These included the Mackintoshes, the Macleans, the MacNeils, the Mackinnons, and the MacLeods.

Meanwhile, the giant Celtic earldoms of eastern Scotland disintegrated and Norman influences from the south became more dominant. Clans whose earliest makeup might have been heavily influenced by Norman bloodlines include Clan Frasier (from the French *des fraises,* because of the strawberry leaves on the family's coat of arms), de Umfraville, and Rose. Other clans adapted their Celtic names, like Clan Robertson (Celtic Clan Donnachaidh) and Clan Campbell (Celtic Diarmid).

Simultaneously, in the Borders between England and Scotland, families and clans with differing sets of traditions and symbols held a precarious power over one of Britain's most heavily contested regions, enduring or instigating raids on their territories from both north and south. But despite the rich traditions of the Lowland and Border clans, it's the traditions of the Highland clans (with their costumes, bagpipes, speech patterns, and grandly tragic struggles) that have captured the imagination of the world.

The clans had broken down long before Sir Walter Scott wrote his romantic novels about them and long before Queen Victoria made Scotland socially fashionable. The clans today represent a cultural rather than a political power. The best place to see the remnants of their tradition in action is at any traditional Highland gathering, although battalions of bagpipers seem to show up at everything from weddings and funerals to political rallies, parades, and civic events throughout Scotland.

3 A Taste of Scotland

FROM ANGUS BEEF TO HAGGIS
For many years, restaurants in Scotland were known mainly for their modest prices, watery overcooked vegetables, and boiled meats. But you need no longer expect a diet of oats, fried fish, and greasy

chips—in the past 20 or so years, there has been a significant improvement in Scottish cookery. There was a time when the Scot going out for dinner would head for the nearest hotel, but independent restaurants are now opening everywhere, often by newly arrived immigrants, along with bistros and wine bars.

More and more restaurants are offering "Taste of Scotland" menus, a culinary program initiated by the Scottish Tourist Board. Scotland's culinary strength is in its fresh raw ingredients, ranging from seafood, beef, and game to vegetables and native fruits.

One of Scotland's best-known exports is pedigree **Aberdeen Angus beef.** In fact, ye olde roast beef of England often came from Scotland. Scottish **lamb** is known for its tender, tasty meat. A true connoisseur can taste the difference in lamb by its grazing grounds, ranging from the coarse pastureland and seaweed of the Shetlands to the heather-clad hills of the mainland.

Game plays an important role in the Scottish diet, ranging from woodcock, red deer, and grouse to the rabbit and hare in the crofter's kitchen. And **fish** in this land of seas, rivers, and lochs is a mainstay, from salmon to the pink-fleshed brown trout to the modest herring that's transformed into the elegant kipper (the best are the Loch Fyne kippers). Scottish smoked salmon is, of course, a delicacy known worldwide.

The good news is that the word "eclectic" now describes many restaurants in Scotland. To cite only an example or two, fresh salads are often given a Thai kick with lime leaves and chile, and stir-fries and chargrill are standard features. Scots today eat better than ever before. Robert Burns would be shocked at some of the new taste sensations creative chefs are devising. But he would be happy to learn that alcohol—especially whisky—is still a favored ingredient in many dishes and sauces.

Of course, it takes a wise chef to leave well enough alone, and many Scottish cooks know the simplest dishes have never lost their appeal, especially if that means **Lismore oysters** or **Loch Etive mussels.** The Scots have always been good bakers, and many small tearooms still bake their own **scones** and buttery **shortbread.** Heather honey is justly celebrated, and jams make use of Scotland's abundant harvest of soft fruit. Scottish raspberries, for example, are said to be among the finest in the world.

You'll definitely want to try some of Scotland's excellent **cheeses.** The mild or mature cheddars are the best known. A famous hard cheese, Dunlop, comes from the Orkney Islands as well as Arran and Islay. One of the most-acclaimed cheeses from the Highlands is Caboc, creamy and rich, formed into cork shapes and rolled in pinhead oatmeal. Many varieties of cottage cheese are flavored with herbs, chives, or garlic.

And, yes, **haggis** is still Scotland's national dish—it's perhaps more symbolic than gustatory. One wit described it as a "castrated bagpipe." Regardless of what you might be told facetiously, haggis isn't a bird. Therefore, you should turn down invitations (usually offered in pubs) to go on a midnight haggis hunt. Cooked in a sheep's paunch (nowadays more likely a plastic bag), it's made with bits and pieces of the lung, liver, and heart of sheep mixed with suet and spices, along with onions and oatmeal. Haggis is often accompanied by single-malt whisky— then again, what isn't?

SINGLE MALT OR BLEND? "It's the only liquor fit for a gentleman to drink in the morning if he can have the good fortune to come by it . . . or after dinner either." Thus wrote Sir Walter Scott of the drink of his country—**Scotch whisky.** Of course, if you're here or almost anywhere in Britain or Europe, you don't have to identify it as *Scotch* whisky when you order. That's what you'll get. In fact, in some parts of Scotland, England, and Wales, they look at you oddly if you order Scotch as you would in the States.

The difference in the Scotch whiskies you may have become accustomed to seeing in bars or liquor stores at home is whether they're blends or single-malt whiskies. Many connoisseurs prefer single malts, whose tastes depend on their points of origin: Highlands, Lowlands, Islay, or Campbeltown on Kintyre. These are usually seen as sipping whiskies, not to be mixed with water (well, maybe soda) and not to be served with ice. Many have come to be used as after-dinner drinks, served in a snifter like cognac.

Blended Scotches came into being both because the single malts were for a long time too harsh for delicate palates and because they were expensive and time-consuming to produce. A shortcut was developed: The clear and almost tasteless alcohol produced in the traditional way could be mixed with such ingredients as American corn, Finnish barley, Glasgow city tap water, and caramel coloring with a certain percentage of malt whiskies that flavored the entire bottle. Whichever you prefer, both the single malts and the blends must be made within the borders of Scotland and then aged for at least 3 years before they can legally be called Scotch whisky.

The making of Scottish **beer**—the ales drunk by the common folk in earlier days—almost died out when palates became more adapted to Scotch whisky and when a malt tax was levied in the 18th century, followed in the 19th century by beer duty. The brewing industry has made a comeback in the last quarter of a century, and Scottish beer, or Scotch ale, is being produced. Real **ale** is beer made from malted barley, hop flowers, yeast, and water, with a fining process (use of an extract from the swim bladders of certain fish) to complete the brewing. Ales are fermented in casks in a series of steps. Scottish ale, either dark or light, is malty and full of flavor.

Index

See also Accommodations and Restaurant indexes, below.

ACCOMMODATIONS

RESTAURANTS

CLOSED
due to
accidental demolition

WEGEN BISSIGEN
EICHHÖRNCHEN GESCHLOSSEN

CERRADO

CABRAS

Κλειστό
Μετεωρίτες

POOL CLOSED

ELECTRIC EELS

プール も

閉鎖中

Hotel
closed for
facelifting

FERMÉ POUR
RAISON
DE GRÈVE
DES BONNES

FECHADO!
POR CAUSA DE
ATAQUES DOS CROCODILOS

— I don't speak
sign language.

A hotel can close for all kinds of reasons.
Our Guarantee ensures that if your hotel's undergoing construction, we'll
let you know in advance. In fact, we cover your entire travel experience.
See www.travelocity.com/guarantee for details.

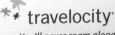

travelocity
You'll never roam alone.